D1590993

EXTERNAL HISTORY
OF THE
ROMANCE LANGUAGES

Foundations of Linguistics Series

Editor:

Charles F. Hockett, Cornell University

Erwin A. Esper,
Mentalism and Objectivism in Linguistics: The Sources of Leonard Bloomfield's Psychology of Language, 1968

Robert A. Hall, Jr.,
External History of the Romance Languages, 1974

C. F. and F. M. Voegelin,
Index of the Languages of the World (in preparation)

COMPARATIVE ROMANCE GRAMMAR

EXTERNAL HISTORY
OF THE
ROMANCE LANGUAGES

Robert A. Hall, Jr.
Cornell University

American Elsevier Publishing Company, Inc.
New York   London   Amsterdam

AMERICAN ELSEVIER PUBLISHING COMPANY, INC.
52 Vanderbilt Avenue, New York, N.Y. 10017

ELSEVIER PUBLISHING COMPANY
335 Jan Van Galenstraat, P.O. Box 211
Amsterdam, The Netherlands

International Standard Book Number 0-444-00136-0
Library of Congress Card Number 73-6088

Library of Congress Cataloging in Publication Data

Hall, Robert Anderson, 1911-
    External history of the Romance languages.

    (Foundations of linguistics series)
    Bibliography: p.
    At head of title: Comparative Romance grammer.
    1. Romance languages--Grammar Comparative.
I. Title. II. Title: Comparative Romance grammar.
PC61.H3   440   73-6088
ISBN 0-444-00136-0

Manufactured in the United States of America

TO CAROL, TERRY, AND JIM

CONTENTS

Preface

Chapter 1. Introduction

Chapter 2. The Romance Languages and Their Distribution

Chapter 3. Latin in Early Italy

Chapter 4. The Spread and Differentiation of Latin

Chapter 11. History of Romance Linguistics

References

Index

ROBERT A. HALL, JR. is Professor of Linguistics at Cornell University, a post he assumed in 1950 after a four-year tenure as Associate Professor in the Division of Modern Languages. Prior to his long-standing association with Cornell, he held the successive positions of Catedrático Auxiliar de Idiomas Extranjeros at Universidad de Puerto Rico, Instructor in Italian at Princeton University, and Instructor and Assistant Professor of Italian at Brown University. Professor Hall received the A.B. degree from Princeton University in 1931, the Doctor in Letters from the University of Rome (Italy) in 1934, and the A.M. degree from the University of Chicago in 1935. His professional affiliations include membership in the Linguistic Society of America, the American Association of Teachers of Italian, the Dante Society of America, and the Modern Language Association of America, and he has twice been appointed a Guggenheim Fellow (1954 and 1970). In addition to the present volume, Professor Hall has authored 33 books and over 400 articles and reviews for professional journals, in addition to several short stories and a novel; he has also composed a Mass on the melody of the Provençal troubadour Jaufré Rudel's song "Lanquan li jorn son lonc en mai".

PREFACE

0.1. Purpose and Scope

It is my intention, in this *Comparative Romance Grammar*, to present a systematic description of the development of the Romance languages (mediaeval and modern) out of their common ancestor Proto-Romance (cf. §§1.5, 1.6) and, farther back in time, out of the common ancestor of Proto-Romance and Classical Latin (cf. §§1.5, 4.31). The material will, according to present plans, be organized in six volumes:

1. External History of the Romance Languages
2. Phonology
3. Inflection
4. Syntax
5. Word-Formation
6. Lexicon

0.2. Techniques of Analysis and Presentation

Analysis and presentation will utilise all those techniques currently available, wherever their use is appropriate. In the description of linguistic structure, tagmemic-odic, transformational, stratificational, and other approaches will be used. In historical matters, the comparative method (including systematic reconstruction of sounds, forms, and constructions attributable to Proto-Romance and to intermediate stages of development) will form the basis of the presentation, but it will be supplemented by all other useful approaches, including the study of internal borrowing (chiefly analogical new-formation) and external borrowing due to cultural and dialectal influences. It must be emphasised, in this connection, that neither our reconstructed Proto-Romance nor any hypothetical intermediate stages are to be regarded as stable, rigid "états de langue," any more than any other language

0.3. Typographical Conventions

A sharp distinction is made between phonetic transcription (using, in general, the symbols of the International Phonetic Alphabet) enclosed in square brackets [ ], and phonemic transcription, enclosed in slashes / /. Virtually all forms are cited in phonemic transcription, with an added phonetic transcription wherever necessary, and with conventional spelling (in italics) following these in the majority of cases, e.g. OFr. /čəválčəθ/ *chevalcheṭ* 'he rides'. As in the example just given, glosses are enclosed in single quotation-marks. The symbols ˆ and ˘, standing alone after a vowel-letter, indicate tense and lax articulation, respectively. The symbol /¢/ stands for [tˢ], /ẓ/ for [dᶻ], /č/ for [tˢ], and /ǧ/ for [dᶻ]. Palatalised consonants are indicated by a comma or cedilla beneath the consonant-letter, e.g. /ṇ/ [ɲ], /ḷ/ [ʎ]. In the citation of bound morphemes, a distinction is made in the phonemic transcription between those which are inflectionally bound and those which are derivationally bound. The former are preceded or followed by a hyphen, e.g. It. /-iámo/ *-iamo* 1.pl. present-ending; the latter, by a raised plus-sign, e.g. seventeenth-century French /⁺iḷə/ *-ille*.

0.4. General Abbreviations

These include the following:

Ar.	Arabic
C	any consonant
Cast.	Castilian
Cat.	Catalan
CL	Classical Latin
Eng.	English
Fr.	French
G	Gallo-
Ger.	German
Gk.	Greek
GrLat.	Gracchan Latin
Ib.	Iberian, Ibero-
I.-E.	Indo-European
It.	Italian, Italo-
Langob.	Langobardic
Lat.	Latin
Lig.	Ligurian

Mex.	Mexican
O	Old
Osc.	Oscan
P	Proto-
PItWRom.	Proto-Italo-Western Romance
PRom.	Proto-Romance
pl.	plural
Port.	Portuguese
pres.	present
Prov.	Provençal
Rom.	Romance
Roum.	Roumanian
sg.	singular
Sp.	Spanish
Tusc.	Tuscan
Umbr.	Umbrian
V	any vowel
Vegl.	Vegliote

For abbreviations of journal-names, cf. References, at end of book.

0.5. Acknowledgments

I am of course deeply indebted to all my predecessors in Romance linguistics and philology, but especially, for both references and examples, to Tagliavini 1947 (1969[5]) and Elcock 1960, as well as to the two long series of annual bibliographies published by the Zeitschrift für romanische Philologie and the Comité International Permanent des Linguistes.

My thanks are due to those who have read and criticised this first volume in a preliminary form, especially Messrs. F. B. Agard, Boni H.-J. Kirstein, Clifford S. Leonard, Jr., Gordon M. Messing, and Ernst Pulgram. Naturally, any errors of fact or interpretation are attributable solely to me.

R. A. H., Jr.

Ithaca, N.Y.

The publication of this book has been aided by a grant from the Hull Foundation of Cornell University.

CHAPTER 1

Introduction

1.1. Purpose and Arrangement

Our purpose in this work is to present the history of the Romance languages[1] in the form of a comparative grammar, tracing their development from the Latin spoken by the Roman populace down to the present time. The development of any language or group of related languages ("language-family") is best treated from two points of view: the history of its use, and that of its structure. The former involves the vicissitudes of its use in the varying political and social conditions which have determined its spread, prestige, and (in some instances) decline or extinction. This is known as its "external" history.[2] Its "internal" history is, by contrast, the development of its structure (sounds, forms, syntactic combinations, lexicon) over the centuries, as known to us from both earlier documentation and reconstruction (cf. §1.5).

In accordance with this distinction, our first volume will treat the external history of the Romance languages, and following volumes the history of their phonology, inflection, syntax, word-formation, and lexicon. Our attention will be devoted primarily to the standard languages, but not excluding the dialects, particularly when the latter cast light on developments which are otherwise difficult to understand. Before taking up the history itself, it will be well to discuss the nature of linguistic structure, the techniques used in analysing and formulating it, the factors at work in its change during time, and the comparative study of a language-family, including the reconstruction of the common source out of which a group of related languages has developed.

1.2. The Nature of Linguistic Structure

There has been, ever since Graeco-Roman antiquity, an inordinate amount of ink spilled on this topic.[3] That language is a means of communication, exclusive to the human race ("species-specific"), and used by humans in society for conveying messages from one person to another, is about all that theoreticians of language can be said to agree on. The present writer's view of linguistic structure[4] can be summed up as follows:

1. A language is a (complicated) set of habits involving the production of sounds on the part of each person who speaks, and their reception by each hearer.

2. These habits are not innate to their users, although the capacity to develop such habits is. What habits any particular speaker learns are wholly conditioned by his experiences as he grows up in a given speech-community.

3. Conscious reflection and purposive behavior are of course present in speakers' use of their language; but their activity in producing sounds and meaningful combinations of sounds, and in associating linguistic forms with their referents, is almost wholly a matter of habit, carried on outside of awareness.

4. The MEANING of a linguistic form is the correlation between a sequence of sounds and some feature of the universe. The feature with which a form is correlated, in the usage of its speakers, is its REFERENT. The correlation (which exists only inside the brain of each speaker) is its SENSE. The referent of a linguistic form (including a grammatical element or construction) can be a feature of the external universe; of the speaker's internal functioning (including his emotions); or of the linguistic context. The last-mentioned type of reference is often termed "grammatical meaning."

5. Significant units of sound (PHONEMES), of form (MORPHEMES), and of longer sequences of forms (SYNTAGMATA) can be established with reasonably clear boundaries between them. Boundaries between meanings, however, cannot be established with similar sharpness of definition, since the senses of linguistic forms exist only inside people's heads and are therefore not accessible to exact observation. It is not possible to establish units of meaning (SEMEMES) with the same kind of precision as is possible for phonemes, morphemes, or syntagmata.[5]

6. Writing is very important for our civilisation and technology, and useful in documenting earlier stages of language. Nevertheless, a written form is not coequal with the corresponding spoken form in its relation to sense and referent. In general, written forms represent spoken forms,[6] and these latter are in their turn correlated with further, mostly non-linguistic referents. Alphabets normally represent features of phonological systems.

7. In linguistic structure, most analysts recognise the existence of at least the levels shown in Table I.[7] The phonological and the morpho-syntactic levels constitute two distinct "articulations," to use Martinet's terminology.[8] On the phonological level, there are a relatively small num-

TABLE I

Levels of Linguistic Structure

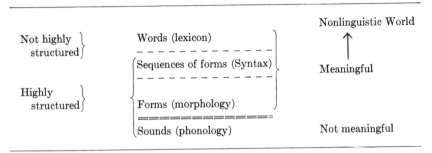

ber (normally between 15 and 40 or 50, for any given language) of non-meaningful units of sound. On the morphological and syntactic levels, there are a much larger number of meaningful units, which are built up, as it were, out of the meaningless phonological units. Morphology and syntax are therefore the levels which are both highly structured and meaningful. Lexicon, although meaningful, is by no means as highly structured as are the other levels. There are, however, even in the phonological and morpho-syntactic levels, inevitable loosenesses in structure, which manifest themselves synchronically as fluctuations in usage, and diachronically as the respects in which change takes place.

Another type of distinction, between "surface" and "deep" structure, is much less tenable.[9] The term *surface structure* normally refers to the actual, observable phenomena of human linguistic activity. *Deep structure* is variously used to refer to a paraphrase from which a syntactic combination is said to be "derived," *e.g.* the active serving as a source from which the passive is transformed; a synonym (word or phrase) from which a word is similarly "derived," *e.g. kill* from 'cause to die'; the meaning of a structural combination or form; or (in phonology) a set of single units serving as an "underlying representation" of which various phonetic phenomena are the "realisations." This approach to linguistics is based on a dualism that is Neo-Platonic and essentially antiscientific. It is preferable to recognize simply the existence of structure as such, together with meaning, both of which are legitimate objects of study, but of which the first is more amenable to scientific examination than the second, and therefore more suited to serve as a starting-point for our analysis.

1.3. The Presentation of Linguistic Structure

It is possible, in presenting linguistic structure, to begin at either the "bottom" or the "top" (in terms of the levels shown in Table I). The order SYNTAX—MORPHOLOGY—PHONOLOGY implies that we can identify and state an abstract "underlying" syntactic kernel for all utterances before we begin to give rules for its "actualisation" in linguistic forms, which in their turn are "realised" in sound. The opposite order, PHONOLOGY—MORPHOLOGY—SYNTAX implies that the sounds of language are the elements of which utterances consist and should be described first, followed by the enumeration of minimum forms and then of longer combination-types, with their meanings. The latter order is more in accord with the observable facts of language, and we shall follow the example of most historical grammars in using it here.

It is customary to distinguish between two axes of linguistic description, the SYNCHRONIC and the DIACHRONIC.[10] The former deals with language as it exists at a given (necessarily fictional[11]) point of time; the latter, with language as it changes over time. The PANCHRONIC approach treats those aspects of language for which the passage of time is not relevant. In a work dealing primarily with linguistic history, the diachronic approach is of necessity predominant. However, inasmuch as such a work always involves the comparison of two or more stages of linguistic structure, synchronic techniques will be used in the description of these latter.

1.4. Factors in Linguistic Change

Linguistic changes are of two kinds: those which arise within the structure of a linguistic system, in its phonology, morphology, or syntax; and those which come from sources outside linguistic structure, *i.e.* are conditioned by such nonlinguistic aspects of human activity as social prestige or political influence.

1.41. STRUCTURAL FACTORS are of two types:

1. Change in the sounds of language, usually referred to as "sound-change" or "phonetic change." The fundamental assumption of historical linguistics is that sound-change would be regular—*i.e.* that when a sound changes, all of its occurrences would show the same change under the same conditions—if it were not for the interference of other factors. Without this assumption, historical linguistics would have no guide-line by which to

separate phenomena due to sound-change from those due to other factors such as analogy (internal borrowing) or external borrowing. It was the absence of this assumption (which is best termed the REGULARIST PRINCIPLE) that impeded the development of valid historical linguistics before the nineteenth century, with few exceptions.[12]

Under the heading of regular sound-change, it is customary to distinguish two subtypes:

a. Nonconditioned, which manifests itself in every or almost every instance of the occurrence of a given sound in an earlier stage, as it undergoes a given change in the transition to a later stage: *e.g.* Lat. long /u·/ > PRom. tense /uˆ/ > French /y/, as in Lat. /mu·ru(m)/ 'wall' > PRom. /múˆru/ > Fr. /myr/ *mur*, and a host of other instances.

b. Conditioned, said of a change which takes place only under certain specifiable, phonetically determined conditions, *e.g.* the diphthongisation of Lat. and PRom. stressed open /é/ in free syllable to /ié/ in Old North French, as in Lat. /béne/ 'well' (adv.) > PRom. /béne/ > ONFr. /bién/. Note that both unconditioned and conditioned sound-changes are specific historical events, each of which has taken place in a particular language or dialect (preliterary ONFr. in the instances just cited), at a particular time (here, ca. seventh to ninth century A.D.). The term *sound-law* is often used to refer to such changes, but they are not general all-inclusive principles like the "laws" of physics.

The term *weak sound-change* has been proposed to cover instances in which a phonetic change has taken place in a particular dialect, but has spread only in part to neighboring dialects or has been overlaid in part by the results of analogical change or borrowing. This term, which implies that there are degrees of "strength" in sound-change, shows confusion between the origin of a phonetic change and its spread (or its over-lay by other factors), and is better avoided.[13]

In addition to regular sound-change, we find various kinds of irregular sound-change, such as often occur in the unmonitored flow of every-day speech as "slips of the tongue." Under this heading come: dissimilation of sounds (*e.g.* the city-name *Bonōnia* > It. *Bologna*, Fr. *Boulogne*)[14]; metathesis, or the interchange of two sounds in their respective positions in a form (as in OIt. *fisolafo* 'philosopher' < *filosafo, filosofo*); haplology, or the loss of one of two successive sounds or syllables (*e.g.* Lat. *nūtrītrīx* 'nurse' > *nūtrīx*). These changes result, for the most part, from the generalisation, through interidiolectal borrowing, of more or less frequent slips of the tongue which spread from one or more individuals to an entire speech-community.

2. The extension of a given feature (of sound, form, or syntactic combi-

nation) from one part of a linguistic structure to another. Such spread is usually termed ANALOGICAL CHANGE. Since it takes place within a particular linguistic structure, it can also be regarded as INTERNAL BORROWING. On the phonological level, the replacement of one phoneme by another, in a given linguistic form, usually takes place under the influence of semantic similarity or contrast. It is often termed CONTAMINATION or CROSSING, symbolised by the mark ✘ written between the two forms involved, as in Lat. /gra·u̯e(m)/ *grāve(m)* 'heavy' ✘ /leu̯e(m)/ *leve(m)* 'light' > PRom. /gréu̯e/ 'heavy'. In some instances, such contamination reflects the re-interpretation of an unfamiliar form or part of a form under the influence of another form with which it has been identified. Such reshapings are often termed "popular etymologies," *e.g.* Fr. /oksipy/ *occiput* 'skull-bone' re-interpreted as /oskipy/ *os qui pue* 'stinking bone',[15] or German (dialectal) /sú·rkrù·t/ 'sauerkraut', reinterpreted as Fr. /šukrut/ *choucroûte* through identification of the first part with /šu/ *chou* 'cabbage' and of the second with /krut/ *croûte* 'crust'.

On the morphological level, single inflectional or derivational forms may be reshaped on the analogy of others (*e.g.* Eng. *arrived* ✘ *drove* > *arrove*, past). Part or all of an entire paradigm may be rehaped, as in the 1.sg. and 2.sg. of the imperfect of Italian verbs, exemplified with a first-conjugation verb (*cantare* 'to sing') in Table II. In the passage from PRom. to OIt., final /-s/ and /-t/ were regularly lost in all positions,[16] and consequently all three persons of the imperfect would have ended in /-va/ in OIt. The 2.sg. had already, by OIt. times, had /-s/ replaced by the more distinctive ending /-i/, from the regular development /-i/ < PRom. /-is/ in the present of verbs of the /i/-stem conjugation, *e.g.* It. /dórmi/ *dormi* 'thou sleepest' < /dórmis/. From the sixteenth century onwards, forms of the 1.sg. imperfect in /-o/, modelled on the distinctive 1.sg. present-tense ending (as in /kánto/ *canto* 'I sing') are more and more frequent, and become part of standard usage in the nineteenth century.

TABLE II

The Imperfect Singular from Proto-Romance to Italian

Meaning	PRom.	OIt.	ModIt.
I was singing	kantába	/kantáva/ *cantava*	†/kantávo/ *cantavo*
thou wast singing	kantábas	†/kantávi/ *cantavi*	/kantávi/ *cantavi*
he was singing	kantábat	/kantáva/ *cantava*	/kantáva/ *cantava*

NOTE: The forms which have been analogically reshaped are preceded by a dagger (†).

In syntactic combinations, likewise, analogical borrowings can lead to the extension of a pattern from one construction to another. Thus, in Italian, one or more procomplements[17] normally follow a positive imperative (*e.g.* /dátemelo/ *datemelo!* 'give it to me!'; but, in earlier usage, they preceded a negative imperative (*e.g.* /nóˆnmelodáte/ *non me lo date!* 'don't give it to me!'). In modern times, however, speakers have been placing the procomplements after negative imperatives as well, on the analogy of their use in this position with the positive imperative: /nóˆndátemelo/ *non datemelo!*.[18]

1.42. NONSTRUCTURAL FACTORS involve primarily the imitation, on the part of users of a given linguistic structure, of patterns which derive from a different variety of speech. Such imitation, for which the term *borrowing* is generally reserved,[19] may perhaps better be termed EXTERNAL borrowing, in contrast to the borrowing within a system which is generally termed ANALOGY (cf. §1.41.2). External borrowing may come from any type of linguistic system, whether closely related, distantly related, or not related at all from the historical point of view. In the case of a very closely related source, the imitation is termed DIALECT-BORROWING, *e.g.* in Spanish /hwérga/ *juerga* 'wild party, spree' from Andalusian, in contrast to /wélga/ *huelga* '(industrial) strike', both from a pre-Spanish */fólga/: */folgar/ < PRom. /follikáre/ 'to bat around aimlessly'.[20] In many instances, such as that just cited, dialectal or other borrowings can give rise to DOUBLETS, pairs of forms deriving from the same ultimate source but having different phonological shape[21] and more or less different meaning.

From languages more distantly related, or not related at all, borrowings usually reflect one type or another of cultural influence. Some scholars[22] divide such borrowing, in general, into "intimate" and more narrowly defined "cultural" subtypes. To the former variety would be assigned borrowings resulting from close symbiosis of two or more speech-communities, as when speakers of Italian in the United States borrowed such terms from American English as /ǧóbba/ < *job*, /štínǧə/ 'miserly' < *stingy*, or (with popular etymology) /olivéˆta/ (which in Italian means 'olive-shaped pearl' < *elevated* (*railroad*)[23]. In the narrow sense, cultural borrowing would reflect less intimate contacts with other speech-communities, and is involved in most transfers of terms from one language to another, *e.g.* Ger. *Blitzkrieg*, Russian *troika*, Span. *tango*, Fr. *comme il faut*, Japanese *kamikaze* 'suicide-pilot', etc., in most modern standard languages. A special case of cultural borrowing is LEARNÈD influence, the taking over of terms from a language which no longer has native speakers and is studied only as a "dead" tongue. For the modern world, Greek and Latin have served for centuries as an almost inexhaustible reservoir for learnèd borrowings, not only of individual words, but also of formative elements which are often

combined to make new expressions, *e.g. tele-* 'far, distant' + *vision* →
television.

The social and political relations involved in external borrowing can be
of any type. Social (including intellectual, artistic, etc.) prestige or political
superiority are often at the base of cultural borrowing, as in the extensive
spread of Italian terminology in the fine arts (*stucco, chiaroscuro*, etc.) and
in military matters (*artiglieria* 'artillery', *capitano* 'captain', *colonnello*
'colonel', etc.) in the Renaissance, and in music (*sonata, cantata; vivace,
andante*, and practically all terms relating to speed and loudness) in the
seventeenth and eighteenth centuries.[24] On the other hand, more favored
groups often borrow terms from less favored, especially to refer to objects
or behavior-patterns with particular characteristics (*e.g.* It. *spaghetti,
pizza, ravioli* in American English, or *guagua* 'Puerto Rican bus' in the
English of Americans living in Puerto Rico).

External borrowings are most frequent on the level of vocabulary: any
word of any language can be imitated by speakers of another language.
How close such a borrowing comes to the phonology of the original, depends on the knowledge that the borrowers have of the source-language.
Borrowing through different channels can lead to different results. Thus,
Eng. *jazz* has been borrowed twice into Italian, once in the 1930's with the
pronunciation /já¢/ based on the interpretation of the spelling according to
the principles of Italian orthography, and a second time in the 1950's as
/ǧés/, with an approximation of American English speech. Syntactic
constructions are often imitated, especially for reasons of prestige, as in
English sequences like *Operation Boot-Straps* (with the modifier following,
not preceding, the noun), *that understands itself* or *that goes without saying*,
or *but certainly!*, all imitated from French. If sufficient forms containing a
derivational element (*e.g.* a prefix or a suffix) are borrowed, the element itself often spreads beyond the words in which it was originally contained.
Thus, Eng. /⁺əǧ/ *-age*, first borrowed in such French loans as *passage,
carriage*, or *homage*, was later extended to such English bases as *spill* or
waste in *spillage, wastage*, etc. Similarly, in seventeenth- and eighteenth-
century French, the suffix /⁺iʃə/ *-ille*, originally a Spanish diminutive-for-
mant /⁺íʃa/ *-illa*, spread from the names of imported cloths based on
names of countries or regions like *brabantille* (: *Brabant*), *hollandille* (: *Hollande*), to new-formations like *écarlatille* 'scarlet cloth' (: *écarlate* 'scarlet')
or *cotonille* 'cotton cloth' (: *coton* 'cotton').[25]

The possibility that external borrowing might be an important factor in
phonological change has been extensively debated. There are at least two
types of situations in which the phonological influence of one language upon
another has been conclusively demonstrated. The first involves the borrowing of so many words from one language into another, introducing a new

sound or a new contrast, that their presence changes the environment in which previous contrasts had functioned. Mexican Spanish has the consonant-cluster /tl-/, unknown in other varieties of Spanish, in a number of words borrowed from Mexican Indian languages, both in place-names like /tlalpán/ *Tlalpán* and in every-day words like /tláko/ *tlaco* 'a coin', /tlapalería/ *tlapalería* 'paint-store'.[26] Before the Norman Conquest, English [f] and [v] were in complementary distribution: [v] occurred only between vowels and [f] elsewhere, forming one phoneme, which could be (and was) written *f* or *v* indiscriminately. The flood of French loan-words containing initial /v-/ (*e.g. very* < OFr. /vərái/ 'true', *vain* < OFr. /váin/ 'empty', etc.) and /-f-/ between vowels (*e.g. offer* < OFr. /ofrír/ *ofrir*) introduced a previously nonexistent contrast between /f/ and /v/.[27]

The other type of situation is that in which speakers of one language give it up in favor of another, but, during the inevitable bilingualism of the transition-period, carry over their previous phonetic habits into their use of the newly acquired phonological system (they "speak with a foreign accent"). If no other models are present, their linguistic descendants imitate what they hear from their predecessors, and continue speaking with the same accent down the generations. It is as such a "relic of a period of bilingualism"[28] that the influence of both sub- and superstratum-languages[29] is to be interpreted.

Change in linguistic behavior under foreign influence can take place, not only in morphology, syntax, and phonology, but also in semantics. A word can undergo a shift in its meaning on the model of an equivalence in another language, as when the Greek noun /ptô·sis/ πτῶσις 'a falling; an inflected form of a noun or adjective' was rendered in Latin grammatical terminology by /ka·sus/ *cāsus*, which had earlier meant only 'a falling'. Similarly, French *réaliser* 'to bring into existence' has, in the mid-twentieth century, undergone a shift of meaning to 'become aware', under the influence of Eng. *realise*. Such a process of reinterpretation is known as a LOANSHIFT, and its result as a CALQUE. On occasion, a newly formed word may consist, in part, of a native term (which often undergoes a loan-shift) and, in part, of a borrowing. The result is a LOAN-BLEND, as in Fr. *bar-serveuse* 'bar-maid', with the first part of the loan-compound kept and with the second part replaced by Fr. *serveuse* 'maid, waitress'.

1.5. The Comparative Method

It has been recognised for centuries (cf. Chapter 11) that languages showing extensive resemblances to each other are to be grouped in "fami-

TABLE III

Sound-Correspondences in Six Romance Morphemes

English Meaning	'sing'	'dog'	'field'	'head'	'meat'	'side'	'earth'
Portuguese	kãtár	kãu	kápu	kábu	kárni	kósta	térra
Castilian	kantár	kán (OSp.)	kámpo	kábo	kárne	kuésta	tiérra
Catalan	kantá	ká	kámp	káp	kárn	kóstə	térrə
OSFr.	kantár	ká(n)	kámp	káp	kárn	kósta	térra
ONFr.	čantǽr	čiǽn	čámp	čiǽf	čárn	kóstə	tér(r)ə
Italian	kantáre	káne	kámpo	kápo	kárne	kósta	térra
Rumanian	kíntá	kí(i)ne	kímpu-	kapu-	kárne	koástə	ɟárə
Sardinian	kantáre	káne	kámpu	kábu	kárre	kósta	térra
PRom.	kantáre	káne	kámpu	kápu	kárne	kósta	térra

lies," and regarded as having developed by successive differentiation out of a common source, for which the term PROTO-LANGUAGE is used. This type of relation is often known by the rather misleading but wide-spread expression GENETIC RELATIONSHIP.[30] Examples of such resemblances are given in Tables III, IV, and V. Note that, to be considered as belonging to the same family, two or more languages must show regular correspondences, not only in sounds or in vocabulary, but in all aspects of linguistic structure[31]:

1. Between sounds, in morphemes having the same meaning or at least having related semantic features;
2. Between inflectional elements having the same or a related grammatical function;
3. Between syntactic combinations with the same or like structures and meanings; and
4. Between a certain number of lexical items of similar meaning.

The reader must not think that such correspondences are always complete or perfect. They can on occasion be overlaid by the effects of analogy or borrowing, so that the actual picture in any given language at any given time can be quite complex. Disagreements can arise as to which development of a given sound is "regular" in a particular area. Thus, in Tuscan we find Latin and PRom. intervocalic voiceless stops (/-p- -t- -k-/) represented by both voiceless stops (as in the past participle endings PRom. /-átu -í^tu -ú^tu/ > Tusc. /-áto -íto -úto/) and voiced stops (in such forms as PRom. /(ụía) stráta/ 'paved road' > Tusc. /stráda/ 'street'). Some scholars maintain that the voiced stops are the "normal" development in Tuscany and that the voiceless stops represent learnèd borrowings from

TABLE IV

The 1.sg. Present-Ending in Three Romance Verbs

English Meaning	'I sing'	'I sleep'	'I sell'
Portuguese	kã́tu	dúrmu	védu
Castilian	kánto	duérmo	béndo
Catalan	kánt	dórm	vén
OSFr.	kánt	dórm	vén
ONFr.	čánt	dór	vént
Italian	kánto	dórmo	vé^ndo
Rumanian	kínt	dórm	vínd
Sardinian	kánto	dórmo	béndo
PRom.	kánto	dórmo	ų̯é^ndo

Latin; others, that the opposite is true, with the voiceless stops having continued as such in popular Tuscan speech since Latin times, and the forms with voiced stops representing North Italian or Gallo-Romance influence.[32] The possibility of such divergent interpretations does not, however, impair the validity of the comparative method itself.[33]

Nor must it be thought that a reconstructed proto-language was of necessity absolutely unified. No language, no dialect, not even any idiolect is wholly consistent or rigid in its structure.[34] Like every other language, a proto-language must be thought of as having inconsistencies and fluctuations between different features, some of which survive in one area and some in another. In the Indo-European languages, for the dative-ablative plural of nouns, some forms point back to an ending /-mos/ and others to /-bhos/

TABLE V

Two Sentence-Types in the Romance Languages

English Meaning	'A	cow	gives	milk'	'it rains'
Portuguese	uma	váka	dá	léiti	šóvi
Castilian	una	báka	dá	léče	ḷučbe
Catalan	unə	vákə	dónə	ḷét	plóu
OSFr.	una	váka	dá	láč	plóu
ONFr.	ynə	váče	dónəθ	láit	pluét
Italian	una	vákka	dá	látte	pióve
Rumanian	o	vákə	dɔ́	lápte	plóу̯ə
Sardinian	una	bákka	dát	látte	pióet
PRom.	una	ų̯ákka	{dát / dó^nat}	lákte	plóу̯et

in the proto-language; likewise, the Proto-IE instrumental plural must be
set up as both /-mis/ and /-bhis/.[35] In Romance, likewise, some forms such
as Ital., Sp. /-ó/ and Port. /-óu/ point back to a stressed diphthong
/áu̯/ in the 3.sg. preterite ending of first-conjugation verbs, whereas Cat.1
Prov., and Fr. /á/ suggest a simple vowel /á/. Such discrepancies, however, are natural, and not to be wondered at.

If two or more languages are similar in only one or two of the respects
mentioned above, they are not necessarily "genetically" related, since
their similarities may have arisen in some other way. Thus, between English
and Spanish, say, there are a number of correspondences in both sound and
meaning in a number of word-groups, *e.g. constitution* and Sp. *constitución*,
destitution and Sp. *destitución*, *institution* and Sp. *institución*, etc. Nevertheless, the inflectional and syntactic systems of English and Spanish are quite
different from each other. We must recognise that the two languages do not
come from an immediate common source,[36] and that the similarities between groups of words such as those listed above must be due to some other
cause. In this case, we can easily identify Eng. *constitution*, Sp. *constitución*
and other words having a similar structure as learnèd borrowings from
Latin.

In the case of the Romance languages, however, all four requirements
listed above are met (not excluding deviations and interferences, as we have
noted), as shown in the sample items listed in Tables III, IV, and V. We
therefore conclude that they must belong to the same family, and have been
differentiated from a common source. For most language-families, the common source, as reconstructed by scholars, lies too far back in time for us
to have written attestations of either the proto-language itself or a variety
of speech which was close to it.[37] Our reconstructed PRom., however,
proves to be quite close to (though not identical with) Latin, of which we
have extensive attestations. These are almost all written in a socially and
intellectually prestigious variety of Latin, which was highly polished, with
a complicated structure (especially in syntax) that was rather different
from that of every-day speech. It is this latter, not the literary Classical
Latin, which was the source of the Romance languages. Our Proto-Romance, as reconstructed on the basis of what has survived into later centuries, is therefore a composite of various features of popular Latin, and
(if we insist on using kinship-terms in a metaphorical sense) a "sister,"
not a "daughter" of Classical Latin.

It is never possible to set exact dates for particular stages of language-
development (cf. note 29). However, the features which we must ascribe
to Proto-Romance place it in the period between ca. 100 B.C. and A.D. 0.
We must set PRom. before the period in which the merger of lax /i/ and
tense /eˆ/, lax /u/ and tense /oˆ/[38] took place, hence before the first century

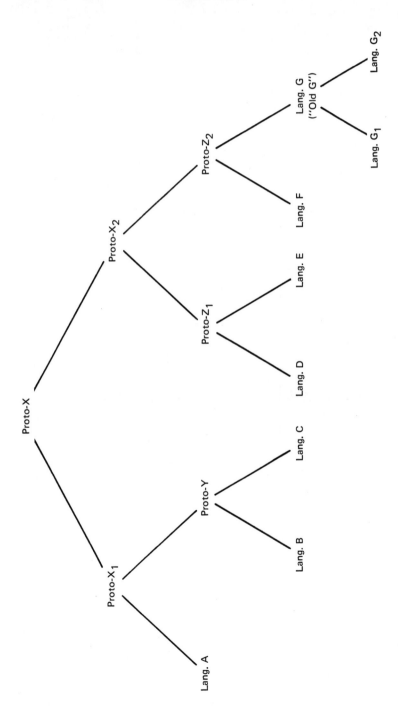

FIG. I. A typical (abstract) family-tree diagram.

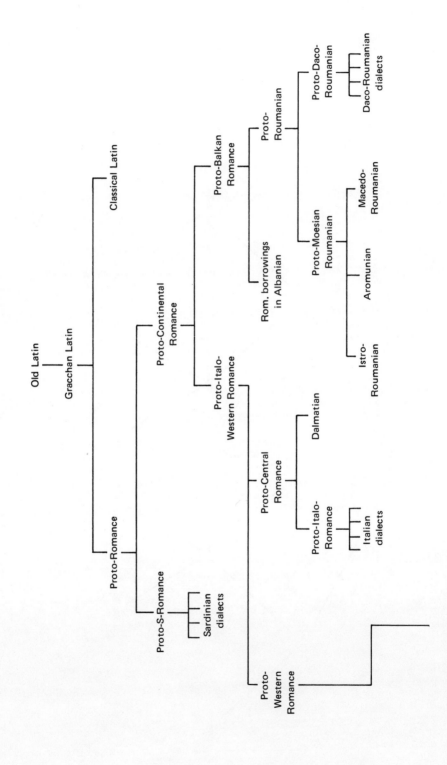

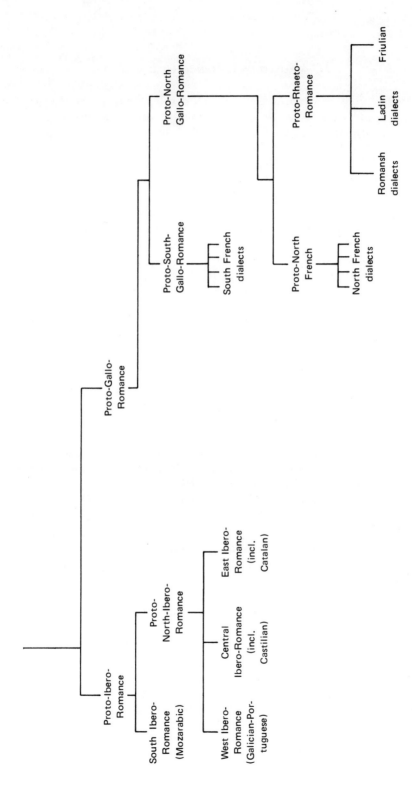

FIG. II. Family-tree of the Romance languages. (Cf. also Chapter 2)

A.D.[39] On the other hand, it is after such developments as the change of Old Latin intervocalic /-s-/ to /-r-/ ("rhotacism," fourth century B.C.[40]) and the monophthongisation of /ei/ to /i·/ and of /ou/ to /u·/, which was completed at about 170–150 B.C.[41] The common ancestor of PRom. and Classical Latin might well be placed in the middle of the second century B.C. This approximate date accords well with what is known concerning the separation of classical literary usage from every-day informal speech,[42] which at the time of the brothers Gracchi (Tiberius, 163–133 B.C., and Caius, 153–122 B.C.) had not yet become as sharp as it was later.[43] For lack of a better term, and assuming that the Gracchi would have used such a kind of Latin in their ordinary speech, especially in addressing their fellow-citizens, we might refer to it as GRACCHAN LATIN (GrL).

1.6. The Reconstruction of Proto-Romance

In many instances, we do not have direct attestations of either a reconstructed proto-language or the intermediate stages of differentiation. This is the case, not only with Indo-European and such of its branches as Germanic, Keltic or Slavic, but even with Romance. The wide-spread opinion that it is not necessary to reconstruct a Proto-Romance because we already have ample attestations of Latin[44] is unjustified. The Romance languages point back (as can be seen in the sample PRom. forms given in Tables II through V in this chapter) to a common source-language which was clearly close to, but by no means identical with, the standard form of Classical Latin. In the process of differentiation, the dialects of various regions developed out of common intermediate "ancestral" stages. This process is often represented, very schematically, in a "Stammbaum" or "family-tree," of the type shown in Figure I.

Such a "family-tree' can and must be reconstructed for Romance.[45] The ideal procedure would be,[46] if time, funds and man-power were available, to start with all the modern standard languages and dialects of the various regions, and to work backwards to the reconstruction, first of each intermediate stage (e.g. Proto-Ibero-Romance, Proto-Gallo-Romance, etc.) and then still further backwards, ending with Proto-Romance itself. Since this is a virtually Utopian program, a first approximation thereto can be reached by using the earliest attested stages of the various languages, with whatever further relevant data can be adduced from modern dialects. With such a procedure, we can set up the rough scheme of relationships for the Romance languages shown in Figure II.

Several caveats need to be entered here, in view of possible misunderstandings:

1. The intermediate stages set up in the form of "nodes" in a "family-tree-diagram" must not be taken to represent sharply distinct "états de langue," even if one believes in the existence of these latter.[47] Such nodes represent only abstract points of division, and may actually stand for periods lasting one or two hundred years or more, with various changes going on during such periods.

2. Neither the intermediate stages nor the ultimate Proto-Romance, as reconstructed, are to be thought of as wholly unified, without any dialectal variation (such as exists at all times, in all languages; cf. §1.5).

3. On many occasions, a form may be considered as having existed in a given stage, because of its presence in related forms of Romance or of Classical or Old Latin. Often, conclusions of this type are reached on the basis of argumentation "over the top," as when we set up a seven-vowel pattern for Old Italian (even though the rhyme-schemes of Old and Modern Italian recognise only five vowels), because we find a contrast between lax /é/ and tense /é^/, lax /ó/ and tense /ó^/, in modern Italian and also in Provençal, Catalan, and Portuguese, in words cognate with those having similar vowels in modern Italian.

4. We must not equate reconstructed Proto-Romance with "Vulgar Latin" nor even with Popular Latin as a whole (cf. §4.32). Proto-Romance is to be defined very strictly as that which can be reconstructed on the evidence furnished by the Romance languages. It unquestionably represents a congeries of features of Popular Latin, not all of which necessarily existed at the same time or in the same place, and which certainly did not form a cohesive "état de langue." Nevertheless, the degree of realism obtainable in reconstructing Proto-Romance, when we compare it with what is known of Latin from other sources (perhaps 95% in phonology, 80% in morphology, 70% in syntax, and 80% or more in basic vocabulary) gives us some basis for interpreting our success in reconstructing other protolanguages such as Proto-Indo-European.[48]

NOTES TO CHAPTER 1

1. The adjectives *Romanic* and *Neo-Latin* are also occasionally used as alternatives to *Romance*. The first-mentioned has the advantage of parallelism to such other names of language-families as *Germanic* and *Slavic*; the second, that of emphasising the fact that the languages involved are the modern continuators of Latin. Both avoid any possible confusion with the noun *romance* 'story, tale; love-affair'. Nevertheless, the use of

Romance, referring to this family of languages, is so wide-spread that it would be futile to attempt to dislodge it.

2. Virtually all works on the development of individual Romance languages devote one or more chapters to the external history of the language in question (cf. references Chapter 2). The external history of the Romance languages as a whole is treated by Groult 1947; Tagliavini 1947; Vidos 1956; Elcock 1960; Posner 1966; Bal 1966; Bec 1970. For more general treatment of linguistic history cf. Sturtevant 1917; Sapir 1921, Chapters 7–9; Jespersen 1922, chapters 16–21; Bloomfield 1933, chapters 18–27; Hockett 1958, chapters 42–62; W. Ph. Lehmann 1962; Hall 1964, chapters 46–66. King 1969 and Kiparsky 1970 have nothing of any value to contribute.

3. For the history of the study of language since ancient times, cf. Steinthal 1863; Robins 1951, 1967; Leroy 1963; Tagliavini 1963; Waterman 1963; Ivić 1965.

4. Set forth at greater length and in more detail in Hall 1968b.

5. Cf. Hall, forthcoming-d.

6. This statement is not to be taken as implying that all writing necessarily represents features of sound. Chinese characters stand for morphemes abstracted from their sound, as do such conventional signs as £ (= *pound* in English, *lira* in Italian) or & (= *and* in English, *et* in Latin, etc.). In many alphabetical systems, some letters stand, not for single phonemes, but for morphophonemic alternations, as do Italian *c* and *g* (= /č ǧ/, respectively, before *e* and *i*, and /k g/ elsewhere; cf. Hall 1971:63–64). In others, looseness of fit between grapheme and phoneme is used to distinguish between two or more homonymous morphemes, *e.g.* Fr. *cet* 'this (m.sg.)', *cette* 'this (f.sg.)', *Cette* or *Sète* 'a town in southern France', *sept* 'seven', and *Seth* 'a man's name', all standing for the sequence of phonemes /set/. None of these phenomena contradicts the basic principle that written forms are representations of one feature or another of spoken forms.

7. Reproduced from Hall 1964:31.

8. Cf. Martinet 1960 (1964), chapter 1.8.

9. Cf. Hall 1968b, chapter 5.

10. This distinction was formulated most rigidly by de Saussure 1916. In its Saussurean form it has given rise to endless and mostly futile debates. More recent discussions (*e.g.* von Wartburg 1943) have tended to emphasise the compatibility of the synchronic and diachronic approaches.

11. Cf. Hall 1965:337–338, 341.

12. Cf. our discussion in §11.5, and references given there.

13. Cf. Hall 1969d.

14. Cf. Grammont 1895; Posner 1961; Togeby 1963/64.

15. Metathesis is also present in this example; cf. Nyrop 1899–1930:1.§533.1.

16. Many scholars maintain that /-as/ and /-es/ > OIt. /-i/ by phonological change, but this view is certainly wrong; cf. Hall 1961/62.

17. That is, unstressed pronouns and similar enclitic forms which take the place of certain types of phrases introduced by prepositions, and of predicate complements; cf. Hall 1952.

18. Cf. Hall 1971:162, fn. 20.

19. Thus virtually all writers on general linguistics, *e.g.* Sapir, Bloomfield, Hockett (cf. fn. 2); but cf. Hall 1964, chapter 54.

20. Cf. Corominas 1954–57:2, 930–932.

21. Which, without the principle of regular phonetic change, it would not be possible to identify as coming from one dialect as opposed to another. Tolomei, in the passage quoted in §11.2, clearly recognised the existence of doublets and identified them on the basis of the phonological developments involved.

22. For example, Bloomfield 1933, chapters 25–27.

23. Examples from Menarini 1947a, chapter 6 ("Sull'italo-americano degli Stati Uniti").

24. Cf. Migliorini 1960:424–428, 495–496, 582–583.

25. Cf. Höfler 1968.

26. It has been pointed out that, even now, /tl-/ occurs only in words of Mexican Indian origin; but this does not invalidate the observation that, for the ordinary speaker of Mexican Spanish, this cluster is a part of his every-day activity on the phonological level.

27. Cf. Hockett 1958:410.

28. Cf. Moulton 1941, especially 19–20; Hall 1949b, 1950b.

29. For these terms, cf. our discussion in §11.6.

30. Cf. the remarks of Nyrop 1899–1930:1.3: "Il n'y a pas de langues filles ni de langues mères: le langage humain va sans cesse en se modifiant, et les transformations se succèdent ordinairement avec une très grande lenteur, sans qu'on puisse séparar nettement les états successifs du développement [. . .]. Aussi est-il impossible de fixer une époque précise où cesse le latin et où commence le français: comme il n'y a eu ni changement subit ni brusque 'dégénération', une telle époque n'existe pas."

31. Adapted from Kent 1932:15.

32. For these two divergent view-points, cf. Urciolo 1965 and Rohlfs 1967b, respectively.

33. Cf. Hockett 1948:125–127.

34. Cf. Hall 1950a:7, fn. 8, and 1964:15–16, 284–288; Hockett 1968, especially chapter 4.

35. Cf. Buck 1933:172–174.

36. They are indeed to be traced to an ultimate common source, Proto-Indo-European, but through different intermediate channels. English is a Germanic language, and Spanish is Romance; the "ancestral" forms of these two groups belonged to the same family. Cf. Buck 1933 or any other manual of Indo-European comparative linguistics.

37. The Old Germanic runic inscription on the horn discovered at Gallehus is, as has often been pointed out (cf. Bloomfield 1933:305–306), very close to our reconstructed Proto-Germanic—perhaps as close as Proto-Romance is to attested Latin.

38. Corresponding to Classical Latin short /i/, long /e:/, short /u/ and long /o:/, respectively.

39. Cf. Väänänen 1963:36–37.

40. Cf. Kent 1932:132–134.

41. Cf. Kent 1932:90–91; Väänänen 1963:38.

42. Cf. Pulgram 1950.

43. As suggested by Devoto's felicitous phrasing "lingua letteraria come derivazione e non come contrapposizione alla lingua parlata" (Devoto 1936, title of chapter 4:7).

44. As suggested by Pei 1965 and many others.

45. Cf. the programmatic statements in Hall 1950a, to which I still adhere unrepentantly, despite such criticisms as those of Roncaglia 1950.

46. As suggested by Trager 1946:463.

47. As I, for one, do not (cf. Hall 1968b).

48. Nineteenth- and twentieth-century criticisms of "rekonstruirtes Phantasielatein" (the term used by Seelmann 1890) are hardly valid, since many such reconstructed forms have later turned up in new attestations.

CHAPTER 2

The Romance Languages and Their Distribution

2.0. The Romance Languages

The Romance languages are a group of related languages (§1.5) which have developed out of popular Latin speech. From being the language of a small area perhaps twenty-five miles in radius around Rome and the Alban Hills, Latin came to be used throughout the Mediterranean basin and surrounding regions, under the late Roman Republic and the Empire. In the past two millennia, and especially since the fifteenth century, the Romance languages have become markedly (though for the most part gradually) differentiated, and have spread to all parts of the world.[1]

The distribution of the Romance languages is best treated under four heads: (1) NATIVE use; (2) OFFICIAL use; (3) use as LINGUE FRANCHE; and (4) use in PIDGINISED and CREOLISED forms. Under the first heading come those situations in which an entire population, or a majority thereof, use a given language in their every-day relations in the region where they are permanently settled, and pass it on to their children as the latter's first language. Under a subdivision of this heading comes the use of a language by emigrant groups, in linguistic "enclaves." If a language is used only in the nonintimate relationships (*e.g.* governmental, bureaucratic, educational, commercial) of a region, and only by a relatively small proportion of the population (whether natively or not), its use can be called OFFICIAL. A *lingua franca* (pl. *lingue franche*) is any language used in common by people of different linguistic back-grounds, whether it be native to any of them or not, as was French in eighteenth- and nineteenth-century diplomacy.[2] In some instances, a language is greatly reduced in both lexicon and grammatical structure, and is used as a lingua franca between speakers to none of whom it is native; such a language is a PIDGIN. If a pidgin comes to be native to a population (*e.g.* of slaves or of plantation-workers of different linguistic back-grounds living together with no common language except a pidgin), it becomes a CREOLE, and is said to be CREOLISED.

Scholars are not agreed on the exact number of Romance languages to be

21

recognised, nor on their classification. In general, the criteria for distinguishing LANGUAGE from DIALECT are not sure.[3] They normally include not only major dialectal boundaries (bundles of isoglosses), but also the existence of an orthographical system ("is it a written language?"), of a standard literary or national variety of usage, of school-grammars and dictionaries, and of language-academies. Both the "man-in-the-street" and many scholars, particularly in Romance-speaking countries, are inclined to follow the folk-lore of our Western European culture in ascribing the status of "language" only to those types of speech which manifest the prestigeful features just mentioned. Here, without regard to social standing, we shall discuss the use of the present and past forms of the Romance languages under each of the headings listed at the beginning of the preceding paragraph, proceeding in each instance from the western end of the Mediterranean (Portuguese-Galician) to the eastern end (Roumanian).

2.1. Native Use

2.11. IBERO-ROMANCE. Under this heading come the languages and dialects of the Iberian peninsula, chiefly Portuguese-Galician, Spanish, and Catalan.[4]

2.111. WESTERN. This group is known collectively as Portuguese-Galician, with its home-territory in present-day Portugal and in Galicia (directly north of Portugal).[5] Portuguese is also used natively in various present or former colonies of Portugal.

    1. Standard languages with a Western Ibero-Romance base are:
    a. Galician, which is linguistically very close to Portuguese and shares with it many characteristic developments (*e.g.* the loss of intervocalic PRom. /-l-/ and /-n-/). The orthography of Galician is based chiefly on that of Spanish, using, for instance, *ll* for /ļ/ and *ñ* for /ņ/, as in /fiļa/ *filla* 'daughter' (Port. *filha*), or /báņu/ *baño* 'bath' (Port. *banho*). Galician is used as a literary language only in Galicia itself.[6]
    b. Portuguese, based on the speech of central Portugal, *i.e.* the territory from Coimbra to Lisbon. It is used in two varieties, which differ only slightly from each other:
        i. Peninsular, in present-day Portugal and its colonies (*e.g.* the Azores, Madeira, Cabo Verde, Portuguese East and West Africa, Macao).[7]
        ii. Brazilian, in most parts of Brazil.[8]
The orthographies of Peninsular and Brazilian Portuguese have, since the

establishment of Brazil as an independent country in 1822, been slightly different from each other, but repeated official decrees have brought the two countries' spelling-systems closer in recent decades.[9]

2. The dialects of Western Ibero-Romance[10] are divided into:

a. Northern, including the Galician subvarieties[11] and those of northern Portugal: Tras-os-Montes,[12] and the dialects of the Entre-Duoro-e-Minho (known as "interamnenses"): Minhoto alto, Minhoto baixo, Durience alto, and Duriense baixo.[13]

b. Central, with the dialect of Beira (Beirão),[14] that of Estremadura,[15] and that of the Lisbon area.

c. Southern, with the dialect of the region immediately south of the Tagus (the Alemtejo or "beyond the Tagus") and that of the Algarve (southernmost Portugal).[16]

d. Extra-peninsular varieties include:

i. Insular (European) Portuguese, in Madeira[17] and the Azores.[18]

ii. Overseas Portuguese, but in general as an official language (cf. §2.21) or in pidginised or creolised form (§2.41).

Dialectal varieties of "full-sized" Portuguese are spoken natively by some groups in former colonies in India (e.g. Goa, Diu, Daman) and widely in Brazil. In the last-mentioned country, there is variation over a wide spectrum between local dialects and the regional standard; the greatest dialectal differentiation is found in the North-East,[19] but there are also marked variants in Rio Grande do Sul[20] and in Rio de Janeiro ("carioca" dialect).[21] There are scattered enclaves of Portuguese settlers in North America, especially in Fall River (Mass.) and neighboring regions.[22]

2.112. CENTRAL. In this group, during the Middle Ages, Castilian, Leonese, Leonese, and Asturian were nearly equal in prestige. Since the Reconquista and Renaissance, the speech of New Castile and especially of Madrid[23] has come to be the dominant variety.

1. The standard language, Spanish,[24] based on modern Castilian, is used in Spain and in virtually all present or former Spanish colonies, in two chief varieties:

a. Peninsular Spanish, for which the term *castellano* 'Castilian' is often reserved,[25] with certain conservative features, especially the preservation of the contrasts between /θ/ and /s/ in such words as /θiénto/ *ciento* '100' vs. /siénto/ *siento* 'I feel', and between /ḷ/ and /j/ in such words as /káḷe/ *calle* 'street' vs. /májo/ *Mayo* 'May'. The use of /θ/ in a word like *ciento* is known as "ceceo"; that of /ḷ/ in a word like *calle*, as "lleísmo".

b. American Spanish,[26] used in most parts of Spanish-speaking America. Normal American Spanish merges /θ/ with /s/ and /ḷ/ with /j/: both *ciento* and *siento* are, therefore /siénto/, *calle* is /káje/, and *Mayo* is

/májo/. The merger of /θ/ with /s/ is termed "seseo"; that of /ĺ/ with /j/, "yeismo".[27]

2. Dialects[28] likewise fall into two main groups: peninsular, including those of the islands near Europe, and extrapeninsular, primarily American.

    a. The peninsular dialects fall into the following approximate divisions:

        i. North-eastern, *i.e.* Aragonese and Navarrese[29];
        ii. Northern and north-western, in the Asturias[30];
        iii. Central, including Leonese[31] and Castilian[32];
        iv. Southern,[33] including Murcian[34] and Andalusian[35];
        v. Western, including Extremaduran[36];
        vi. Insular[37];
        vii. Judaeo-Spanish or "Ladino," the continuator of the Spanish of the Jews expelled from Spain in 1492, as spoken at present in various localities in eastern Europe,[38] northern Africa,[39] and in enclaves in North America.[40]

    b. Extra-peninsular, chiefly American Spanish,[41] spoken in:

        i. The Caribbean islands (Greater Antilles: Puerto Rico[42] [with large numbers of speakers of Puerto Rican Spanish in the New York City area], Santo Domingo,[43] and Cuba[44]);
        ii. Central America, with subvarieties in Mexico[45] (including regions of the United States formerly part of Mexico[46]) and the countries south-east of Mexico[47];
        iii. South America,[48] with subvarieties in the individual countries[49];
        iv. The Philippines, where Spanish is spoken natively together with one of the local languages, by some upper-class families in a bilingual situation.

2.113. Eastern, known collectively as Catalan-Valencian, and spoken in Catalonia and neighboring areas of France (Roussillon) and Spain (the region of Valencia); in the Balearic Isles; and in the city of Alghero (Sardinia). Everywhere that Catalan is spoken, there prevails a diglossic situation, with standard Castilian (§2.112.1.*a*) as official language in territories belonging to Spain, and with Italian as the official language and Sardinian in the surrounding regional speech in Alghero. The most outstanding characteristic of Catalan-Valencian is the development of PRom. initial /l-/ to /ĺ-/, as in /ĺéngua/ *llengua* 'tongue' < /língua/. The position of Catalan with respect to Ibero- and Gallo-Romance has long been a topic of debate[50]: current opinion assigns it to the former group, though with extensive influence from the latter.

1. The standard language, Catalan, is based primarily on the usage of the capital of Catalonia, Barcelona, with certain features of Barcelonese

phonology such as the merger of earlier unstressed /a/ and /e/ in /ə/, e.g. /ənrérə/ enrera 'back'. Slightly differing standards are recognized for Catalan proper[51] and for Valencian[52]; writers from the Balearic Isles will on occasion introduce local features of their own.

2. Dialects[53] fall into four main groups:

a. Northern peninsular, or Catalan-Rossillonese,[54] including the dialect of Andorra[55];

b. Southern peninsular, or Valencian[56];

c. Balearic, spoken in Mallorca[57] and Minorca[58] and neighbouring lesser islands.

d. Algherese, spoken by a relatively small community of Catalan fishermen in the city of Alghero.[59]

2.12. GALLO-ROMANCE includes principally the varieties of Romance spoken in ancient Gaul (modern France).[60] In present-day France, non-Romance tongues are spoken in the south-west (Basque, in the western Pyrenees), in the peninsula of Brittany (Breton, a Keltic language), in an area near the extreme western end of the Franco-Belgian frontier (Flemish) and in parts of Lorraine and Alsace (dialects of German). In Roussillon (extreme eastern end of the Pyrenees), a dialect of Catalan is spoken (§ˇ2.113.2.*a*). Varieties of Gallo-Romance are also spoken in the upper reaches of Piedmontese valleys adjacent to the French frontier in Italy; in French-speaking Switzerland; and in overseas territories, particularly present or former French colonies. Some[61] would include the Rhaeto-Romance languages of Switzerland and northern Italy as part of the Gallo-Romance group.

All scholars recognize a bipartite division in Gallo-Romance, into South French (Provençal) and North French. Most also recognize a third area, in the east-central part of France and in French-speaking Switzerland, usually termed Franco-Provençal.[62]

2.121. SOUTH FRENCH has had three standard varieties, at different stages in its history, and a number of dialects.

1. Of the standard varieties, one was widely used in the Middle Ages, and the other two have arisen in modern times:

a. Old Provençal[63] was the language which the mediaeval troubadour poets used in their lyrics,[64] and was also used by other writers, from the tenth through the fourteenth centuries.[65] After the prosperity of southern France was destroyed in the religious wars of the first half of the thirteenth century, Old Provençal continued to be used as a literary language for a hundred or so more years, but had gone almost wholly out of use by the fifteenth century.

   b. Modern Provençal has had two main standard varieties[66]:

     i. That of the lower Rhône valley and the French Riviera, used extensively in the early part of the nineteenth century by such writers as Jacques Jasmin (1798–1864) and Joseph Roumanille (1818–1891) and rendered best known through the works of Frédéric Mistral (1830–1914) *Mirèio* (1859) and his associates and followers, known as the "Félibriges".[67] This variety, often called "Mistralien," is still used by many modern Provençal authors, but many others, especially those from parts of southern France other than the Rhône valley, have rejected it in favor of

     ii. "Occitan," a somewhat different variety with its base in the usage of Languedoc.[68] Much, but not all, of the difference between "Mistralien" and "Occitan" lies in orthographical details: for instance, the former uses -*o* and the latter uses -*a* to represent final /-a/ [aˑˆ]; in the former, the phonemes /ļ/ and /ŋ/ are spelled (*i*)*ll* and *gn*, respectively, whereas in the latter, they are written *lh* and *nh* (intentionally harking back to Old Provençal orthography).

  Both of these varieties are used only for bellettristic purposes, and largely by small, specialised groups of enthusiasts; the normal standard language throughout southern France is modern French (cf. §2.123).

  2. Local dialects include the following:

    a. "Provençal" in the narrow sense, extending from Menton and Monaco along the Riviera and in the Alpine region north thereof, through the Marseilles region and into the lower Rhone valley[69];

    b. Languedocien, spoken to the west of Nímes, in the valley of the Aude and including the speech of Toulouse, the eastern Pyrenees (with the exception of Roussillon), and the Tarn region north of the Aude valley[70];

    c. Auvergnat, spoken in the region of Auvergne, the Gévaudan, and the Cévennes mountains[71];

    d. Limousin, in the Limoges area, and the related dialects of the Marche (to the north of Limoges) and Périgord[72];

    e. Gascon, in the western part of the Pyrenees and the territory north thereof, extending to the Garonne river.[73] Gascon shows certain markedly distinctive features (*e.g.* the development of PRom. /-ll-/ > /-t/ in final position, as in /béllu/ 'beautiful' > /bét/), so that some have wished to set it up as a separate variety, distinct from the other South French dialects.

2.122. Franco-Provençal is usually defined by the divergence of one pair of isoglosses.[74] It is considered to be the area in which PRom. /á/ is raised or diphthongised in a free syllable after a palatal (*e.g.* /mandukáre/

'to eat' > /mangié/, /mangí/ or the like), but remains unchanged in a free syllable after a nonpalatal (*e.g.* /mánu/ 'hand' > /má(n)/). There is no standard or literary language based on Franco-Provençal. Its subvarieties include:

1. Forézien, or the language of the Forez, including that of Saint-Étienne[75];
2. Lyonnais, used in Lyon and the surrounding area, and the dialects of the near-by Mâcon, Doubs, and Jura regions[76];
3. Dauphinois, spoken in the Dauphiné and Haute Savoie[77];
4. The dialects of the Suisse Romande,[78] or French-speaking Switzerland. The boundary between French and German in Switzerland has been gradually moving westward, in favor of the latter.[79] Individual varieties in the Suisse Romande area include those of the regions of Geneva,[80] Neuchâtel,[81] and Fribourg[82]; the canton of Vaud[83]; and that of Valais.[84]
5. Franco-Provençal dialects spoken in the upper reaches of certain Piedmontese valleys, notably the Val d'Aosta.[85]

2.123. NORTH FRENCH
1. The standard variety of North French has, ever since the Middle Ages, been based on "Francien," *i.e.* the speech of Paris and the surrounding region in the Middle Seine valley known as the Île de France.[86] At first limited to this area in the Old French period,[87] it has spread to the rest of France and is at present the only variety recognised as standard-setting for French usage in general. There are, in actual fact, regional varieties of standard French in metropolitan France, with characteristics carried over from the local dialects on which it has been superimposed (*e.g.* South French /Vn/ where North French has /Ṽ/). Due, however, to strong puristic insistence on a single invariable norm, that of upper-class Parisian usage (especially as codified by the Académie Française[88]), regional standards have not been extensively studied.[89] Jewish communities in the Middle Ages used a slightly different variety, which often casts light on Old French developments.[90]
2. North French dialects[91] have almost wholly disappeared in the area around Paris, where, however, urban speech has developed characteristics of its own.[92] In the out-lying regions of Northern France, the following dialects are still more or less alive:

a. Berrichon, in the Berry region north of the Massif Central[93];
b. Poitevin, in the area of Poitou[94];
c. Saintongeais, in the Saintonge, north of Bordeaux[95];

    d. Vendéen, in the Vendée region in the lower Loire basin[96];

    e. Western French dialects, of Upper Brittany and the Maine[97];

    f. Norman, spoken in Normandy, along the coast and inland on either side of the mouth of the Seine,[98] and in the Channel Islands[99];

    g. Picard, the dialect of Picardy, to the north and east of Normandy[100];

    h. Walloon, spoken principally in the French-language are of Belgium[101];

    j. Lorrain, spoken in the province of Lorraine[102];

    k. Franche-Comté and the upper Saône valley.[103]

    3. Canadian French dialects[104] are spoken, not only in the main area of the lower St. Lawrence valley and the province of Québec, but also in regions to which French Canadians have emigrated, especially Western Canada and New England.[105] The speech of present-day Acadia is rather different from that of the rest of French-speaking Canada.[106]

    4. In the Mississippi valley, French is still spoken in parts of Missouri.[107]

    5. In Louisiana, French is spoken natively by two groups of speakers: those who use the provincial standard,[108] and the "Cajuns" or "Acadians," descendants of the population that was deported from Acadia in 1755.[109] In addition, a third, creolised variety is spoken by members of the Negro population (cf. §2.43.1.*a*).

2.124. RHAETO-ROMANCE tongues[110] are spoken in three separate territories, to the dialect-groups of which are given three different names:

    1. Romansh,[111] in the Grisons region of Switzerland and part of the Ticino, with four main varieties:

        a. Surselvan, in the "Vorderrhein" area above Chur[112];

        b. Sotselvan, in the "Hinterrhein" area[113];

        c. The dialects of the Engadine, divided into "upper" and "lower," in the Inn valley and adjacent regions[114];

        d. In the Ticino, the dialect of the upper Val Bregaglia.[115]

    The several Romansh varieties have been used fairly extensively for literary purposes since the sixteenth century; no such use has been made of

    2. Ladin, spoken in several valleys which open off to the east and the west of the Ãdige (Etsch) river in South Tyrol.[116]

    3. Friulian, spoken in the valley of the Tagliamento river in northeastern Italy, has been used since the Middle Ages as a literary language. At present, the situation is similar to that prevailing in

southern France (§2.121.1), with almost all the population at least bilingual in Friulian and either Venetian or Italian, or (often) trilingual.[117]

2.13. ITALO-ROMANCE, as its name implies, is the ensemble of Romance varieties spoken in Italy, and also in Corsica and Sicily.[118]

1. The Italian literary language, an out-growth of fourteenth-century Tuscan, and more specifically Florentine, is used throughout Italy and its political dependencies.[119] In recent years, the formerly dominant Tuscanising purism has largely yielded before a wave of influence from the dialects, effected largely by neorealism in the cinema and by television; this situation has given rise to extensive popular and scholarly interest in the relation between standard language and dialect.[120]

2. The Italian dialects[121] fall into three main groups:

  a. Northern,[122] with the following divisions:

    i. Piedmontese, spoken in Piedmont, with the exception of the Provençal- and Franco-Provençal-speaking Alpine valleys (§2.121, 2.122)[123];

    ii. Lombard, spoken in the Italian region of Lombardy and the adjacent Ticino canton of Switzerland[124];

    iii. Ligurian, used in the territory east and west of Genoa along the Riviera, and in the mountain hinterland[125];

    iv. Venetian, spoken not only in the city of Venice, but in the area of the Tre Venezie: Venezia Eugànea westward to Verona, southward to the Po, and eastward to the border of the Friuli[126]; Venezia Tridentina, in the Adige valley and neighbouring mountain regions to north of Trent[127]; and Venezia Giulia, east of the Friuli, and including Trieste[128];

    v. Emilian, spoken from the region of Piacenza to that of Ravenna, and between the Po and the Adriatic and the Apennines, in the territories of Emilia[129] and Romagna[130].

During the Middle Ages, a number of groups of emigrants left northern Italy to settle in the south, where their descendants still speak dialects with markedly North Italian characteristics, especially in certain villages in Lucania[131] and Sicily.[132]

  b. Central,[133] south of a heavy bundle of isoglosses running from west to east through the central Apennines from approximately La Spezia to the region of Rìmini. The main Central Italian dialects are:

    i. Marchigiano, spoken in the Marche, on the Adriatic side of the Apennines from approximately Rìmini to south of Ancona[134];

    ii. Tuscan, the dialect of Tuscany, from the Apennines southward to the region of Grosseto and Monte Amiata, and eastward to Arezzo[135];

    iii. Corsican, the local speech of the country-side in Corsica and still of a number of urban residents, although the official language has been French since 1768[136];

    iv. Umbrian, in the central Tiber valley[137];

    v. The dialects of Latium, on either side of Rome in the lower Tiber valley,[138] including the speech of Rome itself.[139]

    c. Southern,[140] extending from the Tiber valley through the east central (Abruzzi) and southern parts of the Italian peninsula, and including Sicily, with the following major dialectal areas:

    i. Abruzzese, in the regions of the Abruzzi and the Molise, along the central Adriatic coast of Italy[141];

    ii. Campanian, in the region of Campania, around and in back of Naples[142];

    iii. Apulian, in the "heel" of Italy, including the Salento peninsula[143];

    iv. Lucanian, in the Basilicata or Lucania, in the "ankle-bone" of Italy, with Potenza as its center[144];

    v. Calabrian, in the "toe" of Italy (Calabria)[145];

    vi. Sicilian, on the island of Sicily.[146]

    3. There are a number of Italian-speaking linguistic enclaves in overseas regions. In general, given the low socio-economic status of the greater part of the Italian emigrants, these "islands" manifest various mixtures of (chiefly southern) dialectal characteristics. They are found primarily in:

    a. North America, in various American cities and in Toronto, Ontario[147];

    b. South America, particularly in the River Plate region (Uruguay and Argentina)[148];

    c. Australia, chiefly in the larger cities.[149]

    4. Judaeo-Italian, now dying out, has been attested in some mediaeval documents, and in scattered remnants in modern Italian dialects.[150] It is most alive, perhaps, at Livorno (Leghorn).[151]

2.14. Sardinian, spoken on the island of Sardinia, was formerly regarded as simply an aberrant dialect of Italian, but is now universally recognised to be an independent variety of Romance.[152] There is no single standard variety of Sardinian, although literary efforts have been made in several of its dialects; it is therefore to be considered an "L-complex," in Hockett's terminology.[153] Its main dialectal subdivisions are:

    1. Central, the most conservative variety, also known as Logudorese

(from one of the regions of the center of Sardinia, the Logudoro), in which, for instance, PRom. lax /í/ has remained as such instead of merging with /é^/, and PRom. /k g/ have retained their occlusive articulation before front vowels (*e.g.* in /píske/ 'fish' < PRom. /píske/, Lat. /piske(m)/; /kélu/ 'heaven' < PRom. /kélu/, Lat. /kaelu(m)/; /gélu/ 'cold' < PRom. /gélu/, Lat. /gelu(m)/).[154]

    2. Southern, including the region of Càgliari and the Gennargentu[155]

    3. Northern, including the region of Sâssari and the Gallura.[156]

2.15. ROUMANIAN, spoken in Roumania and in numerous smaller linguistic enclaves throughout the Balkans. There are two standard languages based on varieties of Roumanian, and four major dialectal groups.

    1. Standard languages are:

        a. Roumanian, based on the Muntenian variety (spoken in the region of Bucureşti) and used as the official language of Roumania itself[157];

        b. Moldavian, based on the variety spoken in the parts of Bessarabia ceded to the U.S.S.R. after the Second World War, and set up by the government of that country as a separate "language," written in an adaptation of the Cyrillic alphabet.[158]

    2. The four dialect-groups[159] of Roumanian are:

        a. Daco-Roumanian, spoken within the territory of Roumania itself and in adjacent territories now under Bulgarian, Jugoslavian, Hungarian, or Russian rule[160];

        b. Megleno-Roumanian, spoken in the upper valley of the Vardar river in Greece and Jugoslavia[161];

        c. Macedo-Roumanian or Aromunian (Roum. *aromîn*), spoken by a number of widely scattered groups in the Balkans, in southern and western Jugoslavia, Albania, and north-western Greece[162];

        d. Istro-Roumanian, spoken by a small number of persons in villages near Abbazia in the Istrian peninsula.[163]

2.2. Official Use

The various Romance languages are used outside the regions where they are natively spoken, for the operations of government, for legally valid actions and documents, and for education (normally in their standard varieties), as follows:

2.21. PORTUGUESE, in all the present Portuguese colonies, and in those parts of Brazil where American Indian languages are spoken natively or where there are enclaves of speakers of other European languages (*e.g.* German).

2.22.   SPANISH, in Catalonia and the Balearic islands, in Galicia, in the colonies of Spain, and in large areas in Central and South America where the native population is Amerindian. It is also officially recognised in the state of New Mexico.

2.23.   FRENCH, in virtually all present and former colonies[164]; in the semi-autonomous Italian region of the Val d'Aosta; and throughout Canada and in Louisiana. In some regions, *e.g.* Haiti, a strong influence is exerted on official French by the local dialect or creole.[165]

2.24.   ITALIAN, in the Gallo-Romance valleys of Piedmont, in South Tyrol, in the Friuli, and in Sardinia.

2.25.   ROUMANIAN, in those parts of Roumania (especially Transylvania) where Hungarian or German is the local native language.

2.3. Use as Lingua Franca

Due to their social or political prestige, certain Romance languages are used in areas where they are not native and have no official standing.

2.31.   FRENCH has been used extensively since the eighteenth century among the upper classes of many European nations, especially Germany (*e.g.* at the courts of Frederick the Great and many lesser princes), Piedmont, Hungary, and eastern Europe. In some countries, such use has diminished or disappeared as a result of nationalistic pressures; in others (*e.g.* Roumania and Greece), it has continued to the present day. From the mid-eighteenth to the early twentieth century, French was recognised as the internationally valid language for diplomatic relations and treaties.[166]

2.32.   ITALIAN was widely used as a lingua franca in the eastern end of the Mediterranean from the sixteenth to the early twentieth century, especially in Greece and Egypt.[167] It has largely gone out of use in this area, except in certain former Italian colonies such as Ethiopia and Libya.

2.4. Pidginised and Creolised Varieties

Certain pidginised and creolised Romance languages are found very widely spread throughout the world.[168] The earliest Romance-based pidgin of which we have any knowledge was the mediaeval Lingua Franca, based on the Italian-Provençal speech of the Riviera from Genoa to Marseilles, and used during and after the time of the Crusades in Palestine and the eastern end of the Mediterranean.[169] The same term was applied also to a variety of pidginised Spanish used in the sixteenth century in the Maghreb (Algeria, Morocco); it is not certain whether this latter was a direct continuator of the earlier Levantine Lingua Franca or not. According to certain (far from universally accepted) theories, these two varieties would have been connected by oral tradition, and would have been the predecessors of West African Pidgin Portuguese, from which all other modern pidgins and creoles would have sprung by a process of "relexification."[170] The chief Romance languages on which pidgins and creoles have been based are:

2.41. PORTUGUESE, the first and perhaps the most widely pidginised. Pidgin Portuguese is attested from 1621 onwards[171]; it is reported that there is or was a pidginised or creolised variety of the language in every present or former Portuguese colony.[172] It is a matter of debate whether the Portuguese dialects of north-eastern Brazil are based on earlier creolised varieties.[173] In some areas, where a Pidgin Portuguese was formerly spoken and later replaced by a pidgin or creole based on another language, more or less extensive traces of Portuguese have remained in the lexicon of the later language.[174]

2.42. SPANISH was probably pidginised, in earlier centuries, fairly widely. There are, at present, only a few varieties of Pidgin Spanish used in trade-contacts in South America and the Philippines[175]; the chief Spanish-based creole is Papiamentu, spoken on the Dutch-owned islands of Curaçao, Aruba, and Bonaire.[176]

2.43. FRENCH is spoken in pidginised or creolised form in:
  1. The Caribbean[177]:
      a. Louisiana (cf. §2.123.5)[178];
      b. Haiti, where French is the official language (cf. §2.23) but Creole is the native language of the entire population[179];
      c. The lesser Antilles, including the islands of Dominica,[180] Martinique,[181] and Trinidad,[182] and French Guiana.[183]

2. The Mascareigne islands[184] to the east of Africa, *i.e.* Mauritius[185] and Réunion.[186]

3. In French Africa, including the Maghreb and central Africa, where one or more kinds of pidginised French (often called "petit-nègre" or "sabir") are or have been used.

2.44. Italian has been pidginised but little in modern times: in Brazil, among the mixed Italian and Negro population,[187] and in Ethiopia during and after the Italian occupation in the 1930's and 1940's.

2.5. Romance Languages No Longer Spoken

2.51. Dalmatian, which was formerly used along the coast of Dalmatia, from Istria to Ragusa (mod. Dubrovnik). By the nineteenth century it survived only on the island of Veglia, off the coast of Croatia south of Fiume (Rijeka). The last native speakers of Vegliote were the parents of a certain Antonio Udina. His first language was a variety of Venetian,[188] but he learned Vegliote as a child by listening to his parents. Udina died in 1898 through stepping on a "land-mine," *i.e.* dynamite intended for blasting. Dalmatian is attested in mediaeval documents from Zara and other cities, and in texts taken down from Udina's dictation by two scholars, Antonio Ive and M. G. Bàrtoli.[189] Further indications of the characteristics of Dalmatian can be gleaned from loan-words surviving in Croatian and Albanian.[190] Dalmatian has often been classified with Roumanian under the heading of "Balkan Romance," but it has been shown to belong, rather, with Italo-Romance in a "Central Romance" group.[191]

2.52. The Lingua Franca, discussed above under pidginised forms of Romance (§2.4). It was an important channel in the transmission of words from eastern languages into Romance and vice versa.[192]

2.53. North African Romance, spoken probably until the ninth or tenth century A.D. in what is now Tunisia and perhaps other parts of the Maghreb, and documented in person- and place-names of Romance origin attested in Arabic sources.[193]

2.54. Anglo-Norman, used by the upper classes in England as their native language and as an official language throughout the English dominions from the Norman Conquest until the thirteenth or fourteenth century, and in legal contexts until the nineteenth.[194]

Other, unidentifiable varieties of Romance or Pre-Romance speech were undoubtedly used in areas once under Roman rule, such as England before the Anglo-Saxon invasions; the Balkans; or the area west of the Rhine and south of the Roman "limes" and the Danube in what is now the Palatinate, Baden, Württemberg, Switzerland, Bavaria, Austria, and Hungary. Proto-Rhaeto-Romance may have been spoken somewhere in southern or western Germany, and its speakers driven southward before the invading Germanic tribes.[195]

NOTES TO CHAPTER 2

1. For the Romance languages in general, cf. Körting 1884–88; Gröber (ed.) 1886–88; Zauner 1900; Meyer-Lübke 1901 (and Meyer-Lübke-Castro 1926); Bourciez 1910; von Wartburg 1936, 1939; Meier 1941; Groult 1947; Tagliavini 1947; Auerbach 1949; Rohlfs 1950–52; Monteverdi 1952; Vidos 1956; Lausberg 1956–62; Elcock 1960; Rohr 1964; Posner 1966; Bal 1966; Battaglia 1967a; Vàrvaro 1968; Bec 1970–71; Deutsehmann 1971. Historical grammar of all the Romance languages: Meyer-Lübke 1890–1902. Etymological dictionaries: Diez 1853 (still useful); Körting 1890–91; Meyer-Lübke 1911. Romance linguistic geography in general: Millardet 1921–23, 1924; Pop 1950 (volume 1), 1956–57, 1960; Álvar 1960; Butler 1965/66. Classification of the Romance languages: Trager 1934; Puşcariu 1937; Alonso 1943c; Hall 1950a; Muljačić 1967. For the history of Romance linguistics, cf. Chapter 11.

2. Closely allied to the function of a lingua franca is the use of a language as a mark of prestige, even through all those using it may have a given other language as their native tongue—as was the case with French in the high society of eighteenth- and nineteenth-century Russia. A large part of the aristocrats' conversation in Tolstoǐ's *War and Peace*, for instance, is in French; Russian editions give the Russian translation in foot-notes at the bottom of each page.

3. The effort of Agard (1971) to establish a distinction in terms of rigid structural criteria can hardly be called successful.

4. Extensive bibliography in Rohlfs 1957. Cf. also Meier 1930; Kuen 1950; Baldinger 1963; Pottier 1957–58. Over-all historical treatments in Entwistle 1936; Tavani 1968. Linguistic atlas of the Iberian peninsula: Navarro Tomás, Balbín et al. (eds.) 1962–   .
Arabic element: Steiger 1932.

5. This is one of the many instances in which political affiliation cannot be taken as indicative of linguistic relationships: Portuguese is used both natively and officially in Portugal, whereas, in Galicia, Galician is the native language by Spanish is official.

6. Cf. García de Diego 1906; Lugris Freire 1922; Carballo Calero 1966. Phonemics: Veiga 1969. Vocabulary: Buschmann 1965; Franco Grande 1968.

7. Cf. Sten 1944; Chaves de Melo 1968. Phonetics: Gonçalves Viana 1883; Mattoso Câmara 1953; Barbosa 1965. Phonemics: Intonation: de Lacerda 1940–44. Historical grammar: Leite de Vasconcelos 1911; Nunes 1919; Said Ali 1931; de Lima Coutinho 1938; Williams 1938; Silva Neto 1952; da Silveira Bueno 1955; Machado 1967; Mattoso Câmara 1972. Etymological dictionaries: Nascentes 1932, 1966; Machado 1952–59; da Silveira Bueno 1963.

8. Brazilian Portuguese in general: Guimarães Daupiás 1925/27; Mendonça 1936; Elia 1940, 1966; Silva Neto 1951; Barbosa Lima 1958; de Lemos 1959; Parentes Fortes

36   COMPARATIVE ROMANCE GRAMMAR

1962; van den Besselaar 1963; Ferreira da Cunha 1968. Phonemics: Jucá 1939; Houaiss 1959. Syntax: Thomas 1969. Lexicon: Piel 1965/66. Slang: Nascentes 1953b.

9. A historical survey of orthographical developments: Monteiro 1954.

10. Over-all surveys in Leite de Vasconcelos 1901; de Paiva Boléo 1942. Sociological position of Portuguese compared with Italian dialects: Lüdtke 1956b.

11. Cf. Carballo Calero 1969.

12. Cf. de Moura Santos 1962–68.

13. For the Miranda region, cf. de Moraes Ferreira 1898; Leite de Vasconcelos 1882, 1900–01; Sletsjoe 1967. For Ervedosa de Douro: Soares de Azevedo 1928/29. Póvoa de Varzim: Krüger 1936.

14. For Monsanto, in the Castelo Branco area of Beira Baixa, cf. Carvalhão Buescu 1961.

15. Cf. Leite de Vasconcelos 1933.

16. Cf. Capela e Silva 1947; Rohner 1938.

17. Cf. Brüdt 1937; de Oliveira Monteiro 1947–49.

18. Cf. da Câmara Borges 1960.

19. Cf. Marroquim 1934; Silva Neto 1955; Seraine 1958; Girão 1967. Linguistic atlas of Bahia region: N. Rossi 1963–   . Possible African elements: Mendonça 1933; Raimundo 1933; Coelho de Senna 1938. Are Brazilian dialects creolised or not?—Révah 1963.

20. Cf. Romaguera Corrêa et al. 1964.

21. Cf. Nascentes 1953a.

22. Cf. Pap 1949.

23. As with the speech of other European capitals (e.g. Paris, London), the modern lower-class usage of Madrid has fallen into disfavor with purists. In such situations, the speech of a smaller city relatively close to the capital is often recommended as a preferable model—for Spanish, that of Toledo.

24. Bibliography: P. C. Hall 1957; Seris 1964; Pottier 1961–64. Phonetics: Navarro Tomás 1918. Phonemics: Trager 1938; Navarro Tomás 1944; Alarcos Llorach 1950; Quilis 1963; J. W. Harris 1969. Intonation: Navarro Tomás 1944. Descriptive grammar: Alarcos Llorach 1951; Pottier 1958; Hadlich 1970. Syntax: Gili Gaya 1943. Lexical frequency: Juilland and Chang-Rodríguez 1964. History: Menédez Pidal 1926; Entwistle 1936; Spaulding 1943. Historical grammars: Menéndez Pidal 1904; Oliver Asín 1938 (but cf. Malkiel 1945); Lapesa 194; García de Diego 1946, 1951; Bolaño e Isla 1959; Ayala 1963. Historical phonology: A. Alonso 1955–69. Historical syntax: M. Alonso 1962. Etymological dictionaries: Corominas 1954–57; García de Diego 1955. Comparison with Italian: Lausberg 1947.

25. Cf. Alonso 1943a.

26. Cf. Henríquez Ureña 1921–31; Rosenblat 1933, 1962, 1967; Alonso 1935; Wagner 1949.

27. The inhabitants of Bogotá (Colombia) are said to pride themselves, rather unrealistically, on the closeness of their speech to Peninsular Spanish, especially in the preservation of "ceceo" and "lleismo."

28. Spanish dialectology in general: García de Diego 1946; Zamora Vicente 1960. Bibliography: Avellaneda et al. 1966–67.

29. Aragonese in general: Álvar 1953. Lexicon: Borao y Clemente 1859; Pardo Asso 1938. Upper Aragonese: Kuhn 1935, 1935–39, 1955; Krüger 1935–39. The boundary between Aragonese and Catalan: Griera i Gaja 1914; Álvar 1956/57. Individual subdialects: Aguaviva: Sanchis Guarner 1949. Alta Ribagorza: Haensch 1960. Campo de Jaca: Álvar 1948. Puebla de Hijar: Monge 1951. Ribagorza: Rubio García 1965. Valle de

Bielsa: Badia i Margarit 1950. Valle de Venasque: Ferraz y Castán 1934. The border between Upper Aragon and Navarre: Bergmann 1934. Navarrese: Iribarren 1952.

30. Asturian: lexicon: de Rato y Hévia 1891. Western Asturian: Krüger 1927; Acevedo y Huelves and Fernández y Fernández 1932; Rodríguez Castellano 1954, 1957; Catalán Menéndez Pidal 1956–58. Individual subdialects: Alto Aller: Rodríguez Castellano 1952. Cabo de Peñas: Díaz Castañón 1966. Cabranes: Canellada 1944. Colunga: Vigón 1896–98; Zamora Vicente 1953. Cuarto de los Valles: Menéndez García 1963–65. Lena: Neira 1955. Oseja de Sajambre: Fernández González 1959. Sisterna: Menéndez García 1950.

31. Leonese in general: Menéndez Pidal 1906. Individual subdialects: Astorga: Alonso Garrote 1909. Babia and Laciana: Álvarez 1949. Cabrera Alta: Casado Lobato 1948. Cespedosa de Tormes: Sánchez Sevilla 1928. La Ribera: Llorente Maldonado de Guevara 1947. Salamanca: de Lamano y Beneite 1916. Sanabria: Krüger 1923, 1925a, 1925b. Villacidayo: Millán Urdiales 1966. Zamora: Castro 1913.

32. Castilian in general: de Múgica 1892; García de Diego 1950. Individual subdialects: La Bureba: González Ollé 1964. Cuellar (Segovia): de la Torre 1951. Cuenca: López Barrera 1912. Pasiego: Penny 1970. Quintanillabón (Burgos): Gonzáles Ollé 1953. Rioja: Magaña 1948; Llorente Maldonado de Guevara 1965. Santander: García Lomas 1922, 1949.

33. Cf. Alther 1935; Álvar 1955.

34. Cf. Sevilla 1919; García Soriano 1932. Dialect of Cartagena: García Cotorruelo 1959.

35. Linguistic boundary: Navarro Tomás et al. 1933. Lexicon: de Toro y Gisbert 1920; Alcalá Venceslada 1933. Linguistic atlas: Álvar et al. (eds.) 1962–65. Individual subdialects: Cabra: Rodríguez Castellano and Palacio 1948. Cádiz: Giese 1937. Cúllar-Baza: Salvador 1957.

36. Cf. Krüger 1914; Santos Coco 1940–44. Individual subdialects: Sierra de Gata: Fink 1929; Bierhenke 1929, 1932. Mérida: Zamora Vicente 1943.

37. Canaries: Catalán Pidal 1960, 1964; Álvar 1965. Tenerife: Álvar 1959, 1966; Catalán Menéndez Pidal 1966.

38. Over-all studies: Wagner 1930; Crews 1935; Renard 1967; Kovačec 1968. Individual varieties: Monastir (Jugoslavia): Luria 1930. Bosnia: Baruch 1930. Constantinople: Wagner 1914. Bucharest: Sala 1970, 1972.

39. E.g. Morocco: Wagner 1931.

40. North American Judaeo-Spanish: Agard 1950. New York City: D. Levy 1952.

41. Bibliography of American Spanish: Solé 1970. American Spanish dialectology: Rona 1958; Lope Blanch 1968. Phonetics: Canfield 1962. Syntax: Kany 1945. Semantics: Kany 1960. Lexicon: de Toro y Gisbert 1912; Malaret 1925; Santamaría 1942–43; Morínigo 1966. Relation to possible Amerindian substrata: Malmberg 1947–48. Relation to Andalusian dialect: Henríquez Ureña 1925, 1932; Wagner 1927; Boyd-Bowman 1956, 1964–68; Guitarte 1958; Lapesa 1963.

42. Puerto Rican Spanish in general: Navarro Tomás 1948; de Granda Gutiérrez 1968 (very politically slanted). Lexicon: Malaret 1937; del Rosario 1965.

43. Dominican Spanish in general: Henríquez Ureña 1940. Lexicon: Tejera 1935.

44. Cuban Spanish in general: Dihigo 1915; Montori 1916. Lexicon: Pichardo 1836; Suárez 1921; Ortíz 1921–22. African element: Ortíz Fernández 1924; López Morales 1964, 1966.

45. General discussion: Henríquez Ureña 1938b. Lexicon: Ramos y Duarte 1895; García Icazbalceta 1905. Individual subdialects: Guanajuato: Boyd-Bowman 1960.

Jalisco: Cárdenas 1967. Mexico City: Marden 1896; Matluck 1951. Coastal regions: Nykl 1929/30.

46. *E.g.* New Mexico: cf. Hills 1906; Espinosa 1930–46. American-Spanish argots in New Mexico: Barker 1958; and in Texas: Coltharp 1965.

47. *E.g.* Guatemala: Batres Jáuregui 1892. Costa Rica: Gagini 1893, 1919; Cuervo 1904; Agüero 1962. Honduras: Membreño 1895. Panamá: Robe 1960; Tejeira 1964.

48. General lexicon: Bayo 1910.

49. *E.g.* Venezuela: Medrano 1883; Calcaño 1897; van Wijk 1946. Colombia: Cuervo 1867–72, Alario de Filippo 1964 and E. González 1964; Flórez 1951a (Bogotá); Flórez 1957 (Antioquia); Flórez 1951b (Segovia and Remedios); Flórez 1965 (Santander). Ecuador: Lemos Ramírez 1920; Toscano Mateus 1953; Boyd-Bowman 1953. Perú: de Arona 1871; Benvenutto Murrieta 1936; Wagner 1939; E. Tovar 1966. Chile: A. Alonso and Lida (eds.), 1940 (general, including articles by Lenz, Bello, and Oroz, and bibliography by Oroz), and Oroz 1966; Rodríguez 1875 and Echeverría y Reyes 1900 (lexicon). Bolivia (Vallegrande): Sanabria Fernández 1965. Bolivia and Argentina: Bayo 1906. River Plate region: Castro 1941 (general); Granada 1889 (lexicon); Meo-Zilio 1965a (Italian influence). Argentina, in general: Alonso 1943b; Borges 1952; Vidal de Battini 1954. Lexicon: Garzón 1910. Foreign elements: Grossmann 1926; Laguarda Trías 1969. Individual subdialects: Buenos Aires: Clemente 1952. San Luís: Vidal de Battini 1949. Uruguay (Montevideo): Guarnieri 1969. The border-dialect between Uruguayan and Brazilian Portuguese: Rona 1965.

50. Cf. Griera i Gaja 1922, 1925; Meyer-Lübke 1925, 1926; Alonso 1926; Hagedorn 1939; Engler 1969.

51. Bibliography: Griera i Gaja 1947. Descriptive grammar: Fabra 1912; Fabra and Coromines 1956. Historical grammar: Griera i Gaja 1931, 1965; Badia i Margarit 1951; Moll 1952. Phonetics: Schaedel 1908; de Lacerda and Badia i Margarit 1948. Lexicon: Alcover 1930–32; Griera i Gaja 1935–47. Etymological dictionary: Coromines, forthcoming.

52. Cf. Sanchis Guarner 1936, 1948, 1950, 1960, 1961. Phonetics of Valencian: Navarro Tomás and Sanchis Guarner 1934. Lexicon: Ferrer-Pastor 1966.

53. Catalan dialects in general: Griera i Gaja 1949; Sanchis Guarner 1956. Linguistic atlas: Griera i Gaja 1923–68. The sociological situation in Barcelona: Badia i Margarit 1969. In Valencia: Ninyoles 1969.

54. Cf. Schädel 1909; Salow 1912. For Rossillon, cf. Fouché 1924a, 1924b.

55. Linguistic atlas: Griera i Gaja 1958.

56. Cf. such studies of individual dialects as Torres Fornés 1903; Barnils Giol 1913.

57. Cf. Amengual 1835; Moll y Casanovas 1960.

58. Cf. Guiter 1943.

59. Cf. Guarnerio 1886; Kuen 1932–34; Scanu 1963.

60. Over-all treatments of the French area: bibliography of dialect-dictionaries: von Wartburg 1934b; von Wartburg et al. 1969. Gallo-Romance dialects: de Tourtoulon 1890; Dauzat 1906b, 1922, 1927; Morf 1911; Brun 1946. The border between Provençal, Franco-Provençal, and North French: de Tourtoulon and Bringuier 1876; Rosenquist 1919; Brun 1936; Escoffier 1956, 1958. Linguistic atlas of central area: Dubuisson 1971–

61. *E.g.* C. Leonard 1964.

62. Beginning with Àscoli 1878. The major dissenter has been the present writer (Hall 1949a).

63. For the word *Provençal*, the present writer learned at the University of Chicago, in the 1930's, the pronunciation /provénsəl/, and has found it convenient to continue

using this pronunciation to refer to the mediaeval language, while using the French sound-sequence /provãsal/ for the modern dialects.

64. First edited and studied systematically by Raynouard (1816, 1821, 1836–44). Since then, there have been a number of editions of individual poets' works, and several anthologies (*e.g.* Crescini 1892; Appel 1895; Hill and Bergin 1942; Hamlin, Ricketts, and Hathaway 1967), in addition to extensive discussion from a literary point of view.

65. For Old Provençal, cf., in addition to the early studies of Raynouard (note 64), such general reference-works as Grandgent 1905; Anglade 1921a; Roncaglia 1965. Extensive additional lexical material in E. Levy 1894–1924; grammatical discussion in Pfister 1958. An example of a study on the language of a single author (Arnaut Daniel): Toja 1969.

66. A general treatment in Bec 1963.

67. Historical grammar: Koschwitz 1894; Ronjat 1930–32. Syntax: Herzog 1900. Lexicon: Mistral 1878.

68. Cf. Alibert 1935; Salvat 1943. For syntax: bibliography in Price 1965. An over-all survey of Old and Modern Provençal syntax, based primarily on "Occitan" but with much other material: Lafont 1967.

69. On individual subdialects: Cagnes and Vence: P. Dubois 1958. Entraunes: Blinkenberg 1939–40. Marseilles: Brun 1931. Menton: Andrews 1875, 1876, 1890/92. Monaco: Arveiller 1967. Nice: Sütterlin 1896; Bàrtoli 1941; Compan 1965, 1967. Rhône valley: Savinian 1882. Dialects in Rhône valley: Arles: Coustenoble 1945. Avignon: Pansier 1924–27.

70. Grammatical studies: Luchaire 1879. Lexicon: Alibert 1965. Linguistic atlas: Guiter 1966. Individual subdialects: Aniane: Zaun 1917. Bethmale valley (Ariège): Schönthaler 1937, Couzou (Lot): Maas 1969. La-Salle-Saint-Pierre (Gard): Fouquet 1884–85. Lézignan: Anglade 1897. Rouergue: Aymeric 1879.

71. Bibliography: Dauzat 1928, Linguistic atlas: Nauton 1957–63. Individual subdialects: Aurillac: Lhermet 1931. Basse-Auvergne: Dauzat 1897, 1900, 1906a, 1913–25. Gévaudan: Camproux 1958, 1962. Langy (Varennes-sur-Allier): Bonin 1956. Saugues (Haute-Loire): Nauton 1948.

72. On Limousin: Chabaneau 1871–75; Roux 1895. On La Creuse (in the Marche): Queyrat 1927–30. Upper Dordogne valley and Périgord: Guillaumie 1927.

73. General treatments: Sarran 1920; Rohlfs 1935. Lexicon: Palay 1932. Linguistic geography: Fleischer 1913. Linguistic atlas: Séguy et al. (eds.) 1954–56. Relation with Languaedocien: Bec 1968. Individual subdialects: Lescun (Basses-Pyrénées): Bendel 1934. The Landes region: Millardet 1910; Dengler 1934.

74. General discussions: Àscoli 1878; Stimm 1952. Bibliography: Sala and Reinheimer 1967–68. Mediaeval Franco-Provençal; Gardette 1968. For the Franco-Provençal of the Waldensians who emigrated to Württemberg, cf. Hirsch 1963.

75. Boundaries of Franco-Provençal in the Forez: Gardette 1939; Escoffiier 1956, 1958. Linguistic geography: Gardette 1941a, 1941b. Linguistic atlas: Gardette et al. (eds.) 1950–68. Individual subdialects: Saint-Étienne: Dorna and Lyotard 1953. Poncins: Gonan 1947.

76. For Lyonnais, cf. Miège 1937. Mâconnais: Violet 1932, 1936. Bournois (Doubs): Roussey 1894. Dombes (Ain): Egloff 1937. Grand 'Combe (Doubs): Boillot 1910. Lantignié-en-Beaujolais (Rhône); Descroix 1946. Nozeroy (Jura): Kjellén 1945. Ruffieux-en-Valromey (Ain): Ahlborn 1946. Vaux-en-Bugey (Ain): Duraffour 1932a, 1932b, 1941.

77. Dauphinois in general: Giese 1932a; Devaux 1935a, 1935b. Individual subdialects: Bozel (Savoie): Hering 1936. Cellefrouin (Savoie): Rousselot 1891–92. Hauteville (Savoie): Martinet 1956. Magland (Haute-Savoie): Osterwalder 1933. Saint-Martin-la-Porte

40   COMPARATIVE ROMANCE GRAMMAR

(Savoie): Kuckuck 1936; Ratel 1956, 1958. Saxel (Haute-Savoie): Dupraz 1938–39. Linguistic atlas of northern Alps and Jura: Martin and Tuaillon 1971– . French in the Val d'Aosta: Rosellini 1970.

78. Bibliography: Gauchat and Jeanjaquet 1912–20. General discussion: Ayer 1878. Phonetic atlas: Gauchat, Jeanjaquet, and Tappolet 1925. Lexicon: Bridel, 1866; Gauchat, Jeanjaquet, Tappolet, and Muret (eds.) 1924– .

79. Cf. Zimmerli 1891–99; Weigold 1943.

80. Cf. O. Keller 1919.

81. Cf. Haefelin 1873.

82. Cf. Haefelin 1879. Dialect of Charmey (Fribourg): Gauchat 1903.

83. Cf. Bertrand 1758; A. Odin 1886. Individual subdialects: Blonay: L. Odin 1910. Ollon and Aigle: Hasselrot 1937. Savièse: Favre and Balet 1960.

84. The relation between German and French in this area: Moulton 1941. Phonetic atlas: Gilliéron 1880b. Individual subdialects: Ardon: Delaloye and Schüle 1964. Bagnes: Bjerrome 1957. Einfisch (Sion): L. Meyer 1914. Hérémence: de Lavellaz 1935. Marécottes: Müller 1961. Martigny: Alf. Dietrich 1945. Montana: Gerster 1927. Val d'Illiez: Fankhauser 1910–11. Vionnaz: Gilliéron 1880a.

85. Cf. W. Walser 1936. For Usseglio (Val Soana): Terracini 1910–22.

86. General historical treatments: Brunot and Bruneau 1905–69; Vossler 1913; Dauzat 1926, 1930; von Wartburg 1934a; Holmes and Schutz 1935; Ewert 1938, 1958; Cohen 1947; R.-L. Wagner 1947 (1955); François 1959. Historical grammars: Brachet 1867; Nyrop 1899–1930; Meyer-Lübke 1908–21; Strohmeyer 1929; Kukeheim 1967– . Historical phonology: Bourciez 1899; Herzog 1913; Buscherbruck 1931; Dauzat 1950; Fouché 1952–61; Borodiná 1961; Mańczak 1962. Historical morphology: Mańczak 1962; Borodiná 1965. Historical syntax: Lerch 1925–34; Sneyders de Vogel 1927; Gamillscheg 1957. Etymological dictionaries: Brachet 1868; Hatzfeld, Darmesteter, and Thomas 1888; Gamillscheg 1928; von Wartburg 1928–71; Bloch and von Wartburg 1932; Dauzat 1938; Picoche 1971.

Descriptive treatments of modern French: Damourette and Pichon 1927–49; Lerch 1933; Gougenheim 1939; Galichet 1947, 1949, 1953; Hall 1948; Togeby 1951; Harmer 1954; Regula 1957; J. Dubois 1965– ; Schane 1968; Zwanenburg 1968. Current tendencies: Richter 1933; Heinimann 1948. Phonetics: Passy 1887; Nyrop 1902 (cf. Hall 1966/67); Bruneau 1927; Gougenheim 1933; Grammont 1938; Martinet 1945; Fouché 1956; Malmberg 1969. Intonation: Coustenoble and Armstrong 1934. Syntax: bibliography: Horluc and Marinet 1908. Descriptive syntax: Sandfeld 1928–43; Le Bidois and Le Bidois 1935–38; de Boer 1947; von Wartburg and Zumthor 1947; Guiraud 1963; Roulet 1969. Dictionaries: a great many, beginning with Littré 1863–73; cf. especially, for phonetically oriented approach, Michaëlis and Passy 1914. French in North Africa: Lanly 1962.

87. Relation of dialect and standard language in Old French: Wacker 1916. Historical grammar: Schwan 1888; Rheinfelder 1937–64. Syntax: Foulet 1919; von Ettmayer 1930–36 (principally on Old French). Lexicon: Godefroy 1881–1902; Tobler and Lommatzsch 1925– ; van Daele 1939; Greimas 1969; Baldinger et al. 1972– .

88. A historical curiosity: the *Grammaire de l'Académie Française* (Hermant 1932), written by a nonlinguist three hundred years after the foundation of the Academy, and roundly criticised by Brunot 1932; (cf. §8.322).

89. For La Grand'Combe, cf. Boillot 1930; for Toulouse, Séguy 1950, for Brussels, Baetens-Beardsmore 1972.

90. Cf. Blondheim 1925; R. Lévy 1932, 1960, 1964.

91. Dialect-texts: Herzog 1906. Linguistic atlas (ALF): Gilliéron and Edmont 1902,

1902–10, 1912. For the several atlases included in the *Nouvel Atlas Linguistique de la France* (NALF), see the various regions.

92. Parisian popular speech: texts: Koschwitz 1893. General discussion: Nisard 1872, 1876; Bauche 1920; Sainéan 1920.

93. Cf. Meunier 1912a, 1912b, 1926a, 1926b.

94. Cf. Scharten 1942; Pignon, 1960; Wuest 1969. Linguistic atlas of Poitevin and Saintongeais: Massignon and Horiot 1971– .

95. Cf. Doussinet 1958.

96. Cf. Svensen 1959; de la Chaussée 1966.

97. For Pléchâtel (Ille-et-Vilaine), cf. Dottin and Langouët 1901. For the Haut-Maine dialect: Verdier 1951.

98. Linguistic atlases: Guerlin de Guer 1903, 1945. Individual subdialects: Percy: de Beaucoudrey 193?. Saint-Pol: Edmont 1887–97. Thaon (Calvados): Guerlin de Guer 1901.

99. Cf. Spence 1960; Sjögren 1964– ; Le Maistre 1966.

100. Amiens region: Debrie 1961, 1965. Beauquesne (Somme): Debrie 1966. Melleville (Seine-Maritime): Vacandard 1964. Mesnil-Martinsart (Somme): Flutre 1955. Thiérache and Laounois region: Chaurand 1968. Vimeu (Somme): Vasseur 1963.

101. The boundary of Walloon dialects: Legros 1948. Phonology: Marchot 1892. Etymological dictionary: Grandgagnage 1845–50. Linguistic atlas: Remacle (ed.) 1953– . Individual subdialects: Cerfontaine: Balle 1963. La Gleize: Remacle 1937. Liège: Haust 1927, 1929–33, 1948.

102. General discussion: Adam 1881. Ardennes region: Bruneau 1913a, 1913b, 1913–26. Hattigny and Ommeray: Callais 1908. Moselle region: Zéliqzon 1922–24; Jungandreas 1967. Metz: Rolland 1873–75.

103. Southern Vosges region: Bloch 1915, 1917a, 1917b, 1921. Individual subdialects: La Baroche and Belmont: Horning 1916. Damprichard: Grammont 1892–1900. Naisey: Alex 1965. Pierrecourt (Haute-Saône): Juret 1913. Ranrupt (Bas-Rhin): Aub-Büscher 1962. Uriménil: Haillant 1886.

104. Bibliography: Geddes and Rivard 1966. General discussion: Dionne 1909; Gendron 1966; Gendron and Straka (eds.) 1968. Lexicon: *Glossaire du parler français au Canada* (1930).

105. For Brunswick, Maine, cf. Locke 1949.

106. Cf. Massignon 1962.

107. Cf. Dorrance 1935; McDermott 1941.

108. Cf. Read 1931; Phillips 1936; Tisch 1959; Conwell and Juilland 1963.

109. Cf. Fortier 1891; Ditchy 1932.

110. Over-all discussions: Böttiger 1853; Schürr 1963; Wunderli 1966; Kuen 1968. Lexicon: *Dicziunari Rumantsch Grischun* (1938–).

111. Bibliography: Widmer 1966. General treatments: Gartner 1883, 1910; Widmer 1965; Borodiná 1969; Prader-Schucany 1970. Linguistic boundaries: Menghius 1898. Lexicon: Vieli and Decurtins 1962.

112. In earlier centuries, Romansh was spoken in Chur and farther down the Rhine valley; cf. Camenisch 1962; Cavigelli 1969. Grammar: Cahannes 1924. The Tavetsch valley: Caduff 1952.

113. Cf. Àscoli 1880/83. Grammar: Cahannes 1924.

114. Historical grammar: Velleman 1915–24. Lexicon: Pallioppi 1895–1902. Individual subdialects: Bergün: Lutta 1923. Celerina-Cresta: Walberg 1907. Müstair: Schorta 1938. Sent: Pult 1897. Surmeir: Grisch 1939.

115. Cf. von Wartburg 1919.

116. General discussions: Schneller 1870; Àscoli 1873a; Alton 1879; Battisti 1910, 1922, 1929, 1931, and a number of other publications down to 1962, expounding the Italian nationalist doctrine that Ladin and the other Rhaeto-Romance languages do not constitute a separate unity, but are only aberrant Italian dialects. Individual subdialects: Badia: lexicon: Martini 1950; Pizzinini 1966. Erto: Gartner 1892. Fassa: Elwert 1943; Mazzel 1968–69. Gardena: phonology: Urzí 1962. Lexicon: Lardschneider-Ciampac, 1933. Gíudicarie: Gartner 1882. Moena: Heilmann 1955. Non: Battisti 1909; Politzer 1967. Sole (Sulzberg): Battisti 1911. Valvestino: Battisti 1913/14. Border dialects between Ladin and Vèneto: Comèlico: Tagliavini 1926, 1942–44. Livinallongo: Tagliavini 1933–34.

117. General: Blanch 1929; Francescato 1970. Grammar: Marchetti 1952. Lexicon: Pirona 1871; Carletti et al. (eds.) 1935. Dialectology: Francescato 1966. Friulian enclaves in Roumania: Iliescu 1964, 1968.

118. Bibliography: Hall 1958a, 1969a.

119. General discussions: Bàrtoli 1936; von Wartburg 1936b; Devoto 1953; Pulgram 1958; Migliorini 1960; Migliorini and Griffith 1966; Battaglia 1967b. Historical grammar: Meyer-Lübke 1890; Grandgent 1927; Tagliavini 1936; Pei 1941; Rohlfs 1949–54. Etymological dictionaries (in addition to the now antiquated Zambaldi 1889 and Pianigiani 1907): Battisti and Alessio 1948–56; Prati 1951; Olivieri 1953; Devoto 1966.

For modern Italian: general descriptions: Panconcelli-Calzia 1911; Spitzer 1922; Regula and Jernej 1965; Hall 1971. Recent developments: Heinimann 1948; Devoto 1956; Hall 1960a; de Mauro 1963. Phonetics: Camilli 1941. Phonemics: G. Porru 1939; Malmberg 1942/43; Saltarelli 1970. Comparison with Spanish: Lausberg 1947.

120. Cf. Prati 1954; G. Pellegrini 1960; Hall 1968a. Regional differences in standard Italian lexicon: Rüegg 1956.

121. Bibliography of dialect-dictionaries: Bacchi della Lega 1876, 1877; Prati 1931; d'Elia 1940. Texts: Zuccagni-Orlandini 1864; Papanti, 1875; Battisti 1914–21. General discussions: Bertoni 1915; Rohlfs 1937c, 1947c, 1967a; Schürr 1938; Battisti 1967; Parlangèli 1969; Cortelazzo 1969. Linguistic atlas (AIS): Jaberg and Jud (eds.) 1928, 1928–40, 1960 (cf. Hall 1942b, 1962a); Scheuermeier 1943–56. Linguistic atlas (ALI): Bàrtoli et al. (eds.), forthcoming.

122. Cf. Biondelli 1853; Haag, 1930.

123. General: Simon 1967; Clivio 1971. Bibliography: Clivio and Clivio 1971. Grammar: Aly-Belfàdel 1933. Lexicon: di Sant'Albino 1859; dal Pozzo 1888; A. Levi 1927. Individual subdialects: Castellinaldo: Toppino 1905–29. Pettinengo: Pautasso 1969. Turin: Viriglio 1897; Soffietti 1949. Valle d'Andorno: Berruto 1970. Val Sesia: general: Spoerri 1918. Lexicon: Tonetti 1894.

124. Relation with German: Wunderli 1968. Syntax: Spiess 1956. Lexicon: Bosshard 1938. Individual subdialects: Bèrgamo: Zappettini 1859; Tiraboschi 1873, 1879; von Ettmayer 1903. Bormio: Longo 1912; Bläuer-Rini 1924. Brescia: Melchiori 1817, 1820. Como: Monti 1845. Crema: Samarani 1852; Bombelli 1940. Cremona: Peri 1847; Fumagalli 1882. Milan: general: Pagani 1945. Phonology: Salvioni 1884. Lexicon: Banfi 1852; Arrighi 1896. Pavia: general: Capioni 1884. Phonology: Heilmann 1961. Lexicon: Galli 1965. Poschiavo: Michael 1905; Salvioni 1906; Tognina 1967. Valle Antrona: Nicolet 1929. Valle Anzasca: Gysling 1929. Val Bregaglia: von Wartburg 1919; Stampa 1934. Valtellina: Livigno: Huber 1960. Voghera: Niccoli 1901.

125. General: Àscoli 1873b; Giusti 1936, 1937; Petracco Sicardi 1965. Individual subdialects: Bordighera and Realdo: Garnier 1898. Genoa: general: Parodi 1905. Lexicon: Gismondi 1955. Lunigiana region (Magra valley): Bottiglioni 1911; Giannarelli 1913. Ormea: Schädel 1903; Parodi 1907. Pigna: Merlo 1938–57.

126. General: Màfera 1958; Battisti 1962; Pellegrini 1965. Phonemics: Lepscky 1962, 1963a. Morphology: Lepscky 1963b. Lexicon: Boerio 1829; Michelàgnoli 1935; Bevilacqua 1949; Frey 1962. Greek influence: Cortellazo 1969. Individual subdialects in Venezia Eugànea: Àgordo- Pellegrini 1954/55. Belluno: Nazari 1873, 1884. Treviso: Ninni 1891. Verona: Bologinini and Patuzzi 1901; Beltramini and Donati 1963. Vicenza: Pajello 1896. Vittorio Vèneto: Zanette 1955. Venetian in overseas regions: Folena 1968/70.

127. General: Tomasini 1957. Individual subdialects: Trent: general: Cesarini-Sforza 1896. Lexicon: Azzolini 1856; Ricci (ed.) 1904; Groff 1955. Valsugana: Prati 1916, 1960.

128. General: Bàrtoli 1910b; Bàrtoli and Vidossi 1945. Lexicon: Rosamani 1958. Individual subdialects: Fiume: Bató 1933. Trieste: Vidossich 1900–01. Lexicon: Kosovitz 1889; Pinguentini 1969. Veglia: Königes 1933. Zara: Wengler 1915.

129. Bibliography: Vincenzi 1968. General: Bottiglioni 1951. Individual subdialects: Bologna: general: Gaudenzi 1889; Mainoldi 1950. Lexicon: Bumaldi 1660; Coronedi-Berti 1869–74; Mainoldi 1967. Jargons: Menarini 1942. Comacchio: Barbagallo 1959. Ferrara: Ferri 1889. Firenzuola: Casellz 1922. Lizzano in Belvedere: Malagòli 1930, 1940, 1941. Mantua: Arrivabene 1891, 1892; Bardini 1964. Miràndola: Meschieri 1876. Mòdena: Bertoni 1905, 1925. Lexicon: Galvani 1868; Maranesi 1892. Novellara: Malagòli 1910, 1918. Parma: phonology: Piagnoli 1904. Lexicon: Peschieri 1827–28; Malaspina 1856–69, 1880; Pariset 1885–92. Piacenza: phonology: Gorra 1890. Lexicon: Foresti 1836, 1842. Reggio: Bellocchi 1966. Spina: Barbagallo 1961.

130. General: Mussafia 1871; Schürr 1917, 1918–19, 1933, 1954. Lexicon: Morri 1840; Ercolani 1960. Individual subdialects: Ìmola: Bottiglioni 1919. Lexicon: Tozzoli 1857.

131. Cf. Rohlfs 1931, 1941a.

132. Cf. G. de Gregorio 1882/83, 1897, 1901, 1910; Piazza 1921; Peri 1950; Petracco Sicardi 1963, 1969; Tropea 1966. Individual varieties: Francavilla: Tropea 1963. Nicosia: La Via 1889, 1902; Finocchiaro 1950. Piazza Armerina: Roccella 1875.

133. Cf. Vaughan 1915; Schürr 1965.

134. General: Neumann von Spallart 1904, 1907; Crocioni 1951; Parrino 1967. Individual subdialects: Ancona: Spòtti 1929. Arcevia: Crocioni 1906. Iesi: Gatti 1910. Macerata: Ginobili 1963, 1965. Tronto valley: Mastràngelo Latini 1966.

135. General: Nencioni 1949. Syntax: Lüers 1942. Lexicon: Fanfani 1863. Individual subdialects: Amiata region: Longo 1942–43; Fatini 1953. Arezzo: Redi 1928. Elba: Diodati Caccavelli 1966–69. Florence: Broglio et al. 1897; Volpi 1932. Lucca: Nieri 1901; Parducci 1947/48. Pisa: Malagòli 1939. Pistoia: Bruner 1894. Siena: historical grammar: Hirsch 1885–86. Lexicon: Gigli 1707; Lombardi et al. 1944; Cagliaritano 1969. Versilia region: Pieri 1904; Cocci 1956–57.

136. General: Guarnerio 1892–98, 1905; Bottiglioni 1926–27; Rohlfs 1941b; Coco 1958. Phonology: Schmeck 1952, 1954. Lexicon: Bottiglioni 1952. Linguistic atlases: Gilliéron and Edmont 1914–15; Bottiglioni 1933–44. Individual subdialects: Niolo: Giese 1932b. Pieve d'Evisa: Ceccaldi 1968.

137. Individual subdialects: Città di Castello: Bianchi 1886. Perugia: Schiaffini 1928. San Sepolcro: Zanchi Alberti 1937–39. Todi: Mancini 1960.

138. Individual subdialects: Amaseno: Vignoli 1926. Castelmadama: Norreri 1905. Castro de' Volsci: Vignoli 1911. Cervara: Merlo 1922. Orvieto and Viterbo: Bianconi 1962. Paliano: Navone, 1922. Rieti: Campanelli 1896. S. Oreste: Elwert 1958. Sora: Merlo 1920. Subiaco: Lindsström 1907. Velletri: Crocioni 1907. Veroli: Vignoli 1925.

139. General: Tallenbach 1909; G. de Gregorio 1912; Merlo 1929; Ernst 1970. Lexicon: Merlo (ed.) 1932; Chiappini 1933; Belloni and Nilsson-Ehle 1957; Vaccaro 1969, 1971.

140. Bibliography: Rohlfs 1925. General: Parlangèli 1960a. Greek element: Morosi

44   COMPARATIVE ROMANCE GRAMMAR

1880; Rohlfs 1924, 1947; Caratzas 1958; Parlangèli 1960b. Comparison with Portuguese dialects: Lüdtke 1956b. Relation to Sardinian: Rohlfs 1937a.

141. General: Giammarco 1958, 1959, 1965. Phonology: Radica 1943/44. Lexicon: Finamore 1880; Giammarco 1967– . Individual subdialects: Agnone: Ziccardi 1910. Lexicon: Cremonesi 1893. Àquila: Rossi-Casè 1894. Campobasso: d'Ovidio 1878. Introdacqua: Giammarco 1964. Loreto Aprutino: Parlangèli 1952. Montella: Marano Festa 1928–33. Scanno: Schlack 1966. Tèramo: Savini 1881, 1895. Vasto: Rolin 1908. Lexicon: Anelli 1901.

142. Individual subdialects: Cilento: Ondis 1932; Rohlfs 1937b. Irpinia: general: de Salvio 1913. Lexicon: Nittoli 1873. Ischia: Freund 1934. Naples: general: Capozzoli 1889; Altamura 1961. Lexicon: Galiani 1789; Puoti 1841; d'Ambra 1873; Malato 1965.

143. Modern texts: M. Melillo 1970. Individual subdialects: Andria: Cotugno 1909. Bari: Lopez 1952. Bisceglie: I. de Gregorio 1939. Lexicon: Còcolo 1925. Cerignola: Zingarelli 1899–1901. Foggia: Bucci 1960–65. Francavilla Fontana: Ribezzo 1911. Gargano peninsula: G. Melillo 1926. Giovinazzo: Maldarelli 1967. Lecce: Morosi 1878. Martina Franca: Gius. Grassi 1925; Prete, 1925. Molfetta: Scardigno 1903, 1963a, 1963b. Salento region: general: Parlangèli 1953. Lexicon: Rohlfs 1956–59; Parlangèli 1958. Tàranto: de Vincentiis 1872.

144. General: de Salvio 1915; Lausberg 1939; Rensch 1964. Linguistic atlas: M. Melillo 1955. Individual subdialects: Matera: Festa 1916; Rivelli 1924.

145. Bibliography: M. V. Li Gotti 1968. General: Scerbo 1886. Lexicon: Rohlfs 1932–38, 1965–67; Longo 1935–40. Greek element: G. de Gregario 1930; Rohlfs 1933; Alessio 1934. Individual subdialects: Catanzaro: Cotronei 1895. Cittanova: Longo 1937. Cosenza: Gentili 1897.

146. General: Avolio 1882; Maccarrone 1915; Pagliaro 1934; Alessio 1946–48; Piccitto 1959; Rohlfs 1963, 1964/65. Phonology: Schneegans 1888; Ducibella 1934. Lexicon: Traina 1868; Piccitto 1967– . Substrata: Parlangèli 1964/65. Greek element: Parlangèli 1958. Arabic influence: Steiger 1932; Pellegrini 1962. Central Sicily: Piccitto 1969. Individual subdialects: Agrigento (Girgenti): Pirandello 1891. Caltagirone: Cremona 1895. Messina: Rohlfs 1962a. Modica: Schiavo-Lena 1908. Noto: Avolio 1875. Palermo: Calvaruso 1929. Ragusa: Piccitto 1941. Sciacca: Sacco 1925. Tortorici: Salvà 1959.

147. Cf. especially Menarini 1947a.

148. Cf. M. L. Wagner 1947; Meo-Zilio 1960, 1965a, b.

149. Cf. Rando 1967, 1968.

150. Cf. Berenblut 1949; Terracini 1951.

151. Cf. Bedarida 1956.

152. General discussion: Guarnerio 1892–98; Bàrtoli 1903; Wagner 1921, 1931; Sanna 1957. Bibliography: Hall 1942c; Maria T. Atzori 1953b. Relation to South Italian: Rohlfs 1937a. Historical phonology: Wagner 1941. Historical morphology: Wagner 1938–39. Historical word-formation: Wagner 1952. Etymological dictionary: Wagner 1960–64 (cf. also Maria T. Atzori 1961–65). Lexicon: Porru 1832, 1866; Maria T. Atzori 1953a. Linguistic atlas: Terracini and Franceschi (eds.) 1964– .

153. Cf. Hockett 1958:323–326.

154. Cf. Hofmann 1885; Campus 1901; Meyer-Lübke 1902. Individual subdialects: Bosa: Biddau 1905. Ìsili: Mario Atzori 1940. Nùoro: Pittau 1956.

155. Historical phonology: Wagner 1907. Lexicon: Atzeni 1897.

156. Cf. Sassu 1951. Lexicon: Muzzo 1953, 1955.

157. General: Puşcariu 1920, 1940; Niculescu 1956, 1965; Rosetti and Cazacu 1961; Daicoviciu, Petrovici, and Ştefan 1963; Graur 1965; Arvinte 1968; Coteanu and Dănăilă 1970. Eastern Romance: Puşcariu 1937; Lozovan 1968. Historical grammar: Densusianu

1901–38; Rosetti 1938, 1968. Historical phonetics: Nandriş 1963; Rothe 1957. Historical morphology: Rothe 1957. Historical syntax: Barbu 1944. Etymological dictionaries: Cihac 1870–79; Puşcariu 1905; Domaschke 1919; Cioránescu 1958– .

Descriptive grammar: Pop 1948; Agard 1958. Phonetics: Lombard 1936. Phonology: Vasiliu 1965; Roceric-Alexandrescu 1968. Morphology: Iordan et al. 1967; Guţu-Romalo 1968. Syntax: Sandfeld and Olsen 1936–62; Drăganu 1945; Budagov 1958. Lexicon: Macrea (ed.) 1958. Frequency: Juilland et al. 1965.

158. Cf. Borsci et al. 1956. For a discussion of the claims of Moldavian to be a separate language, cf. Tagliavini 1947 (1965): §64. Linguistic atlases: Udler et al. 1968.

159. Relation between standard language and dialect: Lăzărescu 1967.

160. Daco-Roumanian in general: Petrovici 1964; Coteanu 1961. Historical phonology: Vasiliu 1968. Linguistic atlases: Weigand 1898–1909; Pop and Petrovici (eds.) 1938–42a, 1938–42b; Cazacu et al. (eds.) 1968– . Individual subdialects: Banat: Weigand 1897, 1899. Bessarabia and Bucovina: Weigand 1904. Dobrudja and Moldau: Weigand 1902. Crisana: Weigand 1896. Maramureş: Papahagi 1925. Muntenia: Popovici 1905. Oltenia: Gamillscheg 1919, 1936. Transylvania: Candrea 1907; Densusianu 1915. Wallachia: Weigand 1888, 1900, 1901. Vrancea: Diaconu 1930.

161. Cf. Capidan 1925–35.

162. General: Weigand 1894–95, 1907; Capidan 1932. Historical phonology: von Miklosich 1881–83; Caragiu-Marioţeanu 1968. Lexicon: Dalametra 1906; Pascu 1925; Papahagi 1963.

163. Texts: Cantemir 1959. General: Popovici 1908–14; Puşcariu et al. 1926–29; Coteanu 1957. Lexicon: Byhan 1899.

164. Cf. Roz 1957. For French in Africa, cf. Bal 1968.

165. Cf. Pompilus 1961a, 1961b.

166. Cf. Roumiguière 1926.

167. Cf. Schiaffini 1943.

168. For general bibliography of pidgins and creoles, cf. Reinecke and Tsuzaki, forthcoming.

169. Cf. Schuchardt 1909.

170. Cf. R. W. Thompson 1961; D. Taylor 1961; Whinnom 1965.

171. Cf. Egerod 1958.

172. Reinecke 1936. For Portuguese pidgins and creoles in general, cf. Coelho 1880–86; Schuchardt 1888–89, 1882–90; Leite de Vasconcelos 1897–99; Valkhoff 1966; Morais-Barbosa (ed.) 1967. Individual varieties: Cabo Verde: Lopes da Silva 1957. Guinea: de Barros 1897/99; Wilson 1962.

173. Cf. Ribeiro 1939; Silva Neto 1949; Révah 1963; Elia 1966.

174. Cf. Silva Neto 1938a for the Portuguese element in Sranan (the English-based creole of Surinam).

175. For the trade-Spanish of the Piñaguero Panare in Venezuela, cf. Riley 1952; for the Philippine contact-languages based on Spanish, cf. McKaughan 1954; Whinnom 1956.

176. Cf. Lenz 1926–27; Navarro Tomás 1953; Wood 1972. Some scholars consider Papiamentu to be of Portuguese rather than Spanish origin (cf. van Wijk 1958); but others (e.g. Rona 1971) reject this theory.

177. Cf. Poyen-Bellisle 1894; Stewart 1962. African substratum in the French-based creoles: Göbl-Gáldi 1933, 1934; Sylvain 1936; Hall 1950c; Goodman 1964; Valkhoff 1969.

178. Cf. Mercier 1880; Lane 1935; Broussard 1942; Morgan 1959, 1960.

179. Cf. Sylvain 1936; Faine 1937, 1939; Pressoir 1947; Hall et al. 1953; Zumthor

1953; Hall 1962b, Social status of Creole: Efron 1954; Valdman 1969. Haitian Creole dialects: Hyppolite 1950.

180. Cf. D. Taylor 1947, 1951.

181. Cf. Turialt 1874; Jourdain 1956a, 1956b.

182. Cf. Thomas 1889; Goodman 1958.

183. Cf. de Saint-Quentin 1872; North 1949.

184. Cf. Ad. Dietrich 1891.

185. Cf. Baissac 1880; Urruty 1950–51.

186. Cf. Focard 1885; Valkhoff 1964.

187. Cf. Nardo Cibele 1900.

188. For the modern Venetian dialect of Veglia, cf. Königes 1933.

189. Cf. Ive 1886; Bàrtoli 1910a.

190. Cf. Bàrtoli 1942. Dalmatian elements in mediaeval Slavic documents: Muljačić 1962.

191. Cf. Hadlich 1965.

192. Cf. Schuchardt 1909; Corominas 1948; Kahane, Kahane, and Tietze 1958.

193. Cf. Lewicki 1951/52.

194. Cf. Vising 1900–02, 1923; Menger 1904. Lexicon: Moisy 1889. Historical grammar: Pope 1934 is strongly oriented towards Anglo-Norman.

195. Cf. C. Leonard 1964.

CHAPTER 3

Latin in Early Italy

3.1. Latin and Its Congeners

The Romance languages have developed, over somewhat more than two millennia, out of Latin. At the beginning of recorded (but still somewhat mythical) history, in the eighth century B.C., Latin was the speech of a small area around the mouth of the Tiber, known as Latium (whence the name *lingua latīna* 'the Latin tongue'). The history of Latin and Romance is that of the gradual spread of the former and its eventual differentiation into the latter.[1]

3.11. LATIN AND INDO-EUROPEAN. Latin was one of the family of *Italic* languages, which included Latin-Faliscan and Osco-Umbrian (see below). This, in its turn, formed part of the Indo-European stock or super-family, which included also the language-groups of Keltic, Germanic, Balto-Slavic, Greek, Albanian, Armenian, Indo-Iranian, Hittite, and Tocharian.[2] The degree of closeness between Latin and the other Indo-European languages can be seen from the comparative lists in Table VI. Proto-Indo-European is known only from comparative reconstruction: there are no written attestations of Proto-Indo-European, nor is it certain where it was spoken. Some scholars place the Indo-European home-land in present-day southern Russia, not far from the Caucasus.[3] It is generally considered that the Indo-European speech-community broke up and that its various sub-groups moved, in relatively large-scale migrations (?),[4] to their earliest attested historical locations beginning around 1500 B.C. The linguistic ancestors of the Latin speech-community are usually thought[5] to have entered Italy from the north ca. 1200 or 1000 B.C.

3.12. LATIN-FALISCAN. Latin itself was at first restricted to an area extending not more than twenty-five miles in any direction from the present city of Rome. The earliest documentation of Latin is by some considered to be an inscription on a brooch dating from the seventh century B.C., found

TABLE VI

Sample Correspondences between Latin and Selected Indo-European
Languages (Greek, Sanskrit, Old Church Slavonic, Gothic, Old Irish)

	"brother"	"carry"	"flee, bend"	"split, bite"	"beech"
Latin	frātr-	fer-	fug-	find-	fāgo-
Greek	φρᾱτρ- "member of a religious brotherhood'	φερ-	φυγ-	φειδ- "save, spare"	φᾱγο- 'a kind of oak'
Sanskrit	bhrātar-	bhar-	bhuj-	bhind-	—
Old Church Slavonic	bratr-	ber- "gather, take"	—	—	—
Gothic	brōþar	ber-	biug-	beit-	OHG buohha OEng. bōc
Old Irish	brāthir	ber-	bocc "bow (n.)"	—	—
Proto-I.E.	*bhrātr-	*bher-	*bhug-	*bhi(n)d-	*bhāgo-

at Palestrina (ancient Praeneste), 20 miles east of Rome: MANIOS
MED FHEFHAKED NUMASIOI.[6] Others[7] regard the Praenestine
brooch-inscription as Oscan, and consider a cippus found in the Roman
Forum and dating from the end of the sixth century B.C.,[8] and a vase from
the beginning of the fifth century B.C., as the earliest attestations of Latin.
Only a few words of the Forum cippus-inscription are intelligible, such as
iouxmenta kapiat 'let him take the draught-animals' (= CL *iumenta capiat*).
Similarly, on the vase the longest intelligible passage is *iouesat deiuos quo
med mitat* 'he who sends me swears [to] the gods' (= CL *iūrat deōs quī mē
mittit*).

The language of ancient Italy most closely related to Latin was Faliscan,[9]
spoken at Falerii, north of Rome near the right bank of the Tiber and on
the western edge of Etruscan territory. Most scholars place Latin and
Faliscan together, as opposed to the "Italic" dialects (Oscan, Umbrian,
etc.; see the next section).

3.13. THE ITALIC DIALECTS. Under this (somewhat misleading) name
are classified a number of tongues which were spoken in central Italy during
the first millennium B.C. They include three main groups:

1. Ancient Umbrian, spoken in the upper Tiber valley.[10]
2. The Sabellic dialects, used by groups living in a semicircle around
Rome: Sabine, in the middle Tiber valley; Paelignian, Marrucin-

ian, Vestine, and Marsic in the central Appennines east of Rome; and Volscian to the south-east, between modern Velletri and Formia. There were Sabine settlements on the Quirinal in the earliest years of Rome (cf. §4.31).

3. Oscan, spoken in a wide area of southern Italy, including Samnium, Campania, and Lucania, as well as Messina in Sicily.[11]

These languages were probably mutually comprehensible. Old Latin would not have been too hard for speakers of the Italic dialects to understand, before Latin intervocalic /-s-/ became /-r-/ and before Latin pretonic vowels were weakened (cf. §§4.121, 4.122); afterwards, mutual comprehensibility was clearly reduced. Among the characteristic features of the Italic dialects were:

a. The preservation of earlier intervocalic /-s-/, as opposed to its development to /-r-/ in Latin ("rhotacism"; cf. §4.121).

b. The development of /-nd-/ > /-nn-/, and of /-mb-/ > /-mm-/. The preservation of /-s-/ and the change of /-nd-/ to /-nn-/ are exemplified in Oscan UPSANNAM = Lat. *operandam* 'to be done', both < Proto-Italic */opusandam/.

c. The passage of Proto-Italic /-bh-/ to /-f-/ in all positions, as opposed to Lat. /f-/ initially and /b/ elsewhere, *e.g.* in Ancient Umbr. *alfu* 'white': Lat. *albo-*, both < PIt. */albho-/.

d. Proto-Italic /kʷ/ > /p/, and /gʷ/ > /b/, as opposed to their preservation in Latin: cf. Osc. *pid* 'what': Lat. /kʷid/ *quid* < PIt. /kʷid/; Ancient Umbr. *umen* 'finger-nail' < */umben/: Lat. /ungʷen/ *unguen* < PIt. */ungʷen/.

3.2. Pre-Latin ("Substratum") Languages[12]

3.21. INDO-EUROPEAN

3.211. KELTIC is the name given to a group of related languages which includes modern Scots Gaelic, Manx Gaelic (now extinct), Irish, Welsh, Cornish (whose last monolingual native speaker died in 1777[13]), and Breton. Since the early Middle Ages, after the Keltic tribes had been driven back by Germanic and other invaders, Keltic languages have been spoken only in marginal areas of western Europe and the western British Isles. In earlier times, Keltic was used over a much wider area. Most scholars consider that, because of certain shared peculiarities (especially the use of an element ending in /-r/ in the formation of the passive), Proto-Italic and Proto-Keltic were more closely related to each other than to other Indo-European languages.[14] Their common ancestor, Proto-Italo-Keltic, is thought by some to have been spoken somewhere east of the Rhine, perhaps in modern Thuringia, whence the linguistic ancestors of the Italic group would have migrated south to Italy, and those of the Keltic group both westwards and eastwards. At one time, just before the dawn of recorded history in Italy (*i.e.* ca. 500–400 B.C.), Keltic languages were spoken over a wide area from Iberia to Asia Minor.[15] Ancient sources mention a people known as Celtiberi living in the first-mentioned region. Most of the territory of ancient Gaul was occupied by speakers of Gallic or Gaulish[16]; most of ancient Britain, by speakers of Brythonic, mutually intelligible with Gaulish. Extensive migrations of Keltic speakers in the centuries before 400 B.C. had carried them as far east as Galatia in Asia Minor, and place-names ascribed to a Keltic substratum are found throughout central Europe, in modern Switzerland, southern Germany, and Austria.[17]

Of especial importance in the history of Latin were the Keltic invasions and settlements in Italy. Successive waves of Keltic tribes led to the occupation of the Po valley by Gauls in the fifth century B.C., and to incursions farther south into the Tiber valley. It was one such invasion, under Brennus, that led to the capture and nearly total destruction of Rome (except for the Capitol) by the Gauls in 390 B.C. The Gauls were later driven back north, but their settlements in the Po valley were permanent. The Romans used the name *Gallia* both for modern France (*Gallia Transalpīna* 'Gaul across the Alps') and the Po valley (*Gallia Cisalpīna* 'Gaul this side of the Alps').

3.212.   Greek was, of the Indo-European languages, the most important one with which speakers of Latin came into contact, from the earliest days of Rome onwards. For them, the prime source of Greek influence was, at first, Etruscan (cf. §3.221) as an intermediary, and, later, direct contacts with the Greeks of the southern part of Italy and eastern Sicily. Here, the coast-line was so extensively settled by Greek colonists as to receive the name of *Magna Graecia* 'Greater Greece'. The often rich and prosperous cities of this region were settled from the Greek home-land principally from the eighth to the sixth centuries B.C.

In Greece itself, in the first half of the first millennium B.C., there was no single dominant variety of speech, but a number of closely related dialects of about equal standing. The Greek states were politically independent of, and often at war with, each other; coöperation against a common enemy, as against the Persians in 490 and 480–479 B.C., was the exception rather than the rule. Of the Greek dialects, the most important were Attic (used in Athens and the surrounding region of Attica), Ionic (in the Greek settlements along the coast of Asia Minor and on the nearby off-shore islands), and Doric (in the northwest of Greece and the Peloponnesus).[18] On Attic, with an admixture of Ionic characteristics, was based Classical Greek, the language of literature and general usage from the fifth century onwards. Attic-Ionic had several peculiarities as against the other Greek dialects, notably the change of /aː/ to /eˑ/, as in /máːteːr/ 'mother' > /méːteːr/ μή τ ηρ, or /máːlon/ 'apple' > /méːlon/ μῆλον. Other dialects, including Doric, preserved /aˑ/ as such, and it was primarily these latter varieties that were carried to Italy and Sicily by the settlers of Magna Graecia.

3.213. PRE-ITALIC DIALECTS is the name given to other varieties of speech used in ancient Italy (whether Indo-European or not) before the spread of Latin. In general, attestations of these languages are very scanty, so that their affiliation is often in doubt.[19] Among those commonly considered to be Indo-European (though in general rather distantly related to Latin) are:

1. Messapic, spoken in what is now Apulia, and perhaps related to Illyrian, which was spoken directly across the Adriatic.[20]
2. Venetic, used around the northern end of the Adriatic.[21]
3. Rhaetic, in the Alps north of present-day Venetia, Lombardy, and Piedmont, and perhaps in the Po valley before the coming of the Etruscans (cf. §3.22.1) and of the Gauls (cf. §3.13).
4. Ligurian, used along what is now the Italian and French Riveria, and perhaps to the north of this area in present-day Piedmont and Savoy.

In the earlier period of Roman history, other Indo-European languages were too far removed geographically to be of any importance for the history of Latin. Proto-Germanic or its predecessor[22] was spoken around the mouth of the Elbe, in Schleswig-Holstein, and in southern Scandinavia. The first incursions of Germanic tribes into the Mediterranean region were those of the Cimbri and Teutones in 102–101 B.C., but Germanic speech became important for the history of Latin only later, in Imperial times.[23] With Balto-Slavic, Indo-Iranian, etc., speakers of earlier Latin had virtually no contact.

3.22. NON-INDO-EUROPEAN LANGUAGES. In the middle and latter part of the first millennium B.C., a number of non-Indo-European languages were spoken in Italy and around the Mediterranean. Most of them are scantily attested, and of some we know nothing but their names.

3.221. ETRUSCAN is one of the most discussed and at the same time the least known of languages. This paradox is due to the fact that a number of Etruscan texts has been preserved, but no satisfactory bilingual inscription or other key to their decipherment is available.[24] Hence only so much can be known as can be deduced from internal evidence in the texts themselves, by the "combinatory" method, with very little information concerning their meaning.

The origin of Etruscan and the Etruscans is quite obscure. Attempts have been made to interpret it as Indo-European, and also as "Mediterranean" and autochthonous in Italy (cf. §3.223).[25] Most scholars, however, consider that the account given by Herodotus (1.94) is substantially accurate, and that the earliest Etruscans came to Italy from Asia Minor, by way of northern Africa.[26] In the earliest historical times, the Etruscans occupied two main regions: Etruria, to the north-west of Rome, in a rather larger area than present-day Tuscany, and a large part of the lower and central Po valley. It is not known whether the one region was settled from the other (presumably the Po valley from Etruria), or the two were the result of separate immigrations.

The sociolinguistic situation in ancient Etruria is also unclear. It is not known whether all strata of the population spoke Etruscan, or (perhaps more likely) Etruscan was spoken only by a small upper-class group in each city-state, while the other city-dwellers and the country-folk used a different tongue, possibly one or more Italic languages.

The Etruscans probably arrived in Italy around 1000–800 B.C., and their power was strongest from 700 to 500 B.C. At its greatest, it extended from the Po valley to the north, down the Tyrrhenian side of Italy, to Campania. For a hundred years or more, in the latter part of the regal period (ca. 600–500 B.C.), Rome was ruled by Etruscans.[27] Even after the Etruscan king Tarquinius (= Etr. Tarχnas) Superbus was expelled (according to traditional history) in 509 B.C., a considerable proportion of the Roman patrician clans were of Etruscan origin. Many Roman names (*e.g. Tarquinius, Larcius, Maecenas*), customs, beliefs, and rites (*e.g.* in their sooth-saying practices) were Etruscan. Many cultural advances (*e.g.* the alphabet, the drama) came to the Etruscans through their contacts with the Greeks in Campania, and passed to Rome through Etruscan intermediaries.

The Etruscans' political power seems to have been based chiefly on loose alliances among separate city-states, rather than on a strong central organization. To this cause is generally ascribed the gradual decline of Etruria after ca. 500 B.C., under the pressure of expanding Roman power from the south and Keltic invasions from the north. How long Etruscan continued to be spoken, is not known. By the time of the emperor Claudius (cf. fn.

24), it may already have been a "dead" language, preserved only in the books of the augurs for ritual use.

3.222. OTHER NON-INDO-EUROPEAN OR DOUBTFUL LANGUAGES. Of these, little is known except their names. In most instances, not enough attestations have survived to enable their affiliation to be determined precisely. In Sicily, the Greek colonists found a language called Sikel.[28] In Sardinia, before the Punic conquest, there were one or more peoples who presumably were the builders of the large stone fortresses known as *nuraghi*, and of whose language some words may survive in modern Sardinian.[29] In Iberia, it is not clear whether the ancient Iberi spoke the ancestor-language of modern Basque, or whether Iberian and pre-Basque were two different tongues,[30] with the latter spoken on both sides of the Pyrenees by groups related to the ancient Aquitani. Thracian, spoken in ancient Thrace and north of there in Dacia and the lower Danube valley, is considered by some, but not by others, to have been Indo-European[31]; it is often invoked as a substratum-language to account for developments in Roumanian.

Of the languages spoken in the eastern end of the Mediterranean, the only group that needs concern us is the Hamito-Semitic stock. To the Hamitic family belonged ancient Egyptian; to the Semitic belonged Arabic, Hebrew, and the language of the Phoenicians along the Mediterranean coast of Palestine. Of this latter tongue, a variety known as Punic was carried by Tyrian colonists to Carthage and its settlements in northern Africa, Sicily, Sardinia, and Iberia.

3.223. "MEDITERRANEAN." Some scholars[32] have searched for more distant and extensive relationships between the early pre-Latin languages of the Mediterranean and those spoken farther east. The sources for such comparisons are particularly Basque and the Caucasian languages. These two groups, being located in marginal zones on either side of the Mediterranean basin, might be expected to be archaic in character, and have certain structural features in common (*e.g.* the use of a special "ergative" case for the subject of a passive verb) which seem to indicate an ultimate genetic relationship. To evidence of this kind are added presumed lexical survivals in Romance and other European languages, particularly place-names and dialectal terms for geographical features, flora, and fauna, which might be expected to have been taken over from the earlier inhabitants by speakers of more lately-arrived tongues. No correspondences systematic enough to establish a comparative grammar have been discovered, but a number of single words have been reconstructed such as *tauru-* 'hill', *ganda* 'scree (slide of gravel down a mountain-side)', *karra* or *garra* 'stone; rocky ground; plant growing thereon', *sala 'slide of earth; channel', or *magŭra 'height, mountain'.[33] Such "Mediterranean" reconstructions are always less certain than forms attested directly or established on the basis of systematic sound-correspondences (cf. Vol. II), but the possibility of pre-Latin survivals in Romance is of course always present.

NOTES TO CHAPTER 3

1. For the language-situation in ancient Italy, cf. Gröber (ed.) 1886–88:1.281–414 ("Die vorromanischen Völkersprachen"; in the 2nd ed., 1.351–497); Buck 1905; Kent 1932:27–29; Pulgram 1958; Haas 1960a.
2. Cf. Meillet 1903; Hirt 1921–37; Pagliaro 1930; Buck 1933; Lehmann 1962; Devoto 1962; Georgiev 1966.
3. Cf. Hirt 1905–07; Carnoy 1921; Bender 1922; Lehmann 1962:207–209.
4. On the analogy of the attested Völkerwanderungen in the times of the late Roman Empire and thereafter; but cf. Pulgram 1958.
5. Cf. Homo 1927:48–52; Devoto 1936, chapter 2; Poultney 1959:9.
6. This sentence would be, in the Classical Latin of seven centuries later, *Manius mē fēcit Numeriō* 'Manius made me for Numerius'. The Praenestine inscription manifests several characteristics of Old Latin: /-s-/ between vowels which had not yet become /-r-/, unstressed pretonic /a/ not yet reduced to /e/, and the dative singular ending /-o:i/ ≠ later /-o:/, all in NUMASIOI; final /-os/ of the nominative singular, not yet become /-us/ in MANIOS; final /-d/ in the accusative pronoun MED; and reduplication of the first syllable of the root in the present perfective FHEFHAKED (as if it were CL *fefēcit*, parallel to *cecinit* 'he has sung', *fefellit* 'he has deceived': *can-* 'sing' and *fall-* 'deceive', respectively).
7. *E.g.* Devoto 1936, chapter 2:5.
8. Usually called the "Duenos vase" from the first words of the inscription, *Duenos med feced* 'Duenos [= CL Bonus] made me'.
9. Cf. G. Giacomelli 1963.
10. Not to be confused with the modern Umbrian dialect of Italian (cf. §2.13.2.b.iv), spoken in a somewhat larger area. Our main source of information for ancient Umbrian is the seven bronze tablets found in 1444 at Gubbio (ancient Iguvium); cf. Devoto 1948, 1954; Poultney 1959; Ernout 1961.
11. For Oscan and Umbrian in general, cf. Buck 1904; Devoto 1951a; Bottiglioni 1954. Oscan and Umbrian are by many considered to have had a common origin with Latin in a Proto-Italic period (cf. Meillet 1928, chapter 4). Some reject this hypothesis, considering the similarities between Latin and the Italic dialects to have been recent cultural borrowings (in Devoto's words [1936, chapter 2:5] "le affinità fra latino e osco-umbro sono recenti; le diversità sono antiche"). In addition to Devoto, cf. Marstrander 1929; Delfino 1958; Pisani 1962, chapter 3; Beeler 1966.
12. Cf., in general, Conway, Whatmough, and Johnson 1933.
13. Cornish is still, however, kept artificially "alive," by a group of literati, native speakers of English who cultivate Cornish as a literary language; cf. Parry 1946.
14. Cf. Meillet 1928, chapter 9; Whatmough 1944:36.
15. Cf. Whatmough 1944:41.
16. Cf. Whatmough 1970.

17. Cf. Whatmough 1944:37–39.

18. For the Greek dialects in general, cf. Buck 1955.

19. For the prae-Italic dialects in general, cf. Conway, Whatmough, and Johnson 1933; Pisani 1952.

20. Cf. Whatmough 1937:320–322. Haas (1962:11–13) opposes this theory. Cf. also Polomé 1966.

21. Cf. Beeler 1949; Polomé 1966; Pellegrini and Prosdòcimi 1967.

22. For a theory that Proto-Germanic may have originated as a creolised version of some Indo-European language (perhaps Venetic), in connection with the prehistoric amber-trade between the Mediterranean and the Baltic, cf. Feist 1932.

23. The language of certain German-speaking communities in the Àdige valley was earlier thought to be of Cimbric origin, but has been shown to be simply an Austro-Bavarian dialect; cf. Tagliavini 1947 (1969ᶠ): §§35, 68.

24. The emperor Claudius (10 B.C.–A.D. 54) is said to have studied Etruscan and written an Etruscan history, but his treatise has unfortunately not survived.

25. Pallottino (e.g. 1936, 1947) is the chief remaining defender of this position. The most recent over-all presentation of Etruscan is Pfiffig 1960.

26. The parallel between the probable settlement-route of the Etruscans and that followed by Aeneas in his legendary journey from Troy to Carthage and Italy is striking. In all probability, Aeneas was originally an Etruscan founder-hero, later taken over by the Romans through the traditions of the Etruscan element of the Roman aristocracy (cf. most recently Alföldi 1957 and 1964:278–287; Georgiev 1966:276–282). Similarly, the legend that Mantua was settled by Antenor, after a voyage from Troy up the Adriatic may be a reflection of the actual settlement-history. These considerations of a nonlinguistic nature have been cited by Georgiev (1962; 1966:262–286) in support of his thesis that Etruscan is related to Hittite, and thereby distantly to Indo-European; but many scholars (e.g. Poultney 1968:340–341) are skeptical of Georgiev's linguistic arguments.

27. Cf. Homo 1927:113–122; Alföldi 1964. Dionysius of Halicarnassus says (Antiquitates Romanae 1.29): "There was a time when the Latins, the Umbrians, the Ausoni, and many others were called Etruscans by the Greeks [. . .]. Many historians even held that Rome was an Etruscan city."

28. Possibly an Illyrian dialect related to Messapic; cf. Whatmough 1937:264.

29. Cf. Wagner 1951, chapter 11.

30. Cf. Jungemann 1955; Schmoll 1959; Tovar 1961.

31. Cf. Duridanov 1969; Haas 1960b, 1964; Hubschmid, 1964; Reichenkron, 1958–60, 1966.

32. E.g. Bertoldi 1931, 1937, 1945, 1950 (cf. also Malkiel 1950); Bouda 1949; Hubschmid 1949, 1951, 1963.

33. Cf. Aebischer 1931; Bertoldi 1931; Alessio 1935–36; Battisti 1933; Pop 1949/50, respectively.

CHAPTER 4

The Spread and Differentiation of Latin

4.1. From Old to Classical Latin

It is traditional to consider the history of Latin as extending from earliest Roman times (ca. 800 B.C.) to the late Roman Empire (ca. A.D. 450), with mediaeval and Renaissance Latin either neglected or relegated to a minor position; and that of the Romance languages as beginning with "Vulgar Latin," which is usually placed in Imperial times.[1] In fact, no sharp break or even relatively rapid transition took place. The roots of Romance developments are to be sought far back in Republican Latin. Certain features absent from Classical Latin but present in Romance[2] are attested as far back as the comedies of Plautus (ca. 250–184 B.C.). We shall therefore give a brief account, in this chapter, of the way in which Latin spread from its place of origin in Rome to its greatest extent under the emperors; in Chapter 5, of the languages which were superimposed on popular Latin speech as a result of post-Imperial migrations; and, in Chapters 6–10, of the rise of new standard languages and their later vicissitudes in Romance territory.

4.11. NON-LATIN INFLUENCES ON OLD LATIN

4.111. SABINE. Before Rome was founded, there were three Latin-speaking villages on the Palatine hill (the original *Roma quadrata* 'square Rome') and four Sabine villages on the Quirinal along the *Alta Sēmita* ('High Path', the present Via del Quirinale and Via Venti Settembre). Rome was formed by the fusion of the settlements on these two hills, with a common gathering-place at the crossing of the intervening brook (the Forum) and a common ritual center on the Capitoline.[3]

In the resultant double city, both Sabine and Latin must have been spoken for a time. They were probably close enough at that time to be mutually intelligible (as were, say, Anglo-Saxon and Danish in eastern England when that area formed part of Denmark in the eighth and ninth centuries A.D.). Sabine eventually yielded to Latin, but not without leaving

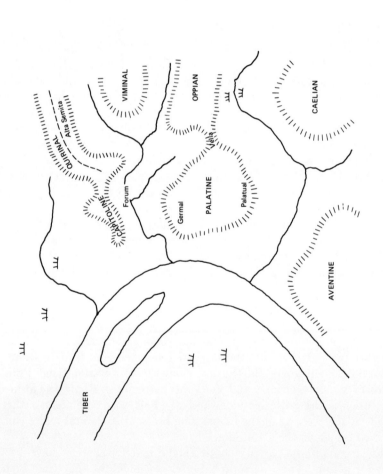

MAP I. Pre-Etruscan Rome (ca. 800 B.C.)

traces in the shape of loan-words, whose nature points to "intimate" borrowing. One of the special characteristics of Sabine was the development of /d/ to /l/. Some Latin words show /l/ where we might, on the basis of their relation to cognates in Latin or other Indo-European languages, expect /d/: e.g. *lingua* 'tongue' instead of OLat. *dingua* (: Eng. *tongue*); *lacrima* 'tear' instead of OLat. *dacruma* (: Gk. δάκρυ, Eng. *tear*); or *olēre* 'to smell' as contrasted with *odor*. Such Latin words are therefore very early Sabinisms.[4]

4.112. ETRUSCAN. During the period of Etruscan domination. Latin received a number of loan-words from that language, mainly in certain special fields, such as religion and sooth-saying (*caerimōnia* 'cremony'; *Angerōna* 'goddess of death'), the drama (*hister, histriō* 'actor', *persōna* 'mask'), and music (*subulō* 'flute-player'), and perhaps others (*e.g. miles milit-* 'soldier'; *servus* 'servant'; *triumphus* 'triumph'; *barō barōn-* 'strong man, lout').[5] The Roman naming-system of *praenōmen* (first name) + *nōmen gentīle* (clan-name) + *cognōmen* (family-name) was of Etruscan origin, as were the names of the three first centuries of Roman *equitēs* or 'knights': *Ramnes, Luceres, Tities*.

4.12. PHONOLOGICAL DEVELOPMENTS

4.121. RHOTACISM. Towards the end of the Old Latin period (ca. 300 B.C.), the change of intervocalic /s/ to /r/ ("rhotacism") already referred to took place. This left Latin with extensive morphophonemic alternations between /-r/ and nonintervocalic /s/. Thus, in the ending of the infinitive, most Latin verbs had /-re/ (*e.g. lavāre* 'to wash', *vidēre* 'to see'), but a few, with zero thematic vowel, had /-se/, as did *es-se* 'to be', *pos-se* 'to be able' (<*pot-se*). In the inflection of certain nouns, and in derivatives based on them, /-r-/ alternates with final or preconsonantal /s/: thus, the root *honōr-* 'honour' has the nominative *honōs* (also *honor* by analogy with the other declined forms) and such derivatives as *hones-tāt-* 'honesty'. Rhotacism was complete before the time of Plautus, and all Romance developments derive from post-rhotacistic Latin.

4.122. REDUCTION OF UNSTRESSED VOWELS. Another characteristic of Old Latin, which lasted somewhat longer, was the extensive and systematic "reduction" (mostly raising) of unstressed short vowels. This followed regular patterns, especially in medial syllables,[6] with a number of specially conditioned changes. The most regular and extensive are exemplified in Table VII.

To this vocalic reduction are due various morphophonemic alternations

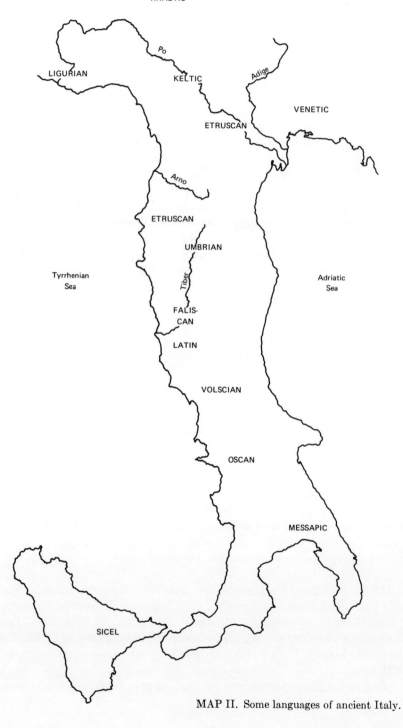

MAP II. Some languages of ancient Italy.

TABLE VII

Samples of Vowel-Reduction in Early Latin

Vowel	Root	Checked Syllable	Free Syllable
a	fac- 'to do'	ef-fect-um 'effected'	ef-fic-ere 'to effect'
a	fall- 'to deceive'	fe-fell-it 'he deceived'	
o	novo- 'new'		novi-tāt- 'newness'
o	onos 'burden'	onustus 'burdensome'	
e	leg- 'to bind'		col-lig-ere 'to bind together'
ou̯	*dē nou̯ōd 'anew'		denuō
au̯	clau̯d- 'to close'		con-clūd-ere 'to close thoroughly, conclude'

in Latin inflection and derivation, *e.g. honos ∼ honestāt-* (cited above). A number of perfective stems and past participles show this type of alternation, *e.g. can-* 'sing' imperfective ∼ *cecin-* perfective. In derivation, we find such relationships as *effic-* 'to effect' (past participle *effect-*): *fac-* 'do'. These patterns of vocalic reduction lasted long enough for them to affect the earliest Greek loan-words (cf. §4.131).

4.123. STRESS. The vocalic "reductions" just discussed are usually ascribed to a heavy stress falling automatically on the initial syllable of each Latin word. This initial stress was later replaced by an (equally automatic) placing of stress on the syllable containing the third mora[7] from the end of the word, counting the last syllable as containing only one mora even through it might be checked or contain a long vowel. Thus, /u̯ide:re/ 'to see' was stressed [u̯i-'de:-re], /u̯ide:bit/ 'he will see' [u̯i-'de:-bit], /kari:na/ 'keel' [ka-'ri:-na], and /kari:na:/ 'from the keel' [ka-'ri:-na:]; but /karmina/ 'songs' ['kar-mi-na], /homini·/ 'to the man' ['ho-mi-ni·], /hominibus/ 'to the men' [ho-'mi-ni-bus]. All the prosodic patterns of Romance go back to this latter type of stress.

4.124. MONOPHTHONGISATION. A further linguistic change in the development from Old to Classical Latin was the monophthongisation of the diphthongs /ei/ and /ou/ to /i·/ and /u·/, respectively, as in /deikerent/ *deicerent* '(that) they should say' > /di·kerent/ *dīcerent*, or /iouksmenta/ *iouxmenta* 'herds' > /iu·menta/ *iūmenta*.[8] This change took place ca. 170–150 B.C. All Romance developments are post-monophthongal.

4.13. THE ROMANISATION OF ITALY took place essentially between the fourth century B.C. and the first century A.D., as Roman power was gradually extended over the whole peninsula.[9] It must not be assumed that Latin was substituted for the language previously spoken, in any given region, immediately on conquest by Rome. On the contrary, it often took centuries for Latin to supplant the local language, and in a few instances outside of Italy, *e.g.* Basque, it never did. Oscan remained extensively enough in use down to the end of the second century B.C. for it to be the official language of the anti-Roman allies in the Social War of 91–88 B.C. It was still being used in Pompeii at the time this city was buried in the eruption of Vesuvius in A.D. 79, at least enough to be used in election-campaign-propaganda scribbled on the walls of houses. Greek continued in very active use in Magna Graecia all throughout the Republic and the Empire. Many scholars[10] consider that the Greek used to the present day in certain small villages in the toe of Calabria and in Apulia goes back to the language spoken in Magna Graecia, and does not represent a reimportation of Greek in later times under Byzantine rule. Those who support this view argue that such forms as /tomálo/ 'the apple' go back, not to the Attic-Ionic koiné (which, by Byzantine times, had replaced all other varieties of Greek except Zaconian, in the region of Sparta), but to the Doric of Magna Graecia (cf. §3.212).

Roman rule was not extended by a simple process of direct and complete annexation of one adjoining territory after another. Rather, Rome entered into different types of alliance with countries and city-states both near and far. In certain situations, when enemy territory had been conquered or allied states had rebelled, Rome took over the entire area and sent out colonists—often retired soldiers or *veteranī*—to whom the land of the vanquished was allotted. The conquered peoples were (after the earliest times) sometimes sold into slavery, sometimes left in their territory in an inferior status. Consequently, at any given time during the expansion of Roman power in the Republican period, the map of Italy looked like a crazy quilt, with directly ruled areas, colonies, allies of varying degrees of closeness in association, and non-Roman territory all jumbled together. As time went on, and especially under the Empire, these distinctions disappeared. In the first century B.C., all inhabitants of Italy were declared Roman citizens, and thenceforth, from a legal point of view, the peninsula was unified.

In language-matters, Roman policy was the opposite of what is considered to be imperialistic practice in modern times. Rome did not impose the Latin language upon conquered peoples or allies. On the contrary, the use of Latin was treated as a special privilege. Latin was then rendered highly desirable, and its use was sought after in what was actually an extended period (at least several centuries) of wide-spread bi- or plurilingualism in Rome and its domains. For instance, the poet Ennius (ca. 239–169 B.C.) spoke of himself as having "three hearts" because he was a trilingual speaker of Greek, Oscan, and Latin.[11]

In this situation, it would hardly be surprising that a number of local populations should learn Latin, speak it with peculiarities carried over from their earlier language (in "accent," grammar, vocabulary), and hand it down to their linguistic descendants with these features. Extensive claims have been made for the influence of the various pre-Latin languages upon the Latin spoken in the different regions of Italy, and hence for the survival of such substrata in modern Italian dialects.[12] Such claims have to be evaluated, not *en bloc*, but according to the conditions prevailing in each instance of a presumed substratum-influence. For us to accept the possibility of such an influence, three conditions must be met for each case, independently of any other cases:

1. The languages involved must be shown to have been in sufficient contact for a period of bilingualism to have existed;
2. The period of bilingualism must have been long enough to have affected one or more generations of speakers;
3. It must be demonstrated that the alleged substratum-language actually had the structural feature(s) ascribed to its influence on the later language.

We may divide the cases of presumed substratum-influence into three types.

Type 1: Those for which the three conditions set forth above are met, and hence a substratum-influence can be considered reasonable: *e.g.* that of the Italic dialects in the development /-nd-/ > /-nn-/ and /-mb-/ > /-mm-/ (cf. §2.13.B) in a wide region of central Italy, exactly where this phenomenon was present in Oscan and Umbrian.[13]

Type 2: Those for which one or two, but not all three of the conditions set forth above can be met, and hence in which a substratum-influence is at best doubtful, as in the alleged survival of Etruscan pronunciation-habits in the "gorgia toscana" (the development of intervocalic allophonds [ɸθχ] for /p t k/). In this instance, condition 1 can be met, but not 2 (there is too long a gap between the last possible use of Etruscan and the first trustworthy attestation of the "gorgia" in the sixteenth century) or 3 (the presence of the letters ɸ, θ and χ in the Etruscan alphabet does not prove that they represent the fricatives which are found in modern Tuscan). At best, we can only say *non liquet*, but the case made so far for an Etruscan substratum is very unconvincing.[14]

Type 3: Those in which none of the conditions 1–3 can be met, and which therefore cannot be considered seriously at all: *e.g.* Merlo's ascription of modern Ligurian weak pronunciation or disappearance of /r/ to an ancient Ligurian or "Mediterranean" substratum, or Millardet's

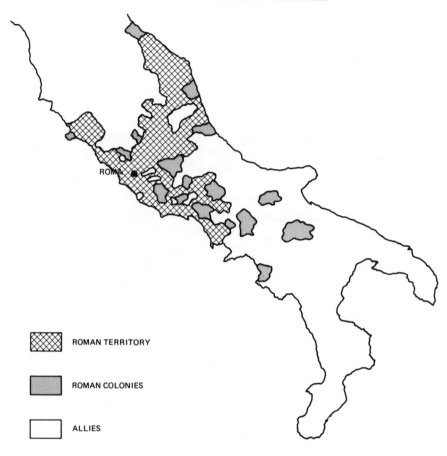

ROMAN TERRITORY

ROMAN COLONIES

ALLIES

MAP III. Central and southern Italy (third century B.C.) (After Devoto, 1936, opp. 192.)

assumption of an unidentified, presumably "Mediterranean" substratum for the cacuminalisation of intervocalic /-ll-/ to /-ḍḍ-/ in Sicilian and other Romance dialects.[15]

4.131. LATIN AND GREEK. After their initial expansion into central Italy, the Romans came into contact with the Greeks of Magna Graecia, beginning with the fourth century B.C. Close contacts with these Greeks, and later with the Hellenic home-land, lasted eight hundred years or more, and constituted the greatest single source of lexical influence on Latin (both popular and learnèd). There were three main stages of this influence: (1) that dating from the late Republican (immediately post-rhotacistic) period; (2)

that of the very end of the Republic and the early Empire; and (3) that of the later Empire. In the first of those stages, the influence of Greek came primarily through direct personal contact, and hence through oral channels. In the second, it was more learnèd, took place especially in such fields as philosophy and rhetoric, and was exerted much more through the written varieties of both languages. In the third, Greek was again influential chiefly through every-day speech, but reflected especially the Hebraeo-Hellenic usage of the Christian community.

From the time of the Punic wars onward, early Roman pride in homely, simple life yielded before the technical and cultural innovations which were imported from the Hellenistic world. Conservative Romans like Cato the Elder (234–149 B.C.) condemned the new-fangled Greek ways as decadent and corrupting; and in Plautus (e.g. Mostellaria 1.1.22, 65) we find such references to what was considered typically Greek behavior as bibite, pergraecāminī 'drink, carouse [lit. act like Greeks]!'.[16] But even old Cato finally gave in, and started to learn Greek in his eighties. The earliest Greek loans in Latin[17] refer particularly to innovations of various kinds, especially those with which the lower classes would come in contact: nautical and other technologies, sports, business, house-hold equipment, and novel foods and items of dress. For instance, the Greek word for a "device" of any kind to work by nonhuman or nonanimal means was /me·khắne·/ μηχάνη, Doric /ma·khána·/ μᾱχάνᾱ. This word, in its Doric form, was borrowed into Latin, and adapted to the phonology of third-century B.C. speech as /makina/ machina. This borrowing reflects earlier Latin initial stress and reduction of the pretonic unstressed vowel from /a/ to /i/ (cf. §§4.123, 124). It also reflects the fact that, at that time, Greek had a series of voiceless aspirates /ph th kh/ (written φθχ), but Latin had, corresponding to them, only /p t k/. Consequently, speakers of Latin reproduced the /kh/ of /ma·khána·/ as /k/. The Latin /makina/ is reflected in PRom. as /mákina/, whence Italian /mắčina/ macina 'mill'. Our modern words such as Sp. /mákina/ máquina, Italian /mákkina/ macchina, French /mašin/ machine (whence Eng. /mašíjn/ machine, Ger. /mašíne/ Maschine etc.) are all learnèd borrowings from Latin; all our forms in mechan-, mechanic- etc. are learnèd loans from Attic Greek.

4.132. LATIN AND THE ITALIC DIALECTS. One of the evils from which late republican Rome suffered was the acquisition of large tracts of land (latifundia) by wealthy absentee land-lords, and the consequent impoverishment and emigration of the yeomen farmers. Most of these latter came to Rome, and merged with the ever-increasing Roman urban proletariat. Many of them were of Italic origin, especially after the Social War of 91–88 B.C. These immigrants from Osco-Umbrian territory brought with them certain rustic terms such as *popīna* 'cook-shop' (with Osco-Umbr. /p/ for /kʷ/, cf. §3.12; the corresponding Latin form would have been **kokui·na/ *coquīna*).[18] It has been claimed[19] that not only these loan-words, but certain structural developments in Romance as well, are to be ascribed to an Osco-Umbrian substratum, *e.g.* the merger of PRom. /i/ and /e^/ into PCRom. /e^/, and that of PRom. /u/ and /o^/ into PITWRom. /o^/ (cf. Vol. 2).

4.14. WEST MEDITERRANEAN EXPANSION. This process began when the Romans extended their rule to Sicily, Sardinia, and Iberia, and thus came into inevitable conflict with the equally expanding power of Carthage. As has been pointed out,[20] the first half of Roman imperialistic expansion, under the later Republic, was primarily maritime, extending farther and farther along the coasts of the Mediterranean, and involving conflicts which took place largely at sea, from the three Punic wars (264–146 B.C.) to Pompey's extermination of the Cilician pirates (67 B.C.). The dates of the organization of the western Mediterranean provinces by Rome are:

241 B.C.	Sicily
238 B.C.	Sardinia, Corsica
197 B.C.	Hispania
167 B.C.	Illyria
146 B.C.	(N.W.) Africa
120 B.C.	Southern Gaul (Provincia Narbonensis)

These are, of course, only the years in which these regions were set up as Roman provinces. Complete Romanisation took centuries more, and in some regions (*e.g.* North Africa) never did come about.[21]

4.141. LATIN AND THE TIME OF COLONISATION. Some scholars[22] have maintained that the differences between the Romance languages in various regions were due to corresponding differences between the Popular Latin of the various epochs at which the provinces were conquered and colonised by the Romans. Against this, it can be argued that (1) all Romance speech goes back to a kind of Latin which had monophthongised /ei/ and /ou/ to /i·/ and /u·/ (cf. §4.124), and certainly such regions as Sicily and Sardinia began to be Latinised before this development took place; and (2) it is perfectly possible for the variety of language originally imported into a region to be completely overlaid by another variety which embodies later developments.

4.142. INFLUENCE OF PRE-LATIN LANGUAGES. The languages spoken in the western Mediterranean regions of course left lexical traces in the Popular Latin and hence in the Romance of their particular territories. Thus, in Iberia, the words for 'left (hand)'—Port. /eské^rdu/ *esquerdo*, Span. /iθkiérdo/ *izquierdo*, Cat. /eskérrə/ *esquerre*—are clearly related to Gascon /(es)kêrr/ and to Basque *ezkerr*, all of pre-Latin origin, since they correspond to nothing in Latin or Romance. Sardinian /ʠíppiri/ 'rosemary' is from Punic *zibbir*.[23] In general, it can be assumed that a word is from a pre-Latin substratum only when no satisfactory etymology can be found for it in Latin or a later language.

The structural influence of pre-Latin languages in these areas is considerably less certain, and there has been considerable debate as to specific instances. In Ibero-Romance certain words show /-mb/- > /-mm-/, as in Span. /palóma/ 'dove' < PRom. /palúmba/. This development has been ascribed by some[24] to an Osco-Umbrian substratum (cf. §4.124, and earlier in this section). This substratum would have been brought to Iberia by colonists of Italic origin, as shown by such place-names as /wéska/ *Huesca* (<*Osca*) in north-eastern Spain. More convincing, perhaps, is the ascription of Old Castilian /h-/ (lost in modern standard Spanish, but preserved in spelling and in some dialects) < PIbRom. and PRom. /f-/,[25] to a Basque substratum. It is argued that speakers of modern Basque do not have /f-/ in their phonemic inventory, and that speakers of pre-Basque would not have had it either. They would have imitated [f] with a bilabial fricative [ɸ], which would, in the usage of their linguistic descendants, have been replaced by a simple aspirate [h]. The area covered by Basque was formerly much larger than it is now, and extended at least as far as the Garonne in Aquitaine, and Burgos or beyond in Spain. It is in just these areas—Gascony and Old Castile—that we find PRom. /f-/ > /h-/.[26] The three conditions mentioned above (§4.13, beginning) for the assumption of a substratum-influence are met in this instance, and a Basque substratum for this development may be regarded as a reasonable assumption.

4.2. The Spread of Latin in the Classical Era

4.21. EAST MEDITERRANEAN EXPANSION. In the eastern end of the Mediterranean, from 148 B.C. onwards, Roman expansion proceeded, from the political point of view, along much the same lines as it had in the west: formation of alliances with kings or city-states, wars, and eventual absorption of allies, at first with retention of nominal independence and then with complete subjection to Roman rule. The cultural and linguistic situation, however, was very different from that in the west. In the east, the Romans were dealing, for the most part, with old-established and deeply entrenched cultures, to which they themselves felt inferior, especially in the case of Greece. Hence the oft-remarked paradox that the Romans vanquished Greece militarily and politically, but the Greeks conquered their conquerors in matters cultural and intellectual.[27] During the late Republic and the Empire, it was *de rigueur* for young upper-class Roman men to learn Greek and, if possible, to spend time studying in Athens. Latin did not even become a lingua franca of administration, to say nothing of the first language of the population, in the eastern Mediterranean as it did in the west. On the contrary, Roman administrators learned and used Greek, which by this time had become a general lingua franca throughout the eastern Mediterranean.

As Roman power made the whole Mediterranean into *Mare Nostrum* 'our sea', more and more Levantines, of all ethnic origins and social levels, crowded into Rome, making it a thoroughly cosmopolitan city. Many Greeks, from both Magna Graecia and Greece proper, were brought— either as slaves or as free persons—to help in the education of upper-class Roman youths. To this class of Greeks and their pupils, especially, is to be attributed the flood of Greek loan-words which now entered Latin, primarily on a literary level.[28] Such words included *philosophīa* 'the love of wisdom' < Gk. /filoso·fí·a·/ φιλοδωφίᾱ,[29] *theatrum* 'theater' < Gk. /θéa·tron/ θέᾱτρον, *odontalgīa* 'tooth-ache' < Gk. /odontalgí·a·/ ὀδονταλγίᾱ, etc. In many instances, Romans made loan-shifts in the meaning of Latin words under the influence of Greek, as in *spīritus* 'breath > spirit' = Gk. /θy·mós/ θῡμός, which had both meanings.

Some claims have been made for the influence of this learnèd Greek adstratum[30] on Latin prosody and morpho-syntax. It has been suggested[31] that the replacement of the Old Latin initial stress by a movable, though still nonsignificant, stress (cf. §4.123) was an imitation of the somewhat similar situation in Classical Greek. In morphology, this latter language had a proclitic definite article /ho he· ton/ ὁ ἦ τον, whereas Latin had neither definite nor indefinite article. Some[32] consider the development of a definite article, based on one of the demonstrative stems /ill-/ or /ips-/ (cf. Vol. 3), to have been like-wise a loan-translation on a Greek basis, and especially under Christian influence.

4.22. WEST EUROPEAN AND NORTH EUROPEAN EXPANSION. The conquest of Greece was completed, and that of the eastern end of the Mediterranean well under way, when Caius Julius Caesar (102–44 B.C.) undertook the first major expansion of Roman power to territories away from the inland sea. His conquest of central and northern Gaul (59–51 B.C.) brought under Roman control a large area which was chiefly Keltic in speech. Caesar made an abortive effort to conquer southern Britain (55, 54 B.C.), which was later successfully carried through under the emperors Claudius and Nero in A.D. 43–61, adding another Keltic-speaking territory to the Roman Empire. By this time, Germanic groups had moved southwards into what is now western Germany, and were attempting to continue their migrations further to the south and west. Caesar and later emperors made a successful effort to halt the Germanic advance; under the Empire, the boundary was more or less stabilized along the Rhine and the Danube. Efforts to extend Roman rule east of the Rhine were less successful, and were definitively ended by the German leader Arminius' total defeat of the Roman legions in the Teutoburg Forest in A.D. 9. Later, Rhaetia, Noricum, and Pannonia— *i.e.* modern Switzerland and much of modern Austria and Hungary—were brought under Roman rule. These regions were probably fairly thinly settled, and little evidence of pre-Indo-European or Keltic speech has survived, save in some place-names, such as the river-names *Dreisam, Traisen, Trisāne* in the Tyrol and the Black Forest (< *trag- [-us -is] + -ēna).[33]

Gaul, on the contrary, was fairly thickly settled, both in the country-side and in a number of flourishing cities. We have very little direct information on the process whereby Latin replaced Gaulish in every-day use. Undoubtedly the language-transfer took centuries to complete. Presumably it took place in the cities earlier than in the country-side, and among the upper classes before it did on lower social levels. Upper-class Gauls were especially eager to send their children to schools where they learned Latin and Greek. As time passed, more and more persons of Gallic origin entered the Roman military and civil service. In the middle and later Empire, many outstanding literary men were of Gallic origin. Gaulish may have continued to be spoken in rural regions as late as the fifth century A.D.[34] Whether Keltic was wholly replaced by Latin in all of Gaul, or whether modern Breton represents a direct survival of ancient Gaulish in an outlying area which was never Latinised, is a moot point.[35]

A number of Keltic words found their way into popular Latin usage in Imperial times, and became part of the common lexicon, surviving in Romance. These terms referred in general to specifically Keltic novelties in transport, food, and dress, which spread into the Roman world: *carrum* 'four-wheeled wagon' (> PRom. /kárru-/ > Sp., It. /kárro/ *carro*, ONFr. /čár/ *char* > Mod.Fr. /šar/); *cammīnus* 'road' (> PRom. /kammíˆnu-/ > Sp. /kamíno/ *camino*, It. /kammíno/ *cammino*, ONFr. /čəmin/ *chemin* > Mod.Fr. /šəmẽ/); *cerevisia* 'beer' (> PRom. /kereu̯ísia/ > OSp. /ȼervéẓa/ *cerveza* > Mod. Sp. /θerbéθa/ and >ONFr. /ȼervóˆizə/ *cervoise*); *camīsia* 'shirt' (> PRom. /kamíˆsi̯a/ > Sp. /kamísa/ *camisa*, It. /kamíča/ *camicia*, ONFr. /čəmízə/ *chemise* > Mod.Fr. /šəmiz/). Other Keltic survivals refer especially to features of country living such as birds, animals, and rustic implements: *e.g. alauda* 'swallow' (> PRom. /aláu̯da/ > ONFr. /aló^ðə/ *aloḍe* and—diminutive with suffixes going back to PRom. /⁺ítta/—/aloétə/ *aloete* > Mod.Fr. /aluet/ *alouette*, and It. /lodolé^tta/ *lodoletta*); *veltragus* 'grey-hound' (> PRom. /véltragu-/ > ONFr. /véltrə/ *veltre*, OIt. /véltro/ *veltro*); *carrūca* 'plow' > PRom. /karrú^ka/ > ONFr. /čarryə/ *charrue* > Mod.Fr. /šary/; etc.

Concerning possible Keltic substratum-influence on structural features of Gallo-Romance and possibly also Ibero-Romance, there has been a great deal of theorising, but with no universally accepted conclusions. Several phonological developments which are wide-spread in western Romance have been ascribed to a Keltic substratum, especially involving a presumably relaxed basis of articulation in contrast to that of Latin. The two most often thought to be of Keltic origin are: (1) the fronting of PRom. /u^/ to /y/ in Gallo-Romance and northern Italo-Romance,[36] and (2) the "lenition" which characterises most, but not all, of western Romance. This latter involves the fricativisation of the intervocalic voiced stops [b d g] to [βðγ], and the voicing of the intervocalic voiceless stops, fricatives, and sibilants [p t k f s ¢] to [b d g v z ẓ].[37] Against this theory of Keltic substratum-influence it has been urged[38] that (1) evidence for the presence, in Keltic, of the structural features in question is at best scanty; and (2) the chronology of phonological development argues against an early enough sound-change for Keltic pronunciation-habits to have been at work.[39] The question is still open, and the case for a Keltic substratum in these developments is by no means as strong as some of those already mentioned (Osco-Umbrian in central Italy, §4.132, or even Basque in Castile and Gascony, §4.142).

4.23. EAST EUROPEAN EXPANSION. Under the Julian-Claudian house and the Antonines, the Empire continued to expand into the Balkans, especially the lower Danube valley, and Dacia. This latter region was conquered under the emperor Trajan in A.D. 101–107, and remained Roman territory for nearly two centuries. That a considerable area south of the Danube was Romanised as well, is shown by the survival of Latin place-names in what is now Slavic-speaking Jugoslavia and Bulgaria. The Slavicist Josef Konstantin Jireček was able to draw a line through the southern part of the Balkans, marking the southernmost extent of Latin-based place-names.[40] This "Jireček-line," as it has been called, presumably indicates the outer limit of the extension of Latin in this region.

Palestine and Egypt came under Roman rule in Caesar's time, and for a while in the second and third centuries A.D. some of the regions beyond Asia Minor and Palestine, extending into Mesopotamia, were more or less Roman-dominated.[41] In these areas, Latin was at best an administrative language, and left little or no trace on local (primarily Hamito-Semitic) Semitic) tongues. In what is now Albania, however, Latin loans were extremely heavy, so that Albanian vocabulary of Latin origin is very useful in determining certain features of early Romance phonology (cf. fn. 51).

Semitic (Hebrew) exerted a certain amount of influence on Popular Latin under the middle and late Empire, in conjunction with late Hellenistic (so-called New Testament) Greek, through the usage of the Christian community from the third century A.D. onwards.[42] To Hebrew are to be traced some direct loans, such as /šabbaθ/ 'Sabbath' > Late Lat. *Sabbatum* > PItWRom. /sábbatu/ > Sp. /sábado/ *sábado*, It. /sábbato/ *sabbato* 'Saturday', and (with unexplained intrusive /m/) various further forms including ONFr. /sámədi/ > Mod.Fr. /samdi/. New Testament Greek furnished a number of direct loans, mostly connected with theology and church-organisation, such as /epískopos/ ἐπίσκοπος 'over-seer' > PItWRom. /epískopu/ > It. /véˆskovo/ *vescovo*, ONFr. /evékə/ *evesque* (>Mod.Fr. /eˆvek/ *évêque*), Sp. /obíspo/ *obipso* etc. Some of these Greek words were, in their turn, loan-translations from Hebrew, such as /ángelos/ ἄγγελος 'messenger, angel', on the model of Hebrew /malax/, which has both meanings. Certain Greek derivational elements were so frequent in these loans that they spread to Latin bases. Thus, the suffix /⁺ízein/ -ίζειν, in such words as /baptízein/ βαπτίζειν 'to dunk > to baptise', was generalised in PItWRom. as /⁺idjáre/ > ONFr. /⁺izær/ -*iser* (> Mod.Fr. /⁺izeˆ/), It. /⁺eǧǧáre/ -*eggiare*, Sp. /⁺iθár/ -*izar*.[43]

4.3. Literary and Popular Latin

4.31. THE EARLIEST SPLITS. The separation between literary and popular Latin became more marked in the first century B.C., from ca. 100 B.C. onwards. Classical usage thenceforth became more and more static, while popular speech kept on developing, as shown in the diagram in Table VIII.[44] Our reconstructed Proto-Romance shows only rhotacism, and only monophthongs in forms having /iˆ/ and /uˆ/ (corresponding to Classical Latin /i·/, /u·/, respectively); it therefore cannot be placed earlier than ca. 150 B.C. On the other hand, its beginning must be assigned to ca. 100–0 B.C., when the split between Classical and Popular Latin began to be serious, but before the first vowel-changes in popular speech (the merger of /í/ and /éˆ/; cf. Vol. 2).[45] Between 150 and 100 B.C., therefore, after rhotacism and monophthongisation, but before the split between Classical and Popular Latin, must be placed the common ancestor of CL and PRom., for which we have already (§1.6) suggested the term GRACCHAN LATIN (Gr.Lat.).

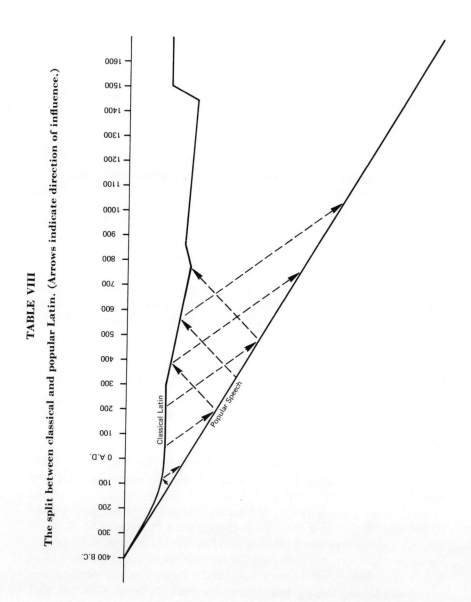

TABLE VIII

The split between classical and popular Latin. (Arrows indicate direction of influence.)

4.32. VARIETIES OF LATIN. From the time of Cicero onwards, rhetoricians and grammarians recognised different varieties of Latin. The more elegant literary language was referred to as *sermō urbānus* 'urban(e) speech', whereas for less prestigious usage they used such terms as *sermō cotidiānus* or *usuālis* 'every-day speech', *sermō plebēius* or *vulgāris* 'the common people's language', or *sermō rūsticus* 'countrified talk'. In Romance linguistics, it is unfortunately almost a universal practice to refer to these latter types of nonprestigious speech, taken together, as "Vulgar Latin" (Fr. *latin vulgaire*, Sp. *latín vulgar*, It. *latino volgare*, Ger. *Vulgärlatein*, etc.).[46] There are several major objections to the term *Vulgar Latin*,[47] and we shall do well to avoid it as too vague and imprecise. For the every-day spoken usage of the Latin-speaking populace, of whatever level or period, we may better use the German term *Volkslatein* 'Latin of the folk' or its English or Romance equivalents (*Popular Latin*, *latin populaire*, etc.), with indication of specific time and social milieu as required. Popular Latin, thus defined, should be kept sharply distinct from, on the one hand, written documentation of any kind (for which the terms *Late Latin* and *Mediaeval Latin* are perfectly adequate, again with indication of time, place, and milieu as needed), and, on the other hand, reconstructed Proto-Romance or intermediate stages in the development of early Romance speech.

The sources for our knowledge of Popular Latin, of whatever epoch, are scanty, and come under the headings of direct and indirect evidence.

1. Direct evidence, of these kinds:

a. Intentional reproduction of nonstandard speech, such as the well-known passage in Petronius' *Satyricon*, usually called the *Cēna Trimalchiōnis* 'Dinner of Trimalchio', in which the rich vulgarian Trimalchio's speech is reproduced with considerable exactitude,[48] as far as morphology, syntax, and lexicon are concerned. Such passages are quite rare. In a few places, we find descriptions of people's speech-traits, as in Catullus' well-known poem (84) mocking a certain Arrius for his misplaced aitches.

b. Non-Classical traits in authors who were presumably trying to write "correct" Latin, but whose "mistakes" are evidence for the presence of features which are later attested in Romance. Of this type are: (1) aspects of certain specific works, such as the *Peregrinatiō Silviae Aetheriae* 'Pilgrimage of Silvia Aetheria', the account of a fourth- or fifth-century nun's trip to the Holy Land[49]; (2) mistakes in inscriptions; (3) stenographers' transcripts in the short-hand known as *notae Tirōniānae* 'Tyronian notes'.

c. Instructions how to avoid errors, of the type "Say Y, not X." The best-known example of such instructions is a collection known as the *Appendix Prōbī*,[50] usually assigned to some Roman school-master of the third or fourth century A.D. It contains 227 items, such as *pauper mulier non paupera mulier* (42), *aper non aprus* (139), or *vetulus non veclus* (5). These mistakes, which the school-master was correcting, afford attestations of such phenomena as the analogical feminine *paupera* 'poor' (> It. /póvera/ *povera*) or the development of the consonant-cluster /-t(u)l-/ to /-kl-/, confirming our reconstruction of a PRom. / u̯éklu/ 'old' for such Romance forms as Port. /véḷu/ *velho*, Span. /biéxo/ *viejo*, ONFr. /viéḷ/ *vieil*, OProv. /véḷ/ *velh*, It. /vékkio/ *vecchio*.

2. Indirect evidence:

a. Borrowings into other languages, *e.g.* Keltic, Germanic, Greek, Slavic, Albanian, Basque, or Berber, datable as having taken place in Imperial times.[51]

b. Reconstruction on the basis of later developments in the Romance languages, *e.g.* PRom. /u̯éklu/ 'old' (cf. the preceding section). On occasion, scholars reconstruct such forms,[52] and these forms are later discovered in previously unknown documents or inscriptions. Thus, on the basis of Roum. /strú¢/ *struṭ* 'ostrich', It. /strú¢¢o/ *struzzo*, Prov. and Cat. /estrús/ *estrus*, and OSpan. /estrú¢/ *estruç*, we would reconstruct a PRom. /strú^ti̯u/; this form has been discovered, written *struthius*, in the late Latin translations of Oribasius.[53] Not only phonological, morphological, and lexical features, but also syntactical ones, are on occasion attested in this way, *e.g.* the construction of Lat. *juvāre* 'to aid, benefit' with a dative which must be assumed as the origin for Italian *giovare a . . .* (with the same meaning): in the Oribasius-translations we find such expressions as *lapides in renes habentibus jubat* 'it benefits those who have stones in their kidneys'.[54]

4.33. GEOGRAPHICAL EXTENT. At its greatest extent, in the fourth century A.D., Popular Latin was used (as far as is now known) in virtually all of Italy, Iberia (except in the Pyrenees and perhaps across the northern mountain-range), Sardinia, Corsica, Gaul (with perhaps the exception of Brittany and a few remaining pockets of Keltic), present-day Switzerland, those parts of Germany south of the Rhine, the Main, and the Danube, southern Austria, present-day Croatia and Serbia, and Dacia. (Cf. Map IV, Greatest Extent of Popular Latin.) It was probably also the first language of groups of Roman colonists (administrators, merchants, etc.) all along the coast of northern Africa, from Cyrenaica westwards. In Greece, Asia Minor, Palestine, and Egypt, Latin was never more than official language, spoken only by Roman administrators and such members of their families as accompanied them.

4.34. PIDGIN LATIN? The varieties of Latin we have discussed, and also our reconstructed Proto-Romance, were "full-sized" languages, *i.e.* they had a complete phonological, morpho-syntactic, and lexical repertory. In

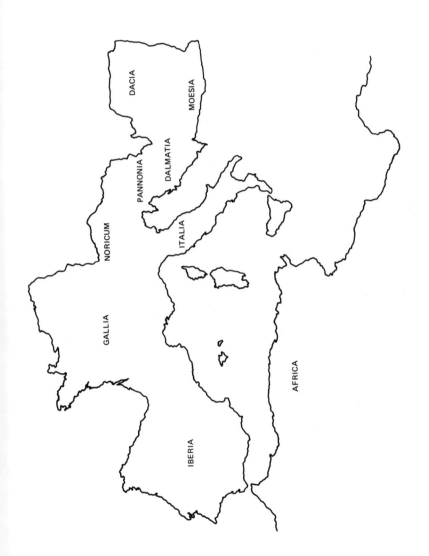

MAP IV. Greatest extent of popular Latin.

addition, there probably existed various pidginised versions of Latin, spoken wherever Romans came into more or less temporary contacts with non-Romans, especially along the borders in military camps and in markets. It would be strange if such pidgins had not arisen. However, we have no direct record of any such, nor can any of the later developments of Latin into Romance be ascribed with any certainty to any kind of Pidgin Latin which later became creolised. All the Romance developments (even such relatively extensive changes as that involved in the Roumanian numeral-system; cf. Vol. 5) could have taken place in the course of normal slow linguistic change over the centuries, without the sudden sharp break and drastic restructuring which is by definition involved in pidginisation.

NOTES TO CHAPTER 4

1. For the history of Latin in general, cf. Stolz and Schmalz 1885; Stolz 1910; Meillet 1928; Devoto 1936; Pisani 1948, 1962; Palmer 1954; Pulgram 1958; Collart 1967.

2. *E.g.* the Latin 3.pl. ending in /-nunt/ > It. /-no/; cf. Förster 1898 (and the replies of d'Ovidio 1899 and Merlo 1909).

3. Cf. Holland 1961 for a thorough discussion of the earliest urban development of Rome, especially from a hydrographic point of view.

4. Cf. Devoto 1936:85–86; Peruzzi 1967; and, for Sabine in general, Tibiletti Bruno 1961–62. Had it not been for the Sabinism *lingua* in Latin, we might now be discussing *dinguistics* or studying les *dangues romanes*, las *denguas románicas*, etc.!

5. Cf. Palmer 1954:46–49. For *triumphus*, cf. Warren 1970. For *barô*, cf. Paschall 1939:12–14; Hall 1947a and forthcoming.

6. Cf. Kent 1932:99–105.

7. *I.e.* unit of length. A mora in Latin prosody consisted of either: (a) a short vowel; (b) the lengthening of a vowel /:/ ; or (c) a consonant or consonants checking a syllable; but a syllable could not contain more than two morae.

8. Cf. Kent 1932:47, 93, 104.

9. Cf. Budinszky 1881; Hammer 1894.

10. Following Rohlfs 1924, 1933, 1950, 1962b, etc., and Caratzas, 1958. Rohlfs' theory of Greek survival from ancient times is accepted by most scholars, except in Italy, where there has been strong opposition to them; cf. especially Battisti 1927; Alessio 1955; Parlangèli 1953, 1960a, b, etc.

11. Aulus Gellius, *Noctes Atticae*, 17.17.1: *Quintus Ennius tria corda habere sese dicebat, quia loqui Graece et Osce et Latine sciebat.*

12. For a general survey, cf. Pulgram 1949; Battisti 1959 (reviewed by Szemerényi 1961/62).

13. Cf. Hall 1950b.

14. Cf. Izzo 1972, for a thorough discussion and demolition of the substratum-theory in this instance.

15. Merlo 1933:6 and 1938:30; Millardet 1933.

16. An ancient commentator defines this verb thus: *pergraecari est epulis et potationibus inservire 'pergraecari* is "to be addicted to banqueting and wine-bibbing" ' (Paul. ex. Fest. 215 [ed. Müller]).

17. Cf. Palmer 1954:49–52, 81–84. For Greek in southern Gaul and its influence on the Latin and Romance of that region, cf. von Wartburg 1952.

18. Cf. Ernout 1909 for this and many similar borrowings.

19. Especially by Devoto 1930.

20. Lüdtke 1965. We are of course using the term *imperialistic* in a broader sense than its narrow reference to the *imperium* of the Caesars, or its modern, often pejorative meaning.

21. For the survival of Latin words in Berber, cf. Schuchardt 1918; Rössler 1962.

22. *E.g.* Gröber 1884–90:1.210–213; Bonfante 1943. The objections of Pei (1945) are equally exaggerated in the opposite direction, that of assuming an impossibly long duration of linguistic unity after the break-up of the Roman Empire.

23. Cf. Bertoldi 1950:42.

24. *E.g.* Menéndez Pidal 1926: §53.3; cf. also Entwistle 1936:63–64, 74–75. For the pre-Latin languages of Iberia, cf. Tovar 1968.

25. In many words, *e.g.* PRom. /fíʌlįu/ 'son' > OCast. /hížo/ *fijo* > Mod.Sp. /íxo/ *hijo*. This thesis, first proposed and vigorously defended by Menéndez Pidal (1926: §41), has been generally accepted among Hispanists (*e.g.* Entwistle 1936:35–36; Lapesa 1942: 27–28).

26. Cf. Clément Marot's description (*Épître* 29:15) of his rascally Gascon valet as a *vénérable hillot* 'venerable fellow', with the Gascon loan-word /hilot/ < PRom. /fílįu/ 'son' + the diminutive-pejorative suffix /-óttu/.

27. Cf. the often-cited verses of Horace:
Graecia capta ferum victōrem cēpit et artēs
Intulit agrestī Latiō
'Greece, though conquered, conquered her barbarous conqueror and brought the arts to rustic Latium' (*Epistles* 2.1.156–159).

28. Cf. especially Weise 1882; Saalfeld 1884; Rebelo Gonçalves 1930; (for early Latin) Friedmann 1937; (for Imperial Latin) Jannaccone 1950.

29. By the first century A.D., the Greek voiceless aspirates /ph th kh/ (cf. §4.131) had become fricatives /f θ x/, a pronunciation which was mirrored in Greek loans in Latin from this time onwards. Cf. Sturtevant 1920:181; Allen 1968:21.

30. Since no political conquest or socially dominant ruling class was involved, many scholars use the term *adstratum* for cultural influences of this type.

31. *E.g.* by F. F. Abbott 1907 (especially 455–458); cf. also Sturtevant 1920, chapter 5 (in 1940 ed., chapter 7), and Buck 1933:167.

32. *E.g.* Wolterstorff 1919 (with references 62–63); Trager 1932; Abel, 1970.

33. Cf. Finsterwalder 1969:387–389.

34. St. Jerome's statement that he found the language used in Galatia similar to that used in the rural areas around Trier is usually taken as referring to Keltic speech in both regions (cf. Whatmough, 1944:71). Cf. also Hubschmid, 1938.

35. Almost all scholars in the last century have considered that Breton represents a reintroduction of Keltic into Gaul by speakers of Keltic emigrating from Great Britain ca. A.D. 500–600 under the pressure of advancing Anglo-Saxon invaders. The Breton scholar F. Falc'hun (1968 and many previous publications) has argued that certain surviving features of French (*e.g.* place-names) show the same linguistic traits as does Breton, and that hence Breton is to be regarded as a direct survival of ancient Gaulish.

36. This theory goes back to Àscoli (1881:19–26). By now, most scholars accept it more or less readily: *c.g.* von Wartburg 1936a (1950:36–51; in the Spanish translation, 52–69); Elcock 1960:192–193; Tagliavini 1947 (1969⁵): §24; etc. Lausberg 1956–62

(in Sp. tr., 1965:235–237), though mentioning the Keltic hypothesis, considers the shift from [uˆ] to [y] to be very old, and suggests the possibility of Greek influence.

37. Cf. Martinet 1952 (reprinted in Martinet 1955, chapter 11).

38. *E.g.* by Meyer-Lübke 1914–19. Against the theory of a relaxed basis of articulation in Keltic, cf. Fowkes 1966 (and the reply of Delattre 1969/70).

39. The fronting of PRom. /uˆ/ to /y/ must have been posterior to that of /á/ in stressed syllable to /ǽ/ (later > /e/) in Old North French, otherwise /kúˆ/ would have given /čý/ as /ká/ gave /čǽ/. But the change of /á/ in stressed free syllable to /ǽ/ cannot have taken place earlier than the seventh century or so A.D., by which time Keltic had long since been replaced by Romance speech everywhere except perhaps in Brittany (cf. Whatmough 1944:76).

40. Jireček 1901–03:1.13–21. For the presumed language of the Thracians, cf. Russu 1959.

41. The program set forth by Hahn (1907) for investigating the interaction between Latin and other languages in the East has unfortunately never been carried out.

42. Some scholars (*e.g.* Mohrmann 1955, 1961–65) have set up a special variety of Late Latin which they term "Christian Latin"—which, however, was characterised only by certain lexical and stylistic features, rather than by any structural differences from Late Latin in general.

43. In almost all the Romance developments of these early Christian loans from Greek and Hebrew, a certain amount of learnèd influence was at work from the very beginning, so that we find numerous exceptions to purely "popular" phonetic developments in words of this kind.

44. Adapted from Pulgram 1950:462.

45. For Classical Latin pronunciation, cf. Sturtevant 1920; Allen 1965.

46. For "Vulgar Latin" in general, cf. Grandgent 1907 (old, but still one of the best manuals, especially in the 1928 Spanish translation); also Meyer-Lübke 1887; Silva Neto 1938b, 1957; Battisti 1949 (poor); Coşeriu 1954; Vossler 1955; Löfstedt 1959; Maurer 1959, 1962; Väänänen 1963; Haadsma and Nuchelmans 1963; Avalle 1965; Campanile 1967.

47. These objections may be summed up under the following heads:

(1) Vagueness of reference to time: the term *Vulgar Latin* has been used to refer to popular speech as far back as the time of Plautus (*e.g.* by Altheim 1932), and to documents written in Latin as late as Charlemagne's time (especially by Muller [1929, 1945] and his followers, *e.g.* P. Taylor [1932], Muller and Taylor [1932], and Pei [1932]).

(2) Vagueness of reference to social level; it has been used to refer to all kinds of Latin, from upper-class colloquial to the most lowly or rustic (cf. Holmes and Schutz 1935).

(3) Confusion with reconstructed Proto-Romance (cf. §1.6).

48. For Petronius, cf. Nelson 1947; Stefenelli 1962; Bonfante 1968; Väänänen 1970.

49. Cf. Bechtel 1902; Anglade 1905; Löfstedt 1911; Klein 1958.

50. Cf. Baehrens 1922; Silva Neto 1938b. The suggestion of Robson (1963), that the *Appendix Probi* was written in the seventh century by an Irish or English monk at Bobbio, and is hence valueless for Imperial Latin, has not won general acceptance.

51. For Keltic, cf. Güterbock 1882; Loth 1892; Vendryes 1902; Lewis 1943. For Welsh: Haarmann, 1970. For Old English: Pogatscher 1888. For German: Frings 1932. For Greek: Viscidi 1944. For Slavic: Romansky 1909; Scheludko 1927; Skok 1931. For Albanian: Jokl 1936, 1942/42; Tagliavini 1943; Mihăescu 1966b. For Basque: Schuchardt 1906; Densusianu 1924; Rohlfs 1927; Caro Baroja 1946; Gamillscheg 1950. For Berber

and North African languages: Schuchardt 1918; Colin 1926–30; Wagner 1936a; Beguinot 1938; Rössler 1962.

52. Of which a considerable number were set up by Gröber 1884–90, and others by Meyer-Lübke and other scholars; cf. Meyer-Lübke's brief discussion in the third edition of the *Romanisches Etymologisches Wörterbuch* (x–xi).

53. Mørland 1932:66.

54. Mørland 1932:114.

CHAPTER 5

Post-Latin ("Superstratum") Languages

5.0. Historical Back-Ground[1]

From the late Republic on, both Rome itself and the rest of the Empire became quite cosmopolitan in social and linguistic structure. Slaves from northern and eastern Europe, from Asia, and from Africa were spread throughout the Mediterranean area. For the first two or three centuries A.D., however, the linguistic processes taking place in western Europe were principally those of Latinization. It was not until the fourth century A.D. that large enough groups of non-Latin speakers entered the Empire, establishing themselves in areas which had become Latin in speech, to preserve their previous languages at least for a time and to exert an influence on the Latin which their linguistic descendants learned. This process started first along the northern frontiers, where Germanic-speaking soldiers were recruited to serve in Roman legions.[2] Not only individual men, but entire tribes were invited to enter Roman territory and settle in the border-areas. The growing number of Germanic soldiers in the Roman army spread certain Germanic words to the rest of the Empire. To this earliest source of Germanic loans are normally ascribed certain military terms, such as Gmc. /werra/ > PItWRom. /gu̯érra/ 'war' (> It. /guérra/, Port., Sp. and OSFr. /gérra/ [all spelled *guerra*], ONFr. /guérə/ *guerre* [> Mod.Fr. /ger/]), which replaced Lat. *bellum* everywhere except in Roumania, which has the Slavic borrowing /rəzbói/ *război*.

The gradual decline and break-up of the Roman Empire lasted roughly two hundred years, from the mid-third to the mid-fifth century A.D. As a definitive end-date, historians usually give the deposition of the boy-emperor Romulus Augustulus by the Germanic king Odoacer in A.D. 476. The causes of the decline were very complex: among those suggested have been exhaustion of the soil, incredibly wasteful luxuries on the part of the imperial court, economic parasitism of the urban proletariat, crushingly heavy taxation of the rest of the population, with resultant loss of will to live, race-suicide, decline in population and economic resources, and unwillingness to defend an oppressive imperial rule. Massive immigrations of large non-Roman nations, on the march in search of new regions in which to live—the so-called "Völkerwanderungen" or "migrations of peoples"— took place without successful opposition from imperial armies or local populations. Rome was captured, first by the Goths under Alaric in A.D. 410, and then by the Vandals in 455. The greatly reduced Eastern or Byzantine empire, with its capital at Constantinople (Byzantium), remained relatively intact for some centuries more, though increasingly weakened by attacks from Germanic, Slavic, Arabic, and Turkic enemies on its frontiers.

Of the new kingdoms established by the Germanic nations in the western part of Europe, almost none were long-lasting. The Visigoths ('western Goths') established themselves for a time in Italy (401–410) and then moved on to southern Gaul (410–507) and to Iberia (456–711). Their place was taken in Italy by the Ostrogoths ('eastern Goths'), whose kingdom lasted from 493 to 555, and was finally destroyed, after long wars, by the Byzantine armies.[3] Alemannic groups migrated up the Rhine valley and into Switzerland and the Tyrol. Another tribe, the Burgundians, were defeated by the Romans in 437, and were resettled in an area centering on Lyons and Geneva; their kingdom later came to include also Vienne, Mâcon, and Besançon. The Langobards invaded Italy in 568 and established their rule in three principal regions: the main kingdom, with its center at Pavia in the upper Po valley; the duchy of Spoleto in the middle Tiber valley; and the duchy of Benevento in the Apennines east of Naples.[4] Meanwhile, the Franks had established a kingdom which, in the seventh and eighth centuries, extended from what is now Bavaria, across the present-day Palatinate, Hesse, and the Rhine-land, to the Low Countries and northern Gaul, with the over-all name of *Frank-ẹa*. The Vandals made their way across Iberia to northern Africa, where they set up a short-lived kingdom (435–534). The rule of the Suebi lasted considerably longer (ca. 411–585) in Galicia, but they were eventually absorbed into the Visigothic kindgom of Spain.

After the passage of the Goths through Dacia and the Balkans in the fourth and fifth centuries, new large-scale migrations of Slavic groups took place in the sixth and seventh centuries. Their incursions extended as far as Greece and the Peloponnesus, and they settled permanently in the Balkans, the central and lower Danube valley, and Dacia. It is not sure whether the Latin-speaking population of Dacia moved en masse to new homes south of the Danube, to escape the on-coming Slavs, or whether they remained north of the Danube, especially in Transylvania, in a close symbiosis with Slavic-speaking groups.[5]

The Byzantine Empire maintained at least a claim to sovereignty over

Sardinia, Corsica, certain parts of Italy (the exarchate of Ravenna and the south), and Sicily, during this period, in addition to its rule over the eastern Mediterranean. There was considerable dissatisfaction with its rule in many of these regions, which accounts at least in part for the remarkable rapidity with which all of Palestine, Egypt, and northern Africa were conquered by Moslem Arabic invaders in the seventh century (632–708). From the Maghreb, the Moslem conquerors were called in by a dissident faction among the Visigoths and invaded Iberia in 711, extending their rule in a few decades to all except the extreme northernmost mountains. The Moslems also invaded Italy and Sicily in the ninth century, establishing themselves for varying periods of time, and ruling over Sicily from 827 to 1016. They never established effective rule in Sardinia, though they made several attacks on that island between 711 and 1016. Carrying their campaigns beyond the Iberian peninsula, the Arabs of Spain established a brief rule in southern France and advanced north, only to be decisively defeated by Charles Martel at Tours in 732. His son Pippin expelled them from Narbonne in 759; but after the eighth century, there were still a certain number of Moslems living in southern French towns. The town of Fraisnet, in the Alps, was held by Moors from 894 to 972, and used by them to prey on commerce along the coast and in the Alps.

Although there were raids into western Europe by roving bands of Huns in the fourth and fifth centuries, and by Hungarians in the ninth and tenth, they resulted in no permanent settlements. The last major wave of incursions to trouble Europe in the Middle Ages took place primarily along the coasts, coming from southern Scandinavia. The Norsemen were extremely active in a combination of trading and looting, from the seventh through the eleventh centuries. Their voyages of conquest took them to Russia, where Rurik established the kingdom of Novgorod in 862; to England, where the eastern part of the island was subject to Denmark from 876 to 920; and to the northern coast of France, where their rule was officially recognized in 901. Those who settled along the French coast soon gave up their North Germanic speech in favor of Gallo-Romance; they became known as Normans, and their region as Normandy. From there, the Normans ranged far afield, conquering Sicily in 1003–1022, Apulia in the 1040's, and England in 1066, and starting to invade the Balkans at Durazzo in 1087. From one point of view, the First Crusade (1096–1099) was a continuation of the Norse expansion of the previous five centuries. During "Frankish" rule in Palestine (1099–1187) and in the Byzantine Empire (1204–1261), French was an official language in those regions.

In the following sections, we shall discuss briefly the main "superstratum"-languages and the effects which they are considered to have had on Romance. To be realistic, without recourse to mysticism or to theories of

genetic transmission of linguistic competences, we must envisage the effect
of a superstratum-language as being exerted through the same process as
that of a substratum-language, namely, the survival of relics of a period of
bilingualism (cf. §4.13). In the case of a superstratum, the later comers
would have acquired the language of the region and spoken it with a foreign
accent. This accent would then have been imitated by others because of the
prestige (in the case of upper-class speakers of Germanic origin) or the
numerical superiority (social equals of Slavic origin) of the linguistic descendants of the supervenient group.[6]

5.1. Germanic

There has been some discussion of the extent of Germanic influence on
Popular Latin in general, before the break-up of the Roman Empire. When
"Vulgar Latin" was thought of primarily as the ancestor of Italian and the
western Romance languages, a number of Germanic loans were ascribed to
the Imperial period, including /wérra/ 'war' (cf. §5.0), /blánku-/ 'white',
/blúndu-/ 'blond', /búrgu-/ 'burg', /drú^du-/ 'lover', and many others.[7]
If, however, Balkan Romance and Sardinian are taken into account, the
number of Germanic loans ascribable to PRom., i.e. to ca. 150–0 b.c., drops
to zero. Ancient authors cite only a few Germanic words, but some (e.g.
framea 'lance', Tacitus, Germania 6.) have not survived at all in Romance,
and others (e.g. vanga 'hoe', Palladius 1.43) have survived only in individual
Romance languages, in this case Italian. The Germanic loans definitely
ascribable to the Popular Latin of the earlier Imperial epoch are quite few.[8]
They include PItWRom. /sapó^n-/ 'a kind of hair-dye > soap' (cited by
Pliny the Elder as sapō-ōnis [Historia Naturalis 28.12.51]), /táksu-/
'beaver' (< WGmc. */θahsu/) and /mártor-/ 'marten' (< WGmc.
*/marθr/).

The chief Germanic languages to be considered as possible superstrata in
the individual regions of Romance speech are, in the approximate order of
their arrival on the Romance scene, the following[9]:

5.11. Gothic, belonging to the East Germanic subgroup. It is attested
principally in the surviving portions of the New Testament as translated
by Bishop Wulfila (ca. 311–381). The chief regions where Gothic loans might
be expected are Italy, southern France, and Spain.[10] There are a number of
Gothic words in the dialects of each of these regions, and in standard
Italian, Old South French, Catalan, Spanish, and Portuguese. Inasmuch
as the Goths were the earliest major Germanic group to enter the Roman
Empire, and traversed it fully from east to west, their lexical influence
shows the greatest geographical extension (though, strangely, there are no

sure Gothic loans in Roumanian). Among Gothic loans are /le:vjan/
lêŵjan 'betray', */gale:vi:ns/ *galêwins* 'betrayal' (> OSp. /alébe/ *aleve*,
OPort. /alé^ive/ *aleive* 'betrayal'); */harihringa/ 'army-ring' (> It.
/arríngo/ *arringo* 'tourney-place', /arringáre/ *arringare* and OSFr. /aren-
gár/ *arengar* 'to harangue'; */bawiθa/ 'hut' (> SFr. /báito/ *baito*, NIt.
/báita/ *baita* 'Alpine cabin'; */flasko/ 'flask' (> It. /fiaskó^ne/ *fiascone*,
taken as an augmentative, whence the back-formation /fiásko/ *fiasco*); and
*/θwahlja/ 'piece of cloth' (> It. /továḷḷa/ *tovaglia* 'napkin, table-cloth',
ONFr. /tuáḷə/ *touaille* > Eng. *towel*). A striking loan-translation of a
Gothic word is PItWRom. /kompanịó^n-/ (nom.sg. /kompánịo/ 'companion' (> It. /kompáṇṇo/ *compagno*, OSFr. /kompáṇo^(n)/ *companho[n]*,
ONFr. /kompaṇón/ *compagnon* > Eng. *companion*, and Sp. /kompaṇ+/
in /kompaṇéro/ *compañero*), on the basis of Gothic /gahleba/ *gahlaiba*
'one who shares the same bread', formed on /hleba/ 'bread' (:Eng. *loaf*).
Some personal names, such as Port. /gimaráis/ *Guimarães* (< *Vimaranis*,
gen.) and Sp. *Alfonso, Fernando, Ramiro*, are of Gothic origin.

In structural features, the only effect of a Gothic superstratum suggested
so far is in Old Spanish anisosyllabic verse. Romance verse is in general
ISOSYLLABIC, *i.e.* the meter of each line depends on its having a specific
number of syllables. But in some of the earliest attested Romance verse,
especially in the Old Spanish *Cantar de myo Çid* and other epic poems, this
principle does not hold, and each line has a given number of stresses, usually four. Such verse is known as ANISOSYLLABIC 'not having an equal
number of syllables'; it is the earliest attested and most wide-spread type
of verse in all Germanic languages. This feature in Old Spanish anisosyllabic
verse suggests that the language of the versifier was stress-timed, as is
universally the case in Germanic, and not syllable-timed, as is usual in
Romance. A Visigothic superstratum is the obvious explanation for this
characteristic.[11]

5.12. VANDALIC AND SUEBIC are to be mentioned only for completeness'
sake, since the kingdoms of both these tribes lasted only relatively short
times, and there are very few sure traces of their languages left.[12] Perhaps
Port. /britár/ *britar* 'break' and Galician /lavérka/ *laverca* 'lark' are from
Suebic. Particularly in North Africa, the Vandalic rulers probably formed
a very thin upper stratum of society, and it is not even known whether they
continued speaking their Germanic language until the reconquest of the
region by the Byzantine empire, or had by that time given it up in favour
of the local Popular Latin.

5.13. BURGUNDIAN influence might be expected to have been greatest in
east central Gaul, where the tribe was resettled in 437 (cf. §5.0). Inasmuch

as Franco-Provençal is spoken in approximately the same area, some[13] have seen the Burgundian superstratum as the source of its phonological peculiarities; others[14] have ascribed them rather to simple borrowing from North French. Certain items of vocabulary in the Franco-Provençal area are probably to be ascribed to Burgundian, but there has been considerable debate as to which[15]: *e.g.* Lyonnais /broǧi/ 'dream' < */brugdjan/; Lyonnais /froǧi/ 'be silent' < */fro:djan/ 'be wise'; Allier (Lyonnais, Forez, etc.) /mase/ 'ant' < */e:maitja/ (: Ger. *Ameise*); Franco-Prov. /fato/ 'pocket' < */fatta/ (: Ger. *Fetzen* 'scrap of cloth').

5.14. LANGOBARDIC. The Langobards' linguistic influence was exerted chiefly in Italy, where there are a certain number of survivals in place-names and proper names, and in the lexicon of both the standard language and the dialects.[16] Like the other Germanic peoples, the Langobards at first lived apart from the Roman population in their kingdom, and a number of their settlements were referred to as *Longobardo -i* or *Lombarda -i*, with or without such nouns as *poggio* 'hill', *guardia* 'watch-house' (*Poggio Lombardello, Guardia Lombardi* and the likes). A Langobard's family-group was his *fara*, and there are quite a number of place-names containing this element, combined either with personal names, as in *Fara San Martino*, or with indications of regions, such as *Fara in Sabina*. Other Langobard elements occurring in place-names are */skulk/ 'look-out' (:*/skulkan/ 'spy'; cf. Eng. *skulk*), */wald/ 'wood, weald', */gahagi/ 'hedge',[17] */stafilo/ 'post, boundary-marker', */snaida/ 'cut (in trees, etc.) indicating a boundary'.[18] Among personal names of clearly Langobardic origin in Italy are *Azzo, Aldo, Guarino,* and *Pandolfo.*

In the lexicon of standard Italian, there are a number of words of Langobardic origin such as *guancia* 'cheek' (< Langob. */wangja/:Ger. *Wange*; cf. §5.0, fn. 4); /stínko/ *stinco* 'shin' and such dialectal cognates as Emilian, Venetian /skínko/ (< Langob. */skinka:/; OIt. /gastáldo/ *gastaldo* 'administrative officer' (< Langob. */gastald/ 'governor of a domain'). In Italian dialects, other Langobard words have survived, *e.g.* */le:ha/ 'sow' in Marchig. /léˆkka/; */skerpfa/ 'trousseau' in Old Comasque *scerfa*; */snarhh(j)an/ 'snore' (cf. Ger. *schnarchen*) in N., Cent. It. /sarnakkiáre/ *sarnac(chi)are*, Molise and southern Latium /sənučǎ́/, /sornakkjá/. The semantic sphere of Langobardic lexical influence was, as might be expected, limited to types of activity for which the Germanic ruling classes had terms not corresponding to anything in Romance speech (cf. *gastaldo*, above); to certain place- and person-names; and, curiously, to rather homely things which must have been associated with the lower classes of Germanic settlers. A Langobardic */stain-berga/ 'stone shelter', perhaps originally used by shepherds watching their flocks, gave It. *stamberga* 'hovel'. Similarly,

Langob. */skranna/ 'cupboard' > It. *scranno*, and Langob. */balko/ > It. *balcone* 'balcony'.

None of the Germanic languages which come into consideration as possible "superstrata" in Romance had the second Germanic sound-shift, except Langobardic. (This sound-shift differentiated Old High German from the other Germanic languages, and still characterises Modern German.) as in Ger. /pfúnt/ *Pfund* 'pound' ⌣ Eng. *pound*; Ger. /¢ín/ *Zinn* 'tin' ⌣ Eng. *tin*;; and Swiss Ger. /kxált/ 'cold' ⌣ Eng. *cold*.) As a result, certain words borrowed from Gothic into Italian, without the second consonant-shift, contrast with cognates taken from Langobardic and showing this shift. Thus, OIt. /táttera/ *tattera* 'long, narrow banner' (:Eng. *tatter*) is clearly from Gothic because of its unshifted /t/-sounds, but It. /¢á¢¢era/ *zazzera* 'tress of unkempt hair' is from Langobardic, by virtue of the shifted /¢/ [ts] sounds. Similarly, It. /¢ólla/ *zolla* 'glebe' (:Ger. *Zoll* 'clod') is from Langobardic, whereas Corsican /tólla/ 'earth' is to be ascribed to a Gothic */tolla/ with unshifted initial /t-/.[19]

In morphology, one derivational suffix in Italian is to be traced to Langobardic forms, particularly in place- or person-names, or adjectives derived therefrom, in /+é^ngo/ *-engo* < Langob. /+ink/, as in the toponym /fiamé^nga/ *Fiamenga* (in Umbria, near Perugia), or in /térragirardé^nga/ *terra Ghirardenga* (attested at Lucca, in 1106).[20] In phonology, it has been suggested[21] that the diphthongisation of open /é/ and /ó/ to /ié/ and /uó/, respectively, in free syllable in Tuscan (and hence in standard Italian) is due to the Langobardic pronunciation of vowels as long in free syllable.

5.15. Frankish was the last Germanic language to appear on the Romance scene in the "Völkerwanderungen," and the one to exert, in certain respects, the greatest influence.[22] It is in northern Gaul that the greatest number of Frankish loans is found (in the dialects and in Old North French even more than in modern standard French), with the widest semantic range, including even the name of the country, *France* (ONFr. /frán¢a/ < /fránk-ja/; cf. §5.0). From this fact, it is usually concluded that the Frankish settlement must have been heaviest in the areas bordering on the Netherlands and the lower and middle Rhine-land.[23] No population-statistics are available, but the speakers of Frankish must have included not only the nobility, but also a large number of people of lesser rank. Nor is it known how long Frankish continued to be spoken. Charlemagne may well have been bilingual in Frankish and Gallo-Romance; the period of bilingualism probably lasted at least two or three centuries.

Frankish loan-words in Romance generally entered through northern Gallo-Romance and spread out from there. They are connected chiefly with court-life, the law, the army and military activities, and also with more homely concerns such as the house, its equipment, and clothing. Many Frankish words underwent extensive semantic shifting. Thus, in Frankish, */marh-skalk/ meant 'horse-servant'—at first, a mere ostler-boy, but later a court-official in charge of the horses. From this meaning, it became generalised to 'an official of the army, a marshal'. Frankish */marh-skalk/ appears in this latter meaning as a borrowing in Old North French, with the typical ONFr. change of /ka/ to /ĕa/; /maresčál/ *mareschal*; and in Old South French as /maneskálk/ *manescalc* (with /-n-/ instead of /-r-/, perhaps under the influence of /mán-/ *man-* 'hand'). The North French form was borrowed into Italian as /marešsállo/ *maresciallo*. The parallel Italian form /mariskálko/ *mariscalco*, and the Spanish and Portuguese /mariskál/ *mariscal* show, by the absence of palatalisation of /k/ before /a/, that they were borrowed from South French. This word is typical of many Gallo-Romance borrowings from Frankish in its semantic shifting and in its later diffusion to other Romance languages.

Other words related to court-life include Frankish */skankjo:/ 'page, cup-boy' > ONFr. /esčanǵón/ *eschançon*, and Frankish */kamerliŋ/ 'room-servant' (in its turn based on */kamer/ 'room' < Lat. *camera*) > ONFr. /čamberlénk/ *chamberlenc*, which passed into English as *chamberlain*. In legal matters, the very term for 'free man' was /fránk/ > ONFr. /fránk/ 'free', which underwent considerable semantic extension, particularly with reference to personality and character, to 'open, straightforward'. 'To call to court' was, in Frankish. */bannjan/, which gave ONFr. /banír/ *ban(n)ir* 'to summon'[24]; crossed with /band-/ 'sign', this verb became /bandír/ *bandir* 'to proclaim'. Among political divisions, the border-region was referred to in Frankish as */marka/ > ONFr. /márčə/ *marche* and OSFr., It., Sp., Cat., Port. /márka/ *marca*.

Many army-terms were taken from Frankish into Gallo-Romance, as was natural in a situation where the upper echelons of the fighting forces were, for several centuries, almost wholly Germanic in origin. In Frankish, 'to watch (over), protect' was */wardo:n/ (: Eng. *ward*) > ONFr. /guardǽr/ *guarder* (>Mod. Fr. /garde^/ *garder*) 'to keep'.[25] From early Gallo-Romance this verb spread to the other western Romance languages, *e.g.* It. /guardáre/ *guardare* 'watch > look', Cat., Sp., and Port. /guardár/ *guardar*. Among expressions referring to equipment were Frankish */helm/ 'helmet' > ONFr. /hélmə/ *hélme* (later /həaumə/, Mod. Fr. /'o^m/ *heaume*), OSFr. /élm/ *elm*; */brand/ 'sword' > ONFr. /bránt/ *brant*, OSFr. /brán/ *bran*; */helt/ 'hilt (of a sword)' > ONFr. /hélt/ *helt*, later /heut/ *heut*; and many others. In the field, the king or commander of the army would sit on a special folding chair, a /faldestuél/ *faldestoël* < Frankish */fald-/ 'fold' + */sto:l/ 'chair'.[26] The terms for the lower ranks of the army were, however, of Romance origin, *e.g.* the 'serving-man' or sergeant, ONFr. /serğánt/ *serjant*) < PRom. /seru̯iénte/ (present participle of /seru̯-/ 'serve', and the mercenary, ONFr. /soldeiǽr/ *soldeier* (whence, of course, Eng. *soldier*): /sóldə/ *solde* 'pay' (<PRom. /sólidu-/ 'solidus [a coin]' + /⁺ eiǽr/-*eier*, noun-forming suffix.

In the house and its surroundings, some types of cooking were of specifically Germanic origin, *e.g.* roasting: Frankish */raustjan/ 'to roast' > ONFr. /rostír/ *rostir*, OSFr. /raustír/ *raustir*[8] the North French form was then borrowed into Italian as /(ar)rostíre/ *(ar)rostire*.[27] Some specifically Germanic types of feminine attire were reflected in French loanwords, such as ONFr. /hývə/ *huve* 'woman's cap' (<Frankish */hu:be/: Mod. Ger. *Haube*, Swiss Ger. /hu:be/); ONFr. /kóˆifə/ *coife* 'a type of hair-do' (<Frankish */kufja/ 'cap'). Many Latin color-terms were replaced in western Romance by words of Germanic origin.[8] Those which are most wide-spread were borrowed from Gallo-Romance into Italo- and Ibero-Romance: */blank/ 'colorless, white' > ONFr, /blánk/ *blanc* (>It. /biánko/ *bianco*. Sp. /blánko/ *blanco*. Port. /bráku/ *branco*); */bru:n/ 'dark' > ONFr. /brýn/ *brun* 'brown' (> It., Sp, /bruno/ *bruno*, still often 'dark' rather than specifically 'brown'); and */gris/ 'gray' > ONFr. /grís/ (> It. /grígo/ *grigio*, Sp. /grís/ *gris*). The only major color-term from Gothic is considered to be */falw/ 'tawny' > Sp. /obéro/ *overo*, Port. /fouvéˆiru/ *fouveiro*.[29]

In some instances, it is possible to assign obviously related Romance words to different Germanic languages, as in the terms for 'tap (of a cask, etc.)'. ONFr. /tapǽr/ *taper* 'to tap' is from Frankish */tappo/; It. /tappáre/ *tappare* and Prov., Cat., Sp., Port. /tapár/ *tapar* 'to shut off', from Gothic *tappa/; It. /ȼáffo/ *zaffo* 'tap', from Langob. */tsapfo/; and Ladin (Val Gardena) /ȼafón/ *tsafon*, because of the cultural relationships and the unlikelihood of an earlier Germanic borrowing, has been ascribed to OHG /tsapfo/ *zapfo*.[30] In other instances, the various Germanic languages had forms so similar to each other that it is not possible to distinguish one possible source from another except on the basis of cultural and historical probabilities, as in the case of WGmc. /mag-/ 'ability, strength' serving as the basis for a Western Romance */eksmagáre/ 'deprive of strength' (>ONFr. /esmaiǽr/ *esmaier* 'dismay' [whence OSFr. /esmaiár/ *esmaiar*], OIt./smagáre/ *smagare*, OPort. /esmagárse/ *esmagarse* 'feel oppressed'), or */re:dan/ 'have provisions' (<ONFr. /(ar)reðǽr/ [*ar*]*reḍer* 'out-fit' [>Eng. *array*]), It. /ar° korredáre/ *ar° corredare*). In such instances as these, it is difficult to tell whether the West Germanic form was borrowed into late Popular Latin and developed from what we would set up as a PItWRom. form, or was taken over independently from the Germanic languages in each region.

In morphology, some have seen, in the late preservation of a two-case-system in Gallo-Romance (cf. Vol. 3), an effect of Germanic inflectional complexity acting as a model for speakers of Romance,[31] especially as manifested in the declension of personal names in /ón/ -on (m.) and /áin/ -ain (f.), e.g. ONFr. /ýk yón/ Huc Huon and OSFr. /úk ugón/ Uc Ugon 'Hugh', or ONFr. /bértə bertáin/ Berte Bertain 'Bertha'.[32] A number of derivational elements were introduced in loan-words from Frankish and then extended to Romance bases. The ONFr. prefix /for(s)+/ for(s)- is probably a conflation of /fórs/ fors 'out' (<PRom. /fóris/ 'outside') with the Germanic pejorative prefix */for+/ 'with undesirable results, badly', in such ONFr. forms as /for(s)fáirə/forsfaire 'to do wrongly', /(séˆi) forveiǽr/ (sei) forveier 'to lose one's way'.[33] A number of Germanic elements are found in personal names, especially such suffixes as ONFr. /+árt/ -art < Frankish /hard/ (e.g. in /ričrát/ Richart. /rənárt/Renart)[8] /+ált/ -alt < Frankish /+ halt/ (as in /rənált/ Renalt, /ǧirált/ Giralt) or /+bert/ -bert < Frankish /+bert/ (e.g. /albért/ Albert, /robért/ Robert etc.).[34] A number of place-names, especially in northern France, are of Frankish origin,[35] e.g. /'eristal/ Héristal (Liège) < */heristal/ 'lord's dwelling-place', /la'e/ la Haye < */hag/ 'hedge', or /busbek/ Bousbecques < */busk/ 'wood' + */bek/ 'brook'.

In syntax, various features of Old North French have been ascribed to Frankish influence: e.g. the placing of verbs at the end of dependent clauses, as in Si com Dix le vaut qui les amans ainme 'as God wills it, who loves lovers' (Aucassin et Nicolete 26.11–12)[36]; the position of color-adjectives before the noun they modified (e.g. ONFr. /blánkfér/ blanc fer 'white iron = tin'; or the habitual placing of a subject-pronoun before its verb, as in /ǧəčánt/ jo chant, modern /žəšát/ je chante 'I sing'.[37] In phonology, French vowel-raising and diphthongisation in stressed free syllables (/á/ > /ǽ/ > /é/, /é/ > /ié/, /ó/ > /uó/ > /ué/, /éˆ/>/éˆi/, and /óˆ/ > /óˆu/) has been ascribed to a presumed Frankish pronunciation of vowels as long in free stressed syllables.[38]

5.15. Norse. Later than the other Germanic languages usually considered as superstrata, and not connected with "Völkerwanderungen," was the language of the Norsemen (cf. § 5.0).[39] This exerted its influence chiefly on the French of Normandy, and through it on the Anglo-Norman of the eleventh through the fourteenth centuries in England (cf. § 2.55). A number of town- and other place-names in Normandy are clearly of Norse origin,[40] especially those containing such elements as /ham/ 'town' (seen in the diminutives Eng. hamlet and Mod. Fr. /'amoˆ/ hameau), e.g. /wistra'am/ Ouistreham < */westerham/ 'western village'. Certain French words show clearly that they were introduced from Norman, since they point to specifically North Germanic features in their phonology. For example, the Scandinavian languages preserved /sk/ as such before front vowels, instead of palatalising it to /š/ as was done in West Germanic (English and German), *e.g.* in /skíp/ 'boat' ⌣ Eng. /síp/ *ship*, Ger. /šif/ *Schiff*. Modern French /e^kipe^/ *équiper* 'to out-fit' < ONFr. /eskipǽr/ *esquiper* 'provide (refl., take ship)' is clearly formed on a Norse base /skíp/.

Other Germanic languages, such as Anglo-Saxon (Old English) and Old High German, which exerted an influence on Romance languages or dialects in preliterary times, did so, not as superstrata through a period of settlement and bilingualism in the speech-community, but through the normal process of borrowing in the course of cultural contacts, and hence will be discussed in later chapters.

5.2. Slavic

The chief Slavic languages involved as possible superstrata in Romance-speaking territory were Old Bulgarian and Serbo-Croatian, both belonging to the South Slavic group. The regions of contact were two: Dacia and Dalmatía.

5.21. OLD BULGARIAN. Whether Proto-Roumanian was formed south or north of the Danube (cf. § 5.0), it was strongly influenced by Slavic, not only in lexicon, but in structural features as well.[41] Since the Eastern Orthodox variety of Christianity prevailed among the Slavs, a number of religious terms were taken into Roumanian from Old Church Slavonic (Old Bulgarian), *e.g.* /pop(u-)/ *pop(u-)* 'priest', /sfínt(u)-/ sfïnt(u-) 'holy, Saint'. Many Roumanian personal names have come from the roster of saints of the Eastern Orthodox church, with Slavonic form even though ultimately of Greek origin, *e.g.* /dimítrie/ *Dimitrie*, /grigóre/ *Grigore*, /geórge/ *Gheorghe*. Nonreligious loan-words are connected with all levels of society, from /stəpín/ *stăpîn* 'over-load' and /bogát(u-)/ *bogat(u-)* 'rich' to /slúg(u-)/ *slug(u-)* 'servant' (with the Slavic derivative /slúžbə/ *slujba* 'service'). All semantic areas and all parts of speech are represented in the Slavic loans in Roumanian, as in /plúg(u-)/ *plug(u-)* 'plow', /slənínə/ *slănină* 'bacon', /grədínə/ *grădină* 'garden', /bríču/ *briciu* 'razor', /greši-/ *greşi-* 'make a mistake'. It has been pointed out[42] that almost all the Slavic loan-words in Roumanian refer to phenomena involving an emotional reaction, as in the examples given above and such words as /iubi-/ *iubi-* 'love', /drág(u-)/ /drág(u-) 'dear', /sláb(u-)/ *slab(u-)* 'weak', /trai-/

trai- 'live', /trúp(u-)/ *trup(u-)* 'body', /boálə/ *boală* 'sickness'. They point to a situation in which speakers of Slavic would have carried over, into newly learned Romance speech, terms which had emotional over-tones for them.

The influence of Slavic structural patterns on Roumanian is undeniable, though scholars differ as to its extent. The most obvious instance is that of the formation of the numerals above 'ten'.[43] In Latin and in the other Romance languages, we find separate cardinal numerals up to 'fifteen' or 'sixteen', and individual forms for 'twenty' and the tens thereafter: *e.g.* Fr. /ˈōz/ *onze* '11', /duz/ *douze* '12', /trez/ *treize* '13', /katorz/ *quatorze* '14', /kēz/ *quinze* '15', /sez/ *seize* '16'; /vēt/ *vingt* 'twenty', /trāt/ *trente* "thirty", etc. Roumanian, on the other hand, has much more transparent formations: /ùnsprezéče/ *unsprezece* '11', literally 'one on ten', /dòuə-sprezeče/ *douăsprezece* '12 (two on ten), etc.; and /dòuəsprezeče/ *două-sprezece* '12 (two on ten)', etc.; and /dòuəzéč/ *douăzeci* '20', literally 'two tens', /trèizéč/ *treizeci* '30 (three tens)', etc. These formations are simply loan-translations of the Slavic patterns represented by Russian /odìnnádsaţ/ одиннадесять 'eleven = one on ten', /dvànádsaţ/ двана-десять 'twelve = two on ten' etc., and similarly /dvádsaţ/ двадесять 'twenty = two tens', /trídsaţ/ тридесять 'thirty = three tens' and so forth. This is the type of loan-translation that one might expect from people who had learned another language tolerably well, but had carried over into it some previous habits of word-formation and syntax. There are also a number of Slavic derivational elements in Roumanian, such as the prefixes /ne⁺/ *ne-* 'not' (as in /nehotərít(u-)/ *nehotărît(u-)* 'indefinite' and /rəs⁺/ *răs-* and /rəz⁺/ *răz-* indicating intensification or repetition, from Slavic /rəz⁺/, as in /rəskoáče-/ *răscoace-* 'to over-cook'. Among suffixes derived from Slavic are /⁺ák(u-)/ *-ac(u-)*, /⁺áč/ *-aci*, /⁺eálə/ *-eală*, /⁺án(u-)/ *-an(u-)*, /⁺ník(u-)/ *-nic(u-)*, /⁺íšte/ *-iște*, /⁺íȼə/ *-ița,* as in /cerneálə/ *cerneală* 'ink' (to the Slavic root /čern-/ 'black').

In inflection, some scholars[44] have ascribed the preservation of the vocative, in Roumanian alone as opposed to the other Romance languages, to the presence of the Slavic declensional model, which also included a vocative element clearly differentiated from the other case-forms. The m.sg. vocative in /-e/ *-e* (as in /rádule/ *Radule!* 'o Radu!', /dómnule/ *domnule!* 'sir!') clearly goes back to the Latin vocative ending *-e,* and so we would set up a PRom. nom. sg. vocative in /-e/. The Roumanian f.sg. vocative in /-o/ *-o* (as in /marío/ *Mario! 'O Maria!'*) has no such obvious source in Latin, in which the f.sg. nominative, ending in *-a,* was also used as a vocative (cf. *Ave Maria* 'Hail, Mary!'). That this /-o/ in Roumanian was a borrowing from the Slavic f.sg. vocative, likewise ending in /-o/, is a tempting hypothesis; but some[45] have preferred to see in the Roumanian simply a fusion of the feminine noun-stem with the exclamation /o/ 'oh!'.

In phonology, the development of the middle series of vowels /ə/ and /ɨ/ can reasonably be traced to the introduction of Slavic loan-words containing the high central-back unrounded [ɨ], e.g. /stəpín/ stapîn 'over-lord', thus bringing into the phonological system a new dimension which served as a model for the development of conditioned sound-changes such as /á/ and /é/ > /ɨ/ before /n/, e.g. PRom. /pauiméntu/ 'floor' > Roum. /pəmínt(u-)/ pamînt(u-) 'ground, earth'; /kánto/ 'I sing' > Roum. /kínt/ cînt. Some varieties of Roumanian, especially the Daco-Roumanian (out of which the modern standard language has grown), manifest an extensive palatalisation of consonants, especially before /i/, and also an extensive replacement of initial /e-/ by /je-/. Thus, modern Roum. /zéče/ zece 'ten' goes back to */dᶻéče/ < *dᶻiéče/ < */diéče/ < PRom. /déke/ (: Lat. dekem/ decem). Word-final /-i/, especially in noun-plurals and verb-forms, has become simply a palatalised articulation of the preceding constant (except in the case of certain clusters): e.g. /bánj-/ bani 'coins' (morphophonemically still//báni//). The normal pronunciation of the verb-forms written e and este 'is' is now /jé/ and /jéste/, respectively; /é(ste)/ is archaic or dialectal. All these palatalisations have, by some,[46] been ascribed to Slavic influence; others,[47] however, have doubted the necessity of assuming a Slavic superstratum in these instances.

5.22. Serbo-Croatian has been invoked[48] as a superstratum to explain the special developments of Dalmatian phonology, particularly Vegliote. To the earliest Serbo-Croatian influence would be ascribed the Vegliote merger of /a/ and open /o/; the loss of phonemic consonant-length and the resultant phonemicisation of vowel-length, which had previously been allophonic; and the further differentiation of vowels in checked as opposed to free syllables. A second stage would have included the fronting of /u/, the loss of phonemic vowel-length, the phonemicisation of /j/ and /w/, and a series of phonemic mergers. The last stage involved primarily various shifts in articulation due to lowering of tongue-position, parallel to similar changes in modern Serbo-Croatian. Some developments in Vegliote have puzzled scholars, e.g. the fact that PRom. /k/ palatalised before lax /e/ but not before tense /eˆ/: thus, /kéˆna/ 'supper' > Vegl. /kájna/, but /kéntu/ '100' > OVegl. /kjénto/ > Mod. Vegl. /čánt/. According to the theory of Serbo-Croatian superstratum, when /č/ and /j/ acquired phonemic significance in Old Vegliote, the outcome of /eˆ/ had already shifted far enough towards its modern position of /a/ so as to condition nonpalatal allophones of preceding /k/ and /g/.

5.3. Arabic

Arabic exerted an extensive influence on the western Romance languages,[49] in part because it was the language of those who ruled over the Iberian peninsula (albeit a gradually diminishing part thereof) for more than seven centuries, and over Sicily for two centuries; and in part because it was a source for commercial and learnèd borrowings in other regions as well during the Middle Ages.

5.31. IBERIAN Arabic furnished a great many loans to Romance,[50] distributed in rough proportion to the extent and intensity of Arabic penetration. In Catalonia, where Muslim rule lasted the shortest time (712–788), there are relatively few loans from Arabic.[51] In Portugal, the process of reconquest was roughly parallel to that in Spain, but was completed earlier (with the conquest of the Algarve in 1253). The Arabic domination was strongest and lasted longest (until the fall of the kingdom of Granada in 1492) in central Iberia; here, the Arabic legacy of vocabulary and place-names is by far the greatest. The Romance-speaking population of "Mozárabes" (< Arabic /must'ara:b/ 'Arabized') were the chief channel of transmission for Arabic loans into Spanish. As the Reconquista proceeded southwards, speakers of Castilian took over from Mozarabic many words which had been borrowed from Arabic.[52] The variety of words and their referents indicate that there must have been a fairly close contact between Mozarabs and Muslims, not only in the cities, but also in the country-side. These contacts must have been, not only official, but also commercial, technological, and social.

As might be expected, a number of the loans are related to government and administration, *e.g.* Sp. /alkálde/ *alcalde* 'mayor' < Ar. /al-ka:di:/ 'the judge'; /valí/ *vali* 'governor' < Ar. /wa:li:/ id.; /albaθéa/ *albacea* 'executor' < Ar. /al-waṣi:ja/ 'something enjoined in a will'. The Arabs' military organization is reflected in such names of ranks and functions as /almiránte/ *almirante* 'admiral' < Ar. /al-'ami:r/ 'the chief', /alféreθ/ *alférez* 'ensign' < Ar. /al-fe:ris/ 'the knight, horseman', and /almogábar/ *almogávar* 'raider, commando-trooper' < Ar. /al-muga:wi:r/ 'the skirmisher'; in names for activities such as /alárde/ *alarde* 'parade' < Ar. /al-'ard/ 'the review (of troops)', the taking of a hostage, in Sp. /reén/, OSp. /rehén/ *rehén* < Ar. /rehén/ 'pledge, security', or the formation of a rear-guard, Sp. /θága/ *zaga* < Ar. /ṣa:qa/; and in names of buildings or parts thereof, such as /alkáθar/ *alcázar* 'fortress' < Ar. /al-kaṣr/ 'the fortress'.

Arabic competence in medicine was renowned in the Middle Ages, and not only persons (*e.g.* /albéitar/ *albéitar* 'veterinarian' < Ar. /al-béĭtar/ 'the veterinarian', ultimately from Gk. /hippiátros/ 'horse-doctor') but maladies (such as /alórre/, earlier /alhórre/ *alhorre* 'skin-rash of new-born babies' < Ar. /al-ḥorr/ 'the inflammation', or /albaráθe/ *albarazo* 'leprosy-like eruption' < Ar. /al-baraṣ/ 'white leprosy') were referred to with Arabic terms.

In matters referring to every-day life, Spanish and Portuguese have hundreds of Arabic loans. The reference of these may range all the way from major necessities of life to quite minor details. A mason is, in Spanish, an /alb níl/ *albañil* (< Ar. /al-banní/ 'the builder'). In the house he builds, there can be a /θaguán/ *zaguán* 'vestibule' (< Ar. /ostowa:n/ 'portico'), on whose floor there is an /alfómbra/ *alfombra* 'rug' (Old. Sp. /alhómbra/ < Ar. /al-ḫúmba 'the rug'), or he may build an /almaθén/ *almacén* 'ware-house' (< Ar. /al-máhzan/, Maghr. /al-mahzén/ 'the storage-place'). For one's quarters, one pays /alkilér/ *alquiler* 'rent' (< Ar. /al-hira:/ 'the rent'). To buy theatre-tickets, one goes to the /takíḷa/ *taquilla* '(ticket-)window', a diminutive on earlier /táka/ *taca* 'window' (< Ar. /ṭa:qa/).

Feminine garb was influenced by Arabic customs, as in the wearing of the /alfárda/ *alfarda* 'bosom-covering' (< Ar. /al-farda/ 'each of two halves [of a piece of cloth]') or the /albánega/ *albáneg* 'hair-net' (< Ar. /al-bani:qa/ 'the coif'), or of decorations or trinkets like an /alfilér/ *alfiler* 'pin', OSp. /alhilél/ (< Ar. /al-ḫile:l/ 'the pin') or an /axórka/ *ajorca* 'bracelet' (< Ar. /aš-šorka/ 'the bracelet'). Materials with names from Arabic include /algodón/ *algodón* 'cotton', Port. /algodáu/, etc. (< Ar. /al-quṭn 'the cotton') and /fustán/ *fustán* 'fustian' (< Ar. /fuṣta:t/ 'tent, tent-cloth').

In cultural life, a number of musical terms have come from Arabic, such as /albóke/ *alboque* 'a kind of flute' (< Ar. /al-bu:q/ 'the trumpet'), /laúθ/ /laúθ/ *laúd*, OSp. /alaúd/ *alaúd* 'lute' (< Ar. /al-ʻud/ 'the lute'), and /r:abél/ *rabel* 'rebec' (< Ar. /rabe:b/ 'a kind of viol'). Recreations included playing /axedréθ/ *ajedrez*, OSp. /ašedréȼ/ *axedreç* 'chess' (< Ar. /al-šiṭráng̃/ 'the chess'), with such pieces as the /r:óke/ *roque* 'rook' (< Ar. /ruḥḥ/ 'cart').

In the country, features of the land-scape with Arabic names included the /r:ámbla/ *rambla* 'sandy or dry ravine' (< Ar. /ramla/ 'sandy place'). The Arabic technique of irrigation brought in a whole new nomenclature, including /aθékia/ *acequia* 'ditch' (< Ar. /aṣ-ṣa:kija/ 'the trench'), /aθúθ/ *azúd* 'dam' (< Ar. /as-sudd/ 'the obstruction'), /albérka/ *alberca* 'reservoir' (< Ar. /al-birka/ 'the tank'), /alxíbe/ *aljibe* 'cistern' (< Ar. /al-ŷubb/ 'the well'), /arkadúθ/ *arcaduz* 'bucket' (OSp. /alkadúȼ/ *alcaduz* < Ar. /al-qa:dus/ 'the bucket'), and /nória/ *noria* /'draw-well' (OSp.

/annória/ *annoria* < Ar. /an-na:'u:ra/ 'the draw-well'). Various vege-
tables and crops included the /aθélga/ *acelga* 'best' (< Ar. /as-silqa/
'the beet'), the /θanaória/ *zanahoria* 'carrot' (OSp. /ǵahanória/ *çahanoria*
< Ar. /safuna:rija/, /arróθ/ *arroz* 'rice' (< Ar. /ruzz/), /alfálfa/ *alfalfa*
(< Ar. /al-faṣgaṣa 'the alfalfa'), and /aθúkar/ *azucar* 'sugar' (< Ar.
/as-sukkar/ 'the sugar'). These last terms are typical of certain Arabic
words referring to food imported from the East, which spread over Western
Europe in the later Middle Ages, and were introduced through more than
one channel of cultural and linguistic borrowing.

Many place-names in the Iberian peninsula are of Arabic origin,[53]
from that of the largest city of Spain, /madríθ/ *Madrid* (< Ar. /maǧríṭ/
'small fortress'), and many of its most important rivers, to those of little
villages. Other city- and town-names include /káθeres/ *Cáceres* (< Ar.
/kaṣr/ 'fortress') and several places containing Ar. /madi:na/ 'town', *e.g.*
Medina del Campo, Medina Sidonia. Some Arabic generic names for smaller
towns or parts of towns also entered Ibero-Romance vocabulary, *e.g.* Sp.
/aldéa/ *aldea* 'town' (< Ar. /al-dei̯ʔa/ 'the town, the field'), /bárrio/
barrio 'a part of town' (< Ar. /barri/ 'exterior'), and /arrabál/ *arrabal*
'suburb, slum' (< Ar. /ar-rabad̦/ 'the suburb').

Many Ibero-Romance river-names contain Ar. /wa:di:/ 'river', some
some with Arabic modifying elements (*e.g.* /gudalkibír/ *Guadalquivir* <
/wa:di:-al-kabi:r/ 'the big river [with the same meaning as our *Mississippi*])
or /guadarráma/ *Guadarrama* < /wa:di:-ar-ramla/ 'river with a sandy
strip of bank'), and others with /wa:di:/ followed by a previously existing
name (such as /guadaléte/ *Guadalete* = /wa:di:-al-léte/ 'river Lethe'). The
Arabic element /ǧabal/ 'mountain' appears in such place-names as
/xibraltár/ *Gibraltar*, OSp. /ǧebeltári/ *Gebeltari*, a Hispanisation of Ar.
/ǧabal-ṭa:riq/ 'the mountain of Ṭariq [the Muslim general who made
the original landing in 711]'. A number of towns in the Valencia region
preserve the indication of the Muslim families whose settlements they
originally were, with the Arabic element /ben/ 'son', as in /benidórm/
Benidorm, /benikaláp/ *Benicalap*.

It will be noted that a great many of these Arabic loans contain the
element /al⁺/ *al-*, from the Arabic definite article.[54] It is not sure whether
this element was included in the borrowed words through the ignorance
of the Mozárabes who took them into Ibero-Romance, or whether, as has
been suggested,[55] the speakers of Arabic from whom the Mozárabes learned
these words were themselves only recently Arabised Berbers, and had
taken them over with the article "frozen into" the words.[55] Beyond this
element, there is little morphological influence of Arabic evident in Ibero-
Romance. In all the Arabic loans, there were a number of prosodic patterns
(*e.g.* oxytone stress, as in /algodón/ *algodón* 'cotton', /marfel/ *marfil*

'ivory', and proparoxytone, as in /almokárabe/ *almocárabe* 'loop-like architectural decorations' [< Ar. /al-muqarbaṣ/ 'the carved adornments']) which rendered these patterns more frequent, and gave Ibero-Romance a greater variety of prosodic features than is the case in other Romance languages.[57] It is also possible that the Castilian palatalisation of PIbRom. fortis (long) /-nn-/ and /-ll-/ to /-ṇ-/ and /-ḷ-/ may have been due to imitation of Arabic "emphatic" articulation.

5.32. SICILIAN. Here, the influence of Arabic was similar to that observed in Ibero-Romance, but lesser in extent.[58] Among ordinary words, we may mention such terms as /(a)mmátula/ 'in vain' (< Ar. /ba:ṭil/ 'useless, vain'[59]), /dágala/ 'low ground' (< Ar. /daga:l[60]), /makalúbbi/ 'mud-volcano' (< Ar./maqlub/ "overturned[61]; and /mafaríta/ 'bucket' (< Maghrebian Ar. /marfad/ 'large drinking-cup, bowl'[62]). A number of Sicilian place- and river-names are from Arabic,[63] *e.g.* /burgilúsa/ *Burgilusa* (< Ar. /bu:rg-al-lu:zah/ 'tower of the almond-tree'), /u-ránnu/' *u Rannu* (< Ar. /rand/ 'laurel'), /a-délia/ *'a Delia* / < Ar. /da:li:ah/, /marsála/ *Marsala* and /marḍamémi/ *Marzamemi*, both containing Ar. /marsa:/ 'beach' (/marsa:-ali:/ 'Ali's beach' and /marsa:-al-hamam/ 'Turtle-dove Beach' respectively), or /u-kássaru/ *'u Cássaru* (< Ar. /kaṣr/ 'castle'). The Arabic words /wa:di:/ 'river' and /ǧabal/ 'mountain' are also found, as in *u Muncibbeddu* 'Etna' (a combination of the Romance and Arabic words for 'mountain', PRom. /mónte/ and Maghrebian Ar. ['dᶻɛbɛl][64]) and /u-vitiḍḍáru/ *'u Vitiḍḍaru* 'the river Elvio' (< Ar. /wa:di:-al-uru/). The town of Caltanissetta derives its name from Arabic /gal'at/ 'castle' plus the earlier name of the town, *Lissa*.

In other parts of Italy and in Sardinia, Arabic rule lasted too short a time to have left much lasting effects on lexicon or toponymy.[65] The Sardinian town of /arbatáš/ *Arbatax*, on the eastern coast, is said to derive its name from the presence of the fourteenth (Ar. /arba'ta:'š/) Muslim watch-tower along the coast.[66] Other Arabic elements in Sardinian are all indirect borrowings.

5.33. INTERNATIONAL ARABISMS came to western Europe primarily through commerce and shipping, and through learnèd channels, but less through direct contact during the Crusades than has sometimes been thought.[67] The Ar. /funduq/ 'inn' is reflected in Italian as /fóndako/ *fondaco*, OSFr. /fóndek/ *fondech*, and ONFr. /fondika/ *fondique* 'foreign merchants' quarter; ware-house' and (with the definite article /al⁺/) in OSp. /alhóndiga/ *alhóndiga* (modern /alóndiga/) 'public wheat-marketing house', Port. /alfádiga/ *alfándega* 'customs-house'. The 'office' or 'registry', Ar. /diwa:n/, was for "Frankish" traders the customs-house, whence the Spanish and Portuguese /aduána/ *aduana*. It. /dogána/ *dogana*, and OFr. /duánə/, Mod. Fr. /dwan/ *douane*. Ships were built and repaired in the /dar-aṣ-ṣina:'a/ 'house of construction' > It. /dársena/ *dàrsena* 'dry-dock' and Ven. /arȼaná/ *arzaná* 'arsenal' (whence It. /arsenále/ *arsenale* and, from Italian, Eng. *arsenal* and related words in other languages).

Learnèd channels, particularly Mediaeval Latin translations of Arabic treatises, on philosophy, mathematics, and science, introduced many Arabic words which have by now become part of our international terminology. Thus, *algebra* is from Ar. /al-ǧa:br/ 'the restoration, reduction (a mathematical operation); *zero*, from Ar. /ṣifr/ 'empty' (whence also *cypher*); *azimut*, from Ar. /as-simu:t/, plural of /as-samt/ 'the direction' (whence also *zenith*); *almanac*, from Ar. /al-manaḥ/ 'calendar', The mediaeval version of chemistry was *alchemy* < Ar. /al-kimija:/ 'philosopher's stone', in its turn from Byzantine Greek /ximía/ χυμέια 'fusion'. Magic powers were ascribed to an *elixir*, from Ar. /al-iksi:r/ 'the philosopher's stone (< Greek /kse:rón/ ξηρόν 'dry'). Our term *alcohol* is from Arabic /al-k-(u)ḥul/ 'the mascara'. All of these terms were borrowed into the different Romance languages at different times and in varying forms, so that no common pattern can be established for their history beyond their Arabic origin and learnèd introduction.

NOTES TO CHAPTER 5

1. The literature on the Roman Empire and its decline and fall is of course immense, beginning with Gibbon 1776–88. For more recent treatments, cf. such works as Seeck 1897–1921; Bury 1923; Homo 1925; Rostovtseff 1926 and 1926–27; Jones 1964, 1966; Downey 1969.

2. For the problem of the earliest Germanic loans in popular Latin, cf. Gamillscheg 1934–36:1.3–39 ("Die ältesten Berührungen zwischen Römern und Germanen"); also Lerch 1947 (questioning the ascription of */wérra/ 'war', *marríre/ 'anger, irritate', and */bastíre/ 'stitch, weave' to "Vulgar Latin") and the reply of Gamillscheg 1948.

3. For Goths, Langobards, and other groups in Italy, cf. the (by now old but still valuable) work of Hodgkin 1880–99; Gamillscheg 1934–36:1.229–338 and 2.3–229; also Gamillscheg 1937. For the Langobards, cf. also Poupardin 1907; Pochettino 1947; Peri 1962.

4. These three focal areas of Langobard influence are still evident in the geographical distribution of Italian loan-words from Langobard, *e.g.* /guánča/ *guancia* 'cheek' < Langob. */wankja/ (Kahane 1941).

5. This question has been hotly debated, not without nationalistic over-tones, by scholars on both sides of the question; cf. the discussion and references in Tagliavini 1947 (1969⁵) §64, and also Gamillscheg, 1964.

6. Instances of a "foreign accent" having prestige and being imitated by native speakers of a language are not unknown in the modern world, *e.g.* the French uvular [ʀ] in modern Italian, or an English accent in Afrikaans. Mack Smith (1968:2.338) reports

that under the British occupation of Sicily from 1806 to 1815, "the salons of Palermo even developed a snobbish affectation of speaking Sicilian with a British accent."

For problems of "superstratum" in general, as applied to Romance, cf. especially von Warrburg 1934c, (1950), 1939a; Valkhoff 1947. A negative opinion was expressed most strongly by Merlo 1939, 1942.

7. Cf. the list of eighty-odd terms given by Brüch 1913:87.

8. Cf. Brüch 1913:16.

9. For Germanic influence on Romance in general, cf. Brüch 1913, 1926 (with bibliography); Gamillscheg 1934–36; Rohlfs 1947b; Gaeng 1968. Germanic military terminology in Romance: Goldschmidt 1902. The Germanic element in French and Provençal; Mackel 1887. In Rhaeto-Romance: Gamillscheg 1934–36:2.267–306. In Italian: Bertoni 1914; Salvioni 1916; Bonfante 1959. In Roumanian: Löwe 1906:297–311; Meyer-Lübke 1906; Gamillscheg 1934–36:2.233–266.

10. For Ostrogothic, cf. Wrede 1891; for Visigothic, Gamillscheg 1932. A list of presumed Gothic loans in Romance is given by Holthausen 1929. The Goths in Spain: Alegre Peyrón 1966; E. A. Thompson 1969.

11. Cf. W. E. Leonard 1928–31, 1931; Hall 1965/66a.

12. For Vandalic, cf. Wrede 1886. The region in southern Iberia where they had their kingdom was called by the Arabs /al-andalu:s/ 'the Vandal territory'; from this term came Mod.Sp. /andaluθía/ *Andalucía*.

13. *E.g.* Gamillscheg 1934–36:3.3–201; von Wartburg 1936a (1950:87–101).

14. *E.g.* Hall 1949a.

15. Cf. Gamillscheg 1934–36:3.48–66; Jud 1937; von Warrburg 1939b.

16. Cf. Sabatini 1963.

17. Cf. Aebischer 1938.

18. Cf. Aebischer 1944.

19. Cf. Rohlfs 1941c.

20. Cf. Aebischer 1941.

21. By von Wartburg 1936a (1950:116–147).

22. For Frankish influence in general, cf. Schmaus 1912; Gamillscheg 1934–36:1.43–295; Frings 1937–39; von Warrburg 1936a (1950:74–87). Words from Frankish borrowed into other Romance languages from Gallo-Romance: Rohlfs 1952a.

23. Cf. Elcock 1960:231–235.

24. Germanic verbs whose infinitives ended in /-jan/ (mostly causatives) were, in general, assigned to the second or /-íre/ conjugation in Romance; cf. our Vol. 3, and Brosman 1962.

25. Germanic verbs in /-o:n/ were normally borrowed into Romance with the endings of the first or /-áre/ conjugation; cf. Vol. 3.

26. From the shape of the chair, with arm-rests, the term was extended to any arm-chair (Mod.Fr. /fo^tœj/).

27. Meier and de Gelós (1968) doubt the Germanic origin of the Romance verbs for 'to roast', but without sufficient reason.

28. Cf. Giacalone Ramat 1967. It is generally considered that most of the Romance color-names of Germanic origin were borrowed in connection with horses.

29. Cf. Gamillscheg 1934–36:1.36–37.

30. Cf. Gamillscheg 1934–36:1.33–34.

31. Cf. Hilty 1968.

32. Cf. Jud 1907.

33. Cf. Barbier fils 1930.

100   COMPARATIVE ROMANCE GRAMMAR

34. For Germanic personal names in the ONFr. epic, cf. Kalbow 1913; in Provençal, cf. Bergh 1941.
35. Cf. Gröhler 1913–33:1.250–354.
36. As suggested by Holmes 1931.
37. Cf. Hilty 1968.
38. By von Wartburg 1936a (1950:84–86), followed by many others.
39. For Scandinavian elements in Norman and French, cf. de Görög 1958.
40. For place-names of Scandinavian origin in Normandy, cf. Joret 1913; Sjögren 1928; Adigard des Gautries 1954.
41. For the Slavic element in Roumanian in general, cf. von Miklosich, 1861; Gaster 1886; Sandfeld-Jensen 1904; Skok 1923; Bărbulescu 1929; Mihăilă 1960. In Aromunian: Capidan 1925. Periods of Slavic loans: Vascenco 1959. Slavic influence on verbs: Křepinský 1938/39. Possible syntactic influences: Seidel 1958.
42. E.g. by Reichenkron 1964:253.
43. Cf. Sandfeld 1930:148–149; Rosetti 1953:23.
44. E.g. Densusianu 1901–38:1.244; Sandfeld 1930:146–148; Rosetti 1953:32; Niculescu 1965:25–29.
45. E.g. Tucker 1944. Schmid (1956) ascribes the preservation and extension of the vocative in Roumanian to its marginal position with respect to the other Romance languages and to Europe in general, with, as a result, what Jaberg (1936:95) termed "exagération périphérique des caractères morphologiques".
46. Especially Petrovici 1956, 1957a, 1957b.
47. E.g. Agard and Fairbanks 1958.
48. By Hadlich 1965 (cf. also Hall 1967a). For another view of the position of Dalmatian in Romance, cf. Muljačić 1962.
49. Arabic influence on the Romance languages: Seybold 1886; Lokotsch 1927; Bertoldi 1932; Steiger 1963; Pellegrini 1972.
50. For Arabic loans in Ibero-Romance in general, cf. Engelmann 1861; Dozy and Engelmann 1869; Eguílaz y Yanglas 1886; Neuvonen 1941. In Portuguese: Machado 1958–61. Mozarabic speech: Steiger 1943.
51. For Arabic loans in Catalan, cf. Corominas 1937.
52. Cf. Neuvonen 1941:29.
53. Spanish place-names of Arabic origin: Asín Palacios 1940.
54. Cf. Solá-Solé 1967/68.
55. Cf. Elcock 1960:280.
56. The element /al⁺/ al- has come to be treated, by naïve speakers of Ibero-Romance, as characteristic of foreign loan-words in general, so that, for instance, Eng. overalls and overcoat were reshaped, in the Portuguese of New England, to /alvirózis/ and /albakóti/, respectively (Pap 1949:101).
57. As pointed out by Elcock 1960:279.
58. Cf. de Gregorio and Seybold 1903; Calvaruso and daAleppo 1910.
59. Cf. Schuchardt 1908.
60. Cf. Wagner 1936b.
61. Cf. de Gregorio 1924.
62. Cf. Wagner 1944.
63. Cf. Avolio 1898; Pellegrini 1961.
64. Cf. Migliorini 1935.
65. For Italy in general, cf. Pellegrini 1963; for Liguria, cf. Pellegrini 1961.
66. Cf. Wagner 1951:177–178.
67. Cf. Tagliavini 1947 (1969⁵): §59. For Arabic borrowings in French, cf. Lammens 1890.

CHAPTER 6

The Rise of Romance Standard Languages

6.1. Pre-Literary Romance

6.10. WHEN DID THE ROMANCE LANGUAGES BEGIN? The history of standard languages is often viewed from the stand-point of the literature written in them. From this point of view, there would seem to be a gap of five centuries or more between the end of Latin as a "living" language and the beginning of the Romance languages. Latin literature—at least of a type and quality considered commensurate with the achievements of the Golden (Augustan) and Silver Ages—is usually considered to have ended by the sixth century A.D.[1] The first substantial literary production in any Romance language is that of Provence, with its earliest surviving monuments dating from the tenth century. The literatures of other West European languages follow at relatively short intervals: North French and Spanish in the eleventh, Portuguese in the twelfth, and Italian and Catalan (lagging markedly behind the rest) in the thirteenth and fourteenth, respectively. Since these early manifestations have been studied primarily by historians of literature, their approach has led them to ask questions like "Why did the Romance standard languages arise so late? What caused the birth of one, Provençal, before the others? Why should Italian have been so far behind the others in achieving literary dignity?"

If we broaden our horizon to include nonliterary documents, we achieve a somewhat different perspective. In general, nonliterary documents antedate those to which some literary value may be ascribed, by anywhere from one to three centuries. The earliest connected sentences in a clearly Romance tongue are the Oaths of Strassburg, pronounced in A.D. 842/43 by Louis the German and by the soldiers of Charles the Bald of France. Due to their connection with a specific historical event, they can be ascribed to an exact date. Other categories of documents of little or no literary value include sermons and little religious poems (the *Jonas* fragment and the *Sequence of St. Eulalia*, both from ninth-century northern France); sentences uttered in juridical contexts (*e.g.* the statements of

101

witnesses concerning land-tenure in Campania, 960 ff.); wills (that of Elvira Sanchiz in Portugal, 1192) and other legal papers; or business-men's records, preserved by chance, like those of a firm of Florentine bankers in 1211. In the absence of literary material from these earliest periods, such documents are often taken as indicating the existence of standards recognised beyond the boundaries of the regions in which they were written.[2] This is, in many instances, a doubtful conclusion.

A still broader perspective can be gained by taking every-day speech, rather than literary usage, as our point of departure, and by considering literature as not only written, but also oral.[3] During the entire "gap" of five or more centuries between the surviving attestations of Classical Latin and Romance literature, people were talking to each other. They were also telling stories and singing songs, either of their own invention or as they had learned them from others, as people do in all societies. From the fact that no attestations of such stories or songs have survived at all, we normally conclude that literate persons did not consider them worth writing down. Nevertheless, we have mentions of the existence of popular songs in various genres even in Latin times, e.g. love-songs,[4] satirical songs,[5] and tales of heroic valour, i.e. epic lays, whether they were long or short.[6] There were, indeed, some persons who could read or write, although literacy is generally considered to have declined between the fourth and the tenth centuries. But every-day life, talking and listening, story-telling and singing, went on all the same.

Inevitably there were some local differences in speech in Latin times. Efforts to identify these, on the basis of inscriptions and other documentation from the various regions have not been very successful.[7] (Similarly, it would be difficult to identify the local variations in, say, American or Australian English on the basis of scanty material written almost wholly in an approximation of standard English.) Nevertheless, since no "language" is ever wholly unified—in fact, each individual's idiolect is different in some respect, however minor, from that of each other individual[8]—local dialects certainly existed throughout the history of Latin. As the centripetal forces of standard Latin grew weaker, and as communication between the parts of the Empire diminished, these differences would inevitably increase. It must not be thought, however, that when the centripetal forces disappeared, the Romance languages immediately sprang into being. No-one rang the church-bells and proclaimed: "Hear ye! Hear ye! Latin is dead, and the Romance languages are now fully differentiated from each other!".

The situation in the late Roman Empire and the early Middle Ages, until ca. A.D. 800, was not unlike that in the modern English- and French-speaking worlds.[9] In each case, we find a single standard language, with a firmly established orthography and grammar taught in schools and recognized officially. No matter what dialectal differences may exist, they are not considered worthy of any recognition or prestige. Even nonnative speakers of the standard will, when they come to read and write, do their best to approximate it. Under these circumstances, only those works which are written in the standard will be considered to have any likelihood, even, of being valuable from a literary point of view. Any poetry, any prose narrative in nonstandard language will simply not be considered worth writing down. It will be passed from one group, one generation, to another, only through oral repetition. As has been repeatedly pointed out,[10] such oral literature inevitably undergoes changes, in form and content, in the course of its transmission.

It is, therefore, wrong to consider either the language or the literature of any given region as having begun with the earliest written material to have survived. Both the epic and the lyric genres of poetry probably had a long tradition of oral composition and repetition behind them. The *Roland* and the *Cid* were probably, not the first, but towards the last monuments of an old-established oral epic tradition which may have been starting to die out at the very time they were given definitive shape in writing.[11] The Provençal lyric, like-wise, probably had a centuries-old history of oral song, in relation to real-life situations of illicit love-affairs and jealousies, before the earliest surviving troubadour-poems—already semistylised and conventionalised—were written down. We must remember, also, that chance has played a very great rôle in the preservation of the earliest texts.[12] We have no way of knowing what other material may have been written down, but lost in the turbulence of following centuries.[13]

The question to be answered in connection with the earliest attestations of mediaeval languages and literatures is, rather, what considerations induced people to write down words or utterances in non-Latin form. For individual words, the two main incentives were: (1) the necessity of providing speakers of other languages with words they could use in the context of local speech; and (2) the impossibility of finding equivalents in Latin. The first type of situation would lead to the compilation of lists of equivalents or GLOSSARIES, such as those of Kassel and Monza (cf. §6.21). To facilitate comprehension of difficult words in Latin texts, scribes or others would often write simpler equivalents between the lines or in the margins of the pages. These words often reflect vernacular speech, either in Latinised shape or in their every-day form. Modern editors have extracted them from their contexts and made lists of them, as in the case of the Glosses of Reichenau, San Millán, or Silos. The second type of situation led historians and keepers of official records to note down the *ipsissima verba* of oaths, *e.g.* those of Strassburg in 842/43, or of witnesses' depositions, as at Capua and other towns in 960 (§6.42).

Short texts were the next type of material to be recorded, either as parts of lyric poetry (the Mozarabic *ḫarǧāt*; §6.43) or in connection with religious matters, such as the narration of saints' lives (*e.g.* the ninth-century Old North French *Cantilène de Sainte Eulalie* or the mid-eleventh-century *Vie de Saint Alexis*; §6.2). Only later were longer, more specifically literary works preserved in writing, with the development of a reading public which had social prestige, affluence, and leisure-time to devote to reading, but (especially among the ladies) no knowledge of Latin.[14]

6.11. How Standards Arise. To a considerable extent, the external history of the Romance languages from ca. A.D. 500–1500 is that of the emergence and rise—and, in some instances, decline—of certain favored varieties. From their function as standard-setters in literary and other types of usage (legal, governmental, educational), such varieties are termed STANDARD languages.

6.111. Koinés. A standard normally has its origin in the dialect of some particular territory, which comes to enjoy superiority over those of neighbouring regions, for nonlinguistic reasons (usually political, less often economic or social, never purely literary). Such a favoured dialect comes to be the common language or KOINÉ (< Gk. κοινή [διαλεκτός] 'common [dialect]') used throughout its region, where it is usually comprehensible to most of the speakers of neighbouring dialects. In the course of its spread, the koiné retains its basic relationship to the dialect on which it is based, but takes in features from related dialects, as in the instance of Span. /xuérga/ *juerga* 'spree' from Andalusian (§1.42), or French *fabliau* 'animal-fable' from Picard (≠ ONFr. *fablel* 'little fable').

6.112. Competition Among Dialects. Later, there ensues a competition between the koinés of different regions (*e.g.* the Île de France, Normandy, Picardy, and Champagne in northern France; Asturias, León, Aragon, Castile, Galicia in Spain), the upshot of which is the eventual victory of one (*e.g.* Francien or Castilian) and the gradual reduction of the others to the status of less favoured dialects. In Italy, for instance, in the thirteenth century, north Italian varieties (Venetian, Lombard, Piedmontese) were used for various types of didactic and moralistic poetry, while Sicilian was the vehicle for courtly love-poetry, at the court of Frederick II Hohenstaufen at Palermo (1225–1250) and later. Towards the end of the century, Guido Guinizelli (ca. 1240–1274) wrote love-poetry in his native Bolognese, and a group of writers collectively known as the poets of the

Dolce Stil Nuovo or "sweet new style" carried on and developed the tradition of courtly love, reaching their highest literary point in the works of Dante Alighieri (1265–1321). Not only the fame of these literary manifestations, but commercial expansion carried Tuscan to other parts of Italy, where it replaced local speech, first for poetry and then, later, for prose.[15]

6.113. COCKNEYS. On occasion, after a koiné has become the language of a whole country, the local dialect from which it arose undergoes further developments which are not accepted as part of the standard language (e.g. the Tuscan "gorgia" in Italian; cf. §4.13.2). The dialect of the political or cultural capital then comes to be looked down on by purists. In London, the speech of the lower classes, who are said to drop their aitches and to interchange *v* and *w*,[16] is called COCKNEY. We may use this as a generic term to refer to any dialect of this type (*e.g.* those of Paris, Madrid, or Florence in the Romance-speaking world). Purists then recommend, for imitation, the speech of some nearby city (*e.g.* Orléans, Toledo, Siena in the three instances just cited) whose slightly archaising usage they consider superior to the cockney of the capital.

6.12. THE "RUSTICA LINGUA ROMANA." For several hundred years after the break-up of the Roman Empire, the normal language for all kinds of writing continued to be Latin (of a sort). No official recognition was given to the increasing difference between the "grammatica," as it was taught in schools, *tant bien que mal*, and the every-day speech of the common people, until 813. The authorities of the Western Church had been growing concerned over the failure of the common people to understand the sermons delivered at Mass, and in that year, at the Council of Tours, an edict was issued that priests should thenceforth translate their sermons *in rusticam romanam linguam aut theotiscam* 'into the rustic Roman or German tongue'. With this edict, official recognition was given to an existing situation, in which popular speech had gradually come to be so different from the official language as to be one or more separate varieties. Note the use of the adjective *romana* in connection with *lingua*; this was the most common term, in that period, for popular Romance speech,[17] and has survived as the name of the language and of the people in Roumania. To speak in the *lingua romana* was *romanice loqui*; from the adverb *romanice* 'in the Roman fashion' derived, not only the name of the Rhaeto-Romance variety called *Romansh* (§2.124.1), but also the Old North French term *romanz*. Used at first as an adverb, referring to language (whence the English word for these languages, *Romance*), it came to be used also as a noun, referring to a story told in the vernacular, *i.e.* a *romance*.[18] The adjective *Latīnus* was also used as the name for some groups and their vernaculars, such as the Ladin dialects of South Tyrol (§2.124.2), the Ladinos or speakers of Judaeo-Spanish in the Balkans (§2.112.2.*a*.vii), and the *ladinos* who were Negroes that had acquired some smattering of Portuguese or Spanish in the slave-trading-days of the sixteenth century (cf. §7.4).

6.121. LATIN AS A SECOND LANGUAGE. The antinomy between Romance and Latin did not imply, as has often been thought, that the latter ceased to be spoken, and survived only as a "dead" language used exclusively for writing and reading.[19] The difference between the two was, at this stage, rather that of native versus nonnative,[20] with the native vernacular almost never used for writing.[21] The "grammatica" was taught to boys in schools—girls almost never received formal schooling of this type—as a second language, which they were expected to speak in school and, as much as possible, outside as well. (Boys were often punished with fines or beatings for using the vernacular, instead of Latin, among themselves in school.) Latin was the regular language of instruction, discussion, and debate, in elementary and advanced learning, in the church, in law-courts, and in the offices of lawyers and notaries.[22] It also served as a lingua franca for learnèd persons, not only in their written correspondences, but in their personal contacts with each other at home or on their travels. In fact, Latin did not wholly cease to have this function until the eighteenth century, and many have regretted that it is no longer so used.[23]

The Latin of the mediaeval schools was, despite the use of the grammars written in late antiquity by Donatus and Priscian and their successors,[24] by no means uniform. As the centuries passed and the phonological systems of the vernaculars became gradually differentiated from each other, local pronunciations of Latin also diverged, with, for example, Latin *ce ci* being rendered as [tse tsi] (later as [se si]) in Gallo- and Ibero-Romance territory, but as [tše tši] in Italy. Grammatical "mistakes," which abounded in early mediaeval Latin, often reflected the developments of local vernacular Romance speech. In Gallo-Romance territory, where the nominative case was kept distinct in form (cf. Vol. 3), but the functions of the various nonnominative cases were merged in the single oblique case, we might expect this phenomenon to be reflected in the local use of Latin. Thus, in the sixth-century Salic law,[25] written down in northern Gaul, we find such sentences as (3. §4) *Si quis vacca cum vitulum furaverit* 'if any-one shall have stolen a cow with a calf', with *vacca* ending in -*a* (not -*am*, accusative) and *vitulum* in -*um* (not -*o*, ablative). In Italy, on the other hand, where the loss of final /-s/ had occurred early on, the nominative is also involved in the confusion with the other cases: *e.g. ad omnes sancti et sancte Deo* 'to all the saints (m). and saints (f.) of God' and *de omnibus sanctis et sancte Dei* of all the saints (m.) and saints (f.) of God'.[26] Local vocabulary-differences come to be reflected in regional use of Latin,[27] as when the Glosses of Reichenau give *sabulo* 'sand' (Fr. *sable*) or *donare* 'to give' (Fr. *donner*).

6.122. LATIN AND EVERY-DAY SPEECH. The relations between the "grammatica" and vernacular usage were by no means unidirectional. From the earliest times of differentiation[28] (cf. the diagram in Table VIII, Chapter 4), not only did writers consciously or unconsciously introduce "vulgar" words and expressions into their works, but conservative or learnèd elements filtered "down" into popular speech. One of the earliest such instances is the West Romance verb for 'to think', for which we can reconstruct a Proto-Italo-Western Romance root /pé^ns-/, based on its occurrence in Ibero-, Gallo-, and Italo-Romance.[29] Our reconstructed Proto-Romance as a whole, however, has no cluster /-ns-/ (cf. Vol. 2). For this root, we can establish a doublet based on the verbs meaning 'to weigh, press', attested in all the Romance languages, with the PRom. shape /pé^s-/, related to CL/pe:nsum/ *pēnsum* 'weight'.[30] The obvious explanation for PItWRom. pé^ns- ('think' (< 'deliberate, weigh (alternatives)')) is that it is a borrowing into popular speech, probably made in Imperial times, from the CL forms which preserved *-ns-* in writing and presumably also in careful pronunciation. In later centuries, there were thousands of such borrowings, identifiable by their preservation of one or more phonological features of Latin. Even in the earliest extant monuments of Romance literature, we find such learnèd words as *element* in the ONFr. *Eulalie* poem (ca. 880), *encenso* 'incense' in the OSp. *Auto de los Reyes Magos* (twelfth century), or *benedictione* in the OUmbr. *Cantico delle Creature* of St. Francis of Assisi (probably ca. 1225). In some instances, the learnèd words were reshaped under one kind of analogical influence or another, as in OSp. *celestrial* "celestial" in the *Auto*.

The early mediaeval relation between Latin and every-day speech, at least in western Europe, was probably not unlike that now prevailing in Haiti between French and Creole. In such a situation, the prestige-language is taught in schools and spoken, in a relatively few families, as a near-native tongue; but all, even the members of the upper classes, speak the vernacular from earliest childhood. Depending on the extent of his schooling and of his exposure to the prestige-language, each individual will speak the vernacular with more or fewer intercalated borrowings (words, phrases, even whole sentences) from learnèd sources.[31] (Conversely, in his use of the prestige-language, the less puristic he is, the more vernacular features he will introduce.) Learnèd borrowings will occur especially in connection with concepts[32] for which no corresponding term is immediately available in the vernacular; but the converse can also occur, especially the use of popular expressions to refer to local phenomena (features of the land-scape, plants, animals, etc.)

The channels of learnèd influence in the Middle Ages were manifold. Church Latin[33] was of course the major source of terms pertaining to religion and philosophy, such as *apostolus* 'apostle', *ecclēsia* and *basilica* 'church', *episcopus* 'bishop', *haereticus* 'heretic' or *philosophus* 'philosopher'. These would filter into every-day speech both from the conversation of priests, monks, and nuns, and from their frequent introduction into sermons.[34] Legal and notarial Latin furnished such expressions as *iustitia* 'justice', *innocens* 'innocent', *auctoritas* 'authority', *criminālis* 'criminal', *opiniō* 'opinion'. Similarly, medical terms came from doctors and dentists. Schools and teachers early acquired a reputation for haughtiness and arrogance, as shown by the popular developments of the learnèd borrowing *grammaticus* 'grammarian'.[35]

There were also more homely borrowings, in such fields as herbal and anatomical nomenclature. Terms used by monks in such activities as gardening and medicine would spread from their usage to the populace at large, either directly or through herbalists and quack doctors. To such influences as these are to be traced a number of learnèd or semilearnèd borrowings (often influenced by popular etymology; cf. §1.41.2),[36] *e.g.* Ligurian *cornabüggia* 'origanum' < *cunula bübula*, under the influence of folk-beliefs concerning the efficacy of this herb against certain diseases of bovines, whence the crossing with *corn-* 'horn'; or terms for 'rosa canina' from *crataegus*, with the first element reinterpreted as if it were related to *grat-* 'scratch' and the second to *cul* 'buttocks', as in NIt. *grata-cul* 'rosa canina [lit. arse-scratcher]'.[37]

6.13. THE PROBABLE SITUATION CA. A.D. 800. If, with the aid of a Wellsian time-machine, we could return to Charlemagne's empire at the beginning of the ninth century, and visit all the Romance-speaking territory, what would we find? Very likely, something like this:

In Iberia, the large majority of the lower classes in city and country, and many of the middle-class people in the cities, speaking a very conservative Ibero-Romance, close to the language of the *ḥaraǧāt* (cf. §6.23; the rulers, governors, urban upper classes, and country land-holders speaking Arabic; in the northern mountains some rather divergent Romance dialects, predecessors of later Castilian, Asturian, Leonese, and Galician; perhaps, among the Christian nobles of Gothic origin in the north, some surviving traces of Gothic, and probably some bilinguals who spoke Romance with a Germanic accent; and in the Pyrenees, extending down as far as Burgos or beyond, speakers of Basque.

In Gaul, virtually every-one speaking Gallo-Romance, which may have extended (by this time, perhaps, only in scattered surviving groups) into the Moselle valley,[38] and across the Palatinate, Baden-Württemberg, Suabia, Bavaria, and into the Swiss mountain-regions and the Vorarlberg; Keltic (Breton) being used in the west, beginning at Rennes or even farther east; Basque, as far north as the Garonne; and the more innovative variety of Francien limited to the region immediately in and around the Île-de-France.

In Italy, local varieties of Italo-Romance throughout the north and center, with an especially conservative variety in the back-water of Tuscany; Greek used extensively in city and country to the south; Arabic as the language of the rulers and at least some bilinguals in the middle and lower classes in Sicily; and some Rhaeto-Romance in South Tyrol and the Friuli.

Along the Dalmatian coast and perhaps inland for some distance, Dalmatian.

In the Balkans, a close symbiosis of groups speaking pre-Roumanian with others speaking Slavic, probably both north and south of the Danube and perhaps in the central Danube valley (in what is now the Alföld).

In Corsica, Sardinia, and some places in North Africa (Tunisia and perhaps farther west as well), very conservative varieties of local Romance.

Latin we would have found usable as a lingua franca throughout the West, but we would have had to use Greek in the Balkans and Sardinia, and Arabic in North Africa as well as with the rulers and upper classes in Sicily and those parts of the Iberian peninsula under Moslem rule.

6.2. Earliest Romance Documents

Individual words of obviously vernacular character, such as *caballicāre* 'to ride a horse' (cf. OSFr. /kabalgár/ *cabalgar*, ONFr. /čavalčǽr/ *chevalchier*) or *avicellus* 'bird' (cf. OSFr. /auẓél/ *auzel*, ONFr. /oiẓél/ *oisel*, It. /uččéllo/ *uccello*), and syntactic constructions like *habet annōs quindecim* 'he is fifteen years old' (= It. *ha quindici anni*, lit. 'he has fifteen years', Fr. *il a quinze ans*, Sp. *tiene quince años*) or *membra ad duōs fratrēs* 'the members of two brothers, lit. to two brothers', inscription on a tomb-stone are to be found in many late Latin documents.[39] Three of the most important collections of such items are the glossaries of Reichenau, Kassel, and Monza. The earliest attestations of complete sentences are to be found, for Gallo-Romance, in the Oaths of Strassburg; for Italo-Romance, in the depositions preserved at Monte Cassino; and for Ibero-Romance, in the Old Spanish glosses.

6.21. EARLY GLOSSARIES

1. The Glossary of Reichenau[40] is a collection of Latin words, occurring principally in the Vulgate of the Bible, explained with other Latin words. Many of these latter repeat synonyms which have occurred in preceding passages of the Vulgate. Some of them either reflect the Latin etymon of modern Romance terms (*e.g. ficatus* for 'liver, glossing *gecor* = CL *iēcur*, no. 932; cf. Sp. *hígado*, It. *fégato*, Mod. Fr. *foie*), or are simply Romance words with Latin endings, such as *cooperīre* 'cover' (= Sp. *cubrir*, It. *coprire*, Fr. *couvrir*). The glosses of Reichenau are generally ascribed to northern France, because of certain forms which are, in later attestations, restricted to that region: *e.g. causare* 'to speak, ask oneself' (= Mod. Fr. *causer* 'to speak, chat').

2. The Glossary of Kassel[41] is a collection of words (plus a few very short sentences) in more or less "barbarous" Latin plus their equivalents in Bavarian German. It is usually ascribed to the early ninth century, and was perhaps written at Freising in Bavaria. It would seem to have been primarily a travellers' conversation-manual for use by Germans in Romance territory, with a purely practical purpose, as shown by such equations as *figido* = *lepara* 'liver', *pulcins* = *honchli* 'chickens', *martel* = *hamar* 'hammer', and such sentences as *implenus est* = *fol ist* 'it is full', *radi me meo colli* = *skir minan hals* 'shave my neck'. Scholars are still in disagreement over the localization of the Kassel glosses.

3. The Glossary of Monza[42] also consists of isolated words plus a few sentences, equating Italian terms with Greek: *gallo* = *aletora* (ἀλέκτορα) 'rooster', *de mandegare* = *desmetinaosefaimo* (δόςμετ ίναῖσαφά[γ]ωμε[ν]) 'give me something to eat'. It was probably written somewhere in northern Italy in the tenth century, with the Green part furnished by some-one from the Greek linguistic islands in southern Italy.

4. There are two major collections of Old Spanish glosses, from the district known as La Rioja: the Glosas Emilianenses, so called from the monastery of San Millán where they were preserved, and the Glosas Silenses,[43] from the monastery of Silos. The former also contain some complete sentences, such as *cono ajutorio de nostro dueno, dueno Christo, dueno Salbatore, qual dueno get* (= /jét/) *eno honore, e qual dueno tienet ela mandatione, cono Patre, cono Spiritu Sancto, enos sieculos elos sieculos. Facanos Deos omnipotes tal serbitio fere ke denante ela sua face gaudioso segamus* (= /sejámus/) 'with the help of our Lord, Lord Christ, Lord

Saviour, the which Lord is in honour, and the which Lord has the dominion, with the Father, with the Holy Spirit, in the centuries and the centuries. May the all-powerful God have us do such service that we may be joyful before his countenance'. In the Glossary of Silos we find such equations as *comburatur = kematu siegat* /kemátu siéjat/ 'that he be burned', *semel = una vece* /úna vé^¢e/ 'once', *usque in finem* 'up to the end' = *ata que mueran* /áta ke muéran/ 'until they die'.

6.22. IPSISSIMA VERBA. As suggested in §6.10, certain sentences in the vernacular were transcribed, in the middle of texts written otherwise in Latin, for the purpose of preserving the exact form of something which had been said.[44] Of this type are the two best known early attestations of Romance speech, the Oaths of Strassburg and the Cassino depositions.

1. The Oaths of Strassburg are four long sentences, two in a variety of Gallo-Romance (called 'romana lingua' in the Latin text) and two in Old High German, preserved in the account which the German historian Nithard (?–844) gives of the meeting of the French king Charles the Bald and the German king Louis the German, together with their armies, at Strassburg in February of 842/43, to form an alliance against their brother Lothair. First Louis took an oath in 'romana lingua', so as to be understood by his brother's soldiers, and similarly Charles swore in German. Then Charles' men took an oath in their own language, followed by the same oath sworn by Louis' soldiers in theirs.

The texts of the two Gallo-Romance oaths have been the object of extensive study and discussion.[45] The actual texts, with my tentative phonemic transcription and a translation, are as follows[46]:

Louis the German's oath:

Pro Deo amur, & pro cristian poblo & nostro comun salvament, d ist di in avant, in quant Deus savir & podir me dunat, si salvarai eo cist meon fradre Karlo, & in aiudha & in cadhuna cosa, si cum om per dreit son fradra salvar dift, in o quid il mi altresi fazet, & ab Ludher nul plaid nunquam prindrai ki, meon vol, cist meon fradre Karle in damno sit.

/pro déə amó^r e pro kristián póblə e nóstre komún salvamént, d é^st dí en avánt, en kuánt déəs savé^r e podé^r mə dó^nat, sí salvarái éə ¢é^st meón frádrə kárlə, ed en aiúda ed en kadúna kósa, sí kó^m óm pər dré^it son frádrə salvár dé^ft, en ó kəd íl mí (mé^?) àltrəsí fá¢et, ed ab lodér núl pláit nó^nkə pre^ndrái kí məón vól ¢é^st məón frádrə kárlə en dámnə sé^t./

'For the love of God, and for the Christian people and our common well-being, from this day onwards, insofar as God gives me knowledge and power, I shall aid this brother of mine Charles, both in [feudal] assistance and in every matter, as a man should by right aid his brother, insofar as he does likewise to me, and with Lothair I will make no agreement which, of my will, should be harmful to this brother of mine Charles.'

Charles the Bald's oath:

Si Lodhuuigs sagrament que son fradre Karle iurat, conseruat, & Karlus meus sendra de suo part non lo s tanit, si io returnar non l int pois, ne io ne neuls cui eo returnar int pois, in nulla aiudha contra Lodhuuig nun li ui er.

/si loduvíks sagramént kə son frádrə kárlə ǧurát, konsérvat, e kárləs méəs séņdrə də só^ə párt nón lə s tánit, si ǧɔ́ rəto^rnár non l e^nt póis, nə ǧɔ́ nə nəúls kúi éə rəto^rnár e^nt póis, en núla aiúda kóntra loduvíg non li vi ér./

'If Louis keeps the oath which he has sworn to his brother Charles, and Charles, my lord, on his part, does not keep his, if I cannot deter him from it, neither I nor any-one whom I can deter from doing so will be of any help to him in it against Louis.'

There has been a great deal of discussion of the phonology reflected in the orthography of the Oaths, and of their localisation in the Gallo-Romance territory. Many commentators, confusing phonetic and phonemic criteria, debate earnestly the extent to which, for instance, the *K* of *Karlus* stands for a palatalised or nonpalatalised [k]. The language of the Oaths has been ascribed to many different regions of France, even as far away as the South-East. My own view is that their language was, even when they were pronounced, so conservative as to be virtually archaising, a kind of nearly undifferentiated pre-North-French, so as to be comprehensible to all the speakers of Gallo-Romance in Charles' army. This is not to deny that there may have been, among those men, some speakers of more advanced varieties, *e.g.* of the Francien reconstructed in our first "contemporary" version given below.

An anonymous speaker of Friulian, ca. 1740, on coming across the Oaths of Strassburg, was so struck by their closeness to his native variety of Rhaeto-Romance that he translated them as follows[47]:

Per l'amor di Dio, e del popul cristian, e nestri comun salvament, da chest di indevant, in quant che Dio mi donarà savè e podè, io salvarai chest mio fradi Carlo, e lo judarai in ogni ciosse, come che om al def salva so fradi, in chel che altri faress per me; e cum Lotari no farai alcune convenzion, che di mio volè a chest mio fradi Carlo sei in dan.

Following his example, it is an interesting exercise to attempt an (admittedly highly tentative, but not speculative) reconstruction of the Oaths in a number of varieties of what we can, with the best available information, consider would have been the Romance vernacular of several other regions as of 842/43. This exercise permits us to see, in an approximate way, how great the mutual comprehensibility between these varieties would have been. Table IX shows, schematically, the main isoglosses (phonological, morphological, lexical[48]) between the conservative varieties of the regions involved. From their distribution it is evident that, if our reconstructions are even to a limited extent valid, the western Romance area (including Sardinia!) still formed a single L-complex,[49] whereas pre-Roumanian was already a separate language by any criterion. In the following paragraphs we give the Oaths in the Old North French of the 880's (when the *Cantilène de Sainte Eulalie* was presumably written down, and following Porter's reconstruction of its phonemics[50]); in both a conservative Italo-Romance of the Cassino area and a more advanced, diphthongising Romance of the Tuscan area; similarly, in a conservative, nonlenited Ibero-Romance and a more advanced, lenited and diphthongising variety thereof; in Sardinian; and in pre-Roumanian.

Old North French[51]:

/por l amó^ur dǽu, e por lə puóvlə krestiǽn, e nóstrə komún salvəmént, də ȼé^st dí en avánt, en kánt kə dǽus mə dónəð savé^ir e poðé^ir, sí salvərái ǧé ȼé^st mién frǽðrə čarlón, en aiúðə eð en časkúnə čózə, sí kóm óm por dré^it son frǽðrə salvǽr dé^it, en kánt keð íl a mé^i àltrəsí fáȼəð, eð ab loð ǽr núl pláit nónkəs prendrái, ki də mé^iə volontǽð a ȼé^st mién frǽðrə čarlón sé^it en dán./

Italo-Romance (Cassino region) as of *843:

/per lu amó^re de déu, e pper lu kristiáno pópulu, e nnóstru komúne salvaméntu, da kkué^stu dí en avánti, en kuántu déu me dá ssapé^re e ppoté^re, si ssalvaráo éu kué^stu fráte mu károlu, e llu aiutaráo en ónne kósa, sí kkó^me per deré^ttu lu ómo dé^ve salváre fráte su, en kuántu é^lli fáȼȼa àltressí pper mé^; e kkon

lotáriu nom faráo mmái nessúnu páttu, ke dde méu voléˆre a kkuéˆ-
stu fráte mu károlu séˆa en dánnu./

*Italo-Romance (Tuscan) as of *843:*

/per l(o) amóˆre di Dío, e pper lo kristiáno puópolo, e nnóstro
komúne salvaménto, da kkuéˆsto díe in avánti in kuánto dío mi dá
ssapéˆre e ppotéˆre, sí ssalvaró io kuéˆsto mío fráte kár(o)lo, e llo
aiutaró in ónne kósa, sí kkóˆme per dirítto l(o) uómo déˆve salváre
súo fráte, in kuánto éˆlli fáčča àltressí pper méˆ; e kkon lotário nom
faró mmái nassún(o) pátto, ke ddi mío voléˆre a kkuéˆsto mío
fráte kár(o)lo sía in dánno./

Isogloss No.	Phenomenon
Phonological (——)	
1	Simplification of long (double) consonants
2	Loss of final vowels (except /-a/) after single consonants, and final /-a/ after clusters > /-ə/
3	/-kt-/ > /-it-/
4	/-kt-/ > /-pt-/
5	/kᵉ,ⁱ/ not palatalised to /č/ or /¢/
6	Lenition of intervocalic /p t k/ to /b d g/, of intervocalic /b d g/ to /v ẟ γ/ (and further developments)
7	Intervocalic /-l-/ > /-t-/
Morphological (— — —)	
8	Preservation of case-system (nom.-acc. vs. gen.-dat.)
9	Preservation of case-system (nom. vs. oblique)
10	Fusion of future-phrase (AUX + INFIN) into FUTURE TENSE
11	Definite article or personal pronoun from /íps-/, not /íll-/
Lexical (- - - - - -)	
12	Replacement of /amóˆre/ 'love' by /liubíre/
13	Loss of /kommúne/ 'common'
14	Replacement of /ómne/ 'every' by formations with /káta-/
15	Replacement of /ómne/ 'every' by phrase /fíe-káre/ 'be it whichever'
16	Replacement of /per/, /pro/ or /por/ by /péntru/ 'for'
17	Replacement of /skíre/ 'to know' by /sapéˆre/
18	Replacement of /káusa/ 'thing' by /lúkru/
19	Absence of forms < /ab ánte/ 'before'
20	Replacement of /dáre/ 'to give' by /donáre/
21	Replacement of /fráte/ 'brother' by /iermánu/
22	Loss of /dámnu/ 'harm'
Syntactic (—O—O—O—)	
23	Definite article comes in second, not first, slot in noun-phrase
24	Preposition used before 'personal' direct object
25	Possessive adjective follows kinship-term it modifies

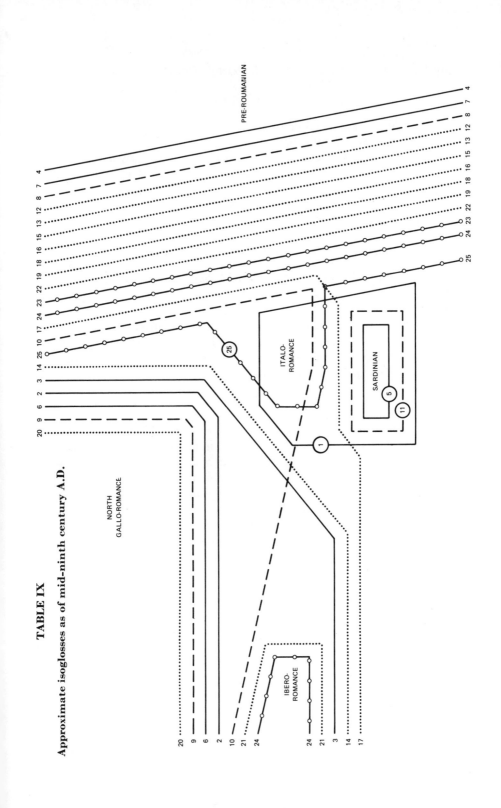

TABLE IX

Approximate isoglosses as of mid-ninth century A.D.

PRE-ROUMANIAN

4 7 8 12 13 15 16 18 19 22 23 24 25

4 7 8 12 13 15 16 18 19 22 23 24 17 10 26 14 3 2 6 9 20

ITALO-
ROMANCE

25

SARDINIAN

5

11

1

NORTH
GALLO-ROMANCE

IBERO-
ROMANCE

20
9
6
2
10
21
24

24
21
3
14
17

*Ibero-Romance (conservative) as of *843:*

/por el amóˆr de déus, e por el kristiánu póplu, e nóstru komún salvaméntu, de ak(u)éˆstu día en adelánte, en kuántu déus me dá sapéˆre e potéˆre, assí eˆsalvár ad ak(u)éˆstu méu i̯ermánu kárlu e éˆ aiudár lu en káta kósa, assí kóˆmu por deréxtu el ómne déˆve salvár súu i̯ermánu, en kuántu el fáȼa àltrusí para mí; e kon lotár nóˆ éˆ tomár nekún pláitu, ke de méa volontáde a ak(u)éˆstu méu i̯ermánu kárlu séˆa en dánnu./

*Ibero-Romance (advanced, lenited), as of *843:*

/por el amˆóˆr de déus, e por el kristiánu puéblu, a nuéstru komún salvaméntu, de akéˆstu día en adelánte, en kuantu deus me da saveˆre e podeˆre, asi salvar eˆ ad akéˆstu méu i̯ermánu kárlu, e aiudár lu eˆ en káda kóza, así kóˆmu per deréitu el ómre déˆve salvár sú(u) i̯ermánu, en kuántu él fáȼa àltrusí para mí; e kon lotár nó tomár éˆ negún pléitu ke de méa volontáde a akéˆstu méu i̯ermánu kárlu seˆa en dánnu./

*Sardinian, as of *843:*

/pro su amóre de déus e ppro su pópulu kristiánu e nnóstru komúne salbaméntu [?], da ístu díe in ántes, in kántu déus dáetmi* iskíre e ppotére, sí áppo salbáre [?] ístu méu fráte károlu et in aiutóru et in ónnia káusa, sí kkómo su ómine per diréttu débe aiutáre súu fráte, in kántu ísse átteru tántu mi fákat, ek kum lutáru non áppo fákere núllu páttu ki de méu bólere ad ístu méu fráte károlu síat dannárdiu./

* unstressed /mi/, dative, in contrast with /me/, accusative.

*Pre-Roumanian, as of *843:*

/péntru liubíre-a dùm(i)nediéu-lui si péntru popóru-lu kresčínu si tráiu-lu búnu nóstru de tóti, de la ačeástə díe in aínte, dákə dùm(i)nediéu me da sčíre si puteáre, asiá vóliu ağutáre ačéstu fráte méu kárulu, si in ağutóru sí in fìe-káre lúkru, kúmu ómu-lu trébuie sə ağúte fráte-lu séu, dákə iélu fáče asémenea péntru míne, si ku lutáru nú(n) vóliu fáčere níci úna invoíre če de vóia méə ačéstui fráte méu kárulu fíe rə̀u-fəkətoáre./

2. The Cassino depositions, so called because the manuscripts in which they are preserved form part of the library of the monastery of Monte Cassino (southeast of Rome), are four short sentences uttered by witnesses

involving the monastery's claim to various holdings of land: in Capua in
March of 960, in Sessa Aurunca in March of 963, and in Teano in July and
October of that year.[52] The texts of two of these depositions read as
follows:

(Capua, 960) Sao ko kelle
terre, per kelle fini que ki
contene, trenta anni le pos-
sette parte Sancti Benedicti.

'I know that those lands, with
those boundaries which are contained herein, were possessed for
thirty years by the monastery of
St. Benedict.'

(Teano, 963) Kella terra,
per kelle fini que bobe mos-
trai, Sancte Marie è, et
trenta anni le posset parte
Sancte Marie.

'That land, with those boundaries which I showed you, belongs
to St. Mary's, and the monastery
of St. Mary posssessed them for
thirty years.'

The phonology of these depositions has given rise to little or no discussion, since it is, by and large, fairly clear (including the Campanian merger
of PRom. /b/ and /ụ/ in a single phoneme, here mostly written with b,
as in bobe 'to you' (< /ụoˑbis/). Despite certain efforts to interpret the
language of the depositions as reflecting an already wide-spread Italian
koiné,[53] most commentators agree that it is a faithful reflection of local
tenth-century Campanian speech.[54]

6.23. THE MOZARABIC ḫaraǧāt [sg. ḫarǧa]. These are bilingual refrains, in
Ibero-Romance vernacular, of bilingual poems (muwaššāt, sg. muwaššaḫ),
with verses in Hebrew or Arabic, composed and written down in those parts
of the Iberian peninsula which were under Moslem rule; the earliest date
from the eleventh century, but probably represent a much older tradition.[55]
These poems were love-songs, with the refrain always put in the mouth of a
woman who often apostrophises her lover, whom she calls by the Arabic
term habībī 'my friend'. Two examples, of these refrains, one from a Hebrew
poem, the other from an Arabic poem,[56] follow:

Gar, si yes devina,
e devinas bi-l-haqq
garme cuand me vernad
mio ḥabībī Išaq.

'Tell, if you are a sooth-sayer,
and foretell, in truth,
tell me when will come to me
my friend Isaac.'

Amān, yā habībi!
al-waḥs no me farás.
Bon, beža mi bokella;
lo sé que te no irás.

'Please, o my friend,
abandoned you will not make me.
Handsome man, kiss my little mouth;
I know that you will not go away.'

Since the Hebrew and Arabic scripts, in which these poems are written, do not in general indicate the vowels /e/ and /o/, the reconstruction of these is somewhat tentative. There has been extensive discussion of the phonological characteristics of these ḫaraǧāt[57]; it is fairly sure that their language is quite archaic, especially in preserving final /-t/ and, in the earliest ones, unlenited intervocalic stops.

6.3. The Rise of Literary and National Standards

Literary and national standards began in the eleventh century, with Old South French, and have lasted down to the present time, with three major periods during which new standard languages were developing: the later Middle Ages, the period of the Reformation, and the nineteenth and twentieth centuries. We shall describe very briefly the rise of the various Romance standard languages during these three periods,[58] and then shall discuss (§6.4) the various factors involved in their development.

6.31. THE MIDDLE AGES. The period from roughly 1000 to 1400 saw the establishment of the major literary and national languages of western Europe, most of which have retained their dominant position down to the present.[59]

6.311. OLD SOUTH FRENCH (OLD PROVENÇAL) was the first to achieve standing as a literary language, though it never became the national language of any major political entity.[60] The first literary work in Old Provençal to have been preserved is the *Boeci* (probably composed soon after the year 1000)—a fragment, 257 lines long, of a highly fictionalised narrative poem recounting the life and death of the late Roman philosopher Boëthius (ca. 480–524). Perhaps slightly later (ca. 1030–1070) was the *Chanson de Sainte Foi d'Agen*, a 593-line hagiographical poem on the martyrdom of a certain Saint Fides at the end of the third century A.D. From the end of the eleventh and the beginning of the twelfth century dates the lyric poetry of the first troubadour, Guilhem de Peitieu (William of Poitou, 1071–1127). The twelfth century and the first part of the thirteenth was the *Blütezeit* of the Provençal troubadour lyric. A troubadour normally put together both words and music for his own songs, whether he sang them himself or had a professional minstrel sing them for him. Courtly love was the main theme of the most outstanding of these poets, such as Jaufré Rudel,[62] Bernart de Ventadorn, Arnaut Daniel, Peire Vidal, Folquet de Marselha, and Giraut de Borneil. Other subjects than courtly love were also treated in verse, especially in political poems (*sirventés*) by such troubadours as Bertran de Born.[63] Both troubadours and minstrels circulated widely from one nobleman's castle to another, and sang their songs in a koiné based, not specifically on any one dialect of South French, but on a mixture of dialects which allowed of considerable fluctuation (*e.g.* /fáč/ *fa*[*c*]*h*, /fáič/ *faich* or /fáit/ *fait* for 'done').

The so-called "Albigensian Crusade" (1209–1229)—in actuality a war using the extirpation of heresy as a pretext, conducted by the North French kings against the nobility of southern France—ruined the latter and destroyed the economic and social basis for the aristocratic culture which had been the support of the troubadours. The 'last of the troubadours' was Giraut Riquier (fl. ca. 1252–1294). With their local livelihood gone, many troubadours emigrated to neighbouring lands, and Provençal poetry continued to be written and sung for a time in Aragon, Galicia, and Italy. It served as a model for the thirteenth-century *trouvère* poetry of northern France[64] and for *Minnesang* in Germany.[65] Some native speakers of other Romance languages poetised in Provençal, *e.g.* Sordello of Goito (Mantua) and Lafranc Cigala in Italy, Berenguer de Palol in Catalonia, and Raimón de Miraval in Spain.[66] Nonlyric poetry continued to be produced in Provençal in the thirteenth century, including the Arthurian romance *Jaufré* and the versified novel *Flamenca*. Among nonfiction, the treatise on falconry by Daude de Pradas, *Dels auzels cassadors* 'Concerning hunting-birds' is outstanding. The use of the language came to be more and more artificial, as exemplified in the founding (1324) of the Academy of the *Jocs Floraus* ('Floral Games', often referred to by its French name, *Jeux Floraux*) in Toulouse. Such grammatical treatises as the *Leys d'Amors* 'Rules of Love' and the *Donatz proensals* (cf. §11.1) also date from this period. From the fourteenth century onward, Provençal is normally considered to have undergone a marked decline in the quality of its literature and in its social standing, until finally, in 1513, French was admitted to the *Jeux Floraux* and in 1680 Provençal itself was banned from them. In the Renaissance and the baroque period, Provençal was little more than a congeries of local dialects, until its revival in the nineteenth century (cf. §6.331).

6.312. NORTH FRENCH, most often referred to simply as "French," had its chief source in Francien, the dialect of the Île de France (the region around Paris). Beginning with the dynasty of Hugues Capet (king from 987 to 996) and his descendants, Paris came to be more and more the political and administrative center of, first northern France, and then the entire country. The earliest literary productions of importance were epics, the most outstanding of which is the *Chanson de Roland* 'Song of Roland' (ca. 1100).[67] This and a number of other epics deal with the heroic deeds of the early French kings, Charlemagne and his successors, in the ninth century, in the *matière de France* ('French cycle'). From Keltic sources came the *matière de Bretagne* ('Breton cycle'), which formed the subject-matter of numerous romances in the twelfth century and later, beginning with the poems of the first major identifiable French author, Chrétien de Troyes (mid-twelfth century), such as *Cligès, Erec, Yvain, Lancelot,* and *Perceval.* A third *matière* was that of Rome, *i.e.,* ancient history in general, retold in such cycles as that of Alexander. In lyric poetry, the *trouvères*[68] of the late twelfth and of the thirteenth century imitated the love-songs and other genres developed by the Provençal troubadours (§6.311). Later poems included the semicourtly, semibourgeois *Roman de la Rose* 'Romance of the Rose' (begun by Guillaume de Lorris ca. 1225–1230, and continued by Jean de Meung ca. 1270), and the satirical *Roman de Renart* 'Romance of Reynard the Fox', an animal allegory representing a thoroughly bourgeois view-point. Prose works in the fields of didactic treatises and history, and religious dramas ('miracle-plays') became frequent from the thirteenth century onwards. In all these works, Francien was the predominant dialect, but many works and authors show dialectal features as well. Thus, the Oxford manuscript of the *Roland* and also numerous other works show Anglo-Norman features, and one of the most attractive Old French works, the "chante-fable" *Aucassin et Nicolete,* is in Picard.

During the Old French period, the language used in literature was relatively stable, with a number of characteristics distinguishing it from the more conservative Old South French (Provençal). In phonology, extensive changes in the vowel-system came about as a result of raising and diphthongisation under stress in free syllables, and a number of special conditioned changes, most of which did not take place in the south. In the consonants, like-wise, marked changes in the phonemic shape of words were brought about by the palatalisation of /k/ and /g/ to /č/ and /ǧ/, respectively, before /a/, and by the fricativisation and eventual loss, under certain circumstances, of intervocalic /-b- -d- -g-/. Thus, PRom. /kadé^re/ 'to fall' > ONFr. /čaðé^ir/, later /čaé^ir/ *chaeir* and then /čəoir/ *cheoir* ∼ OSFr. /kadé^r/ *cader* (in some dialects, /kazé^r/ *cazer*); PRom. /kaballikáre/ 'to ride on a horse' > ONFr. /čəvalčiér/ *chevalchier,* later /čəvaučiér/ *chevauchier,* modern Fr. /šəvo^še^/ *chevaucher* ∼ OSFr. /kabalgár/ *cabalgar.* Both Old Provençal and Old North French preserved, in contrast to the other western Romance languages, a full two-case-system, with a distinction between nominative and oblique.

Even before the beginning of the Hundred Years' War (usually dated 1346–1451), further changes had begun to take place in North French, especially the conditioned loss of /s/ before consonant, later generalised to most word-final positions, and the resultant weakening and disappearance of the contrast between nominative and oblique, which depended largely on the distribution of final /-s/ in the different case-forms. The disorganisation and chaos prevailing during the Hundred Years' War accelerated the spread of these changes, so that standard French in the latter half of the fifteenth century was very different from what it had been two hundred years previously. During this time, the only major French author was François Villon, the "bohemian" scholar of the Parisian Left Bank and one of France's greatest lyric poets. With the return of order after the defeat and expulsion of the English in 1451, the French monarchy and its administration became even more centralised at Paris than before, with Parisian usage assuming an increasingly dominant position.

6.313. SPANISH. In the twelfth and thirteenth centuries, the dialects of Aragon, Asturias, León, Castile, and Galicia were about equal to each other in prestige for administrative and literary use.[69] For a time, as in ancient Greece,[70] certain dialects were thought to be more suited than others for particular literary genres, e.g. Galician for courtly love-poetry and Castilian for the epic. The most important mediaeval Spanish poem preserved for us is the anonymous epic *Cantar de myo Çid* (Song of My Lord the Cid'), usually dated ca. 1140. Other major mediaeval Spanish poems include the *Auto de los Reyes Magos* ('Play of the Magi'), from approximately the same period or a little later; the religious poems of Gonzalo de Berceo (first half of the thirteenth century); and the Libro de Alixandre (mid-thirteenth century). Under King Alfonso X "The Wise" of Castile (reigned 1252–84), Castilian replaced Latin as the language of public documents. Under his patronage—and, in some instances, his personal authorship—a number of legal codes, encyclopaedic works in prose, and religious poems were produced. In following centuries, both prose and poetry were extensively cultivated, the former by Don Juan Manuel (1282–ca. 1349) in his collection of tales *El Conde Lucanor* 'Count Lucanor', and the latter in the *Libro de buen amor* 'Book of True Love' of Juan Ruiz, arch-priest of Hita (ca. 1283–1350). Also worthy of mention are *El Laberinto de Fortuna* 'The Labyrinth of Fortune' (ca. 1444) of Juan de Mena, and the picaresque comedy *La Celestina* (late fifteenth century).

Concomitantly with the Reconquista, the Castilian dialect became the standard for the regions which came under Castilian rule, gradually overlaying the other regional koinés such as Asturian, Leonese, Aragonese, and the conservative Mozarabic spoken in the central area.[71] Originally based on the speech of Burgos, Castilian manifested such special characteristics as the diphthongisation of lax /e/ and /o/ in both free and checked stressed syllables (e.g. PRom. /pérdit/ 'he loses' > /piérde/ *pierde*; PRom. /pórta/ 'gate' > /puérta/ *puerta*); PRom. /-kt-/ > PIbRom. /-xt-/ > /-i̯t-/ >

/-č-/, and /f-/ > /h-/, as in PRom. /fáktu/ 'done' > OCast. /héčo/ *fecho*, modern /éčo/ *hecho*. In the course of its expansion, Castilian took over various elements from the dialects it replaced, such as /pléita/ *pleita* 'plaited strand of esparto-grass' from Mozarabic /pléxta/, or /plómo/ *plomo* 'lead' from Aragonese or Catalan (in which /pl-/ remains as such, in contrast to the Castilian development of /pl-/ > /ḷ-/ *ll-*). In the mid-thirteenth-century Fuero Juzgo, there are such Leonesisms as *voaltas* for Cast. *vueltas* 'turns, times' and *encuantra* for Cast. *encuentra* 'meets'. Spanish forms with initial /f-/ not followed by /r/ or /u/ in hiatus must be either Latinisms (*e.g.* /férbido/ *fervido* 'fervid') or borrowings from other Ibero-Romance varieties which did not change /f-/ to /h-/, *e.g.* /fúrnia/ *furnia* 'under-ground store-room; drain' from Leonese.

At the very end of the mediaeval period, following on the completion of the Reconquista by the taking of the Kingdom of Granada in 1492, the Spanish Jews were expelled by Ferdinand and Isabella, and took refuge in northern Europe (Holland, Hamburg) and in eastern Europe (Turkey). Their Judaeo-Spanish (§2.112.2.*a*.vii), thus sharply separated from the rest of Ibero-Romance, has retained certain markedly archaic features down to the present day, and is therefore a valuable aid for the reconstruction of the Spanish spoken just before the expulsion of the Jews.[72] It preserves, for instance, the contrast between /s/ and /z/, as in /kasár/ 'to hunt' (< OSp. /kaçár/ *caçar*) ∼ /kazár/ 'to marry' (< OSp. /kazár/ *casar*). Old Spanish /h/ and the palatal sibilants are preserved, as in /hížo/ *fijo* 'son', /lešos/ *lexos* 'far'. Since the separation, Judaeo-Spanish, especially that used in the Balkans, has developed along its own lines, with many borrowings from Hebrew, Greek, and Turkish.

6.314. GALICIAN-PORTUGUESE. As already mentioned (§6.313), the earliest bellettristic use of Galician was for courtly lyric poetry, which reached its peak in the early fourteenth century.[73] Several collections of poetry and music embody the extant corpus of these lyrics: three *Cancioneiros* ('Song-Books')—those known by the names of Ajuda, the Vaticano, and the Colocci-Brancuti—and the *Cantigas de Santa Maria* ('Songs of St. Mary') collected by Alfonso the Wise. Most of the remaining mediaeval literary production in Portuguese was in prose, dealing with history, morals, and practical matters; in fiction, the Keltic legends of the Breton cycle (§6.312) were especially popular.

As with Castilian, the extension of Galician followed the Reconquest in its southward path. After the political power and the language had become established farther south, Portuguese split from Galician in the fourteenth century. With the growing subordination of Galicia to Spain, the Portuguese standard lost its connection with the north, and came to be based, rather, first on the usage of Coimbra and then on that of Lisbon. The major innovations of Galician and Portuguese are the loss of inter-vocalic /-n-/ and /-l-/, and the development—in many instances resulting from loss of an intervocalic /-n-/—of a system of nasalised vowels, as in /mãu/ *mão* 'hand' (< PRom. /mánu/), /lã/ *lã* 'wool' (< PRom. /lána/), and /máu/ *mau* 'bad', fem. /má/ *má* (< PRom. /málu/, /mála/).

6.315. ITALIAN. The earliest documents in Italian with any bellettristic pretenses date from the first part of the thirteenth century, when poets at the court of the Hohenstaufen emperor Frederick II at Palermo, from 1125 to 1250, produced imitations of Provençal lyric, in a kind of "siciliano illustre."[74] Early thirteenth-century lyric poets in northern Italy began by composing their songs in Provençal, as did Sordello and Lanfranc Cigala (§6.311); later, however, mid-century poets wrote in their own local vernacular, *e.g.* Guittone d'Arezzo (ca. 1230–1294) in Aretine, Guido Guinizelli (ca. 1230–1276) in Bolognese, and Guido Cavalcanti (ca. 1255–1300) in Florentine. The last-mentioned and others associated with him—of whom the greatest was Dante Alighieri (1265–1321)—developed the lyric style and poetic content of the Provençal troubadours into the ex-pression of lofty spirituality known as the *Dolce Stil Nuovo* ('Sweet New Style'), culminating in Dante's *Vita Nuova* ('New Life,' ca. 1295) and *Divina Commedia* ('Divine Comedy,' ca. 1298–1320). During the same period, Tuscany became the cloth-weaving, commercial, and banking center of Italy. Its traders and bankers travelled throughout the peninsula and western Europe. The gold florin, first minted in Florence in 1252, became the standard coin of all Europe.

After Dante, two other major authors served as models for literary usage: Francesco Petrarca (1304–1374) in lyric poetry, and Giovanni Boccaccio (1313–1375) in prose narrative, especially in his *Decameron* (ca. 1350–1360). A number of other fourteenth-century writers, most but not all of them from Florence or Tuscany, established a corpus of vernacular literature which set the standard for the use of Tuscan, at least in poetry. In prose,[75] however, regional koinés survived much longer for both bellettristic writing (*e.g.* the *Novellino*, a collection of short stories made by Masuccio of Salerno and published in 1476) and practical documents (*e.g.* the reports of the Venetian republic's ambassadors; merchants' records; histories; etc.[76]).

Tuscan was distinguished from the other Romance standards, from the out-set, by its remarkable conservatism, especially in its phonological sys-tem, virtually unchanged from that of Proto-Italo-Western Romance. Tuscany had remained a back-water, isolated during the late Roman Em-pire and the early Middle Ages.[77] The only major change in the phonology was the diphthongisation of stressed lax /é/ and /ó/ of PitWRom., in free nonfinal syllables, to /ié/ and /uó/ respectively, as in /péde/ 'foot' > /piéde/, /sónat/ 'he sounds' > /suóna/. In morphology and syntax, also, Tuscan remained quite close to Proto-Italo-Western Romance.

6.316. Catalan-Valencian. In Catalonia, as in northern Italy, the earliest surviving bellettristic endeavor was in the courtly lyric, which—clearly because of the geographical and cultural closeness of southern France—was in Provençal through the middle of the thirteenth century.[78] The first major Catalan authors to use the local language were Ramon Llull (1235–1315) in his religious and didactic poetry, and several outstanding chroniclers, including Jayme I of Catalonia (1213–1276), Ramon Montaner (1265–1336), Bernat Desclot, and King Peter III (1319–1387). The fifteenth-century literature of this region was primarily in Valencian, with the poems of Jordi de Sant Jordi (ca. 1395–1440) and Ausiás March /márk/ (ca. 1414–1460), and with the chivalric romance *Tirant lo Blanc* (1490, but composed 1460 ff.) by Joan Martorell. From 1474 onwards, however, after the union of Aragon (and hence of Catalonia) with Castile, the use of Catalan in prestige-literature fell into a decline until the nineteenth century.

Specific linguistic features of Catalan include the palatalising of initial /l-/ to /ḷ-/, as in PItWRom. /lé^ngua/ 'tongue' > Cat. /ḷéngua/ *llengua*; the development of intervocalic /-d-/, when it became final, to /u/, as in PItWRom. /péde/ 'foot' > Cat. /péu/ peu; and the exchange of laxness and tenseness in PItWRom. /é/ > Cat. /é^/, whereas PItWRom. /é^/ > Cat. /é/.

6.32. The Reformation was a major factor in bringing about the first literary use of two Romance varieties which had, throughout the Middle Ages, been simply congeries of dialects used by normal people in every-day speech: Rhaeto-Romance, especially Romansh, and Roumanian.

6.321. Romansh. Apart from a few scattered attestations ascribed to the tenth or eleventh centuries,[79] the earliest major material in Romansh was called forth by the religious situation prevailing in the sixteenth century.[80] Upper Engadinese was used by the Protestant poet Gian Travers (1483–1563) in his composition in 704 verses *Chansun de la guerra dalg Chiasté d'Müsch* and by Jachiam Bifrun (1506–?) in his translation of the New Testament (1560), as well as by various Catholic propagandists. Lower Engadinese was used in the translation of the Psalms (1562) of Durich Chiampel (ca. 1520–1583); Surselvan in the seventeenth century by both Catholic and Protestant apologists. No single variety of Romansh emerged, at this time or later, as an over-all standard for the entire region.

6.322. ROUMANIAN, like-wise, received its first extensive literary cultivation in connection with the Reformation, in Psalm-translations ascribed by some of the Hussite movement of the fifteenth century, but by others to Lutheranism in the sixteenth.[81] A Protestant-oriented catechism printed at Braşov by Deacon Coresi in 1559 and a Calvinist song-book printed in Transylvania ca. 1570 were among other early manifestations. Most of these works were written in Cyrillic characters, of Slavic origin (for which reason it was long thought that Roumanian was a Slavic, not a Romance language); only the Calvinists used Roman letters. A relatively thin trickle of literary production continued through the seventeenth century, but it was not until the eighteenth, with the work of the Latin-oriented "Transylvanian School" (*Şcoala Ardeleană*)[82] that Roumanian began to be used more extensively. Due to the political and cultural domination of the Muntenian-Oltenian region, with the country's capital at Bucharest (*Bucureşti*), the dialect of this area has served as the base of the standard language.

6.33. AUTONOMISTIC IMPULSES. During the seventeenth and eighteenth centuries, western European and cultural life was in general dominated by strong centralising and (in many regions) authoritarian currents. These were conducive to establishing and maintaining the ideal of a single standard for any given political unit, in language as well as in nonlinguistic matters.[83] In this situation, certain varieties of Romance which, during the Middle Ages, had enjoyed the status of literary standards—notably Provençal and Catalan—sank in standing to the level of local patois. In the nineteenth century, however, impulses towards local autonomy (in culture, and, on occasion, also in politics), which had never wholly disappeared but which had continued more or less "underground," came to the surface again. In Catalonia (including the Valencian region) the same variety of language was used with no substantial break in tradition; but in Provence, a new tradition was started, and therefore merits separate consideration.

6.331. MODERN PROVENÇAL began to be cultivated extensively again in the first half of the nineteenth century, in the work of Jacques Jasmin (1796–1864) of Agen, Joseph Roumanille (1818–1891) of Saint-Rémy, Victor Gelu (1806–1885) of Marseilles, and Théodore Aubanel (1829–1886) from Avignon.[84] The greatest impetus to the renewed popularity of Provençal came, however, from the poetry of Frédéri Mistral (1830–1914), as well as his intensive propaganda on behalf of the language and the regional culture of Provence, carried on in his personal activity as orator and in his philological work (Mistral 1878). His enormously popular idyllic poem *Mirèio* ("Mireille," 1859) was widely read, in the original or in translation, throughout the French-speaking world.[85] Under his leadership, the group known as the Félibriges (founded 1854) cultivated both poetry and prose in modern Provençal. Their standard language was based, not on the usage of the mediaeval troubadours, but on that of contemporary speech in the lower Rhône valley, especially the region of Avignon, Arles, and the river-delta. Orthographically, their usage was close to that of standard French, especially in the representation of /u/ by *ou*, of /ɲ/ by *gn* and /ʎ/ by *il(l)*, and of the final low back vowel [ɑ>] by *-o*. This standard, which has come to be known as *mistralien* 'of Mistral', was at first adhered to by almost all writers of modern Provençal, and is still followed by twentieth-century authors from the Rhône valley region such as Henrieto Dibon ("Farfantelo").[86]

In the twentieth century, and especially after the Second World War, a number of speakers of Provençal from the Languedoc and more westerly regions have opposed to "mistralien" a somewhat different standard, which they often prefer to call "Occitan."[87] In addition to a few grammatical and syntactic peculiarities, Occitan differs from Mistralien in orthography, through a conscious effort on the part of its practitioners to reattach their usage to that of Old Provençal. Thus, they use *nh* and *lh* for /ɲ/ and /ʎ/ respectively, /u/ is spelled *u*, and final [ɑ>] is represented with *-a*. This of course renders Occitan superficially much more similar to Old Provençal (and also to Catalan) than to Mistralien; but the structural differences are slight.

With the spread of standard French throughout the nation, Provençal as a first language has become limited to outlying country areas, and mono-lingual native speakers of dialect are by now a rarity. Only in 1951 was the Deixonne law passed in France, allowing bilingual instruction using regional languages (*e.g.* Breton, Basque, Provençal) in elementary schools; to date, it has apparently had little effect on the use of Provençal in the class-room, because of the far greater prestige of standard French. Unlike speakers of Catalan, the proponents of literary Provençal have repeatedly, ever since Mistral himself, stressed their political faithfulness to the central government, and their aim to establish only a degree of cultural autonomy. The use of both varieties of modern Provençal is becoming more and more restricted to literary groups which cultivate it more or less artificially, often using French in their every-day contacts, with Provençal spoken only at official literary gatherings.

6.332. FRIULIAN has been used more or less sporadically for literary purposes since the Middle Ages, but no concerted effort to establish it as a standard was made before the nineteenth century. Since that time, there has been a modest tradition of often attractive but relatively minor bellet-

tristic activity.[88] As in the case of Modern Provençal, there has been no
move to set up Friulian as the language of an autonomous political entity,
even though in post-Second-World-War Italy certain regions are officially
bilingual (e.g. the Val d'Aosta with Italian and French, and the South
Tyrol with Italian and German).[89]

Ladin and Sardinian have never developed officially or unofficially
recognized unified standards.[90]

6.333. CREOLES AS STANDARDS.[91] Although the political independence of
Haiti was achieved in 1804, the only standard language recognised there
was French, until Haitian Creole was admitted by law to nominal parity in
1962. Some bellettristic efforts have been made in Creole, including Georges
Sylvain's early efforts at paraphrasing classical-type fables, and Félix
Morisseau-Leroy's adaptation of the *Antigone* story to the Haitian situation.
Similarly, Papiamentu has been accorded recognition in Curaçao, Bonaire,
and Aruba in the Dutch West Indies, and some literary endeavour has taken
place. Other Romance-based creoles have as yet not received official recognition, and have been used only desultorily for literary or other prestigious
purposes.

6.4. Factors in the Rise and Spread of Standards

Especially in histories of literature, it is customary to consider only the
prestige of individual authors as "creating" or spreading the use of a
standard language. That no single writer "creates" a language, is by now
axiomatic in linguistics[92]; it must also be recognised that, in general, the rise
and spread of a standard variety of usage is due to more than one factor.
The chief factors creating language-unity are political, economic, and social.

6.41. POLITICAL factors are probably the most important. In comparing
the development of the various Romance and other European standard
languages, we see that in most cases it was correlated with the rise of a
central political power. In the Middle Ages, regional dukedoms, principalities, and kingdoms developed their local varieties of speech into koinés, as
in the instances of Galician, Leonese, Asturian, Castilian, Aragonese, and
Catalan across the north of the Iberian peninsula; those of Francien, Norman, Picard, Walloon, Champenois, and Burgundian in France; or those of
Northumbrian, Mercian, and Kentish in the Old English period. Later,
with the unification of countries under a single dominating government—
typically, a monarchy in the sixteenth and seventeenth centuries—the

language of the capital city and its region became dominant: that of Paris in France, of Madrid in Spain, of Lisbon in Portugal, or of London in England. In countries where no political unification took place, the spread of an officially recognised and universally adopted standard was correspondingly delayed, as was the case in Italy and Roumania.

6.42. Economic factors are also important. They normally accompany the political aspects of government by making the use of a dominant standard advantageous, as in the instances just cited. In other situations, they can on occasion spread the prestige of a language through the advantage of economic relationships, *e.g.* with Tuscany in fourteenth- and fifteenth-century Italy. The coinage of the gold florin in 1252 (§6.315) was certainly as important a factor in the spread of Tuscan to the rest of Italy as was the literary achievement of any one author.

6.43. Literary factors are neither all-important nor devoid of importance. Even though unifying political forces may be absent, literary works can nevertheless assist the establishment of a standard by their prestige.[93] However, this prestige is normally effective only with that segment of the population interested in such works, and only in the range of usage for which a literary monument can set the style. It is highly significant that, as already pointed out (§6.112), the adoption of Tuscan as a literary language in poetry antedated its extension to prose by two centuries or more. In other words, a kind of di- or even triglossia could prevail, as was the case in fourteenth- and fifteenth-century Italy[94]; Latin was used for theological, philosophical, and scientific works; Tuscan was the language of elegant poetical expression; and the regional koiné (Lombard, Venetian, etc.) served for more matter-of-fact written communication.

NOTES TO CHAPTER 6

1. Thus virtually all histories of Latin literature, ranging from Bergeron 1840, through such works as Fowler 1905, to recent treatments like Grant 1954 or Cazzaniga 1962.

2. Thus, for Italian, Donadoni (1923) 1969:5, to the effect that in the thirteenth century "Italy must have had a language that was common to the whole nation." Cf. also Bàrtoli 1944/45.

3. For the general theory of literature in relation to language, cf. Hockett 1958, chapter 63. On the importance of oral transmission (and hence inevitable variation in texts in the course of time), cf. Lord 1960.

4. Such as that mentioned by Horace (*Satires* 1.5.15–17), in which a boatman *absentem* [. . .] *cantat amīcam* 'sings of his absent lady-friend'.

5. Such as those sung by Caesar's soldiers, as reported by Suetonius (*Dīvus Iūlius* 49, 51) and by many others (cf. Bardon 1952:19).

6. Even if Niebuhr's theory that complete Latin epic poems once existed is no longer held, nevertheless there is plenty of evidence that songs or lays were sung to celebrate the deeds of ancient heroes (cf., for example, Cicero's *Tusculanae Disputationes* 4.2; *Brutus* 19.75).

7. Cf. Löfstedt 1959:39–58 ("Local Variation in Latin"); Mihăescu 1960 (and Messing 1963); Tovar 1964; Herman 1965; Väänänen 1968; Gaeng 1968.

8. Cf. Hall 1964:19–21.

9. As recognised by Muller (1929), but with exaggerated emphasis on the unity of popular speech, and with excessive faith in the dependability of written documents.

10. Most recently and cogently by Menéndez Pidal (1959, 1960).

11. Cf. my remarks in Hall 1965/66a:232.

12. Cf. Elcock's remarks (1960:375–376) on the circumstances attendant on the survival of the *Chanson de Sainte Foi d'Agen*.

13. It would be interesting and valuable to have a work on lost Romance literature parallel to Bardon 1952 for Latin literature, or R. M. Wilson 1952 for Old English.

14. Cf. Ewert 1938:8–9.

15. For the importance of economic factors in the spread of Tuscan, cf. Hall 1942a. The spread of Tuscan in poetry before prose: Kristeller 1946.

16. *E.g.* in the speech of Sam Weller and his father in Dickens' *Pickwick Papers*.

17. On the terms *romana lingua, romanice, Romania*, cf. Paris 1872; Crescini 1910; Muller 1923; Zeiller 1929; Ruggieri 1967.

18. Ruggieri (1967) regards ONFr. and OSFr. *romanz* as a 'cultismo relativamente tardo'; but no matter what its origin, it referred at the outset to the vernacular as opposed to the "grammatica."

19. This is why the use of the terms "spoken" and "written" Latin seems inadvisable. "Learnèd" or "grammatical" versus "vernacular" would be a better contrast.

20. Cf. Lehmann 1929.

21. Sabatini (1968:328–335) suggests that some of the "vernacularisms" we find in early mediaeval Latin texts (*e.g. tonica* 'cloak', *panni* 'clothes', *bacce* 'cows', *capre* 'goats', and the use of a single case-form in a Lucanian document from 823) may have been intentional, to represent every-day speech either as heard from ordinary people or in order to make it more comprehensible to them. Of course, there may have been humorous compositions or casual annotations which have not survived.

22. Cf. P. Lehmann 1929.

23. *E.g.* Martin 1966 and many others like her.

24. Cf. Robins 1967:56–72.

25. In the Merovingian version (published by Eckhardt 1955–61, vol. 1).

26. In clearly Latin expressions in the 12th-century *Formula di confessione umbra* (published by Flechia 1880/83).

27. Cf. Klein 1965.

28. Beginning in the seventh and eighth centuries; cf. Löfstedt 1959:50–53.

29. *E.g.* Port. /pēsár/, Sp. and Cat. /pensár/, all spelled *pensar*; Fr. /pãse^r/ and Romansh /pensér/ *penser*; Friulian /pensá/ *pensa*; Ital. /pensáre/ *pensare*. Cf. Meyer-Lübke (1911) 1936³: §6391.3.

30. Port. /pezár/, Sp. /pesár/, Cat. and Prov. /pezár/, all *pesar*; Fr. /pəze^r/ *peser*; Romansh /peér/ *peer*; It. /pesáre/ *pesare*; Sardinian /pezáre/ 'to weigh'; Roum. /pəsá/ *păsa* 'to cause worry (to)'. cf. Meyer-Lübke (1911) 1936³. §6391.1, 2.

31. The introduction of Latin words, expressions, and sentences into the Old North French of the tenth-century *Jonas* fragment had its exact parallel in a sermon I heard at Port-au-Prince in 1949, delivered in Creole by a young Haitian preacher who interlarded

his Creole with numerous items in a standard French which was strongly influenced by Creole in its pronunciation and grammatical features.

32. I use the term *concept* to refer to a linguistic form and its meaning with no mentalistic or philosophico-psychologistic implications.

33. For the influence of the mediaeval church on the development of Romance in the West, cf. Maurer 1951. For mediaeval Latin pronunciation, cf. Bonioli 1962.

34. To this type of influence are to be ascribed the nonpopular characteristics of such words as Old French /dǽus/ *Deus* 'God' (probably ['dɛ:-us], with long open [ɛ] as it would have been pronounced from the pulpit),/ángələ/ *angele* 'angel',or /diáulə/ *diaule* 'devil'; or such semipopular, semilearnèd forms as Sp. /kabíldo/ *cabildo* 'chapter-house' < Lat. *capitulu(m)*, with /i/ instead of /éʌ/ < Lat. short /i/.

35. Cf. Wahlgren 1936 for the semantic development of *grammaticus* to 'fussy, pedantic; arrogant; no-good'.

36. Cf. Bertoldi 1926, especially 151–154 ("Il contatto reciproco tra materiale dotto e materiale popolare").

37. Cf. Bertoldi 1929.

38. Where, according to some, Romance speech survived into the twelfth century.

39. Cf. Löfstedt 1959, for detailed discussion and exemplification.

40. A complete edition and discussion of previous work in Klein and Labhardt 1968.

41. There is no modern edition of the Kassel glosses similar to Klein and Labhardt 1968, for those of Reichenau; but cf. Marchot 1895; Pirson 1902; Titz 1923; and Roncaglia 1959.

42. Cf. Bischoff and Beck 1963; Sabatini 1963/64.

43. For the texts of these two sets of glosses, cf. Menéndez Pidal 1926.

44. For discussion of the problems of reading out loud that were involved in these transcriptions, cf. Wunderli 1966.

45. Cf. Hall 1953, 1965/66b and bibliographies there given; also Nelson 1966; Hilty 1966.

46. The sign used for "and" in the manuscript is like our numeral 7; for typographical convenience, we are substituting an ampersand (&) for it.

47. Reproduced in d'Aronco 1960:203–204. The anonymous translator (possibly one Gian Giuseppe Liruti) clearly misunderstood the passage *in o quid il mi altresi fazet,* and gave, as an equivalent, a clause meaning 'just as some-one else would do for me'.

48. Only a few syntactic isoglosses have been included, since there is strong suspicion (cf. Ewert 1935 and Elcock 1960:336–339) that the syntax of the oaths may have been strongly influenced by their having been translated from a Latin *Vorlage.*

49. Hockett's term (1958:323–326) for "any idiolect plus all other idiolects which are linked (by a chain of mutual intelligibility) both to the first and consequently to each other."

As is often the case, Ibero-Romance and Roumanian, due to their marginal position, have certain characteristics in common; cf. Iordan 1964.

50. Porter 1960.

51. Note the marked difference between the ONFr. (as reconstructed here) and the graphic shape of the text of the Oaths, due especially to the raising and diphthongisation of all stressed vowels except /i u/ in free syllable, and the palatalisation of /k/ before /a/. To try to force the oaths into the phonology of Francien involves considerable distortion, as I have suggested elsewhere (Hall 1953, 1965/66).

52. Reproduced in Inguanez 1942.

53. *E.g.* by Bàrtoli 1944/45.

54. Cf. the general discussions of Fiorelli 1960 and Sabatini 1962.

55. Cf. Stern 1953 and Heger 1960 (with extensive bibliography ix–xvii).

56. Reproduced from Tagliavini (1947) 1969[5]: §81.

57. Cf. the discussion in Baldinger 1958.

58. For detailed descriptions, reference should be made to the various histories of the individual languages, indicated in the foot-notes to Chapter 2.

59. For the comparative history of the Romance literatures, cf. Gröber (ed.) 1886–88, vol. 2; Morf (ed.) 1909; Iorga 1919; Jauss ahd Köhler (eds.) 1968– .

60. For Old Provençal literature, cf. Anglade 1921b; Jeanroy 1934, 1945; Viscardi 1952; Camproux 1953. On courtly literature in general, see Bezzola 1958–60.

61. Eng. and Fr. *troubadour* is an adaptation of Prov. /trubadúr/ < OProv. /trobadóˆr/ *trobador* 'poet', a derivative of /trobár/ *trobar* 'to find, invent (poetry, music)'. For semantic parallels, cf. Gk. /poie:té:s/ ποιητής 'poet, maker' (: /poiéin/ ποιέιν 'to make'), and mediaeval Scottish *makere* 'poet'.

62. Due to his extensive use of the word /lóˆŋ/ *lonh* 'distant, far' and its derivatives in a number of his poems, Rudel became the subject of a legend concerning his love for a lady in a distant country, treated by many later authors, especially Edmond Rostand in his romantic play *La Princesse Lointaine* ('The Distant Princess', 1895).

63. Bertran de Born was considered, because of the emphasis on war and conflict in his poems, to have had far more effect on political developments than he actually had. A legend arose that Bertran had set Henry I of England and his sons against each other. Dante therefore put Bertran de Born in Hell (*Inferno* 28.128–142) and had him say *Io feci il padre e'l figlio in sé ribelli* 'I made the father and the son hostile to each other'.

64. Cf. Viscardi 1952.

65. As recognised by all historians of mediaeval German literature, from Scherer (1884) onwards.

66. Cf. Milá y Fontanals 1861; López Estrada 1952:134–136.

67. For the history of French literature in general, cf. Lanson 1894; Nitze and Dargan 1922; Bédier and Hazard 1923–24; Brereton 1954; Cazamian 1955; and many other school-texts. For mediaeval French literature, see Holmes 1938; Viscardi 1952; Zumthor 1954.

68. ONFr. /truverə/ *trouvére* was an adaptation of OSFr. /trobadóˆr/, standing in the same relation to ONFr. /truver/ *trouver* 'to find' as did the OSFr. term to /trobár/ (cf. note 60).

69. For Spanish literary history in general, cf. Northup 1925; Valbuena Prat 1937; Díez-Echarri and Roca Franquesa 1960; Alborg 1966– ; and many other texts. For mediaeval Spanish literature: Millares Carlo 1950; López Estrada 1952; Deyermond 1971.

70. For the literary use of dialects in ancient Greece, cf. Buck 1955, especially 14–16.

71. Cf. the imaginative discussion by Malkiel 1964.

72. For Judaeo-Spanish in its relation to mediaeval and pre-Renaissance Spanish, cf. Wagner 1907, 1930; Crews 1935:7–45; Marcus 1962. On Judaeo-Spanish literature: Molho 1960.

73. For Portuguese literary history, cf. Bell 1922 (second edition 1970, with a sub-chapter on modern Galician literature 347–357); Saraiva and Lopes 1954; and other texts. Mediaeval Portuguese literature: Rodrigues Lapa 1952.

74. There has been extensive discussion of the exact linguistic relationships of the language of the "Scuola Siciliana" (*e.g.* Cesareo 1924:175–316; Bonfante 1969). Most scholars agree that it was based essentially on a generalised Sicilian koiné, with heavy influence from Latin in phonology and from Provençal in lexicon (especially terms dealing

with courtly love; cf. Baer 1939) and in some aspects of morphology. For Italian literary history, cf. V. Rossi 1899; Hauvette 1906; Hall 1951; Wilkins 1954; Whitfield 1960.

75. Cf. Kristeller 1946.

76. Cf. Luzzatto 1958:248–249.

77. Cf. Devoto 1951b.

78. For Catalan literary history, cf. Ruiz i Calonia 1954. On mediaeval Catalan literature: Denk 1893; de Riquer 1964. On the nineteenth-century revival: Amade 1924.

79. *E.g.* a sentence from the ninth or tenth century *Diderros ne habe diege muscha* 'Desiderius does not have ten flies' (published by Bischoff and Müller 1959); a sermon with Romansh characteristics preserved at Einsiedeln, dating from ca. 1100; and other items. Cf. Tagliavini 1947 (1969[5]): §83.

80. For Romansh literature, cf. Gartner 1910.

81. Cf. the discussion of Tagliavini 1947 (1969[5]): §87, and references there given. Roumanian literature: Munteanu 1943; Lupi 1955; Schroeder 1967.

82. For the "Transylvanian School" and its theories concerning the relation of Roumanian to the Romance languages and Latin, cf. Macrea 1969.

83. As expressed in the well-known seventeenth-century French slogan *Un roi, une loi, une foi* 'one king, one law, one faith', in what I have termed elsewhere the "Authoritarian Reaction" (Hall 1951, chapter 15.1).

84. For modern Provençal literature, cf. Ripert 1917; Camproux 1953. The beginnings of revival in the early seventeenth century: Lafont 1970. The attitudes of scholars and public towards regional speech: Roche 1954:117–149 (chapter V, "The Question of Dialects").

85. It achieved such immediate popularity as to form the subject of Gounod's opera *Mireille* (1864).

86. Cf. Bec 1963:102–110.

87. Cf. Bec 1963:110–119; Price 1964.

88. Cf. d'Aronco 1960; Hall 1962/63.

89. Cf. Bàrtoli 1927; Tagliavini 1947 (1969[5]): 394–395.

90. Significantly, the two major discussions of Sardinian literature (Siotto-Pintor 1843–44; Alziator 1954) have titles which do not imply the existence of a unified literary language. Cf. also Scano 1901.

91. Cf. Hall, forthcoming-b.

92. Cf. Hockett 1958:563–564; Hall 1964:406.

93. Cf. the remarks of Voorhoeve (1967:105): "I think that only the poets can really convince the general public that these languages [*i.e.* pidgins and creoles] are worth sincere admiration"—an observation which is probably valid for any other variety of nonprestigious speech as well.

94. Cf. Devoto 1953, especially 19–54, 101–114.

CHAPTER 7

Humanistic Influences and Cultural Interchanges

7.1. Early Latin Influence on Romance

The ever-increasing differentiation between the nascent Romance languages and a relatively static Latin by no means implied a sharp separation between the two. As shown by the dotted lines in the diagram in Table VIII (Chapter 4), influences were continually exerted in both directions. The men who made the earliest transcriptions of Romance vernaculars (§§6.122) virtually all knew Latin and had presumably acquired their first literacy in that language. It would come naturally to them, therefore, to introduce Latin features, particularly orthographical and lexical, into their writing of the vernacular whenever a problem of expression arose.[1]

7.11. ORTHOGRAPHY. The regional learnèd language—Old Church Slavonic in the case of Roumanian, Latin elsewhere—afforded the chief orthographical model for writing local speech. The exact extent of Latin influence on the earliest surviving attestations of Romance has long been a matter of debate. Were the Oaths of Strassburg, for instance, written in a heavily Latinised spelling, as some would maintain, or with little or no orthographical Latinism, as others consider?[2] The same type of problem arises in connection with the Glosses of San Millán and of Silos, especially the nonlenition of intervocalic consonants indicated by such graphs as *kematu* 'burned', *sapiendo* 'knowing', *aplekat* 'arrives'. Earlier commentators[3] considered the intervocalic *-p- -t- -k-* of these and similar writings as mere Latinisms, standing for /b d g/ as in modern Sp. /kemádo/ *quemado*, /sabiéndo/ *sabiendo*, /ĺéga/ *llega* respectively. In view of the extensive attestation of nonlenited intervocalic consonants in modern Upper Aragonese[4] and in the earliest Mozarabic material,[5] it seems rather more likely that the *-p- -t- -k-* of the glosses actually represented voiceless stops, and are thus valuable evidence for the relatively late spread of lenition into Ibero-Romance.

In other respects, the model of Latin served to set the basic patterns of Romance orthography, for instance the use of *c* to represent a palatalised or assibilated consonant (/č/ or /¢/) before a front vowel /e i/, and of *c* plus some further graphemic element (*e.g. h* in Italian) or else of *qu* to represent /k/ in that position. Thus, in the words for '100', from Lat. *centum*, PRom. /kéntu/, we find *c* standing for /č/ in It. *cento* /čénto/, and for /¢/ in OSp. *ciento* /¢iénto/, OSFr. /¢én/ *cen*, and ONFr. *cent* /¢ént/. In Italian, *ch* was used for /k/ in such words as *chinare* /kináre/ 'to bend over', whereas OSp., OSFr., and ONFr. *qu* represented /k/ in, say, *que* for OSp., OSFr. /ke/, ONFr. /kə/ 'that'. It was only where Latin did not have the phonological feature in question—such as a series of palatal consonants—that orthographical innovations were introduced. These were at first quite variegated and fluctuating, even within the same language, *e.g.* the use of simple *n*, of *nh*, of *in*, and of (*i*)*gn*(*i*) for palatal /ṇ/, and similar combinations with the letter *l* for /ḷ/. Only in the later Middle Ages and Renaissance did usage become definitively fixed (independently for each Romance standard language) with regard to /ṇ/ and /ḷ/.

7.12.   Lexical Borrowings from Latin began almost as soon as the writing down of Romance material. There were two main channels for the introduction of lexical Latinisms:

7.121.   Original Compositions. Any author, whether clerical or lay, could use whatever Latin words he might have learned directly from Latin or heard from others who knew that language. As early as the ONFr. *Eulalie*, from the 880's, we find obvious Latinisms like *pulcella* 'maiden' (probably standing for /py¢élə/), *anima* 'soul' (/ánəmə/?), and *figure* 'shape' (/figyrə/). The OSp. *Auto de los Reyes Magos* has *december, oriente, occidente*, and other obvious Latinisms. Even the Florentine bankers of 1211 used such expressions as /imperiáli/ *imperiali* 'imperial ducats' and /kalénde/ *calende* 'Calends', which were clearly part of every-day parlance by their time.

7.122.   Translations became increasingly frequent during the later part of the Middle Ages, from the thirteenth century on. Even before the time of Alfonso the Wise (1221–1284), there existed in Spain, at Toledo, a group of scholars known as the *Escuela de Toledo* or "Toledo School." Their activity was directed at first towards rendering learnèd Arabic works into Latin, but later towards the use of Castillian for their translations from both Arabic and Latin. Like King Alfred of England, Alfonso himself engaged in translation-work, and gathered around him a group of men who both translated and compiled encyclopaedic collections of material on law (the *Siete partidas* 'Seven Codes'), history (the *Crónica general* or 'General Chronicle', and the *General e grant Estoria* 'General and Great History'), and science. In the course of this work these translators inevitably introduced a great many words from Latin and (through Latin) from Greek.

Parallel to the work of these Spaniards, translations of the *Historia adversum paganos* ('History against the Pagans') of Paulus Orosius (fifth century A.D.) were made in France by Jean de Meung and in Italy by Bono Giamboni, in the second half of the thirteenth century. Giamboni was especially active as a translator, rendering numerous classical works into Italian (such as the *Epitome rei militaris* 'Summary of Military Science') of Flavius Vegetius (fourth century A.D.), and also the *Roman de la Rose* of Guillaume de Lorris (cf. §6.312). A contemporary of Giamboni (and teacher of Dante) in the latter half of the thirteenth century was Brunetto Latini (ca. 1220–1294), who translated several orations and rhetorical treatises by Cicero.

The number of translations increased even more in the fourteenth century, with the activity in France of Jean de Berçuire (whose version of part of Livy's history dates from 1356) and, in the latter part of the century, Nicolas Oresme, with his translation of Aristotle,[6] of Petrarch's *De remediis utriusque fortunae* 'On the remedies for good and for bad fortune', etc. In Italy, a certain Andrea Lancia, in the first half of the century, rendered Valerius Maximus' stories of Roman history (first century A.D.) into Italian under the title *De' fatti e detti degni di memoria dèlla città di Roma e delle stranie genti* 'Concerning the Memorable Deeds and Sayings of the City of Rome and of Foreign Peoples'. Sallust's historical works (first century B.C.) were translated by one Bartolomeo da San Concordio, and a fourteenth-century version of Livy in Italian has been ascribed to Giovanni Boccaccio (1314–1375).[7]

Latinisms are inevitably frequent in the works of all these translators. Where possible, they would use words common in the contemporary vernacular, such as It. /agé^vole/ *agevole* 'easy' instead of /fáčile/ *facile*, or /óste/ *oste* 'army' instead of /esérčito/ *esercito*, to cite only two instances in which the later language has generalised the Latinism. On many occasions, however, the vernacular simply had no equivalent, or the Latin form had changed so much as to acquire a different phonetic shape and meaning. Thus, we find in the mediaeval Spanish translations such forms as /finžir/ *fingir* 'to feign' (≠ /hennír/ *heñir* 'to knead' < PRom. /fíngere/), or /artíkulo/ *articulo* 'article' (≠ /artéžo/ *artejo* 'knuckle' < PRom. /artíkulu/). Among the Alfonsine Latinisms we find words like /tiráno/ *tirano* 'tyrant', /estúdio/ *estudio* 'study', and /ʒodíako/ *zodiaco* 'zodiac'[8]; other Spanish translators introduced such words as /žustiȼia/ *justicia* 'justice', /omiȼídio/ *homicidio* 'homicide', /diáblo/ *diablo* 'devil'. In French, Oresme went so far as to make lists of learnèd words, such as /anarčiə/ *anarchie* 'anarchy', /melodiə/ *melodie* 'melody', /poemə/ *poeme* 'poem',

/politikə/ *politique* 'politics'. To other mediaeval French translators are due such borrowings as /inosãt/ *innocent*, /ynite^/ *unité* 'unity', /ve^rite^/ *vérité* 'truth'. Italian translators introduced, for example, /stúdio/ *studio* 'study', /líbro/ *libro* 'book', /melodía/ *melodia* 'melody', /veráče/ *verace* 'true', /čibo/ *cibo* 'food'.

Most of these borrowings are fairly easily recognisable, because they preserve some or all of the phonological features of their Latin source, except for adaptation of their endings to the morphological patterns of whatever Romance language they were borrowed into.[9] Thus, a Latin final /-a/ will be kept in Italian and Spanish, but replaced by /-ə/ *-e* in French; Latin /-us -um/ will be represented by /-o/ in Italian and Spanish, but by /-ə/ or nothing in French (cf. the examples given above). In some instances, the borrowings were reshaped, especially in Italian: for instance, Guittone d'Arezzo has /adifikáre/ *adificare* (≠ later /edifikáre/ *edificare* < Lat. *aedificare* 'to build'); we also find such forms as /arismétika/ *arismetica* or /arismétrika/ *arismetrica* (≠ later /aritmétika/ *aritmetika* < Lat. *arithmetica* 'arithmetic' (< Gk. /arithme:tiké:/ ἀριθμητική). In some instances, popular humor may have played a part in the reshaping, as when *scrutinium* 'a scrutiny [of popular sentiment]', applied to plebiscites held in open-air meetings in mediaeval Italy, became /skuittíno/ *squittino* (probably influenced by /skuittíre/ *squittire* 'to shriek, yell').

7.2. Mediaeval Cross-Romance Borrowings

It must not be thought that western European speakers of Romance made borrowings only from Latin. There were, for the times, very active cultural currents flowing from one Romance-speaking area to another, and particularly from Gallo-Romance to Ibero- and Italo-Romance. These last-mentioned influences were correlated with the growing prestige, first of the Provençal courts of the eleventh and twelfth centuries, and, only slightly later, of the North French court.[10] French came to be regarded as the most elegant of the Romance languages. Not a few mediaeval authors used French, even when it was not their native tongue, as did Brunetto Latini for his encyclopaedic miscellany *Li livres dou Tresor* 'The Book of the Treasure'. To explain why he had done so, he said:

> Et se aucuns demandoit por quoi cist livres est escriz en romans selonc le langage des François, puisque nos somes Ytaliens, je diroie que ce est por ij. raisons: l'une, car nos somes en France, et l'autre por ce que la parleüre est plus delitable et plus commune a toutes gens.

'And if any-one were to ask why this book has been written in French, since we are Italian, I should say that it is for two reasons: one, because we are in France, and the other because the [French] language is more agreeable and more common to all people'.

Likewise, the Venetian Martino da Canale wrote his *Cronique des Venitiens* ('Chronicle of the Venetians') in French,[11] and the Tuscan Rusticiano da Pisa used French both for his compilations of Arthurian tales (the *Meliadus*) and for transcribing Marco Polo's account of his Far Eastern travels, which the latter dictated to him (ca. 1254–1324).[12] Some of the translators mentioned in §7.122 made versions of French, as well as Latin, works: *e.g.* Bono Giamboni translated Brunetto Latini's *Tresor* into Italian, and a certain Ser Durante (probably not Dante Alighieri) reworked the first part of the *Roman de la Rose* into a sequence of 232 sonnets, entitled *Il Fiore* ('The Flower').

Not only in learnèd circles, but also among the common people, French influence was strong. Singers travelled through northern Italy in the thirteenth century reciting the *chansons de geste*, particularly those of the Carolingian cycle—at first, in the original French (which at that time was not so different from North Italian dialects as to be totally incomprehensible). Soon, however, the epic poems began to be reworked in a mixed dialect, Franco-Venetian.[13] This term covers various types of language, ranging from simple "bad French" concocted by Italians who knew no better, to a truly hybrid language intentionally based on Old French but covered with a patina of North Italian sounds and forms in order to make it more intelligible to Italian hearers. Naturally, Franco-Venetian had no single standard, and varied from one work and probably one minstrel to another. Current French modes set the style in central and southern Italy as well, and were reflected even in the life and teachings of St. Francis of Assisi, who preached the principles of self-sacrifice and poverty in terms of contemporary fashion, devoting himself, in Provençal manner, to *madonna Povertà* 'my lady Poverty'. Minstrels and street-singers carried the French heroic legends to the populace throughout Italy and Spain, retelling them in verse or in prose.

Of the various cross-currents of inter-Romance borrowing in this period, therefore, that carrying Gallo-Romance lexicon was strongest. The earliest Spanish, Galician, and Italian literature is full of Gallicisms,[14] *e.g.* OSp. /trobár/ *trobar* 'find', /paráže/ *paraje* 'nobility', /folía/*follia* 'madness', /kólpe/ or /gólpe/ *colpe, golpe* 'blow'; OIt. /ǧuǧǧáre/ *giuggiare* 'to judge' (< OProv. /ǧuǧár/ *jutjar* or ONFr. /ǧuǧiǽr/ *jugier* < PRom. /judikáre/), /tósto/ *tosto* 'quickly' (< OProv., ONFr. /tóst/ *tost* < PRom. /tóstu/ 'heated, toasted'), /manǧáre/ *mangiare* 'to eat' (< ONFr. /manǧiǽr/

mangier < PRom. /mandukáre/ 'to chew, chomp', /ǧóˆrno/ *giorno* 'day'
(< OProv., ONFr. /jóˆrn/ *jorn* < PRom. /di̯úrnu/ 'pertaining to the
day').¹⁵ As has been pointed out,¹⁶ the French loans often had special
over-tones of elegant or lofty sentiment, in contrast to the every-day terms
which developed normally in local speech. Thus, OIt. /fiordalíso/ *fiordaliso*
'lily, fleur-de-lis' is used in contexts where the lily symbolises purity and
chastity, as opposed to normal /ǧíḷḷo/ *giglio* (< an intermediate */i̯íˆli̯u/
< PRom. líˆḷu/).

As with Latin borrowings, translators would often introduce French
words when they could find no exact vernacular equivalent. The anonymous
early Italian translation of Livy, which was clearly based on a (now lost)
French version,¹⁷ has such crude Gallicisms as /uno oráǧe/ *uno orage* 'a
storm' (< ONFr. /oraže/ *orage*, /požoˆne/ *pogione* 'poison' (< ONFr.
/poizon/ poison), or /semblábile/ *semblabile* 'similar' (< ONFr. /sembl-
ablə/ *semblable*). At one point, he introduces the French word /faldəstol/
faldestol to explain a Latin term: *si fece rechare suo faldestol el quale l'uomo
chiama sella curule* 'he had them bring him his arm-chair, which one calls
curule chair'. (Note also the French-style use of *l'uomo* '[the] man' for
'one, people in general'). Loan-shifts, too, were frequent: in the same translation from Livy, we find /diféndere/ *difendere* 'defend' > forbid' /assaǧ-
ǧáre/ *assaggiare* 'to taste > to try, attempt', or /fermáre/ *fermare* 'to
stop > to close', all on French models.

Naturally, the currents of borrowing were not all in one direction. French
took various terms from Italian in the thirteenth, fourteenth, and fifteenth
centuries,¹⁸ especially in connection with types of cloth, *e.g.* OFr. /bom-
bazin/ (Mod. Fr. /bõbazẽ/) *bombasin* < It. /bam° bombažíno/ *bam°
bombagino* 'bombazine cloth', and with nautical matters, *e.g.* /arsenal/
arsenal (with variants /aršenal/ *archenal* and /arsenak/ *arsenac*) < It.
/arsenal/ *arsenale*, Ven. /arǵaná/ *arzanà* (< Ar. /dar-aṣ-ṣina:'a/ 'house of
construction', §5.33). As this latter example shows, Italian was a channel
for the transmission of Orientalisms from the eastern Mediterranean, where
Genoese, Venetians, Pisans, and other Italians were active in trade. Such
terms include ONFr. /koton/ *coton* 'cotton' < It. /kot(t)óˆne/ *cot(t)one*
< Ar. /quṭu:n/; fifteenth century Fr. /kandi/ *candi* 'candy' < It. /kan-
díto/ *candito* 'candied [sc. with sugar]' < Ar. /qandi:/:/qand/ 'sugar-
cane'; or fifteenth century Fr. /žirafə/ *girafe* 'giraffe' < It. /ǧiráffa* <
Ar. /zara:fa/. Italian trading and commercial leadership was reflected in
the words for 'bank'—ONFr. /bankə/ *banque*, Sp. /bánko/ *banco* < It.
/banko °a/ *banco* (m.) *banca* (f.) 'bench, [banker's] table'—and for various
coins, *e.g.* the Florentine florin (OIt. /fioríno/ *fiorino*), the Neapolitan
carlino (OIt. /karlíno/ *carlino*), and the Venetian ducat (OIt. /dukato/
ducato).¹⁹

COMPARATIVE ROMANCE GRAMMAR I:
EXTERNAL HISTORY OF THE ROMANCE
LANGUAGES, by Robert A. Hall

pub. date: 1974
price: $18.50

This book
is being sent
     to you
for review.

May we ask you
   to send us
three tear sheets
of your review.

American Elsevier Publishing Company, Inc.
52 Vanderbilt Avenue · New York, N.Y. 10017
Telephone: (212)MU 6-5277

These borrowings often contained suffixes or other elements which were so frequent as to introduce new word-formants into the recipient languages, particularly Italian, Spanish, and Portuguese. In this way, Fr. /⁺ážə/ (spelled -age in the North, -atge or -atje in the South) > It. /⁺áǧǧo/ -aggio, OSp. /⁺áže/ (> Mod. Sp. /⁺áxe/) -aje, at first in such terms as OIt. /liṇṇáǧǧo/ lignaggio, OSp. /lináže/ linaje 'lineage' < ONFr. /liṇaǧe/ lignage; OIt. /serváǧǧo/ servaggio 'servitude, slavery' < ONFr. /servaǧə/ servage; It. /koráǧǧo/ coraggio 'courage', OSp. /koráže/ coraje, originally 'state of one's heart', from OSFr. or ONFr. /koráǧe/ cora(t)ge. Such formative elements eventually become extended to other bases, as in It. /magaẓẓináǧǧo/ magazzinaggio 'storage-fee' (:/magaẓẓíno/ magazzino 'warehouse') or /ankoráǧǧo/ ancoraggio 'anchorage' (:/ánkora/ ancora 'anchor').

7.3. The "Revival of Learning"

This term, often used[20] to refer to the humanistic study of Latin and Latin and Greek during the period commonly called the Renaissance (fifteenth and sixteenth centuries in Italy, sixteenth century elsewhere), contains an element of truth but also some exaggeration. Learning had by no means been as dead in the Middle Ages as it was at one time thought to have been. The Renaissance did not lead men's minds *hors de cette épaisse nuit gothique* 'out of this thick Gothic night,' as Du Bellay put it, because such a *nuit gothique* had never existed. Yet there was indeed a change, both in the corpus of ancient literature available and in the attitudes of scholars and general public towards Latin and Greek.

A certain number of Latin authors (Vergil, Horace, Ovid) had been read and studied in the Middle Ages, but the works of a great many others had been lost either in part (*e.g.* Livy) or completely (*e.g.* Quintilian, Lucretius). In many instances, all or part of their works have remained lost; in others, they were rediscovered, especially during the fifteenth century. Such men as Niccolò de' Niccoli (1364–1437) of Florence, Antonio Loschi (1368–1441) of Verona, Pier Paolo Vergerio from Capodistria (1370–1444), the Sicilian Giovanni Aurispa (1369–1459), and the most active of all, the Florentine Poggio Bracciolini (1380–1459), devoted a major part of their energies to seeking out forgotten manuscripts in out-of-the-way libraries. The work of Humanism proper may be divided into four main stages, those of rediscovery, establishment, codification, and interpretation of the documents of ancient literature. In addition to Latin, Greek now became, for the first time since antiquity, a major factor in intellectual life. This aspect of classical studies, which had been growing in importance since the time of the Greek scholar Manuel Chrysoloras (ca. 1350–1415), was given major impetus by the influx of refugee Greek intellectuals after the fall of Constantinople in 1453. In addition to its effect on purely scholarly activity, Humanism was a major influence in the recasting of education, with the abandonment of the mediaeval curricula of the *trivium* and *quadrivium*,[21] and the establishment of classical studies as the center of an educated person's training.

7.31. Humanism and Philology. The increase in knowledge of Latin and Greek works immediately led scholars to recognise the need for establishing complete and accurate texts.[22] This need was made more acute by the invention and rapid spread of printing with movable types, usually considered to have originated with Johann Gutenberg of Mainz in the 1450's.

7.311. Channels of Influence. Most of the works contained in incunabula (*i.e.* books printed before 1500) were in Latin or Greek. Hence the abilities required for supervising their production involved first of all a good knowledge of both of these languages—their grammar, style, and lexicon—and familiarity with the process of printing and the tastes of the reading public. Many famous early printers, such as Aldo Manuzio (1450–1515) in Venice, and Geoffroy Tory (1485–1533) and Robert Estienne (1503–1559) in France, were able classical scholars in their own right. When printers began to publish books in the Romance vernaculars, very often the production of these would be supervised by the same editors who oversaw the preparation of books in Latin and Greek for the press. These classically trained scholars of course tended to apply to their text-editing the same criteria they used for books in the ancient languages. When they themselves came to make translations or write original works in the vernacular, it came natural to them to transfer, not only words, but constructions from the classical languages into the modern.[23]

7.312. Ciceronianism is the name given to the "purifying" tendency found in the works and attitudes of a number of classical scholars in the sixteenth century. It consisted principally of an emphasis on the imitation of a very few authors of antiquity, in the writing of Latin. That a creative writer should follow earlier models, had been a doctrine of classicism ever since Horace had said, in his *Ars Poetica* ('Art of Poetry', 268–269):

> [. . .] vōs exemplāria graeca
> nocturnā versāte manū, versāte diurnā

'Turn over your Greek models in your hands by night and by day'. The Ciceronians, however, insisted on restricting the models to Cicero in prose, and to Vergil, Ovid, and Horace in poetry. Their insistence on this point was so strong and intimidatory that, as it permeated the teaching of Latin, it created an ideal which was virtually impossible of fulfillment.[24] At the same time, it inhibited full use of Latin to deal with contemporary situations, especially in a period of tremendous new discoveries in geography and science. Erasmus' satire in his *Cicerōniānus* ('The Ciceronian', 1528) helped to diminish the excesses of the movement. Its effects remained, however, both in the permanent (though gradual) impairment of Latin as a flexible instrument for international communication, and in the establishment of a narrow, restrictive ideal for correct usage.

7.313. Hellenism on the contrary, was on the whole a positive force in sixteenth-century intellectual life. The revival of Greek studies (cf. §7.3) brought to classical scholarship a much wider intellectual horizon, expressed in a much richer literature, than was available in Latin alone. The newly awakened enthusiasm for the Hellenic world is expressed in Ronsard's ecstatic sonnet beginning *Je veux lire en trois jours l'Iliade d'Homére* 'I want to read in three days the Iliad of Homer'. In language, the chief influence of Greek was felt in vocabulary. A new, extensive source of borrowings became available, which has been utilised ever since the Renaissance in a host of pan-European borrowings, such as Fr. *phénomène*, It., Sp., Port. *fenómeno*, Eng. *phenomenon* < Gk. /phainómenon/ φαινόμενον 'something appearing [in the experience of the senses]'; Fr. *rhumatisme*, It., Sp., Port. *reumatismo*, Eng. *rheumatism* < Gk. /rheumatismós/ ῥευματισμός; Fr. *hygiène*, It. *igiene*, Sp. *higiene*, Eng. *hygiene* < Gk. /higieiná/ ἱγιεινά 'pertaining to health'.

Some Renaissance writers, especially Ronsard and the Pléiade in France, attempted to imitate Greek patterns of word-formation, as in /brizə-gren/ *brise-grain* 'grain-breaker = mild', /donə-vin/ *donne-vin* 'wine-giver = summer', or /šasə-nyə/ *chasse-nue* 'cloud-chaser = wind'. These efforts were, however, by and large unsuccessful.

7.32. "Humanism in the Vernacular." The patterns of classicism, as established by the humanists of the fifteenth and early sixteenth centuries, were carried over into the cultivation of the vernacular tongues, as these latter grew in importance during the rest of the 1500's. Not only editors and polygraphs (cf. fn. 22), but independent men of letters, of all social ranks, who had been given their schooling in Latin and Greek, went over in their maturity to writing in the vernacular. Outstanding examples of men who made this shift were Pietro Bembo (1470–1547) and Lodovico Ariosto

(1474–1533, author of the romance *Orlando Furioso* 'Roland Gone Mad') in Italy; Michel Eyquem de Montaigne (1533–1592) in France[25]; and Antonio de Nebrija (ca. 1442–1522) in Spain. For men such as these, and others who imitated their use of the vernaculars, certain problems arose and had to be solved.

7.321. WHAT LANGUAGE FOR LITERATURE? This was the first question that had to be answered. To begin with, there was the opposition between Latin itself (Greek hardly came into consideration) and the writer's native speech. Where vested interests were at stake, the pressures to keep using Latin could be quite strong (cf. §7.51); in their absence, however, it came to be a matter of individual choice. To reach the ever-growing reading public that knew no Latin, use of the vernacular was obviously indicated. Against this trend, the protests of old-line humanists (*e.g.* a certain Ròmolo Amaseo [1481–1552] in his oration *Dē linguae latīnae usū retinendō* 'On the need for preserving the use of Latin', delivered at Bologna in 1530), were of no avail.[26]

Once the use of the vernacular was decided on, there were still various choices to be made. Since both humanism and its application to the vernacular begain in Italy, it was there that the major debates first took place. Parallel discussions in other countries followed, in general, the same lines, and were often initiated by persons who had lived in Italy and had come in contact with the discussions of the *Questione della Lingua* or "language-question," as the debates were called there.

There were, basically, three axes along which discussion ranged in Italy,[27] two of them reflecting real problems and one of them involving only the name to be given to the language ("Italian," "Tuscan," or "Florentine"?). The others were: (1) that between Tuscan usage and broader standards, and (2) that between imitation of earlier authors who were set up as "classic" models—especially Petrarch for verse and Boccaccio for prose (cf. §6.315)—on the one hand, and current usage on the other "(archaising" vs. "antiarchaising"). The resultant four possibilities can be shown in a diagram:

Pro-Tuscan archaising	Pro-Tuscan antiarchaising
Anti-Tuscan archaising	Anti-Tuscan antiarchaising

Each of these four positions was reflected in the writings of a number of authors:

1. Pro-Tuscan and archaising: Pietro Bembo (1470–1547) in his dialogue *Prose della volgar lingua* ('On the Vernacular'; ca. 1506–1512, published 1526).
2. Pro-Tuscan and antiarchaising: Niccolò Machiavelli (1470–1527) in his *Diàlogo della lingua* ('Dialogue on the Language'; ca. 1505), and the phonetician Claudio Tolomei (1492–1555; cf. §11.2) in his dialogue *Il Cesano* (ca. 1535).
3. Anti-Tuscan and antiarchaising: Count Baldassar Castiglione (1478–1529) in his *Libro del Cortegiano* ('Book of the Courtier'; ca. 1508–1516, published 1526), and Gian Giorgio Trissino (1478–1550) in the dialogue *Il Castellano* ('The Keeper of the Castle'; 1527).
4. Anti-Tuscan and archaising (a relatively uncommon combination): Giròlamo Muzio (1496–1576) in his *Battaglie in difesa dell'Itàlica lingua* ('Battles in Defense of the Italian Language'; 1530–1536).

The *Diàlogo delle lingue* ('Dialogue on Language'; ca. 1530) of the literary critic Sperone Speroni (1500–1588) reflects all points of view, but seems to give the victory, so far as literary usage is concerned, to Bembo and his puristic view-point. This is certainly what happened, especially in bellettristic Italian.

In Italy, these problems were posed in the sixteenth century, but were not resolved until the nineteenth, because the political and economic conditions were not favourable to the establishment of a unified and officially supported standard.[28] In France, Spain, and Portugal, there was an equally intensive battle to be fought against Latin on behalf of the vernaculars. The *Deffense et illustration de la langue Françoyse* ('Defense and Ennoblement of the French Language'; 1548) of Joachim du Bellay (1524–1560); the *Diálogo de la lengua* ('Dialogue on the Language'; ca. 1535, pub. 1737) of the Spaniard Juan de Valdés (ca. 1470–1541); and the *Diálogo em louvor da nossa lingoa* ('Dialogue in Praise of Our Language'; 1540) of the Portuguese João de Barros (1496–1570) all had as their main purpose to show how their respective vernaculars were equal to the classical languages or, if they were not, could be made so. Both Du Bellay and de Valdés spent a large proportion of their lives in Italy, and all three of these authors used much the same arguments as the Italian discussants to urge the claims of the mother tongue. There were, however, two major differences. National unity and hence the use of a single standard language was more advanced in France and Spain than it was in Italy.[29] On the other hand, Spanish and especially French had changed much more rapidly in recent centuries than had Italian. Hence mediaeval literature was less known[30] and could not be considered as a model for imitation. For these men and their contemporaries, the prime problem was to "ennoble" their language by increasing its potentialities, drawing on all possible sources, but especially those of the classical languages, in lexicon and to a certain extent in structure.

7.322. LEXICAL INFLUENCE. In the sixteenth century, the lexical influence of the classical languages on the western Romance vernaculars differed from that of earlier periods in three ways: in quantity, in the semantic fields involved, and in the source-languages (Greek as well as Latin).

There are, to the best of my knowledge, no statistical studies of the text- or even of the list-frequency of classical loan-words in Italian, French, Spanish, or Portuguese during the Renaissance. All historians of these languages[31] are agreed, however, that the number of words was far greater than it had previously been. In 1529, in his *Le Champ Fleury* ('The Flowery Field'), Geoffroy Tory made fun of those who used an excessive quantity of Latinisms, saying:

> Quand Escumeurs de Latin disent: Despumons la verbocination latiale et transfretons la Sequane au dilucule et crepuscule; puis deambulons par les Quadrivies et Platees de Lutece; et comme verisimiles amorabundes, captivons la benevolence de l'omnigene et omniforme sexe feminin, me semble qu'ils ne se moquent seulement de leurs semblables, mais de leur personne.

> 'When skimmers of Latin say: "Let us despumate [skim off] the Latial verbocination and let us transfrete [cross] the Sequana [Seine] at the dilucule [dawn] and crepuscule [dusk]; then let us deambulate through the quadrivia [cross-roads] and plateas [squares] of Lutetia; and, like verisimilar amorabunds [lovers], let us captivate the benevolence of the omnigenous and omniform feminine sex," it seems to me they are making fun, not only of their fellow-men, but also of themselves.'

The humorist François Rabelais (ca. 1483–1554) took this sentence (which may have been a traditional piece of wit among students) and, adapting it slightly, put it into the mouth of the *écolier limousin*, the student from Limoges whom Pantagruel (II.6) hears comically overloading his sentences with Latinisms, and finally frightens nearly to death and forces to speak Limousin dialect. But Rabelais himself was a mighty "skimmer of Latin." In the immediately following chapter (II.7) he uses such words as *déliberer* 'to deliberate, decide'; *applicquer* 'to apply'; *un inconvénient* 'an inconvenient aspect'; *campanes* 'bells'; *magnifique* 'magnificent'. Gargantua's letter to his son Pantagruel, expounding his ideal of a humanistic education (II.8), is not much less packed with Latinisms than is the speech of the Limousin student. In this incongruous mixture, Rabelais was following the example of the Italian humorous poet Teòfilo Folengo (1491–1544), the foremost writer in macaronic Latin, *i.e.* Latin mixed with elements of one or more other languages for comic effect,[32] who, in his macaronic mock-epic *Baldus* (1529), had made an inextricable medley of Latin, standard Italian, and North Italian dialect, the whole decked out with Latin endings and meter, as in the passage describing the rogue Cingar (2.417–424):

> Alter erat Baldi compagnus, nomine Cingar,
> Accortus, ladro, semper truffare paratus;
> Scarnus enim facie, reliquo sed corpore nervis
> Plenus, compressus, picolinus, brunus, et atrox,
> Semper habens nudam testam, rizzutus et asper.
> Iste suam traxit Marguti a sanguine razzam,
> Qui ad calcagnos sperones ut gallus habebat
> Et nimio risu simia cagante morivit.

> 'There was a second companion of Baldus, by name Cingar, alert, thievish, always ready to cheat; for he was thin of face, but in the rest of his body sinewy, stocky, short, dark, and violent, always bare-headed, curly-haired, and rough. He had his racial origin from the blood of Margutte, who had spurs on his heels like a rooster, and died from excessive laughter at a defecating ape.'

In this passage, *compagnus* is a Latinisation of Ital. *compagno* 'companion', *accortus* of *accorto* 'alert', and so forth; *truflare* is simply the Italian verb for 'to cheat'; and *rizzutus* and *cagante* show North Italian dialectal features (/-¢¢-/ -zz- : standard Italian /-čč-/ -cci- and lenition), corresponding to It. *ricciuto* 'curly-haired' and *cacante* 'defecating'.

The waves of Latinism did not, of course, hit all Romance languages at the same time or with equal strength.[33] In general, for each tongue, there was a rising curve of borrowings, beginning with the early Middle Ages (cf. §7.1) and increasing as time went on, reaching a peak in the first enthusiasm for the new humanism (fifteenth century in Italy, sixteenth in France, Spain, and Portugal), and then falling off somewhat thereafter in semantic fields pertaining to the humanities, but continuing strongly in scientific and technological matters. It follows that any given Latinism might make its first appearance in one country in a particular century, but at a later date in other countries. Usually (though by no means always), Renaissance Latinisms appeared first in Italy, and somewhat later in the other western countries. This phenomenon was probably due to the cultural fact that use of and familiarity with Latin had been greater in Italy than elsewhere, all through the Middle Ages, and to the linguistic fact that Italian had remained structurally closer to Latin, so that borrowing was easier than was the case with the other West Romance languages. Thus, we find such words as /pátria/ *patria* 'father-land', /intelliǧénǂa/ *intelligenza* 'intelligence', /eččeǂió^ne/ *eccezione* 'exception', /persuadé^re/ *persuadere* 'persuade' appearing in Italy in the fourteenth century, whereas the corresponding forms—Fr. /patriǝ/ *patrie*, Sp. /pátria/ *patria*; Fr. /inteližansǝ/ *intelligence*, Sp. /inteližénǂia/ *inteligencia*; Fr. /eksepsion/ *exception*, Sp. /eǂepǂión /ecepción³⁴; Fr. /persyade^/ *persuader*, Sp. Sp. /persuadir/ *persuadir*—appear in the sixteenth. In other instances, a Latinism will appear in all three major West European Romance languages in the same century, normally the sixteenth, *e.g.* the forms for 'paradox': It. /paradósso/ *paradosso*, Fr. /paradoksǝ/ *paradoxe*, Sp. /paradošo/ *paradoxo*.

Most of the Renaissance Hellenisms and Latinisms met new needs, to refer to freshly introduced concepts, and hence did not collide with or duplicate already existing lexical items. In some instances, however, a learnèd word would reïntroduce, in its earlier phonetic shape, a morpheme which had undergone normal development in popular speech. This phenomenon was especially common in French, where phonological change had rendered many words quite different from their Latin etyma. Often there had been a semantic shift as well in popular speech, and the Latinism reïntroduced the earlier meaning. In such cases both forms of the doublet (cf. §1.42) usually survived together, as in the French pairs /natif/ *natif* 'native' ∼ /naif/ *naïf* 'naïve' (< PRom. /nati^ṷu/); /kaptif/ *captif* 'captive' ∼ /še^tif/ *chétif* 'feeble' (< /kaptí^ṷu/); /navige^/ *naviguer* 'to navigate' ∼ /naže^/ *nager* 'to swim' (< /naṷigáre/); /posion/ *potion* 'drink' ∼ /pwezon/ *poison* 'poison' (< /potió^ne/), and a number of others. We have already mentioned (§7.122) similar pairs of doublets in Spanish.

In other instances, the learnèd word has the same meaning as the popular development and replaced it, as in Fr. /le^gymǝ/ *légume* 'vegetable' (≠ /ly:n/ < earlier /lǝyn/ *leün* < PRom. /legú^me/); /de^bitœr/ *débiteur* (≠ /detœr/ *detteur*³⁵ < PRom. /debito^re/); /širyržien/ *chirurgien* 'surgeon' (≠ /syržien/ *surgien* < PItWRom. /kirurg-/ + /⁺iánu/); /interože^/ *interroger* 'to interrogate' (≠ /anterve^/ *enterver* < PRom. /interrogáre/). This latter type of situation was found in Italian and Spanish also, with Latinisms replacing older popular developments: *e.g.* It.

/arǧénto/ *argento* 'silver' (≠ OIt. /ariénto/ *ariento* < PRom. /argéntu/),
/kirúrgo/ *chirurgo* 'surgeon' (≠ OIt. /čerusiko/ *cerusico*), /elefánte/
elefante 'elephant' (≠ OIt. /lionfánte/ *lionfante*), or /lóǧiko/ *logico* 'logical,
logician' (≠ OIt. /lóiko/ *loico*); Sp. /ámbos/ *ambos* 'both' (≠ SOp. /ámos/
amox < PRom. /ámbos/), or /ábe/ *ave* 'bird' (≠ OSp. /áu¢e/ *auce* <
PRom. /áu̯ike/).

In the above paragraphs we have mentioned only words that have survived to the present time in their respective languages. Many other Renaissance learnèd borrowings have not survived, or else have survived in one
language but not in another (for English, cf. fn. 35). Among such words are
French /angystiǝ/ *angustie* 'anguish' (< Lat. /angustia/ *angustia* 'nar-
rowness'), /myliebrǝ/ *muli è bre* 'womanish' (< Lat. /muliebrem/ *mulie-
brem*), /pristin/ *pristin* 'pristine' (< Lat. /pristi:num/ *pristīnum*); It.
/kakinnáre/ *cachinnare* 'to laugh' (< Lat. /kakinna:re/ *cachinnāre*),
/ékuore/ *equore* 'water' (< Lat. /aiku̯orem/ *aequorem*), /élego/ *elego*
'elegiac verse' (< Gk. /élegos/ ἔλεγος 'lament'). In some instances,
troublesome homonymy arose as a result of a learnèd borrowing duplicating
an already existing word, so that the innovation was unsuccessful or, at
best, survived only marginally: for instance, Lat. /ko:pia/ *cōpia* meant
'abundance', and It. /kópia/ *copia*, in this sense, is now used principally
in the expression /ingránkópia/ *in gran copia* 'in great abundance'; but Fr.
/kopiǝ/ and Sp., Port. /kópia/ *copia*, in this meaning, did not survive the
competition with homonyms meaning 'copy'.[36]

7.323. STRUCTURAL INFLUENCES on sixteenth-century Romance languages
from Latin and Greek were relatively slight, not affecting their grammatical
core.[37]. A few classical influences can be discerned in certain respects:

1. Inflectional changes under Graeco-Latin influence were fairly rare.
In a few instances, writers tried to change the gender of words to agree with
that of an ancient language, as in Renaissance Italian /ilparé^te/ *il parete*
'the wall' and /iltígre/ *il tigre* 'the tiger', both masculine to correspond with
Lat. /parie:tem/ *pariētem* and /tigrem/ *tigrem*, respectively, or /ladialétto/
la dialetto 'the dialect', feminine (< Gk. /he: diálektos/ ἡ διάλεκτος). In sixteenth-century French, some used certain words in /⁺œr/ *-eur*, *e.g.* /erœr/
'error', as masculines, for the same reason, since their Latin etyma (such
as /erro:rem/ *errörem*) were of that gender. Such efforts always remained
restricted to individual authors, without ever catching on in normal usage.

2. In derivation, certain sixteenth-century authors attempted to introduce compounds modeled on those of Greek, such as Du Bartas' /portǝ-
flambǝaus/ *porte-flambeaux* 'torch-bearing' (*La Semaine* 1.1), or those introduced by Ronsard and the Pléiade (cf. §7.313); but none of these were
successful.

3. Syntactic patterns were occasionally imitated from Latin or Greek:

a. Of those which did catch on, the most outstanding is the "absolute" construction, with NOUN (or PRONOUN) + ADJECTIVE, in imitation of the Latin ablative absolute (e.g. /ho:k fakto:/*hōc factō* 'this having been done', /akie: instrukta:/ *aciē instructā* 'with the battle-line drawn up', in its origin an ablative of condition). In the absence of the category of case in the Romance literary languages, this construction had to involve simple juxtaposition of elements, in the same order. It occurs quite early on in Spanish, as in *la oración fecha* 'when the prayer had been said' (*Cid*, 366); but it becomes most common in the sixteenth century, especially in Italian and French. It was a favorite construction with Machiavelli, e.g. *ragunata assai gente pisana e lucchese* 'having gotten together a number of Pisan and Lucchese people' (*Vita di Castruccio*, 2). Not infrequently, Italian Renaissance writers left the adjective or past participle in the masculine, even with a noun in the feminine: e.g. *lasciato parte delle sue genti* 'having left part of his people' (Machiavelli, *Il Prìncipe*, 8); *usato ogni industria* 'having used all industry' (*ibid.*, 12); *restato la femmina* 'the woman having remained' (A. F. Doni).[38] In Spanish, we find, say, Juan de Mena (fifteenth century) using such absolute constructions as

> Desque sentida la su proporción
> de umana forma non ser discrepante,
> el miedo pospuesto, prosigo adelante

> 'Its proportion once having been perceived to be not discrepant from human shape, fear having been put aside, I continue on' (Lab., 22.abc).

Such constructions have remained primarily in fixed locutions, e.g. Fr. /səfe/ *ce fait*, It. /fáttočó/ *fatto ciò*, Sp. /éčoésto/ *hecho esto*, all meaning 'this having been done'.

b. The replacement of a subordinate clause with finite verb, by a construction of NOUN or PRONOUN (acc.) + INFINITIVE. This was a normal construction in Latin, especially with verbs referring to saying, thinking, perceiving, or requesting: e.g. *Locūtus est* [. . .] *Diviciācus* [. . .] *Galliae totīus factiōnēs esse duās* 'Diviciacus said that there were two factions [lit. there to be two factions] in all Gaul' (Caesar, *Dē Bellō Gallicō*, 1.31). We find in Renaissance French such imitations of the "accusative with infinitive" construction as *ils demandoient les cloches leur estre rendues* 'they were asking for the bells to be returned to them' (Rabelais, *Pantagruel*, 1.68) or *montrer l'excellence de nostre langue estre si grande* 'to show that the excellence of our language is [lit. the excellence of our language to be] so great' (H. Estienne). A similar construction is exemplified for Spanish by *la su proporción* [. . .] *non ser discrepante* in the passage just quoted from

Juan de Mena. It was a very popular construction in Renaissance Italian,[39] with such authors as L. B. Alberti and N. Machiavelli: *e.g. si vedrà quelli avere sicuramente e gloriosamente operato* 'it will be seen that these men acted with sureness and glory' (*Il Principe*, 12).

c. A favorite rhetorical device, which for a time was thought to be especially attractive, was HYPERBATON, or the displacement of elements from their normal syntactic position, as in Sp. *con una manera de voces extraña* 'with a strange kind of voices' (Juan de Mena) or *de la prisión no pienso huir mía* 'I do not think to flee from my prison' (Herrera); It. *Le prime adunque parti del dipingere* 'The first, therefore, parts of painting' (Alberti). On occasion, such separation can lead to ambiguity, as in Sp. *O matador de mi hijo cruel* (Juan de Mena): does *cruel* modify *matador* ('O cruel killer of my son') or *hijo* ('O killer of my cruel son')?

d. Other syntactic Latinisms, which were popular for a time but later disappeared, were:

  i. Use of the imperfect subjunctive instead of the conditional: *e.g.* Fr. *il pensoit qu'ils s'en allassent* 'he thought that they would go away'; It. *Quale austero uomo non fuggisse questi sollazzi?* 'What austere man would not shun these amusements?' (Alberti).

  ii. Use of a subjunctive instead of an indicative: *e.g.* It. *vedesi [. . .] che l'amicitia sia* (≠ *è*, indic.) *utilissima ai poveri* 'one sees that friendship is very useful to the poor'.

  iii. Avoidance of the normal Romance construction involving the double negative: *e.g.* (*i filosofi*) *della materia lasciano adrieto nulla* '(philosophers) leave behind nothing of material' (Alberti).

3. Phonological influences were exerted primarily through the channel of orthography.

a. In many Latinisms (and Hellenisms introduced through Latin), writers, editors, and type-setters often kept the original spelling, especially in the main or "contentive" part of a word, using, for instance, *ai, ae,* or *oe* for /e/, *œu* for /ø/, *au* for /o/, *y* for /i/, *ph* for /f/, and preserving a number of orthographic features (mostly consonant-clusters) which had phonemic value in Latin, but whose corresponding sounds had either been lost or had divergent developments in Romance: *pt, ct, bd, gd, mn,* etc., and also *x* for /ks/, and silent *h*. Double consonant-letters had always been written (though not always with complete consistency) in Italian; they were re-introduced widely into French and Portuguese orthography, less widely into Spanish. The resultant double or multiple possibilities for representation of sounds were greatest in French, where most of them have remained down to the present day: *e.g.* /fis/ *fils* 'son', but /filolog/ *philologue* 'philologist'; /œžen/ *Eugène* 'Eugene', but /œvr/ *oeuvre* 'work'; /amer/ *amer* 'bitter', but /kler/ *clair* 'clear'; /oˆteˆ/ *ôter* 'to take off', but /poˆvr/ *pauvre* 'poor'; /õⁿ/ *on* 'one (indef.)', but /om/ *homme* 'man'.[40] In some instances, the divergent or extra spellings thus introduced represented false etymologies, as when /le/ *lais* 'legacy' (:/leseˆ/ *laisser* 'leave') was re-spelled *legs*, as if it were in some way related to Lat. *lēgāre* 'to bequeath'. Similarly, from the fifteenth to the early nineteenth century, /savwer/ 'to know' was spelled *sçavoir*, under the delusion that it was derived from Lat. *scīre* instead of *sapere* (PRom. /sapeˆre/).[41]

A few such multiple possibilities for representation of sounds were present in Renaissance Italian, such as /direꝗꝗióˆne/ spelled *direptione* when meaning 'theft', but *directione* when meaning 'direction'; or /órto/ spelled *orto* in the meaning of 'arisen', but *horto* in that of 'garden'. However, the possibility of distinguishing homonyms by orthographical divergences was reduced to a minimum when, towards the end of the sixteenth century, Italian orthography was replaced on an almost wholly phonemic basis.[42] A similar situation prevailed in Spanish[43] from the sixteenth century onwards.

b. In many instances, especially in French, the Latinising spellings introduced in this way remained purely orthographic, without influencing pronunciation, as in *respect* for /respe/, or sixteenth-century *faict, dict* for /feᵗ/ 'done' and /diᵗ/ 'said' (modern spellings *fait, dit* respectively). But in others, the spelling influenced pronunciation so much as to bring back into the modern language various clusters of consonants which had not been present since Latin times, such as /lpt/ in /skylptyrə/ *sculpture*, /kt/ in /aktə/ *acte* 'act', or /pt/ in /aptə/ *apte* 'apt'. Initial clusters which had previously been absent were introduced, such as /mn-/ in words from Greek /mne:monikós/ μνημονικός 'pertaining to memory': Fr. /mneˆmonik/ *mnémonique* 'mnemonic' and its cognates in Italian and Spanish /mnemóniko/ *mnemónico*. Sometimes, from the misreading of unfamiliar sequences of letters in spelling, new pronunciations arose, especially in sixteenth-century French. The stock example is the family-name /ləfevrə/ *Lefèvre* '(the) Smith'. In its earlier spelling, this name was perfectly clear; but when the letter *b* was intercalated in the spelling of the name, to make clear its relation to Latin *faber* 'smith', the resultant graph *Lefebvre* could be, and by some people was, respelled as *Lefebure*—whence the spelling-pronunciation /ləfebyrə/.

7.4. Religion and Language

Concern with the interpretation of the Bible and its availability to all believers had characterised many sectarian movements in Western Christianity since the Middle Ages. The Waldensians of south-eastern France (later, of the Piedmontese valleys) were known especially for their carrying copies of the Bible around with them and constantly citing it as an authority. The problem of the availability of the Bible to the public at large increased to crisis-proportions soon after the diffusion of printing with movable types, which made books much cheaper and more easily accessible to wider strata of the population. Those who—inside or outside the Roman church— wished to see the Bible more widely known were faced with two problems, both of them intimately connected with the vernacular languages: the provision of literature, especially the Bible, and literacy.

7.41. Religious Literature. There had of course been translations of the Bible before 1500, such as John Wycliffe's in England (ca. 1382–1397). With the sixteenth century and the Reformation, however, came a much greater number of translations. As mentioned earlier (§6.32), it was the impulse to provide the speakers of Romansh and Roumanian with materials either favouring or opposing the reformed faith that led to their first extensive use as incipient standards. Not only Bible-translations, but treatises on religion, hagiographical and similar writings, and popular tracts, contributed to this effort. It has often been pointed out that, whereas John Calvin (1509–1564) published his *Institution of the Christian Religion* first in Latin (1536), the revised, expanded version was published in French (1541). Inevitably, Latin exerted an influence on the vernacular style and vocabulary of Calvin's *Institution* and similar works, in the same way as it did on translations of classics (§7.222) or on other works inspired by humanism (§7.32).

7.42. Literacy. For the material prepared by both sides to reach previously illiterate persons, it was of course necessary for these latter to be taught to read and write, in as easy a way as possible.[44] Some theorists took a strictly egalitarian stand on the rights of even dialectal speakers to think for themselves in their own language, *e.g.* the philosopher Pietro Pomponazzi (1462–1525) as represented in Speroni's *Diàlogo delle Lingue* (§7.321), saying, in a debate with the humanist Làscari over the use of the vernacular languages for philosophising:

> Più tosto vo' credere ad Aristotile, ed alla verità, che lingua alcuna del mondo (sia qual si voglia) non possa aver da se stessa privilegio di sígnificare i concetti del nostro animo; ma tutto consista nello arbitrio delle persone, onde chi vorrà parlar di filosofia con parole Mantovane, o Milanesi, non gli può esser disdetto a ragione.

'I would rather believe Aristotle, and the truth, that no language of the world (whatever it be) can have in itself the privilege of signifying the concepts of our mind; but [that] everything consists in the judgment of individuals, wherefore, if any-one wishes to speak of philosophy with Mantuan or Milanese words, it cannot reasonably be forbidden him [to do so]'.

In general, there were few theorists of language who took such an extreme stand. However, by and large, those favoring the diffusion of knowledge, and particularly that of the Bible, were partisans of a straightforward phonemically or morphophonemically based orthography. A system with descriptively unmotivated etymological spellings (*e.g.* French *doigt* = sixteenth century /dwe^t/ 'finger', or *poids* = sixteenth century /pwe/ 'weight'), or other arbitrary irregularities, tended to be favoured by those who wished to keep literacy as a possession of the learnèd. It is rare to find this latter point of view formulated explicitly, but in the *Dialogue de l'Ortografe*[45] (1555) of Jacques Peletier du Mans (1517–1582), we find one of the discussants, the humanist Théodore de Bèze, stating explicitly (Book I):

Il faut qu'il i ęt quelqué diferancé antré la manieré d'ecriré des g'ans doctés, et des g'ans mecaniqués: Car sęroèt cé reson d'imiter lé vulgueré, léquel sans jugément metra auβi tót un *g* pour un *i*, e un *c* pour un *s*, comme un mot pour un autré: brief, qui né gardéra ni reglé ni gracé an son Ecrituré, non plus qu'an son parler ni an ses fęz? ęt cé ręson qu'un Artisan qui né saura qué liré e ecriré, ancoré assez mal adroęt, e qui n'an antant ni les ręsons ni la congruité, soęt estimé auβi bien ecriré, commé nous qui l'auons par etudé, par reglé, et par excęrcicé? Séra il dit qu'a uné fammé qui n'ęt point autrémant lętreé, nous concedons l'art et vreyé pratiqué de l'Ortografé? S'il sé fęsoèt einsi, il faudroèt diré qué l'Ecrituré gít au plęsir, e non point an eleccion. Il faudroèt diré qu'il sufit d'ecriré dé telé sorté qu'on lé puissé liré. N'ètcé pas le meilheur de garder la majeste d'uné Ecrituré lé plus antierémant qué lon peùt?

'There has to be some difference between the way of writing of learned persons and mechanical[46] folk: For would it be reasonable to imitate the vulgar, who without any judgment will just as soon write a *g* for a *j*, and a *c* for an *s*,[47] as one word for another: in short, who will preserve neither rule nor grace in their writing, any more than in their speech or their actions? Is it right that a hand-worker who will know only how to read and write, and quite clumsily at that, should be thought to write as well as us who have it [*i.e.* knowledge of how to write] through study, through rule, and through practice? Shall it be said that to a woman who is by no means in any other way learnèd, we shall grant the art and true practice of orthography? If it were thus, one would have to say that writing is a matter of whim, not of choice [*i.e.* between right and wrong spelling]. One would have to say that it is enough to write in such a way that it can be read. Is it not best to preserve the majesty of a writing-system as completely as possible?'

On the opposite side, we find a certain number of spelling-reformers, anxious to make orthography conform to contemporary every-day speech. Movements for spelling-reform arose most easily in connection with languages having more phonemes than there were letters available in their alphabets, and where there were marked discrepancies in the fit between grapheme and phoneme.[48] Among the leaders of such movements were Gian Giorgio Trissino (1478–1550) in Italy; in France, Louis Meigret (ca. 1510–1558) and Jacques Peletier from Le Mans; and in England, John Hart (?–1574). Many of the new systems proposed involved the use of existing letters in new functions such as *j* for /ž/ or /ǧ/ and *v* for /v/, to distinguish them from *i* /i/ and *u* /u/; or of extra letters such as Greek ε and ω (Trissino) for open /e/ and /o/ in Italian, and ¢ for /ə/ in French (Peletier) or ẹ for French open /e/ (Peletier, Meigret). The extensive and consistent use of accent-marks in French, Italian, and Spanish orthography also began in the Renaissance, though the present usage was not fully established until the nineteenth century. Of the proposed reforms, those not involving changes in familiar letter-shapes stood the best chance of adoption (the inertia of printers and public being what it was—and still is). The introduction of strange shapes or non-Greek diacritics aroused a great deal of hostility and polemics. It also met with opposition from printers, who did not want to make the extra investment in special types that would be required. The use of *j* and *v* (the so-called *lettres ramistes*, from one of their chief advocates, the philosopher-humanist Pierre de la Ramée [1515–1572]) and of accent-marks eventually won general acceptance. The more radical reforms of excessively consistent systematisers like Trìssino, Meigret, Peletier, and Hart failed to catch on, and have remained historical curiosities.

7.43. LEXICAL INFLUENCE from the Bible-translations and other religious literature of the Reformation depended largely on the extent to which they entered into the every-day life of the speakers of any given language. In general, it was stronger in those areas where Protestantism prevailed, and

in the works of those authors who embraced the reforms. Thus, we find
Agrippa d'Aubigné (1552–1630) using, in his long poem *Les Tragiques*
(1616) such loan-translations from the Hebrew as /dan/ *dan* 'damnation
> judgment', such borrowings as /žəenə/ *gehenne* 'Gehenna > torment',
and a high proportion of Old Testament names like /oreb/ *Oreb* 'Horeb',
/že^de^on/ *Gédéon* 'Gideon', or /madian/ *Madian* 'Midian'.

7.5. Science and Language

The sixteenth century witnessed the beginnings of a new approach to
human knowledge of the world we live in. This approach, usually termed
"scientific," involves principally the adoption of an objective view-point,
with dependence on observation and (as far as possible) experimental veri-
fication rather than on aprioristic, untestable dogmas as a basis for study
(cf. §11.0). This new approach had certain implications for linguistic matters, affecting the choice, not only of new terms, but also of the language to
be used in making discoveries known.

7.51. Monopoly versus Diffusion of Knowledge. As long as the
vernaculars were used primarily for bellettristic purposes, their acceptance
was only a matter of social and intellectual prestige (cf. §6.1). Nor was it
a matter of concern to professional men whether merchants kept their records in one language or another. However, when professional secrets might
be revealed by the use of a tongue comprehensible to any "man in the
street," it was a different matter. Priests, lawyers, and doctors all had
specialised knowledge, which many of them did not wish to have made
generally accessible. They had a common language, Latin, which served
them very well for professional cryptolalia. To expound trade-secrets in
the vernacular was to betray one's cause and one's fellow-practitioners.
Consequently, during the sixteenth century, various ordinances were
passed against the writing of medical or legal treatises in any language except Latin. The great sixteenth-century French surgeon, Ambroise Paré
(ca. 1510–1590) was strongly criticised for publishing his works in French,
and was brought to court by his fellow-doctors for doing so.

7.52. Lexical Innovations. With scientific discoveries and their practical
applications, there always comes a need for new words to refer to them.
During the Middle Ages, Arabic (§5.3) had been a major source for scientific
terminology. In the Renaissance, and ever since then, Greek and Latin
have, as already pointed out (§7.322), served as an almost inexhaustible

reservoir for both complete words and elements which can be combined in new-formations. Among the derivational elements most widely adopted were such prefixes as *a-* (negative) < Gk. /a-/ *'α-*, *e-* or *ex-* 'out' < Lat. /e:- eks-/ *ē- ex-*, *pre-* 'before' < Lat. /prai-/ *prae-*, *post-* 'after' < Lat. /post/ *post*, etc., and such suffixes as Fr. /⁺emə/ *-ème*, Sp., It. /⁺éme/ *-ema* < Gk. /⁺e:ma/ *-ήμα*; Fr. /⁺ablə ⁺iblə/ and Sp. /⁺áble ⁺íble/, both spelled *-able -ible*, and It. /⁺ábile ⁺íbile/ *-abile -ibile* < Lat. /⁺a:bile ⁺ibile/ *-ābile -ibile*; and Fr. /⁺ikə/ *-ique*, It. and Sp. /⁺ɨiko/ *-ico* < Lat. /⁺ikus/ *-icus*. These and similar elements have continued in ever-expanding use down to the present.

7.6. The Expansion of Romance

At no time since the break-up of the Roman Empire had the extent of Romance-speaking territory been really static. During and after that troubled period, it was primarily shrinking, with the disappearance of Latin as an official language and of the earliest popular Romance speech from such areas as North Africa, the northern part of the Balkans, southern Germany and Switzerland, and Britain; and with the superposition of Arabic as official language in most of the Iberian peninsula and (for a time) in Sicily. The first major extension of Romance began with its introduction into England in the form of Anglo-Norman (§2.55) as the native language of the rulers and as an official language for all others, after the Norman Conquest in 1066. Anglo-Norman was, however, relatively short-lived, and by 1400 at the latest it was no longer the native language of any considerable element of the English population.

A far greater extension of Romance began with what has been termed "the expansion of Europe" in the fifteenth, sixteenth, and later centuries.[49] Accidents of history and geography made the two major Ibero-Romance languages, Spanish and Portuguese, the ones to be carried most widely to the new colonies, in the wake of the *conquistadores*. Portuguese was also carried far along the coast of West Africa, especially in connection with the slave-trade.[50] French did not begin to spread similarly until the seventeenth century, with the settlements in Canada and the Mississippi Valley. Apart from minor instances (*e.g.* the foundation of the Catalan colony in Alghero in 1355), the other Romance languages were not greatly involved in the process of colonisation until the nineteenth century. When the ban on emigration from Italy was lifted in 1860, large numbers of speakers of Italian (mostly peasants from southern Italy and Sicily) settled in the United States and Canada, and in the temperate areas of South America (southern Brazil, Uruguay, and Argentina, especially the River Plate region). During Italy's rule over Libya, Tripolitania, and Ethiopia in the early twentieth century, Italian was an official language in those regions, but no large permanent groups of native speakers of Italian were established there.

7.61. SOURCES OF DIALECTAL DIFFERENTIATION. Not infrequently, the speech of colonised areas shows a relatively close resemblance to that of some particular region in the home-land. Thus, Australian English has certain features (notably /aj/ < /ej/, as in /ðədájlijmájl/ *the Daily Mail*) in common with lower-class London English, for which reason it is often (erroneously) described as "pure Cockney." Similarly, virtually all varieties of American Spanish share *seseo* (/s/ instead of /θ/ < OSp. /¢/) and *yeismo* (/l̢/ > /j/ or further developments thereof) with south Spanish dialects, particularly Andalusian. Furthermore, the Spanish of the circum-Caribbean low-lands, of the River Plate region, and of Chile, has in common with Andalusian the development of syllable-final /s/ to /x/ or /h/, as in /éhte/ 'this' ∼ Castilian /éste/ *este*. After extensive debate pro and con,[51] these features can definitely be regarded as of Andalusian origin, since the settlement-history of the sixteenth and later centuries shows that a predominant portion of the population, particularly of the women, came from Andalusia. Seville thus played the same rôle in channelling emigration and in exerting a major influence on over-seas dialectal development as did Canton on that of emigrant Chinese, or Naples on Italian in the Americas.[52]

7.62. PIDGINS AND CREOLES. Whether the mediaeval Lingua Franca of the eastern Mediterranean (§§2.4, 2.52) was directly continued in the pidgin of the same name used along the northern coast of Africa (Tunisia, Algeria, Morocco) in the sixteenth century, is an open question, as is the direct continuation of this in the Pidgin Portuguese that arose in connection with the West African slave-trade.[53] From the sixteenth century onwards, a large number of pidgins arose in the Europeans' dealing with the native populations in the newly colonised regions, by a process of stimulus-diffusion.[54] The wide-spread notion among Europeans that the only way to speak to "primitive" peoples was to simplify one's native tongue by such devices as using only infinitives for verbs and making no variations in the form of nouns and adjectives; the natives' attempts at reproducing what they had heard from Europeans; the Europeans' amused or contemptuous reproduction of the "nytives'" efforts; and the latter group's taking this seriously—all of these factors were involved. A pidgin is thus the result of the freezing of the language-learning-process at an early stage. Further developments take place on the basis of analogical extension of the reduced patterns that have been taken into the initial pidgin.[55]

Of the early pidgins, some were certainly based on Portuguese and others on Spanish. By and large, those of Portuguese origin have survived longer, together with the Portuguese colonial régimes themselves, than have those of Spanish origin (cf. §§2.41, 2.42). Pidgins of both Spanish and Portuguese origin became creolised in a number of regions, surviving particularly in the Papiamentu of Curaçao, Aruba, and Bonaire,[56] and in the Creole Portuguese of Cabo Verde, Guiné, and other regions in Africa.[57] It is not possible to assign specific dates for the creolisation of these pidgins, except to say that, in general, it probably occurred within two or three generations after the pidgins themselves began to be used in settled, permanent communities (chiefly plantations) where pidgin-users of more than one linguistic back-ground were brought together, mated, and had children.

French was a late starter in the pidgin- and creole-language-field, as in that of colonisation. It is a matter of debate whether the various French-based pidgins and creoles of the New World and the Mascareignes go back to a single Proto-Pidgin-French used in the West African slave-trade,[58] or had their origin in the separate regions settled by French-speaking plantation-owners.[59] The two theses are not incompatible. It is possible that a rudimentary type of Pidgin French may have begun in Africa and been carried by some slave-traders and some of their victims, and then picked up and developed further by others in the New World—including native speakers of French who knew, by stimulus-diffusion (cf. above), how one was expected to reduce one's language in talking to underlings.

Many Caribbean colonies changed hands a number of times in the seventeenth and eighteenth centuries, in the reshuffling of possessions that went on over the conference-tables at each major European peace-settlement. Consequently, the official languages of the colonies often changed each time there was a new European overlordship, so that the local creoles underwent varying lexical influences. In the French Antilles, for example, where France kept its colonies or remained as the chief cultural model (*e.g.* in Haiti), French has been the dominant source for lexical expansion, as shown by such words as HC /kõtribisjõ/ 'contribution = tax', /mwajen/ 'average', /vwajaž/ 'trip', /ofisiel/ 'official', /ofisielmã/ 'officially', /miltipliê/ 'multiply', /deꞈkuražeꞈ/ 'discourage', /brileꞈ/ 'burn', /tradwi/ 'translate' and a host of others. In other languages, however, such as Papiamentu, the dominant lexical influence in later centuries has come from a non-Romance language, in this case Dutch, *e.g.* /ferwónder/ 'astonish', /dóbel/ 'double', /brúg/ 'bridge', /kérki/ 'church', /dánki/ 'thank you'.

7.63. CONTACTS WITH NATIVE LANGUAGES. The Romance languages carried to new areas, particularly but not exclusively the Americas, exerted (as might be expected) a degree of lexical influence ranging from mild to very strong. The variation in influence depended on several factors: intensity of contact, structural characteristics of the native language involved, and attitudes of the local population (receptivity or hostility to outside influences). The Malayo-Polynesian languages of the Philippines, for instance, have a large number of Spanish loans: in Maranao, we find[60] /orador/ 'orator, spokesman' (< Sp. /oradór/ 'orator'), /oras/ 'hour, time, clock, watch' (< Sp. /óras/ *horas* 'hours'), /opirasion/ 'operation' (< Sp. /operasión/ *operación*), etc. The extreme in receptivity is found in Chamorro, the Malayo-Polynesian language of Guam, where well over 95 per cent of the lexicon is said to be of Spanish origin,[61] even to the numerals. In the Americas, certain words (*e.g.* Sp. /kabáļo/ or /kabájo/ *caballo* 'horse') were taken over early and spread very widely[62]; other words are more scattering in their distribution, but there are borrowings from Spanish in virtually every Amerindian tongue in regions where Spanish was or is the official language.[63] Certain words spread quite far, *e.g.* Spanish /mantéka/ *manteca* 'lard' > Eskimo /mantekaq/ (probably through Filipino laborers in canning-factories in Alaska)[64]; and French /(la)sup/ (*la*) *soupe* 'soup' and /bujabes/ *bouillabaisse* to Algonquian *nasaump* and *napōpi*, respectively.[65]

In some instances, loans from Spanish or Portuguese in native languages preserve features or contrasts which were present at the time of borrowing but have disappeared from the source-language since then, such as the /b/ ~ /v/ contrast shown in Araucanian /kapra/ 'goat' < sixteenth-century Sp. /kábra/ *cabra* vs. /jawi/ 'key' < /jáve/ < /ļáve/ *llave*. However, that (at least for some speakers) the merger of /b/ and /v/ had already taken place or else overlaid the earlier distinction, is shown in Amerindian words from Sp. /kabájo/ *caballo* 'horse', in which the native languages show uniformly /w/ or other developments from [β], not [b].[66]

There were, of course, lexical influences in the opposite direction as well. Spanish, Portuguese, and French borrowed words from the local tongues to refer to fauna, flora, artifacts, and customs which were new to Europeans. Many of these words spread throughout the European languages,[67] normally through the initial mediation of the Romance variety used by the colonisers of the region in which the source-language was spoken. Central American and Caribbean languages have furnished, through Spanish,[68] /maís/ *maís* 'corn', /batáta/ *batata* '(sweet) potato', /tomáte/ *tomate* 'tomato', /čokoláte/ *chocolate*, /kasíke/ *cacique* 'Indian chief > political boss), and a great many others. From South American Indian languages have come, *e.g.* /pámpa/ *pampa* 'prairie', /činčíļa/ *chinchilla*, /gáučo/ *gaucho* 'cow-boy', /púma/ *puma*, etc. A few words entered from Malayo-Polynesian, *e.g.* Sp. /práo/ *prao* 'a kind of Oriental canoe'.[67] In addition to words of this type, there were a great many local borrowings which have remained restricted to the individual languages (especially from the Tupí-Guaraní of South America in Portuguese and River Plate Spanish, and from Quechua in Spanish, *e.g.* /máte/ *mate* 'Paraguayan tea'), and even to specific regions.[70] Surprisingly, despite the intensive contacts between French voyageurs and settlers and Algonquian or Iroquoian Indians in Canada, virtually no words have come into French from Amerindian sources, except through eighteenth- or nineteenth-century English (*e.g.* *moccasin, squaw, wigwam; scalper* 'to scalp').

7.7. Inter-Romance Borrowings

Within Europe, also, cultural interchange was increasing during the fifteenth and sixteenth centuries, both among the speech-communities of Romance stock and between these and speakers of non-Romance languages. The resultant linguistic influences (mostly, but not wholly lexical) were due in part to upper-level contacts between cultured and learnèd persons— often in the form of correspondence or the reading of books—and in part to homely, lower-level intercourse between travellers, sailors, or soldiers in invading armies, and the local populations, in one region or another. The latter type of influence is often detectable through phonological or semantic features.

7.71. LEXICAL BORROWINGS. In the late fifteenth and early sixteenth centuries, the chief source of inter-Romance borrowings was Italy, from which loan-words spread out on both the intellectual level (due to the strong pan-European influence of Italian-based classicism and humanism; cf. §7.2) and that of more earthy activities (since Italy was a major battle-field between French and Imperial forces in the first half of the sixteenth century). In the latter half of this century, however, Spain replaced Italy as the chief focus of diffusion of Romance borrowings, because of its new political and economic strength derived from its colonies in the Americas and elsewhere.

7.711. ITALIAN INFLUENCE was, naturally, exerted in those fields in which Italy was predominant,[71] and through such channels as the following:
   1. Learnèd activity, in areas like:
   a. The fine arts, with such words as /faččáta/ *facciata* 'face (of a building)' > Fr. /fasadə/ *façade*, Sp. /fačáda/ *fachada*; /piedestállo/ *piedestallo* 'pedestal' > Fr. /pie^destal/ *piedestal*, Sp. /pedestál/ *pedestal*; /balkó^ne/ *balcone* 'big beam > balcony' > Fr. /balkon/ *balcon*, Sp.

/balkón/ *balcón*; /grotté^sko/ *grottesco* 'grotto-like, unbalanced, mis-shapen' > Fr. /groteskə/ *grotesque*, Sp. /grotésko/ *grotesco*.

    b. Literature, as with /soné^tto/ *sonetto* 'sonnet' > Fr. /sonet/ *sonnet*, Sp. /sonéto/ *soneto*; /makkeróniko/ *maccheronico* 'macaronic' (cf. §7.322) > Fr. /makaronikə/ *macaronique*, Sp. /makaróniko/ *macarónico*; /pedánte/ *pedante* 'pedant' > Fr. /pe^dan^t/ *pédant*, Sp. /pedánte/ *pedante*; /makiavélliko/ *machiavellico* 'Machiavellian' > Fr. /makiave^likə/ *machiavélique*, Sp. /makiabéliko/ *maquiavélico*.

    c. Music, *e.g.* in /fúga/ *fuga* 'flight > fugue' > Fr. /fygə/ *fugue*, Sp. /fúga/ *fuga*; /madrigále/ *madrigale* 'Madrigal' > Fr. /madrigal/ and Sp. /madrigál/, both *madrigal*; /pavána/ *pavana* 'Paduan dance' > Sp. /pabána/ *pavana* > Fr. /pavanə/ *pavane*.⁷²

    2. Courtly life, in matters pertaining to:

    a. Function and position, *e.g.* /kortiğáno/ *cortigiano* 'of, pertaining to the court; courtier; courtesan,⁷³ > Fr. /kurtisan/ *courtisan*, Sp. /korte-sán/ *cortesán*.

    b. Elegance: *e.g.* /profúmo/ *profumo* 'perfume' > Fr. /parfyᵐ/ *parfum*, Sp. /perfúme/ *perfume* (with related verbs in /-áre/ etc.); /pomáta/ *pomata* 'pomade' > Fr. /pomadə/ *pomade*.

    3. Commerce and finance, *e.g.* in /bánka/ *banca* 'bench > bank' > Fr. /bankə/ *banque*, Sp. /bánka °o/ *banca -o*; /taríffa/ *tariffa* 'tariff' > Fr. /tarif/ *tarif*, Sp. /tarifa/ *tarifa*.

    4. Military activities, with regard to:

    a. Ranks and groups, such as /soldáto/ *soldato* 'paid fighter, merce-nary > soldier' > Fr. /solda^t/ *soldat*, Sp. /soldádo/ *soldado*; /kaporále/ *caporale* 'head-man, corporal' > Fr. /kaporal/, Sp. /kaporál/, both *caporal*; /kolonnéllo/ *colonnello* 'officer in charge of a column, colonel' > Fr. /kolonel/ *colonel*, Sp. /koronél/ *coronel*⁷⁴; /(in)fantería/ *(in)fanteria* 'infantry' > Fr. /anfantəriə/ *enfanterie*, later reshaped to /infantəriə/ *infanterie*, and Sp. /infantería/ *infantería*; /battaḷḷó^ne/ *battaglione* 'big battle > battalion' > Fr. /bataḷon/ *battalion*, Sp. /bataḷon/ *batallón*.

    b. Functions and activities, like /sentinélla/ *sentinella* 'guard, senti-nel' > Fr. /sentinel/ *sentinel*, Sp. /sentinéla/ sentinela (later reshaped to /ɵentinéla/ *centinela*; /imboskáta/ *imboscata* 'ambush (lit. en-woods-ment)' > Fr. /ambyskadə/ *embuscade*, Sp. /emboskáda/ *emboscada*.

    c. Technological innovations, such as /parapétto/ *parapetto* 'chest-protection, parapet' > Fr. /parape^t/ *parapet*, Sp. /parapéto/ *parapeto*; /kâsamátta/ 'movable house, gun-shelter > casemate' > Fr. /kazəmatə/ *casemate*, Sp. /kasamáta/ *casamata*.⁷⁵

    5. Nautical terminology, as in /bússola/ *bussola* 'compass' > Fr. /busolə/ *boussole*, Sp. /brúšula/ *brúxula* (with /-r-/ probably under the influence of /brúšo/ *bruxo* 'wizard'); /tramontána/ *tramontana* 'north wind' > Fr. /tramontanə/ *tramontane*, Sp. /tramontána/ *tramontana*.

6. Miscellaneous fields, such as:

a. The Commedia dell'Arte, in the names of various 'masks' or stock characters, such as the 'zany', Ven. /ʒáni/ 'Johnny' > It. /ʒánni/ *Zanni* and Fr. /zani/ *Zani*, or 'Pantaloon', It. /pantaló^ne/ *Pantalone* > Fr. /pantalon/ *Pantalon*.

b. Foods, such as the by now ubiquitous /makkeró^ni/ *maccheroni* > Fr. /makarons/ *macarons* (later Italianised to /makaroni/ *macaroni*), Sp. /makarónes/ *macarones*; NIt. /artičóko/ 'artichoke' (≠ standard It. /karčófo/ *carciofo*) > Fr. /artičoᵗ/ *artichaut*; or such kinds of sausage as /červelláta/ *cervellata* 'brain-sausage' > Fr. /servəlaᵗ/ *servelat* and /mortadélla/ *mortadella* > 'a kind of sausage' Fr. /mortadelə/ *mortadelle*.

c. Low life, with words referring to inelegant activities such as 'getting infatuated', It. /amoraččare/ *amoracciare* (: amoráččo/ *amoraccio* 'bad, unworthy love') > Fr. /amuraše^r/ *amouracher*, or to dishonest types of people, such as the 'charlatan', It. /čarlatáno/ *ciarlatano* 'fair-barker, trickster'[76] > Fr. /šarlatan/ *charlatan*, Sp. /čarlatán/ *charlatán*, or the 'lout'. It. /fakkíno/ *facchino* 'porter' > Fr. /fakin/ *faquin*, Sp. /fakín/ *faquín*. The Italian insult /koḷḷo^ne/ *coglione,* "testicle > fool', in its NIt. form /kojón/, gave Fr. /koion/ *coīon* (alongside of /kuḷon/ *couillon* 'testicle').

7.712. FRENCH INFLUENCE, during the Renaissance, was stronger in Italy than in Spain.

1. In Italy, French borrowings were evident mainly in the fields of military activities (especially certain French technological innovations) and court-life, the two fields where Italians had the most to learn from Frenchmen:

a. Military terms include Fr. /artiḷəriə/ *artillerie* 'artillery' > It. /artiḷḷería/ *artiglieria*; /approšə/ *approche* 'approach-trench' > /appróččo/ *approccio*; /pe^tardə/ *pétarde* 'petard' > /petárdo/ *petardo*; /trenšeə/ *trenchee* 'trench' > /trinčéa/ *trincea*; and /marše^/ *marcher* 'to march' > /marčáre/ *marciare*. A 'slaughter', Fr. /masakrə/ *massacre*, was Italianised as /massákro/ *massacro*.

b. Various items of clothing, of the elegant type used by courtiers, were borrowed with their names: e.g. Fr. /šapəron/ *chaperon* 'a kind of cape' > It. /čapperó^ne/ *ciapperone*. The 'livery' worn by servants, Fr. /livreə/ *livrée* > It. /livréa/ *livrea*; the edge or 'fringe' of a garment, Fr. /franžə/ *frange* > It. /franǧa/ *frangia*. For elegant dressing itself, the French verb /abiḷeʳ/ *habiller* 'to dress' was borrowed into Italian as /abbiḷḷáre/ *abbigliare*.

c. A few names of wines and the likes were borrowed, such as /klareᵗ/ *claret* > It. /klaré^tto/ *claretto*.

2. In Spain, French influence was relatively slight, with a few borrow-

ings, some from the same sources as mentioned above for French loans in
Italian (*e.g.* /trinčéa/ *trinchea* 'trench', /marčár/ *marchar* 'to march'),
and a scattering of others, such as /gaḷardo/ *gallardo* 'brave, upstanding'
< Fr. /gaḷart/ *gaillard* or Prov. /gaḷárt/ *galhart*, and /rindibú/ *rindibú*
'rendezvous' < Fr. /rende^vu/ *rendezvous* (It. /rendevósse/ *rendevosse* in
the seventeenth century).

7.713. IBERIAN INFLUENCE (mostly from Spanish) was strongest in the
latter part of the century, when to a considerable extent Spanish ways replaced French as a model for aristocratic behaviour. Due to the presence and
hegemony of Spain in Italy, especially after the treaty of Câteau-Cambrésis
(1559), Spanish influence was much stronger in Italy than in France. In
both countries, however, it reached its peak in the following century.

1. Italian Hispanisms in the late fifteenth and in the sixteenth centuries[77]
are connected with such semantic fields as:

a. Courtly life, including new standards of behaviour: Sp. /kreánᶜa/
creanza 'upbringing' > It. /kreánᶜa/ *creanza*; Sp. /puntílo/ *puntillo* 'point
of honor, punctilio' > It. /puntíḷḷo/ *puntiglio*; Sp. /sosiégo/ *sosiego* 'calm
> haughty behaviour' > It. /sussiégo/ *sussiego*. The quarters of a nobleman
were referred to in Spanish as his /apartamiénto/ *apartamiento* 'apartment'
> It. /appartaménto/ *appartamento*.

b. Soldiers' life: /kamaráda/ *camarada* 'group of men living in the
same room; comrade' > It. /kameráta/ *camerata*. The boastful soldier
might be called in Spanish a /fanfarrón/ *fanfarrón* > It. /fanfarró^ne/
fanfarrone.

c. Inelegant terms included cuss-words like /marráno/ *marrano*
'renegade convert from Judaism' > It. /marráno/ *marrano* 'scoundrel'.[78]

2. French Hispanisms were even fewer, including such words as /kama-
radə/ *camarade* 'comrade' and /fanfarron/ *fanfarron* 'boaster' (from the
etyma mentioned above); /matamorə/ *matamore* 'swaggering soldier' <
/matamóros/ *matamoros* 'Moor-killer'; and /musə/ *mousse* 'cabin-boy' <
/móᶜo/ *mozo*.

7.72. STRUCTURAL INFLUENCES were slight, but a few were present:

1. A new consonant-cluster was introduced from Italian into French
in /sbírro/ ['zbir-ro] *sbirro* > Fr. /zbirə/ *sbirre*, the name for the hated
soldier of the petty tyrant.

2. Morphological imitation of Italian in French is perhaps to be seen in
Brantôme's use of the preterite third-person plural of the first conjugation
in /-arət/ *-arent* instead of the normal /-erət/ *-erent*.[79]

3. Syntactic imitation of Spanish in Italian is found in certain phenom-

ena:

a. The use of third-person verbal forms to refer to the person spoken to, with the corresponding use of the third-person feminine pronoun[80] as substitute for /vóstrasiṇṇoría/ *Vostra Signoria* 'Your Lordship', /vóstra-alté^ȼȼa/ *Vostra Altezza* 'Your Highness' and the like, *i.e.* the use of /é^lla/ *ella* 'she' and /léi/ *lei* 'her', and of the corresponding unstressed pronoun-forms /la/ *la* 'her (acc.)' and /le/ *le* 'to her (dat.)' in direct address with third-person agreement, in imitation of the Spanish formal mode of address with /ustéd/ *usted*.[81]

b. Scattering syntactic combinations such as /loke/ *lo che* 'that which', imitating the same sequence in Spanish, /loke/ *lo que*; or the definite article /la/ *la* as a pronoun, as in /lavítadiğesúkkrísto elládimaríavé^rğine/ *la vita di Gesù Cristo e la di Maria Vergine* (Pietro Aretino), also imitating a similar Spanish construction.

7.8. Non-Romance Influences

Non-Romance influences came mostly from German and Dutch, rather less from more easterly languages.

7.81. GERMAN borrowings came to a considerable extent from the contacts of Romance speakers with German soldiers, as in /ráiter/ *Reiter* 'horseman, cavalryman [: Eng. *rider*]' > Fr. /reitrə/ *reître*, It. /ráitro/ *raitro*; /lántsknèxt/ *Landsknecht* 'mercenary soldier' > It. /lanȼikenékko/ *lanzichenecco*,[82] Fr. /lanskənet/ *lansquenet*; /bríṇdírs/ *bring dir's* '(I) bring it to you' > It. /bríndisi/ *brindisi* 'toast (in drinking)', Fr. /brində/ *brinde*, Sp. /bríndis/ *brindis* (whence the verb /brindár/ *brindar* 'to toast'). The older Keltic term for 'beer' (ONFr. /ȼervó^izə/ *cervoise* > OIt. /červó^ğa/ *cervogia*) was replaced in French and Italian by /bierə/ *bière* and /bir(r)a/ *bir(r)a*, respectively, from Ger. /bí:r/ *Bier*. The German institution of the burgomaster, Ger. /búrgmàister/ *Burgmeister*, was referred to in French as /burgmestrə/ *bourgmestre*, in Italian as /bòrgomástro/ *borgomastro*. The Swiss Protestants, who had formed an alliance as /áitgenòssen/ *Eidgenossen* 'oath-companions', were called in French /ygənot/ *Huguenot*, whence Italian /ugonótto/ *Ugonotto*.

7.82. DUTCH words were of the type of /kérkmèsse/ *Kerkmesse* 'fair' > Fr. /kermesə/ *kermesse*, It. /karaméssa/ *caramessa*; /spríṇstòk/ *springstock* 'a kind of pike-like weapon' > Fr. /brindəstok/ *brindestoc* > It. /bràndi-stókko/ *brandistocco* (seventeenth century); /máttegenò:t/ *mattegenoot* 'mat-fellow' > Fr. /matənot/ *matenot*, later /matelot/ *matelot* 'sailor'.

7.83. EASTERN borrowings,[83] referring mostly to innovations of Oriental or East European origin, from such languages as:
1. Greek, in It. /mustákkio/ *mustacchio*, Fr. /mustašə/ *moustache* < /mustáki/ μουστάκι.[84]
2. Hungarian, in It. /kókkio/ *cocchio* 'coach', Fr. /košə/ *coche* (> Sp. /kóče/ *coche*) < /koči/ *kocsi*.
3. Turkish, as in It., Sp. /turbánte/ *turbante* 'turban' < /tylbent/ *tülbent*; It. /sorbé^tto/ *sorbetto* 'sherbet', Fr. /sorbeᵗ/ *sorbet*, Sp. /sorbéte/ *sorbete* (seventeenth century) < /šerbet/ < Ar. /šarba:t/, pl. of /šarba/ 'drink'.

7.9. Romance Influence on Non-Romance Languages

English and the languages of northern, eastern and south-eastern Europe came into increased contact with France, Italy, and Spain during the Renaissance. The resultant borrowings came mainly—as might be expected—through contacts with the countries which were geographically nearest, and in some instances through direct experiences of learnèd men, soldiers, and travellers, particularly in Italy.

7.91. ITALIAN[85] had its most extensive sphere of influence in the Adriatic, the Balkans, and the Near East, chiefly through Venetian.[86] For instance, Greek borrowings of this period include such words as /kantína/ καντίνα 'basement', /sofíto/ σοφίτο 'attic', /vázo/ βάζο 'vase', /sardéla/ σαρδέλα 'sardine', /artelaría/ ἀρτελαρία 'artillery', /tramontána/ τραμοντάνα 'tramontane (wind)'. Italian loans in the German of that time[87] include /kapúʒe/ *Kapuze* 'hood' < /kappúčo/ *cappuccio*, NIt. /kapúʒo/ *capuzo*; /makaró:nen/ *Makaronen* 'macaroni' < /makkeró^ni/ *maccheroni*; /kássa/ *Kassa* 'cash-box, cashier's office' < /kássa/ *cassa* 'strong-box'; /rísiko/ *Risiko* 'risk' < /rísiko/ *risico*; /sáldo/ *Saldo* 'balance (left over)' < /sáldo/ *saldo* 'solid'. English received many words from Italian during the Renaissance,[88] some through direct contacts (*e.g. capricio* 'caprice' < /kapríčo/ *capriccio* 'goat-like jump', *grotto* < /gró^tto/ *grotto*, *portico* < /pórtiko/ *portico*, *violin* < /víolíno/ *violino* 'little viol') and others through the intermediary of French (*e.g. ambuscade, mustache, battalion, grotesque*; cf. §7.711). In instances, words of clearly Italian origin entered various European languages through different channels, as in the case of the terms for 'orange'[89]; standard Italian /pomaránča/ *pomarancia* gave Ger. /pomaránʒe/ *Pomeranze* and Polish /pomaranča/ *pomarancza*, whereas Hungarian /naranč/ *narancs* and Greek /naránʒa/ ναράντζα are from Ven. /naránʒa/ *naranza*.

7.92. FRENCH had considerable lexical influence on Renaissance English,[90] in such words as *entrance, equip, essay, genteel, progress,* and many others; and on German,[91] in commercial terms like /akít/ *Acquit* 'receipt' < /akit/ *acquit* 'acquitted', /falíːren/ *fallieren* 'default, go bankrupt' < /falwer/ *falloir* 'fail', or /returníːren/ *retournieren* 'return' < /rəturneˆ/ *retourner.* There were also a number of French loans in Dutch.[92] Among these we find such words as *pistolet* 'pistol', *inkorrekt* 'incorrect', /likíde/ *liquide,* and /depešeːren/ *depescheren* 'to despatch'.

7.93. SPANISH exerted a direct influence, outside of the Romance field, chiefly on English,[93] with a large number of words, many of them referring to phenomena with which the English first came into contact through Spanish-speaking channels, *e.g. alligator* < /ellagárto/ *el lagarto* 'the lizard', *hurricane* < /urakán/ *huracán, mosquito* < /moskito *mosquito* 'little fly', *maize* < /maís/ *maís, Negro* < /négro/ *negro* 'black',[94] *mulatto* < /muláto/ *mulato, sombrero* < /sombréro/ *sombrero* 'shade-giver'. In some instances Elizabethan English changed the endings, as in *armado* ≠ Sp. /armáda/ *armada* (and in a number of other words with *-ado* representing Sp. /⁺ada/ *-ada*), or adapted the forms to English phonology, as in /pǽvən/ *pavan* < Sp. /pabána/ *pavana* (< It. /pavána/ *pavana,* cf. §7.711.1.*c*).

NOTES TO CHAPTER 7

1. On Roumanian, however, there was very little Latin influence during the Middle Ages, due to lack of contact with the West. Influence from Slavic (cf. §5.21) and Greek (cf. Mihăescu 1966a) was much stronger.
2. Cf. most recently the debates between Nelson (1966) and Hilty (1966), and between Lüdtke (1962/63, 1965/66) and Hall (1965/66b).
3. *E.g.* Ford 1906:77–98.
4. Cf. Elcock 1938.
5. Cf. Entwistle 1936:123.
6. Based on a Latin translation, from the Arabic, from the Greek. Only later, in the fifteenth and sixteenth centuries, did Greek itself become sufficiently accessible to western European scholars for direct translations to be made.
7. For the thirteenth- and fourteenth-century Italian translators, cf. Maggini 1952.
8. For any given word, our dating of its first occurrence (*e.g.* in the Alfonsine works) is of necessity tentative, because it is always possible that an earlier occurrence may turn up. One of the minor, but interesting, activities of word-historians is the "back-dating" of the earliest attestations of lexical items.
9. In Italian, whose phonology is, as we have seen (§6.315), quite close to that of Late Latin, it is possible to set up a system of regular correspondences into which almost all Latinisms fit; cf. Hall 1971:405–408.
10. For the spread of French in Italy in the Middle Ages, cf. P. Meyer 1904; in English, Mackenzie 1939. A detailed study of reciprocal lexical influences between French and Italian: Hope 1971.

11. On Martino da Canale, cf. Catel 1938–40.

12. Marco Polo and Rusticiano were cell-mates in a Genoese prison in 1298, both having been captured by the Genoese. Marco Polo dictated the account of his travels to Rusticiano (presumably in Venetian), and the latter put it down, not in his native Tuscan, but in French.

13. For Franco-Venetian in general, cf. Pellegrini 1956; Ruggieri 1961a, 1961b. Editions of some individual texts are listed in Hall 1958a: §§5078–5084.

14. For Old French influence on Old Spanish, cf. De Forest 1916, and Berns 1964; on Old Italian, cf. P. Meyer 1904; Bezzola 1924.

15. That It. /ğó^rno/ giorno is a very early Gallicism, as against the indigenous /dí^x/ di (< PRom. /dí^e/), has been recognised for a long time (cf. Ringenson 1936); there have been, nevertheless, some excessive and unnecessary polemics on this point, e.g. Bonfante 1944 (cf. Hall 1946b).

16. Cf. Hope 1971:1.66–147.

17. Cf. Maggini 1952:54–64.

18. Cf. Hope 1971:1.27–66.

19. The ducat (first minted 1284) had the effigy of a duke on it; the florin (1252) derived its name from the flower (/fió^re/ fiore) of the lily which symbolised Florence; and the carlino (1278) was named for Charles I (/kárlo/ Carlo) of Anjou, king of Naples (1226–1283).

20. By such authors as Burckhardt 1860 (Part III, "The Revival of Antiquity") and Symonds 1875–86 (Book II, "The Revival of Learning"), from whom the concept has passed into general currency.

21. The trivium consisted of grammar, rhetoric, and logic; the quadrivium, of arithmetic, music, geometry, and astronomy.

22. The establishment of accurate texts led to the study of Latin style, as in the Elegantiae linguae latīnae 'Fine Points of the Latin Language' (1444) of Lorenzo Valla (1407–1457). This, in its turn, occasionally had unexpected results, e.g. Valla's demonstration (in his Dē falsō crēditā et ēmentītā Constantīnī dōnātiōne 'On the Falsely Believed and Forged Donation of Constantine', 1440) that the so-called "Donations of Constantine," on which the Papacy had based its claim to temporal sovereignty, was a mediaeval forgery. This was the first instance of the application of scientific principles to the philological examination of historical documents.

23. In the sixteenth century, a number of writers known as polygraphs met the growing demand for printed reading-matter by providing the public with books on all manner of subjects, both literary and practical, in a popularising vein. Among these men were the Italians Pietro Aretino (1492–1556), Niccolò Franco (1515–1570), and several who contributed to the debates on the language-question (cf. §7.321), including Giròlamo Ruscelli (1500–1566), Lodovico Dolce (1508–1568), and Anton Francesco Doni (1513–1574).

24. One unfortunate scholar, the Belgian Christophorus Longolius (1488–1522), worked so hard at becoming an "ape of Cicero" that he went into a decline and died.

25. Montaigne was actually a native speaker of Latin. He tells (Essais 1.26) how his parents had him brought up by a tutor who spoke Latin to him in his earliest years, and even insisted that the servants learn and use Latin with him. From his description, it is clear that they pidginised it to a certain extent; he says:

> C'estoit une regle inviolable que ny luy mesme, ny ma mere, ny valet, ny chambriere, ne parloyent en ma compaignie qu'autant de mots de Latin que chacun avoit appris pour jargonner avec moy.

It was an unbreakable rule that neither he himself [M's father], nor my mother, nor any servant or chamber-maid, spoke in my company anything but as many Latin words as each had learned in order to yabber with me.'

26. For the relation of Latin and Italian in the Renaissance, cf. Klein 1957; Grayson 1960; R. Fubini 1961. Italian humanists and the vernacular: Dionisotti 1968. On Spanish theories of the relation of Latin to Spanish, and the "defense of the language" in the sixteenth century, cf. Romera Navarro 1929; Pastor 1929; Meier 1935; Bahner 1956; García Blanco 1967. In France: Gerighausen 1963.

27. Cf. Vivaldi 1894–98; Labande-Jeanroy 1925; Hall 1942a; Migliorini 1949; Faithfull 1953; Sozzi 1955; Vitale 1960; Façon 1962a.

28. Cf. Hall 1942a, chapter 5.

29. The Ordinance of Villers-Cotterets (1539) provide that edicts and court-procedures should be *prononcez, enregistrez et deliurez aux parties en langaige maternel françois* 'pronounced, registered, and delivered to the parties in the French mother-tongue'. Most historians of French agree that this meant standard French, not the local dialects. In Spain, Castilian had been used officially since the time of Alfonso the Wise (cf. §6.313).

For discussions of sixteenth-century French, cf. Gougenheim 1951; Rickard 1968.

30. For du Bellay, François Villon, who had lived less than a century previously, was "Old French" in his language.

Du Bellay, incidentally, was by no means consistent in living up to the program he had set forth in the *Deffense et Illustration*; cf. Keating 1971/72.

31. *E.g.* for French, Nyrop 1899–1930:1.45–52; Cohen 1947:169–170; etc. For Italian: Migliorini 1960:301–305, 402–408. For Spanish: Entwistle 1936:191–200.

32. For Folengo's macaronic Latin, cf. Paoli 1959; Migliorini 1968.

33. For partial lists of Renaissance Latinisms in Italian, cf. Migliorini 1960:301–305, 402–408. In French: Brunot and Bruneau 1905–69:2. In Spanish: Entwistle 1936:196–200.

34. Later respelled *excepción* and, on the basis of the spelling, given the pronunciation /eksθepθión/.

35. Some of these now obsolete Romance words seem normal to speakers of English, since they have continued in use after they became archaic in the source-language, *e.g.* Eng. /détər/ *debtor*, /sə́rǧən/ *surgeon*, from the two words cited here.

36. Mediaeval Latin *copia* 'copy' was a back-formation from *copiare* 'to reproduce in abundance'. The Portuguese 17th-cent. Italianism *copia* 'couple' (<It. /kó‸ppia/ coppia < PRom. /kó‸pula/ 'joining, pair') came into collision with *copia* meaning both 'copy' and 'abundance', and hence was "thwarted" in its acceptance (cf. Knowlton 1969/70).

37. It has been wisely observed that not even Dante could have made Italian into a tone-language—nor, we might add, have changed it in fundamental respects like case or voice.

38. Where the participle is derived from a transitive verb, one might be tempted to interpret such a construction as involving the ellipsis of an auxiliary verb-form like /avéndo/ *avendo* 'having', *e.g.* **avendo usato ogni industria*. But such a derivation would not be possible for, say, *restato la femmina*, where the supposedly omitted auxiliary would have to be /esséndo/ *essendo* 'being', and the full construction would be **essendo restata la femmina* 'the woman having [lit. being] remained', with agreement between the past participle and the noun in any case.

39. Cf. Schwendener 1923.

40. Cf. Beaulieux 1927. French Renaissance orthography: Catach 1968.

41. As early as the sixteenth century, it was perfectly well known that the spelling with *sç* was unjustified. In his *Dialogue de l'Ortografe* (Porter [ed.] 1966:95), Peletier has his interlocutor Dauron say:

> [. . .] tous les ecriuains Françoęs sǿ montrer beaucoup sauoȩr, e pour garder a toute rigueur leur Etimologie, ȯnt tous obstinemant ecrit cǿ mot *scauoir* par un c an la prǿmierǿ, pansant qu'il vint dǿ *scire*; combien qu'il viegnǿ regulierǿmant e au vrai de *sapere*: comme rǿcǿuoȩr, dǿcǿuoȩr, de *recipere, decipere:* einsi qu'on peut voȩr par l'italien, qui dit męmǿs *sapere* an l'infinitif, pour *sauoȩr.*

> '[. . .] all the French writers, to show that they know a lot, and to preserve their etymology at all costs, have all obstinately written this word *scavoir* with a *c* in the first syllable, thinking that it came from *scire*, although it comes regularly and truly from *sapere*, like *recevoir, decevoir*, from *recipere* and *decipere*, as one can see from Italian, which even says *sapere* in the infinitive, for "to know".'

42. Cf. Zambaldi 1892; Hartmann 1907. On Renaissance orthography: Migliorini 1955. On the rôle of Pier Francesco Giambullari in regularising Italian spelling: Fiorelli 1956.

43. Cf. Brusiloff 1945.

44. The same problem is faced nowadays by those who wish to bring the Bible or other material to preliterate tribes; cf. Gudschinsky 1953.

45. Reproduced in Porter (ed.) 1966:52. For the social basis of the opposition to easily learned spelling, cf. Hall 1960b.

46. We must remember that, up to the eighteenth century, what was mechanical was thought base, and vastly inferior to what was nonmechanical (cf. Altieri Biagi 1965)—an attitude which has survived in some quarters down to the present time. In Shakespeare's *Julius Caesar* (Act I, Sc. 1), in the opening speech, Flavius berates the commoners as "idle creatures" and asks them "Know you not that, being mechanical, you ought not walk upon a labouring day without the sign of your profession?".

47. In Peletier's system of spelling, the "semivowel" letters *j* and *v* are not distinguished from the vowel-letters *i* and *u*. He is clearly referring here to pairs like *iug'emant* /žyžəmant/ 'judgment' and *g'ans* /žanˢ/ 'people', and to pairs like *cent* '100' and *sant* 'feels', both /sanᵗ/.

48. Cf. Hall 1964, chapter 5.

49. Cf. W. C. Abbott 1918 and many other historians.

50. From the mid-fifteenth century onwards, Negroes with some knowledge of Spanish or Portuguese were termed *ladinos*, and fetched especially good prices in the slave-trade (cf. §6.12). On April 30, 1569, William Fowler, a merchant of Ratcliffe, deposed as follows (quoted in Donnan 1930:1.72):

> "[. . .] if a negro be a Bossale that is to say ignorant of the spanishe or Portugale tongue then he or she is commonlye soulde for iiiiᵉ and iiiiᵉ L [450] pesos. But if the Negro can speake anye of the foresaide languages any thinge indifferentlye (whiche is called Ladinos) then the same negro is commonlye soulde for vᵉ and viᵉ pesos as the negro is of choise and yonge of yeres [. . .]."

This meaning of *ladino* was a development of its use in the phrase *moro ladino* 'Romance-speaking Moor' in the Iberian peninsula in the Middle Ages; cf. Corominas 1954–57: 3.9–10; da Silveira Bueno 1963–67:5.2073.

51. Cf. most recently Boyd-Bowman 1956, 1964–68.
52. Cf. Menéndez Pidal 1962a; Boltz 1967/68.
53. Cf. Whinnom 1956:9.
54. Cf. R. W. Thompson 1961, especially 112–113.
55. Cf. Hall 1965, chapter 8.
56. For the debate as to whether Papiamentu is of Spanish or Portuguese origin, cf. Hesseling 1933; Navarro Tomás 1953; van Wijk 1958; Rona 1970.
57. Cf. Valkhoff 1966:51–145.
58. As suggested, for instance, by Goodman 1964.
59. As suggested by Sylvain (1936:8): "À mon avis, le créole haïtien est probablement né dans l'Île de la Tortue au cours du XVIIIe siècle, du jour où un esclave nègre s'est avisé, pour se faire comprendre du flibustier français, son maître, d'essayer de lui parler dans sa langue."
60. Opening at random to two pages (286–287) of McKaughan and Macaraya 1967.
61. Cf. Safford 1905.
62. Cf. Bright 1960 for this and other animal-names of Spanish origin in American Indian languages.
63. An extensive but confused over-all survey of scholarly work on Spanish influence on American Indian languages, with bibliography, in Malkiel 1968b. General discussion: Kiddle 1952a, 1952b. Spanish influence on individual North American Indian languages: Taos: Trager 1944. Keresan: Spencer 1947. Central California in general: Shipley 1962/ 63. Acoma: Miller 1959–60. Patwin: Bright and Bright 1959/60. Pomo: McLendon 1969/ 70. Wappo: Sawyer 1964/65. On Central American languages: Aztec: Bright and Thiel 1964/65. Maya: Malkiel 1948. Nahautl: Boas 1930. Pame (San Luís Potosí): Olson 1963. The Island Carib of Honduras: D. Taylor 1962/63. On South American languages: Waunana (Colombian Chaco): Loewen 1960. Guaraní: Morínigo 1931. Mapuche: Giese 1948/ 49, Rabanales 1952/53.
64. Cf. A. Taylor 1962/63.
65. Cf. Geary 1945.
66. Cf. Hall 1947b.
67. For general listings of words of native American origin, cf. Friederici 1926; Lokotsch 1926.
68. Cf. Entwistle 1936:239–247 for a general survey. For native (in general Amerindian) words in Spanish, cf. Henríquez Ureña 1938b; Casullo 1964; Buesa Oliver 1965; Suárez 1966/67.
69. For words of this type which entered Italian and other European languages through Spanish, cf. Zaccaria 1905, 1908, 1927.
70. E.g. for Chile: Lenz 1905–10.
71. For Italian influence on French, cf. Kohlmann 1901; Tracconaglia 1907; Klemperer 1914; Saarauw 1920; Wind 1928; Hope 1971:1.141–248. On Spanish: Terlingen 1943.
72. Cf. Messedaglia 1942/43.
73. The pejorative development of It. /kortiǧána/ cortigiana 'lady of the court > harlot' took place very early, and was followed in other languages.
74. As is well known, Eng. /kə́rnəl/ colonel has the French spelling and the Spanish pronunciation.
75. Cf. Hall 1962c.
76. Cf. Malkiel 1948/49.
77. Cf. Beccaria 1968.
78. Cf. Marinelli 1925.
79. For Italian influence on Brantôme, cf. Price 1967:160–163.

80. For the history of this type of formal address in Italian, cf. Grand 1930; Migliorini 1946.

81. It used to be thought that Sp. /ustéd/ *usted* was a contraction of /buéstramerǵéd/ *Vuestra Merced* 'your Mercy'; it is more likely however, that it was a late fifteenth-century borrowing from Maghrebian Arabic /usta:θ/ [us'tɛ:θ] 'master; sir' (cf. Krotkoff 1963/64), later confused with *Vuestra Merced*.

82. For the pidginised variety of Italian, called "Lanzi," used by the Lanzichenecchi in Italy, cf. Coates 1969.

83. Cf. Lokotsch 1927; Steiger 1963.

84. Cf. Maher 1971.

85. For Italian lexical influences on other languages in general, cf. Vidos 1932; Battisti 1942.

86. Cf. Folena 1968/70.

87. Cf. Wis 1955.

88. Cf. Praz 1929; Baugh 1935:280.

89. Cf. Migliorini 1960:427.

90. Cf. Mackenzie 1939.

91. Cf. Waterman 1966:120–127.

92. Cf. Salverda da Grave 1906, 1913. Direct Italian influence on Dutch did not begin to any extent until the seventeenth century (cf. Francescato 1966).

93. Cf. Baugh 1935:280–281.

94. This word has had two reflexes in English: /níjgròw/, a direct adaptation and spelling-pronunciation from the Spanish; and /nígər/, through oral channels from seventeenth-century French /negrə/ *nègre*.

CHAPTER 8

Purism and Academicism

The post-Renaissance period in the West European Romance languages—roughly the seventeenth and eighteenth centuries, with spill-overs into the nineteenth—was characterised by continuing developments along the lines described in Chapters 6 and 7, and also by certain new trends, involving emphasis on presumed purity of language, as codified by academies and taught in prescriptive grammar-books and dictionaries. These new trends had their roots in changed political and social conditions, beginning in the latter part of the sixteenth century.

8.1. The Authoritarian Reaction

The "authoritarian reaction" is a convenient term[1] for a complex of attitudes which arose in the mid-sixteenth century and became dominant, in varying degrees, in the following two hundred and fifty years. These attitudes embodied a reaction against the spirit of freedom, independent inquiry, and change which was embodied in the progressive aspects of the Renaissance and the Reformation. Many conservative-minded persons, especially in the ruling classes and the Church, were alarmed at the spread of liberal or progressive ideas, and attempted to stop them by returning to the doctrines of the Middle Ages and by enforcing obedience to authority.[2] Governments and churches sought to inculcate universal and unquestioning obedience to absolute rule, based on emotional acceptance of and attachment to the principle of established authority as a good in itself. This reaction manifested itself in almost all spheres of human activity, but especially in those of politics, religion, literature, and (our main concern here) language.

In politics, this reaction took the shape of absolute rule and the principle of the "divine right of kings," as practised by the monarchs of Spain in the sixteenth century and as seventeenth-century kings tried to institute it elsewhere, successfully in some countries (*e.g.* France, parts of Germany) and unsuccessfully elsewhere (*e.g.* England). In religion, it appeared as what is usually called the "Counter-Reformation," in which the Roman Church met the challenge of the Protestant Reformation by a parallel purification in moral standards, combined with a reaffirmation of the doctrines of mediaeval Western Christianity on a wholly intransigent, ultra-conservative basis as set forth in the pronouncements of the Council of Trent (1545–1563). In literature, the genres and precepts of classical writers, particularly those of Aristotle in his *Poetics* and of Horace in his *Ars Poetica*, were set up as absolutes, and literary production was judged according to whether it measured up to these absolutes. The language of literature (and, in some instances, even that of every-day speech) was likewise regarded as subject to regulation in the name of "purity" and "correctness," according to the model set by the "best" writers and codified by grammarians in books of rules.

8.11. POLITICAL ABSOLUTISM was dominant in virtually all regions of Romance speech in this period. It did not become supreme without considerable opposition, particularly from previously powerful regional feudal lords, in Spain in the sixteenth century, and in France in the latter part of the sixteenth and the first part of the seventeenth centuries, up through the time of the Fronde.[3] It was perhaps most completely successful in Italy, where republican rule (even though oligarchical in its true nature) survived only in Venice and Genoa. Lombardy was ruled directly by Spain, and the other states of the peninsula were under the sway of kings, princes, dukes, or lesser potentates, whose rule was nominally independent but in reality dependent on the favor of Spain. Under this type of rule, government was wholly by absolute authority, with a single, in theory all-powerful monarch at the top and an obedient hierarchy of nobles below him, lording it over an adoring, servile populace.[4] His government derived a large part of its power and revenue from conferring privileges and monopolies on favored individuals or groups. Opposition to any aspect of absolute rule, or disagreement with any dogma set forth in theoretical matters, was regarded as little short of high treason, and was put down by means of strong disfavor, imprisonment, or death. Architecture and city-planning reflected the dominant pattern of life in the Baroque period, with showy, costly buildings along broad, straight avenues designed to facilitate the movement of troops and the sweep of offensive weaponry, but with poverty-stricken and disease-ridden slums in back of the glittering façades of the main thoroughfares.[5]

8.12. INSECURITY AND PURISM. Naturally, those who ventured to hold views at variance with official doctrines, even in such matters as literature or the study of language, were rendered highly insecure. Especially in religious affairs, very strong pressure was brought on dissenters to change their views and to adhere to whatever denomination might be the established one (Catholicism in almost all the Romance-speaking territory; one kind or another of Protestantism in England, Scandinavia, and parts of Germany). Not only converts, but members of families which included or had, in previous generations, included heretics felt especially insecure and under a special obligation to prove their right-mindedness. In language-matters, speakers of nonstandard varieties felt impelled, not only by social pressures but by official dogma, to "purify" their usage and make it conform to new standards of "correctness."[6] No-one, even in seventeenth-century France, was jailed or executed for "incorrect" language; but one could be, and many people were, subjected to ridicule and mockery for any expression of independent thought or judgment in such matters. To put down any disagreement, orthodoxy was enforced in the name of "pure" language and "good" literature, which (it was claimed) could be legislated by rule.

8.2. Absolutism and Authoritarianism in Language

These Baroque ideals of conformism were enforced, in language and literature, by the promulgation of ideals of purity, of several types:

8.21. INDIVIDUAL AUTHORITY is, perhaps, the simplest of all kinds: the *ipse dixit* of a single person ("it's right because I say it's right"), by whose dicta his pupils and disciples swear (whence the Latin expression *jurāre in verba magistrī* "to swear by the words of the master"). In sixteenth-century Italy, Cardinal Bembo played the rôle of literary and linguistic arbiter (cf. §7.32), but with less arbitrariness and dogmatism than did François de Malherbe (1555–1628) in the following century in France. Born of a Protestant family in Caen, Malherbe early abjured his family's heresy and became a Catholic. His first forty-five years were spent in Provence and in Normandy. In 1605 he moved to Paris, receiving the favour of King Henry IV because of an adulatory ode, and established himself in the capital and at court. His poetical production was scanty in quantity and even scantier in quality. However, it was exactly in tune with current fashions in lyric poetry, which embodied a strong reaction against the richness and (to early seventeenth-century tastes) excessive classicism of such sixteenth-century poets as Ronsard and his chief follower Philippe Desportes (1546–1606). Malherbe's personality was anything but agreeable; he was crotchety, ill-tempered, and insolent to any-one who differed from his views. (Note that he was both a convert from Protestantism and of dialectal back-ground in speech, two facts which probably explain much of his self-defensive harshness and unpleasantness.) However, such was the insecurity of his contemporaries, that, by sheer force of personal aggressiveness, he was able to impose his out-look on language and literature on a whole generation.[7]

Malherbe's purism[8] was essentially restrictive in nature, embodying at their fullest the "three I's of purism": insecurity, ignorance, and insensitivity. His method was chiefly to "proscribe" words, on the grounds of their being obsolete (e.g. *ains* 'on the contrary', *moult* 'very', *ores* 'now'), dialectal (*maint et maint* 'very many' as Gascon, *poursuivir* 'pursue' as Norman), foreign (*alme* 'beloved') or Latin (*opportun* 'opportune'), diminutive (*sagette* 'little and wise'), or newly-coined.[9] In grammar and versification, likewise, he objected to even the slightest freedom of construction and to the permissibility of alternative options, e.g. in the use of the subjunctive, or in hiatus and *enjambement* in verse. Malherbe's main concern seems to have been that poetry should be understandable to all native speakers, even the most naïve or ignorant. His disciple Racan tells us that Malherbe used to regard the *crocheteurs du Port au Foin*, the porters in the Haymarket, as his 'masters in language'—not, obviously, for their coarse or vulgar talk, but as representing the strata of the people to whom words should be intelligible (as opposed, say, to the learnèd folk conversant with Latin, Greek, and Italian, as were the Pléiade, Desportes, and Montaigne).

Malherbe's doctrines were popular with the court fops and light versifiers, and were continued and extended by his disciples such as François Maynard (1582–1646) and Honorat de Bueil, Marquis de Racan (1589–1670). Due to their influence, even such outstanding earlier poets as Villon, Ronsard, and Du Bellay came to be regarded as hopelessly outdated and their language as obsolete, so that Nicolas Boileau-Despréaux (1636—1711), was able, in his *Art Poétique* (1674) to write the notorious verses (1.131–134):

> Enfin Malherbe vint, et, le premier en France,
> [. . .] réduisit la Muse aux règles du devoir.

> 'Finally Malherbe came, and was the first in France [. . .] to reduce the Muse to the rules of duty.'

Chiefly through Malherbe's influence (aided by the servility of later generations) the "classical" French literary language of the seventeenth and eighteenth centuries was sharply reduced, to the point of impoverishment, in vocabulary and syntax.

There were, indeed, a few who opposed Malherbe's purism in his time.

Chief among these were the satirist Mathurin Régnier (1575–1613) and Montaigne's "adoptive daughter," the Demoiselle Marie le Jars de Gournay. (1565–1645). Régnier[10] attacked Malherbe, in part for the latter's intrinsic short-comings but also in part because of his disrespect towards Régnier's uncle Desportes. In his Ninth Satire (56–66), Régnier criticises Malherbe and his on-hangers because they are concerned only with

> [. . .] regratter un mot douteux au jugement,
> Prendre garde qu'un *qui* ne heurt une diphtongue,
> Espier si des vers la rime est brève ou longue,
> Ou bien si la voyelle, à l'autre s'unissant,
> Ne rend point à l'oreille un vers trop languissant,
> Et laissent sur le verd le noble de l'ouvrage.
> Nul esguillon divin n'eslève leur courage;
> Ils rampent bassement, foibles d'inventions,
> Et n'osent, peu hardis, tenter les fictions,
> Froids à l'imaginer: car s'ils font quelque chose,
> C'est proser de la rime et rimer de la prose.

'scratching out a word which in their judgment is doubtful, guarding against a *qui* clashing with a diphthong, spying out whether the rhyme of verses is short or long, or whether the vowel, joining with the other, does not render a verse too languishing, and they neglect the nobility of the poem. No divine goad spurs on their courage; they crawl basely, and, weak in invention, and short on boldness, cold in imagination, they do not dare to attempt fictions; for, if they do anything at all, it is putting rhyme into prose and prose into rhyme.'

Malherbe's and his followers' finickiness and pedantry, coupled with their lack of inspiration, were what aroused Régnier's ire. Marie de Gournay, on the other hand, objected especially to the condemnation of old and—to her way of thinking—valuable words and turns of speech.[11] Her admiration for Ronsard and the Pléiade, and above all for Montaigne (whose literary executrix and chief seventeenth-century defender she was) led her to consider that, in eliminating so many older but still useful expressions, the purists were diminishing the richness of the language. Unfortunately, by the time the battle with Malherbe was joined, she was already in her forties, and when the French Academy was founded (1634; cf. §8.322) she was nearly seventy. Frivolous but popular mockery of her and of her ideas on language has led later critics to consider Marie de Gournay simply an old-maidish defender of antiquated words and attitudes.[12] In fact, she was one of the most intelligent of the early seventeenth-century French thinkers on the topic of language.

8.22. Usage as a determinant of "correct" language was defended primarily by the seventeenth-century courtier Claude Favre de Vaugelas (1585–1650).[13] He too considered that there was a highly important distinction to be made between good and bad language; but he considered that the "good" was to be found, as he put it (*Remarques*, preface II.3), in *la façon de parler de la plus saine partie de la Cour, conformément à la façon d'escrire de la plus saine partie des Autheurs du temps* 'the manner of speaking of the best balanced part of the Court, in accordance with the manner of writing of the best balanced part of the authors of the time'. Note that he lays emphasis on the adjective-phrase *la plus saine* 'the best balanced' (as opposed to frivolous or silly members of the court, or to ephemeral authors), and also on agreement between speakers and writers. On the debate between reason and usage as determinants of language (cf. §8.23), Vaugelas said:

> C'est une erreur [. . .] en matière de langues vivantes, de s'opiniastrer pour la Raison contre l'Usage. [. . .] On a beau invoquer Priscien, et toutes les puissances grammaticales, la Raison a succombé, et l'Usage est demeuré le maistre; *communis error facit jus*, disent les jurisconsultes.

> 'It is an error [. . .], with regard to living languages, to take a stubborn stand on behalf of Reason against Usage. [. . .] There is no use invoking Priscian and all the grammatical powers, Reason has lost, and Usage has remained master of the field; if every-one is wrong, their error becomes right, as the lawyers say.'

Vaugelas claimed that he was only an observer, not a law-giver. He set down his observations in his *Remarques sur la langue françoise* (1647), a series of discussions with no fixed plan or order, expounding his reactions, favourable or unfavourable, to current alternatives in various moot points of usage.

Despite his disclaimers, Vaugelas did act, in many respects, as an arbiter, with an essentially puristic point of view. To Vaugelas, it seemed that French had already reached a peak of perfection, at which it had to be kept by conscious effort. He was opposed, as Malherbe had been, to neologisms, whether borrowed from other modern languages or formed on Latin bases, and he gave only grudging acceptance to new-formations on existing French words. His view-point was strictly aristocratic, disdaining the low talk of *la lie du peuple* 'the dregs of the populace'. Vaugelas' out-look on language was so close to that of the great majority of aristocrats and socially climbing bourgeois of the time that it was almost universally adopted,[14] and talking "pure" French was referred to as *parler Vaugelas* 'speaking Vaugelas'.

8.23. REASON was, in the French seventeenth century, widely regarded as the final arbiter in all problems, not only of real life, but of language. René Descartes (1596–1650), the philosopher and scientist, said in his *Discours de la Méthode de bien conduire sa Raison* 'Discourse on the Way to Guide One's Reason Rightly' (1636) that *le bon sens est la chose du monde la mieux partagée* 'reason is the most widely shared thing in the world'. The general public soon equated Descartes' *bon sens* with ordinary "common sense," using Cartesian rationalism as a justification for upholding traditional attitudes, as recognised in both grammarians' dicta and popular folk-lore, towards language. This pseudorationalism was at the base of the influential *Grammaire de Port-Royal* (1660), published anonymously but the work of the philosopher-logician Antoine Arnauld (1612–1694) and the language-teacher Claude Lancelot (1615–1695). We shall discuss the rôle of the Port-Royal grammar in the history of linguistics in §11.3. Here, it is enough to observe that this work was the initiator of a long tradition of discussion of language on a presumed basis of "reason," actually of Latin grammar as applied to French, and claiming to discover fundamental principles and to set up rules for all human language on a universal basis.

In the latter part of the seventeenth century and in the eighteenth, these three streams of purism fused into a single current of worship of the French language as the supposed embodiment of everything that was most noble, polished, and reasonable in human speech. The most notorious expression of this attitude was the superficial but extremely influential prize-essay of one Antoine de Rivarol (1753–1801), the *Discours sur l'universalité de la langue française* ('Discourse on the Universality of the French Language', 1784), asserting the supremacy of French over all other languages, and containing the widely repeated dictum *Ce qui n'est pas clair n'est pas français* 'Whatever is not clear, is not French'.[15] In reality, of course, the French language is no clearer or less clear (more rational or less rational, more pure or less pure, etc.) than any other language. It was the success of French armies in the seventeenth and early eighteenth centuries, and the glamour of French court- and society-life, that caused the French language and French literary styles to have prestige and be imitated throughout the rest of Europe in that period. It was the success of French diplomacy (backed up, naturally, by French arms) that caused French to be used as the international lingua franca of diplomats on through the nineteenth century into the early twentieth.

8.3. Institutionalised Authority: Academicism

In the Renaissance, one of the most attractive features of intellectual life was the growth and spread of discussion-groups, which gathered, at first in private houses, to take up problems of all kinds connected with literary creation and scientific investigation. Some of these groups were devoted simply to diversions ranging from parlor-games to buffoonery; others were more serious. As they assumed an increasingly important rôle in each country's intellectual development, these groups were often granted official status and converted into ACADEMIES, with their own rooms or buildings, and a regular organisation and schedule of meetings. By the seventeenth century, academies pullulated throughout western Europe; some, like the Royal Academy of England and the Accademia dei Lincei of Rome, have continued as major forces in scientific work down to our time. On occasion, the discussions in the academies became inflated, empty, or futile, and this situation has caused a somewhat pejorative or contemptuous connotation to become attached to the adjective *academic*. In general, however, the academies performed a highly meritorious service in advancing research and furthering its publication.

8.31.   THE ITALIAN ACADEMIES were, like other Italian manifestations of Renaissance humanism, the earliest on the scene.[16] The first academy of note was the famous Platonic Academy of Florence, founded ca. 1441 by Còsimo de' Mèdici. Others were founded by the humanists Giovanni (Gioviano) Pontano in Naples (ca. 1440), Pomponio Leto in Rome (ca. 1470), and Aldo Manuzio in Venice (1500). Soon every town had one or more academies, ranging from the frivolous to the serious. In general, these groups took fanciful names (*e.g.* the *Sonnacchiosi* or 'Sleepy-heads' and the *Storditi* or 'Dazed Ones' of Bologna, the *Insensati* or 'Mad-men' of Perugia, the *Ùmidi* or 'Damp Ones' of Florence), and their members assumed equally fanciful names by which they were known and addressed in the gatherings of the coterie.

8.32.   LANGUAGE-ACADEMIES. Of the academic groups specifically devoted to language, the first was like-wise founded in Italy, and its example was followed later in France and Spain. They all had in common the purpose of furnishing men of letters an opportunity to discuss problems connected with the use of the literary languages. Their common ideal was the neo-classical belief that for each language and its literary manifestations there was an ideal fixed for all time, already reached by the classical writers of Greece and Rome, and which could be attained in modern days only by setting up similar models of perfection. They viewed language itself as something unruly and unserviceable for the lofty purposes of culture and literature unless tamed and "reduced to rule," like a high-strung but wayward colt.

8.321. ITALY. In Florence, a group of literary men used to meet in the gardens of the Rucellai family in the mid-1500's. Like absolutist rulers in general, the Mèdici dukes regarded such private gatherings with suspicion. In this case, Duke Còsimo I sought to render the group subservient to the state by constituting it an officially-sponsored Academy in 1572. In the Italian academic tradition, it took a fanciful name, the Accademia della Crusca or 'Bran-Academy', which is usually interpreted as referring to its task of separating out the pure grain of the language from the useless husks or bran.[17] Originally, its members also took academic names referring to various aspects of the grain-milling process. Its task was to "purify" the language, to codify it in a grammar and dictionary, and to pass judgment on contemporary works—as it did, for instance, by publishing the animadversions of one of its leading members, Lionardo Salviati (1540–1589) on the romantic poem *Gerusalemme Liberata* ('Jerusalem Freed') of Torquato Tasso (1544–1595). It never published a grammar, but its members set to work vigorously on the dictionary, which was prepared in the years 1591–1610, and which appeared at Venice in 1612. Later editions came out in 1623, 1691, 1729–38, and 1843–1922.[18] Beginning in 1815, the Crusca has published a long series of *Testi di lingua* 'texts of the [literary] language', starting with Bono Giamboni's translation of Vegetius (§7.122).

The Crusca vocabulary was the first and in some ways the best of the great academic dictionaries, with plentiful exemplifications based on mediaeval and modern texts. Its chief fault lies in the quality of the editing done on the texts used. In too many instances, the editors did not hesitate to change spellings and forms in earlier documents to agree with what they thought was proper usage. Because of the Crusca's pretensions to purity of language and its claim of exclusive authority for Florentine usage, however, there was a certain amount of opposition, even in the seventeenth century, from such writers as Paolo Beni (ca. 1552–1625) in his *Anti-Crusca* (1612), and Alessandro Tassoni (1565–1635),[19] and, in the eighteenth, from the eccentric but perceptive Sienese lexicographer Girolamo Gigli (1660–1722).[20] By the nineteenth century, after the anti-Cruscan satires of Vincenzo Monti (1754–1828), in his *Proposta di alcune correzioni ed aggiunte al Vocabolario della Crusca* ('Proposal for Some Corrections and Additions to the Crusca Vocabulary,' in seven volumes, 1817–26), and of Monti's son-in-law Giulio Perticari (1779–1822), the Crusca was pretty much of a spent force in the determination of standard Italian usage.

8.322.   FRANCE. As in Italy, various coteries of learnèd men (and ladies) formed unofficial groups to discuss language-problems; some have even considered the sixteenth-century Pléiade as a kind of language-academy. There were several such groups in the early seventeenth century, including that of Marie de Gournay (cf. §8.2) and another, in part overlapping, *cénacle* which met at the house of one Valentin Conrart (1603–1675).[21] Also as in Italy, the rulers looked askance at such independent groups, and the efficient dictator Cardinal Richelieu (who had literary ambitions himself) converted Conrart's coterie into an official body. Founded in 1634 as the Académie Française, this self-perpetuating group of forty men (the "forty Immortals") was intended by Richelieu to exert absolute power, under his close supervision, over literature and language.[22] The Academy's first trial of strength came in 1637, when it condemned the highly popular new play *Le Cid* ('The Cid', 1636) of Pierre Corneille (1606–1684) by the Cardinal's orders.[23] Ever since Richelieu's time, the Académie Française has been above all a state institution, enjoying a veneration, at all levels of French society, far out of all proportion to its merits.[24] There have been, beginning in the seventeenth century, a number of attacks on the Academy,[25] none of which have been really successful in deflating its pretensions or diminishing its prestige, which has been maintained down to the present day through the French school-system.

The Academy was entrusted with the tasks of preparing an official dictionary, grammar, and treatise on rhetoric. It was given a legal monopoly on its dictionary, which took sixty years to prepare, and did not appear until 1694. One of the Academy's members, Antoine Furetière (1619–1688),[26] had already been working on a vocabulary, which he proposed to publish before that of the Academy. For this, he was expelled in 1685; his *Dictionnaire universel* was published posthumously in 1690, in Holland. (It had later editions in 1701–02 and 1708, and served as the base for the *Dictionnaire de Trévoux*, which had numerous editions from 1704 onwards.) The Academy's dictionary was, even on its first appearance, manifestly an inferior job, as might be expected from a group of dilettantes with no competence or training as lexicographers. Nevertheless, it has gone through a number of editions, and is still regarded with superstitious veneration, as an infallible authority, in many quarters in France. As for the grammar, the task of writing it was assigned to Vaugelas in 1635, and later to various others, but it was never completed. For the third centenary of the Academy, it was decided to publish a grammar, which was entrusted to one Abel Hermant (1862–1950), a novelist and dramatist. The task proving beyond his forces, he sublet the job to a lycée-professor; the resultant grammar (Hermant 1932) was such a scandalously poor piece of work that even the

Academy's prestige could not save it from immediate and total condemnation.[27]

8.323. SPAIN was the last of the three major Romance-speaking countries to have its official Academy, the Real Academia Española, founded in 1714.[28] The history of the Spanish Academy has been much quieter than that of the Crusca or the Académie Française, and it has been, on the whole, less pretentious but more successful in its work. The *Diccionario* (1726–29) of the Spanish Academy came out more quickly and with less fanfare than the other two, but is probably the best of the three.[29] It was the only one of the major language-academies to prepare a reasonably accurate grammar.

8.4. Centralisation

The prime goal of most seventeenth- and eighteenth-century governments was centralisation. Linguistic purism[30] aided them in matters concerning language, by setting up a single, unified ideal for usage, which could be prescribed for official documents, legislative and judicial activities, and could be taught in schools and used as a touch-stone in judging literature. The rising middle classes, especially in seventeenth-century France and eighteenth-century England,[31] found a command of the standard language a major help in establishing and consolidating their social position. Molière mocked, in his comedy *Le Bourgeois Gentilhomme* ('The Bourgeois as Gentleman,' 1670), the efforts of Monsieur Jourdain to learn grammar as well as the other social graces of dancing and fencing; but many a contemporary of Monsieur Jourdain learned elegant language and—more important—had it taught to his children as part of proper behaviour. The extent to which language-behaviour was actually standardised among the upper and middle classes differed from one country to another. It was most strongly uniform in France, nearly as much so in Spain, but much less so in Italy (where the political fragmentation of the country left local dialects much more strongly entrenched than elsewhere).

8.41. GOVERNMENT, by the seventeenth and eighteenth centuries, was normally using the national language, rather than Latin, in the writing and promulgation of laws, in courts, and in the rapidly growing bureaucracies which served as enforcement-agencies for the decrees of the central government. This came to be the case also in alloglottic territories which came under the rule of one country or another: thus, French, rather than

German, was the official language in Alsace and Lorraine, after these regions came under French rule in 1648–84 and 1756, respectively. Significantly, in the Rossillon area, which became subject to the French crown in 1659, the local variety of Catalan was at first continued as the official language, but was replaced by French in 1738, at the height of the drive for centralisation under Louis XV. In Spain, like-wise, Castilian was strongly favoured over Catalan and Galician, reducing them to the status of patois. The over-lay of Castilian caused a markedly diglossic situation to arise in both Galicia and Catalonia.[32] Some of the features of the Valencian type of pronunciation known as /apičát/ *apitxat*, involving devoicing of intervocalic sibilants, are probably to be traced to imitation of Castilian speech-habits, since the *apitxat* accent arose precisely in this period. In Italy, a rather conservative, even archaising variety of standard Italian was official in most regions, but French was the dominant language in Piedmont, and Venetian was still widely used in administrative affairs in Venice and its main-land holdings.[33]

8.42. EDUCATION came, like-wise, to be conducted primarily in the major national languages. Latin and Greek were still taught as vehicles of learning, and were still used in some scientific writings, but were rarely used for oral communication outside of certain specialised types of class-room-instruction (theology, medicine). Grammars based on puristic doctrines were written and came to be used more and more widely.[34] Command of "good" language, in accord with the conservative teachings of national academies, came to be a hall-mark of learning and social acceptability.

8.43. LITERATURE was, according to the neoclassical doctrines dominant in the Baroque period, restricted to the approved standard language, with of course complete observation of all the grammatical niceties prescribed by academies or other "authorities," and avoiding any features of grammar or vocabularies that might be considered inelegant. Such restrictions on literary usage were most completely observed in France, rather less so in Italy and Spain. In certain literary genres, especially comedy, nonstandard usage might be introduced for special effect, *e.g.* the rusticisms and malapropisms of Molière's house-maids, or the countrified speech which Michelàngelo Buonarroti the Younger (1568–1646) deliberately introduced to exemplify Tuscan dialect in his comedies *La Fiera* ('The Fair') and *La Tancia*.[35] Dialect as a vehicle for literary efforts was strictly banned in neoclassical theory. In practice, it was used on occasion, but chiefly by local enthusiasts who wished to defend their regional speech, as did, say, the Gascon Pey de Garros (ca. 1525–1583) or the Provençal poet Pierre Goudoulin (Peire Godolí, 1580–1649). A modestly flourishing school of poets used the Franco-

Provençal dialect of St.-Étienne (Forez) in the eighteenth and nineteenth centuries.[36] Dialect-literature could also serve as a kind of protest against the dominance of academicism in the standard language, as a means of attaining greater self-expression; this was the case with several Italian authors of dialect-works in the seventeenth and eighteenth centuries, *e.g.* the Milanese Carlo Maria Maggi (1630–1699) and Carlo Porta (1775–1821), and the Sicilian Giovanni Meli (1740–1815). Even here, the genres of literature attempted in dialect were, in general, those traditionally regarded as less serious, especially the comedy and the satire.[37]

8.5. Cultural Interchanges

During the seventeenth and eighteenth centuries, cultural exchanges continued and even increased despite the opposition of purists.

8.51. LATINISMS AND HELLENISMS. Beginning with the development of the microscope and the telescope in the early 1600's, scientific investigation brought an increasingly wide range of hitherto unknown phenomena into human ken. To refer to these, and to render scientific discussion of them possible, a correspondingly increasing number of new terms were coined, for the most part on Greek or Latin bases. These terms normally spread fairly rapidly, setting the modern pattern for quick acceptance of new scientific formations. Since most scientists of the time had had a fairly thorough grounding in Latin and Greek, it came naturally to them to combine elements from those languages in new-formations. Among such formations we may cite It. /konóide/ *conoide* 'cone-shaped' (:/kón-/ *con-* 'cone'); It. /rarefaϕió^ne/ *rarefazione*, Fr. /rare^faksjon/ *raréfaction*, Sp. /rarefakθión/ *rarefacción* 'rarefaction = a making thinner' < Lat. /rar-/ *rar-* 'thin' + /faktio:n-/ *factiōn-* 'a making'; or the French philosopher Gassendi's /mole^kylə/ *molécule* (> It., Sp. /molékula/ *molécula*), lig. 'a little mass' (:Lat. /mol-/ *mol-* 'mass' + the diminutive suffix /:kul-/ *-cul-*). In some instances, we know the specific scientists who invented or borrowed terms, as is the case with Francis Bacon's Latin word *selenographia* 'description of the moon', borrowed into Italian by Galileo as /selinografía/ *selinografia*. Also from this period are such formations as *telescope* (Fr. /te^le^skopə/, It., Sp. /teleskópio/ *telescopio*) and *microscope* (Fr. /mikroskope/ *microscope*, It., Sp. /mikroskópio/ *microscopio*). Due to the presence of elements like *tele-* 'far' and *micro-* 'small' in a great many such words, these formants came to acquire considerable independence and latitude in their use in neologisms. They have appropriately been termed "prefixoids," and elements added onto the end of words (*e.g. -scope*) have been called "suffixoids."[38]

The flood of straight borrowings from Latin also continued unabated, in such fields as botany and physiology (*e.g. antenna, cellula* > Fr. /antenə/ *antenne*, It. /anténna/ *antenna*, Sp. /anténa/ *antena* and Fr. /selylə/ *cellule*, It. /čéllula/ *cellula*, Sp. /θélula/ *celula*, respectively); astronomy (*e.g.* Gk. /apógaia/ ἀπόγαια [n.pl.] '[a planet's greatest distance] from the earth, apogee' > Fr. /apože^ə/ *apogée*, It. /apogéo/ and Sp. /apoxéo/ *apogeo*); and biology (*e.g.* Lat. /krustakeu-/ *crustaceu-* > Fr. /krystase^/ *crustacé*, It. /krostáčeo/ *crostaceo*,[39] Sp. /krustáθeo/ *crustáceo*). Here, too, certain scientists were particularly active in the process of introducing learnèd terms into the vernacular, as were Galileo Galilei (1564–1642), Francesco Redi (1626–1698), and Marcello Malpighi (1628–1694) in Italy.[40] By and large, due to the restrictive effects of neoclassicism and purism, the scientific part of the lexicon and the humanistic part flowed in nearly wholly separate channels for most of this period; only in the latter part of the eighteenth century did interpenetration begin, as it did, for instance, in the works of the Italian satirist Giuseppe Parini (1729–1799).[41]

8.52. HISPANISMS. The crest of the wave of Spanish influence on the customs and vocabulary of western Europe came in the first part of the seventeenth century, in the period which historians of Spanish literature and culture term the *Siglo de Oro* or 'Golden Age'. The Spanish theater was at its height, as exemplified especially in the plays of Lope de Vega Carpio (1562–1635), Tirso de Molina (1584–1648), and Pedro Calderón de la Barca (1600–1681). Spanish manners, behaviour (especially at court), dress, and foods were widely imitated. The influence of Spain was perhaps strongest in Italy, both in the north (where Lombardy was under direct Spanish rule) and in the south (where the Kingdom of the Two Sicilies was nominally independent, but in actuality a Spanish satellite); it was also strong in France, despite opposition on nationalistic grounds. In bureaucracy and government; in military and maritime activities; and in matters pertaining to court-life, a number of Spanish loans spread to Italian, French, and English in this time.[42]

In the field of bureaucracy and government, Spanish borrowings were of course most frequent in the regions under Spanish rule or hegemony: *e.g.* Sp. /abrigo/ *abrigo* 'protection' > It. id.; /alistár/ alistar 'to enroll (recruits)' > It. /allistáre/ *allistare*; /beedór/ *veedor* 'supervisor' > It. /veedó^re/ *veedore*; /papéles/'papers, documents' > It. /papéli/ *papeli*. Spanish military and naval organization was reflected in some loan-words, *e.g.* Sp. /gerríḷa/ *guerrilla* 'little war' > It. /guerríḷḷa/ guerriglia (Fr.

/gerija/ or /geriḷa/ *guerrilla* was not borrowed until the Napoleonic Wars in the nineteenth century); /flotíḷa/ *flotilla* > It. /flottíḷḷa/ *flottiglia*, Fr. /flotiḷa/ *flotille*; /embargo/ *embargo* > Fr. It. id.

In court-life, such titles as Sp. /infánta/ *infanta* 'princess' > It. id., Fr. /enfantə/ *infante*, and the proclitic /don/ *don* 'Sir' > Fr., It. id.[43] The corresponding full feminine form /duéɲa/ *dueña* 'lady, mistress' was used for a chaperon, who was referred to in seventeenth-century French and Italian as a /dyeɲe/ *duègne* and a /duéɲɲa/ *duegna*, respectively. Unconcerned behaviour or ease in doing something was called in Spanish /desembueltúra/ *desenvueltura* (: /desembuélto/ *desenvuelto* 'disinvolved') > Fr. /de^zenvoltyrə/ *désinvolture*, It. /disimvoltúra/ *disinvoltura*. 'Boldness' or 'daring', Sp. /atrebimiénto/ *atrevimiento* (:/atrebérse/ *atreverse* 'to dare') > It. /attreviménto/ *attrevimento*, whence the back-formation in Italian /attrevíre/ *attrevire* 'to dare'.[44] Several Spanish games were popular in the rest of Europe, *e.g.* /ómbre/ *hombre* > Fr. /ombre/ *(h)ombre*, It. /ómbre/ *hombre*, and /tokadíḷa/ *tocadilla* > Fr. /tokadiḷə/ *tocadille*, It. /tokkadíḷḷo :tíḷḷa/ *toccadiglio -tiglia*.[45] Certain types of dress and the words for them spread outwards from Spain, especially the mantilla (Sp. /mantíḷa/ > Fr. /mantiḷə/ *mantille*, It. /mantíḷḷa/ *mantiglia*). The custom of taking a nap after the mid-day meal, at the 'sixth hour', Sp. /siésta/, was imitated, with the word giving Fr. /siestə/ *sieste*, It. /siésta/ *siesta*.

In art, the key term for the style of the first part of the seventeenth century, *baroque*, was a borrowing from Portuguese /barró^ku/ *barroco* > Sp. /barruéko/ *barrueco*, It. /barókko/ *barocco*, Fr. /barokə/ *baroque*, whence the English term.[46] Several musical terms spread from Spain, including the names for instruments like the guitar (Sp. /gitárra/ *guitarra* > It. /kitárra/ *chitarra*, Fr. /gitarə/ *guitare*) and the castanets (Sp. /kastaɲétas/ *castañetas* 'little chestnuts' > Fr. /kastaɲetəᶻ/ *castagnettes*, It. /kastanné^tte/ *castagnette*). The pavane spread from Spain to France, accompanied by such other dances as the saraband (Sp. /θarabánda/ *zarabanda* > Fr. /sarabandə/ *sarabande*, It. /sarabánda/ *sarabanda*) and the chaconne (Sp. /čakóna/ *chacona* > Fr. /šakonə/ *chaconne*, It. /čakkó^na/ *ciaccona*).

Certain Spanish foods were popular in the rest of Europe, such as the olla podrida (Sp. /óḷapodrída/, lit. 'rotten pot' > It. /óḷḷapodrída/ *oglia podrida*) and the tortilla (Sp. /tortiḷa/ > Fr. /tortiḷə/ *tortille*, It. /tortíḷḷa/ *tortiglia*). Such flavors as vanilla came into Europe through Spain and hence spread with their Spanish names: Sp. /bainíḷa/ *vainilla* > Fr. /vaniḷə/ *vanille* (whence the English word), It. /vainíḷḷa/ *vainiglia*.

It will be noted that a number of these loans contain the Spanish diminutive suffix /⁺íḷa/ *-illa*, which is reflected in French /⁺iḷə/ *-ille* and Italian /⁺íḷḷa/ *-iglia*. This suffix acquired a certain independent productivity of its own, as pointed out in §1.42 à propos of such words as Fr. /brabantiḷə/ *brabantille* 'a kind of cloth'. The presence of this suffix is presumptive (though, of course, not conclusive) evidence of a Spanish borrowing. In some instances, with this suffix and with other forms already cited, a certain amount of reshaping took place, blending a Spanish borrowing with a native base, as in the case of /pekadíḷo/ *pecadillo* 'little, venial sin' > Fr. /pekadiḷə/ *peccadille*, but (crossed with native /pekkát-/ *peccat-* 'sin') It. /pekkatíḷḷo/ *peccatiglio*.

8.53. Gallicisms. In the latter half of the seventeenth century, the cultural hegemony of Spain began to wane, with French manners and words taking the place of Spanish. The prestige of France and its culture reached its height in the mid-eighteenth century. In the earlier period (roughly 1660–1760), the elegant, glittering court-life of the Louvre and Versailles was the cynosure of all aristocratic eyes throughout Europe, and Parisian graces were imitated all over the continent.[47] In the latter part of the eighteenth century, to this continuing influence was added the strong intellectual impact of the Enlightenment, and especially of the Encyclopaedists. At the end of that century and the beginning of the nineteenth, the French Revolution and the Napoleonic era (1789–1815) brought still further Gallicisms in the wake of the new institutions which were imposed on countries "liberated" or conquered by France.

In social life, the organisation of French house-holds was reflected in, say, the seventeenth-century term /lake/ *laquais* 'lackey' > Sp. /lakájo/ *lacayo*, It. /lakkéˣ/ *lacchè*. Eighteenth-century borrowings in this sphere include the polite forms of address /madamə/ *madame* > Sp., It. /madáma/ *madama* and /madəmweselə/ *mademoiselle* > It. /madamosélla/ *madamosella* (or, crossed with the earlier French borrowing /damiǧélla/ 'damsel', /madamiǧélla/ *madamigella*). Ladies' flirtatious behaviour could be characterised as /koketeriə/ *coquetterie* > It. /kokettería/ *cochetteria* (Sp. /koketa/ *coqueta* is eighteenth-century, with /koketería/ *coquetería* attested from the nineteenth). A popular French dance was the /bureˆ/ *bourrée* > It. /buréˣ/ *burè*.

For elegant fashions in clothing, the very term /modə/ *mode* was taken over in Italian and Spanish as /móda/ *moda*. However, French styles, to judge from the number of loan-words, seem to have been imitated more readily in Italy than in Spain, e.g. /lenžəriə/ *lingerie* 'linens' > It. /linǧería/ *lingeria*[48]; /manto/ *manteau* 'cloak' > It. /mantóˣ/ *mantò*; Fr. /syrtu/ *surtout* 'over-coat' > It. /surtúˣ/ *surtù*. Popular etymology entered into the reïnterpretation of Fr. /žystokor/ *justaucorps* 'form-fitting waistcoat, lit. just [fitting] to the body' > It. /ǧustakuóre/ *giustacuore*, with /kuóre/ *cuore* 'heart'. The 'toilet,' in the various senses of the term, passed from Fr. /tweletə/, /twaletə/ *toilette* to It. /to(e)lé^tta/ *to(e)letta*, /twalé^tta/ *toaletta*.[49] Items of furniture included the buffet, Fr. /byfe/ > It. /bufé^x/ *bufè*; the canapé, Fr. /kanape^/ > It. /kanape^x/ *canape;* the bureau, Fr. /byro/ > It. /buró^x/ *burò*; the curtain, Fr. /rido/ *rideau* > It. /ridó^x/ *ridò*; and the bath-room-fitting, the bidet, Fr. /bide^/ > It. /bidé^x/, Sp. /bidé/, both spelled *bidé*.

Various means of transport spread from France to other countries, including the train (first of animal-drawn vehicles, later of steam-cars), Fr. /tren/ *train* > Sp. /trén/ and Braz. Port. /trẽ/ *tren*, It. /tré^no/ *treno*; and the convoy, Fr. /konvoi/ *convoi* > Port. /kombóiu/ *comboio* ('train'), It. /komvóḷḷo/ *convoglio* (with over-correction to It. /ḷḷ/ = Fr. /j/). A number of military terms of French origin included the seventeenth-century borrowings of the names for the platoon, Fr. /ploton/ *ploton* > It. /plotó^ne/ *plotone*; the regiment, Fr. /re^žimanᵗ/ > It. /reǧǧiménto/ *reggimento*, Sp. /reximiénto/ *regimiento*; the bivouac, Fr. /bivwak/[50] > It. /bivákko/ *bivacco*; the gendarme, Fr. /žandarmə/ > It. /ǧendárme/ *gendarme*; and, among items of equipment, the platform, Fr. /platəformə/ > It. /piattafórma/ *piattaforma*, Sp. /platafórma/ *plataforma*. In the eighteenth century, such innovations as the bayonet, the grape-shot, the picket, and the manoeuver were reflected in Fr. /baionetə/ *baionette* > It. /baioné^tta/ *baionetta*, Sp. /bajonéta/ *baioneta*; Fr. /mitraḷə/ *mitraille* 'grape-shot' > It. /mitráḷḷa/ *mitraglia*, Sp. /metráḷa/ *metralla*; Fr. /pikeᵗ/ *piquet* > It. /pikké^tto/ *picchetto*, Sp. /pikéte/ *piquete*; Fr. /manøvrə/ *manoeuvre* > It. /manóvra/ *manovra*, Sp. /manióbra/ *maniobra*.

During the eighteenth century, French culinary items and terms spread, *e.g.* the cutlet, the ragoût, the dessert, and champagne: Fr. /kotəletə/ *cotelette* > It. /kotolé^tta/ *cotoletta*; Fr. /ragu/ > It. /ragú^x/ *ragù*; Fr. /deser/ > It. /desér/ *dessert*; Fr. /šampaṇa/ > It. /šampáṇṇa /*sciampagna*, Sp. /čampáṇa/ *champaña* or /čampán/ *champán*. In music, theatre, and entertainment, French fashions led to the adoption of such terms as Fr. /parterə/ *parterre* 'ground-floor (of a theater)' > It. /par: pertérra/ *parperterre;* /marionetə/ *marionette* > It. /marioné^tta/ *marionetta*; /uvertyrə/ *ouverture* 'opening (piece of music), overture' > It. /overtúra/ *overtura*, Sp. /obertúra/ *obertura*; /obwe/ *hautbois* 'oboe' > It., Sp. /oboé/ *oboé*. French dances popular in the rest of Europe included the minuet, Fr. /mənueᵗ/ *menuet* > It. /minué^tto/ *minuetto*, Sp. /minué *minué*; and the rigaudon, Fr. /rigodon/ > It. /rigodó^ne/ *rigodone*, Sp. /rigodón/ *rigodón*. The term for a 'gaming house, casino', It /kasíno/ *casino* (lit. 'little house') had been borrowed into French as /kasino/ [ka-si-'no]; with French accentuation, and in this special meaning, it was then borrowed back into Italian as /kasinó^x/ *casinò*.[51]

Even some general terms spread from French into other languages at this

time, such as the participle /alarmanᵗ/ *alarmant* 'alarming' > It. /alar-
mánte/ *allarmante*,[52] Sp. /alarmánte/ *alarmante*; the term of endearment
/papa/ [pa-'pa] > It. /papáˣ/ *papà*, Sp. /papá/ *papá*; and such verbs as
/rəgreteᶜʳ/ *regretter* 'to regret' > It. /regrettáre/ *regrettare* and /remplaseᶜʳ/
remplacer 'to replace' > It. /rimpiaȼȼáre/ *rimpiazzare*, Sp. /reemplaθár/
reemplazar. Loan-shifts took place in the meanings of a number of words,
on French models, *e.g.* It. /feličitáre/ *felicitare*, Sp. /feliθitár/ *felicitar*
'to make happy > to congratulate', on the pattern of French /feᶜlisiteᶜʳ/
féliciter, itself a seventeenth-century neologism in French; It. /preǧudíȼio/
pregiudizio, Sp. /prexuíθio/ *prejuicio* 'earlier judgment > prejudice',
following Fr. /preᶜžyže^/ *préjugé*; 'public' as a noun, It. /púbbliko/
pubblico, Sp. /públiko/ *público*, Port. /públiku/ *público*, on the model of
Fr. /ləpyblik/ *le public*; or It. /superfičále/ *superficiale*, Sp. /superfiθiál/
superficial in the transferred meaning, imitating Fr. /syperfisiel/ *superficiel*;
etc.[53]

8.54. Italianisms were, during the seventeenth and eighteenth centuries,
markedly fewer than in the Renaissance, and restricted, in general, to terms
referring to music, the arts, the theatre, or specifically Italian phenomena.
In the Baroque and post-Baroque period, Italian commercial activity was
in a sharp decline, and Italy's main exports were music and the *commedia
dell'arte*. Italian players (especially on stringed instruments, whose quality
was notably improved by seventeenth-century Italian violin-makers such
as Antonio Stradivari of Cremona [ca. 1644–1737]), singers, and actors
toured Europe, and established Italian dominance in their specialties.[54]
The opera (at first referred to as /óperainmúsika/ *opera in musica* 'work
set to music') developed in the early seventeenth century in Italy and spread
throughout the Continent. Those who sang it were, according to the pitch
of their voices, referred to as *soprano* 'topmost', *alto* 'high', *contralto*
'counter-high', /tenó^re/ *tenore* 'tenor' (a term inherited from mediaeval
music) and /básso/ *basso* 'low'. A person with especial ability (It. /virtúˣ/
virtù) was a /virtuóso -a/ *virtuoso -a*. The names for the new stringed instruments were derived from /vióla/ *viola*, *e.g.* the 'little viol' or /violíno/
violino, or 'little big viol', /violončéllo/ *violoncello*. Indications of speed,
such as /adáǧo/ *adagio* 'with ease', /gráve/ *grave* 'serious', /largo/ *largo*
'broad', etc., in the seventeenth-century, were followed in the eighteenth
by "expression-marks," such as /alléᶜgro/ *allegro* 'merry', /mésto/ *mesto*
'sad', and /espressívo/ *espressivo* 'with expression'.[55] The major new types
of composition in the seventeenth century were developed in Italy, *e.g.*
the piece to be played, It. /sonáta/ *sonata* and that to be sung, It. /kantáta/
cantata (both forms being nouns based on the past participles of the verbs
/sonáre/ *sonare* 'to sound' and /kantáre/ *cantare* 'to sing', respectively);

the oratorio (It. /oratório/); or shorter pieces, such as the boat-song (of Venetian origin), It. /barkaróla/ *barcarola* 'barcarolle' (the English spelling shows the French channel of transmission).

In the theatre, various further 'masks' or stereotyped characters of the *commedia dell'arte* (cf. §7.711.6.*a*) spread, such as 'Punch', It. /pulčinélla/ *Pulcinella* > Fr. /polišinelə/ *Polichinelle*; 'Columbine', It. /kolombína/ *Colombina* > Fr. /kolombinə/ *Colombine*; or the Molière character Scapin < It. /skappíno/ *Scappino* (:/skappáre/ *scappare* 'to run away').⁵⁶ 'To improvise,' as was the habit in both theatrical and musical performances, passed from It. /improvvisáre/ *improvvisare* to the rest of Europe, as did the habit of shouting /brávo/ *bravo* 'excellent!' to a performer.⁵⁷ A person who 'took delight' in art or other aesthetic manifestations, It. /dilettánte/ *dilettante*, came to be thought of elsewhere as superficial and 'dilettantish'. Italy came to be thought of in other countries as the land of /dólčefárni-énte/ *dolce far niente* 'sweet inactivity, lit. doing nothing',⁵⁸ with amusements including the /ǧirándola/ *girandola* 'merry-go-round' (> Fr. /žirandolə/ *girandole*) and the festival-parade of boats or gondolas (Ven. /regáta/ > It. /regátta/ *regatta* > Fr. /reˆgatə/ *régate*, Sp. /regáta/ *regata*, Eng. /rəgǽta/ *regatta*). Many an eighteenth-century lady had her gigolo or /čičisbéo/ *cicisbeo* (>Fr. /sižisbeˆ/ *sigisbé*), and many a tourist in Italy was shown the sights by a guide known (at first satirically) as a 'Cicero', It. /čičeróˆne/ *Cicerone*.

Aside from these (fairly extensive) borrowings, only a few Italianisms penetrated the rest of Europe in the seventeenth and eighteenth centuries. A few referred to Italian foods, such as 'celery', It. /séˆdano/ *sedano* > Fr. /seˆləri/ *séleri* > Eng. /séləri/, or the thin noodles known as /vermi-čélli/ *vermicelli*, lit. 'little worms'. One or two terms referred to commercial contacts, such as /áǧo/ *agio* 'discount < ease' or /fattúra/ *fattura* 'invoice' (> Fr. /faktyrə/ *facture*, Ger. /faktúːr/ *Faktur*). Wide-spread epidemics arising in Italy in the late eighteenth century brought with them the (rather vague) Italian name of /influénȼa/ *influenza* 'influence'.

8.55. ANGLICISMS. Beginning in the mid-eighteenth century, the influence of English culture became more and more felt on the Continent, growing to an "Anglomania." The English philosophers Thomas Hobbes (1588–1679) and John Locke (1632–1704), and the theoreticians of politics the Earl of Shaftesbury (1671–1713) and Lord Bolingbroke (1678–1751), came to be regarded as path-finders in developing a more liberal out-look than had prevailed in authoritarian despotisms of the Baroque period (cf. §8.1). In politics and government, therefore, borrowings and loan-shifts on English models began to be made, *e.g.* Eng. /párləmənt/ *Parliament* > Fr. /parlə-manᵗ/ *parlement* (previously 'high court'), It. and Sp. /parlaménto/

parlamento; /ǧúwrij/ *jury* > Fr. /žyri/ > It. /ǧurí^x/ *giurì* (whose stress betrays its French channel of transmission).[59]

In the latter part of the century, English literature and manners became widely known in Europe, particularly through such sentimental novels as those of Samuel Richardson (1689–1761) and the out-pourings of "Ossian" (James MacPherson [1736–1796]). Through reading about them and coming in contact with them as tourists, the European public became familiar with /milór(d)/*my Lord* and /miléjdij/ *my lady*, who came to symbolise riches and luxurious living. A sect peculiar to England were the Quakers (> Fr. /kwakrə/ *coacre*, It. /kuákkero/ *quacchero*).

Fashionable clothing included the 'riding-coat' (> Fr. /rədengotə/ *redingote*, It. /redengótto/ *redengotto*). Foods new to Europe included the 'pudding' (> Fr. /buden/ *boudin*, It. /pudin(g)o/ *pudin[g]o* or, crossed with the French form, /budino/ *budino*), the 'punch'[60] (> Fr. /ponš/ *ponche*, It. /pónče/ *ponce*), and the 'toast' (> Fr. /tost/ *toast*, It. /tósto °e/ *tosto -e*). Society people might form a club (> Fr. /klyb/ or /klœb/), from which undesirables might be black-balled (> Fr. /blakbule^r/ *blackbouler*). One might read about the most recent political or social events in a 'pamphlet' (> Fr. /panfle^t/ *pamphlet*, It. /pamflé^tto/ *panfletto*) or in a 'magazine' (>Fr. /magazen/ *magasin*, It. /magaẓẓíno/ *magazzino*, previously 'ware-house'). Towards the end of the century, during the Napoleonic period, England began to take the lead over the Continent in industrial and technological development; but the flood of Anglicisms that accompanied the diffusion of these innovations did not get thoroughly under way until the nineteenth century.

8.56. OTHER INFLUENCES. As Europeans' knowledge of the rest of the world increased, borrowings began to be made from other cultures' ways of living and artifacts, along with the vocabulary relative thereto. German furnished such words as that for the 'coffee-house', /káfe: + hàws/ *Kaffeehaus* (> It. /kafeáus/ *caffeàus*) and the names of several minerals, such as 'cobalt' (> It. /kobálto °ólto/ *cobalto °olto*) and 'nickel' (> Fr. /nikel/ *nickel*, It. /níkel/ *nichel*). Russia was beginning to be known to the outside world, in at least the names of its rulers the Tsar and Tsarina, and its coins, the ruble and the kopeck. From India came the name of the rich potentate or 'nabob' (> Fr. /nabab/, It. /nabáb/ *nabab*). Here, too, the really large influx of exotic terms began in the nineteenth century, with its greatly extended and improved communications.

NOTES TO CHAPTER 8

1. Cf. the extensive discussions in Symonds 1875–86, Book 6; also Mumford 1961, chapter 12. My sections 8.1–3 are largely a reworking of chapter 15.1 of Hall 1951 and chapter 62 of Hall 1964, with some additional material.

2. Mumford (1961:356–360) suggests that the success of the authoritarian principle, from the sixteenth century onwards, may have been due to the tipping of the balance of power in favor of offensive military action which resulted from the invention, not of gun-powder itself, but of dependable and transportable gun-powder in the sixteenth century, and from consequent greatly increased fire-power.

3. These local magnates, however, were themselves, in many instances, so tyrannical that the centralised rule of absolute monarchy was regarded by the common people and the rising middle classes of this period as a relief from the abuses of the decaying feudal system. The best expression of this attitude is found in Lope de Vega's play *Fuenteovejuna* (ca. 1612–1614, according to Morley and Bruerton 1940:200–201).

4. Cf. the observations of Mumford (1961:366–367) on the deification of the ruling prince, especially as typified by the "Sun-King" Louis XIV.

5. As remarked by Mumford 1961:367–371, 386–391.

6. That non-native speakers often devote more care and attention to "correct" usage than do native speakers, had of course been noticed long before the Baroque period of authoritarianism. In his *Dialogue de l'Ortografe*, Peletier du Mans has one of his interlocutors, Denis Sauvage, justify the intervention of the Provençal, Dauron, in the discussion by saying:

E puis on voęt assez souuant qué ceus qui n'ont point uné chose dé naturé, la font quelquéfoęs mieus valoęr qué les autrés: Car l'afeccion qué nous auons d'i ateindré, fęt qué nous i amassons toutés nos forcés, e i régardons dé si pręs, que nous nę lęβons rien derrieré: la ou quand nous auons quelqué chosé chez nous, il nous samblé qu'elé nę nous peùt jamęs falhir: e bien souuant nę nous chaut dé la cultiuer.

'And, then, one sees quite often that those who do not have a given thing from their birth, often set more store by it than do others; for the desire that we have of attaining it, makes us concentrate all our strength on it, and pay so close attention to it that we leave nothing out of consideration; whereas, when we have something as a birth-right, it seems to us that it can never desert us, and often we do not care to cultivate it.'

7. For Malherbe's life and works, cf. Gosse 1920; de Celles 1937; Fromilhague 1954.

8. For Malherbe's doctrines, cf. especially Brunot 1891.

9. Cf. Nyrop 1899–1930:1.66–68, 70–71.

10. For Régnier, cf. Vianey 1896.

11. For Marie de Gournay's attitudes towards language-matters, cf. Ilsley 1963:130–136, 217–231.

12. Cf. the discussion of satires in which Marie de Gournay was held up to ridicule for her defense of old words, in Ilsley 1963, chapter 16.

13. On Vaugelas, cf. Moncourt 1851.

14. Among Vaugelas' few opponents one may mention a friend of Marie de Gournay, François de La Mothe le Vayer (1585–1675), with his *Lettres touchant les Nouvelles Remarques sur la Langue Françoise* 'Letters Concerning the New Remarks on the French Language' of 1647, and the essay *La Liberté de la langue française dans sa pureté* 'The Liberty of the French Language in Its Purity' (1651) of Scipion Dupleix (1600–1661).

15. On Rivarol, cf. Curmier 1858; Le Breton 1895; Latzarus 1926; Jünger 1956; Loiseau 1961. The legend of French "clarity" has persisted down to the present (*e.g.* Bourgaux 1963, and many similar writings).

16. Cf. Maylender 1926–30.

17. For the history of the Accademia della Crusca, cf. Zannoni 1848; Reumont 1853–

57:6.144–225; Maroncini 1910; Maylender 1926–30:2.122–146; de Lollis 1922. On its Vocabulary: Duro 1962; Vitale 1966; Devereux 1968.

18. The fifth edition of the Crusca vocabulary proceeded very slowly, stopping at the letter O in 1923. The preparation of a sixth edition, based on modern principles of lexicography and utilizing new material excerpted from adequately edited texts, has been under way since the 1960's.

19. Cf. Renda 1908.

20. Cf. Migliorini 1940.

21. For Conrart's life and work, cf. Bourgoin 1883; Mabille de Poncheville 1935.

22. A number of books have been written on the history of the Académie Française, most of them naïvely laudatory, e.g. Mesnard 1857; Vincent 1901; Robertson 1910; Masson 1912; Académie Française 1935; Gaxotte 1965; Cardahi 1967. The only really critical over-all survey is Bellamy 1939. The Academy in the seventeenth and eighteenth centuries: François 1905; Boissier 1909; Albert-Buisson 1960. In the twentieth century: R. Peter 1949.

23. Cf. Searles (ed.) 1916. Corneille replied to the Academy's criticisms, but he showed thereafter that he had learned his lesson, by following the Academy's official neoclassical line in the language, structure, and content of his plays.

24. Some interesting, but little known, details with regard to the membership of the Académie Française: at any given time, not over fifty per cent of its members have been even professional writers. The rest of its membership has consisted of such types as nobles, military men, and clergy. It has never admitted women. Only two men with competence in philology or lexicography have ever been members of the Academy: Antoine Furetière, whom it expelled (cf. below) and Gaston Paris (1839–1903).

25. Among those who satirised it may be mentioned the Seigneur de Saint-Évremond (1613–1703) and Gilles Ménage (cf. §11.3) in the seventeenth century; and, in the eighteenth, the wit Alexis Piron (1689–1773). The last-mentioned wrote an epitaph for his own tomb:

> Ci-gît Piron, qui ne fut rien,
> Pas même académicien

'Here lies Piron, who was nothiug—not even a member of the Academy'.

26. Cf. Fischer 1937; Gégou 1962.

27. Cf. Brunot 1932; Baudry de Saunier 1932; Laronde 1933.

28. Cf. Molíns 1870.

29. For the aims of the three great Academy dictionaries of the seventeenth and eighteenth centuries, cf. Viscardi et al. 1959. For the history of French dictionaries in general, cf. Matoré 1967.

30. For the concepts of *purism* and *purist*, cf. Vitale 1964.

31. Our notions of "correctness," as applied to English, go back to the eighteenth century; cf. S. A. Leonard 1929. A similar work for French or any other Romance language has yet to be done.

32. For Valencian diglossia, from the sixteenth century onwards, cf. Ninyoles 1969.

33. Cf. Migliorini 1960:448–450.

34. For the history of grammar in France, cf. Kukenheim 1962; in Italy, Trabalza 1908; in Spain, from Nebrija to the present, Malaret 1948.

35. Cf. Poggi Salani 1969, 1971.

36. Cf. Straka (ed.) 1964.

37. Cf. Elwert 1970.

38. For "prefixoid," cf. Migliorini 1935.

39. First borrowed as /krustáčeo/ *crustaceo* by Redi; cf. Migliorini 1960:489.

40. For Galileo, cf. Altieri Biagi 1965a; for Redi, Altieri Biagi 1968; for Malpighi, Altieri Biagi 1966.

41. Cf. M. Fubini 1969.

42. For Spanish influence on Italian, cf. Croce 1895; Beccaria 1968. On French: Schmidt 1914; Ruppert 1915.

43. The use of proclitic *Don* (and the corresponding full feminine form *Donna*) with a given name or a full name (*e.g. Don Nunzio; Donna Angelina Lauro*), after the Spanish fashion, has survived in southern Italy and Sicily. On other parts of Italy, only *Don* has survived, but used with a last name alone, as well, and only when referring to a priest, *e.g. Don Giovanni Bosco* or *Don Bosco*.

44. Cf. Hall 1960c; Beccaria 1968:20. From the examples quoted by the latter, it is clear that the Italian verb must be a back-formation, as can be seen from the thematic vowel /-i-/ (if the verb had been borrowed directly from Spanish, it would have been */attrevé⌣rsi/ *attreversi*) and from the nonreflexive use.

45. Cf. Hall 1958b.

46. The ultimate origin of *baroque* and its congeners is not clear (cf. Hall 1962d and references given there), but we are sure that it was of Portuguese origin and referred to something uneven, distorted, or twisted.

47. In 1765, for instance, when the young Goethe went to Leipzig, he found it entirely given over to imitation of French manners, so much so that it was called *Klein-Paris* 'Little Paris'.

48. The French word /linžaᶻ/ *linges* 'linens' had been borrowed into Italian as /línǧi/ *lingi*, by Machiavelli; but this form is a hapax legomenon and did not catch on (cf. Mazzoni 1939).

49. Cf. Altieri Biagi 1963.

50. Itself a loan from Alsatian German /bí + và:xe/ *Biwache* = Ger. /báj + và:xe/ *Beiwache*, lit. 'by-watch'.

51. In Italy, mean-while, the word /kasíno/, with Italian-type stress, became specialised in the meaning 'house of ill fame, brothel'.

52. Fr. /alarme^r/ *alarmer* was formed on the noun /alarmə/ *alarme*, itself a sixteenth-century loan from the Italian cry /allárme/ *all'arme* 'to (the) arms!'.

53. The lists given by Migliorini (1960:576–578) could, in general, be paralleled for Spanish and Portuguese. For the Spanish reaction against eighteenth- and early nine-teenth-century Gallicisms, cf. Rubio 1937. For eighteenth-century French influence on Venetian, cf. Zolli 1971.

54. So much so that the typical "common practice" in west European music from ca. 1600 to ca. 1915, the melodic line, and the base of articulation in singing favored by vocal teachers and choir-masters, was derived from seventeenth-century Italian speech-charac-teristics; cf. Hall, forthcoming-c. Hence, understandably enough, the folkloristic notion that Italian is an "especially musical language."

55. For the detailed history of *espressivo*, cf. W. W. Austin 1954.

56. In the title of Molière's play, *Les Fourberies de Scapin* (1671), both contentives are Italian loans, with /furbəriə/ *fourberie* < It. /furbería/ *furberia* 'rascality' (:/fúrbo/ *furbo* 'rascally').

57. In Italian, as is well known, the gender and number of an adjective used in this way varies with the sex and number of the persons addressed; in the languages into which the expression *bravo* was borrowed, however, it has remained invariable.

58. Cf. Praz 1927 for this and similar expressions which either were never current in their language of presumed origin (like *dolce far niente*) or which have preserved earlier meanings that have become obsolete in the source-language (*e.g.* Eng. *smoking* as a noun, meaning 'smoking-jacket, tuxedo').

59. Many of these Anglicisms had, in their turn, been borrowed into Middle English from French, such as *parliament* and *jury*.

60. Itself a loan-word from an Indic form related to Sanskrit /paṇča/ 'five', because, we are told, the drink originally contained five ingredients.

CHAPTER 9

Changes in Social Structure

In the nineteenth and twentieth centuries, the external history of the Romance languages has been related chiefly to changes which have taken place in two main aspects of modern life: social structure and channels of communication. These will accordingly form the topics of this and the following chapter. Against the back-ground of these changes, the officially recognised literary languages inherited from the Renaissance and Baroque periods (cf. Chapters 7, 8) have undergone various modifications and expansions, and have seen the rise of new subvarieties and of competitors for the function of standards. The major changes in social structure were brought about by industrialisation and its consequences involving altered relations between classes, political organisations, and emigrant groups.

9.1. Industrialisation

Industrialisation was by no means an absolute novelty in the nineteenth century; its early origins date far back in the Middle Ages.[1] However, it did not really begin to develop rapidly until the latter part of the eighteenth century in England, and until the nineteenth century on the European continent. As is universally recognised,[2] it brought with it manifold and rapid changes in almost all aspects of living, which were reflected in language, particularly in lexicon and in the relative prestige of different types of usage.

9.11. TECHNOLOGICAL CHANGE AND LEXICON. The initial impact of the "Industrial Revolution" lay in the introduction of a great many new ways of manufacturing both already well-known objects of consumption and new items; new ways of marketing them; and new ways of transporting both merchandise and people. This expansion of technology, and the corresponding development of theoretical and applied science, inevitably brought about a corresponding increase of terms to refer to the new phenomena, in many fields. Systematically organised terminologies were introduced during the French Revolution for the months, the days of the week, and the measurement of length, area, and weight.[3] These sets of terms were invented *ex novo*, almost wholly on Graeco-Latin bases, and in accordance with pre-determined theories, especially use of the decimal system (not only in the metric measurements, but also in Fabre d'Églantine's substitution of the "décade" or period of ten days in place of the seven-day week). The Revolutionary calendar did not survive, but the metric system did, and has by now been adopted in a large part of the world. Most terminologies, however, did not develop in so systematic a way. In any given field, we find, for the most part, a mixture of terms, of various origins.[4] In the early stages of a new technology, there was usually fluctuation among the terms employed, until one or another became generalised, out-distancing its competitors, which might then either disappear entirely or remain as old-fashioned, literary, or even poetical synonyms.[5] Thus, in the early and middle nineteenth century, Italian had a number of expressions for 'railroad', consisting mostly of terms for road' (*strada, cammino, via*) with phrases indicating the material, iron, of which it was made (*di ferro* 'of iron', *in ferro* 'in iron', *ferrato* '[of] iron', *ferraio* 'pertaining to iron', *ferràbile* 'connected with iron') or the rails involved (*e.g. a canali* 'with channels', *a striscie* 'with strips', *a guide* 'with guides', *a rotaie* 'with rails'). All of these were eventually replaced by the compound *ferrovia* 'iron road', except that *strada ferrata* has survived as a rather high-sounding literary or juridical term.[6]

The countries from which most terminological innovations came were England and France, with contributions ranking in that order. In certain fields (*e.g.* railways and horse-drawn vehicles), English furnished most of the items. In others (*e.g.* air-transport, automobiles), French was a more important source, since many of the earliest developments took place in France. Italian, Spanish, Portuguese, and especially Roumanian were, in general, passively receptive in technical terminology. Only occasionally do we find one of these latter languages serving as a source for lexical innovations in technological matters, as did Italian with the adjective /ferroviário/ *ferroviario* 'pertaining to railways' (> Sp. id., Fr. /ferovjer/ *ferroviaire*[7]).

One of the most important reservoirs, linguistically speaking, for new technical and scientific terms was the lexicon of Latin and Greek.[8] In such fields as chemistry, physics, and astronomy, by far the largest number of terms were coinages utilising Graeco-Latin elements as prefixoids (*e.g. hydro-* 'water', *oxy-* 'sharp', *poly-* 'many'), derivational bases (*e.g. ferr-* 'orn', *stann-* 'tin', *cupr-* 'copper') or suffixes (*e.g.* Gk. /$^+$ikós/ -ικός 'pertaining to' > Fr. /$^+$ik/ *-ique* and It., Sp. /$^+$' iko/ and Port. /$^+$' iku/ -*ico*; Lat. /$^+$o:su-/ -*ōsu-* '-ous' > Fr. /$^+$ø$^$/ -*euse -eux* and It. /$^+$ó$^$so/, Sp. /$^+$óso/, Port. /$^+$ó$^$zu/ -*oso*). Often hybrid compounds resulted, as in Eng. *ferric*,

Fr. /ferik/ *ferrique*, etc., or Fr. /syrkostal/ *surcostal* 'supercostal'. The practice of making such formations has continued down to the present times, in ever increasing proportions, in theoretical fields like nuclear physics (cf. *electron, neutron, proton*) and also in applied fields such as electronic transmission and reproduction of sound, e.g. *radiophony* (abbr. *radio* in almost all European and other languages), *heterodyde, superheterodyne, phonograph, gramophone, disc* (and compounds such as *discography* [on the model of *bibliography*] and Fr. /diskotek/ *discothèque* 'collection of records'[9]), *monophonic, stereophonic, quadriphonic*, etc.

It is very rare for a term to be coined wholly *ex novo* (the stock examples are van Helmont's *gas* [ca. 1600] and George Eastman's *kodak* [1888][10]), but when a science or a technology is in its infancy, already existing words are likely to be used in transferred meanings. In certain fields of inquiry, this has been the source of most new terminology, as in economics (with expressions like *value, interest, marginal*, and their Romance equivalents). In the abortive development of railways in pre-Revolutionary France,[11] and in French descriptions of developments in England, we find 'rail' represented by /ornjer/ *ornière* 'rut' (1803), /gid/ *guide* 'guide' (1776), /bãd/ *bande* 'band' (1784), and /baro/ *barreau* 'bar'. In some instances, if a parallel technology has developed a set of terms, one or more of these can be transferred. Thus, canal-transport, which was a serious competitor of railways in the early nineteenth century, furnished such terms in French as /por/ *port* (1821) or /porsek/ *port sec* 'dry port' (1828), /ãbarkader/ *embarcadère* 'landing-stage' (1834), and /gar/ *gare* 'mooring-place' (1830's), in addition to /stasjõ/ *station*, for the place along a railway-line where passengers could get on or off trains.[12] For the cars, early French terms included /šarjo/ *chariot* and /furgõ/ *fourgon* 'truck'; for the 'tender', /alež/ *allège* '(towed) barge' was at first widely used.[13] Circumlocutions, in the form of phrases, are also not uncommon, especially at the out-set of a new technology. We have already mentioned It. *strada* (*cammino, via*) *ferrata* 'iron road', etc., and one may also cite the parallel French phrases /šəmẽferê^/ *chemin ferré* (1780) and /vwaferê^/ *voie ferrée* (1784) which preceded /šəmẽtfer/ *chemin de fer*.

The proportion of loan-words, often international in their extent, became very large in the course of the nineteenth century in the applied sciences and technologies. In French, for instance, the terms for 'rail' mentioned above were replaced, in the first half of the century, by the English borrowing *rail*, at first often pronounced /rel/, but later /raj/. In Spain, where the institution of railways came towards the middle of the century, Eng. *rail* was borrowed as /rél/ *rel*, later reshaped to /riél/ *riel*. Among the various terms used at first in Italy, English *rail* was represented by /rél/, pl. /réli/ *rail -i*, and by an imitation of the French /raj/ as /ráḷḷo/ *raglio*.

This last-mentioned form was, unfortunately, homonymous with the word for 'bray (of a donkey)', and has long since been replaced in general usage by /rotáia/ *rotaia* (:/ruóta/ *ruota* 'wheel'). The derivatives /dereḷḷáre/ *deragliare* 'to derail' and /deraḷḷaménto/ *deragliamento* 'derailment', however, were not so obviously related to /ráḷḷo/ *ragiio* 'bray', and have survived. Among other wide-spread English loans in this field were *wag(g)on* > Fr. /vagõ/ (spelled also *vag[g]on, vaguon*[14]), It. /vagó^ne/ *vagone*, Sp. /bagón/ *vagón*; tunnel (itself a loan-word from OFr. /tonelə/ *tonnelle*) > Fr. /tynel/ and It., Sp. /túnel/ *túnel*; *tram(way)* > Fr. /tram(we)/, It. /tram(vái)/ *tram, tramway, tranvai* (also half-Italianized to /tramvía/ *tranvia*); and *locomotive* > Fr. /lokomotiv/, It. /lokomotíva/ and Sp. /lokomotíba/ *locomotive*.[15]

Examples of French terminology spreading with new inventions are such words for parts of aeroplanes as /elrõ/ *aileron* > Eng. /éjləràn/, It. /aleró^ne/ *alerone*, Sp. /alerón/ *alerón*; and for parts of automobiles or people connected with them as *automobile* itself. (Fr. /o^tomobil/ > It. /automóbile/ *automobile* and Sp. /automóbil/ *automovil*, with the abbreviations formed with the element *auto-* used alone[16]); /karbyratœr/ *carburateur* 'carburettor' (> It. /karburató^re/ *carburatore*, Sp. /karburadór/ *carburador*); and /šofœr/ *chauffeur*, originally 'heater, fireman' (> It. *id.*, Sp. /čófer/ *chófer*). Here, likewise, individual terms had different fates in different countries: *chauffeur* was replaced in Italian by /autísta/ *autista* (cf. §9.12), but has become the normal term in Spanish.

9.12. PRESTIGE-FACTORS IN USAGE. In many instances, the use of novelties, in artifacts and in vocabulary, was accompanied by an increase in prestige, and hence the introduction of foreign terms had considerable snob-value. This factor was at the base of the spread of many Anglicisms in the nineteenth century, especially those related to elegant life, such as new types of (horse-drawn) carriages like the *brougham* (> It. /brúm/ *brum*, whence also /brumísta/ *brumista* 'driver') or the *tilbury*. Socially prestigious activities, also, were known by their English names, *e.g.* Fr. /ləfivoklok/ *le five o'clock* 'afternoon tea',[17] /lə'iglif/ *le high-life*, and such garb worn by gentlemen as /ləsmokiŋ/ *le smoking* 'the tuxedo'. Knowledge of the pronunciation of foreign languages spread widely enough, on occasion, to introduce new phonemes (*e.g.* Eng. /ŋ/ in words ending in *-ing*) or to reïntroduce features of phonology which had previously been lost (*e.g.* consonant-doubling in French, practised in imitation of Italian, especially after prefixes like /il+ in+ im+/ *il- in- im-*, as in /illyzjõ/ *illusion*, /immobil/ *immobile*, /inne^/ *inné* 'innate'). In the case of Roumanian, the prestige of French was so great as to introduce thousands of French words—a process which is still going on—and to make much of the Roumanian vocabulary consist simply of French lexicon with Roumanian endings. Thus we find (opening the dictionary at random) such Gallicisms as /glasá/ *glasa* 'to glaze (candies, etc.)' < Fr. /glase^r/ *glacer*; /eksistá/ *exista* 'to exist' < Fr. /egziste^/ *exister*; /ekspertízə/ *expertiză* 'expert knowledge' < Fr. /ekspertiz/ *expertise*; /modérn/ *modern* < Fr. /modern/ *moderne*; etc.

As might be expected, opposition to foreignisms has frequently arisen, on both linguistic and nonlinguistic grounds. Self-appointed guardians of linguistic "purity" have often protested, ever since Baroque times (cf. Chapter 8), against the introduction of non-native words, alleging that they were unnecessary and harmful to the language.[18] On occasion, especially with the aid of the publicity afforded by modern mass-media, purists have attracted wide popular attention with their campaigns, such as that which René Etiemble mounted, in the 1950's and 1960's, against what he termed /ləfrãgle/ *le franglais*.[19] In the long run, such campaigns are never effective, since need for new terminology and prestige-values will always outweigh considerations of "purity" with normal speakers of a language, and Frenchmen, say, will go on leaving their automobiles in /ləparkiŋ/ *le parking* next to /ləbildiŋ/ *le building* where they are giving an interview to improve /ləstãdiŋ/ *le standing*, while their wives are having a /šãpwẽ/ *shampooing* at the beauty-parlor,[20] no matter what any purist may say. In the short run, purists can do a certain amount of harm,[21] and can bring about results opposite to those which they wish to achieve, by intervention in situations concerning which they have little or no first-hand knowledge. Thus, in Italian, the car immediately following a steam-locomotive and carrying coal and water was known among railway-men as a /(vagó^nedi) skórta/ (*vagone di*) *scorta* 'supply-car', whereas the most widely used word among nonprofessionals was the English loan *tender*. In their opposition to *tender*, the Italian nineteenth-century purists suggested all kinds of confusing and ambiguous substitutes, *e.g.* /magaȼȼíno/ 'ware-house', /dispénsa/ *dispensa* 'pantry', or /serbatóio/ *serbatoio* 'tank', all of which were useless because they were already preëmpted in other meanings. But the purists did not know *scorta* and hence failed to recommend it. *Tender*, therefore, won out in standard Italian despite puristic opposition, because it was the only available completely unambiguous term.[22]

In a few minor instances, puristic authorities, particularly the Académie Française, were consulted and gave advice. When a small group of speakers initiated the linguistic novelty and the innovation spread from such a focus, it stood a good chance of being adopted. Thus, in the early twentieth century, when a group of Parisian cab-drivers began to use fare-meters in their vehicles, they wanted to call their cabs /taksametr/ *taxamètre = taxe à mètre* 'fare by meter'.[23] They consulted the Académie Française, and were told that the form ought, rather, to be /taksimetr/ *taximètre*—the form which they adopted and which has served as the base for the world-wide abbreviation *taxi*. In the 1950's, the Italian linguist Bruno Migliorini suggested certain equivalents for English terms, such as /spoḷḷaré^llo/ *spogliarello* (:/spoḷḷársi/ *spogliarsi* 'to undress') as a substitute for *strip-tease*, and /ragáẹẹaskuíllo/ *ragazza squillo* 'girl [ready to answer the] ring [of the telephone]' to replace Eng. *call-girl*. These terms were popularised by the Italian radio, television, and film-industry. On the other hand, a decision made by the speech-community as a whole (and largely outside of awareness) can never be influenced by the dicta of some "authority," whether an academy or an individual. On its introduction, Fr. /o^tomobil/ *automobile* was decreed by the Académie Française to be masculine; but, in the French-speaking world, speakers have universally made it feminine, without respect for any academic pronouncements.

Puristic hostility to foreignisms can, on occasion, be taken over by political movements, and made part of nationalistic antiforeign propaganda. In Italy, the Fascist government (1922–1945) undertook a strong campaign against loan-words from French and English, calling on speakers of Italian to replace, for instance, /otél/ *hôtel* by /albérgo/ *albergo* 'inn', /garáǧe/ *garage* by /àutorimé^ssa/ *autorimessa* 'auto-storage-place', /šofœr/ *chauffeur* by /autísta/ *autista* 'auto-driver', /demarráǧe/ *démarrage* 'starting' by /avviaménto/ *avvimento* 'getting under way', /ferrovía/ *ferrovia* 'railway' by /strádaferráta/ *strada ferrata* (cf. §9.11), or /lokomotíva/ *locomotiva* f. by /lokomotó^re/ *locomotore* m.[24] In some instances, these attempts to "purify" the language were successful, as with the words cited above for 'garage' and 'chauffeur'. In others, especially in sports-terminology, they were quite unsuccessful, and /gól/ *gol* 'goal', /básket/ *basket*, etc., have continued in normal (especially oral) use, despite all efforts to replace them by /ré^te/ *rete* 'net', /čésta/ *cesta* 'basket', and the likes. Still other Fascist coinages have survived, but apparently with no political over-tones, *e.g.* the term for 'internal-combustion-engined rail-car', /littorína/ *littorina* (:/littó^r-/ *littor-* 'lictor'), as opposed to the learnèd term /automotríče/ *automotrice*.

9.2. Political Changes

Beginning with the French Revolution in 1789, and continuing down to the present day, there has been a series of changes in the political organisazation of virtually all nations, resulting in large-scale reorientation of traditional values and attitudes, with respect to language as well as to many other matters.

9.21. THE TRANSFER OF POWER. In the Baroque period, throughout the Romance-speaking world (as in many other regions), power was concentrated in the hands of a small upper class, normally the hereditary aristocracy.[25] During the nearly two centuries following the French Revolution this situation has very largely been altered, with the rise of a middle class between the old aristocracy and the plebs, and with great increase in upward mobility. The linguistic effects of this transfer have included a great loosening of standards of usage, inevitable in a situation where many previously condemned features of speech have come to be used by persons enjoying new power and prestige. The most notorious instance of such a change is the replacement, in early nineteenth-century French standard speech, of earlier /we/ by the lower-class pronunciation /wa/, as in *loi* 'law', earlier /lwe/ > /lwa/, and a host of other forms with the spelling *oi*.[26] Similarly, and at much the same time, an earlier palatal lateral /l/ was replaced by the previously lower-class pronunciation /j/ (as in *fille* /filə/ 'daughter' > /fij/). Such developments can of course result in structural changes, as when the last-mentioned shift introduced a new semiconsonant /j/, and, parallel to this, there developed also the corresponding semiconsonants /w/ and /ɥ/.

Not only new governments, but, in some instances, new nations resulted from the transfer of power. This was especially true in one region of Romance speech in the Old-World—Roumania—and in the whole of Spanish- and Portuguese-speaking America. The territorial fortunes of these regions shifted during the nineteenth and twentieth centuries, but without basically affecting the linguistic situation. In Roumania, the principalities of Walachia and Moldavia were united in 1859, with the capital at Bucureşti (Bucharest), whose speech soon became the standard. Until after the First World War, the western portion of the Roumanian dialect-area remained under Austro-Hungarian rule; since 1919, with only a brief interruption, this region has formed part of Roumania. (Bessarabia, on the other hand, with its own variety of Roumanian, was part of Roumania proper only from 1919 to 1945, after which it was ceded to the U.S.S.R. and "Moldavian" was set up as a separate officially recognised language [cf. §2.15.1.*b*].) Roumanian was then faced with the problem of attaining, in a short time, the lexical extent and variety necessary for it to function as a national standard—a stage which it had taken the Romance literary languages of western Europe several hundred years to reach. A national academy was set up, and many words were introduced, especially from French (cf. §9.12)—a process which has gone on continuously ever since.[27]

In the Americas, the situation was markedly different, in that the areas of Spanish and Portuguese speech had formerly been colonies, and, despite their new political independence (achieved by stages throughout the nineteenth century), they remained closely dependent culturally upon the mother-countries. In every Latin American country, there has been a continual tension between imitation of Peninsular models, in language as well as in literature, and recognition of local divergences from Castilian or Portuguese standards.[28] In some places, especially Bogotá (Colombia), local speakers with any pretense to social prestige pride themselves on adherence to Castilian norms, even when in actual usage they do not usually observe them.[29] Spanish spelling, although relatively consistent, nevertheless has some ambiguities, which have given rise to unrealistic notions on the part of many speakers and have led to artificial pronunciations.[30] As yet, however, despite increasing recognition of local variations, there has been no movement favouring the establishment of separate norms and hence of a diglossic situation in Spanish American countries or in Brazil. In only one country (Paraguay) has there been *de jure* recognition of an existing bilingual situation, in this case the coexistence of Spanish and Guaraní, both of which are now recognised as national languages.[31]

9.22. INTELLECTUAL ATTITUDES. The shift of power from the old aristocracy to either the proletariat or the plutocracy had inevitable repercussions in speakers' attitudes towards language. These could vary anywhere from enthusiastic acceptance of new features (especially in lexicon) to disdain and rejection. Both of these attitudes were present in nineteenth-century France, Spain, and Italy. The Romantic movement of the 1820's and 1830's drew upon both. The Romantics tended to reject what they considered the "vulgarity" of the new bourgeois and plutocratic world, and to turn their attention to (often idealised) exotic regions and times, especially the Orient and the Middle Ages. On the other hand, particularly in France, where the heavy hand of restrictive neoclassical purism had resulted in an etiolated literary language, the Romantics, with Victor Hugo at their head, advocated far greater freedom in grammar, vocabulary, and metrics. Hugo said of himself (*Les Contemplations* 1.7.41–185):

> Les mots, bien ou mal nés, vivaient parqués en castes;
> Les uns, nobles, hantaient les Phèdres, les Jocastes [. . .]
> Les autres, tas de gueux, drôles patibulaires,
> Habitant les patois, quelques-uns aux galères
> Dans l'argot; dévoués à tous les genres bas,
> Déchirés en haillons dans les halles; sans bas,
> Sans perruque, créés pour la prose et la farce [. . .]
> [. . .] je montai sur la borne Aristote,
> Et déclarai les mots égaux, libres, majeurs,
> Je nommai le cochon par son nom; pourquoi pas? [. . .]

J'ai dit a Vaugelas: "Tu n'es qu'un mâchoire!"
J'ai dit aux mots: "Soyez république!"

'Words, high- or low-born, lived separated in castes; the ones, noble, frequented the Phaedras and the Jocastas [*i.e.* were used in lofty tragedy]; the others, gangs of rascals, hang-dog louts, living in dialects, and some imprisoned in slang; condemned to all the low genres, in tatters and rags in the market-places; without stockings, without wigs, created for prose and farce. [. . .] I expelled Aristotle, and declared all words equal, free, and of age. I called the hog by his right name; why not? [. . .] I said to Vaugelas: "You are only a jaw-bone!".[32] I said to words: "Be a republic!".'

Archaisms, dialectal terms, words from foreign and exotic languages, in short all the types of vocabulary which the purists (whether of Malherbe's or Vaugelas' stamp; cf. §8.2) had banned, were reïntroduced by the French Romantic writers.[33] Nevertheless, particularly in the free use of suffixation, French structure had permanently lost its flexibility in contrast with the other Romance languages.

In Italy, Spain, and Portugal, Romanticism was less specifically associated with linguistic iconoclasm, at least in part because the strangle-hold of neoclassicism had been somewhat less strong in those countries. In Italy, the prime thrust of such Romantic authors and linguistic theorists as Alessandro Manzoni (1785–1873)[34] was, rather, towards the revivification of the literary language by a *rapprochement* with the living usage of the linguistic center, Florence, on whose speech the original standard had been based five centuries previously. After Manzoni's time, the current favouring the use of modern Tuscan gradually became associated with a somewhat affected purism, typified in the writings of Manzoni's chief follower, Edmondo de Amicis (1846–1908).[35] The anticlassical movement was even weaker in the Ibero-Romance countries, where there had never been any really serious opposition to the literary language's keeping step with the times.

9.23. REGIONALISM. Partly as a reaction against excessive centralisation, the local subcultures of such countries as France and Spain came to be the object of special study and cultivation in the middle part of the nineteenth century and after. In literature, as part of the general movement towards greater realism, such French authors as George Sand (Aurore Dupin, 1804–1876), René Bazin (1853–1932), and Maurice Barrès (1862–1923) treated their home regions of Berry, Alsace, and Lorraine, respectively. In Spain, a whole school of "costumbristas" or portrayers of regional customs included José María de Pereda (1832–1905), Juan Valera (1827–1905),

Benito Pérez Galdós (1843–1920), and Armando Palacio Valdés (1853–1938). Spanish American writers, from Mexico to Chile and Argentina, have perforce had to deal with the life and customs of their own regions in order to portray their own experience adequately. The two chief Italian representatives of this approach were Giovanni Verga (1840–1922) and Antonio Fogazzaro (1842–1911), whose tales dealt largely with their native Sicily and Vicenza, respectively. But the most regionalist movement, which went beyond the use of the standard language and restored that of local speech to public estem, was the Félibre of southern France, under the leadership of Frédéri Mistral (of. §6.331).

Not all regionalist efforts were exclusively literary. In Catalonia, the "Renaixença" or renaissance of Catalan literature (cf. §6.316) coïncided with a strong drive towards political autonomy, if not actual independence from Spain. In 1859 the *Jocs Florals* ('Floral Games') were reïnstated in Barcelona, serving as a focus for both literary and political aspirations. Among the leading Catalan authors of the nineteenth and twentieth centuries were the poets Jacint Verdaguer (1854–1902), Joan Alcover (1854–1926), Joan Maragall (1860–1911), Josep Carner (1884–   ); the novelists "Victor Català" (Catalina Albert y Paradis, 1873–1966), and Carles Soldevila (1892–1967); and the dramatist José Ma. Sagarra (1894–1961). The close parallelism in literary and cultural aims between the Catalan drive for regional autonomy and that of the Provençal Félibre aroused such concern in France that Mistral and the Félibriges had to go to great lengths to reassure their fellow-Frenchmen that they had no intention of seeking political autonomy or independence as well. In more recent time, the difference in aims has become even more obvious. Catalan is still, despite the encroachment of Castilian, widely used in every-day speech and in as many printed manifestations as the government will allow (books, magazines, but—as of 1972—not daily news-papers). Modern Provençal or "Occitan" is, on the other hand, all but moribund in every-day speech outside of remote country regions, and is used only as a consciously culti-vated literary vehicle by small groups of intellectuals.

In their linguistic effects, the regionalisms of the different countries varied widely. By and large, there was a correlation between the prevalence of centralised normativism in language-matters, and the avoidance of markedly divergent regional speech-characteristics in the established stand-ard languages. In France, such writers as Sand, Barrès, and Bazin made only timid use of a few words of dialect in their stories. In Italy, Verga and Fogazzaro each introduced dialectal features, but in rather different ways. Verga wrote in almost straightforward standard Italian, with Sicilian dialect represented primarily by syntactic and stylistic peculiarities.[36] Fogazzaro was far bolder in reproducing his characters' dialogue directly, even where it was in Venetian, Lombard, Tuscan, or Roman dialect, and used it largely for comic or heightened emotional effect.[37] With Spanish, Spanish American, and Brazilian authors, no single over-all tendency can be identified, each one using dialectal features according to his own style. Perhaps the most extreme example of the use of dialectal elements in standard Portuguese is found in *Os Sertões* (usually entitled in English 'Rebellion in the Back-lands'; 1902) of the Brazilian Euclides da Cunha (1866–1909). In Argentina, the gauchos, or cow-boys of the frontier regions, developed a variety of Spanish with markedly divergent lexicon and with many morphological and syntactic features of lower-class speech. This *lengua gauchesca* or 'gaucho talk' was used for literary purposes in the latter part of the nineteenth century, especially by José Hernández (1834–1886) in his outstanding frontier-epic *Martín Fierro* (1872–78).[38] In later writings purporting to use the same style, the *gauchesco* dialect became artificial and came to have less resemblance to the original gauchos' actual usage (as also happened in the English of North American "Westerns").[39]

9.3. Class-Structure and Usage

Usage and class-structure were very closely linked, especially in the shifts which took place during the nineteenth century. There were three main parameters along which attitudes towards language were ranged: the degree of social standing, the extent of education, and the presumably intrinsic excellence of the language which an individual speaker or writer might use.

9.31. ARISTOCRATIC VERSUS POPULAR. This opposition continued the Baroque correlation of social position with merit, in language as in other matters. Although often unacknowledged as such, it was at the base of much nineteenth-century purism, especially in the rejection of "vulgarisms," as taught in school-books and grammars. This attitude was carried so far that such a homely word as French /mušwar/ *mouchoir* 'handerchief' caused a near-riot when it was used in the translation of Shakespeare's *Othello* by Alfred de Vigny (1797–1863), performed in 1829—it was too vulgar, especially because it suggested the verb /səmuše^/ *se moucher* 'to blow one's nose'.

9.32. EDUCATED VERSUS NONEDUCATED. As universal primary and later secondary education spread—in France and Switzerland in the nineteenth century, in other Romance-speaking countries in the twentieth—the type of language taught in schools was regarded as characteristic of educated people, and, as such, superior to that of the uneducated. In France, particularly, most school-grammars were based on the doctines of the "universal grammar" which prevailed from the time of Port-Royal (1660) to the *Grammaire des grammaires* ('Grammar of Grammars', 1811 and many later editions) of Charles-Pierre Girault-Duvivier (1765–1832),[40] coupled with an uncritical admiration for the Académie Française and slavish submission to its pronouncements. Beginning with the French Revolution, republican doctrine considered the local dialects as having been fostered by the aristocracy with the deliberate intent of keeping the peasantry of different regions from understanding each other. One of the projects warmly advocated during the French Revolution was the abolition of dialects, through universal education, which was to bring to every-one the "good" language which had previously been reserved for the *aristos*. The first investigation of dialects undertaken in France was that made by the curé Henri-Baptiste Grégoire (1750–1831), with the aim of getting precise information to be used in their extirpation, as envisaged in his *Rapport sur la nécesisté de détruire les patois* ('Report on the Necessity of Destroying Dialects,' 1794). From the same year dated a decree providing for the presence of a teacher of French in every province where it was not already spoken.[41]

In other Romance-speaking countries, such officially sponsored measures of repression and extinction were not taken against dialects, but the gradual spread of education had, as its inevitable effect, their replacement by the national standard language. As this latter, in each country, became better known and more widely used, and more necessary for every-day living, the local dialects came to be studied in greater detail than before, either for the purpose of comparing them with the standard and thus aiding dialect-speakers to avoid mistakes, or as relics of former times to be preserved before they finally disappeared (cf. §11.3).

9.33. "GOOD" VERSUS "BAD" LANGUAGE. Some conservative purists of the nineteenth century, in both France and Italy, justified their aversion to change on the grounds of presumed inherent excellence of earlier usage. This was essentially the position of such Italian purists as the Marchese Basilio Puoti (1782–1847) of Naples, in his opposition to Gallicisms.[42] Organisations for "the defence of the language" are still being founded and fostered, especially in French-speaking regions.[43] Needless to say, such attitudes often have hidden roots in their holders' aversion to modern developments or to change in general, rather than in any objectively provable merit of conservative usage in itself.

9.4. Emigration and Intergroup Contacts

The nineteenth century, with its greatly improved transport-facilities and with a more liberal policy on the part of European governments towards emigration, witnessed a great increase in the mobility of populations, particularly from southern Europe to the Americas. Large numbers of Spaniards, Portuguese, and Italians moved themselves and their families to homes in the New World. Brazil, particularly the southern part, received immigrants from Portugal and Italy; the River Plate area (Uruguay and Argentina), from Spain and Italy. In North America, the United States had a massive wave of Italian immigration from the 1870's to the early 1900's[44]; Canada, a considerably smaller influx, concentrated primarily in Toronto, Ontario. On arrival, these groups tended to form closely knit communities, set apart from the surrounding speakers of other languages. Assimilation to the customs and speech of the new country normally took place fairly rapidly, with the native language of the original immigrants being replaced by that of the new country within three or, at the most, four generations.[45] Features of the earlier immigrant tongues remained, however, so that Romance languages functioned as new substrata, while the languages of the host countries formed new superstrata.

9.41. New Superstrata. The languages of the new countries (Portuguese in Brazil, Spanish in Uruguay and Argentina, English in the United States and Canada) all furnished numerous loans, in vocabulary and also in syntax, to the speech of the immigrants. In the Italo-American of the United States,[46] a host of lexical items reflected the new environment, *e.g.* /kékka/ 'cake', /pinótto/ 'peanut' (pl. /pinóȼȼi/ < *peanuts*), /rúmmu/ 'room', /búkku/ 'book', /tíčča/ ('teacher', /ǧóbba/ 'job', /veššetúbbu/ 'wash-tub', /bakkáusu/ 'toilet' (< /bǽk + hàws/ *'back-house'*),[47] etc. Various exclamations were taken over from English, such as /aȼȼapurigúddu/ 'That's pretty good!', /aȼȼoráiti/ 'That's all right!', /uaȼȼamarauaččú/ 'What's the matter with you?', /goraélli/ 'Go to hell!', /sanemagónna/ 'Son of a gun, ya!' and /sanemabíčča/ 'Son of a bitch, ya!'.[48] Many forms showed a partial adaptation to Italian patterns, especially in suffixation, as in /pressató^re/ 'presser (*e.g.* of pants)', /bordánte/ 'boarder', or (with Neapolitan /nkóppǝ/ 'up') /nkòppastéssa/ 'upstairs' and /nkòppatáuna/ 'uptown'. Some Italian words were reïnterpreted semantically, under the influence of phonetically similar English words, *e.g.* /árto/ 'limb (of the body) > heart', /stíma/ 'esteem > steamer', /bósso/ 'box(wood) > boss', /grossería/ 'rude behavior, insult > grocery', /olivé^tta/ 'olivette (olive-shaped artificial pearl) > elevated (railroad)', /ǧórǧo/ 'George > judge'.

The same kind of borrowings are found in the speech of Italian emigrants to Australia and New Zealand.[49]

Similar developments took place in the language of Italian immigrants in the River Plate area and in Brazil.[50] Here, due to the similarities between Italo- and Ibero-Romance, the lexical borrowings from Spanish and Portuguese into the immigrants' speech were perhaps fewer than in North America, but structural cross-currents were greater. In the *cocoliche* or Italian immigrants' language in Argentina, we find such words as /máte/ 'Paraguayan tea', /bombíǧ(ǧ)a/ 'thermos-like container for *mate*' (< River Plate Spanish /bombíja/ [bom-'bi-ža]), /čurrásko/ 'filet mignon', /čé/ 'exclamation of familiarity', /makanúdo/ 'very good'. Some loan-shifts took place under Spanish influence, such as /assúnto/ 'assumed > affair, matter' (Sp. /asúnto/ *asunto*); /dispáččo/ 'despatch > office' (Sp. /despáčo *despacho*); /portáre/ 'to carry > to be . . . old', with an indication of a number of years, *e.g.* /kuántiánnipórtaɨ/ 'how old is he?', on the model of Sp. /kuántosáŋosjébaɨ/ *¿cuántos años lleva?*, lit. 'how many years does he carry?'. We also find loan-blends like /desprevenúto/ 'unprepared' < Sp. /desprebenído/ *desprevenido* ∼ It. /⁺úto/ -*uto* past part.

Many features of local Spanish pronunciation have been carried over into the *cocoliche*, *e.g.* the replacement of nonprevocalic /s/ by /h/, as in /finísko/ 'I finish' > /finíhko/; the development of voiced fricatives as intervocalic allophomene of voiced stops, *e.g.* /vábéne/ (without syntactic doubling after /vá/!) ['va-βene 'all right, lit. it goes well']; or the use of /rr/ in word-initial position, as in /rrósa/ 'rose'. Morphosyntactic influence is evident in such Hispanisms as the use of the Spanish plural-suffix /-s/, as in /fučíles/ 'guns' (normal Italian /fučíli/ *fucili*); shift in gender, *e.g.* from masculine to feminine in words like /lalátte/ 'the milk' or /lamiélə/ 'the honey' (modelled on Sp. /laléče/ *la leche* and /lamiél/ *la miel*, respectively); the borrowings of the Spanish "neuter" pronoun /lo/, as in /lokevuói/ 'that which you wish'; or the use of the auxiliary (tené^re/ 'to hold' instead of /avé^re/ 'to have' in perfect phrases, *e.g.* /téngoportáto/ 'I have carried' (Standard It. /ópportáto/ *ho portato*).

An analogous situation is found in the language of the Portuguese immigrants to New England, particularly in the Massachusetts cities of Fall River and New Bedford.[51] Here, we find straight loans from English of the type of /dáipas/ 'diapers', /kárič̌i/ 'cottage', /tomé^ina/ 'tomato' (of course with American English /éj/), /alpestéris/ 'upstairs', /šutár/ 'to shoot', and many others. Loan-shifts, some of them amusing or disgusting to native speakers of standard Portuguese, include changes of meaning like those involved in /grosería/ 'rude behavior > grocery', /rrúmu/ 'a ship's course > room', /kráka/ 'furrow > cracker, biscuit', or /bordár/ 'to embroider > board (*e.g.* in a boarding-house)'.

In Canadian French, likewise, Anglicisms have been and are still making great head-way, despite much puristic opposition.[52] Although the French-speaking immigrants arrived in the province of Quebec in the seventeenth and eighteenth centuries, their migration to other parts of Canada (e.g. in the neighborhood of Winnipeg, Alberta) and to parts of New England took place only later, and, in general, their situation vis-à-vis speakers of English has been very similar to that of Italian or Portuguese immigrant. There are a host of English lexical borrowings in Canadian French, such as /gazolin/ *gazoline* (≠ Fr. /esãs/ *essence*), /katš/ *catch* (≠ Fr. /seryr/ *serrure* 'latch'), /min/ 'mean' (≠ Fr. meskē/ *mesquin* 'contemptible'), /staf/ 'staff' (≠ Fr. /personel/ *personnel*), and also of loan-shifts like /kase^/ *cassé* = Eng. *broke* 'without money', /komersjel/ *commerciel* 'commercial (on radio, television, etc.)'. A similarly heavy penetration of Anglicisms is to be observed in the Spanish of Puerto Rico,[53] Colorado,[54] New Mexico, Arizona, and southern California, with a multitude of borrowings like /bloféro/ 'bluffer', /suíče/ 'switch', /tróle/ 'trolley', /parkeár/ 'to park', /čekeár/ 'to check', and of course a great many terms from /béisbol/ 'base-ball', /fútbol/ 'foot-ball' and other sports.

9.42. NEW ROMANCE SUBSTRATA. In certain countries where speakers of Romance languages have settled, they have not only borrowed features from the local "superstratum," but their speech has acted as a "substratum," introducing lexical and (in some instances) also structural innovations into the language which their descendants have grown up speaking. In North America, Italian influence has been almost wholly lexical: especially names of Italian foods, such as *pizza, spaghetti, macaroni*, and *vermicelli* have come into every-day use.[55] In the River Plate area, there are similar lexical borrowings, like /espagétis/ *espaguetis*, /rrabiólis/ *raviolis*, /pȧsta/ 'macaroni', but the influence of Italian has extended to structure as well. These borrowings have come from not only the current colloquial language, as in /čáu/ *chau* 'so long!'[56] (< It. /čáo/ *ciao* < Venetian /šao/ *sciao* '[your] servant'; cf. the use of Lat. *šervus* in this function in Austria and Hungary), but also from Italian dialects (e.g. /eskašáto/ 'broken, crushed' < SIt. /skaššáto/) and argots (e.g. /kána/ 'prison, police' < Venetian slang /kána/). Certain Italian suffixes have been borrowed and have become productive in River Plate Spanish, e.g. /+éli/, diminutive and contemptuous, as in /pesadéli/ 'sort of heavy', /lokatéli/ 'crazy, batty, cuckoo'; this suffix is thought[57] to have been extracted from the Italian surname /lokaté^lli/ *Locatelli*, due to its chance similarity to the Spanish word /lóko/ *loco* 'crazy'. In Brazil, likewise, the Italian immigrants' speech has left some traces.[58]

Spanish has furnished some expressions to North American English, coming in particularly through the usage of ranchers and other settlers and workers in the old South-west: *e.g. vamoose* 'leave, esp. in a hurry' < Sp. /bambós/ *vamos* 'let's go!', *calaboose* 'jail' < Sp. /kalabóso/ *calabozo, lasso* < Sp. /láso/ *lazo* 'loop' or *loco* 'crazy' < Sp. /lóko/ *loco*. A few names of foods have entered as well, *e.g. tamales* < Sp. /tamáles/ *tamales* pl. (with a new singular *tamale* [≠ Sp. /tamál/] being formed in English), *arroz con pollo* < Sp. /arróskompójo/, id. 'chicken with rice', or *chile con carne* < Sp. /čílekonkárne/ id. 'chili with meat'.

NOTES TO CHAPTER 9

1. For the Middle Ages, cf. especially White 1962; for the Renaissance, Nef 1954, 1958.

2. Cf. especially Dietz 1927 and Henderson 1961.

3. In addition to the discussions of railway-terminology in Swann 1918 and Wexler 1955 (for France) and Peter 1969 (for Italy), and of the prefixoids *auto-* and *aero-* in Swann 1918, cf. Troeger 1928 for the terminology of tanning; Zastrow 1963 for that of lighter-than-air transport in France; Guilbert 1965 for aviation in France and Guilbert 1967 for astronautics; and R. Giacomelli 1952 for aeronautical terms in Italian.

4. Cf. Swann 1918, chapters 4 and 5.

5. As Wexler points out (1955:113–114), legal documents, such as companies' charters and franchises, were often influential in fixing usage.

6. Cf. Peter 1969, chapter 1.

7. Cf. Peter 1969:44–46.

8. Cf. Migliorini 1956.

9. Taken over into English in the 1960's with the inexplicable shift of meaning 'record-collection > noisy night-club'.

10. As has often been pointed out, not even formations like *gas* or *kodak* are really "created" *ex nihilo*, since they consist of already existing phonemes of the inventor's language; they fit into its morphological and syntactic patterns; and they bear at least some resemblance to other lexical features (for instance, van Helmont's *gas* /xas/ is similar to the Dutch pronunciation of *chaos* (/xaos/).

11. Cf. Wexler 1955, chapter 2.

12. Cf. Wexler 1955, chapter 8.

13. Cf. Wexler 1955, chapter 10.

14. Cf. Wexler 1955:118–119.

15. On occasion, in such borrowings, strange combinations are made which are foreign to the source-language, *e.g.* Fr. /watman/ *wattman* 'motorman (of a street-car)'.

16. Sometimes, abbreviations of this type can lead to semantic collision. In Italian, for instance, /áuto/ *auto* for the vehicle is homonymous with the prefixoid /auto:/ 'self'. Humourous effects can result from unguarded new-formations with such elements, as in It. /áutodemoliƥió^ne/ *autodemolizione* 'demolition of automobiles' but also 'self-demolition' (cf. Cordié 1963). Similarly, after the Florence flood of 1966, owners of flood-damaged vehicles were referred to as /àutoalluvionáti/ *autoalluvionati* (:/alluvionáto/ *alluvionato* 'flooded'), a term which could also mean 'self-flooded'.

17. With the shift to the meaning of 'afternoon tea', or simply 'tea' as a meal, this term has lost its reference to a specific time, so that one can speak of /ləfivoklokdəkatrœr/ *le five o'clock de quatre heures* 'four o'clock tea'. It is reported that one restaurant advertised /fivoklok atutzœr/ *five o'clock à toutes heures* 'tea at all hours'.

18. Cf. the amusing examples of nineteenth-century French protests against Anglicisms cited in Nyrop 1899–1930:1.94–99.

19. Cf. Étiemble 1964.

19. Cf. Étiemble 1964.

20. And will use the verb /šǎpwine^r/ *champouiner* 'to shampoo', on the analogy of /badine^r/ *badiner* 'to jest':/badē/ *badin* 'jesting', etc.

21. Cf. Devoto 1970.

22. Cf. Peter 1969:130–143.

23. This early formation still survives in the Swedish abbreviation /táksa/ *taxa* 'taxi'.

24. These campaigns were accompanied by (often highly inaccurate) statements concerning the foreignisms which were to be eliminated. As a foreigner learning Italian, I was told in 1933–34 that, for instance, *ferrovia* 'railway' was an ugly Germanism, a calque on Ger. /áizen + bà:n/ *Eisenbahn* (whereas it was actually, in its historical origin, a back-formation on /ferroviário/ *ferroviario* 'pertaining to railways'; cf. Petre 1969:44–46), and that the noun /lokomotíva/ *locomotiva* 'locomotive' was an effeminate Gallicism.

25. The classical description of the French pre-Revolutionary situation is of course Taine 1875–94.

26. The story is told (cf. Nyrop 1899–1930:1.178) that a woman was accused of being a royalist, during the Revolution, because it was alleged that she had said /ilfotoērwe/ *Il faut un roi* 'we need a king'. Her defense was that she had said, not *un roi* 'a king', but *un rouet* 'a spinning-wheel'; both would have been, in the old pronunciation, /oērwe/. After a few such experiences, people would soon learn to say /rwa/ rather than /rwe/ for *roi* 'king'.

27. Especially since the Second World War, the Roumanian Academy has been very active in promoting an etymological dictionary, a descriptive dictionary, a historical grammar, and various dialectal studies (including a new linguistic atlas), done according to modern criteria, but unfortunately not free of political bias.

28. Hence there has been extensive discussion, centered mostly around "the defence of the language" (as in Salinas 1944 and many similar works). Cf. also such writings as Herrero Mayor 1943 and those collected in Presente y Futuro (cf. the list of abbreviations in the References).

29. For instance, many conservative speakers from Bogotá are thoroughly convinced that they make a distinction between /b/ [b] *b* and /v/ [v] *v*, and insist on teaching this distinction to foreign learners, even through in actual practice no-one makes it in the entire Spanish-speaking world, themselves least of all.

30. Cf. Rosenblat 1963.

31. Cf. Rubin 1968.

32. An obvious reference to Judges 15.15.

33. Cf. Brunot and Bruneau 1905–1969, vol. 12.

34. Manzoni rewrote his novel *I Promessi Sposi* ('The Betrothed', 1827) by going to live in Florence and substituting, wherever he considered it necessary, expressions of current Florentine speech for Lombardisms or archaisms that he had used in the first edition. The second, definitive edition (1840–42) was thus the result of his having gone to, as he put it, *risciacquare i panni in Arno* 'rinse out his clothes in the Arno'. He also wrote a number of discussions of the entire problem of the Italian standard language, favoring the adoption of contemporary Florentine usage, though he never got around to completing the extensive treatise on the *questione della lingua* which he intended to write. For Manzoni's linguistic writings, cf. Reynolds 1950. For the penetration of Manzonian doctrines into school-curricula, cf. Raicich 1966.

35. Cf. Gigli 1962.

36. Cf. Raya 1962.
37. Cf. Hall 1967b, chapter 6.
38. Cf. Tiscornia 1930.
39. Cf. Rona 1963.
40. For Girault-Duvivier, cf. Levitt 1968.
41. On the treatment of French dialects during and after the Revolution, cf. Pop 1950:1.9–13.
42. Cf. Rosiello 1958.
43. Cf. Bengtsson 1968.
44. Cf. Tomasi and Engel (eds.) 1970.
45. For the situation among Italian immigrants in a typical not-so-large American city (Rochester, N.Y.), cf. Mangione 1943.
46. For Italo-American in general, cf. Livingston 1918; Vaughan 1925–26; Prezzolini 1939; Menarini 1947a, b, chapter 6; Timiras 1955; von Raffler-Engel 1957; Simoncini 1959.
47. Some of these words were taken back to the home-land by returning emigrants. A few examples among many: /bakkáusu/ 'toilet', /ué^čənə/ '(ticket-) agent', /émmərə/ 'hammer', /gélla/ or /gérla/ 'girl', /fakraisék/ 'for Christ's sake¡', /serióla/ 'town-hall' (< *City Hall*); cf. Menarini 1947a, b:180–200. In the AIS (Jaberg and Jud [eds.] 1928–40), at point 668 (Morrone nel Sannio), for 'miserly' (*avaro*, map 711), we find /štíŋǧə/ < Eng. *stingy*.
48. These two last-mentioned expressions can be used either as exclamations of surprise or disgust, or as attributes modifying nouns, e.g. /ké^ttémposanemabíčča/ 'what dreadful weather!'. The title of Livingston 1918 is derived from this latter use of /sanemagóŋŋa/. Cf. also Scalia 1950.
49. For Italian immigrants speech in Australia and New Zealand, cf. Rando 1967 1968; Andreoni 1969.
50. For Italian immigrants' speech in the River Plate region, cf. Donghi de Halperín 1925; M. L. Wagner 1947; Meo-Zilio 1955a, 1955b, 1955c, 1956a, 1956b, 1964a. Italians in Costa Rica: Francheschi 1970.
51. Cf. Pap 1949, especially chapters 4 and 5.
52. *E.g.* Dionne 1909; Barbeau 1963; Dagenais 1967; Dulong 1968; and continual animadversions in news-papers, popular magazines, and radio-broadcasts. Anglicisms in Acadian French seem to be relatively few; cf. Massignon 1962:750–751.
53. Cf. Alfaro 1950; Malaret 1937 (1955²); de Granda Gutiérrez 1968 (heavily slanted politically); del Rosario 1970:92–93; Pérez Sala 1973.
54. Cf. Trager and Valdez 1937.
55. Cf. Pyles 1952:211–212.
56. With the diminutive /čausíto/, formed on the model of other uses of the diminutive-suffix /:íto/ attached to formulas of greeting, as in /adiosíto/ '(little) good-bye': /adiós/ *adios* id., or, in Puerto Rico, /okeíto/ 'all right' : /oké/ 'O.K.'. For Italian influence on River Plate Spanish, cf. Meo-Zilio 1958, 1959, 1960, 1961, 1962, 1964b, 1965a, 1965b. General discussion of River Plate and Buenos Aires Spanish: del Valle 1966; Terrera 1968 (amateurish but with interesting data).
57. By Meo-Zilio 1958.
57. By Meo-Zilio 1958.
58. Cf. Nardo Cibele 1900; Leoni 1963; da Silveira Bueno 1964.

CHAPTER 10

Changes in Channels of Communication

In the twentieth century, in addition to the factors discussed in preceding chapters, the development of the Romance languages has been influenced by changes in channels of communication. These changes have led, in general, to greater emphasis on oral, as opposed to written, communication as a determinant of usage. They have been accompanied by a marked increase in both the frequency and the intensity of contacts between groups of speakers. The rate of change, particularly in lexicon, has thereby been augmented. The effects of these innovations have been cumulative, affecting both the existing standard languages (in themselves and in their relation to nonstandard or regional standard usage) and newly arisen standards.

10.1. Personal Contacts

In the twentieth century personal contacts have greatly increased, especially since the Second World War. They have developed along several lines, particularly through wide-spread tourism (extending, in the 1960's and 1970's, to previously nontravelling classes of the population, such as workers and students); the growth of longer-term exchange-programs, at both the college- and the high-school-level; and the marked increase in the frequency and accessibility of international exhibitions. On the other hand, the relatively short-term engagement of Spaniards, Italians, and other groups as *Gastarbeiter* in Switzerland, Germany, and other North European countries seems to have had little or no effect on their respective languages.

The effects of these contacts have been felt especially in two sectors of linguistic structure: phonetics and lexicon. Speakers of various languages have become considerably more proficient than previous generations in imitating sounds which they have heard directly from foreigners. In French, for instance, the sounds [ŋ] and [ʌ], previously absent from the phonetic inventory of the language, have become wide-spread in many speakers' usage, in words like /ləparkiŋ/ *le parking* 'the parking-space', /ləkampiŋ/

le camping 'the camping-ground' (and a large number of other loans from English ending in /-iŋ/ *-ing*) and /ləpikʌp/ *le pick-up*. In Italian, by now all except the most die-hard upholders of Tuscan "prestigious incompetence" have no difficulty in pronouncing final consonants in words like /náilon/ *nailon* 'nylon', /kámion/ *camion* 'truck', or /kílovat/ *kilo- chilowatt*. Especially in regions close to the United States, *e.g.* Mexico and Puerto Rico, the newest generation of speakers of Spanish have learned /θ/ in words like *thumb-tack* and /š/ in words like *shock* (alongside of the Gallicism /čóke/ *choque* 'shock') or the name of the drink *Crush* /krúš/.[1]

It is too early to say what will be the ultimate effect of such oral borrowings on the phonological systems of the receptor languages. In some instances, as with /θ/ in Spanish, the sounds are already present in other varieties of the language (in this case, Castilian). In other instances, the sounds were completely absent (*e.g.* /š/ from Spanish, /ŋ/ from French, or consonants in word-final position in Italian) in words inherited from earlier generations. At present, they occur only in loans (which are, of course, marked as such by the very presence of these features), but it is not impossible that they may be extended to elements of the inherited stock of the language.[2]

With extended travel and with the exhibition of foreign products at expositions, the general public in most modern countries has become acquainted with a much wider range of artifacts than were previously known in any given culture. Not only modern industrial products (especially labor-saving devices) but formerly exotic types of fabrics, clothes, items of furniture, and other objects useful in every-day living, have become familiar even to members of less financially advantaged classes. In certain instances, it is possible to date the introduction of a particular artifact or technique quite accurately in connection with a specific international fair. Thus, at the Exposition of 1900 in Paris, the Javanese /batik/ *batik* technique of textile-dyeing first became widely known in France.[3] Not only did the noun spread rapidly, but a new French verb was derived therefrom, /batikeˆ/ *batiquer* 'to weave batik'.

10.2. Audio-Visual Channels

In the twentieth century, various mechanical means of reproducing sound were added to the effects of purely personal contact, which had previously been the only channel for auditory influences on speech.[4]

10.21. Sound-Recordings, particularly on phonograph-records, were available, at first on an experimental basis, beginning with the inventions of Thomas A. Edison (1847–1931) in 1877 and of Emile Berliner (1851–1929) in 1887.[5] They became available commercially to any great extent, however, only in the early years of the twentieth century, and have spread very widely since then (supplemented, since the 1940's, by tape-recordings). Mechanically reproduced sound, often of quite high quality, has served to make the phonetics of any given language available to speakers of any other. This influence has been strongest, not through formal language-teaching,[6] but through popular song, where the immense vogue of American jazz and "rock" music throughout the world has led to its imitation by many speakers of Romance and other languages, especially by teen-agers. The "juke-box" itself has become a feature of many places of entertainment, and has been known by the American English word, e.g. /lədžukboks/ in French, /ilǧubbósse/ il giubbosse in Italian. In popular music, the situation has become remarkably parallel to that which prevailed in western Europe in the twelfth and thirteenth centuries with respect to Old Provençal (§6.311): a foreign language (Provençal then, English now) sung widely in many countries, and learned and imitated—often very successfully—by professional musicians and lay audiences alike. In modern times, the sounds of English have become much more familiar, even to speakers of (say) Romance, who know nothing of its grammatical structure, than in earlier times. In some instances, changes in pronunciation of English loan-words have taken place as a result of closer acquaintance: thus, the word jazz itself was pronounced in the 1920's and 1930's as /žaz/ in French and /já¢/ in Italian, with a spelling-pronunciation; but at present one hears normally /džaz/ or even /džæz/ in French, and /ǧés/ in Italian.

10.22. Films, since the introduction of talking pictures in the late 1920's, have played an increasingly important rôle through their sound-tracks. Here, again, American English has been the main source of innovation, both phonological and lexical. Certain actors have been particularly influential, e.g. Stan Laurel and Oliver Hardy, whose intentionally affected, partly British accents have been imitated in sound-tracks "dubbed" in Italian and Spanish for their films. Here, too, youthful admirers have been remarkably successful in imitating their pronunciation, and /stǽnlio/ Stanlio and /álio/ Ollio have become house-hold names in Italy.[7] Some comic characters' names, e.g. Fatty /fǽti/ (Arbuckle)[8] have come to be used as general nick-names, in this case for any fat man.

The "dubbings" have, in many instances brought about the use and spread of various linguistic forms and even shifts of meaning. The English adjective pixilated 'mildly and amusingly crazy', apparently coined by the film Mr. Deeds Goes to Town (1936), was reproduced in Italian by the new-formation /pikkiatéllo/ picchiatello (a diminutive on the past participle

/pikkiáto/ *picchiato* 'struck'), which fitted excellently both semantically and in its phonetic and articulatory characteristics (so that the sounds would correspond to the movements of the speakers' faces on the screen).[9] Such English titles as *Miss* /mís/ have become common throughout Europe. English nick-names such as *Bob* have become familiar from the names of such actors as Bob Hope; for instance, the chief male character in the novel *Le Ragazze di San Frediano* 'The Girls of San Frediano' (1949) by Vasco Pratolini (1913–   ) has this nick-name, specifically as part of his imitation of American movie-fashions. On occasion, words of this kind are used in ways foreign to the language of origin, as in Fr. /ynmis/ *une miss* or It., Sp. /unamís/ *una miss* 'a young woman', or It. /bíg/ *big* used as an independent noun, e.g. /ibíg delmó^ndodellefinánȼe/ *i big del mondo delle finanze* 'the big-shots of the world of finance'. The motion-pictures have undoubtedly played a part in some loan-shifts, e.g. the passage of Fr. /re^alize^/ *réaliser*, It. /realiʒʒáre/ *realizzare*, Sp. /realiθár/ *realizar* from 'to bring into existence' to 'to become aware'.[10] Names of fashionable garments have been chosen from the titles of films, e.g. It. /rebékka/ *rebecca* 'a kind of sweater' under the influence of the name of Daphne du Maurier's novel *Rebecca* (1938), filmed in 1940.[11]

The Italian cinema has been particularly influential, in the decades following the Second World War, in spreading the vogue of "neorealism," in which every effort is made to reproduce situations and characters taken directly from real life, even to the casting of nonprofessionals to represent particular social or regional types.[12] In the sound-tracks of such films, the use of purely standard language would be highly unrealistic and even jarring. Hence, neorealistic producers have made extensive use of local dialect, which has proven highly efficacious in spite of the loud protests of conservative speakers.[13] Often, the dialects have been chosen to correspond to pre-conceived notions on the part of audiences, e.g. Abruzzese for a house-maid or Florentine for an "uppity" nurse-maid. Some dialect-words, such as Judaeo-Roman /fasúllo/ *fasullo* 'fake',[14] have achieved national currency in this way and have become permanently established in the standard language.

In other Romance countries, the use of local dialect in sound-tracks of films has been much less wide-spread than in Italy. French film-makers have made very little use of dialect, aside from some rather watered-down Parisian argot in pictures dealing with metropolitan low-life, and a rather stereotyped South French accent in certain comedies, such as those of the actor Fernandel or those by Marcel Pagnol (1895–   ) dealing with life in Provence. In Spanish-speaking regions, local accents and some lexical regionalisms have been inevitable in films made in, say, Mexico or Argentina. The influence of purism, and the absence of a strong neorealistic movement in countries of French and Spanish speech, have combined to keep the language of film-sound-tracks considerably closer to the official standards.

10.23. RADIO, in its earlier years (the 1920's and 1930's) was expected to serve as a strong unifying force making for standardisation of pronunciation, especially where (as in most European countries) almost all broad-casting was in the hands of governmental agencies. Considerable pressure was brought on radio-announcers to avoid strong regional accents or other features diverging from a fairly rigid standard.[15] For various reasons, probably associated with relatively small amounts of time spent listening and with low interest-level, the radio has not been as strong a unifying force as it was originally expected to be. Since the Second World War, less emphasis has been laid on avoidance of regionalisms, except perhaps in France.

10.24. TELEVISION, on the other hand, has been a major factor in spreading knowledge of nation-wide behavior-patterns, in language as in many other respects.[16] A high interest-level, many hours spent per day watching television, and the addition of visual as well as auditory models, may account in part for the greater influence of television as compared with radio. As with films, younger speakers are especially given to imitation of television-stars and -announcers or "emcees." Television has thus been an especially potent force in breaking down old unitary standards of usage, even in France.

10.3. Written Material

Especially since the Second World War, written material has come to lose its uncontested primacy as a channel for transmission of linguistic innovations in standard languages, since auditory and visual stimuli are now reproducible, and they approach (if not surpass) written and printed matter in ubiquitousness. The twentieth century has nevertheless seen a tremendous proliferation of written material, due to improvements in techniques of reproduction and to the availability of inexpensive paper. Consequently, the volume of reading-matter has swollen to a super-flood and, with the extension of schooling even in previously "backward" regions, has reached a far larger proportion of the population than ever before. The demands of this enlarged reading-public have exerted a considerable influence upon style and vocabulary, and even somewhat upon structural features of the Romance standard languages, both in books and in journalistic material.

10.31. BOOKS. In the world of books, two main but opposing tendencies have manifested themselves. On the one hand, there has been a great increase in the production of works aimed at lower-class and lower-middle-class readers, with relatively little or no literary back-ground, and serving primarily as "escape-literature." The intellectual content of such works is low; they embody chiefly the naïve wish-fulfillments of an untutored ex-*Lumpenproletariat*.[17] The authors of such works make a curious mélange of simple sentence-structure and vocabulary with occasionally oversophisticated constructions or single words, with which to impress their untrained readers.

As a reaction against the increasing prevalence and popularity of what they consider "trash," a number of avant-garde authors in various countries have turned out works which go as far in the opposite direction as possible. As far back as the 1910's, the Italian and French "futurists," under the leadership of Filippo Marinetti (1876–1944), proclaimed for their productions a linguistic ideal involving "words set free" and the "destruction of syntax."[18] In practice, this meant the avoidance of verbs and verbal predicates, with a correspondingly heavy predominance of nouns and noun-phrases, used chiefly in elliptical or exclamatory constructions, with a certain number of onomatopoetic or non-sense expressions (often consisting of unfamiliar or even unpronounceable sequences of letters in print), as in the following programmatic passage from Marinetti (*Lang-tumb-tuum*, 1914):

> Correzione di bozze + desideri in velocità Nessuna poesia prima di noi colla nostra immaginazione senza fili parole in libertà vivaaaaᴀAA il FUTURISMOfinalmente finalmente finalmente finalmente finalmente FINALMENTE poesia NASCERE treno treno treno treno tren tron tron tron (ponte di ferro: tatatluuuntlin) sssssssiii ssiissii ssii sssssiii treno treno

> 'Proof-correcting + desires at speed No poetry before us with our wireless imagination words set free hooraaaAY for FUTURISM finally finally finally finally finally FINALLY poetry BORN train train train train tren tron tron tron (iron bridge: tatatluuuntlin) sssssssiii ssiissii ssii sssssiii train train.'

This direction was followed also by the French "Dada" school of the 1920's, led by Tristan Tzara (1896–   ),[19] which went even farther in the use of disconnected, nearly meaningless sequences of individual words and phrases, as in the following ("Maison Flake"):

> déclenchez clairons l'annonce vaste et hyaline animaux du service maritime

forestier ǽrostatique tout ce qui existe chevauche en galop de clarté
la vie
l'ange a des hanches blanches (parapluie virilité)

'Unloose bugles the vast and glassy announcement animals of the
maritime service
aerostatic forest-ranger all that exists rides at a gallop of clarity
life
the angle has white hips (umbrella virility).'

Among the various "experimental" writers of the 1940's, 1950's, and
1960's were the French authors Raymond Queneau (1903–   ),[20] Jacques
Prévert (1900–   ),[21] and the Italian Carlo Emilio Gadda (1893–   ).[22]
All three showed an extreme readiness to play in all kinds of unusual ways
with their respective languages. In his best-known work, the novel *Zazie
dans le Métro* ('Zazie in the Subway', 1959), Queneau introduces all kinds
of Anglicisms and part-Anglicisms (*e.g. le policehomme* 'the policeman'),
dialectalisms and slang terms (*e.g. notre bled* 'our neck of the woods', with
bled 'region' from Maghrebian Arabic) and quasi-phonetic spellings, *e.g.*
meussieu for /məsjø/ *monsieur* 'sir', or *vzêtes* for /vzet/ *vous êtes* 'you are'.
Zazie is only the best-known manifestation of Queneau's all-pervading interest in matters of language, with a much more antitraditionalist view-
point than is general in late twentieth-century France, and extending even
to (rather sporadic and unpredictable) advocacy of spelling-reform and
phonetic transcription. Another, in some ways even more remarkable,
tour de force on Queneau's part was his *Exercices de style* ('Exercises in
Style', 1947), a series of 99 different accounts of the same happening, told
on 99 different levels of style varying according to dialect and functional
variety.

Gadda made use of various types of dialect in several of his novels, including *L'Adalgisa* (1944) with Milanese, and *Quer Pasticciaccio Brutto de
Via Merulana* ('That Nasty Mess in Via Merulana', 1957, with even the
title in Roman dialect). In the latter, Gadda uses a number of different
dialects, not only in the conversation but in the narration as well, giving
somewhat of a Joycean stream-of-consciousness-effect.[23] Other Italian
authors besides Gadda have, following the impulse given by the neorealistic
cinema (cf. §10.22), made more or less extensive use of dialect in their
stories, especially P. P. Pasolini.[24] In these writers' work, however, dialect
is mostly restricted to direct reporting of conversation (as it would be in a
film), rather than being put to somewhat surrealistic use in narration as
well, à la Gadda.

10.32. JOURNALISM has, in the middle of the twentieth century, also tended to be a follower rather than a leader, adopting styles made popular by other mass-media. However, because of the wide diffusion of news-papers and periodicals (especially illustrated weeklies), journalists have exerted a certain influence, especially through their popularisation of previously esoteric knowledge in such fields as medicine and the sciences.[25] The snob-value of foreignisms, especially Anglicisms, has been broadened by their wide-spread use in journalism. Some, such as *baby-sitter, teen-ager,* or *test,* have apparently achieved permanent international acclimatisation. Sports-writers, in particular, seem given to use of (often ill-suited) learnèd terminology (*e.g.* It. /ivirğiliáni/ *i virgiliani* 'the Vergilians = the Mantua foot-ball-team') and high-falutin' phrases (*e.g.* It. /téssere letrámedunníti-doğóko/ *tessere le trame d'un nitido gioco* 'weave the plot of a spotless game').[26]

10.4. The Nature of Standard Languages

Up to the end of the nineteenth century and even beyond, there was little question as to the prime determining factor in the establishment of a standard language: it was the usage of the upper classes and of "good" authors, more or less according to the principles enunciated by Vaugelas for seventeenth-century French (cf. §8.22). In the twentieth century, however, the situation has changed markedly, with regard to two problems: the basis of the standard, and the relation of this latter to spatial and social variations.[27]

10.41. LITERARY OR NATIONAL? Especially since the Second World War, the literary foundation of standard languages has become eroded, as a result of two phenomena: aberrations on the part of *littérateurs* in their usage, especially in "avant-garde" writing; and the extension of the standard to greater segments of the population. It can no longer be said that the language of such authors as Samuel Beckett (1906–   ), Eugen Ionescu (1912–   ), or Raymond Queneau (cf. §10.31), who are widely considered as being in the fore-front of literary achievement, serves to set any kind of standard for the French-speaking community as a whole.[28] Similar observations can be made concerning contemporary Italian, Spanish, or Portuguese authors of the "experimental" school.[29] The leading rôle in determining usage is passing to more impersonal agencies, particularly schools (with predominantly conservative, puristic texts and teachers), the armed forces, government-offices, and secretarial schools.[30] Thus, the increased frequency of the order FAMILY-NAME + GIVEN NAME (*e.g.* /dyräpjer/ *Durand Pierre* or It. /biánkiğovánni/ *Bianchi Giovanni*, rather than /pjerdyrã/ *Pierre Durand* or /ğovánnibiánki/ *Giovanni Bianchi*, respectively) is directly traceable to its occurrence in official lists, and especially in the files of the national vital-statistics-bureaux.[31]

10.42. OLD DIALECTS AND NEW REGIONAL VARIETIES. With the great extension of education to which we have already alluded (§9.32), the local dialects of Romance have been constantly retreating, being replaced by the national standard of whatever country was involved. This process is nearly complete in France, where strongly differentiated local speech prevails only in marginal areas such as the Pyrenees, the Massif Central, and out-lying regions of the north.[32] It is not so far along in other Romance areas, but it has become markedly accelerated since the First World War in Italy,[33] and since the Second in Spain. Perhaps the greatest differentiation still prevails in Switzerland, where the local varieties of Rhaeto-Romance are cultivated with particular attention to their distinguishing characteristics. It is for this reason that dialectologists have, ever since the beginning of the twentieth century, felt an increasing need for the recording of Romance dialects before they disappear because of the continual encroachment of standard languages.

Nevertheless, complete uniformity has by no means been achieved simply through the spread of national standards. This is because, when the speakers of any given dialect learn the standard language, they normally— unless they are given careful instruction—carry over features of their dialect into the newly learned "Hochsprache." In this respect, the dialect forms a "substratum," functioning exactly in the same way as the pre-Latin languages are presumed to have done when they were replaced by Latin (cf. Chapters 3, 4). For instance, speakers of Provençal, not having nasalised vowels in their local speech, often use /Vn/ instead of /Ṽ/ in their standard French, and preserve /ə/ in positions (particularly word-final) where French has lost it, saying /pandrə/ for /pãdr/ *pendre* 'to hang', /ben/ instead of /bẽ/ *bain* 'bath', or /milə/ instead of /mil/ *mille* '1000'. North Italians do not have double consonants in their dialect; consequently the more naïve dialect-speakers will simply reproduce standard Italian /CC/ with /C/, whereas the more educated North Italian will pronounce /CC/ where it is written, but not where the Tuscan or South Italian has "syntactic doubling." Standard Italian /fátto/ *fatto* 'done' will thus be rendered, by the naïve North Italian dialect-speaker, as /fáto/ (with short stressed vowel), and by the educated North Italian as /fátto/; but both will pronounce /vá×béne/ = /vábbéne/ 'very well (lit. it goes well)' as /vábéne/, since it is written as two words, *va bene*.[34]

In this way, new regional varieties are being formed, which, while not "dialects" in the old sense of speech-types confined to narrowly circum-scribed, independent areas, are nevertheless different enough from the old locally-based standards to constitute separate subdivisions within the national language as a whole. Since they are based on the old standards, they are mutually comprehensible. They serve, however, to identify their speakers' regional origin, without necessarily marking them as socially inferior. Especially in Italy and the Spanish-speaking world, little or no stigma attaches to the use of a regional standard. It has well been observed that, whereas Manzoni went to Florence to "rinse out his clothes in the Arno," linguistically speaking (cf. §9.22, fn. 33), no twentieth-century author (*e.g.* the Sicilian Giovanni Verga [1840–1922] or the Triestine Italo Svevo [1862–1928]) would have dreamed of doing the same.[35] In France, however, regional standards (*e.g.* those of Brussels, Lyon, Toulouse, Geneva, or Marseilles) are still regarded as inferior to Parisian French; there is a corresponding unwillingness, among many students of the language, to admit their existence or to examine them objectively.[36]

10.5. New Standard Languages

In addition to the old established Romance standards, new ones have arisen in the course of the twentieth century. Although they have already been enumerated briefly in Chapter 2, it will be valuable to mention them again here so as to place them in historical perspective. Most of them are former dialects which have come to be used as literary languages without restructuring (apart from some inevitable borrowings from already domi-nant national languages); others have grown out of creoles, which have undergone such extensive changes as to have acquired completely separate linguistic structures.

10.51. NON-RESTRUCTURED

1. Friulian (§2.124.3) has had a rather meagre literature since the Middle Ages, and a modest literary flowering in the nineteenth and twen-tieth centuries.[37] Its orthography is based on that of Italian, from which it has a number of loan-words. Despite the support of the semi-official literary and linguistic "G. I. Àscoli" Academy of Údine, Friulian at present leads a somewhat precarious existence, constantly threatened by Italian on the literary level and by Venetian on the oral.

2. Romansh (§2.124.1) has been established as the fourth national lan-guage of Switzerland since 1938, when this recognition was accorded it largely for political reasons (to counter the claims of the Fascist régime

that Romansh was simply an aberrant Italian dialect and, as such, formed a basis for Italian territorial claims to the Engadine as well as to the Italian-speaking Ticino). No one area is recognised as standard-setting, and the use of Romansh is restricted to the Engadine itself. Even there, bilingualism (Romansh-German, Romansh-Italian) is very wide-spread, and in every-day speech Romansh is gradually receding before German.[38] Its use in literature and journalism is quite modest.

3. Moldavian (§2.15.1,*b*) is only officially a separate language, since it is in actuality a not very divergent variety of Roumanian.

10.52. RESTRUCTURED

1. Haitian Creole is the native language of virtually all Haitians, and it has been officially recognised since 1962 as the second national language of Haiti. Nevertheless, it is not used extensively for prestigious purposes, this rôle being reserved almost exclusively for French. After considerable fluctuation with regard to orthography,[38] a compromise between an accurate phonemically-based spelling and the French writing-system has been made official. The future of Haitian Creole is, despite recent advances in the recognition afforded it, by no means secure; there are strong pressures, both from socially dominant Francophile elements in Haiti itself and from French-oriented foreign linguists,[40] towards extensive Gallicisation. It is not unlikely that a situation may develop like that attested for Jamaica,[41] in which, rather than two separate languages, there may develop an entire spectrum ranging between two poles, with the original Creole on one end and a regional standard variety of the European language on the other.

2. Papiamentu (§2.42) is also recognised, in the Dutch islands of Curaçao, Aruba, and Bonaire, as a vehicle for education and government. Its literary development has not, as yet, been markedly flourishing.

NOTES TO CHAPTER 10

1. Cf. Gili Gaya 1966, chapter 12.

2. As has happened many times in linguistic history, as in the introduction of /h-/ into Old North French in words of Germanic origin and its later spread to a few words of Romance stock, such as /hált/ *halt* 'high' (<PRom. /áltu/); or the introduction of /ɨ/ into Roumanian in words of Slavic origin, *e.g.* /stəpɨn/ *stăpîn* 'over-lord'.

3. The word is first attested in French in 1845 (cf. Dauzat, Dubois, and Mitterand 1964:77), but its spread dates from 1900 (cf. Bloch and von Wartburg 1932:72).

4. For the effects of mass-communication-media in Italy, cf. Sobrero 1971.

5. Before the invention of phonographic recording, many people were acutely aware of the absence of any way of preserving sound; the first part of Alfred de Musset's *Stances à la Malibran* (1836) is simply a lament to the effect "we have no phonograph!".

6. Despite its extensive use in the 1940's and following decades, there is little evidence

that the recorded sound of foreign languages in the language-laboratory has had much effect on popular reproduction of loan-words from foreign languages.

7. Cf. Menarini 1955:148, 155.
8. Cf. Menarini 1955:99.
9. Cf. Menarini 1955:175–178.
10. Cf. Menarini 1955:155.
11. Cf. Menarini 1955:94–95.
12. The most articulate of these nonprofessional actors was the linguist Carlo Battisti, chosen by Vittorio de Sica to enact the title-rôle in *Umberto D.* (1952). Battisti has told of his experience as an actor, especially from the linguistic point of view (Battisti 1952).
13. For the relation between standard language and dialect in the neorealistic film, cf. Menarini 1955:162–168; Pucci 1959.
14. Cf. Tagliavini 1956.
15. In Italy, under Fascism, an attempt was made to establish a "Rome-Florence linguistic axis" for setting a uniform standard in pronunciation, and various scholars were called in to establish norms, as in Bertoni and Ugolini 1939a, 1939b. For the general relation between radio and the national language in Italy, cf. Fracastoro Martini 1951; Camilli 1951.
16. For the influence of television on Italian usage, cf. Medici 1961; de Mauro 1968.
17. This type of material has been with us since the nineteenth century and even earlier. It is known in English as "bilge-literature," in German as "Trivialliteratur," and in Italian as *letteratura di consumo* 'literature for (mass-) consumption'. Even the names of its chief practitioners, such as Marie Corelli in England, "Delly" in France, or "Liala" in Italy, bring either smiles or (especially in Germany) frowns to the faces of literary critics (cf. Schmidt-Henkel [ed.] 1964). For the linguistic aspects of nineteenth-century Italian bilge-literature, cf. Melis Freda 1968.
18. Cf. Vaccari 1959; Briosi 1969.
19. Cf. Petersen 1971.
20. Cf. Quéval 1960; Bens 1962; Bergens 1963; Guicharnaud 1965; Borie 1966; Gayot 1967; Michelson, forthcoming.
21. Cf. Miclău 1966; Greet 1968.
22. Cf. Pucci 1958; S. Pellegrini 1970.
23. Cf. Hall 1961.
24. Cf. Pucci 1958; Façon 1962b; S. Pellegrini 1970.
25. Most discussions of journalistic style and vocabulary have been puristic in their approach and hence sharply critical. For French, cf. Puchet 1965. For Italian, cf. Lupi 1940; Venturini 1942; Aliprandi 1962; Fucci 1962; Bascetta 1964; Lenzi 1965. On publicity: Castagnotto 1970. For Brazilian press-usage: Hampejs 1961.
26. Cf. the animadversions, for Portuguese, of Joda 1967. For Italian, cf. Devoto 1939; de Felice 1941; Medici 1959; Bascetta 1962. For Roumanian, cf. Trofin 1967. For Spanish sports-terminology, cf. Pfändler 1954.
27. For modern French in general, cf. Galichet 1949; Cohen 1950, 1963, 1966; Darbelnet 1963; Harmer 1965; Doppagne 1966. For French popular usage: Bauche 1920; Frei 1929; Guiraud 1965. For modern Italian, cf. Hall 1960a; de Mauro 1963. For modern Spanish, cf. Beinhauer 1930; Muñoz Cortis 1958; Lorenzo 1966; M. Alonso 1968; Carniver 1969; Stevenson 1970. For modern Roumanian, cf. Coteanu 1962; Grauer 1968.
28. It has frequently been observed that, particularly in France, many of the avant-garde writers, such as Samuel Beckett and Eugen Ionescu, have been foreigners who have achieved a native-like command of French, only to push the resources of the language to their limits and beyond, in striving for novel and attention-catching effects.

29. This is not true of countries where official doctrines of "socialist realism" stand in the way of voluntary individual variations.

30. For the effect of secretaries' insecurity on spelling and usage in English, cf. Joos 1960:252. No similar study has been made, to the best of my knowledge, for any Romance language.

31. For this construction in Italian, cf. Hall 1956; Leone 1956. On occasion, the bureaucrats in government-agencies exert a certain restrictive influence on usage, as when an employee in an Italian vital-statistics-bureau forbade a family to name its daughter *Esther* on the grounds that that name, ending in a consonant, could not be considered a permissible Italian name!

32. Cf. Brun 1946.

33. Cf. G. B. Pellegrini 1960; Migliorini 1963; G. B. Pellegrini 1963; Hall 1968a; Berruto 1971; Rosiello 1971. For regional lexical variants in modern standard Italian, cf. Rüegg 1956. Some efforts were made in the Fascist period to use local dialects as a point of departure for elementary education in the public schools, but this endeavour was abandoned in the anti-Fascist reaction after 1945; cf. Mazzotta 1969.

34. The story is told of the North Italian school-master who wanted his pupils to emphasise the double consonants, and told them /ragási, batételedópie/ *Ragasi, batete le dopie!* 'Kids, hit the longs hard!', with a strong regional accent (himself using /C/ instead of /CC/, and also the typical North Italian merger of /s/ and /¢/) instead of the standard pronunciation /ragá¢¢i, batté^teledó^ppie/ *Ragazzi, battete le doppie!*.

35. Dionisotti 1962/63:58: "A nessuno è passato o passa per la testa l'idea che debbano essere risciacquati in Arno *I Malavoglia* o la *Coscienza di Zeno* ('No-one has thought or thinks that [Verga's] *The Malavoglia Family* or [Svevo's] *The Conscience of Zeno* needed to be rinsed out in the Arno').

36. Cf. my remarks in Hall 1966/67.

37. Cf. d'Aronco 1960.

38. For instance, Chur, the capital of the canton of the Grisons, formerly Romansh in speech, has been German-speaking since the fifteenth century, and villages to the east of it have been gradually giving up Romansh since then; cf. Cavigelli 1969.

39. Cf. Hall 1953:25–27 for a discussion and table of the various orthographies that have been proposed for Haitian Creole. The one finally adopted as official is quite close to the Pressoir adaptation of McConnell-Laubach.

40. *E.g.* Berry 1969; Valdman 1968, 1969.

41. Cf. DeCamp 1962.

CHAPTER 11

History of Romance Linguistics

11.0. Definitions of Linguistics

The term *linguistics* has been used in various senses. The three which need concern us here are[1]:

1. Speculation concerning language in general, from a philosophical or theological point of view.[2]
2. The description of language for practical purposes, to enable native speakers to attain command of a prestigious variety or type of usage, or nonnative speakers to learn a foreign linguistic system.
3. The application of scientific methods to the study of language, from either a diachronic, a synchronic, or a panchronic point of view, and regardless of questions of social prestige or philosophical preconceptions.

Related to linguistics, but by no means identical with it, is *philology*, the study of a culture (especially ancient or mediaeval) through its written texts. Especially, historical linguistics is an essential adjunct to philology, and philology to historical linguistics; but the field of the latter extends also to the study of ancient manuscripts (palaeography), to stylistics, and to literary and cultural history.

Our concern, both in this book as a whole and in this chapter, is primarily with linguistics$_3$ or "scientific linguistics." However, since the origin of linguistics$_3$ is closely related to the development of linguistics$_{1,2}$, it will be necessary to take these varieties of language-study into account in tracing the history of Romance linguistics.

11.1. The Middle Ages

That the Romance languages were somehow different from the (relatively) standard Latin used in the Church and in legal affairs, was recog-

227

nized at least from the ninth century onwards. Some scholars, in this connection, ascribe especial importance to the use of the term *rustica romana lingua* 'the rustic Roman tongue' in the Edict of Tours (813), which provided for the use of popular speech rather than Latin in sermons.[3] For some centuries more, however, the vernaculars, although they gradually rose in prestige and came to be used in works having greater or lesser literary pretensions, were not made the objects of analytical study.

The first attempts to describe a Romance language originated in the efforts of mediaeval students of literary Old Provençal to codify it, in such works as the *Leys d'Amors* 'Rules of Love' or the *Donatz proensals* 'Provençal Grammar' (§6.311), so that it might be more easily learned by would-be poets, native speakers of either related dialects or foreign languages.[4] Among the earliest works dealing with other Romance languages were those aimed at helping English speakers to learn French, *e.g.* the fourteenth-century *Orthographia gallica*[5] and Jean Barton's *Donait français* (ca. 1400) and various vocabularies and phrase-books for travellers and merchants.[6]

The closest approach in the Middle Ages to our linguistics, as applied to the Romance languages, was made by Dante Alighieri (1265–1321), in his unfinished *De vulgari Eloquentia* ('On poetry in the vernacular', ca. 1290–1300).[7] The intellectual basis of Dante's theories was primarily mediaeval theological speculation concerning language.[8] The *De v. E.* begins with an extremely abstract discussion of the reasons for the existence of human language and the history of its development as set forth in the Old Testament. Dante then discusses the different languages of Europe, especially the Romance tongues, among which he identifies three, distinguishing them by the favorite mediaeval criterion of the words for 'yes': *oc*, *oïl*, and *sì*.[9]

Dante recognises that there is a relation between Latin and the Romance languages, but ascribes the existence of the former (the *grammatica* par excellence, as he and other mediaeval writers termed it) to an act of deliberate invention on the part of philosophers, the result of an intentional consensus directed towards avoiding the confusions that might arise from the diversity of the vernaculars. Italian he considers the noblest of all the latter, *quia magis videtur inniti grammaticae* 'because it is evident that it rests more upon Latin' (*De v.E.* 1.10.4).[10] In order to discover a variety of Italian suitable for literary endeavour, he passes in review the dialects of the peninsular, fourteen in all, but finds none of them adequate. To some he applies highly opprobrious terms, such as *non vulgare, sed potius tristi-loquium* 'not a vernacular, but, rather, a base form of speech' and *ytalorum vulgarium omnium . . . turpissimum* 'of all the vernaculars of Italy, the most shameful' for Roman, and considers that the Sardinians are *grammaticam, tamquam simiae homines, imitantes* 'imitating Latin, as apes do men' (De v. E. 1.11.7). Having rejected all the Italian dialects, he sets up an

ideal *vulgare illustre, cardinale, aulicum et curiale* 'an ennobled, fundamental, courtly, and norm-setting vernacular' (*De v. E.* 1.17.1), standing
to the Italian dialects in the same relation as does Latin, in his view, to
Romance.

11.2. The Renaissance

Several factors contributed to the marked increase in grammatical
studies, as applied to the Romance languages, and to the development of
linguistics in the Renaissance. A general improvement of communication,
both in travel and in the diffusion of books, led to a wide-spread demand
for the knowledge of foreign languages. From the sixteenth century date,
therefore, the first extensive grammars of French, Italian, and Spanish for
foreigners.[11] One of the earliest dictionaries of a Romance tongue was the
Lexicon a sermone latino in ispanicum ('Latin-Spanish dictionary', 1492)
of the Spaniard Antonio de Nebrija (ca. 1446–1522).

The extension of humanistic learning and its conflict with the vernaculars
led the partisans of the latter to defend them, not least by demonstrating
that popular speech was "grammatical" and could be reduced to rule. The
earliest descriptions of Romance tongues—cast, inevitably, in the mould of
Latin grammar—were those of Leon Battista Alberti (ca. 1404–1472) for
Italian,[12] and of Nebrija for Spanish,[13] both from the latter part of the
fifteenth century. French was first extensively described in the sixteenth
century, in such works as the *In linguam gallicam Isagωge* ('Introduction
to the French language', 1531–32) of Jacques Dubois ("Sylvius Ammianus,"
1478–1555; the *Tretté de la grammęre françoęse* ('Treatise on French grammar', 1550) of Louis Meigret (ca. 1510–1558); the *Traicté de la grammaire
françoise* ('Treatise on French grammar', 1557) of Robert Estienne (1499–
1559)[14]; the *Gramęre* ('Grammar', 1562; second ed., 1572) of Pierre de la
Ramée ("Petrus Ramus," 1515–1572); the *Grammatica gallica* ('French
grammar', 1570) of Antoine Cauchie; and others.[15] The introduction and
diffusion of printing brought increased attention to the accuracy of texts,
and therewith the observation of norms in spelling and grammatical structure.

From these various sources arose a concern with the nature and the name
of the language to be used as a literary standard, giving rise to extensive
debates in the sixteenth century, first in Italy and then in Spain, Portugal,
and France. In Italy, the *Questione della lingua* ('language-problem'), as it
came to be known,[16] revolved mainly around two chief points of difference:
(1) should literary usage be restricted to the language of Tuscany, and

more specifically to that of Florence, out of whose fourteenth-century dialect it had grown, or should non-Tuscan lexical and grammatical features be admitted? (2) Should writers restrict themselves to the words and constructions found in the "Golden Age" of the fourteenth century (especially Petrarch and Boccaccio), as Latinists were doing vis-à-vis Vergil and Cicero, or should modern usage, especially that of the newly arisen court-life, set the norm? In specifically literary work, the Tuscanising and archaising tendency, as set forth in the *Prose della volgar lingua* ('On the vernacular', ca. 1506–12, pub. 1526) of Pietro Bembo (1470–1527), came to dominate the field.[17] The other three possible points of view were also extensively represented in the debate. The anti-Tuscan/anti-archaising attitude is best expressed in the works of Gian Giorgio Trìssino (1478–1550; *Il Castellano*, ca. 1527), and the Tuscan/antiarchaising in those of Claudio Tolomei (1492–1555; *Il Cesano*, ca. 1530). A dialogue presenting the various points of view, without reaching a specific conclusion, was the *Dialogo delle lingue* ('Dialogue on languages', ca. 1530) of the literary critic Sperone Speroni (1500–1588).

The polemic works produced during the Italian debates served as a reservoir for the arguments set forth in similar discussions at a slightly later date in other Romance-speaking countries, whose languages were facing similar problems in their use, not only in literature, but also in such fields as medicine, law, religion, and science, which had previously been reserved for Latin. The safe-guarding and ennoblement of French was the concern of a number of mid-sixteenth-century writers, particularly of Joachim du Bellay (1524–1560) in his *Deffense et illustration de la langue françoyse* ('Defence and ennoblement of the French language', 1548) and of Henri Estienne (1531–1598) in his *Précellence du langage françois* ('Superiority of the French language', 1579).[18] Du Bellay, especially, drew heavily on his Italian predecessors, in particular on Speroni, for his argumentation.[19] The Spaniard Juan de Valdés (ca. 1470–1541), who spent a good part of the 1520's and 1530's in Italy, likewise reflects the atmosphere of the Italian *Questione della lingua* in his *Diálogo de la lengua* ('Dialogue on the language', ca. 1535; pub. 1737). The same may be said of the *Diálogo em louvor da nossa linguagem* ('Dialogue in praise of our language', 1540) of the Portuguese João de Barros (1496–1570).

Related to these debates over the nature and name of the literary languages were those concerned with the standardisation of orthography. This had not been a great problem in the Middle Ages, when books and their readers were alike few, and copying was done by hand. With the advent of printing, the literate public and the number of books grew markedly, and the average person's rate of reading likewise increased. An initial result of the changed situation was a demand for consistent orthography, more in conformity with current pronunciation than had been the case earlier (when etymological spellings and silent letters had been introduced by learnèd men and scribes, *e.g. doubte* for Fr. /dutə/ 'doubt', or *philosophia* for It., Sp., Port. /filosofía/ 'philosophy'). The phonemically based orthographies, including special letters taken from Greek and elsewhere, proposed by Trissino for Italian and by Meigret for French, did not catch on, because of the printers' objection to the expense of new characters, and, even more, the reading public's resistance to innovations.[20] In certain countries, however, particularly Italy and Spain, by the end of the sixteenth century a relatively consistent orthography was established, free from most ambiguities of the types which have persisted to the present day in the spelling of French and English.

In the course of the debates over the standard languages and their orthographies, a considerable number of scattered but important advances were made in linguistic theory. Especially in Italy, a number of scholars recognised the independence of language from writing, its relation to social organisation, and the connection of language-development with history. A few fifteenth-century scholars, *e.g.* Flavio Biondo (1388–1463), had considered the modern idiom to be the direct continuation, unchanged, of popular Latin; but others, beginning with Poggio Bracciolini (1380–1459) and Leonardo Bruni (1370–1444), saw that the modern Romance tongues, including Roumanian, were the result of linguistic change as it had affected Latin.[21] Most attempts at etymological investigation were still influenced by mediaeval attitudes towards linguistic change, admitting any kind of substitution in the sounds of a word, so that such cautious theorists as Benedetto Varchi (1503–1565), in his dialogue *L'Ercolano* (written ca. 1550–60), were skeptical of the results of etymology. But at least one scholar, Claudio Tolomei, perceived the necessity of postulating an underlying regularity in sound-change as a basis for etymological work. Tolomei's clear and unequivocal statement in the *Cesano* deserves to be known as the first formulation of the "regularist" principle. A propos of the regularity of the development of Latin *pl-* to Italian *pi-*, he says:

> [. . .] e ardirei dire che nel primo e puro parlar degli uomini toscani questa fosse universale e verissima regola, e tutti quei vocaboli, che ora altrimenti s'usano e scritti si trovano, come *plora*, *implora*, *splende*, *plebe e* simili, non fussero presi dal mezzo delle piazze di Toscana; ma poste innanzi dagli scrittori, e da qualche ingegno, che volse la lingua arricchire, che gli parse usargli, come nelle stampe latine gli trovò, senza dar loro forma di toscan parlare [. . .] perchè senza dubbio il comune uso di quel secolo averebbe, se egli avesse quei vocaboli ricevuto, *piora*, *impiora*, *spiende e pieve* detto, come

di questo ultimo ne abbiamo manifesto segno, che volgarmente
Pieve si chiama quella sorte di chiesa ordinata alla religione di una
plebe.

'[. . .] and I would be so bold as to say that in the original and pure
speech of Tuscans, this was a universally valid rule, and that all those
words which are now spoken and written differently, such as *plora*
'he weeps', *implora* 'he implores', *splende* 'it is resplendent', *plebe*
'populace' and the like, were not taken from the middle of the town-
squares of Tuscany [*i.e.* from every-day speech], but were set up by
writers, and by some wit who wished to enrich the language, pre-
ferring to use them in the form in which he found them written in
Latin, without giving them the form of Tuscan speech [*i.e.* without
substituting *pi-* for *pl-*] [. . .] because without a doubt the common
usage of earlier times would, had it inherited these words, have said
piora, impiora, spiende, and *pieve,* and we have manifest evidence
of this latter in that in the vernacular we call *pieve* a church devoted
to the religious services of the common people.'

11.3. The Seventeenth and Eighteenth Centuries

Unfortunately, Tolomei's work remained relatively unknown and without influence. In Italy, he had one follower, Celso Cittadini (1553–1627),[22]
whose *Trattato della vera origine, e del processo, e nome della nostra lingua*
('Treatise on the true origins, development, and name of our language',
1061) might have been a valuable history of Italian had Cittadini been
more consistent in applying Tolomei's principle of regular sound-change
and in avoiding fantastic etymologies.

In seventeenth-century Spain and France, likewise, interest in linguistic
history and etymology were in evidence, for instance in the *Tesoro de la
lengua castellana* ('Thesaurus of the Castilian language', 1611) of Sebastián
de Covarrubias (1539–1613), and the etymological dictionaries of the
Frenchman Gilles Ménage (1613–1692): *Origines de la langue françoise*
('Origins of the French language', 1650) and *Origini della lingua italiana*
('Origins of the Italian language', 1669).[23] Both of these scholars admitted
irregular, even wild, phonological developments, so that some of their
etymologies were completely fantastic. Ménage, for instance, derived Fr.
haricot 'string-bean' from Lat. *faba* 'bean' (which had actually given *fève*
'bean', quite regularly, in French), or It. *alfana* 'steed' from Lat. *equus*
'horse'. Covarrubias' dictionary has enjoyed uninterrupted favor as a
source for mediaeval Spanish lexicography. Ménage's work, on the other

hand, has fallen into undeserved oblivion, both because it was eclipsed in public interest by the "general grammar" movement (cf. below) and because Ménage's wrong derivations (28% in one sample) were so obviously ludicrous as to discredit the much larger proportion of valid and often ingenious etymologies in his work.[24]

The development of a scientific approach to the study both of the Romance tongues and of language in general was checked for nearly a century and a half, from ca. 1660 to ca. 1810, by the "general grammar" movement, beginning with the *Grammaire générale et raisonnée* ('General and reasoned grammar', 1660; later editions, 1664, 1669) of Claude Lancelot (1615–1695) and Antoine Arnauld (1612–1694).[25] Since Lancelot and Arnauld were connected with the Port-Royal (Jansenist) movement, this book is often referred to as the *Grammaire de Port-Royal* or 'Port-Royal grammar'. It was intended to be a comparison of Latin and French grammar for students on the intermediate level, and as such was moderately successful in its aim. However, Lancelot and Arnauld interpret many features of French in terms of Latin grammar, *e.g.* in seeing an "ablative" in every phrase introduced by a preposition other than *de* 'of' or *à* 'to'. Even worse, they make claims for wider applicability of their formulations than simply to these two tongues. They attempt to set up certain principles having universal validity for all languages, *e.g.* that every verb implies a subject in the nominative, or that all verbs other than "be" are to be interpreted as equivalent to "be" plus a present participle, *e.g.* Lat. *Petrus vivit* or Fr. *Pierre vit* 'Peter lives' = *Petrus est vivens* or *Pierre est vivant* 'Peter is living'. The unwary reader is likely to accept these identifications as valid unless he realises that they are based on insufficient data (French and Latin afford only a small and unrepresentative sample of the world's languages), and that Latin grammar is inadequate as a mould into which to force the facts of all other linguistic structures.

The grammarians of the later seventeenth and of the eighteenth centuries were extensively influenced by Port-Royal and by "general grammar," so that their work was marked more by abstract theorising and philosophising than by attention to actual phenomena of language. The most notable of these eighteenth-century grammarians were César Chesneau du Marsais (1674–1756)[26] and Nicolas Beauzée (1717–1789), whose *Grammaire générale ou exposition raisonnée des éléments necessaires du langage, pour servir de fondement à l'étude de toutes les langues* ('General grammar, or reasoned exposition of the necessary elements of language, to serve as a foundation for the study of all languages', 1767) sums up in its title the pretensions of the whole movement. The obsession of seventeenth- and eighteenth-century grammarians with panchronic "general grammar" impeded further advances along the line of historical linguistics, so that Turgot, in his article

"Étymologie" for the *Encyclopédie* (1756) had to recognise that there was still lacking a firm guide-line for the study of sound-change.[27]

The seventeenth and eighteenth centuries marked also the beginning of major lexicographical work on the standard Romance languages. This was closely tied in with the foundation of language-academies, which were official, governmentally supported bodies intended to "govern" the use of the language (at least in prestigious uses such as literature), to promulgate rules for correct usage, and to prepare dictionaries giving the accepted meanings of words.[28] The Italian Accademia della Crusca ('Bran-Academy', so called because it was intended to separate out the "bran" from the flour of language) was founded in 1546; the Académie Française, in 1634; the Real Academia Española in 1712. The dictionaries of these three academies were slow in appearing: that of the Crusca came out in 1612, that of the Académie Française in 1694, and the *Diccionario de la lengua castellana* ('Dictionary of the Castilian language') in 1726–39. In general, these dictionaries were in large (folio) format, with careful definitions and extensive supporting quotations. However, their choice of words was often limited by puristic considerations, and the texts from which the quotations were taken had often been rendered untrustworthy by unjustified emendations intended to ensure their "correctness."

Aside from Dante's discussion in the *De vulgari Eloquentia* (cf. §11.1), little or no attention was paid to dialects in mediaeval and Renaissance linguistic theory, except to dismiss them as "corruptions" of good language, used only by the basest strata of the populace. Except for a few word-lists designed for practical use by traders, the first dialectal dictionaries began to appear in the sixteenth century (Nicola Valla's Latin-Agrigento vocabulary, 1500; L. Cristòforo Scobar's Sicilian dictionary, 1519–20). Really extensive dialect-studies date from the seventeenth and eighteenth centuries, with the *Vocabolista bolognese* ('Bolognese vocabulary', 1660) of G. A. Bumaldi, and the abbé Ferdinando Galiani's study *Del dialetto napoletano* ('On the Neapolitan dialect', 1779). With the spread of the standard languages, especially in France, more attention was paid to dialects, either to condemn them (as was done officially by the National Convention in France in 1792[29]) and to help dialect-speakers to learn the standard language, or else to preserve the dialects as relics of an earlier age. The first extensive dialectal investigation, carried out by the abbé Henri-Baptiste Grégoire in France in 1790, was essentially a fact-finding study carried out as a prelude to an antidialectal campaign.

11.4. The Early Nineteenth Century

Not until the beginning of the nineteenth century, with the renewed interest in the Middle Ages and the modern survivals of mediaeval phenomena which was awakened by the Romantic movement, did further advances in linguistics[3] take place. The name of "father of Romance philology" has often been given to François Raynouard (1761–1836), for his fundamental work on Old Provençal in his anthology *Choix des poésies originales des Troubadours*[30] ('Selection of original poems of the troubadours', 1816–21), including a grammar of Old Provençal in the first volume and a *Grammaire comparée des langues de l'Europe latine* ('Comparative grammar of the languages of Latin Europe') in the sixth, and in his *Lexique roman ou dictionnaire de la langue des Troubadours* ('Romance lexicon, or dictionary of the language of the troubadours', 1838–44). These works have remained indispensable for the study of Old Provençal. Unfortunately, Raynouard's view of the relationships of the Romance languages was erroneous. It was widely thought, in the early nineteenth century, that Sanskrit was the direct ancestor of the other Indo-European languages, rather than simply one of the several tongues which had developed out of an unattested Proto-Indo-European. Similarly, Raynouard considered Old Provençal to be the *langue romane par excellence*, out of which all the others had developed. In fact, of course, they all, including Old Provençal, are to be traced back to spoken Latin.

If Raynouard was the "father of Romance philology," the title of "founder" of Romance linguistics" should be given to Friedrich Diez (1794–1876), professor at the University of Bonn from 1820 onwards. Diez began as a philologist. He studied and published, in accord with then prevalent Romantic interests, a collection of Old Spanish romances (*Altspanische Romanzen*, 1818) and then, acting on a suggestion from Goethe, he turned his attention to the Old Provençal material recently published by Raynouard. In this field, Diez published his *Die Poesie der Troubadours* ('The poetry of the troubadours', 1826) and *Leben und Werke der Troubadours* ('Lives and works of the troubadours', 1829). His more specifically linguistic works came later, with his *Grammatik der romanischen Sprachen* ('Grammar of the Romance languages', 1836–43) and his *Wörterbuch der romanischen Sprachen* ('Dictionary of the Romance languages', 1854). Both of these latter books went through several editions, and were the standard reference-works for Romance linguistics during the rest of the nineteenth century.

Diez' method was essentially the same as that of his contemporaries Rasmus Rask (1787–1832), Jakob Grimm (1785–1863), and Franz Bopp (1791–1867) in Indo-European comparative linguistics. He rightly saw that Old Provençal was simply the earliest attested of the Romance languages, not their common ancestor; and his prime concern was to establish correlations between Romance developments and their Latin sources. His dictionary is arranged, not by Latin etyma nor yet by sememes, but by individual languages: first a section containing "Gemeinromanische

Wörter" (words common to all or most of the Romance languages), then separate sections on Italian, Spanish, and French. This latter is also the order (clearly reflecting their relative degree of differentiation from Latin) in which Diez gives the words in the individual entries. He includes words from Rhaeto-Romance, but pays very little attention to Roumanian. Diez of course recognised popular, rather than classical, Latin as the source of the Romance languages; but he made little use of the concept of "Vulgar Latin" in his approach to historical linguistics, citing normally only Latin forms and their Romance equivalents. Since, for the most part, his Latin material was already attested, he was very little concerned with reconstructing intermediate stages—an attitude which has persisted down to the present in almost all scholars' approach to Romance linguistics.

Before further work could be done on the history and comparison of the Romance languages, the extensive but still unpublished mediaeval text-material had to be made available for study. This philological work, begun by Raynouard and Diez, was the main concern of Romance scholars in the first part of the nineteenth century, first in France and somewhat later in Italy, Spain, and Portugal (as well, of course, as in Germany). The École des Chartes, devoted to the study of French mediaeval manuscripts, was founded in 1821. An increasing number of dialect-dictionaries and -grammars was published, beginning in Sardinia with Vissentu Porru's *Saggio di grammatica sul dialetto sardo meridionale* ('Grammatical essay on the South Sardinian dialect', 1829); in Italy with Giuseppe Boerio's *Dizionario veneziano* ('Venetian dictionary', 1829); and in France with Hyppolite Jaubert's Berrichon dictionary (*Vocabulaire du Berry*, 1838).[31] There were relatively few works on the history of individual languages produced in this period. Such as did appear, *e.g.*, for French, Jean Ampère's *Histoire de la formation de la langue française* ('History of the formation of the French language', 1841), H. du Méril's *Essai philosophique sur la formation de la langue française* ('Philosophical essay on the formation of the French language', 1852), or Auguste de Chevallet's *Origine et formation de la langue française* (Origin and formation of the French language', 1853), were of little value. Some scholars were still inclined to consider, say, French as a Keltic language spoken with Latin words, or to establish far-fetched relationships between French and distant languages such as Sanskrit.

11.5. The Later Nineteenth Century

In the 1860's and 1870's, scholars in Indo-European linguistics came to be more and more concerned with the questions of the comparative method and of the regularity of linguistic change, which was at the time discussed primarily as involving *Ausnahmslosigkeit der Lautgesetze* ('absence of exceptions to sound-laws').[32] The philologist August Schleicher (1821–1867), under the influence of his avocational interest in botany and in the Darwinian approach, viewed languages as living organisms, whose relationship to each other could be represented in the form of a *Stammbaum* or family-tree. This technique, which is highly useful as a schematic representation of over-all relationships, was widely criticised as being too rigid and abstract, and as implying too sudden and sharp a differentiation at the individual nodes of the family-tree. A number of scholars, more or less independently, came to operate with a fairly strict criterion of regularity of phonetic change, without which it would be impossible to establish any principles of historical development at all. Tolomei's regularist principle (§11.1) was thus rediscovered three and a half centuries after it was first stated. It received its most explicit statement in the works of the Indo-Europeanist Karl Brugmann (1849–1919) and the Slavicist August Leskien (1840–1916), in the 1870's. The briefest and most drastic formulation was Leskien's affirmation, in 1876, that *Die Lautgesetze kennen keine Ausnahmen* ('phonetic laws admit of no exceptions'). A more accurate way of stating the principle would have been "Sound-change would be regular if there were no interfering factors"—an affirmation of fundamental regularity which enables the investigator to identify both normal developments and factors which have interfered with them.

Because of their tenacity in affirming this principle and their apparent rigidity in adhering to it, Brugmann, Leskien, and their followers received the nick-name of *Junggrammatiker* or 'Neo-Grammarians', at first as a term of opprobrium but later used by their disciples as well. Opposition to the Neo-Grammarians' declaration of *Ausnahmslosigkeit der Lautgesetze* was expressed immediately, both by older scholars such as Georg Curtius (1820–1885) and by younger men such as the Indo-Europeanist Johannes Schmidt (1843–1901), who advanced his "wave-theory," according to which linguistic innovations spread from centers like waves, as a substitute for the Neo-Grammarian principle.[33]

In the Romance field, Graziadio Isaìa Àscoli (1829–1907) criticised the Neo-Grammarians in his *Due léttere glottologiche* ('Two linguistic letters', 1882, 1886), not for the regularist principle itself (to which he also adhered), but for having acted as if they had been the first to discover it. The Romance scholar whose opposition to the Neo-Grammarians was most influential was Hugo Schuchardt (1842–1929). He had made his début with an extensive and highly detailed study of the vowels of Vulgar Latin (*Der Vokalismus des Vulgärlateins*, 1866–68); the sequel, on the consonants, never appeared. Schuchardt's criticism of the Neo-Grammarians, in his *Über die Lautgesetze: gegen die Junggrammatiker* 'On sound-laws: against the Neo-

Grammarians', 1885), was based on several misunderstandings, especially (1) the literal interpretation of Neo-Grammarian doctrine as implying that exceptions to sound-laws are nowhere to be found, whereas every historical grammar can cite hundreds of them; and (2) the observation that each word has its own history. The latter point is valid enough, but has been misapplied by Schuchardt and his followers. In the history of each word, various factors are at work, including sound-change; but in the history of sounds, the phonological system constitutes a separate level, whose changes proceed independently of morphological, syntactic, or semantic developments.

The success of the Neo-Grammarians' work in the Indo-European field and its branches was such that their principles were soon applied in Romance linguistics as well.[34] Gustav Gröber (1844–1911) was not only the founder of the *Zeitschrift für romanische Philologie* ('Journal of Romance philology', 1877 ff.) and the editor of the first encyclopaedic survey of the field,[35] but also the first major scholar to apply the comparative method to the reconstruction of unattested "Vulgar Latin" words. In a long series of articles[35] (never published in book-form), Gröber set up many hypothetical forms (conventionally marked with an asterisk, hence often called "starred forms") which must have been, in popular Latin speech, the sources from which later Romance words developed. A number of the forms which Gröber and others set up, by the technique of comparative reconstruction, have since then turned up in actual inscriptions or other written sources, *e.g. abantiare* 'to go ahead' (: Lat. *ab ante* 'in front') > It. *avanzare*, Fr. *avancer*, Sp. *avanzar*, etc. The method itself has thus been proven valid, despite some over-reliance on "starred forms" for which its practitioners have been excessively criticised.

Diez' etymological dictionary, with its inconvenient arrangement, was replaced, first by the (not very satisfactory) *Lateinisch-romanisches Wörterbuch* ('Latin-Romance dictionary', 1890–91) of Gustav Körting (1845–1913), and later by the *Romanisches etymologisches Wörterbuch* ('Romance etymological dictionary', often abbreviated *REW*; 1911–20) of Wilhelm Meyer-Lübke (1861–1936). The *REW* was preceded by the *Grammatik der romanischen Sprachen* ('Grammar of the Romance languages, 1890–1902) of the same author, an extensive four-volume work covering all aspects of Romance historical linguistics, and based on all the major Romance languages (including Rumanian and Sardinian). Meyer-Lübke was also the author of a general *Einführung in das Studium der romanischen Sprachwissenschaft* ('Introduction to the study of Romance linguistics[37]'), and a number of works on the historical grammar of individual Romance languages, particularly Italian (*Italienische Grammatik* ['Italian grammar'], 1890), French (*Historische Grammatik der französischen Sprache* ['Historical grammar of the French language'], 1908), and Catalan (*Das Katalanische*, 1925).

Meyer-Lübke's work was characterised by sobriety and balance, with exceptional solidity in detail but with an over-all sense of systematicity. He has frequently been criticised for adhering excessively to Neo-Grammarian principles. In fact, however, he continually took into account all new developments in linguistic geography and word-history, as the great linguistic atlases and other works appeared.

The work of editing and publishing mediaeval Romance texts went on apace, especially in such series as those of the Société des anciens textes français ('Society for Old French texts', 1875 ff.). The increased availability of text-materials made it possible for scholars to begin large new dictionaries for earlier stages of the Romance languages, intended to be fuller treatments than had previously been available, e.g. Frédéric Godefroy's Dictionnaire de l'ancienne langue française ('Dictionary of the Old French language', 1880–1902). Unfortunately, in many instances the financial support available for such projects was meagre, and it often took decades for a multivolume work to appear, as in the case of E. Levy's supplement to Raynouard's Old Provençal dictionary.[38]

Not only practical, but also scholarly considerations brought about a great expansion in dialectal studies in the latter part of the nineteenth century. In addition to the large numbers of (often very extensive) dialectdictionaries, grammars of local speech-varieties began to appear.[39] These were in some instances brief descriptions cast in the mould of Latin grammar; in others, comparisons of dialectal peculiarities with the corresponding features of the standard language, intended especially to aid dialect-speakers in overcoming their "mistakes"; and in still others, historical treatments outlining the development of Latin sounds and forms in individual dialects. On the basis of such studies, new classifications of dialects were on occasion proposed, such as Àscoli's identification of a separate area in Gallo-Romance which he, and virtually all scholars since his time, have termed Franco-Provençal,[40] or his recognition of a separate group of Romance languages, the Rhaeto-Romance, in the Swiss and Italian Alps.[41]

The study of dialects also received further impetus from the theoretical debates over the assumption of *Ausnahmslosigkeit der Lautgesetze* (cf. above). It was not hard to disprove Leskien's flat assertion that *Die Lautgesetze kennen keine Ausnahmen*, taken literally. Even in a single family, there exist differences between the generations in their speech, as shown by the phonetician abbé Pierre Rousselot (1846–1924) for the usage of a Savoyard family.[42] This was confirmed later for a Franco-Provençal village in French-speaking Switzerland.[43] To this debate was due also the beginning of linguistic geography and the preparation of linguistic atlases. In the nineteenth century, especially under the influence of the Romantic doctrine that civilisation was corrupt and the "folk" were pure, it was widely thought that folk-speech would of necessity preserve original linguistic conditions in less altered form than would literary language.

Under the influence of this conception, a certain supporter of the Neo-Grammarians, the German Georg Wenker (1852–1911), began an extensive investigation of German dialects to prove that they preserved the results of regular sound-change intact. His investigations, whose findings were recorded in the form of a series of maps (begun in 1876, but not published until 1926–58), proved the exact opposite, namely that dialects show fully as much mixture of linguistic phenomena and criss-crossing of isoglosses as do standard languages. Work along similar lines in the Romance field was begun by the Swiss French scholar Jules Gilliéron (1854–1916) in the late 1870's with his *Petit atlas phonétique du Valais roman* ('Little phonetic atlas of French-speaking Valais [a region of Switzerland]', 1880). In the 1890's, Gilliéron undertook the preparation of an atlas for all of France, for which his collaborator and field-worker Edmond Edmont (1848–1926) collected the materials in 1897–1901; but the work was not published until the next decade (cf. §11.6).[44]

The middle and latter part of the nineteenth century witnessed the foundation of a number of journals devoted to modern-language-study, the earliest of which was R. Herrig's *Archiv für das Studium der neueren Sprachen und Literaturen* ('Archive for the study of modern languages and literatures', abbr. *ASNS*; 1846 ff.). Specifically devoted to the Romance languages were the *Revue des langues romanes* ('Romance language review', abbr. *RLR*; 1870 ff.), the *Romania* (1872 ff.), the *Zeitschrift für romanische Philologie* (cf. above; abbr. *ZRPh.*; 1876 ff.), and the *Romanische Forschungen* ('Romance investigations', abbr. *RF*; 1883 ff.).

11.6. The Early Twentieth Century

A reaction against what was erroneously taken to be excessive rigidity and materialism on the part of the Neo-Grammarians (cf. §1.5) set in towards the end of the nineteenth and the beginning of the twentieth century.[45] The Italian philosopher Benedetto Croce (1866–1952) expounded, in his influential *Estetica come scienza dell'espressione e linguistica generale* ('Aesthetics as the science of expression and general linguistics', 1902), the doctrine that linguistics was a valid subject-matter only as a branch of aesthetics, inasmuch as all language was only an expression of the individual's perception of and reaction to each specific situation. The same general approach was taken by the German scholar Karl Vossler (1872–1949)—unlike Croce, a professional philologist in the Romance field—but with sharper criticisms directed specifically against the Neo-Grammarians, particularly in his *Positivismus und Idealismus in der Sprachwissenschaft* ('Positivism and idealism in linguistics', 1904). This aestheticising approach, when applied to linguistic history, led to serious distortions and misrepresentations, *e.g.* in Vossler's *Frankreichs Kultur im Spiegel seiner Sprachentwicklung*.[46]

To the doctrine of language as aesthetic expression (hence not subject to scientific investigation) was added an element of metaphysical dualism, adhered to as a theological doctrine (cf. fn. 2 to this chapter) and defended almost as a religion by its devotees, who regarded language as the expression of an inaccessible, unobservable "spirit" which had absolute primacy over mere matter. In the question of sound-laws, it was therefore assumed *a priori* that changes in purely material phenomena, such as sounds, could not possibly have any priority in determining the development of the more "spiritual" aspects of language, especially syntax and meaning; but that, on the contrary, these latter must be the ultimately determining factors in what happened in the rest of language. This view-point was propounded by the Italian philologist and dialectologist Giulio Bertoni (1878–1942) and by the German stylisticians Leo Spitzer (1887–1960)[47] and Eugen Lerch (1888–1952).

Linguistic geography, which had already begun in the nineteenth century (cf. §1.5), received a strong impulse from the publication of Gilliéron and Edmont's *Atlas linguistique de France* ('Linguistic atlas of France', abbr. *ALF*; 1902–10) and of Gilliéron's monographs based thereon.[48] Gilliéron became the teacher of a group of enthusiastic students in Paris, many of them from other countries, who planned similar works on a nationwide scale for their home-lands. Of these, the only major one to be completely carried out and published was the *Atlante linguistico-etnografico dell'Italia e della Svizzera meridionale* (German title *Sprach- und Sachatlas Italiens und der Südschweiz* 'Linguistic and ethnographic atlas of Italy and southern Switzerland', abbr. *AIS*) of the two Swiss linguists Karl Jaberg (1877–1958) and Jakob Jud (1882–1952). The atlas itself appeared in eight volumes between 1928 and 1940, and supplementary volumes were published later.[49] The Italian linguist Gino Bottiglioni (1887–1963) carried through a similar, though smaller, project for Corsica.[50]

Other atlases on a national scale were seriously delayed in their publication, as were A. Griera's for Catalonia, T. Navarro Tomás' for the Iberian peninsula, and that of Sextil Puşcariu (1877–1948) for Rumania.[51] The worst delayed of all was the *Atlante linguistico italiano* ('Italian linguistic atlas', abbr. *ALI*), an Italian atlas covering much the same territory as the *AIS*, planned by Matteo Giulio Bàrtoli (1873–1946), originally in coöperation with Jaberg and Jud, but forced into competition with them under Fascist pressure in the 1920's and 1930's.[52] Gustav Weigand's early Roumanian atlas, whose approach differed from that of Gilliéron in a number of important respects,[53] remained isolated and without influence. As each atlas or portion of one appeared, its materials served as the basis for numerous studies in onomasiology ('The words for . . . in . . .') and in semasiology ('The semantic development of . . . in . . .').

In discussions of theory, the findings of Gilliéronian linguistic geography were used to buttress the anti-Neo-Grammarian arguments of the 'idealistic' school (cf. above). Gilliéron himself attacked[54] the type of etymology which was too narrowly based on phonetic developments alone. His pupil Bàrtoli specifically combined linguistic geography with Crocean and Bertonian idealism, and, in his doctrine of "Neolinguistica,"[55] set up a series of six "norms" or statistically based predictions concerning the geographical distribution of linguistic phenomena which were intended to replace the principle of regularity in sound-change.[56] For a time it was almost obligatory to preface every treatise on linguistic geography, no matter how far removed from problems of sound-change, with *boutades* against the Neo-Grammarians and their supposedly pernicious doctrine of phonetic law. The chief exceptions to this phenomenon were the well-balanced works of Jaberg and Jud and their trainees,[57] which combined carefully documented considerations of geographical distribution with solid historical and comparative study completely in the regularist tradition. The Italian linguist Pier Gabriele Goidànich (1868–1953) and the dialectologist Clemente Merlo (1879–1960) also professed adherence to the Neo-Grammarians' principles, but in an unimaginative and doctrinaire fashion.

The example of Meyer-Lübke's work was followed in a considerable number of historical grammars and histories of individual languages (cf. Chapter 2, for listings of the main works).[58] Of these, some were extensive, detailed treatments, such as Nyrop's historical grammar of French, and Brunot and Bruneau's history of the literary language. Others were compendia, ranging from extensive but unoriginal compilations all the way to mere reproductions of lecture-notes. At their best, these works afforded clear, penetrating presentations of the development of linguistic systems over two millennia. At their worst, their unimaginative rigidity reïnforced the hostility which littérateurs felt towards linguistics and seemed to justify the idealists' condemnation of what they presented as the Neo-Grammarian approach.

Not only the recognised literary languages, but also hitherto neglected varieties of Romance began to receive more extended attention than they had previously. Sardinian, thanks mainly to the life-long work of Max Leopold Wagner (1880–1962),[59] came to be recognised as a separate Romance language, not merely an aberrant dialect of Italian. The claims of

Friulian to recognition as a literary language were upheld by the "Àscoli" Philological Society of Ùdine, especially through its active support of the *ALI* and other dialectological projects. Latin-American and Franco-Canadian speech received increasing attention in its own right, not merely as the object of condemnation from Spanish, Portuguese, or French purists. Schuchardt had studied a number of Romance-based pidgin and creole languages,[60] in woefully inadequate attestations, for the purpose of demonstrating the untenability of the Neo-Grammarian principle in the case of so-called "mixed" languages. In the 1920's and 1930's, more extensive studies of this type of language—at first, for reasons extraneous to linguistics, of Haitian Creole—began to be made, partly on a basis of traditional European-style grammar,[61] but partly also with phonetic or phonemic transcription and with adequate attention to social and historical factors.[62]

From the Renaissance onward, it has been evident to Romance scholars that the languages spoken earlier in the areas conquered by the Romans, where Latin "took root" and developed into the Romance tongues, must have left some traces in the speech of these regions. Such languages have, with a not wholly fortunate geological metaphor, been termed the "substrata" underlying the Romance languages. By an extension of the same metaphor, the languages of later conquering groups (especially Germanic and Slavic), which are thought to have exerted influences on Romance, have been called "superstrata"; and those of groups existing at the same time (*e.g.* Greek in Roman times) have been termed "adstrata." Interest in sub-, super-, and adstrata has grown markedly since ca. 1900. All agree that their influence is evident in certain parts of linguistic structure, especially lexicon and word-formation, as evidenced by such substratum-loans as Fr. *charrue* 'plow' < Keltic *carrūca*, or such superstratum-borrowings as Fr. *fauteuil* 'arm-chair' < OFr. *faldestoel* 'curule chair' < Gmc. **falda-stōl* 'folding stool'.

Concerning other levels of structure, especially phonetics and morphology, scholars are not all agreed. Some, the "substratomaniacs," see the effects of a sub- or a superstratum-language in every otherwise unexplained phenomenon, *e.g.* the French /y/-sound from Latin /u:/, as in Fr. *mur* /myr/ 'wall' < Lat. *mūru(m)* (a change often ascribed to Keltic substratum) or Old French and Old Italian diphthongisation, as in OFr. *nuef* 'new', It. *nuovo* < Lat. *novu(m)* (ascribed to Germanic superstratum). Among the extreme advocates of wide-spread substratum-influence were Clemente Merlo, Gino Bottiglioni, and Benvenuto Aron Terracini (1886–1968) in Italy, and Ramón Menéndez Pidal (1869–1968) in Spain. Others, more conservative, were ready to admit the possibility of a sub- or superstratum-influence where it could be shown, but not otherwise, e.g. the German

Gerhard Rohlfs (1892–   ), the Swiss Siegfried Heinimann (1917–   ) and the present writer. Very extensive substratum-connections have been suggested by some, especially for relations between Basque, the Caucasian languages, and a presumed pre-Latin "Mediterranean" substratum. Chief among such scholars have been Hugo Schuchardt, Alfredo Trombetti (1866–1929), and Johannes Hubschmid (1916–   ).

A number of new reviews devoted wholly or primarily to Romance philology were founded in the first half of the twentieth century, including the American *Romanic Review* (abbr. *RR*; 1910 ff.) and *Romance Philology* (abbr. *RPh.*; 1947 ff.); the German *Volkstum und Kultur der Romanen* (abbr. *VKR*; 1928 ff.) and *Romanistisches Jahrbuch* (abbr. *RJb.*; 1947 ff.); and the Swiss *Vox Romanica* (abbr. *VR*; 1936 ff.) with its monograph-series *Romanica Helvetica* (abbr. *RH*). Devoted specifically to Italian dialectology is *L'Italia Dialettale* (abbr. *ID*; 1925 ff.); to the study of the Italian language, *Lingua Nostra* (abbr. *LN*; 1939 ff.) and *Studi Linguistici Italiani* (abbr. *StLI*; 1960 ff.); and to that of modern French, *Le Français moderne* (abbr. *FM*; 1936 ff.). The only journal exclusively devoted to Romance linguistics is the *Revue de Linguistique Romane* (abbr. *RLiR*; 1925 ff.)

11.7. The Mid-Twentieth Century

Linguistic geography was the last novel approach to language to originate or receive its first major development in the Romance field. Some further changes in direction took place in Romance linguistic geography after the Second World War. The large national atlas-projects were obviously so subject to long-term delays and unforeseen vicissitudes that scholars began to turn their attention to projects more easily realisable in a relatively short period. These mostly took the form of less ambitious regional atlases,[63] or, in some instances, of groups of regional projects designed to cover an entire country.[64] In the technique of gathering and editing material, almost all Romance linguistic geographers remained faithful to the Rousselot-Gilliéron tradition of the face-to-face interview with native dialect-speakers, the recording of unprompted immediate responses in a very narrow phonetic transcription, and their publication in cartographic form.

Towards other approaches to linguistic description and history, most Romance linguists remained aloof, when not actively hostile. The historical-comparative frame-work established by Meyer-Lübke was often deprecated, but remained in practice the only basis accepted in the field. Attempts to make explicit statements of the comparative method, in its application to Romance, were met with rejection,[65] even from those who practised it in their own work. There were scattered efforts to apply structurally oriented techniques of description to Romance, especially the well-established literary languages, but these attempts likewise went uncomprehended or rejected.[66] In the field of pidgins and creoles, with a less rigidly established grammatical tradition, structural descriptions were somewhat less unwelcome.[67] Of the various attempts made to interpret the history of the Romance languages in structural terms,[68] only Martinet's *Économie des changements phonétiques* ('Economy of phonetic changes', 1955) had any extensive influence.

The transformational-generative movement of the 1960's had a more immediate impact,[69] primarily because it combined a deceptive modernity in quasi-mathematical formulation with a basically mediaeval, theological type of underlying philosophy (cf. fn. 2) and an approach to grammar which required from the adept no advance beyond the Renaissance type of analysis taught in elementary schools.[70] To counter wide-spread criticisms of Romance linguistics as an essentially backward and unoriginal field, some scholars[71] took a defensive stand, rejecting the structural approach as not fitted for "languages of civilisation," and regarding the Schuchardtian tradition as a contribution of the field to linguistics rather than as an impediment to the further development of Romance studies.

NOTES TO CHAPTER 11

1. Cf. Hall 1969c.
2. We are defining, for our purposes, a *theology* as a set of statements brooking no contradiction (DOGMAS), concerning forces or beings (*e.g.* deities, spirits, devils, souls) which are not accessible to human observation in any controllable or verifiable fashion, but whose existence, paramount importance, and supreme power is assumed *a priori* and is considered an undeniable, irrefutable factor which has to be taken into account as determining everything else in the study or discussion of the universe; and a *science* as a method for arriving at statements which brook contradiction, concerning only phenomena which are accessible to human observation or are deducible on the basis of observation; whose existence is assumed only on the basis of hypotheses which can be tested, checked, and confirmed (or disconfirmed) by procedures accessible to all observers; and whose function in the study or discussion of the universe is never considered permanently undeniable or irrefutable.
3. Cf. Pulgram 1958:404–405; Elcock 1960:329–331; and most other discussions of the earliest differentiation of Romance from Latin.
4. Cf. Stengel 1878.
5. Cf. Stengel 1879; Stürzinger 1884.
6. Cf. Brunot and Bruneau 1905–69:1.392–394; Kukenheim 1962 (1966²).
7. Especially in connection with the seven-hundredth anniversary of Dante's birth, in 1965, a number of studies of Dante's contribution to linguistics were made, of which the most important are Francescato 1965; Bahner 1965; Grayson 1965. Among earlier

studies, cf. also Casella 1925; Ewert 1940; Pagliaro 1947; Pabst 1952; Pellegrini 1960; Ruffini 1962. For a complete listing of studies on Dante's views of language, cf. Hall 1958a: §§6710–6734 and 1969a: §§9289–9309.

8. Cf. Rotta 1910 and Robins 1951.

9. From the context, it is clear that by *(il) bel paese là dove il sì suona* 'the fair country where *sì* is heard' *(Inferno* 33.80), and hence also in the *De v. E.*, Dante meant only Italy; in the latter work and elsewhere he pays no attention to Spain or Portugal, so far as language is concerned.

10. Cf. Terracini 1952.

11. Cf. Kukenheim 1932. On the French grammars of Palsgrave and others written for Englishmen, cf. Brunot and Bruneau 1905–69:1.123–128; for the first French grammars for Germans, cf. Streuber 1964–69.

12. The "Grammatichetta vaticana," the first known grammar of Italian, has now definitely been shown to be by Alberti; cf. Colombo 1962 and Grayson 1964. For the history of Italian grammars in general, from the sixteenth to the nineteenth century, the only survey is the rather unsatisfactory work by Trabalza (1908).

13. On Nebrija, cf. especially A. Alonso 1952.

14. For R. Estienne's influence on sixteenth-century French lexicography, cf. Brandon 1904.

15. Cf. Brunot and Bruneau 1905–69:2.133–159; Kukenheim 1932; Neumann 1959.

16. Cf. Labande-Jeanroy 1925; Hall 1942; Migliorini 1949; Sozzi 1955; Vitale 1960; Façon 1962a.

17. Cf. Petrocchi 1959; Santàngelo 1961.

18. Cf. Brunot and Bruneau 1905–69:2.157–159.

19. Cf. Villey 1908. To one who knows the Italian materials, Du Bellay's *Deffense et Illustration* reads almost like a cut-and-paste job.

20. In Meigret's case, dialectal differences between his (originally Lyonnais) speech and that of Paris seem also to have played a part; cf. Shipman 1953.

21. For the problem of "Vulgar Latin" in general in the fifteenth and sixteenth centuries, cf. Klein 1957. For Poggio Bracciolini, cf. Walser 1914.

22. Cf. Vannini 1920.

23. For Ménage's work on Italian, cf. Zehnder 1938. No over-all reëvaluation of Ménage as a linguist has yet appeared.

24. Ménage was addicted to social life, so that his etymological divagations became well known in elegant Parisian circles; the pedant Vadius in Molière's *Les Femmes savantes* (1672) is thought to be a satirical portrait of Ménage. The quatrain of the Chevalier d'Aceilly on the etymology *alfana* < *equus* is worthy of mention: *"Alfana* vient d'*equus* sans doute; / Mais il faut avouer aussi / Qu'en venant de là jusqu'ici / Il a bien changé sur la route" ('*Alfana* comes from *equus*, without a doubt; but one must also admit that, while coming from there to here, it has certainly changed along the way').

25. Cf. Donzé 1966; Hall 1969c; Aarsleff 1970, 1971. For linguistic theory in the Enlightenment in general, cf. Rosiello 1967.

26. An excellent discussion in Sahlin 1928.

27. Cf. Piron's edition (1961) and my notice thereof (Hall 1964/65). The guide-lines whose lack Turgot recognised had already been stated by Tolomei over two centuries previously (cf. above), but the principle of regularity in sound-change had been lost sight of in the mean-time.

28. For a discussion of academicism and purism in general, cf. Hall 1964, chapter 62.

29. Cf. Pop 1950:1.xxix, 12–13.

30. The adjective *originales* in Raynouard's title emphasised the contrast between the

poems contained in his anthology and those produced in the mid-eighteenth century as a factitious imitation, in the lyrics of the "genre troubadour."

31. For a detailed listing and discussion of nineteenth-century dialect-dictionaries and other works on Romance dialects, cf. Pop 1950:1.xxx–xliv.

32. The best presentation of the history of these questions is in Pedersen 1931. For their relevance to modern linguistic theory, cf. particularly Bloomfield 1933, chapter 13; Hockett 1958, chapter 57; Hall 1964, chapter 60.

33. In actuality, there is no contradiction between the two; cf. Pulgram 1953.

34. It used to be maintained, especially by the "idealistic" school (cf. below, §11.6), that G. I. Àscoli, because of his criticism of the Neo-Grammarians, was antiregularist. The inaccuracy of this claim was shown by Merlo 1929 and Goidànich 1929.

35. Gröber (ed.) 1886–88.

36. Gröber 1884–90. Note that Gröber's term *substratum* refers to reconstructed or attested ancestral forms of Romance words, not to languages spoken at earlier times in regions where Latin was imported and developed into Romance (see below, §11.6).

37. The second Spanish translation, by Américo Castro, is the most profitable to consult, since it contains numerous bibliographical additions and observations, often significant, by the translator.

38. E. Levy 1894–1924. In some instances, the rate of publication of dictionaries for older stages of a language or for dialect-areas (*e.g.* Sganzini [ed.] 1952– â€ƒ) has been such that, if continued, the complete work would not appear until the twenty-second or twenty-third century!

39. Cf. the historical sketch given by Pop (1950:1.xxxv–xliv), and the detailed discussion of many dialect-studies in the sections of his first volume devoted to the individual Romance languages and their dialects.

40. Àscoli 1878; but cf. also Hall 1949a.

41. Àscoli 1873a. The validity of Rhaeto-Romance as a separate subgroup has been vigorously denied by Battisti (1922, 1929, 1931, 1962, etc.) and many other Italian scholars.

42. In the village of Cellefrouin, not far from Culoz; cf. Rousselot 1891–92.

43. Cf. Gauchat 1905.

44. Cf. Pop 1950:1.113–136 for a detailed history and description of the Gilliéron atlas.

45. Cf. the general discussion in Hall 1963.

46. Vossler 1913; reworked as *Frankreichs Kultur und Sprache* ('The Culture and Language of France', 1929).

47. For a somewhat arrogant, but basically valid, evaluation of Spitzer's work, cf. Malkiel 1960/61.

48. *E.g.* Gilliéron and Mongin 1905; Gilliéron 1918.

49. Scheuermeier 1943, 1956; Jaberg and Jud 1960.

50. Bottiglioni (ed.) 1933–44.

51. Griera i Gaja 1923–68; Navarro Tomás et al. (eds.) 1962–. The history of the Roumanian atlases has been exceptionally complicated; cf. Pop 1950:1.709–732.

52. Bàrtoli et al. (eds.), forthcoming. As of 1972, over fifty years after the inception of the project, two sample maps had been printed and distributed. For the detailed history of the ALI, cf. Pop 1950:1.598–610, and Butler 1965/66.

53. Weigand 1898–1909. His material was apparently collected by much the same technique of choosing representative informants and interviewing them on the spot; but his maps give, not the phonetic transcription of the actual responses, but a schematised

representation of the distribution of individual features. For the history of Roumanian lexicography, cf. Seche 1966.

54. Especially in Gilliéron 1919.

55. Set forth primarily in Bàrtoli 1925; Bàrtoli and Bertoni 1925. For the history of Romance philology in Italy in this period, cf. Ruggieri, 1969.

56. Cf. the criticisms of Hall 1946a and the reply thereto of Bonfante 1947.

57. *E.g.* Jaberg 1926 and Jud 1946, 1948.

58. For a general, though not unbiased, survey of work in this field, cf. Malkiel 1960.

59. From his earliest work on South Sardinian (1907) through his etymological dictionary of Sardinian (1960–64), Wagner changed the status of Sardinian from one of the least known of the Romance languages to one of the best known. Y. Malkiel, in his obituary (Malkiel 1962/63), gives a perceptive but somewhat tendentious evaluation of Wagner's achievement.

60. In a long series of articles published from 1882 to 1914; cf. Hall 1965:173–174 for a complete bibliography.

61. *E.g.* Göbl-Gáldi 1933, 1934; Faine 1937, 1939.

62. *E.g.* S. Sylvain 1936.

63. Such as M. Melillo 1955 for Lucania in Italy, or Álvar 1961–65 for Andalucía in Spain. Cf. Álvar 1960 for a general discussion of developments in the 1940's and 1950's.

64. *E.g.* the *Atlas linguistique de la France par régions* ('Linguistic Atlas of France by Regions'), first planned in the 1920's and 1930's by Albert Dauzat (1877–1955) as a means of filling the lacunae of the ALF (cf. Pop, 1950:1.136–151). It was continued in the post-Second-World-War period with the publication of such works as Gardette et al. (eds.) 1950–68 for the Lyonnais region; Nauton 1957–63 for the Massif Central: Séguy et al. (eds.) 1954–1956 for Gascony; Guiter 1966 for the Eastern Pyrenees; Bourcelot 1968– for Champagne and Brie; and Remacle 1953– , for the Walloon area. A series of eight linguistic atlases for the various regions of Roumania, under the direction of Boris Cazacu (1919–) was begun in the 1960's (Cazacu [ed.] et al. 1968–).

65. For instance, Hall 1950a, and such discussions thereof as Roneaglia 1950.

66. Thus, for French, Hall 1948 and Togeby 1951; for Italian, Hall 1971; for Spanish, Alarcos Llorach 1950, 1951. Cf. also such criticisms as those of Martinet 1949 and Messing 1951.

67. As in the case of D. Taylor 1947 and 1951 for Dominican Creole; Hall 1953 and d'Ans 1968 for Haitian Creole; and Valkhoff 1966, for Portuguese-based creoles in Africa. Traditional-style treatments of creolised languages still continued to appear, however, *e.g.* as theses written under the direction of conservatively oriented purists, for instance, Jourdain 1956a, b; cf. R. Hall 1957.

68. *E.g.* Haudricourt and Juilland 1949 for French; Goodman 1964 for French-based creoles; or, for Romance as a whole, Lüdtke 1956a.

69. As evidenced in such works as Schane 1968 for French; Costabile 1967 and Saltarelli 1970 for Italian; Harris 1969 and Hadlich 1970 for Spanish.

70. Cf. such criticisms as those of Uhlenbeck 1967; Buyssens 1969; or Hall 1969b.

71. *E.g.* Malkiel 1968b.

References

The following list contains only those works cited in the main text of the notes of this volume. It is in no wise intended to be a complete bibliography of Romance linguistics or of any part thereof.

The listing of each item contains: author's name, year of publication, title, and place (city, in the case of books; journal-, volume-, and page-numbers for articles or reviews). A period following a number, in a journal-reference, indicates pages in a volume; a colon indicates a separate number within a volume. Thus, 6.228–341 means "Volume 6, pages 228 to 341"; 53:3.9–12 = "Volume 53, number 3, pages 9 to 18." In the listing of years of publication, a dash connects the numbers referring to the first and last years of a period over which the publication of a work extended: thus, Mohrmann 1961–65 refers to a work by Mohrmann whose publication began in 1961 and ended in 1965. A slash indicates the years covered by a given volume of a periodical or other publication: for instance, Krotkoff, 1963/64, refers to an article published, in this case in Romance Philology, Volume 17, which extended from 1962 into 1963.

Abbreviations and Collection-Volumes

A William Cameron Townsend en el vigésimoquinto aniversario del Instituto Lingüístico de Verano. México, D.F., 1961.
AAA = Archivio per l'Alto Adige.
AAColombaria = Atti dell'Accademia Fiorentina "La Colombaria".
AAPalermo = Atti dell'Accademia di scíenze, lettere ed arti de Palermo.
AATorino = Atti dell'Accademia delle scienze di Torino.
AAVerona = Atti dell'Accademia di scienze e lettere di Verona.
AbhBAW = Abhandlungen der bayrischen Akademie der Wissenschaften.
AbhBerlin = Abhandlungen der Akademie der Wissenschaften zu Berlin.
AbhMainz = Abhandlungen der Akademie der Wissenschaften und der Litteratur in Mainz.
ACILFR^n = Atti del [n] Congresso Internazionale di Linguistica e Filologia Romanza.
ACISS = Atti del congresso internazionale di scienze storiche. Roma, 1904–07. 12 vols.
AcJut. = Acta Jutlandica.
AcLHa. = Acta Linguistica (Hafniensia). København.
ACLHu. = Acta Linguistica Hungarica. Budapest.

ACSR = Atti del congresso di studî romanzi.
AEM = Anuario de Estudios Medievales.
AFLBari = Annali della Facoltà di Lettere dell'Università di Bari.
AGI = Archivio Glottologico Italiano.
AGIS = Archivio Glottologico Italiano—Supplementi Periodici.
ACIL^n = Actes du [n] congrès international de linguistes.
AION-Ling. = Annali dell'Istituto Orientale di Nàpoli. Sezione Linguistica.
AIVeneto = Atti dell'Istituto Veneto di scienze, lettere ed arti.
ALLG = Archiv für lateinische Lexicographie und Grammatik.
AnL = Anthropological Linguistics.
AnzWien = Anzeiger der philosophisch-historischen Klasse der k. Akademie der Wissenschaften, Wien.
AOR = Anuari de l'Oficina Romànica.
AR = Archivum Romanicum.
ArFA = Archivo de Filología Aragonesa.
AS = American Speech.
ASAT = Annuario della Società degli Alpinisti Tridentini.
ASCL = Archivio Storico per la Calabria e la Lucania.
ASNS = Archiv für das Studium der neueren Sprachen und Literaturen.
ASS = Archivio Storico Siciliano.
ASSO = Archivio Storico per la Sicilia Orientale.
ASTP = Archivio per lo Studio delle Tradizioni Popolari.
ATr. = Archeografo Triestino.
AUCh. = Anales de la Universidad de Chile.
AUTosc. = Annali delle Università Toscane.

BA = Balkan-Archiv.
BAAL = Boletín de la Academia Argentina de Letras.
BAE = Boletín de la (Real) Academia Española.
BALI = Bollettino dell'Atlante Linguistico Italiano.
BALM = Bollettino dell'Atlante Linguistico Mediterraneo.
BAR = Biblioteca dell'Archivum Romanicum.
BBF = Biblioteca Brasileira de Filologia.
BBG = Bayrische Blätter für das Gymnasialschulwesen.
BBRPh. = Berliner Beiträge zur romanischen Philologie.
BCDI = Bollettino della Carta dei Dialetti Italiani.
BCSic. = Bollettino del Centro di Studî Filologici e Linguistici Siciliani.
BDC = Butlletì de Dialectologia Catalana.
BDH = Biblioteca de Dialectología Hispánica.
BDR = Bulletin de Dialectologie Romane.
BÉHÉ = Bibliothèque de l'École des Hautes Études. Sciences historiques et philologiques.
Behrens-Festschrift. Leipzig, 1929. (ZFSL Supplementheft no. 13.)
Beiträge Förster = Beiträge für romanische und englische Philologie. Festgabe für Wendelin Förster. Halle/S., 1902.
BFE = Boletín de Filologia Española.
BF-Lisb. = Boletim de Filologia (Lisboa).
BFUCh. = Boletín de Filología (Universidad de Chile).
BH = Bulletin Hispanique.
Bhft. = Beiheft.

BICC = Boletín del Instituto Caro y Cuervo.
BLN = Biblioteca di Lingua Nostra.
BM = Bündnerisches Monatsblatt.
BMér. = Bibliothèque Méridionale.
BNF = Beiträge zur Namenforschung.
BRAE = Boletín de la Real Academia Española.
BRH = Biblioteca Románica Hispànica.
BRPh. = Beiträge zur romanischen Philologie.
BRPhM = Beiträge zur romanischen Philologie des Mittelalters.
BSBS = Bollettino Storico-Bibliografico Subalpino.
BSDM = Beiträge zur schweizerdeutschen Mundartforschung.
BSGL = Boletim da Sociedade de Geografia de Lisboa.
BSL = Bulletin de la Société de Linguistique de Paris.
BSSA = Bollettino della Società di Storia Patria "Anton Lodovico Antinori" negli Abruzzi.

CaQ = Caribbean Quarterly.
Centenary Essays on Dante. Oxford (England), 1965.
CeSC = Cultura e Scuola.
CIELB[n] = Coloquio International de Estudos Laso-Brasileiros.
CIF = Cuadernos del Instituto de Filología de la Universidad de Buenos Aires.
CJ = Classical Journal.
CLS = Creole Language Studies.
CN = Cultural Neolatina.
COIR = Collezione di Opere Inedite o Rare.
CP-CDI = Convegno per la preparazione della Carta dei Dialetti Italiani. Messina, 1965.
CPh. = Classical Philology.
CSSH = Comparative Studies in Sociology and History.
CUBA = Facultad de filosofía y letras de Buenos Aires. Cuadernos.
CuC = Cuba Contemporanea.
Current Trends in Linguistics. The Hague, 1965– .

Donum Natalicium Carolo Jaberg messori indefenso sexagenario. Zürich and Leipzig, 1937.
DsWien = Denkschriften der k. Akademie der Wissenschaften, Wien. Philosophisch-historische Klasse.

ES = Essays and Studies by members of the English Association.
Estructuralismo e Historia. Miscelánea Homenaje a André Martinet. Tenerife (Canarias), 1957–62. 3 vols.
Estudios Menéndez Pidal = Estudios dedicados a Menedez Pidal. Madrid, 1950–57. 8 vols.

FdaM = Le Français dans le Monde.
Festgabe Gamillscheg = Festgabe Ernst Gamillscheg zu seinem fünfundsechzigsten Geburtstag [. . .] überreicht. Tübingen, 1952.
Festschrift Gauchat = Festschrift Louis Gauchat. Aarau, 1926.
Festschrift Kretschmer = Festschrift für [. . .] Paul Kretschmer. Wien, 1926.
Festschrift Morf = Aus romanischen Sprachen und Literaturen. Festschrift Heinrich Morf [. . .] dargebracht. Halle/S., 1905.

Festschrift W. von Wartburg zum 80. Geburtstag. Tübingen, 1968. 2 vols.
FM = Le Français Moderne.
FMLS = Forum for Modern Language Studies.
FRom. = Filologia Romanza.

GCI = Giornale della Cultura Italiana.
GL = General Linguistics.
GRM = Germanisch-Romanische Monatsschrift.
GSLI = Giornale Storico della Letteratura Italiana.
GSLLig. = Giornale Storico e Letterario della Liguria.

Homenaje a D. Alonso = Studia Philologica. Homenaje ofrecido a Dámaso Alonso [. . .]. Madrid, 1960. 3 vols.
Homenaje a Menéndez Pidal = Homenaje ofrecido a Menéndez Pidal. Madrid, 1925. 3 vols.

ID = L'Italia Dialettale.
IF = Indogermanische Forschungen.
L'Insegnamento dell'italiano in Italia e all'estero. Atti del Quarto Convegno Internazionale di Studî (Roma, 1-2 giugno 1970). Roma, 1971.
IQ = Italian Quarterly.
Italia e Croazia. Roma, 1942.
Italiani nel mondo. Firenze, 1942.

JAAC = Journal of Aesthetics and Art Criticism.
JAZU-Rad = Jugoslovenska Akademija Znanosti. Umjetnoski—Rad.
JbGLGA = Jahrbuch der Gesellschaft für lothringische Geschichte und Altertumskunde.
JbHWA = Jahrbuch der hamburgischen wissenschaftlichen Anstalten.
JbIRSʟ = Jahrbuch des Instituts für rumänische Sprache in Leipzig.
JEAS = Journal of East Asiatic Studies.
JL = Janua Linguarum.
JL-SMin. = Janua Linguarum, Series Minor.
JL-SP = Janua Linguarum, Series Practica.

KrJber. = Kritischer Jahresbericht über die Fortschrijte der romanischen Philologie. Die Kultur Südosteuropas. Wiesbaden, 1964.
KZ = Zeitschrift für vergleichende Sprachforschung ("Kuhns Zeitschrift").

LB = Linguistique Balkanique—Balkansko Ezikoznanie.
LBijdr. = Leuvense Bijdragen.
LE = Le Lingue Estere.
LN = Lingua Nostra.
LPosn. = Lingua Posnaniensis.
LRSt. = Leipziger romanistiche Studien.
LSc. = Language Sciences.
LT = Levende Talen.
LUÅ = Lunds Universitets Årsskrift.

MA = Medium Aevum.
MAR = Memorie Academiei Române. Secția literară.
MCLIⁿ = Memoria del [n] Congreso [. . .] de Literatura Iberoamericana.
Medium Aevum Romanicum. Festschrift für Hans Rheinfelder. München, 1963.
Mél. Duraffour = Mélanges A. Duraffour. Zürich, 1939. (RH no. 14.)

Mél. Roques = Mélanges de linguistique et de littérature romane dédiés à Mario Roques. Bade, 1950–52. 3 vols.

Mélanges Linguistiques. Bucarest, 1957.

MFTorino = Miscellanea della Facoltà di Lettere e Filosofia della (r.) Università di Torino.

MIL = Memorie del (r.) Istituto Lombardo di scienze (Classe di lettere, scienze storiche e morali).

Mille. I dibattiti del Circolo Linguistico Fiorentino, 1945–70. Firenze, 1970.

Misc. Fabra = Miscel·lanea Fabra. Buenos Aires, 1943.

Misc. Griera = Miscelánea filológica dedicada a Antonio Griera. Barcelona, 1955. 2 vols.

Misc. Hortis = Miscellanea di studî in onore di Attilio Hortis. Trieste, 1910.

Misc. Said Ali = Miscelânea em honra de Said Ali. Rio de Janeiro, 1938.

Misc. Tassoniana = Miscellanea Tassoniana di studî storici e letterarî pubblicata nella Festa della Fossalta. Bologna-Roma, 1967.

Miscellanea Dantesca. Utrecht, 1965.

MLJ = Modern Language Journal.

MLR = Modern Language Review.

MPh. = Modern Philology.

MRA = Münchener romanistische Arbeiten.

MRAE = Memorias de la Real Academia Española.

MSL = Mémoires de la Société de Linguistique de Paris.

MSNH = Mémoires de la Sociéte Néophilologique de Helsinki.

NA = La Nuova Antologia.

NArg. = Nuovi Argomenti.

NF = Neue Folge.

NM = Neuphilologische Mitteilungen.

NRFH = Nueva Revista de Filología Hispánica.

NRMI = Nuova Rivista Musicale Italiana.

NS = Nuova Série; Nouvelle Série; New Series.

NTS = Norsk Tidskrift for Sprogvidenskab.

PADS = Publications of the American Dialect Society.

PagIl. = Páginas Ilustradas.

PBB = Beiträge zur Geschichte der deutschen Sprache und Literatur ("Paul und Braunes Beiträge").

PDS = Prager deutsche Studien.

PeM = Parole e Metodi.

PFLUT = Pubblicazioni della Facoltà di Lettere dell'Università di Torino.

PFMUT = Pubblicazioni della Facoltà di Magistero dell'Università di Torino.

PICC = Publicaciones del Instituto Caro y Cuervo.

PICC-SMin. = Publicaciones del Instituto Caro y Cuervo, Series Minor.

PILRL = Publications de l'Institut de Linguistique Romane de Lyon.

PKLC = Papers from the . . .th annual Kansas Linguistics Conference.

PM = Petermanns Mitteilungen aus Justus Perthes' geographischer Anstalt.

PMLA = Publications of the Modern Language Association of America.

La poesia rusticana nel Rinascimento. Roma, 1969.

PP = La Parola del Passato.

Presente y futuro de la lengua española = Actos de la Asamblea de Filología del I. Congreso de Instituciones Hispánicas. Mad4id, 1964. 2 vols.

PRF = Publications Romanes et Françaises.

Problemi e orientamenti critici di lingua e letteratura. Milano, 1948–49. 3 vols.
Protimēsis—Scritti in onore di V. Pisani. Lecce, 1969. (= StLSa. 2.)
PSA = Papeles de Son Armadans. Madrid and Palma de Mallorca.
PSb. = Philologus. Supplementband.

QFSCGV = Quellen und Forschungen zur Sprach- und Culturgeschichte der germanischen Völker.
QIGUB = Quaderni dell'Istituto di Glottologia dell'Università di Bologna.
QR = Quaderni di Roma.

RABM = Revista de Archivos, Bibliotecas y Museos.
RAItalia = Rendiconti dell'Accademia d'Italia (Classe di scienze morali e politiche).
RBC = Revista Bimestre Cubana.
RBF = Revista Brasileira de Filologia.
RBPhH = Revue Belge de Philologie et d'Histoire.
RCCM = Rivista di Cultura Classica e Medioevale.
RCEE = Revista del Centro de Estudios Extremeños.
RDR = Revue de Dialectologie Romane.
RDyTP = Revista de Dialectología y Tradiciones Populares.
Recueil Lovanium = Recueil commémoratif du Xe anniversaire de la Faculté des Lettres de l'Université Lovanium [Kinshasa]. Louvain-Paris, 1968.
RÉL = Revue des Études Latines.
RER = La Rivista Emilia-Romagna.
RERoum. = Revue des Etudes Roumaines.
RÉS = Revue des Etudes Slaves.
RESEE = Revue des Études Sud-Est Européennes.
RF = Romanische Forschungen.
RFE = Revista de Filología Española.
RFIC = Rivista di Filologia e d'Istruzione Classica.
RFLCUH = Revista de la Facultad de Letras y Ciencias de la Universidad de la Habana.
RFRG = Revista de Filologie Romanică și Germanică.
RGoth. = Romanica Gothoburgensia.
RH = Romanica Helvetica.
RGua. = Revue Guadeloupienne.
RHi. = Revue Hispanique.
RIbL = Revista Iberoamericana de Literatura.
RIEB = Revue International des Études Basques (Revista Internacional de los Estudios Vascos).
RII = Rivista Ingauna e Intemelia.
RIL = Rendiconti del (r.) Istituto Lombardo di scienze e lettere.
RIS = Revue de l'Institut de Sociologia (Montréal).
RJb. = Romanistisches Jahrbuch.
RLI = Rassegna della Letteratura Italiana.
RLing. = Ricerche Linguistiche.
RLiR = Revue de Linguistique Romane.
RLR = Revue des Langues Romanes.
RLus. = Revista Lusitana.
RMI = La Rassegna Mensile di "Israel".
RNC = Revista Nacional de Cultura (Bogotá, Colombia).
Rom. = Romania.
Romanica (Festschrift für Gehard Rohlfs). Halle/S., 1958.

ROr. = Rocznik Orientalistyczny.
RPF = Revista Portuguêsa de Filologia.
RPGR = Revue des Patois Gallo-Romans.
RPh. = Romance Philology.
RR = Romanic Review.
RRL = Revue Roumaine de Linguistique.
RRom. = Revue Romane.
RSO = Rivista degli Studî Orientali.
RTSS = Revue Tunisienne de Sciences Sociales.

Sache, Ort und Wort. Festschrift Jakob Jud. Zürich, 1943.
SbBayr. = Sitzungsberichte der bayrischen Akademie der Wissenschaften (Philoso-
    phisch-historische Klasse).
SbWien = Sitzungsberichte der (k.) Akademie der Wissenschaften in Wien (Philoloso-
    phisch-historische Klasse).
SEER = Slavonic and East European Review.
Serta Eusebiana. Genova, 1958.
SiL = Studies in Linguistics.
Silloge Àscoli = Silloge linguistica dedicata alla memoria di Graziadio Isaia Àscoli.
    Torino, 1929.
SJA = Southwestern Journal of Anthropology.
SMLV = Studî Mediolatini e Volgari.
SPRF = Sociéte des Publications Romanes et Françaises.
SRU = Studia Romanica Upsaliensia.
SSUF = Språkvetenskapliga Sällskapets i Uppsala Förhandlingar.
StCL = Studii și Cercetări Lingvistici.
StE = Studî Etruschi.
StFI = Studî di Filologia Italiana.
StFR = Studî di Filologia Romanza.
StFR. = Studî Francesi.
StGI = Studî Glottologici Italiani.
StLI = Studî Linguistici Italiani.
StLing. = Studia Linguistica.
StLLSp. = Studî di Lingua e Letteratura Spagnola. Torino, 1965.
StLSa. = Studî Linguistici Salentini.
StM = Studî Medioevali.
StN = Studia Neophilologica.
StP = Studies in Philology.
StR = Studî Romanzi.
StREN. = Studies in the Renaissance.
StRic. = Studî e Ricerche.
StSa. = Studî Sardi.
Studî A. Era = Studî storici e giuridici in onore di Antonio Era. Padova, 1963.
Studî Deanović = Studî offerti a M. Deanović. Firenze, 1970. (= BALM 10./12.)
Studî Fiorentini. Firenze, 1949.
Studî Levi della Vida = Studî orientalistici in onore di Giorgio Levi della Vida. Roma,
    1956. 2 vols.
Studî Schiaffini = Studî in onore di Alfredo Schiaffini. Roma, 1965. 2 vols. (= RCCM 7.)
Studî V. Pisani = Studî linguistici in onore di Vittore Pisani. Brescia, 1969. 2 vols.
SUBB = Studia Universitatis Babeș-Bolyai, Philologia. Cluj.

TCLC = Travaux du Cercle Linguistique de Copenhague.
TCLP = Travaux du Cercle Linguistique de Prague.
Televisione e Vita Italiana. Torino, 1968.
TLL = Travaux de Linguistique et de Littérature (Strasbourg).
TMIFR = Testi e Manuali dell'Istituto di Filologia Romanza (Roma).
TNTL = Tijdschrift voor nederlandse Tall- en Letterkunde.
Todd Memorial Volumes. New York, 1930. 2 vols.
TPr. = Terzo Programma.

UCPL = University of California Publications in Linguistics.
UCPMPh. = University of California Publications in Modern Philology.
UMSLL = University of Minnesota Studies in Language and Literature.
UNCSRLL = University of North Carolina Studies in the Romance Languages and Literature.
UUÅ = Uppsala Universitetets Årsskrift.
UWSLL = University of Wisconsin Studies in Language and Literature.

VKAW = Verhandelingen van de Koninklijke Akademie van Westenskapen.
VKR = Volkstum und Kultur der Romanen.
VLGU = Vestnik Leningradskogo gosudarstvennogo Universiteta.
VR = Vox Romanica.

WRA = Wiener romanistische Arbeiten.
WS = Wörter und Sachen.
WZHU = Wissenschaftliche Zeitschrift der Humboldt-Universität zu Berlin.

ZFSL = Zeitschrift für französische Sprache und Literatur.
ZNU = Zeitschrift für neusprachlichen Unterricht.
ZRPh. = Zeitschrift für romanische Philologie.

Authors and Titles

Aarsleff, Hans. 1970. The history of linguistics and Professor Chomsky. Language 46.570–585.
———. 1971. "Cartesian Linguistics"; History or fantasy? LSc. 17.1–12.
Abbott, F. F. 1907. The accent in Vulgar and Formal Latin. CPh. 2.444–460.
Abbott, Wilbur Cortez. 1918. The expansion of Europe. A history of the foundations of the modern world. New York. 2 vols.
Abel, Fritz. 1970. Die Ausbildung des bestimmten Artikels und der deiktischen Systeme der romanischen Sprachen untersucht an der Sprache der lateinischen Bibel. Glotta 48.229–259.
Académie Française. 1935. Trois siècles de l'Académie Française, par les Quarante. Paris.
Acevedo y Huelves, Bernardo, and Marcelino Fernández y Fernández. 1932. Vocabulario del bable de Occidente. Madrid.
Adam, Lucien. 1881. Les patois lorrains. Nancy-Paris.
Adigard des Gautries, J. 1954. Les noms de personne scandinaves en Normandie de 911 à 1066. Lund.
Aebischer, Paul. 1931. Le catalan turò et les dérivés romans du mot prélatin taurus. BDC 18.193–216.
———. 1938. Les dérivés italiens du mot gahagi et leur répartition d'après les chartes médiévales. ZRPh. 58.51–62.

———. 1941. Pour l'histoire d'un suffixe d'origine langobarde: -ing dans l'Italie centrale. ZRPh. 61.114–121.

———. 1944. *Sinaita*: l'aire de dispersion et le développement sémantique du mot dans le latin médiéval d'Italie. ZRPh. 64.380–388.

Agard, Frederick Browning. 1950. Present-day Judaeo-Spanish in the United States. Hispania 33.203–210.

———. 1958. Structural sketch of Roumanian. Baltimore. (Language Monograph no. 26.)

———. 1971. Language and dialect. Linguistics 65.1–24.

———, and Gordon H. Fairbanks. 1958. Review of Petrovici 1957. Language 34.297–303.

Agüero, Arturo. 1962. El español de América y Costa Rica. San José de Costa Rica.

Ahlborn, Gunnar. 1946. Le patois de Ruffieux-en-Valromey, Ain. Göteborg.

Alarcos Llorach, Emilio. 1950. Fonología del español. Madrid. (2nd ed., 1954; 3rd ed., 1961.)

———. 1951. Gramática estructural según la escuela de Copenhague y con especial atención a la lengua española. Madrid.

Alario de Filippo, Mario. 1964. Léxicon de colombianismos. Cartagena (Colombia).

Albert-Buisson, François. 1960. Les Quarante au temps des lumières. Paris.

Alborg, Juan Luïs. 1966– . Historia de la literatura española. Madrid.

Alcalá Venceslada, Antonio. 1933. Vocabulario andaluz. Andújar. (2nd ed., Madrid, 1951.)

Alcover Sureda, Antoni Maria, and Francisc de B.' Moll i Casanovas. 1930–62. Diccionari català-valencià-balear. Palma de Mallorca. 10 vols.

Alegre Peyrón, José Ma. 1966. La España visigoda. Proceso de germanisación de una provincia romana. RRom. 1.1–23.

Alessio, Giovanni. 1934. Il sostrato latino nel lessico e nell'epo-toponomastica della Calabria meridionale. ID 10.111–190.

———. 1935–36. La base preindoeuropea *kar(r)a/*gar(r)a 'pietra'. StE 9.133–151 (1955); 10.165–189 (1936).

———. 1946–48. Sulla latinità di Sicillia. AAPalermo IV.7:2.287–510 (1946/47); IV.8.73–155 (1947/48).

———. 1955. Il fondo latino dei dialetti romanzi del Salento. AFLBari 2.1–44.

Alfaro, Ricardo J. 1950. Diccionario de anglicismos. Panamá.

Alföldi András. 1957. Die trojanischen Urahnen der Römer. Basel.

———. 1964. Early Rome and the Latins. Ann Arbor.

Alfonsi, Tommaso. 1932. Il dialetto corso nelle parlate balanine. Livorno.

Alibert, Louis. 1935. Gramatica occitana, segon los parlars langadocians. Toulouse.

———. 1965. Dictionnaire occitan-français d'après les parlers languedociens. Toulouse.

Aliprandi, Giuseppe. 1962. Voci giornalistiche. LN 23.62–65.

Alex, Paul. 1965. Le patois de Naisey, canton de Roulans, arrondissement de Besançon. Paris.

Allen, W. Sidney. 1965. Vox Latina. A guide to the pronunciation of Classical Latin. London.

———. 1968. Vox Graeca. A guide to the pronunciation of Classical Greek. Cambridge (England).

Alonso, Amado. 1926. La subagrupación románica del catalán. RFE 13.1–38, 225–261. Reprinted in Alonso 1951:11–100.

———. 1935. El problema de la lengua en América. Madrid.

——. 1943a. Castellano, español, idioma nacional. Buenos Aires. (2nd ed., 1948.)

——. 1943b. La Argentina y la nivelación del idioma. Buenos Aires.

——. 1943c. Partición de las lenguas románicas de occidente. Misc. Fabra 81–101.

——. 1949. Examen de las noticias de Nebrija sobre la antigua pronunciación española. NRFH 3.1–82.

——. 1951. Estudios lingüísticos: temas españoles. Madrid.

——. 1955–69. De la pronunciación medieval a la moderna en español. Madrid. 2 vols. Vol. 1: 1955. Vol. 2: 1969.

——, and Raimundo Lida (eds.). 1940. El español en Chile. Trabajos de Rodolfo Lenz, Andrés Bello y Rodolfo Oroz. Buenos Aires.

Alonso, Martín. 1962. Evolución sintáctica del español. Sintaxis histórica del español desde el iberorrománico hasta nuestros días. Madrid.

——. 1968. Gramática del español contemporaneo. El lenguaje del hombre de hoy, actualizado con autoridades de los escritores de nuestra época, españoles e hispano-americanos. Madrid.

Alonson Garrote, Santiago. 1909. El dialecto vulgar leonés hablado en Maragatería y Tierra de Astorga. Astorga.

Altamura, Antonio. 1957. Dizionario dialettale napoletano. Nàpoli.

——. 1961. Il dialetto napolitano. Nàpoli.

Altheim, Franz. 1932. Die Anfänge des Vulgärlateins. Glotta 20.153–171.

Alther, A. 1935. Beiträge zur Lautlehre südspanischer Mundarten. Aarau.

Altieri Biagi, Maria Luisa. 1963. Schede per *toilette—toeletta—toletta—teletta—tavoletta*. LN 24.102–113.

——. 1965. Galileo e la terminologia tecnico-scientifica. Firenze. (BAR II.32.)

——. 1965b. *Vile meccanico*. LN 26.1–12.

——. 1966. *Struttura e modello* nel lessico di Malpighi. LN 27.37–47.

——. 1968. Lingua e cultura di Francesco Redi, medico. AAColombaria NS.19. (= 33.) 189–304.

Alton, Johann. 1879. Die ladinischen Idiome in Ladinien, Gröden, Fassa, Buchenstein, Ampezzo. Innsbruck.

Álvar, Manuel. 1948. El habla del Campo de Jaca. Salamanca.

——. 1953. El dialecto aragonés. Madrid.

——. 1955. Las hablas meridionales de España y su interés para la lingüística comparada. RFE 39.284–313.

——. 1956/57. Catalán y Aragonés en las regiones fronterizas. BDE 34.737–778.

——. 1959. El español hablado en Tenerife. Madrid. (RFE Anejo no. 69.)

——. 1960. Los nuevos atlas lingüísticos de la Romania. Granada.

——. 1965. Notas sobre el español hablado en la isla de la Graciosa (Canarias Orientales). RFE 48.293–320.

——. 1966. El español de Tenerife. Cuestión de principios. ZRPh. 82.507–548.

——, et al. (eds.). 1962–65. Atlas lingüístico y etnográfico de Andalucía. Granada.

Álvarez, Guzmán. 1949. El habla de Babia y Laciana. Madrid.

Álvarez Fernández-Cañedo, Jesús. 1963. El habla y la cultura popular de Cabrales. Madrid. (RFE Anejo no. 76.)

Aly-Belfadel, Arturo. 1933. Grammatica piemontese. Noale (Venezia).

Alziator, Francesco. 1954. Storia della letteratura in Sardegna. Càliari.

Amade, Jean. 1924. Origines et premières manifestations de la renaissance littéraire en Catalogne au XIXe siècle. Toulouse and Paris.

Amengual, Juan José. 1835. Gramática de la lengua mallorquina. Palma. (2nd ed., 1872.)

Andreoni, G. 1969. Alcuni verbi dell'Australitalian. Te Reo 12.72–75.

Andrews, James Bruyn. 1875. Essai de grammaire du dialecte mentonais. Nice.

———. 1876. Vocabulaire français-mentonais. Nice.

———. 1890/92. Il dialetto di Mentone, in quanto egli tramezzi ideologicamente tra il provenzale e il ligure. AGI 12.97–106.

Anelli, Luigi. 1901. Vocabolario vastese. Vasto.

Anglade, Joseph. 1897. Le patois de Lézignan (Aude) (dialecte narbonnais). RLR 40.145–176, 289–345. (Also sep.: Montpellier, 1897).

———. 1905. De latinitate libelli qui inscriptus est Peregrinatio ad Loca Sancta. Parisiis.

———. 1921a. Grammaire de l'ancien provençal ou ancienne langue d'oc. Paris.

———. 1921b. Histoire sommaire de la littérature méridionale au Moyen Âge. Paris.

Appel, Carl. 1895. Provenzalische Chrestomathie. Leipzig.

Arrighi, Cletto. 1896. Dizionario milanese-italiano. Milano.

Arrivabene, Ferdinando. 1891. Vocabolario mantovano-italiano. Màntova.

———. 1892. Vocabolario italiano-mantovano. Màntova.

Arveiller, R. 1967. Étude sur le parler de Monaco. Monaco.

Arvinte, Vasile. 1968. Die Entstehung der rumänischen Sprache und des rumänischen Volkes im Lichte der jüngsten Forschung. ASNS 204.1–25.

Àscoli, Graziadio Isaia. 1873a. Saggi ladini. AGI 1.1–537.

———. 1873b. Del posto che spetta al ligure nel sistema dei dialetti italiani. AGI 2.111–160.

———. 1878. Schizzi franco-provenzali. AGI 3.61–120.

———. 1880/83. Annotazioni soprasilvane. AGI 7.406–602.

———. 1881. Lettere glottologiche. Prima lettera. RFIC 10.1–71.

Asín Palacios, M. 1940. Contribución a la toponimia árabe de España. Madrid-Granada.

Atzeni, Emilio. 1897. Vocabolario sardo-meridionale-italiano. Càgliari.

Atzori, Maria Teresa. 1953a. Glossario del sardo antico. Parma.

———. 1953b. Bibliografia di linguistica sarda. Firenze.

———. 1961–65. Aggiunte al Dizionario Etimologico Sardo di M. L. Wagner. RPF 11.113–118 (1961); 13.263–278 (1964/65).

Atzori, Mario. 1940. Saggio sulla fonetica del dialetto di Ìsili. StSa. 4.106–148.

Aub-Büscher, Gertrud. 1962. Le parler rural de Ranrupt (Bas-Rhin). Paris.

Auerbach, Erich. 1949. Introduction aux études de philologie romane. Frankfurt/M. (Eng. tr.: Introduction to Romance languages and literature, New York, 1961. It. tr.: Introduzione alla filologia romanza, Torino, 1965.)

Austin, William Weaver. 1954. Espressivo. JAAC 12.509–517.

Avalle, d'Arco Silvio. 1965. Protostoria delle lingue romanze. Torino.

Avellaneda, Maria R., et al. 1966–67. Contribución a una bibliografía de dialectología española y especialmente hispanoamericana. BRAE 46.335–369, 525–555 (1966); 47.125–156, 311–342 (1967).

Avolio, Corrado. 1875. Canti popolari di Noto. Noto.

———. 1882. Introduzione allo studio del dialetto siciliano. Noto.

———. 1898. Saggio di toponomastica siciliana. AGLS 6.71–118. (2nd ed., Noto, 1937.)

Ayala, Juan Antonio. 1963. Imagen de la lengua española. Introducción histórica. Monterrey, N.L.

Ayer, Cyprien. 1878. Introduction à l'étude des dialectes du pays romand. Neuchâtel.

Aymeric, Josef. 1879. Dialecte rouergat: phonétique, morphologie. ZRPh. 3.321–358.

(Also sep.: Halle/S., 1879).

Azzolini, G. B. 1856. Vocabolario vernacolo-italiano pei distretti roveretano e trentino. Venezia.

Bacchia della Lega, Alberto. 1876. Bibliografia de' vocabolarî ne' dialetti italiani. Bologna.

———. 1877. Appendice alla Bibliografia de' vocabolarî ne' dialetti italiani. Bloogna.

Badia i Margarit, Antoni. 1950. El habla del Valle de Bielsa (Pirineo Aragonés). Barcelona.

———. 1951. Gramática histórica catalana. Barcelona.

———. 1969. La llengua dels barcelonins: resultats d'una enquesta sociologico-linguistica. Barcelona.

Baehrens, W. A. 1922. Sprachlicher Kommentar zur vulgärlateinischen Appendix Probi. Halle/s.

Baer, Gertrud. 1939. Zur sprachlichen Einwirkung der altprovenzalischen Troubadourdichtung auf die Kunstsprache der frühen italienischen Lyrik. Zürich.

Baetens-Beardsmore, H. 1972. Le français régional de Bruxelles. Bruxelles.

Bahner, Werner. 1956. Beitrag zum Sprachbewusstsein in der spanischen Literatur des 16. und 17. Jahrhunderts. Berlin. (Sp. tr.: La lingüística española del siglo de oro, Madrid, 1966.)

———. 1965. Dantes theoretische Bemühungen um die Formung der italienischen Literatursprache und die "Sprachenfrage". BRPh. 4:2.29–35.

Baissac, Charles. 1880. Étude sur le patois mauricien. Nancy.

Bal, Willy. 1966. Introduction aux études de linguistique romane. Paris.

———. 1968. Introduction aux recherches de linguistique romane en rapport avec l'Afrique noire. Recueil Lovanium 7–34.

Baldinger, Kurt. 1955. Die sprachliche Gliederung der Pyrenäenhalbinsel und ihre historische Begründung. WZHU 4.5–34.

———. 1958. Die Herausbildung der Sprachräume auf der Pyrenäenhalbinsel. Berlin.

———. 1963. La formación de los dominios lingüísticos en la península ibérica. Madrid.

Baldinger, Kurt, Jean-Denis Gendron, and Georges Straka. 1972– . Dictionnaire étymologique de l'ancien français. Tübingen and Paris.

Balle, Arthur. 1963. Contribution au dictionnaire du parler de Cerfontaine. Liège.

Banfi, Giuseppe. 1852. Vocabolario milanese-italiano. Milano. (3rd ed., 1870.)

Barbagallo, Salvatore. 1959. Il dialetto di Comacchio. Bologna. (2nd ed., 1960.)

———. 1961. Il Basso Po (territorio di Spina): problemi linguistici. Bologna.

Barbeau, Victor. 1963. Le français au Canada. Montréal.

Barbier fils, Paul. 1930. A contribution to the history of a Germanic prefix in French and the French dialects. RLiR 6.210–305.

Barbosa, Jorge M. 1965. Études de phonologie portugaise. Lisboa.

Barbosa Lima, Alexandre José. 1958. A língua portuguêsa e a unidade do Brasil. Rio de Janeiro.

Barbu, N. 1944. Sintaxa limbii române după metoda istorico-stilistică. Bucureşti.

Bărbulescu, Ilie. 1929. Individualitatea limbii române şi elementele slave vechi. Bucureşti.

Bardini, Mario. 1964. Vocabolario mantovano. Màntova.

Bardon, Henry. 1952. La littérature latine inconnue. Paris.

Barker, George Carpenter. 1958. Pachuco, an American-Spanish argot and its function in Tucson, Arizona. Tucson.

Barnils Giol, Pere. 1913. Die Mundart von Alacant. Beitrag zur Kenntnis des Valencianischen. Barcelona.

Bàrtoli, Matteo Giulio. 1903. Un po' di sardo. ATr. III.1.129–156.

——. 1910a. Das Dalmatische: altromanische Sprachreste von Veglia bis Ragusa und ihre Stellung in der appenino-balkanischen Romania. Wien. 2 vols.

——. 1910b. Alle fonti del neolatino. Misc. Hortis 889–913.

——. 1925. Introduzione alla neolinguistica. Genève. (BAR II.12.)

——. 1927. L'Italia linguistica: abbozzo dell'Italia dialettale e alloglottica. Torino.

——. 1936. Caratteri fondamentali della lingua nazionale italiana e delle lingue sorelle. MFTorino 1936.69–106.

——. 1941. La posizione del dialetto nizzardo rispetto al provenzale, all'italiano e al francese. RII 7.147–200.

——. 1942. Dalmatico e albanoromanico: reliquie romaniche nel croato e nell' albanese. Italia e Croazia 109–185.

——. 1944/45. Sao ko kelle terre . . . . LN 6.1–6.

Bártoli, Matteo Giulio, and Giulio Bertoni. 1925. Breviario di neolinguistica. Mòdena.

——, and Giuseppe Vidossi. 1945. Alle porte orientali d'Italia. Dialetti e lingue della Venezia Giulia (Friuli ed Istria) e stratificazioni linguistiche in Istria. Torino.

——, et al. (eds.). Forthcoming. Atlante Linguistico Italiano (ALI).

Baruch, K. 1930. El judeo-español de Bosnia. RFE 17.113–154.

Bascetta, Carlo. 1962. Il linguaggio sportivo contemporaneo. Firenze.

——. 1964. Giornalismo e tipografia. Roma.

Bató Mária. 1933. A fiumei nyelvjárás. Bevezetés és hangtörténet. Budapest.

Batres Jáuregui, Antonio. 1892. Vicios de lenguaje y provincialismos de Guatemala. Guatemala.

Battaglia, Salvatore. 1967a. Introduzione alla linguistica romanza. Nàpoli.

——. 1967b. La formazione dell'italiano. Nàpoli.

Battisti, Carlo. 1909. Die Nonsberger Mundart: Lautlehre. Wien. (SbWien 160:3.)

——. 1910. Lingua e dialetti nel Trentino. Pro Cultura 1.178–205.

——. 1911. Zur Sulzberger Mundart: ein Reisebericht. AnzWien 16.189–240.

——. 1913/14. Die Mundart von Valvestino. Wien. (SbWien 174:1.)

——. 1914–21. Testi dialettali italiani in trascrizione fonetica. Halle/S. 2 vols. (ZRPh. Bhft. nos. 49, 56.)

——. 1922. Studî di storia linguistica e nazionale del Trentino. Firenze.

——. 1927. Appunti sulla storia e sulla diffusione dell'ellenismo nell'Italia meridionale. RLiR 3.1–91.

——. 1929. Sulla pretesa unità ladina. Silloge Àscoli 409–444.

——. 1931. Popoli e lingue nell'Alto Àdige. Firenze.

——. 1933. La voce prelatina sala e le sue possibili sopravvivenze. StE 7.267–277.

——. 1942. Risonanze italiane nel vocabolario europeo. Italiani nel mondo 389–415.

——. 1949. Avviamento allo studio del latino volgare. Bari.

——. 1952. La lingua e il cinema: impressioni. LN 13.29–34.

——. 1959. Sostrati e parastrati nell'Italia antica. Firenze.

——. 1962. Le valli ladine dell'Alto Adige e il pensiero dei linguisti italiani sulla unità dei dialetti ladini. Firenze.

——. 1967. Nuovi indirizzi collettivi della dialettologia italiana. BCDI 2.53–71.

——, and Giovanni Alessio. 1948–56. Dizionario etimologico italiano. Firenze.

Bauche, Henri. 1920. Le langage populaire: grammaire, syntaxe et dictionnaire du français tel qu'on le parle dans le peuple de Paris, avec tous les termes d'argot usuel. Paris.

Baudry de Saunier, Charles Louis. 1932. Gaîtés et tristesses de la Grammaire de l'Académie Française. Paris.

Baugh, Albert Croll. 1935. A history of the English language. New York.

Baylon, Ch. 1965. Description du parler provincial alpin de Beuil. Montpellier.

Bayo, Ciro. 1906. Vocabulario de provincialismos argentions y bolivianos. RHi. 14.241–564.

———. 1910. Vocabulario criollo-español sud-americano. Madrid.

Beau, Albin. 1937. Nation und Sprache im portugiesischen Humanismus. VKR 10.65–82.

Beaulieux, Charles. 1927. Histoire de l'orthographe française. Paris. 2 vols.

Bec, Pierre. 1963. La langue occitane. Paris. ("Que sais-je?" no. 1059.)

———. 1968. Les interférences linguistiques entre Gason et Languedocien dans les parlers du Comminges et du Couserons. Paris.

———. 1970. Manuel pratique de philologie romane. Paris.

Beccaria, Gian Luigi. 1968. Spagnolo e Spagnoli in Italia. Riflessi ispanici nella lingua italiana del Cinque e del Seicento. Torino.

Bechtel, Edward. 1902. Sanctae Silviae Peregrinatio: the text and a study of the Latinity. Chicago.

Bedarida, Guido. 1956. Ebrei di Livorno: tradizioni e gergo in 180 sonetti giudaico-livornesi. Firenze.

Bedier, Joseph, and Paul Hazard. 1923–24. Histoire de la littérature française illustrée. Paris. 2 vols. (New edition, entitled "Littérature française," Paris, 1948–49.)

Beeler, Madison S. 1949. The Venetic language. Berkeley and Los Angeles.

———. 1966. The interrelationships within Italic. In Birnbaum and Puhvel (eds.) 1966:51–58.

Beguinot, Francesco. 1938. Di alcune parole di linguaggi nord-africani derivate dal latino. Roma 16.460–463.

Beinhauer, Werner. 1930. Spanische Umgangssprache. Berlin. (2nd ed., 1956. Sp. tr. [of 2nd ed.]: El español coloquial, Madrid, 1963. 2nd ed. of Sp. tr., 1968.)

Bell, Aubrey F. G. 1922. Portuguese literature. Oxford (england). (2nd ed., 1970.)

Bellamy, Henry. 1939. L'Académie Française. Paris. (Crapouillot: Numéro spécial, Mars 1939.)

Bellocchi, Ugo. 1966. Il "volgare" reggiano. Reggio Emilia. 3 vols.

Belloni, P., and Hans Nilsson-Ehle. 1957. Voci romanesche. Lund.

Beltramini, Gino, and Elisabetta Donati. 1963. Piccolo dizionario veronese-italiano. Verona.

Bendel, Hugo. 1934. Beiträge zur Kenntnis der Mundart von Lescun (Basses-Pyrénées). Tübingen.

Bender, Herman H. 1922. The home of the Indo-Europeans. Princeton.

Bengtsson, Sverker. 1968. La défense organisée de la langue française. Étude sur l'activité de quelques organismes qui depuis 1937 ont pris pour tâche de veiller à la correction et à la pureté de la langue française. Uppsala. (SRU no. 4.)

Bennett, Charles Edwin. 1907. The Latin language: a historical outline of its sounds, inflections, and syntax. Boston.

Bens, Jacques. 1962. Queneau. Paris.

Benvenutto Murrieta, Pedro M. 1936. El lenguaje peruano. Lima.

Berenblut, Max. 1949. A comparative study of Judeo-Italian translations of Isaiah. New York.

Bergens, Andrée. 1963. Raymond Queneau. Genève.

Bergeron, Pierre. 1840. Histoire analytique et critique de la littérature romane. Bruxelles.

Bergh, Å. 1941. Études d'anthroponymie provençale. Göteborg.

Bergmann, W. 1934. Studien zur volkstümlichen Kultur im Grenzgebiet von Hocharagon und Navarra. Hamburg.

Berns, Klaus. 1964. Die lautliche Behandlung der galloromanischen Lehnwörter im Spanischen. Erlangen.

Berruto, Gaetano. 1970. Dialetto e società industriale nella Valle d'Andorno. Torino. (BALI Suppl. no. 1.)

――――. 1971. Per una semiologia dei rapporti tra lingua e dialetto. PeM 1.45–58.

Berry, Paul. 1969. Literacy and the question of Creole. In R. Schaedel (ed.) 1969: 204–280.

Bertoldi, Vittorio. 1926. Parole e idee. Monaci e popolo, "calques linguistiques" e etimologia popolare. RLiR 2.137–162.

――――. 1929. Dal lessico botanico. Una fortunata etimologica popolare. AR 13.370–373.

――――. 1931. Problèmes de substrat. Essai de méthodologie dans le domaine préhistorique de la toponymie et du vocabulaire. BSL 32:1.93–175.

――――. 1932. Regionalismi arabi nel romanzo. RSO 13.367–376.

――――. 1937. Contatti e conflitti di lingua nell'antico Mediterraneo. ZRPh. 57.137–169. (Reprinted in PP 8.407–448 [1953]).

――――. 1945. La parole quale testimone del passato. Nàpoli.

――――. 1950. Colonizzazioni nell'antico Mediterraneo occidentale alla luce degli aspetti linguistici. Nàpoli.

Bertoni, Giulio. 1905. Il dialetto di Modena. Torino.

――――. 1914. L'elemento germanico nella lingua italiana. Gènova.

――――. 1915. Italia dialettale. Milano.

――――. 1925. Profilo storico del dialetto di Modena. Genève. (BAR II.11.)

――――. 1940. Profilo linguistico d'Italia. Mòdena. (TMIFR no. 16.)

―――― and Francesco A. Ugolini. 1939a. L'asse linguistico Roma-Firenze. LN 1.25–27.

―――― and ――――. 1939b. Prontuario di pronuncia e di ortografia. Milano-Roma.

Bertrand, Élie. 1758. Recherches sur les langues anciennes et modernes de la Suisse, et principalement du pays de Vaud. Genève.

Bevilacqua, G. 1949. Dizionario veneto-italiano. Vicenza.

Bezzola, Reto R. 1924. Abbozzo di una storia dei gallicismi italiani nei primi secoli (750–1300). Saggio storico-linguistico. Zürich-Heidelberg.

――――. 1958-60. Les origines et la formation de la littérature courtoise en Orient (500–1200). Paris.

Bianchi, Bianco. 1886. Il dialetto e la etnografia di Città di Castello con raffronti e considerazioni storiche. Pisa.

Bianconi, Sandro. 1962. Ricerche sui dialetti d'Orvieto e di Viterbo nel medioevo. StLI 3.3–175.

Biddau, Giuseppe. 1905. Studio sul dialetto di Bosa. Torino.

Bierhenke, W. 1929. Das Dreschen in der Sierra de Gata. VKR 2.20–82.

――――. 1932. Ländliche Geräte der Sierra de Gata. Sach- und wortkundliche Untersuchungen. Hamburg.

Biondelli, Bernardino. 1853. Saggio sui dialetti gallo-italici. Milano.

Birnbaum, Henrik, and Jaan Puhvel (eds.). 1966. Ancient Indo-European dialects. Berkeley and Los Angeles.

264   COMPARATIVE ROMANCE GRAMMAR

Bischoff, Bernhard, and H. G. Beck. 1963. Das italienisch-griechische Glossar der Handschrift e 14 (127) der Biblioteca Capitolare in Monza. Medium Aevum Romanicum 49–62.

Bischoff, Bernhard, and I. Müller. 1959. Eine rätoromanische Sprachprobe aus dem 10./11. Jahrhundert. VR 14.137–146.

Bjerrome, Gunnar. 1957. Le patois de Bagnes (Valais). Stockholm. (RGoth. no. 6.)

Bläuer-Rini, Ambrosina. 1924. Giunte al "Vocabolario di Bormio," con note introduttive sul dialetto di Bormio. Studî di dialettologia altoitaliana 97–165 (Genève [BAR II.8]).

Blanch, V. G. 1929. Linguaggio friulano. S. Daniele del Friuli.

Blasi, Ferruccio. 1936–38. Il dialetto di Preta (Rieti) (saggio fonetico lessicale). ID 12.35–57 (1936); 14.59–77 (1938).

Blinkenberg, Andreas. 1939–40. Le patois d'Entraunes. Aarhus. 2 vols. (AcJut. 11:1, 12:1.)

———. 1948. Le patois de Beuil. Aarhus. (AcJut. 20:3.)

Bloch, Oscar. 1915. Lexique français-patois des Vosges méridionales. Paris.

———. 1917a. Atlas linguistique des Vosges méridionales. Paris.

———. 1917b. Les parlers des Vosges méridionales: étude de dialectologie. Paris.

———. 1921. La penetration du français dans les parlers des Vosges méridionales. Paris. (BÉHÉ no. 232.)

——— and Walther von Wartburg. 1932. Dictionnaire étymologique de la langue française. Paris. 2 vols. (Later eds. in 1 vol.; 5th ed., 1968.)

Blondheim, David Simon. 1925. Les parlers judéo-romans et la Vetus Latina, étude sur les rapports entre les traductions en langue romane des Juifs au moyen âge et les anciennes versions. Paris.

Bloomfield, Leonard. 1933. Language. New York.

Boas, Franz. 1930. Spanish elements in modern Nahuatl. Todd Memorial Volumes 1.85–89.

Boerio, Giuseppe. 1829. Dizionario del dialetto veneziano. Venezia. (3rd ed., 1867).

Böttiger, Carl Wilhelm. 1853. Rhetoromanska språkets dialekter. Upsala.

Boillot, F. 1910. Le patois de la commune de la Grand'Combe (Doubs). Paris.

———. 1930. Le français regional de la commune de La Grand'Combe. Paris.

Boissier, Gaston. 1909. L'Académie Française sous l'ancien régime. Paris.

Bolaño e Isla, Amancio. 1959. Manual de historia de la lengua española. México, D.F.

Bolognini, G. and A., and G. L. Patuzzi. 1901. Piccolo dizionario del dialetto moderno della città di Verona. Verona.

Boltz, William G. 1967/68. Canton: the Seville of China. RPh. 21.171–174.

Bombelli, A. 1940. Dizionario etimologico del dialetto cremasco e delle località cremasche. Crema. (2nd ed., 1943.)

Bonfante, Giuliano. 1943. L'origine des langues romanes. Renaissance 1.573–588.

———. 1944. Neogrammarians and neolinguists: Ital. giorno. PMLA 59.877–881.

———. 1947. The neolinguistic position. Language 23.344–375. (It. tr.: La dottrina neolinguìstica—teoría e pràtica, Torino, 1970.)

———. 1959. Latini e Germani in Italia. Genova. (3rd ed., Brescia, 1965.)

———. 1968. Quando si è cominciato a parlare italiano? Festschrift W. von Wartburg 1.21–46.

———. 1969. Il "volgare illustre" di Dante e il volgare dei lirici siciliani. BCSic. 10.18–28.

———, and Maria Luisa Porzio Gernia. 1964. Cenni di fonetica e di fonematica, con particolare riguardo all'italiano. Torino.

Bonin, Marcel. 1956. Glossaire du patois de Langy. Saint-Aubin-le-Monial (Allier).

Bonioli, Maria. 1962. La pronuncia del latino nelle scuole dall'antichità al Rinascimento. Torino. (PFLUT 13:3.)

Borao y Clemente, Gerónimo. 1859. Diccionario de voces aragonesas. Zaragoza. (3rd ed., 1908.)

Borges, Jorge Luís. 1952. El idioma de los Argentinos. Buenos Aires. (Reprinted in Clemente and Borges, 1963.)

Borie, Jean. 1966. Raymond Queneau: poésie et français parlé. RR 57.41–55.

Borodiná, Melitina Aleksandrovna. 1961. Phonétique historique du français. Leningrad.

——. 1965. Morphologie historique du français. Moskva-Leningrad.

——. 1969. Sovremennyĭ literatyrnyĭ jazyk Šveĭcarii [A contemporary literary language of Switzerland]. Leningrad.

Borsci, A. T., N. G. Cîrlateanu, and V. P. Soloviov. 1956. Curs de limbă moldovenească literară contemporană. Chișinau.

Bosshard, Hans. 1938. Saggio di un glossario dell'antico lombardo. Firenze. (BAR II.23.)

Bottiglioni, Gino. 1911. Dalla Magra al Frigido. Saggio fonetico. RDR 3.77–143.

——. 1919. Fonologia del dialetto imolese.

——. 1926–27. La penetrazione toscana e le regioni di Pomonte nei parlari di Corsica (saggio di ricostruzione linguistica). ID 2.156–210 (1926), with 11 maps; 3.1–69 (1927), with 10 maps.

—— (ed.). 1933–44. Atlante linguistico etnografico italiano della Corsica (ALEIC). Pisa.

——. 1951. Parlate emiliane e romagnole. RER 2.35–38.

——. 1952. Dizionario delle parlate corse. Mòdena.

——. 1954. Manuale dei dialetti italici. Bologna.

Bouda, K. 1949. Baskisch-kaukasische Etymologien. Heidelberg.

Bourcelot, Henri. 1966– . Atlas linguistique et etnographique de la Champagne et de la Brie. Paris.

Bourciez, Édouard. 1899. Précis historique de phonétique française. Paris. (Revised ed.: Bourciez, Édouard and Jean: Phonétique française: étude historique, Paris, 1967.)

——. 1910. Éléments de linguistique romane. Paris. (4th ed., 1946.)

Bourgaux, Louis. 1963. Clarté et prestige de la langue française. Gembloux.

Bourgoin, Auguste. 1883. Un bourgeois de Paris lettré au XVIIᵉ siècle. Valentin Conrart, premier secrétaire perpétuel de l'Académie Française, et son temps. Sa vie, ses écrits, son rôle dans l'histoire littéraire de la première partie du XVIIᵉ siècle. Paris.

Bouzet, J. 1928. Manuel de grammaire béarnaise. Pau.

——. 1963. Syntaxe béarnaise et gasconne. Pau.

Boyd-Bowman, Peter M. 1953. Sobre la pronunciación del español en el Ecuador. NRFH 7.221–233.

——. 1956. The regional origins of the earliest Spanish colonists of America. PMLA 71.1152–1172.

——. 1960. El hablar de Guanajuato. México, D.F.

——. 1964–68. Índice geográfico de cuarenta mil pobladores españoles de América en el siglo XVI. Bogotá (Colombia).

Brachet, Auguste. 1867. Grammaire historique de la langue française. Paris. (Eng. tr. by G. W. Kitchin: A historical grammar of the French tongue, Oxford [Eng.], 1869

[3rd ed., 1874]. Eng. tr. by Paget Toynbee: A historical grammar of the French language, Oxford [Eng.], 1896.)

———. 1868. Dictionnaire ètymologique de la langue française. Paris. (5th ed., 1872. Eng. tr.: The etymological dictionary of the French language, Oxford [Eng.], 1873 [2nd ed., Oxford, 1878].)

Brandon, Edgar Ewing. 1904. Robert Estienne et le dictionnaire français au XVIᵉ siècle. Baltimore. (Reprinted, Geneva [Switzerland], 1967.)

Brazeau, Jacques. 1968. La question linguistique à Montréal. RIS 1.31–52.

Brereton, Geoffrey. 1954. A short history of French literature. Harmondsworth, England. (Peguin Books no. A-297.)

Bridel, Philippe Cyriaque. 1866. Glossaire du patois de la Suisse romande. Lausanne.

Bright, William. 1960. Animals of acculturation in the California Indian languages. UCPL 4:4.215–246.

———, and Elizabeth Bright. 1959/60. Spanish words in Patwin. RPh. 13.161–164.

———, and Robert A. Thiel. 1964/65. Hispanisms in a modern Aztec dialect. RPh. 18.444–452.

Briosi, Sandro. 1969. Marinetti. Firenze.

Broglio, Emilio, G. B. Giorgini, et al. 1897. Nuovo vocabolario della lingua italiana secondo l'uso di Firenze. Firenze.

Brosman, Paul W., Jr. 1962. Morphological correspondences among Germanic verbs in Romance. StP 59.593–604.

Broussard, James Francis. 1942. Louisiana Creole dialect. Baton Rouge.

Brüch, Josef. 1913. Der Einfluss der germanischen Sprachen auf das Vulgärlatein. Heidelberg.

———. 1926. Die bisherige Forschung über die germanischen Einflüsse auf die romanischen Sprachen. RLiR 2.25–98.

Brüdt, Käte. 1937. Madeira, estudo lingüístico-etnográfico. BF-Lisb. 5.59–91, 289–349.

Brun, Auguste. 1931. Le français de Marseille: étude de parler régional. Marseille.

———. 1936. Linguistique et peuplement. Essai sur la limite entre les parlers d'oïl et les parlers d'oc. RLiR 12.165–251.

———. 1946. Parlers régionaux: France dialectale et unité française. Paris-Toulouse.

Bruneau, Charles. 1913a. Etude phonétique des parlers d'Ardenne. Paris.

———. 1913b. La limite des dialectes wallon, champenois et lorrain en Ardenne. Paris.

———. 1913–26. Enquête linguistique sur les patois d'Ardenne. Paris. 2 vols. (BÉHÉ nos. 207, 248.)

———. 1927. Manuel de phonétique. Paris.

Bruner, James Dowden. 1894. The phonology of the Pistoiese dialect. PMLA 9.463–549.

Brunot, Ferdinand. 1891. La doctrine de Malherbe d'après son commentaire sur Desportes. Paris.

———. 1932. Observations sur la Grammaire de l'Académie Française. Paris.

———, and Charles Bruneau. 1905–69. Histoire de la langue française des origines à nos jours. Paris. 13 vols.

——— and ———. 1933. Précis de grammaire historique de la langue française. Paris.

Brusewitz, V. 1905. Étude historique sur la syntaxe des pronoms personnels dans la langue des Félibres. Stockholm.

Brusiloff, Constant. 1945. La evolución y la reforma de la ortografía española. RNC 1945:52.15–32.

Bucci, Oreste A. 1960–65. Vecchia Foggia. Foggia. 5 vols.

Buchmann, Jean. 1924. Il dialetto di Blenio. Saggio fonetico-morfologico con un'appendice lessicale. Parigi.

Buck, Carl Darling. 1904. A grammar of Oscan and Umbrian. Boston. (2nd ed., 1928.)

————. 1905. The general linguistic conditions in ancient Italy. CJ 1.99–110.

————. 1933. Comparative grammar of Greek and Latin. Chicago.

————. 1955. The Greek dialects. Chicago.

Buckenmaier, August. 1934. Die Mundart von Camarès (Aveyron). Laut- und Formenlehre. Tübingen.

Budagov, Ruben Aleksandrovič. 1958. Etjudy po sintaksisu rumynskogo jazyka. Moskva.

Budinszky, Alexander. 1881. Die Ausbreitung der lateinischen Sprache über Italien und die Provinzen des römischen Reiches. Berlin.

Buesa Oliver, Tomás. 1965. Indoamericanismos léxicos en español. Madrid.

Bumaldi, Giovanni Antonio. 1660. Vocabolista bolognese. Bologna.

Bunse, Heinrich A. W., and Mário S. Klassman. 1969. Estudos de dialetologia no Rio Grande do Sul: problemas, métodos, resultados. Pôrto Alegre.

Burckhardt, Jakob. 1860. Die Cultur der Renaissance in Italien. Leipzig. (Eng. tr.: The Civilization of the Renaissance in Italy, London, 1878.)

Bury, John Bagnall. 1923. History of the later Roman Empire. London. 2 vols.

Buscherbruck, K. 1931. Einführung in die historische Lautlehre des Französischen. Berlin-Bonn.

Buschmann, Sigrid. 1965. Beiträge zum etymologischen Wörterbuch des Galizischen. Bonn.

Butler, Jonathan. 1965/66. Some new regional linguistic atlases (viewed in concention with the ALS). RPh. 19.460–468.

Buyssens, Eric. 1969. La grammaire générative selon Chomsky. RBPhH 47.840–857.

Byhan, A. 1899. Istrorumänisches Glossar. JbIRL 6.174–398.

Caduff, Léonard. 1952. Essai sur la phonétique du parler rhétoroman de la Vallée de Tavetsch. Bern.

Cagliaritano, Ubaldo. 1969. Vocabolario senese. Siena. 2 vols.

Cahannes, B. G. 1924. Grammatica romontscha per Surselva e Sutselva. Mustér.

Calcaño, Juan. 1897. El castellano en Venezuela. Caracas.

Callais, J. 1908. Die Mundart von Hattigny und die Mundart von Ommeray nebst lautgeographischer Darstellung der Dialektgrenze zwischen Vosgien und Saunois (Lothringen). JbGLGA 20.302–422.

Calvaruso, G. M. 1929. 'U Baccagghiu. Dizionario comparativo etimologico del gergo parlato dai bassifondi palermitani. Catania.

————, and G. M. da Aleppo. 1910. Le fonti arabiche del dialetto siciliano. Vocabolario etimologico. Roma.

Camenisch, Werner. 1962. Beiträge zur alträtoromanischen Lautlehre auf Grund romanischer Orts- und Flurnamen im Sarganserland. Zürich.

Camilli, Amerindo. 1929. Il dialetto di Servigliano (Àscoli Piceno). AR 13.220–271.

————. 1941. Pronuncia e grafia dell'italiano. Firenze. (BLN no. 2.) (3rd ed., 1965.)

————. 1951. La radio e la pronuncia. LN 12.25–26.

Campanelli, Bernardino. 1896. Fonetica del dialetto reatino. Torino.

Campanile, Enrico. 1967. Appunti sul latino preromanzo. Nàpoli.

Camproux, Charles. 1953. Histoire de la littérature occitane. Paris.

———. 1958. Etude syntaxique des parlers gévaudanois. Paris-Montpellier.

———. 1962. Essai de géographie linguistique du Gévaudan. Montpellier. 2 vols.

Campus, G. 1901. Fonetica del dialetto logudorese. Torino.

Candrea, I. A. 1907. Graiul din Țara Oașului. București.

Canellada, María Josefa. 1944. El bable de Cabranes. Madrid. (RFE Anejo no. 31.

Canfield, Delos Lincoln. 1962. La pronunciación del español en Améerica. Bogotá (Colombia). (PICC no. 17.)

Cantemir, Th. 1959. Texte istroromîne. București.

Capela e Silva, J. A. 1947. Estudos alentejanos. A linguagem rústica no concelho de Elvas. Lisboa.

Capidan, Th. 1925. Elementul slav în dialectul aromân. MAR III.2.25–116.

———. 1925–35. Meglenromâni. București. 3 vols.

———. 1932. Aromânii: dialectul aromân. București.

Capioni, C. 1884. Saggio di uno studio sul dialetto pavese. Pavia.

Capozzoli, Raffaele. 1889. Grammatica del dialetto napoletano. Nàpoli.

Caragiu-Marioțeanu, Matilda. 1968. Fono-morfologia aromână. Studiu de dialectologie structurală. București.

Caratzas, S. C. 1958. L'origine des dialectes néo-grecs de l'Italie méridionale. Paris.

Carballo Calero, Ricardo. 1966. Gramática elemental del gallego común. Vigo.

———. 1969. Sobre los dialectos do galego. Grial 23.1–15.

Cardahi, Choucri. 1967. Regards sous la Coupole: histoire et petite histoire de l'Académie Française. Paris.

Cárdenas, Daniel N. 1967. El español de Jalisco. Madrid.

Carletti, E., and G. B. Corgnali (eds.). 1935. Il nuovo Pirona. Vocabolario friulano. Udine.

Carminati, M., and G. G. Viaggi. 1906. Piccolo vocabolario bergamasco-italiano. Lovera.

Carniver, Ramón. 1969. Sobre el lenguaje de hoy. Madrid.

Carnoy, Albert. 1921. Les Indo-Européens: préhistoire des langues, des moeurs et des croyances de l'Europe. Bruxelles-Paris.

Caro Baroja, J. 1946. Materiales para una historia de la lengua vasca en su relación con la latina. Salamanca.

Carvalhão Buescu, Maria Leonor. 1961. Monsanto: etnografia e linguagem. Lisboa.

Cadado Lobato, María Concepción. 1948. El habla de la Cabrera Alta: contribución al estudio del dialecto leonés. Madrid. (FRE Anejo no. 44.)

Casella, Mario. 1922. Studî suí dialetti della Valdarda. Fonologia del dialetto di Firenzuola. StR. 17.5–71.

———. 1925. Il "volgare illustre" di Dante. GCI 1.33–40.

Castagnotto, Ugo. 1970. Semantica della pubblicità. Roma.

Castellani, Arrigo. 1956. Fonotipi e fonemi in italiano. StFI 14.435–453.

Castro, Américo. 1913. Contribución al estudio del dialecto leonés de Zamora. Madrid.

———. 1941. La peculiaridad lingüística rioplatense y su sentido histórico. MCLI[2] 85–154. Also sep.: Buenos Aires, 1941.

Casullo, Fernando Hugo. 1964. Voces indígenas en el idioma español. Buenos Aires.

Catach, Nina. 1968. L'orthographe française à l'époque de la Renaissance: auteurs, imprimeurs, ateliers d'imprimerie. Genève.

Catalán Menéndez Pidal, Diego. 1956–58. El asturiano occidental: examen sincrónico y explicación diacrónica de sus fronteras fonológicas. RPh. 10.71–92 (1956/57); 11.120–158 (1957/58).

———. 1960. El español canario. Entre España y América. BF-Lisb. 19.317–337.

———. 1964. El español de Canarias. Presente y futuro 1.239–280.

———. 1966. El español en Tenerife. Problemas metodológicos. ZRPh. 82.467–506.

Catanelli, L. 1967. Raccolta di voci perugine. Perugia-Gubbio.

Catel, Paulette. 1938–40. Studî sulla lingua della "Cronique des Veniciens." RIL II.72.305–348 (1938/39); II.73.39–63 (1939/40).

Cavigelli, Pieder. 1969. Die Germanisierung von Bonaduz in geschichtlicher und sprachlicher Schau. Frauenfeld. (BSDM no. 16.)

Cazacu, Boris (ed.), et al. 1968– . Noul atlas lingvistic român pe regiuni. București.

Cazamian, Louis François. 1955. A history of French literature. Oxford (England).

Cazzaniga, Ignazio. 1962. Storia della letteratura latina. Milano.

Ceccaldi, Mathieu. 1968. Dictionnaire corse-français (Pieve d'Evisa). Paris.

Cesareo, Giovanni Alfredo. 1924. Le origini della poesia lirica siciliana. Palermo.

Cesarini Sforza, Lamberto. 1896. Il dialetto trentino confrontato col toscano e coll'-italiano propriamente detto. ASAT 12.21–123.

Chabaneau, Camille. 1871–75. Grammaire limousine. RLR 2.167–222 (1871); 3.369–381 (1872); 4.62–79, 407–423, 650–670 (1873); 5.171–196, 435–481 (1874); 6.171–205, 452–475 (1874); 7.145–178 (1875); 8.152–208 (1876). Also sep.: Paris, 1876.

Chaurand, Jacques. 1968. Les parlers de la Thiérache et du Laounois. Aspects phonétiques et morphologiques. Méthodologie et lexicologie dialectal. Paris.

Chaves de Melo, Gladstone. 1968. Gramática fundamental da língua portuguêsa. Rio de Janeiro.

Chiappini, Filippo. 1933. Vocabolario romanesco. Edizione postuma dalle schede a cura di Bruno Migliorini. Roma.

Cihac, Alexandru. 1870–79. Dictionnaire d'étymologie daco-romane. Francfort s/M. 2 vols.

Ciorănescu, Alejandro. 1958– . Diccionario etimológico rumano. Tenerife-Madrid.

Clemente, José Edmundo. 1952. El idioma de Buenos Aires. Buenos Aires. (Reprinted in Clemente and Borges 1963.)

———, and Jorge Luís Borges. 1963. El lenguaje de Buenos Aires. Buenos Aires.

Clivio, Amedeo, and Gianrenzo P. Clivio. 1971. Bibliografia regionata della lingua regionale e dei dialetti del Piemonte e della Val d'Aosta e della letteratura in piemontese. Torino.

Coates, William A. 1969. The German Pidgin Italian of the 16th-century Lanzichenecchi. PKLC⁴ 66–74.

Cocci, Gilberto. 1956–57. Vocabolario versiliese. Firenze.

Coco, Francesco. 1958. L'antico italiano nei parlari di Corsica. StRic. NS.3.1–74.

Còcolo, Francesco. 1925. Vocabolario dialettale biscegliese-italiano. Trani.

Coelho, F. Adolpho. 1880–86. Os dialector românicos ou neolatinos na África, Asia e América. BSGL 2.129–196 (1880/84); 3.451–478 (1882); 6.705–755 (1886). Also sep.: Lisboa, 1881–83.

Coelho de Senna, Nelson. 1938. Africanos no Brasil (estudos sobre os nêgros africanos e influências afro-nêgros sobre a linguagem e costumes do povo brasileiro). Bello Horizonte.

Cohen, Marcel. 1947. Histoire d'une langue: le français. Paris.

———. 1950. Regards sur la langue français. Paris.

———. 1963. Nouveaux regards sur la langue française. Paris.

———. 1966. Encore des regards sur la langue française. Paris.

————. 1970. Toujours des regards sur la langue française. Paris.

Colin, G. S. 1926–30. Étymologies magribines. Hespéris 6.55–82 (1926); 7.85–102 (1927); 10.125–127 (1930).

Collart, Jean. 1967. Histoire de la langue latine. Paris. (Collection "Que sais-je?" no. 1281.)

Colombo, Carmela. 1962. Leon Battista Alberti e la prima grammatica italiana. StLI 3.176–187.

Coltharp, Lurline Hughes. 1965. The tongue of the Tirilones. A linguistic study of a criminal argot. University, Alabama.

Compan, André. 1965. Grammaire niçoise. Nice.

————. 1967. Glossaire raisonné de la langue niçoise. Nice.

Conway, Robert S., Joshua Whatmough, and Sarah Elizabeth Johnson. 1933. The pre-Italic dialects of Italy. Cambridge, Mass.

Conwell, Marilyn T., and Alphonse Juilland. 1963. Louisiana French grammar. The Hague. (JL-SP no. 1.)

Cordié, Carlo. 1963. Autodemolizione. LN 24.22.

Corominas (Coromines), Juan (Joan, John). 1937. Mots catalans d'origen aràbic. BDC 24.1–81.

————. 1948. The origin of Spanish ferreruelo, Ital. ferraiuolo, and the importance of the study of the Lingua França for Romance etymology. PMLA 63.719–726.

————. 1954–57. Diccionario crítico etimológico de la lengua castellana. Madrid. 4 vols.

————. 1965. El que s'ha de saber de la llengua catalana. Palma de Mallorca.

————. Forthcoming. Diccionari etimològic català.

Coronedi-Berti, Carolina. 1869–74. Vocabolario bolognese-italiano. Bloogna. 4 vols.

Cortelazzo, Manlio. 1969. Avviamento critico alla dialettologia italiana. Problemi e metodi. Pisa.

Coșeriu, Eugenio. 1954. El llamado "latín vulgar" y las primeras diferenciaciones romances. Montevideo.

Costabile, Norma. 1967. Le strutture della lingua italiana. Bologna.

Coteanu, I. 1957. Cum dispare o limbă: istroromîna. București.

————. 1961. Elemente de dialectologie a limbii române. București.

————. 1962. Caractere generale ale limbajului popular. LbR 11.242–247.

———— and I. Dănăilă. 1970. Întroducere în lingvistica și filologia românească. București.

Cotronei, Raffaele. 1895. Vocabolario calabro-italiano. Catanzaro.

Cotugno, Riccardo. 1909. Lessico dialettale andriese-italiano. Andria.

Coustenoble, Hélène N. 1945. La phonétique du provençal moderne en terre d'Arles. Hertford (England).

————, and Lilias Armstrong. 1934. Studies in French intonation. Cambridge (England).

Cremona, A. 1895. Fonetica del caltagironese. Acireale.

Cremonesi, G. 1893. Vocabolario del dialetto agnonese. Agnone.

Crescini, Vincenzo. 1892. Crestomazia provenzale. Verona. (Later eds. entitled "Manuale per l'avviamento agli studî provenzali.")

————. 1910. Romana lingua. Misc. Hortis 441–451.

Crews, Cynthia Mary. 1935. Recherches sur le judéo-espagnol dans les pays balkaniques. Paris.

Croce, Benedetto. 1895. La lingua spagnuola in Italia. Roma.

————. 1902. Estetica come scienza dell'espressione e linguistica generale. Bari.

Crocioni, Giovanni. 1906. Il dialetto di Arcevia (Ancona). Roma.

———. 1907. Il dialetto di Velletri e dei paesi finitimi. StR 5.27–88.

———. 1951. La gente marchigiana nelle sue tradizioni. Milano.

Cuervo, Rufino José. 1867–72. Apuntaciones críticas sobre el lenguaje bogotano con frecuente referencia al de los países de Hispano-América. Bogotá (Colombia). (9th ed., 1955.)

———. 1904. El español en Costa Rica. Pag Il. (Reprinted as "Prólogo" in Gagini 1919:11–35, and in BDH 5.237–276 [1938].)

Curmier, Léonce. 1858. Rivarol: sa vie et ses oeuvres. Paris.

d'Ambra, Raffaele. 1873. Vocabolario napoletano-toscano domestico d'arti e mestieri. Nàpoli.

d'Ans, André-Marcel. 1968. Le créole français d'Haïti. Étude des unités d'articulation, d'expansion et de communication. The Hague. (JL-SP no. 106.)

d'Aronco, Gianfranco (ed.). 1960. Nuova antologia della letteratura friulana. Udine.

d'Elia, Alberto. 1940. Bibliography of Italian dialect dictionaries. Chapel Hill, N.C. (UNCSRLL no. 2.)

d'Ovidio, Francesco. 1878. Fonetica del dialetto di Campobasso. AGI 4.145–184.

———. 1899. Ancora sulla etimologia delle forme grammaticali italiane *amano dicono* ecc. ZRPh. 23.313–320.

da Câmara Borges, Nair Odette. 1960. Influência anglo-americana no falar da ilha de S. Miguel (Açores). Coimbra. (RPF Suplemento no. 2.)

da Silveira Bueno, Francisco. 1955. A formação histórica da língua portuguêsa. Rio de Janeiro and São Paulo.

———. 1963. Grande dicionário etimológico-prosódico da língua portuguêsa. São Paulo.

———. 1964. Influências italianas no português do Brasil. Orbis 13.240–252.

Dagenais, Gérard. 1967. Dictionnaire des difficultés de la langue française au Canada. Québec-Montréal.

Daicoviciu, Constantin, Emil Petrovici and Ch. Stefan. 1963. La formation du peuple roumain et de sa langue. Bucureşti.

dal Pozzo, Giuseppe. 1888. Glossario etimologico piemontese. Torino.

Dalametra, I. 1906. Dicţionar macedo-român. Bucureşti.

Dalgado, Sebastião Rodolpho. 1900. Dialecto indo-português de Ceilão. Lisboa.

———. 1906. Dialecto indo-português do Norte. RLus. 9.142–166, 193–228.

Damourette, Jacques, and Édouard Pichon. 1927–49. Des mots à la pensée: essai de grammaire de la langue française. Paris. 8 vols. (Reprinted 1968–69.)

Darbelnet, J. 1963. Regards sur le français actuel. Montréal.

Dauge, G. 1905. Grammaire gasconne. Dax.

Dauzat, Albert. 1897. Études linguistiques sur la Basse-Auvergne: Phonétique historique du patois de Vinzelles (Puy-de-Dôme). Paris.

———. 1900. Morphologie du patois de Vinzelles. Paris.

———. 1906a. Géographie phonétique d'une région de la Basse-Auvergne. Paris.

———. 1906b. Essai de méthodologie linguistique dans le domaine des langues et des patois romans. Paris.

———. 1913–25. Glossaire étymologique du patois de Vinzelles. RLR 56.285–412 (1913); 57.1–112, 425–472 (1914); 63.101–109 (1925).

———. 1922. La géographie linguistique. Paris. (2nd ed., 1944.)

———. 1926. La langue française: sa vie, son évolution. Paris.

———. 1927. Les patois: évolution—classification—étude. Paris. (4th ed., 1946.)

————. 1928. Les parlers auvergnats anciens et modernes: bibliographie critique jusqu'en 1927. RLiR 4.62–119, with 1 map.

————. 1930. Histoire de la langue française. Paris.

————. 1938. Dictionnaire étymologique de la langue française. Paris. (Revised ed. [with Jean Dubois and Henri Mitterand]: Nouveau dictionnaire étymologique de la langue française, Paris, 1964.)

————. 1950. Phonétique et grammaire historique de la langue française. Paris.

de Arona, Juan. 1871. Diccionario de peruanismos. Lima. (2nd ed., Lima, 1883. 3rd ed., Paris, 1938.)

de Barros, Marcelino Marques. 1897/99. O Guinèense. RLus. 5.174–181, 271–300.

de Beaucoudrey, R. G. 193?. Le langage normand au début du XXᵉ siècle. Noté sur place dans le canton de Percy (Manche). Paris.

de Boer, Cornelis. 1947. Syntaxe du français moderne. Leiden.

de Camp, David. 1962. Social and geographical factors in Jamaican dialects. CLS 2.61–85.

de Celles, Jean. 1937. Malherbe: sa vie—son caractère—sa doctrine. Paris.

de Felice, Emidio. 1941. La terminologia del pugilato. LN 3.56–60.

de Forest, John B. 1916. Old French borrowed words in the Old Spanish of the twelfth and thirteenth centuries. RR 7.369–413.

de Fourvières, Xavier. 1941. Grammaire provençale. Avignon.

de Görög, Ralph. 1958. The Scandinavian element in French and Norman. New York.

de Grande Gutiérrez, Germán. 1968. Transculturación e interferencia lingüística en el Puerto Rico contemporaneo. Bogotá (Colombia).

de Gregorio, Giàcomo. 1882/83. Fonetica dei dialetti gallo-italici di Sicilia. AGI 8.304–316.

————. 1890. Saggio di fonetica siciliana. Palermo.

————. 1897. Sulla varia origine dei dialetti gallo-italici di Sicilia. ASS NS.22.391–439.

————. 1901. Ancora per il principio della varietà d'origine dei dialetti gallo-italici di Sicilia. StGl. 2.247–301.

————. 1910. Il dialetto sanfratellano ha elementi speciali [. . .]. StGl. 5.54–125.

————. 1912. Il dialetto romanesco (tipo di Roma). StGl. 6.78–167.

————. 1924. Etimologia del sic. macalubbi. ZRPh. 44.96–100.

————. 1930. La grecità del dialetto calabrese. ZRPh. 50.676–731.

———— and Chr. Seybold. 1903. Glossario delle voci siciliane di origine araba. StGl. 3.225–251.

de Gregorio, Iolanda. 1939. Contributo alla conoscenza del dialetto di Bisceglie (Bari). ID 15.31–51.

de La Chaussée, François. 1966. Les parlers du centre-ouest de la Vendée. Paris.

de la Torre, Alfonso. 1951. El habla de Cuellar (Segovia). BRAE 31.133–164, 501–513.

de Lacerda, Armando. 1940–44. Características da entoação portuguesa. Biblos 16.143–187, 473–566 (1940); 17.241–319, 441–514 (1941); 19.89–166 (1943); 20.157–319 (1944). Also sep.: Coimbra, 1941–48. 2 vols.

————, and Antoni Badia i Margarit. 1948. Estudios de fonética y de fonología catalanas. Madrid.

————, and María Josefa Canellada. 1942–44. Comportamientos tonales vocálicos en español y portugués. RFE 26.171–220, 469–485 (1942); 27.256–288 (1943); 28.190–256 (1944). Also sep.: Madrid, 1945 (RFE Anejo no. 32.)

de Lamano y Beneite, José. 1916. El dialecto vulgar salmantino. Salamanca.

de Lavallaz, L. 1935. Essai sur le patois d'Hérémence (Valais-Suisse): phonologie, morphologie, syntaxe, textes et glossaire. Paris.

de Lemos, Virgilio. 1959. A língua portuguêsa no Brasil. Salvador.

de Lima Coutinho, Ismael. 1938. Ponto de gramática histórica. Rio de Janeiro. (6th ed., 1968.)

de Lollis, Cèsare. 1922. Crusca in fermento. Firenze.

de Mauro, Tuillo. 1963. Storia linguistica dell'Italia unita. Bari. (3rd ed., 1968.)

——. 1968. Lingua parlata e TV. Televisione e vita italiana 247–294.

de Moraes Ferreira, Albino J. 1898. Dialecto mirandés. Lisboa.

de Moura Santos, María José. 1962–68. Os falares fronteriços de Tras-os-Montes. RPF 12.509–565 (1962/63); 13.65–261 (1964/65); 14.213–415 (1966/68). Also sep.: Coimbra, 1968.

de Múgica, Pedro. 1892. Dialectos castellanos: montañés, vizcaino, aragonés. I. Fonética. Berlin.

de Oliveira Monteiro, María de Lourdes. 1947–49. Porto Santo: monografia linguística, etnográfica e folclórica. RPF 1.340–390 (1947); 2.28–92 (1948); 3.90–151 (1949).

de Paiva Boléo, Manuel. 1942. O estudo dos dialectos e falares portugueses. Coimbra.

de Rato y Hévia, Apolinar. 1891. Vocabulario de las palabras y frases bables que se hablaron antiguamente y de las que hoy se hablan en el principado de Asturias. Madrid.

de Riquer, Martìn. 1964. Història de la literatura catalana. Part antiga. Barcelona. 3 vols.

de Saint-Quentin, Alfred. 1872. Introduction à l'histoire de Cayenne, comprenant une grammaire créole. Antibes.

de Salvio, Alfonso. 1913. Studies in the Irpina dialect. RR 4.352–380.

——. 1915. Studies in the dialect of Basilicata. PMLA 30.788–820.

de Santis, Giuseppe. 1857. Saggio di vocabolario vernacolo barese-italiano. Bari.

de Saussure, Ferdinand. 1916. Cours de linguistique générale. Lausanne. (Later eds. Paris.)

de Toro y Gisbert, Miguel. 1912. Americanismos. Paris.

——. 1920. Voces andaluzas. RHi 49.313–647.

de Tourtoulon, Charles. 1890. Des dialectes, de leur classification et de leur délimitation géographique. RDR 34.130–175. Also sep.: Paris, 1890.

——, and Octave Bringuier. 1876. Étude sur la limite géographique de la langue d'oc et de la langue d'oïl. Paris.

de Vincentiis, Domenico Ludovico. 1872. Vocabolario del dialetto tarantino. Tàranto.

Debrie, René. 1961. Lexique picard des parlers nord-amiénois. Arras. (CSLP no. 5.)

——. 1965. Supplément au lexique picard des parlers nord-amiénois. Abbeville.

——. 1966. Petit lexique du parler de Beauquesne (Somme). Grandvilliers (Oise).

del Rosario, Rubén. 1965. Vocabulario puertorriqueño. Sharon, Connecticut.

——. 1970. El español de América. Sharon, Connecticut.

del Valle, Enrique Ricardo. 1966. Lunfardología. Buenos Aires.

Delaloye, Louis, and Ernest Schüle. 1964. Lexique du patois d'Ardon. Sion.

Delare, O. 1883. Les Normands en Italie. Paris.

Delattre, Pierre. 1969/70. La théorie celtique et les substrats. RPh. 23.480–491.

Delfino, Maria Giovanna. 1958. Il problema dei rapporti linguistici tra l'osco e il latino. Serta Eusebiana 27–86.

Dengler, Berthold. 1934. Die Mudart von St. Vincent de Tyrosse und Umgebung (Landes). Tübingen.

Denk, V. M. Otto.   1893.   Einführung in die Geschichte der altcatalanischen Litteratur von deren Anfängen bis zum 18. Jahrhundert. München.
Densusianu, Ovidiu.   1901–38.   Histoire de la langue roumaine. Paris. 2 vols.
——.   1915.   Graiul din Țara Hategului. București.
——.   1924.   Elemente latine ale limbii basce. Craiova.
Descroix, Joseph Marie.   1946.   Glossaire du patois de Lantignié-en-Beaujolais, Rhône. Paris. (SPRF no. 24.)
Deutschmann, Olaf. Lateinisch und Romanisch. München.
Devaux, François-André.   1935a.   Les patois du Dauphiné: I. Dictionnaire des patois des Terres Froides, avec des mots d'austres parlers dauphinois. Lyon.
——.   1935b.   Les patois du Dauphiné: II. Atlas linguistique des Terres Froides. Lyon.
Devereux, Robert.   1968.   The Crusca academy and its Vocabolario. IQ XI:44.67–86.
Devoto, Giácomo.   1930.   Il fondamento del sistema delle vocali romanze. RIL II. 63.593–605.
——.   1936.   Storia della lingua di Roma. Bologna. (German translation: Geschichte der Sprache Roms, Heidelberg, 1968.)
——.   1939.   Lingue speciali: le cronache del calcio. LN 1.17–21.
——.   1948.   Le tavole di Gubbio. Firenze.
——.   1951a.   Gli antichi Italici. Firenze.
——.   1951b.   Protostoria del fiorentino. LN 12.29–35.
——.   1953.   Profilo di storia linguistica italiana. Firenze.
——.   1954.   Tabulae iguuinae. Romae.
——.   1956.   La lingua letteraria italiana e la sua (im)popolarità. NA 467.145–156. (Eng. tr.: The Italian literary language and its [un]popularity, IQ I:1.54–68.)
——.   1962.   Origini indoeuropee. Firenze.
——.   1966.   Avviamento alla etimologia italiana. Dizionario etimologico, Firenze.
——.   1970.   Curatori e medici. Corriere della Sera (Milan), July 16, p. 3.
Deyermond, M. A. D.   1971.   A literary history of Spain: the Middle Ages. London and New York.
di Domenico, Ferdinando.   1922.   Vocabolario napolitano-italiano. Nàpoli.
di Sant'Albino, Vittorio.   1859.   Gran dizionario piemontese-italiano. Torino.
Diaconu, I.   1930.   Tinuțul Vrancei: etnografie, folklor, dialectologie. București.
Díaz Castañón, María del Carmen.   1966.   El habla del Cabo de Peñas. Oviedo.
Dicziunari Rumantsch Grischun. Chur, 1938–   .
Dietrich, Adlophe.   1891.   Les parlers créoles des Mascareignes. Rom. 20.216–277.
Dietrich, Alfred.   1945.   Le parler de Martigny, Valais, et son rayonnement dans l'évolution des patois du Bas-Valsis. Bienne.
Dietz, Frederick Charles.   1927.   The industrial revolution. New York.
Diez, Friedrich.   1853.   Etymologisches Wörterbuch der romanischen Sprachen. Bonn. (5th ed., 1887.)
Díez-Echarri, Emiliano, and José María Roca Franquesa.   1960.   Historia de la literatura española e hispano-americana. Madrid.
Dihigo, Juan Miguel.   1915.   El habla popular a través de la literatura cubana. RFLCUH 20.53–100.
Diodati Caccavelli, Marilisa.   1966–69.   Vocabolario dell'Isola d'Elba. ID 29.78–112 (1966); 30.167–180 (1967); 31.38–91 (1968); 32.63–131 (1969).
Dionisotti, Carlo.   1962/63.   Per una storia della lingua italiana. RPh. 16.41–58.
——.   1968.   Gli umanisti e il volgare fra Quattro e Cinquecento. Firenze.
Dionne, N. E.   1909.   Le parler populaire des Canadiens français, ou lexique des

canadianismes, acadianismes, anglicismes, américanismes, mots anglais les plus en usage au sein des familles canadiennes et acadiennes françaises. Québec.

Ditchy, Jay K. 1932. Les Acadiens louisianais et leur parler. Paris. (SPRF no. 7.)

Domaschke, W. 1919. Der lateinische Wortschatz des Rumänischen. JbIRSL 21/25.65–173.

Donadoni, Eugenio. 1923. Breve storia della letteratura italiana. Roma. (Eng. tr.: A history of Italian literature, New York and London, 1969.)

Donghi de Halperín, Renata. 1925. Contribución al estudio del italianismo en la República argentina. CUBA 1.183–198.

Donnan, Elizabeth (ed.). 1930. Documents illustrative of the history of the slave trade in America. Washington, D.C. (Carnegie Institution of Washington, Publication no. 409.)

Donzé, Roland. 1966. La grammaire générale et raisonnée de Port-Royal, Berne.

Doppagne, Albert. 1966. Trois aspects du français contemporain. Paris.

Dorna, Louis, and E. Lyotard. 1953. Le parler gaga: essai de lexique des mots et locutions du terroir stéphanois. Paris.

Dorrance, Ward Allison. 1935. The survival of French in the old district of Sainte Geneviève. Columbia, Missouri. (UMoSt. 10:2.)

Dottin, Georges, and J. Langouët. 1901. Glossaire du parler de Pléchâtel (canton de Bain, Ille-et-Vilaine). Rennes.

Doussinet, Raymond. 1958. Le parler savoureux de Saintonge. Introduction au patois saintongeais. La Rochelle.

Downey, Glanville. 1969. The late Roman Empire. New York.

Dozy, Reinhart Pieter Anne, and W. H. Engelmann. 1869. Glossaire des mots espagnols et portugais dérivés de l'arabe. Leyde-Paris. (2nd ed. of Engelmann 1861.)

Drăganu, N. 1945. Elemente de sintaxă a limbii române. Bucure ti.

Dubois, Jean. 1965– . Grammaire structurale du français. Paris.

Dubois, Pierre. 1958. Position des parlers de Cagnes et de Vence par rapport au Provençal et au Niçard. Aix-en-Provence.

Dubuisson, Pierrette. 1971– . Atlas linguistique et ethnographique du Centre. Paris.

Ducibella, Joseph William. 1934. The phonology of the Sicilian dialects. Washington, D.C.

Dulong, Gaston. 1968. Dictionnaire correctif du français au Canada. Québec.

Dupraz, J. 1938–39. Notes sur le patois de Saxel (Haute-Savoie). RLiR 14.279–330 (1938); 15.87–151 (1939).

Duraffour, Antoine. 1932a. Phénomènes généraux d'évolution phonétique dans les dialectes franco-provençaux d'après le parler de Vaux-en-Bugey (Ain). Gernoble.

———. 1932b. Description morphologique avec notes syntaxiques du parler franco-provençal de Vaux (Ain) en 1919–1931. Grenoble.

———. 1941. Lexique patois-francais du parler de Vaux-en-Bugey (Ain). Grenoble.

Durand, Bruno. 1932. Grammaire provençale. Aix-en-Provence.

Duridanov, I. 1969. Die thrakischen und dakisch-baltischen Sprachbeziehungen. Sofia. (= LB 13.2.)

Duro, Aldo. 1962. I vocabolarî nella storia della lingua: le prime quattro edizioni della Crusca. TPr. 1962:1.138–146.

Echeverría y Reyes, Aníbal. 1900. Voces usadas en Chile. Santiago de Chile.

Eckhardt, Karl August. 1955–61. Die Gesetze des Merowingerreiches 481–714. Göttingen-Berlin-Frankfurt/M. 2 vols.

Edmont, Edmond. 1887–97. Lexique saint-polois. Part 1: RPGR 1.51–96. 209–224

(1887); 2.113–125 (1888); 3.221–236, 304–307 (1890); 4.40–62, 265–269, 273–282 (1891); 5.9–44, 50–94, 102–125, 130–144 (1891). Part 2: Saint-Pol and Mâcon, 1897.

Efron, Edith. 1954. French and Creole patois in Haiti. CaQ 3.199–214.

Egerod, Søren. 1958. Pidgin Portuguese a.d. 1621. T'oung Pao 46.111–114.

Egidi, Francesco. 1962. Dizionario dei dialetti piceni fra Tronto e Aso. Montefiore dell'Aso.

Egloff, Wilhelm. 1937. Le paysan dombiste: étude sur la vie, les travaux des champs et le parler d'un village de la Dombe, Versailleux (Ain). Paris. (SPRF no. 20.)

Equílaz y Yanglas, L. 1886. Glosario etimológico de las palabras españolas (castellanas, catalanas, gallegas, mallorquinas, portuguesas, valencianas y bascongadas) de origen oriental (árabe, hebreo, malayo, perso y turco). Granada.

Elcock, William Dennis. 1938. De quelques affinités phonétiques entre le béarnais et l'aragonais. Paris.

————. 1960. The Romance languages. London and New York.

Elia, Silvio. 1940. O problema da língua brasileira. Rio de Janeiro. (2nd ed., 1962.)

————. 1966. A difusão das linguas europeias e a formaçãao das variedades ultramarinas, em particular dos crioulos (aplicação especial ao português do Brasil). CIELB[5] 3/5.217–256.

Elwert, W. Theodor. 1943. Die Mundart des Fassa-Tals. Heidelberg. (WS NF Bhft. no. 2.)

————. 1958. Die Mundart von S. Oreste. Romanica (Rohlfs) 120–158.

————. 1970. Letterature nazionali e letterature dialettali nell'Europa occidentale. Paideia 25.169–192.

Engelmann, Willem Hermann. 1861. Glossaire des mots espagnols et portugais dérivés de l'arabe. Leyde.

Engler, Winfried. 1969. Die Diskussion um die Zuordnung des Katalanischen. NSpr. 18.24–29.

Entwistle, William James. 1936. The Spanish language, together with Portuguese, Catalan, and Basque. London. (2nd ed., 1962.)

Ercolani, Libero. 1960. Vocabolario romagnolo-italiano. Monte di Ravenna.

Ernout, Alfred. 1909. Les éléments dialectaux du vocabulaire latin. Paris. (2nd ed., 1928.)

————. 1961. Le dialecte ombrien. Paris.

Ernst, Gerhard. 1970. Die Toskanisierung des römischen Dialekts im 15. und 16. Jahrhundert. Tübingen. (ZRPh. Bhft. no. 122.)

Escoffier, S. 1956. La rencontre de la langue d'oïl, de la langue d'oc et du francoprovençal entre Loire et Allier: limites phonétiques et morphologiques. Paris. (PILRL no. 11.)

————. 1958. Remarques sur le lexique d'une zone marginale aux confins de la langue d'oïl, de la langue d'oc et du francoprovençal. Paris. (PILRL no. 12.)

Espinosa, Aurelio Macedonio. 1930–46. Estudios sobre el español de Nuevo Méjico. Buenos Aires. 2 vols. Vol. 1, 1930. Vol. 2, 1946.

Étiemble, René. 1964. Parlez-vous franglais? Paris.

Ewert, Alfred. 1935. The Strassburg oaths. TPS 1935.16–35.

————. 1938. The French language. New York and London.

————. 1940. Dante's theory of language. MLR 35.355–366.

————. 1958. Of the precellence of the French tongue. Oxford (England).

Fabra, Pompeau. 1912. Gramática de la lengua catalana. Barcelona.

————, and Joan Coromines. 1956. Gramática catalana. Barcelona. [In Cat.]

Façon, Nina. 1962a. Problemele limbii literare în cultura italiană. București.

———. 1962b. Notă cu privire la raportul între limba națională și dialect în Italia de azi. RFRG 6.169–170.

Faine, Jules. 1937. Philologie créole. Études historiques et étymologiques sur la langue créole d'Haïti. Port-au-Prince.

———. 1939. Le créole dans l'univers. Études comparatives des parlers français-créoles. Port-au-Prince.

Faithfull, R. Glynn. 1953. The concept of "living language" in Cinquecento vernacular philology. MRL 48.278–292.

Falc'hun, François. 1968. Gaulois et gallo-roman dans la toponymie de la France. Onoma 13.371–378.

Fallen, J. 1936. Grammaire provençale. Aix-en-Provence.

Fanfani, Pietro. 1863. Vocabolario dell'uso toscano. Firenze.

———. 1878. Storia politica dell'Accademia della Crusca. Firenze.

Fankhauser, Franz. 1910–11. Das Patois von Val-d'Illiez (Unterwallis). RDR 2.198–344 (1910); 3.1–76 (1911).

Fanti, Renata. 1938–39. Note fonetiche e morfologiche su dialetto d'Ascrea (Rieti). ID 14.201–218 (1938); 15.101–135 (1939).

———. 1940. Note fonetiche, morfologiche e lessicali sul dialetto di Paganico (Rieti). ID 16.172–189.

Fatini, Giuseppe. 1953. Vocabolario amiatino. Firenze.

Fausch, Georg. 1962. Testi dialettali e tradizioni popolari della Garfagnana. Zurigo.

Favre, Christophe, and Zacharie Balet. 1960. Lexique du parler de Savièse. Berne. (RH no. 71.)

Feist, Sigmund. 1932. The origin of the Germanic languages and the Indo-Europeanising of North Europe. Language 8.245–254.

Fernández González, Ángel R. 1959. El habla y la cultura popular de Oseja de Sajambre. Oviedo.

Ferraz y Castán, V. 1934. Vocabulario del dialecto que se habla en la Alta Ribagorza. Madrid.

Ferreira da Cunha, Celso. 1968. Língua portuguêsa e realdade brasileira. Rio de Janeiro.

Ferrer-Pastor, Francesc. 1966. Vocabolario castellà-valencià i valencià-castellà. Valencia.

Ferri, Luigi. 1889. Vocabolario ferrarese-italiano. Ferrara.

Festa, Giovanni Battista. 1916. Il dialetto di Matera. ZRPh. 38.129–162, 257–280.

Finamore, Gennaro. 1880. Vocabolario dell'uso abruzzese. Livorno. (2nd ed., Città di Castello, 1893.)

Fink, O. 1929. Studien über die Mundarten der Sierra de Gata. Hamburg.

Finocchiaro, Mary Bonomo. 1950. The Gallo-Italian dialect of Nicosia. New York.

Finsterwalder, Karl. 1969. Die Flusznamen *Trisanna*, *Rosanna* und die Sprachelemente *trag-*, *trog-* in Ortsnamen und Appellativen des Alpenraums. BNF NS.4.380–390.

Fiorelli, Piero. 1956. Pierfrancesco Giambullari e la riforma dell'alfabeto. StFI 14.177–210.

———. 1960. Marzo novecentosessanta. LN 21.1–16.

Fischer, Hildegard. 1937. Antoine Furetière (1618–1688), ein französischer Literat des 17. Jahrhunderts. Versuch eines Beitrags zur Wesenskunde des französischen Menchen. Berlin. (RSE no. 41.)

Fishman, Joshua A., Charles A. Ferguson, and J. Das Gupta (eds.). 1968. Language Problems of Developing Nations. New York.

Flagge, Ludwig. 1935. Provenzalisches Alpenleben in den Hochtälern des Verdon und der Bléone: ein Beitrag zur Volkskunde der Basses-Alpes. Firenze.

Flechia, Giovanni. 1880/83. Confessione latino-volgare (1000–1200). AGI 7.121–129.

Fleischer, Fr. 1913. Studien zur Sprachgeographie der Gascogne. Halle/S. (ZRPh. Bhft. no. 44.)

Flórez, Luis. 1951a. La pronunciación del español en Bogotá. Bogotá (Colombia).

———. 1951b. El español hablado en Segovia y Remedios. BICC 7.18–110.

———. 1957. Habla y cultura popular en Antioquia. Bogotá (Colombia).

———. 1965. El español hablado en Santander. Bogotá (Colombia). (PICC no. 21.)

Flutre, Fernand. 1955. Le parler picard de Mesnil-Martinsart (Somme). Phonétique, morphologie, syntaxe, vocabulaire. Genève. (SPRF no. 51.)

Focard, Voisy. 1885. Du patois créole de l'Île de Réunion. St. Denis (Réunion).

Förster, Wendelin. 1898. Die toskanische Endung -a/ono der 3. Pluralis Praesentis. ZRPh. 22.521–525.

Folena, Gianfranco. 1968/70. Introduzione al veneziano "de là de mar". Studî Deanovic (= BALM 10./12.) 331–376.

Ford, H. E. 1921. Modern Provençal phonology and morphology studied in the language of Frédéric Mistral. New York.

Ford, Jeremiah Dennis Mathias. 1906. Old Spanish readings. Boston.

Foresti, Lorenzo. 1836. Vocabolario piacentino-italiano. Piacenza.

———. 1842. Supplemento al vocabolario piacentino-italiano. Picenza.

Fortier, Alcée. 1891. The Acadians of Louisiana and their dialect. PMLA 6.1–33.

Fouché, Pierre. 1924a. Phonétique historique du roussillonais. Toulouse. (BMér. II.21.)

———. 1924b. Morphologie historique du roussillonais. Toulouse. (BMér. II.22.)

———. 1952–61. Phonétique historique du français. Paris. 3 vols.

———. 1956. Traité de prononciation française. Paris.

Foulet, Lucien. 1919. Petite syntaxe de l'ancien français. Paris.

Fouquet, ? ("Le pasteur Fouquet"). 1884–85. Monographie du sous-dialecte langue-docien du canton de La-Salle-Saint-Pierre (Gard). RLR 25.53–76 (1884); 26.53–76 (1885).

Fowkes, Robert A. 1966. English, French and German phonetics again and the substratum theory. Linguistics 21.45–53.

Fowler, Harold N. 1905. A history of Roman literature. New York and London.

Fracastoro Martini, Ornella. 1951. La lingua e la radio. Firenze. (BLN no. 9.)

Francescato, Giuseppe. 1965. Teoria e realtà linguistica in Dante. Miscellanea Dantesca (Utrecht) 128–137.

———. 1966. Contributo allo studio degli elementi italiani in olandese. StFI 24.443–607.

———. 1967. Dialettologia friulana. Ùdine.

———. 1970. Studî linguistici sul friulano. Ùdine.

Franceschi, Temistocle. 1970. Lingua e cultura di una comunità italiana in Costa Rica. Firenze.

Franco Grande, Xosé Luís. 1968. Diccionario galego-castelan e Vocabulario castelan-galego. Vigo.

François, Alexis. 1905. La grammaire du purisme et l'Académie Française au XVIIIᵉ siècle. Paris.

———. 1959. Histoire de la langue française cultivée des origines à nos jours. Genève. 2 vols.

Françon, Marcel. 1957. La question de la langue en France au XVI⁶ siècle: opposition aux études du latin et du grec. StFr. 1.257–259.

Frei, Henri. 1929. La grammaire des fautes. Geneva-Leipzig-Paris.

Freund, Ilse. 1934. Beiträge zur Mundart von Ischia. Leipzig.

Frey, Hans-Jost. 1962. Per la posizione lessicale dei dialetti veneti. Venezia-Roma.

Friederici, Georg. 1926. Hilfswörterbuch für den Amerikanisten. Lehnwörter aus Indianersprachen und Erklärungen altertümlicher Ausdrücke, deutsch-spanisch-englisch. Halle/S.

Friedmann, B. 1937. Die jonischen und attischen Wörter im Altlatein. Helsinki.

Frings, Theodor. 1932. Germania romana. Halle/S.

———. 1937–39. Französisch und Fränkisch. ZRPh. 57.193–210 (1937); 59.257–283 (1939).

Fromilhague, René. 1954. La vie de Malherbe: apprentissages et luttes, 1555–1610. Paris.

Fubini, Mario. 1969. Elementi scientifici nel lessico poetico del Parini. GSLI 146.212–238.

Fubini, Riccardo. 1961. La coscienza del latino negli Umanisti. "An latina lingua Romanorum esset peculiare idioma." StM III.2.505–550.

Fucci, F. 1962. Dizionario del linguaggio giornalistico. Milano.

Fumagalli, C. 1882. Il nuovo Peri: vocabolario manuale cremonese-italiano. Cremona.

Gaeng, Paul. 1967. An inquiry into local variations in Vulgar Latin, as reflected in the vocalism of Christian inscriptions. Chapel Hill, N.C. (UNCSRLL no. 77.)

———. 1968. An inquiry into the influence of the Germanic superstratum on the vocabulary and phonetic structure of Gallo-Romance. Upper Montclair, N.J.

Gagini, Carlos. 1893. Diccionario de barbarismos y provincialismos de Costa Rica. San José de Costa Rica.

———. 1919. Diccionario de costarriqueñismos. San José de Costa Rica.

Galiani, Ferdinando. 1789. Vocabolario delle parole del dialetto napoletano che più si scostano dal dialetto toscano. Nàpoli.

Galichet, Georges. 1947. Essai de grammaire psychologique du français moderne. Paris. (2nd ed., 1950.)

———. 1949. Physiologie de la langue française. Paris. (2nd ed., 1964.)

———. 1953. Méthodologie grammaticale: étude psychologique des structures. Paris.

Galli, Ettore. 1965. Dizionario pavese. Pavia.

Galvani, Giovanni. 1868. Saggio di un glossario modenese. Mòdena.

Gamillscheg, Ernst. 1919. Oltenische Mundarten. Wien. (SbWien 190:3.)

———. 1928. Etymologisches Wörterbuch der französischen Sprache. Heidelberg. (2nd ed., 1968.)

———. 1932. Historia lingüística de los Visigodos. RFE 19.117–150, 229–260.

———. 1934–36. Romania Germanica. Sprach- und Siedlungsgeschichte der Germanen auf dem Boden des alten Römerreichs. Berlin and Leipzig.

———. 1936. Die Mundart von Şerbaneşti-Tituleşti (Gerichtsbezirk Olt, Kreis Vedea). Jena and Lepizig. (BBRPh. 6:1–2.)

———. 1937. Immigrazioni germaniche in Italia. Leipzig.

———. 1948. Germanische Wörter im Vulgärlatein. RF 61.212–224.

———. 1950. Romanen und Basken. AbhMainz 1950:2.19–50.

———. 1957. Historische französische Syntax. Tübinge.

———. 1964. Zur rumänischen Frühgeschichte. Die Kultur Südosteuropas 45–73, with 4 maps.

García Blanco, Manuel. 1967. La lengua española en la época de Carlos V, y otras cuestiones de lingüística y filología. Madrid.

García Cotorruelo, Emilia. 1959. Estudio sobre el habla de Cartagena y su comarca. Madrid. (BRAE Anejo no. 3.)

García de Diego, Vicente. 1906. Elementos de gramática histórica gallega. Burgos. (2nd ed., Madrid, 1920.)

———. 1946. Manual de dialectología española. Madrid. (2nd ed., 1959.)

———. 1950. El castellano como complejo dialectal y sus dialectos internos. RFE 34.107–124.

———. 1951. Gramática histórica española. Madrid. (2nd ed., 1961.)

———. 1955. Diccionario etimológico español e hispanico. Madrid.

García Icazbalceta, Joaquín. 1905. Diccionario de mejicanismos. México, D.F. [Only A—G.]

García Lomas, Gervasio Adriano. 1922. Estudo del dialecto popular montañés. Fonética, etimologías y glosario de voces. San Sebastián.

———. 1949. El lenguaje popular de las Montañas de Santander. San Sebastián.

García Rey, Verado. 1934. Vocabulario del Bierzo. Madrid.

García Soriano, Justo. 1932. Vocabulario del dialecto murciano. Madrid.

Gardette, Pierre. 1939. Limites phonétiques du franco-provençal au pays du Forez. Mél. Duraffour 22–36.

———. 1941a. Géographie phonétique du Forez. Mâcon. (PILRL no. 4.)

———. 1941b. Études de géographie morphologique sur les patois du Forez. Mâcon. (PILRL no. 5.)

———. 1968. Le francoprovençal écrit en Lyonnais et en Forez au moyen âge. RLiR 32.70–99, with 2 maps.

——— et al. (eds.). 1950–68. Atlas linguistique et ethnographique du Lyonnais. Lyon.

Garnier, Christian. 1898. Deux patois des Alpes-maritimes italiennes. Grammaires et vocabulaires méthodiques des idiomes d Bordighera et de Realdo. Paris.

Gartner, Theodor. 1882. Die judikarische Mundart. SbWien 100.803–884.

———. 1883. Raetoromanische Grammatik. Heilbronn.

———. 1892. Die Mundart von Erto. ZRPh. 16.183–209, 308–371.

———. 1910. Handbuch der rätoromanischen Sprache und Literatur. Halle/S.

Garzón, Tobías. 1910. Diccionario argentino. Barcelona.

Gaster, M. 1886. Die nichtlateinischen Elemente im Rumänischen. In Gröber (ed.) 1886–88:1.406–414.

Gatti, Riccardo. 1910. Il dialetto di Jesi. ZRPh. 34.675–700.

Gauchat, Louis. 1903. Gibt es Mundartgrenzen? ASNS 111.365–403.

———. 1905. L'unité phonétique dans le patois d'une commune. Festschrift Morf 175–232.

———, and Jules Jeanjaquet. 1912–20. Bibliographie linguistique de la Suisse romande. Neuchâtel. 2 vols.

———, ———, and Ernst Tappolet. 1925. Tableaux phonétiques des patois suisses romands. Neuchâtel.

———, ———, ———, and E. Muret (eds.). 1924– . Glossaire des patois de la Suisse romande. Neuchâtel.

Gaudenzi, Augusto. 1889. I suoni, le forme, e le parole dell'odierno dialetto della città di Bologna. Torino.

Gaxotte, Pierre. 1965. L'Académie Française. Paris.

REFERENCES 281

Gayot, Paul. 1967. Raymond Queneau. Paris.

Geary, James A. 1945. Algonquian *nasaump* and *napōpi*: French loanwords? Languaz 21.40–45.

Geddes, James, Jr., and Adjutor Rivard. 1966. Bibliographie du parler français au Canada. Paris and Québec. [Original ed., 1906].

Gégou, Fabienne. 1962. Antoine Furetière, abbé de Chalivey, ou la chute d'un immortel. Paris.

Gendron, Jean-Denis. 1966. Le français rural du Canada. TLL 4:1.173–189.

——, and Georges Straka (eds.). 1968. Étude de linguistique franco-canadienne. Québec and Paris.

Gentili, Angelo. 1897. Fonetica del dialetto cosentino. Milano.

Georgiev, Vladimir I. 1962. Die hethitische Herkunft der etruskischen Sprache. Sofia.

——. 1966. Introduzione alla storia delle lingue indeuropee. Roma.

——. 1970. Etruskische Sprachwissenschaft. Sofia. 2 vols. (= LB 14:1 and 15.)

Gerighausen, Josef. 1963. Die historische Deutung der Nationalsprache im französischen Schrifttum des 16. Jahrhunderts. Bonn.

Gerster, Walter. 1927. Die Mundart von Montana (Wallis) und ihre Stellung innerhalb der frankoprovenzalischen Mundarten des Mitterwallis. Aarau.

Giacalone Ramat, Anna. 1967. Colori germanici nel mondo romanzo. AAColombaria 32. (= NS.18.) 105–211.

Giacomelli, Gabriella. 1963. La lingua falisca. Firenze.

Giacomelli, Raffaele. 1952. Evoluzione della terminologia aeronautica. LN 13.5–11.

Giammarco, Ernesto. 1958. Grammatica dei dialetti abruzzesi. Pescara. (2nd ed., 1960.)

——. 1959. Dialetti d'Abruzzo. Lares 25.355–375.

——. 1964. Analisi fonematica della parlata d'Introdacqua. Abruzzo 2.354–371.

——. 1965. Appunti per la classificazione delle parlate abruzzesi e molisane. Abruzzo 3.105–114.

——. 1967– . Dizionario abruzzese e molisano. Roma.

Giannarelli, D. 1913. Studî sui dialetti lunigianesi compresi fra la Magra e l'Appennino Reggiano. RDR 5.261–311.

Gibbon, Edward. 1776–88. The history of the decline and fall of the Roman Empire. London. 6 vols. (Many later eds.)

Giese, Wilhelm. 1932a. Volkskundliches aus den Hochalpen des Dauphiné. Hamburg.

——. 1932b. Die volkstümliche Kultur des Niolo (Korsika). WS 14.109–145.

——. 1937. Nordost-Cádiz: ein kulturwissenschaftlicher Beitrag zur Erforschung Andalusiens. Halle/S. (ZRPh. Bhft. no. 89.)

——. 1948/49. Hispanismos en el mapuche. BFUCh. 5.115–132.

Gigli, Girolamo. 1707. Vocabolario cateriniano. Roma. (Reëdition, Firenze, 1866.)

Gigli, Lorenzo. 1962. Edmondo de Amicis. Torino.

Gili Gaya, Samuel. 1943. Curso superior de sintaxis española. México, D.F. (5th ed., Barcelona, 1955.)

——. 1966. Nuestra lengua materna. San Juan de Puerto Rico.

Gilliéron, Jules Louis. 1880a. Patois de la commune de Vionnaz (Bas-Valais). Paris. (BÉHÉ no. 40.)

——. 1880b. Petit atlas phonétique du Valais roman (sud du Rhône). Paris.

——. 1918. Généalogie des mots qui désignent l'abeille. Paris.

——. 1919. La faillite de l'étymologie phonétique. Neuveville (Berne).

——, and Edmond Edmont. 1902. Atlas linguistique de la France. Notice servant à l'intelligence des cartes. Paris.

—— and ——. 1902–10. Atlas linguistique de la France. Paris.

—— and ——. 1912. Table de l'Atlas linguistique de la France. Paris.

—— and ——. 1914–15. Atlas linguistique de la France. Corse. Paris.

——, and J. Mongin. 1905. *Scier* dans la Gaule romane du sud et du sud-est. Paris.

Ginobili, Giovanni. 1963. Glossario dei dialetti di Macerata e Petriolo. Macerata.

——. 1965. Appendice al Glossario dei dialetti di Macerata e di Petriolo, con aggiunte di soprannomi e patronimici. Macerata.

Girão, Raimundo. 1967. Vocabolário popular cearense. Fortaleza (Brazil).

Gismondi, Alfredo. 1955. Nuovo vocabolario genovese-italiano. Torino.

Giusti, Antonio. 1936. Appunti sul dialetto ligure. GSLLig. NS.12.99–106, 166–174.

——. 1937. Appunti sul dialetto ligure. ASLL 13.35–41.

Glossaire du parler français au Canada. Québec, 1930.

Godefroy, Frédéric. 1881–1902. Dictionnaire de l'ancienne langue française et de tous ses dialectes. Paris. 10 vols.

Göbl-Gáldi László. 1933. Problemi di sostrato nel creolo francese. RLiR 9.336–345.

——. 1934. Esquisse de la structure grammaticale des patois français-créoles. ZFSL 58.257–295.

Goidànich, Pier Gabriele. 1929. L'Àscoli e i Neogrammatici. L'Àscoli e lo Schuchardt. Silloge Àscoli 611–626.

Goldschmidt, M. 1902. Germanisches Kriegswesen im Spiegel des romanischen Lehnwortes. Beiträge Förster 49–70.

Gonçalves Viana, Aniceto dos Reis. 1883. Essai de phonétique et de phonologie de la langue portugaise d'après le dialecte actuel de Lisbonne. Rom. 12.29–98. (Reprinted in BF-Lisb. 7.161–243 [1941].)

Gonon, Marguerite. 1947. Lexique du parler de Poncins. Paris.

González, Euclides Jaime. 1964. Contribución al vocabulario de colombianismos. Cúcuta (Colombia).

González de la Calle, Pedro Urbano. 1963. Contribución al estudio del bogotano. Orientaciones metodológicas para la investigación del castellano en América. Bogotá (Colombia). (PICC-SMin. no. 9.)

González Ollé, Fernando. 1953. El habla de Quintanillabón. RDyTP 9.3–65.

——. 1964. El habla de la Bureba: introducción al castellano actual de Burgos. Madrid. (RFE Anejo no. 78.)

Goodman, Morris F. 1958. On the phonetics of the French Creole of Trinidad. Word 14.208–212.

——. 1964. A comparative study of French creole dialects. The Hague. (JL-SP no. 4.)

Gorra, Egidio. 1890. Fonetica del dialetto di Piacenza. ZRPh. 14.133–158.

Gosse, Edmund. 1920. Malherbe and the classical reaction in the seventeenth century. Oxford (England).

Gougenheim, Georges. 1933. Éléments de phonologie française. Strasbourg.

——. 1939. Système grammatical de la langue française. Paris.

——. 1951. Grammaire de la langue française du seizième siècle. Lyon.

Grammont, Maurice. 1892–1900. Le patois de la Franche-Montagne et en particulier de Damprichard (Franche-Comté). MSL 7.461–477 (1892); 8.52–90, 316–347 (1892/93); 10.167–206, 290–323 (1897/98); 11.52–72, 130–144, 198–216, 285–296, 362–368, 402–436 (1899/1900). Also sep., Paris, 1901.

——. 1895. La dissimilation consonantique dans les langues indo-européennes et dans les langues romanes. Dijon.

——. 1938. Traité pratique de prononciation française.

Granada, Daniel. 1889. Vocabulario rioplatense. Montevideo. (3rd ed.: Vocabulario rioplatense razonado, Montevideo, 1957.)

Grand, Camille. 1930. *Tu, voi. Lei*: étude des pronoms allocutoires en italien. Ingenbohl.

Grandgagnage, Charles. 1845–50. Dictionnaire étymologique de la langue wallonne. Liège.

Grandgent, Charles Hall. 1905. An outline of the phonology and morphology of Vulgar Latin. Boston.

———. 1907. An introduction to Vulgar Latin. Boston. (Spanish tr.: Introducción al latín vulgar, Madrid, 1928.)

———. 1927. From Latin to Italian. Cambridge, Massachusetts.

Grant, Michael. 1954. Roman literature. Cambridge (England).

Grassi, Giuseppe. 1925. Il dialetto di Martina Franca. Martina Franca.

Graur, Alexandru. 1965. La romanité du roumain. Bucarest. (English tr.: The Romance character of Roumanian, Bucharest, 1967.)

———. 1968. Tendințele actuale ale limbii române. București.

Grayson, Cecil. 1960. A Renaissance controversy: Latin or Italian? Oxford (England).

———. 1964. Leon Battista Alberti: la prima grammatica della lingua volgare. Bologna.

———. 1965. "Nobilior est vulgaris." Centenary Essays on Dante 54–76.

Greet, Anne H. 1968. Jacques Prévert's word games. Berkeley and Los Angeles.

Greimas, Algirdas Julien. 1969. Dictionnaire de l'ancien français jusqu'au milieu du XIVe siècle. Paris.

Griera i Gaja, Antoni. 1914. La frontera catalano-aragonesa. Estudi geografico-lingüístic. Barcelona.

———. 1922. Afro-romànic o ibero-romànic? BDC 10.34–53.

———. 1923–68. Atlas lingüístic de Catalunya (ALC). Barcelona (later Abadia de Sant Cugat del Vallés).

———. 1925. Castellà—Català—Provençal. ZRPh. 45.198–254.

———. 1931. Gramàtica històrica del català antic. Barcelona.

———. 1935–47. Tresor de la llengua, de les tradicions i de la cultura popular de Catalunya. Barcelona.

———. 1947. Bibliografía lingüística catalana. Barcelona.

———. 1949. Dialectología catalana. Barcelona.

———. 1958. Atlas lingüístic d'Andorra. Andorra.

———. 1965. Gramática histórica catalana. Abadía de San Cugat del Vallés.

Grisch, Mena. 1939. Die Mundart von Surmeir (Ober- und Unterhalbstein). Beitrag zur Kenntnis einer rätoromanischen Sprachlandschaft. Zürich. (RH no. 12.)

Gröber, Gustav. 1884–90. Vulgärlateinische Substrate romanischer Wörter. ALLG 1.204–254, 539–557 (1884); 2.100–107, 276–288, 424–443 (1885); 3.138–143, 264–275, 506–531 (1886); 4.116–136, 422–454 (1887); 5.125–132. 234–242, 453–486 (1888); 6.117–149, 377–397 (1889); 7.25–64 (1890). (Never reprinted separately.)

——— (ed.). 1886–88. Grundriss der romanischen Philologie. Strassburg. (2nd ed., 1904–06.)

Groff, Lionello. 1955. Il dialetto Trentino. Trento.

Gröhler, Hermann. 1913–33. Über Ursprung und Bedeutung der französischen Ortsnamen. Heidelberg.

Grossmann, Rudolf. 1926. Das Ausländische Sprachgut im Spanischen des Rio de la Plata. Ein Beispiel zum Problem der argentinischen Nationalsprache. Hamburg.

Groult, Pierre. 1947. La formation des langues romanes. Tournai-Paris.

Guarnerio, Pier Enea. 1886.   Il dialetto catalano di Alghero. AGI 9.261–364.
———. 1892–98.   I dialetti odierni di Sassari, della Gallura e della Corsica. AGI 13.125–140 (1892); 14.131–200 (1897); 14.385–422 (1898).
———. 1905.   Il sardo e il corso in una nuova classificazione delle lingue romanze. AGI 16.491–516.
Guarnieri, Juan Carlos. 1969.   El lenguaje popular que hablamos: páginas sobre sus orígines y su historia. Montevideo.
Gudschinsky, Sarah Caroline. 1953.   Handbook of literacy. Norman, Oklahoma.
Guerlin de Guer, Charles. 1901.   Le parler populaire dans la commune de Thaon (Calvados) (phonétique—morphologie—syntaxe), suivi d'un lexique alphabétique de tous les mots étudiés. Paris. (BÉHÉ no. 136.)
———. 1903.   Atlas dialectologique de la Normandie. Paris.
———. 1945.   Introduction à l'Atlas Linguistique de la Normandie, du Maine et du Perche. FM 13.19–68, 249–269.
Guicharnaud, Jacques. 1965.   Raymond Queneau. New York.
Guilbert, Louis. 1965.   La formation du vocabulaire de l'aviation. Paris.
———. 1967.   Le vocabulaire de l'astronautique. Paris.
Guillaume, Gaston. 1927.   Contribution à l'étude du glossaire périgourdin (canton de Saint-Pierre-de-Chignac), précédée d'un essai de délimitation phonétique des parlers de la Dordogne. Paris.
Guimarães Daupiás, Jorge. 1925/27.   Ensaio dialectológico. RLus. 26.186–210.
Guiraud, Pierre. 1963.   La syntaxe du français. Paris.
———. 1965.   Le français populaire. Paris.
Guitarte, G. L. 1958.   Cuervo, Henríquez Ureña y la polémica sobre el andalucismo de América. VR 17.363–416.
Guiter, Henri. 1943.   Étude de linguistique historique du dialecte minorquin. Montpellier.
———. 1966.   Atlas linguistique des Pyrénées orientales. Paris.
Güterbock, B. 1882.   Bemerkungen über die lateinischen Lehnwörter im Irischen. Leipzig.
Guţu-Romalo, Valeria. 1968.   Morfologia structurală a limbii române. Substantiv, adjectiv, verb. Bucureşti.
Gysling, Fritz. 1929.   Contributo alla conoscenza del dialetto della Valle Anzasca. AR 13.87–190, with 1 map and 5 plates.

Haadsma, R. A., and J. Nuchelmans. 1963.   Précis de latin vulgaire, suivi d'une anthologie annotée. Groningen.
Haag, Karl. 1930.   Die Sprachlandschaften Oberitaliens. GRM 18.458–478.
Haarmann, Harald. 1970.   Der lateinische Lehnwortscharz im Kymrischen. Bonn. (RVV no. 36.)
Haas, Otto. 1960a.   Das frühitalische Element. Versuch über die Sprache der ersten Indogermanen Italiens. Wien.
———. 1960b.   Die phrygische Sprache im Lichte der Glossen und Namen. LB 2.25–68, with 1 map.
———. 1962.   Messapische Studien: Inschriften mit Kommentar, Skizze einer Lautlehre. Heidelberg.
———. 1964.   Das Phrygische und die Sprachen der Balkanländer. Die Kultur Südosteuropas 76–89.
Hadlich, Roger L. 1965.   The phonological history of Vegliote. Chapel Hill, N.C. (UNCSRLL no. 52.)
———. 1970.   Spanish transformational grammar. Honolulu.

Haefelin, Franz. 1873. Abhandlungen über die romanischen Mundarten der Süd-westschweiz. Erste Abtheilung: Die Mundarten des Cantons Neuenburg. KZ 21. (= NF.1.) 289–340, 481–541.

———. 1879. Les patois romans du canton de Fribourg: grammaire, choix de poésies populaires, glossaire. Leipzig.

Haensch, Günther. 1960. Las hablas de la Alta Ribagorza (Pirineo aragonés). ArFA 10/11.57–193; 12/13.117–250. Also sep., Zaragoza, 1960.

Hagedorn, Maria. 1939. Die Stellung des Katalanischen auf der iberischen Halbinsel. ZNU 38.209–217.

Hahn, Ludwig. 1907. Zum Sprachenkampf im römischen Reich bis auf die Zeit Justinians. Psb. 10.675–718.

Haillant, Nicholas. 1886. Essai sir un patois vosgien (Uriménil), dictionnaire phonétique et étymologique. Épinal.

Hall, Pauline Cook. 1957. A bibliography of Spanish linguistics. Articles in serial publications. Baltimore. (Language Dissertation no. 54.)

Hall, Robert A., Jr. 1942a. The Italian Questione della Lingua: an interpretative essay. Chapel Hill, N.C. (UNCSRLL no. 4.)

———. 1942b. Review of Jaberg and Jud 1928–40. Language 18.282–287.

———. 1942c. Bibliography of Sardinian linguistics. Italica 19.133–157.

———. 1946a. Bàrtoli's "Neolinguistica." Language 22.273–283.

———. 1946b. Italian guglia, giorno and the Neo-Grammarians. RR 37.244–246.

———. 1947a. Proto-Romance baró-ne strong man. SiL 5.65–68.

———. 1947b. A note on Taos k'owena horse. IJAL 13.117–118.

———. 1948. Structural Sketch no. 1: French. Baltimore. (Language Monograph no. 24.)

———. 1949a. The linguistic position of Franco-Provençal. Language 25.1–14.

———. 1949b. A note on "gorgia toscana." Italica 26.64–69.

———. 1950a. The reconstruction of Proto-Romance. Language 26.6–27. (Reprinted in Joos [ed.] 1957:303–314.)

———. 1950b. Nasal + homorganic plosive in Central and South Italian. ArL 1.151–156, with 1 map.

———. 1950c. The genetic relationships of Haitian Creole. RLing. 1.194–203.

———. 1951. A short history of Italian literature. Ithaca, N.Y.

———. 1952. Terminologia linguistica: pro-complementi. LN 13.22–24.

———. 1953. The oaths of Strassburg: phonemics and classification. Language 29.317–321.

———. 1956. Ancora del sintagma cognome + prenome. LN 17.27.

———. 1957. Review of Jourdain 1956a, 1956b. Language 33.226–231.

———. 1958a. Bibliografia della linguistica italiana. Firenze. 3 vols.

———. 1958b. Toccadiglio e toccatiglia. LN 19.18.

———. 1960a. Developments in modern Italian. MLJ 44.339–343.

———. 1960b. Thornstein Veblen and linguistic theory. AS 35.124–130.

———. 1960c. Hapax legomena seicenteschi. LN 21.90.

———. 1961. Standard Italian and dialect in Gadda's "Pasticciaccio." A William Cameron Townsend 449–454.

———. 1961/62. Latin -s (-ēs, -ās, -ōs) in Italian. RPh. 15.234–244.

———. 1962a. Review of Scheuermeir 1943, 1956, and of Jaberg and Jud, 1960. Language 38.76–79.

———. 1962b. The determination of form-classes in Haitian Creole. ZRPh. 78–172–177.

———. 1962c. The etymology of Italian casamatta. Language 38.270–273.

————. 1962d.   Meditation on a Baroque theme. MLJ 46.3–8.

————. 1962/63.   Review of d'Aronco (ed.) 1960. RPh. 16.235–237.

————. 1963.   Idealism in Romance linguistics. Ithaca, N.Y.

————. 1964.   Introductory linguistics. Philadelphia, Penna.

————. 1964/65.   Notice of Piron (ed.) 1961. RPh. 18.511–512.

————. 1965.   Pidgin and creole languages. Ithaca, N.Y.

————. 1965/66a.   Old Spanish stress-timed verse and Germanic superstratum. RPh. 19.227–234.

————. 1965/66b.   Graphie und Phonologie in den Strassburger Eiden. ASNS 202.437–439.

————. 1966/67.   Review of Nyrop 1902 (1963[8]). RPh. 20.96–98.

————. 1967a.   Review of Hadlich 1965. Language 43.564–566.

————. 1967b.   Antonio Fogazzaro e la crisi dell'Italia moderna. Firenze.

————. 1968a.   Language standard et dialectes en Italie. RTSS 13.49–53 (with discussion 54–62).

————. 1968b.   An essay on language. Philadelphia, Penna.

————. 1969a.   Bibliografia della linguistica italiana: primo supplemento decennale (1956–1966). Firenze.

————. 1969b.   Some recent developments in American linguistics. NM 70.192–227.

————. 1969c.   Some recent studies on Port-Royal and Vaugelas. AcLHa. 12.207–233.

————. 1969d.   Review of Malkiel 1968. GL 9.185–195.

————. 1971.   La struttura dell'italiano. Roma.

————. Forthcoming-a.   It. *baro, barone* e parole affini—poligenesi o monogenesi? To appear in Parlangèli Memorial Volume.

————. Forthcoming-b.   Pidgins and creoles as standard languages. To appear in J. Pride and J. Holmes (eds.); Readings in sociolinguistics.

————. Forthcoming-c.   La struttura della musica e del linguaggio. To appear in NRMI.

————. Forthcoming-d.   Why a structural semantics is impossible. To appear in LSc.

————, S. Comhaire-Sylvain, H. O. McConnell, and A. Métraux. 1953.   Haitian Creole: grammar, texts, vocabulary. American Anthropological Association (Memoir no. 74; also issued as American Folklore Society Memoir no. 43.)

Hamlin, Frank R., Peter T. Ricketts, and John Hathaway. 1967.   Introduction à l'étude de l'ancien provençal. Genève. (SPRF no. 96.)

Hammer, Martin. 1894.   Die lokale Verbreitung frühester romanischer Lautwandel im alten Italien. Halle/S.

Hampejs, Zdeněk. 1961.   Para o estudo da linguagem da imprensa brasileira contemporânea. RBF 6:1.51–114.

Harmer, L. C. 1954.   The French language today: its characteristics and tendencies. London.

————. 1965.   The present state of French. FMLS 1.250–265, 376–390.

Harris, James W. 1969.   Spanish phonology. Cambridge, Massachusetts.

Hartmann, Gottfried. 1907.   Zur Geschichte der italienischen Orthographie. RF 20.199–283.

Hasselrot, Bengt. 1937.   Étude sur les dialectes d'Ollon et du district d'Aigle (Vaud). Uppsala.

Hatzfeld, Adolphe, Arsène Darmesteter, and Antoine Thomas. 1888.   Dictionnaire général de la langue française depuis le commencement du XVIIe siècle jusqu'à nos jours. Paris.

Haudricourt, André, and Alphonse Juilland. 1949.   Essai pour une histoire structurale du phonétisme français. Paris.

Haust, Jean. 1927. Le dialecte wallon de Liège. Liège.

———. 1929–33. Dictionnaire liégeois. Liège.

———. 1948. Dictionnaire français-liégeois. Liège.

Hauvette, Henri. 1906. Littérature italienne. Paris.

Heger, Klaus. 1960. Die bisher veröffentlichten ḫarǧas und ihre Deutung. Tübingen. (ZRPh. Bhft. no. 101.)

Heilmann, Luigi. 1955. La parlata di Moena nei suoi rapporti con Fiemme e con Fassa. Saggio fonetico e fonematico. Bologna.

———. 1961. Strutturalismo e storia nel dominio linguistico italiano: il vocalismo di una parlata tipica pavese. QIGUB 6.45–58.

Heinimann, Siegfried. 1948. Tendenze recenti nell'evoluzione delle lingua italiana e francese. LN 9.49–53.

Henderson, William Otto. 1961. The industrial revolution in Europe, 1815–1914. Chicago.

Henríquez Ureña, Pedro. 1921–31. Observaciones sobre el español en Méjico. RFE 8.357–390 (1921); 17.277–284 (1930); 18.120–148 (1931).

———. 1925. El supuesto andalucismo de América. CIF 1.117–122.

———. 1932. Sobre el problema del andalucismo dialectal de América. Buenos Aires and Madrid.

———. 1938a. Para la historia de los indigenismos. Buenos Aires.

———. 1938b. Datos sobre el habla popular en Méjico. BDH 5.277–324.

———. 1940. El español en Santo Domingo. Buenos Aires. (= BDH 5.)

Hering, Werner. 1936. Die Mundart von Bozel (Savoyen). Leipzig and Paris. (LRSt. I:14.)

Herman József. 1965. Aspects de la différenciation territoriale du latin sous l'Empire. BSL 60:1.53–70.

Hermant, Abel. 1932. Grammaire de l'Académie Française. Paris.

Herrero Mayor, Avelino. 1943. Presente y futuro de la lengua española en América. Buenos Aires.

Herzog, Eugen. 1900. Materialien zu einer neuprovenzalischen Syntax. Wien.

———. 1906. Neufranzösische Dialekttexte, mit grammatischer Einleitung und Wörterverzeichnis. Leipzig. (2nd ed., 1914.)

———. 1913. Historische Sprachlehre des Neufranzösischen. Heidelberg.

Hesseling, Dirk C. 1933. Papiamento en Negerhollands. TNTL 52.265–288.

Hill, Raymond T., and Thomas G. Bergin. 1942. Anthology of the Provençal Troubadours. New Haven, Connecticut.

Hills, Elijah Clarence. 1906. New-Mexican Spanish. PMLA 21.706–753. (Spanish tr., El español de Nuevo Méjico, BDH 5.1–73 [1938].)

Hilty, Gerold. 1966. Die Romanisierungen in den Strassburger Eiden. VR 25.227–235.

———. 1968. Westfränkische Superstrateinflüsse auf die galloromanische Syntax. Festschrift W. von Wartburg 493–517.

Hirsch, Ernst. 1963. Beiträge zur Sprachgeschichte der württembergischen Waldenser. Stuttgart.

Hirsch, L. 1885–86. Laut- und Formenlehre des Dialekts von Siena. ZRPh. 9.512–570 (1885); 10.56–70, 411–446 (1886).

Hirt, Hermann. 1905–07. Die Indogermanen: ihre Verbreitung, ihre Urheimat, und ihre Kultur. Strassburg.

———. 1921–37. Indogermanische Grammatik. Heidelberg.

Hockett, Charles Francis. 1948. Implications of Bloomfield's Algonquian studies. Language 24.117–131.

——. 1958. A course in modern linguistics. New York.

——. 1968. The state of the art. The Hague. (JL-SMin. no. 73.)

Hodgkin, Thomas. 1880–99. Italy and her invaders. Oxford (England). 7 vols. (2nd ed., 1892–1916, 8 vols.)

Höfler, Manfred. 1968. Ein spanisches Lehnsuffix im Französischen des 18. Jahrhunderts. ZRPh. 84.582–585.

Hofmann, Gustav. 1885. Die logudoresische und campidanesische Mundart. Marburg.

Holland, Louise Adams. 1961. Janus and the bridge. Rome.

Holmes, Urban Tigner, Jr. 1928. The Vulgar Latin question and the origin of the Romance tongues: notes for a chapter of the history of Romance philology prior to 1849. StP 25.51–61.

——. 1931. Germanic influence on Old French syntax. Language 7.194–199.

——. 1938. A history of Old French literature, from the origins to 1300. New York.

——, and Alexander H. Schutz. 1935. A history of the French language. Columbus, Ohio.

Holthausen, Ferdinand. 1929. Gotische Wörter im Romanischen. Behrens-Festschrift 106–109.

Homo, Léon. 1925. L'empire romain. Paris.

——. 1927. Primitive Italy and the beginnings of Roman imperialism. London. (Reprinted, New York, 1968.)

Honsa, Vladimir. 1965. La extensión de la influencia francesa sobre la estructura del castellano medieval. AEM 2.497–504.

Hope, Thomas E. 1971. Lexical borrowing in the Romance languages. New York. 2 vols.

Horluc, Pierre, and Georges Marinet. 1908. Bibliographie de la syntaxe du français. Lyon-Paris.

Horning, Adolf. 1916. Glossare der romanischen Mundarten von Zell (La Baroche) und Schönenberg im Breuschtal (Belmont) in den Vogesen. Halle/S. (ZRPh. Bhft. no. 65.)

Horth, Auguste. 1949. Le patois guyanais. Cayenne.

Houaiss, Antonio. 1959. Tentativa de descrição do sistema vocálico do português culto na área dita carioca. Rio de Janeiro.

Huber, Joseph. 1960. Verhältnis der Mundart von Livigno zu den Mundarten der näheren und ferneren Umgebung. VR 19.1–81, with 2 maps.

Hubschmid, Johannes. 1938. Sprachliche Zeugen für da späte Aussterben des Gallischen. VR 3.48–155.

——. 1949. Praeromanica. Zürich. (RH no. 10.)

——. 1951. Alpenwörter romanischen und vorromanischen Ursprungs. Bern.

——. 1963. Thesaurus praeromanicus. Bern.

——. 1964. Substrate in den Balkansprachen. Die Kultur Südosteuropas 90–102.

Hyppolite, Michelson. 1950. Les origines des variations du Créole haïtien. Port-au-Prince.

Ibáñez, Estéban. 1961. Supervivencia de voces latinas en el dialecto bereber del Rif. Orbis 10.447–455.

Iliescu, Maria. 1964. Zu den in Rumänien gesprochenen friaulischen Dialekten. RRL 9.67–78.

——. 1968. Graiurile friulanilor din România. StCL 19.375–415, with 1 map.

Ilsley, Marjorie Henry. 1963. A daughter of the Renaissance: Marie le Jars de Gournay—her life and works. The Hague.

Inguanez, Mauro. 1942. Documenti cassinesi dei secoli XI–XIII con volgate. Montecassino.

Iordan, Iorgu. 1932. Întroducere în studiul limbilor romanice. Evoluția si starea actuală a lingvisticii romanice. Iași. (2nd ed.: Lingvistica romanică: evoluție, curente, metode, București, 1962. English tr. [by J. Orr]: An introduction to Romance linguistics, its schools and scholars, London, 1937. 2nd ed. of Eng. tr., 1970 [with supplement by R. Posner, "Thirty Years On"]. German tr. of 2nd ed.: Einführung in die Geschichte und Methoden der romanischen Sprachwissenschaft, Berlin, 1962.)

———. 1964. Romîna și spaniola, arii laterale ale latinității. StCL 15.7–14. (French tr.: Le roumain et l'espagnol, aires latérales de la latinité, RRL 9.5–14 [1964].)

———, Valeria Guțu-Romalo, and Alexandru Niculescu. 1967. Structura morfologică a limbii române contemporane. București.

Iorga, Nicolae. 1919. Istoria literaturilor romanice în dezvoltarea și legăturile lor. București. 3 vols. (2nd ed., 1968.)

Iribarren, José María. 1952. Vocabulario navarro. Pamplona.

Ive, Antonio. 1886. L'antico dialetto di Veglia. AGI 9.115–187.

Ivić, Milka. 1965. Trends in linguistics. The Hague. (JL-SMin. no. 42.)

Izzo, Herbert. 1972. Tuscan and Etruscan: the problem of substratum influence in central Italy. Toronto.

Jaberg, Karl. 1926. Una pera mezza. Festschrift Gauchat 52–67.

———. 1936. Aspects géographiques du langage. Paris.

———, and Jakob Jud. 1928. Der Sprachatlas als Forchungsinstrument. Kritische Grundlegung und Einführung in den Sprach- und Sachatlas Italiens und der Südschweiz. Halle/S.

——— and ———. 1928–40. Atlante linguistico-etnografico dell'Italia e della Svizzera meridionale (Sprach- und Sachatlas Italiens und der Südschweiz). Zofingen.

——— and ———. 1960. AIS Index. Bern.

James, Herman, and Julio Ricci. 1967. The influence of locally spoken Italian dialects on River Plate Spanish. FoI 1.48–59.

Jannaccone, S. 1950. Recherches sur les éléments grecs du vocabulaire latin. Paris.

Jauss, Hans Robert, and Erich Köhler (eds.). 1968– . Grundriss der romanischen Literaturen des Mittelalters. Heidelberg.

Jeanroy, Alfred. 1934. La poésie lyrique des troubadours. Toulouse and Paris. 2 vols.

———. 1945. Histoire sommaire de la poésie occitane des origines à la fin du XVIIIᵉ siècle. Toulouse.

Jespersen, Otto. 1922. Language. London.

Jireček, Josef Konstantin. 1901–03. Die Romanen in den Städten Dalmatiens während des Mittelalters. Wien. (DsWien 48:3; 49.1, 2.)

Joda, Lydia Y. G. 1967. A linguagem da imprensa: observações sôbre o léxico da linguagem do fútebol. Alfa 12.227–240.

Jokl, Norbert. 1936. Zu den lateinischen Elementen des albanischen Wortschatzes. Glotta 25.121–134.

———. 1941/42. Albanologische Beiträge zur Kenntnis des Balkanlateins. VR 6.207–232.

Jones, Arthur Hugh Martin. 1964. The later Roman Empire. Oxford (England).

————. 1966.   The decline of the ancient world. London.

Joos, Martin (ed.).   1957.   Readings in linguistics. Washington, D.C.

————. 1960.   Review of A. Wijk: Regularized English. Language 36.250–262.

Joret, Charles, 1913.   Les noms de lieu d'origine non romane et la colonisation germanique et scandinave en Normandie. Rouen.

Jourdain, Élodie.   1956a.   Du français aux parlers créoles. Paris.

————. 1956b.   Le vocabulaire du parler créole de la Martinique. Paris.

Jucá, Cándido.   1939.   A pronúncia brasileira. Rio de Janeiro.

Jud, Jakob.   1907.   Recherches sur la genèse et la diffusion des accusatifs en -*ain* et en -*on*. Halle/S,

————. 1937.   Zum burgundischen Wortgut des Franko-provenzalischen. VR 2.1–23.

————. 1946.   Zur Geschichte der romanischen Reliktwörter in den Alpenmundarten der deutschen Schweiz. VR 8.34–109.

————. 1948.   Altfrz. *estuet*, bündnerrom. *stuver*, *stuvair*. VR 10.29–56.

Jünger, Ernst.   1956.   Rivarol. Frankfurt/M.

Juilland, Alphonse G., and E. Chang-Rodríguez.   1964.   Frequency dictionary of Spanish words. The Hague.

————, P. M. H. Edwards, and Ileana Juilland.   1965.   Frequency dictionary of Rumanian words. The Hague.

Jungandreas, Wolfgang.   1967.   Die Entdeckung des Moselromanischen. LBijdr. 56.154–158.

Jungemann, Fredrick Henry.   1955.   La teoría del sustrato y los dialectos hispano-romances y gascones. Madrid. (BRH no. 7.)

Juret, Étienne Abel.   1913.   Glossaire du patois de Pierrecourt (Haute-Saône). Halle/S.

Kahane, Henry Romanos.   1941.   Designations of the cheek in Italian dialects. Language 17.212–222.

————, Renée Toole Kahane, and Andreas Tietze.   1958.   The Lingua Franca in the Levant. Turkish nautical terms of Italian and Greek origin. Urbana, Illinois.

Kalbow, Werner.   1913.   Die germanischen Personennamen des altfranzösischen Heldenepos und ihre lautliche Entwicklung. Halle/S.

Kany, Charles E.   1945.   American-Spanish syntax. Chicago. (2nd ed., 1951.)

————. 1960.   American-spanish semantics. Berkeley and Los Angeles.

Keating, L. Clark.   1971/72.   Promise and performance: Du Bellay's *Deffence et illustration de la langue françoyse*. FR 45.77–85.

Keller, Oskar.   1919.   Der Genfer Dialekt, dargestellt auf Grund der Mundart von Certoux. Zürich.

Kent, Roland Grubb.   1932.   The sounds of Latin. Baltimore. (3rd ed., 1945.)

Kiddle, Lawrence Bayard.   1952a.   The Spanish language as a medium of cultural diffusion in the Age of Discovery. AS 27.241–256.

————. 1952b.   Spanish loanwords in American Indian languages. Hispania 35.179–184.

King, Robert D.   1969.   Historical linguistics and generative grammar. Englewood Cliffs, N. J.

Kiparsky, Paul.   1970.   Historical linguistics. In Lyons (ed.) 1970:302–315.

Kjellén, Oskar.   1945.   Le patois de la région de Nozeroy (Jura). Paris.

Klein, Hans-Wilhelm.   1957.   Latein und Volgare in Italien. München. (MRA no. 12.)

————. 1958.   Zur Latinität des Itinerarium Egeriae (früher Peregrinatio Aetheriae). Romanica (Rohlfs) 243–258.

————. 1965.   Der romanische Anteil an den Reichenauer Glossen. ZRPh. 81.217–249.

———— and André Labhardt. 1968. Die Reichenauer Glossen. München. (BRPhM no. 1.)

Klemperer, Victor. 1914. Italienische Elemente im französischen Wortscharz zur Zeit der Renaissance. GRM 6.664–677.

Knowlton, Edgar C., Jr. 1969/70. Copia 'couple', a thwarted 17th-century Italianism in Portuguese. RPh. 23.54–55.

Königes Celta. 1933. Veglia mai olasz nyelvjárása. Budapest.

Körting, Gustav. 1884–88. Encyklopädie und Methodologie der romanischen Philologie mit besonderer Berücksichtigung des Französischen. Heilbronn. (2nd ed.: Handbuch der romanischen Philologie, Leipzig, 1896.)

————. 1890/91. Lateinisch-romanisches Wörterbuch. Paderborn.

Kohlmann, G. 1901. Die italienischen Lehnworte in der neufranzösischen Schriftsprache (seit dem XVI. Jahrhundert). Vegesack.

Koschwitz, Eduard. 1893. Les parlers parisiens [. . .]: anthologie phonétique. Paris. (Later eds., Marburg.)

————. 1894. Grammaire historique de la langue des Félibres. Greifswald.

Kosovitz, Em. 1889. Dizionario vocabolario del dialetto triestino e della lingua italiana. Trieste.

Kovačec, August. 1968. Les Séphardim en Yougoslavie et leur langue (d'après quelques publications yougoslaves). SRAZ 25/26.161–177.

Křepinský, Maximilian. 1938/39. Influence slave sur le verbe roumain. Slavia 16.1–49, 220–268, 481–534. (Also sep., Prague, 1941.)

————. 1952. L'élément slave dans le lexique roman. Mél. Roques 4.153–162.

Kristeller, Paul Oskar. 1946. The origin and development of the language of Italian prose. Word 2.50–65. (Reprinted in Kristeller 1956:473–493. Italian tr.: L'origine e lo sviluppo della prosa volgare italiana, CN 10.137–156 [1950].)

————. 1956. Studies in Renaissance thought and letters. Rome.

Krotkoff, George. 1963/64. A possible Arabic ingredient in the history of Spanish usted. RPh. 17.328–332.

Krüger, Fritz. 1914. Studien zur Lautgeschichte westspanischer Mundarten. Hamburg. (JbHWA 31., 7. Bhft.)

————. 1923. El dialecto de San Ciprián de Sanabria (Zamora). Madrid. (RFE Anejo no. 4.)

————. 1925a. Die Gegenstandskultur Sanabrias und seiner Nachbargebiete. Hamburg.

————. 1925b. Mezcla de dialectos. Homenaje a Menéndez Pidal 2.121–166, with 1 map.

————. 1927. Die nordwestiberische Volkskultur. WS 10.45–137. (Spanish tr.: El léxico rural del Noroeste ibérico, Madrid, 1947 [RFE Anejo no. 36].)

————. 1935–39. Die Hochpyrenäen. Hamburg. 6 vols.

————. 1936. Notas etnogràfico linguísticas da Póvoa de Varzim. BF-Lisb. 4.109–182.

Kuckuck, Edith. 1936. Die Mundarten von Saint-Martin-la-Porte und Lanslebourg im département Savoie, arrondissement Saint-Jean-de-Maurienne. Jena and Leipzig. (BBRPh. 5:3.)

Kuen, Heinrich. 1932–34. El dialecto de Alguer y su posición en la historia de la lengua catalana. AOR 5.121–178 (1932); 7.41–112 (1934).

————. 1950. Die sprachlichen Verhältnisse auf der Pyrenäenhalbinsel. ZRPh. 66.95–125.

————. 1968. Einheit und Mannigfaltigkeit des Rätoromanischen. Festschrift W. von Wartburg 1.47–69, with 3 maps.

Kuhn, Alwin. 1935. Studien zum Wortschatz von Hocharagon. ZRPh. 55.561–634.
———. 1935–39. Der hocharagonesische Dialekt. RLiR 11.1–312 (1935); ZRPh. 59.73–82 (1939).
———. 1955. Sintaxis dialectal del Alto Aragón. Misc. Griera 2.7–22.
Kukenheim, Louis. 1932. Contribution à l'histoire de la grammaire italienne, espagnole et française à l'époque de la Renaissance. Amsterdam.
———. 1962. Esquisse historique de la linguistique française et de ses rapports avec la linguistique générale. Leiden. (2nd ed., 1966.)
———. 1967– . Grammaire historique de la langue française. Leiden.

La Via, Mariano. 1899. Vocalismo del dialetto gallo-italico di Nicosia in Sicilia. StGl. 1.222–234.
———. 1902. Il consonantismo del dialetto gallo-italico di Nicosia in Sicilia. StGl. 2.115–128.
Labande-Jeanroy, Thérèse. 1925. La question de la langue en Italie. Strasbourg.
Lafont, Robert. 1967. La phrase occitane. Essai d'analyse systématique. Montpellier.
———. 1970. Renaissance du Sud. Essai sur la littérature occitane au temps de Henri IV. Paris.
Laguarda Trías, Rolando A. 1969. Afronegrismos rioplatenses. BRAE 49.27–116.
Lammens, Henri. 1890. Remarques sur les mots français dérivés de l'arabe. Beyrouth.
Lamouche, L. 1942. Grammaire languedocienne (dialectes de Montpellier et de Lodère). Montpellier.
Lane, George Sherman. 1935. Notes on Louisiana French. II. Negro-French dialect. Language 11.5–16.
Lanly, A. 1962. Le français d'Afrique du Nord. Étude linguistique. Paris.
Lanson, Gustave. 1894. Histoire de la littérature française. Paris.
Lapesa, Rafael. 1942. Historia de la lengua española. Madrid. (2nd ed., 1950.)
———. 1963. El Andaluz y el español de América. Presente y futuro 2.173–182.
Lardschneider-Ciampac, A. 1933. Wörterbuch der Grödner Mundart. Innsbruck.
Laronde, André. 1933. Choix d'inadvertances de la première édition de la Grammaire de l'Académie. Paris.
Latzarus, Louis. 1926. La vie paresseuse de Rivarol. Paris.
Lausberg, Heinrich. 1939. Die Mundarten Südlukaniens. Halle/S. (ZRPh. Bhft. no. 90.)
———. 1947. Vergleichende Characteristik der italienischen und der spanischen Schriftsprache. RF 60.106–122.
———. 1956–62. Romanische Sprachwissenschaft. Berlin. 4 vols. (Sammlung Göschen, nos. 128/128a, 250, 1199, 1200/1200a. 2nd ed., 1967– . Spanish tr.: Lingüística románica, Madrid, 1965– .)
Lăzărescu, Paul. 1967. În legatură cu raporturile dîntre limba standard și graiurile locale. StCL 18.187–201.
Le Bidois, Georges, and Robert Le Bidois. 1935–38. Syntaxe du français moderne. Paris. 2 vols.
Le Breton, André Victor. 1895. Rivarol: sa vie, ses idées, son talent d'après des documents nouveaux. Paris.
Le Maistre, Frank. 1966. Dictionnaire jersiais-français. Le parler normand à Jersey. Jersey, Channel Islands.
Legros, Élisée. 1948. La frontière des dialectes romans en Belgique. Liège.
Lehmann, Paul. 1929. Vom Leben des Lateinischen im Mittelalter. BBG 65.65–82. (Reprinted in P. Lehmann 1941:62–81.)

――――. 1941. Erforschung des Mittelalters. Leipzig.

Lehmann, Winfred Philipp. 1962. Historical lniguistics: an introduction. New York.

Leite de Vasconcelos, José. 1882. O dialecto mirandés. Porto.

――――. 1897–99. Dialectos crioulos portugueses de África (Contribuições para o estudo da dialectologia portuguesa). RLus. 5.241–261.

――――. 1900–01. Estudos de philologia mirandesa. Lisboa. 2 vols.

――――. 1901. Esquisse d'une dialectologie portugaise. Paris.

――――. 1911. Lições de filologia portuguêsa. Lisboa. (5th ed., Rio de Janeiro, 1959.)

――――. 1933. O Português dialectal da região de Xalma (Espanha). RLus. 28.87–244.

Lemos Ramírez, Gustavo R. 1920. Semántica o ensayo de lexicografía ecuatoriana. Guayaquil.

Lenz, Rodolfo. 1905–10. Diccionario etimológico de voces chilenas derivadas de lenguas indígenas americanas. Santiago de Chile.

――――. 1926–27. El papiamento, la lengua criolla de Curazao. La gramática más sencilla. AUCh. II.4.695–768, 1021–1030 (1926); II.5.287–327 (1927). Also sep., Santiago de Chile, 1928.

Lenzi, Mario. 1965. Dizionario di giornalismo. Milano.

Leonard, Clifford S., Jr. 1964. Proto-Rhaeto-Romance and French. Language 40.23–32.

Leonard, Sterling Andrus. 1929. The doctrine of correctness in English usage, 1700–1800. Madison, Wisconsin. (UWSLL no. 25.)

Leonard, William Ellery. 1928–31. La métrica del Cid. RABM 32.334–352 (1928); 34.16–40 (1930); 35.195–210, 302–328, 401–421 (1931). Also sep., Madrid, 1931.

――――. 1931. The recovery of the metre of the Cid. PMLA 46.289–306.

Leone, Alfonso. 1956. La sequenza cognome + nome. La Lucerna 11:6.25–27.

Leoni, Giulio Davide. 1963. Appunti per uno studio delle influenze del portoghese sui dialetti italiani a São Paulo del Brasile. Orbis 12.212–220.

Lepscky, Giulio C. 1962. Fonemantica veneziana. ID 25.1–22.

――――. 1963a. The segmental phonemes of Venetian and their classification. Word 19.53–66.

――――. 1963b. Morfologia veneziana. ID 26.129–144.

――――. 1964. Note sulla fonematica italiana. ID 27.53–67.

――――. 1966. I suoni dell'italiano: alcuni studî recenti. ID 29.49–69.

Lerch, Eugen. 1925–34. Historische Syntax der französischen Sprache. Leipzig. 3 vols.

――――. 1933. Französische Sprache und Wesensart. Frankfurt/M.

――――. 1947. Germanische Wörter im Vulgärlatein? (werra, marrire, bastire) RF 60.647–684.

Leroy, Maurice. 1963. Les grands courants de la linguistique moderne. Brussels. (2nd ed., 1971.)

Lespy, Vastin. 1858. Grammaire béarnaise. Pau. (2nd ed., Paris, 1880.)

Leumann, Manu. 1960. "Urromanisch" und "vulgärlateinisch." LPosn. 8.1–11.

Levi, Attilio. 1927. Dizionario etimologico del dialetto piemontese. Torino.

Levitt, Jesse. 1968. The Grammaire des grammaires of Girault-Duvivier, a study of nineteenth-century French. The Hague. (JL-SMin. no. 19.)

Levy, Denah. 1952. El sefardí esmirniano de Nueva York. México, D.F.

Levy, Emil. 1894–1924. Provenzalisches Supplementwörterbuch. Leipzig. 8 vols.

Lévy, Raphaël. 1932. Recherches lexicographiques sur d'anciens textes français d'origine juive. Baltimore.

――――. 1960. Contribution à la lexicographie française d'après d'anciens textes d'origine juive. Syracure, N.Y.

294   COMPARATIVE ROMANCE GRAMMAR

———. 1964.   Trésor de la langue des juifs français au moyen âge. Austin, Texas.
Lewicki, Tadeusz.   1951/52.   Une langue romane oubliée de l'Afrique du Nord. ROr. 17.415–480.
Lewis, H.   1943.   Yr elfen ladin yn yr iaith Gymraeg. Caerdydd.
Lhermet, J.   1931.   Contribution à l'étude du dialecte aurillacois. Paris.
Li Gotti, Maria V.   1968.   Bibliografia dialettale calabrese. BCDI 3.131–268.
Lindsström, A.   1907.   Il vernacolo di Subiaco. StR 5.237–300.
Littré, Émile.   1863–73.   Dictionnaire de la langue française. Paris. 4 vols. and supplement. (Many later eds.)
Livingston, Arthur A.   1918.   La Merica sanemagogna. RR 9.206–226.
Llorente Maldonado de Guevara, Antonio.   1947.   Estudio sobre el habla de La Ribera. Salamanca.
———. 1965.   Algunas características lingüísticas de la Rioja en el marco de las hablas del Valle del Ebro y de las comarcas vecinas de Castilla y Vasconia. RFE 48.321–350.
Locke, William Nash.   1949.   Pronunciation of the French spoken at Brunswick, Maine. Greensboro, N.C. (PADS no. 12.)
Löfstedt, Einar.   1911.   Philologischer Kommentar zur Peregrinatio Aetheriae. Uppsala.
———. 1959.   Late Latin. Oslo.
Löwe, Richard.   1906.   Altgermanische Elemente der Balkansprachen. KZ39. 263–334
Loewen, Jacob A.   1960.   Spanish loanwords in Waunana. IJAL 26.330–344.
Loiseau, Yvan.   1961.   Rivarol. Paris.
Lokotsch, Karl.   1926.   Etymologisches Wörterbuch der amerikanischen (indianischen) Wörter im deutschen, mit steter Berücksichtigung der englischen, spanischen und französischen Formen. Heidelberg.
———. 1927.   Etymologisches Wörterbuch der europäischen (germanischen, romanischen und slavischen) Wörter orientalischen Ursprungs. Heidelberg.
Lombard, Alf.   1936.   La prononciation du roumain. SSUF 1934/36.103–176. (UUÅ 1936.)
———. 1954–55.   Le verbe roumain: étude morphologique. Lund.
Lombardi, A., P. Bacci, F. Jacometti, and G. Mazzoni.   1944.   Raccolta di voci e modi di dire in uso nella città di Siena e nei suoi dintorni. Siena.
Lombardo, G.   1901.   Saggio sul dialetto nisseno. Caltanisetta.
Longa, Glicerio.   1912.   Vocabolario bormino. Roma. (= StR 9.1–350.)
Longo, Vincenzo.   1935–40.   Postille e correzioni al "Dizionario dialettale delle Tre Calabrie" di G. Rohlfs. ID 11.61–85 (1935); 16.9–30 (1940).
———. 1937.   Saggio fonetico sul dialetto di Cittanova in provincia di Reggio Calabria. ID 13.127–153, 173–206.
———. 1942–43.   Saggio di lessico dei dialetti dell'Amiata. ID 18.167–188 (1942); 19.51–84 (1943).
Lope Blanch, Juan M.   1968.   El español de América. Madrid. (English tr.: Hispanic dialectology. Current Trends in Linguistics 4.106–157 [1968].)
Lopes da Silva, Baltasar.   1957.   O dialecto crioulo de Cabo Verde. Lisboa.
Lopez, Davide.   1952.   La voce e le forme del dialetto barese. Bari.
López Barrera, Joaquín.   1912.   Estudios de semántica regional. Barbarismos y arcaísmos de la provincia de Cuenca. Cuenca.
López Estrada, Fr.   1952.   Introducción a la literatura medieval española. Madrid.
López Morales, Humberto.   1964.   El supuesto "africanismo" del español de Cuba. Archivum 14.202–211.
———. 1966.   Elementos africanos en el español de Cuba. BFE 6.27–43.

Lord, Albert Bates. 1960. The singer of tales. Cambridge, Massachusetts.

Lorenzo, Emilio. 1966. El español de hoy: lengua en ebullición. Madrid. (BRH II.89.)

Loth, J. 1892. Les mots latins dans les langues britanniques (gallois, armoricain, cornique). Paris.

Lovett, Gabriel. 1962. Notes on every-day Spanish, Madrid, 1962. Hispania 45.738–742.

Lozovan, Eugène. 1968. La Romania extrême-orientale. Festschrift W. von Wartburg 75–85.

Luchaire, A. 1879. Études sur les idiomes pyrénéens de la région française. Paris.

Lüdtke, Helmut. 1956a. Die strukturelle Entwicklung des romanischen Vokalismus. Bonn. (RVV no. 2.)

————. 1956b. Die soziologische Stellung der Mundart in Portugal und in Süditalien: ihre Bedeutung für die Sprachgeschichte. Orbis 5.123–130.

————. 1962/63. Zum Problem der Strassburger Eide. ASNS 199.391–393.

————. 1965. Le vie di comunicazione dell'impero romano e la formazione dei dialetti romanzi. ACILFR¹⁰ 1103–1109.

————. 1965/66. Nochmals zum Problem der Strassburger Eide. ASNS 202.436–437.

————. 1968. Geschichte des romanischen Wortschatzes. Freiburg i/Br. 2 vols.

Lüers, Margarete. 1942. Beiträge zur Syntax der toskanischen Umgangssprache. Hamburg.

Lugris Freire, M. 1922. Gramática do idioma galego. A Cruña.

Lugton, Robert C., and Milton G. Saltzer (eds.). 1970. Studies in honor of J. Alexander Kerns. The Hague—Paris. (JL-SMa. no. 44.)

Lupi, Gino. 1940. Lingua di giornalisti. LN 2.18–20.

————. 1955. Storia della letteratura romana. Firenze.

Luria, Max A. 1930. A study of the Monastir dialect of Judeo-Spanish based on oral material collected in Monastir, Yugo-Slavia. RHi. 89.323–584. Also sep.: New York, 1930.

Lutta, Martin. 1923. Der Dialekt von Bergün und seine Stellung innerhalb der rätoromanischen Mundarten Graubündens. Halle/S. (ZRPh. Bhft. no. 71.)

Luzzatto, Gino. 1958. Breve storia economica d'Italia. Torino.

Lyons, John (ed.). 1970. New horizons in linguistics. Harmondsworth (Middx., Eng.) and Baltimore.

Maas, Utz. 1969. Untersuchungen zur Phonologie und Phonetik der Mundart von Couzou (Dept. Lot). Freiburg i/Br.

Mabille de Poncheville, André. 1935. Valentin Conrart, le père de l'Académie Française. Paris.

Maccarrone, Nunzio. 1915. La vita del latino in Sicilia fino all'età normanna. Firenze.

Machado, José Pedro. 1952–59. Dicionário etimológico da língua portuguêsa. Lisboa. (2nd ed., 1967.)

————. 1958–61. Influência arábica no vocabolário português. Lisboa. 2 vols.

————. 1967. Origens do português. Lisboa.

Mack Smith, Denis. 1968. A history of Sicily. London. 2 vols.

Mackel, Emil. 1887. Die germanischen Elemente in der französischen und provenzalischen Sprache. Heilbronn.

Mackenzie, Fraser. 1939. Les relations de l'Angleterre et de la France, d'après le vocabulaire. Paris.

Macrea, Dimitriu (ed.). 1958. Dicționarul limbii romîne moderne. București.

————. 1969. Şcoala ardeleană şi probleme de lingvistică romanică. CL 14.7–13.

Màfera, Giovanni. 1958. Profilo fonetico-morfologico dei dialetti da Venezia a Belluno. ID 22.131–184.

Magaña, J. 1948. Contribución al estudio del vocabulario de la Rioja. RDyTP 4.266–303.

Maggini, Francesco. 1952. I primi volgarizzamenti dei classici latini. Firenze.

Maher, John Peter. 1971. Italian *mostaccio*. ZRPh. 87.320–333.

Mainoldi, P. 1950. Manuale dell'odierno dialetto bolognese: suoni e segni, grammatica, vocabolario. Bologna.

————. 1967. Vocabolario del dialetto bolognese. Bologna.

Malagòli, Giuseppe. 1910. Studî sui dialetti reggiani. Fonologia del dialetto di Novellara. AGI 17.29–197; 18.368–383.

————. 1918. Fonologia del dialetto di Novellara. Appendice: Saggio di testi dialettali. AGI 18.368–383.

————. 1930. Fonologia del dialetto di Lizzano in Belvedere (Appennino bolognese). ID 6.125–196.

————. 1939. Vocabolario pisano. Firenze.

————. 1940. Appunti di morfologia e di sintassi del dialetto di Lizzano in Belvedere. ID 16.191–211.

————. 1941. Lessico del dialetto di Lizzano in Belvedere. ID 17.195–228.

Malara, Giovanni. 1909. Vocabolario dialettale calabro-reggino-italiano. Reggio Calabria.

Malaret, Augusto. 1925. Diccionario de americanismos. Mayagüez, P.R. (2nd ed.: San Juan de P.R., 1931. 3rd ed.: Buenos Aires, 1942–44.)

————. 1937. Vocabulario de Puerto Rico. New York and San Juan de P.R. (2nd ed., 1955.)

————. 1948. Cambios del idioma. BAAL 17.161–207.

Malaspina, Carlo. 1856–59. Vocabolario parmigiano-italiano. Parma.

————. 1880. Aggiunte e correzioni inedite al vocabolario parmigiano-italiano. Parma.

Malato, Enrico. 1965. Vocabolarietto napolitano. Nàpoli.

Maldarelli, Donato. 1967. Lessico giovinazzese-italiano. Molfetta.

Malkiel, Yakov. 1945. Review of Oliver Asín 1938. Language 21.113–120.

————. 1948. On analyzing Hispano-Maya blends. IJAL 14.74–76.

————. 1948/49. Italian *ciarlatano* and its Romance off-shoots. RPh. 2.317–326.

————. 1949/50. Review of Vidal de Battini 1949. RPh. 3.191–201.

————. 1950a. Culture history through linguistics. Italica 27.330–343.

————. 1950b. The hypothetical base in Romance etymology. Word 6.42–73.

————. 1960. A tentative typology of Romance historical grammars. Lingua 9.321–416. (Reprinted in Malkiel 1968a:71–164.)

————. 1960/61. Necrology: Leo Spitzer. RPh. 14.362–364. (Reprinted in Sebeok [ed.] 1966:2.522–526.)

————. 1962/63. Necrology: Max Leopold Wagner. RPh. 16.281–289. (Reprinted in Sebeok [ed.] 1966:2.463–474.)

————. 1964. Some diachronic implications of fluid speech communities. AA NS.66.177–186. (Reprinted in Malkiel 1968a:19–31.)

————. 1968a. Essays on linguistic themes. Berkeley and Los Angeles.

————. 1968b. Hispanic philology. Current Trends in Linguistics 4.158–228.

Malmberg, Bertil. 1942/43. À propose du système phonologique de l'italien. AcLHa. 3.34–43.

————. 1947/48. L'espagnol dans le Nouveau Monde. StLing. 1.79–116; 2.1–36.

————. 1969. Phonétique française. Malmö.

Mancini, Francesco. 1960. Vocabolario del dialetto todino. StFI 18.319–377.

Mańczak, Witołd. 1962. Phonétique et morphologie historiques du français. Łódz-Warszawa.

Mangione, Jerre. 1943. Mount Allegro. New York.

Maranesi, Ernesto. 1892. Vocabolario modenese-italiano. Módena.

Marano Festa, Olga. 1928–33. Il dialetto irpino di Montella. ID 4.168–185 (1928); 5.95–128 (1929); 8.87–116 (1932); 9.172–202 (1933).

Marchetti, Giuseppe. 1952. Lineamenti di grammatica friulana. Ûdine.

Marchot, Paul. 1892. Phonologie détaillée d'un patois wallon: contribution à l'étude du wallon moderne. Paris.

————. 1895. Les gloses de Cassel. Le plus ancien texte rétl-roman. Fribourg.

Marcus, Simon. 1962. A-t-il existé en Espagne un dialecte judéo-espagnol? Sefarad 22.129–149.

Marden, Charles Carroll. 1896. The phonology of the Spanish dialect of Mexico City. PMLA 11.85–150. (Spanish tr.: La fonología del español en la ciudad de Méjico, BDH 4.87–187 [1938].)

Marinelli, Arturo. 1925. *Marrano* (storia d'un vituperio). Genève. (BAR II.10.)

Maroncini, C. 1910. L'Accademia della Crusca dalle origini alla prima edizione de Vocabolario. Pisa.

Marroquim, Mário. 1934. A língua do Nordeste (Alagôas e Pernambuco). São Paulo. (2nd ed., 1945.)

Marstrander, Carl. 1929. De l'unité italo-celtique. NTS 3.241–259.

Martin, J.-B., and G. Tuaillon, 1971– . Atlas linguistique et ethnographique du Jura et des Alpes du nord (Francoprovençal central). Paris.

Martin, Marie-Madeleine. 1966. Le latin immortel. Paris-Bruxelles.

Martinet, André. 1945. La prononciation du français moderne. Paris. (2nd ed., Genève, 1971.)

————. 1949. About structural sketches. Word 5.13–35.

————. 1952. Celtic lenition and Western Romance consonants. Language 28.192–197.

————. 1955. Économie des changements phonétiques. Berne. (2nd ed., 1964.)

————. 1956. La description phonologique, avec application au parler franco-provençal de Hauteville (Savoie). Genève. (SPRF no. 56.)

————. 1960. Éléments de linguistique générale. (English tr.: Elements of general linguistics, London and Chicago, 1964.)

Martini, G. S. 1950. Vocabolario badiotto-italiano. Firenze.

Massignon, Geneviève. 1962. Les parlers français d'Acadie. Paris.

————, and Brigette Horiot. 1971– . Atlas linguistique et ethnographique de l'Ouest (Poitou, Aunis, Saintonge, Angomois). Paris.

Masson, Frédéric. 1912. L'Acdémie Française, 1629–1793. Paris.

Mastràngelo Latini, Giulia. 1966. Caratteristiche fonetiche dei parlari della bassa valle del Tronto. ID 29.1–48.

Matluck, Joseph H. 1951. La pronunciación en el español del Valle de México. Ciudad de México.

Matoré, Georges. 1967. Histoire des dictionnaires français. Paris.

Mattoso Câmara, Joaquim, Jr. 1953. Para o estudo da fonêmica portuguêsa. Rio de Janeiro. (Coleção "Rex," no. 11.)

————. 1972. The Portuguese language. Chicago.

Maurer, Theodoro Henrique, Jr. 1951. A unidade da Românía ocidental. São Paulo.
———. 1959. Gramática do latim vulgar. Rio de Janeiro. (BBF no. 16.)
———. 1962. O problema do latim vulgar. Rio de Janeiro. (BBF no. 17.)
Maylender, Michele. 1926–30. Storia delle accademie d'Italia. Bologna.
Mazzel, Massimiliano. 1968–69. Dizionario ladino (fassano e moenese)—italiano. Fassa and Moena.
Mazzoni, Guido. 1939. Strani francesismi del Machiavelli. LN 1.12–13.
Mazzotta, Giuseppe. 1969. Lingua e dialetto nei programmi delle scuole elementari (1923–1955). Protimēsis (= StLSa. 2.) 139–155.
McDermott, John Francis. 1941. A glossary of Mississippi Valley French, 1673–1850. St. Louis, Missouri.
McKaughan, Howard P. 1954. Notes on Chabacano grammar. JEAS 3.205–226.
———, and Batua A. Macaraya. 1967. A Maranao dictionary. Honolulu.
McLendon, Sally. 1969/70. Spanish words in Eastern Pomo. RPh. 23.39–53.
Medici, Mario. 1959. Dalle cronache del calcio. LN 20.24–26.
———. 1961. Alcuni aspetti del linguaggio televisivo. LN 22.119–121.
Medrano, José D. 1883. Apuntaciones para la crítica del lenguaje maracaibero. Maracaibo (Venezuela). (2nd ed., 1886.)
Meier, Harri. 1930. Beiträge zur sprachlichen Gleiderung der Pyrenäenhalbinsel. Hamburg.
———. 1935. Spanische Sprachbetrachtung und Geschichtsschreibung im 15. Jahrhundert. RF 49.1–20.
———. 1941. Die Entstehung der romanischen Sprachen und Nationen. Frankfurt/M.
———, and Sigrid de Gelós. 1968. Zur Problematik des germanischen Einflusses auf den romanischen Sprachschatz. Wortfamilien im Bereich des Brennens, Sengens, Röstens und Bratens. ASNS 205.257–288.
Meillet, Antoine. 1903. Introduction à l'étude comparative des langues indo-européennes. Paris. (7th ed., 1934.)
———. 1928. Esquisse d'une histoire de la langue latine. Paris. (Many later eds.)
Melchiori, G. B. 1817. Vocabolario bresciano-italiano. Brescia. 2 vols.
———. 1820. Appendice e rettificazioni al dizionario bresciano-italiano. Brescia.
Melillo, Giàcomo. 1920. Il dialetto di Volturino (Foggia). Saggio fonetico-morfologico. Perugia.
———. 1926. I dialetti del Gargano (saggio fonetico). Pisa.
Melillo, Michele. 1955. Atlante fonetico lucano. Roma.
———. 1970. La parabola del figliuol prodigo nei dialetti italiani: i dialetti di Puglia. Roma.
Melis Freda, Rossana. 1968. Alcuni aspetti linguistici della "letteratura di consumo" dell'Ottocento. LN 29.4–13.
Membreño, Alberto. 1895. Hondureñismos. Tegucigalpa. (3rd ed., Méjico, D.F., 1912.)
Menarini, Alberto. 1942. I gerghi bolognesi. Módena.
———. 1947a. Sull'italo-americano degli Stati Uniti. In Menarini 1947b:145–208.
———. 1947b. Ai margini della lingua. Firenze. (BLN no. 8.)
———. 1955. Il cinema nella lingua; la lingua nel cinema. Milano.
Mendonça, Renato. 1933. A influência africana no português do Brasil. Porto. (3rd ed., 1948.)
———. 1936. O português do Brasil: origens, evolução, tendências. Rio de Janeiro.

Menéndez García, Manuel. 1950. Cruce de dialectos en el habla de Sisterna. RDyTP 6.355–401.

———. 1963–65. El cuarto de los Valles (un habla del occidente asturiano). Oviedo. 2 vols.

Menéndez Pidal, Ramón. 1904. Manual elemental de gramética histórica española. Madrid. (Many later eds.; from 4th ed., without adjective *elemental*.)

———. 1906. El dialecto leonés. RABM 10.128–172, 294–311. Also sep.: Madrid. (Reprinted in Menéndez Pidal 1962b.)

———. 1926. Orígenes del español. Madrid. (RFE Anejo no. 1. 4th ed., 1956.)

———. 1959. La chanson de Roland y el neotradicionalismo. Madrid.

———. 1960. La chanson de Roland et la tradition épique des Francs. Paris.

———. 1962a. Seville frente a Madrid: algunas precisiones sobre el español de América. Estructuralismo e Historia 3.99–165.

———. 1962b. El dialecto leonés. Oviedo.

Menger, Louis Emil. 1904. The Anglo-Norman dialect. New York.

Menghius, Martin Clemens. 1898. Die Sprachgrenzen in Graubünden und im Tessin, nach den Ergebnissen der Volkszählungen von 1860, 1870, 1880 und 1888. PM 44.97–105.

Meo-Zilio, Giovanni. 1955a. Influenze dello spagnolo sull'italiano parlato nel Río de la Plata. LN 16.16–22.

———. 1955b. Fenomeni lessicali dell'italiano rioplatense. LN 16.53–55.

———. 1955c. Contaminazioni morfologiche nel cocoliche rioplatense. LN 16.112–117.

———. 1956a. Interferenze sintattiche nel cocoliche rioplatense. LN 17.54–59.

———. 1956b. Fenomeni stilistici del cocoliche rioplatense. LN 17.88–91.

———. 1958. Un morfema italiano con funzione stilistica nello spagnolo rioplatense. LN 19.58–64.

———. 1959. Una serie di morfemi italiani con funzione stilistica nello spagnolo dell'Uruguay. LN 20.49–54.

———. 1960. Sull'elemento italiano nello spagnolo rioplatense. LN 21.97–103.

———. 1961. Appunti di onomastica rioplatense (comportamenti grafici e fonetici dei cognomi italiani nel Plata). AMCISO[7] 3.227–239.

———. 1962. Canali e veicoli dell'italianismo in Uruguay. LN 23.116–121.

———. 1964a. El "Cocoliche" rioplatense. BFil-Mont. 16.61–119.

———. 1964b. Algunos septentrionalismos italianos en el español rioplatense. RJb. 14.197–301.

———. 1965a. Italianismos generales en el español rioplatense. Bogotá (Colombia).

———. 1965b. Notas de español americano. El elemento jergal italiano en el rioplatense popular. StLLSp. (= PFMUT 31.) 411–428.

Mercier, M. 1880. Études sur la langue créole en Louisiane. CRAL 1.373–381.

Merlo, Clemente. 1909. Gli italiani *amano, dicono* e gli odierni dialetti umbro-romaneschi. StR 6.69–83.

———. 1920. Fonologia del dialetto di Sora. AUTosc. 38.121–282.

———. 1922. Fonologia del dialetto di Cervara in provincia di Roma. Roma. (DRL no. 2.)

———. 1929. G. I. Àscoli e i cànoni della glottologia. Silloge Ascoli 587–610.

——— (ed.). 1932. Raccolta di voci romane e marchiane riprodotte secondo la stampa del 1768. Roma. (DRL no. 6.)

———. 1933. Il sostrato etnico e i dialetti italiani. ID 9.1–36.

——. 1938–57. Contributi alla conoscenza dei dialetti della Liguria odierna. ID 14.23–58 (1938); 17.1–16 (1941); 18.1–32 (1942); 19.143–176 (1954); 20.1–28 (1955/56); 21.1–47 (1956/57).

——. 1939. Il latino nelle provincie dell'Impero e il problema delle lingue romanze. Romana 3.1–14.

——. 1942. L'Italia linguistica odierna e le invasioni barbariche. RAItalia VII.3.63–72.

Meschieri, E. 1876. Vocabolario mirandolese-italiano. Bologna.

Mesnard, Paul. 1857. Histoire de l'Académie Française depuis sa fondation jusqu'en 1830. Paris.

Messedaglia, Luigi. 1942/43. La pavana: danza non spagnuola, ma padovana. AAVerona V.21.91–103.

Messing, Gordon Myron. 1951. Structuralism and literary tradition. Language 27.1–12.

——. 1963. Review of Mihăescu 1960. Language 39.673–677.

Meunier, Jean-Marie. 1912a. Monographie phonétique du parler de Chaulgnes, canton de la Charité-sur-Loire (Nièvre). Paris.

——. 1912b. Index lexicographique. Supplément de la Monographie phonétique du parler de Chaulgnes (Nièvre). Paris.

——. 1926a. Étude morphologique sur les pronoms personnels dans les parlers actuels du Nivernais. Paris.

——. 1926b. Atlas linguistique et tableaux des pronoms personnels du Nivernais. Paris.

Meyer, Leo. 1914. Untersuchungen über die Sprache von Einfisch. RF 39.470–652.

Meyer, Paul. 1904. De l'expansion de la langue française en Italie pendant le moyen âge. ACISS 4.61–105. Also separately: Roma, 1904.

Meyer-Lübke, Wilhelm. 1887. Die lateinische Sprache in den romanischen Ländern. In Gröber (ed.) 1886–88:1.351–352. (In 2nd ed.: 1.451–497.)

——. 1890. Italienische Grammatik. Leipzig. (Italian tr.: Grammatica storico-comparata della lingua italiana e dei dialetti toscani, Torino, 1901, with several later eds.)

——. 1890–1902. Grammatik der romanischen Sprachen. Leipzig. 4 vols. (French tr.: Grammaire des langues romanes, Paris, 1890–1906; 4 vols.; reprinted, New York, 1925.)

——. 1901. Einführung in das Studium der romanischen Sprachwissenschaft. Heidelberg. (2nd ed., 1909, with Spanish tr.: Introducción al estudio de la lingüística romance, Madrid, 1914, and Portuguese tr.: Introducção ao estudo da glotologia românica, Lisboa, 1916. 3rd ed., 1920, with Spanish tr. by Américo Castro: Introducción a la lingüística románica, Madrid, 1926.)

——. 1902. Zur Kenntnis des Altlogudoresischen. Wien. (SbWien 145:5.)

——. 1906. Altgermanische Elemente im Rumänischen? KZ 39.593–599.

——. 1908–21. Historische französische Grammatik. Heidelberg. 2 vols.

——. 1911. Romanisches tymologisches Wörterbuch. Heidelberg. (3rd ed., 1936; 4th ed., 1968.)

——. 1914–19. Zur u—ü Frage. ZFSL 41.1–7 (1914/15); 44.75–84 (1916/17); 45.350–357 (1917/19).

——. 1925. Das Katalanische, seine Stellung zum Spanischen und Provenzalischen. Heidelberg.

——. 1926. Afro-romanisch und ibero-romanisch. ZRPh. 46.116–128.

Michael, Johann. 1905. Der Dialekt des Poschiavotals (Poschiavo—Brusio—Campocologno). Halle/S.

Michaëlis, Hermann, and Paul Passy. 1914. Dictionnaire phonétique de la langue française. Hannover.

Michelàgnoli, Alfredo. 1935. Vocabolario veneziano-italiano, etimologico, storico, grammaticale, biografico. Venezia.

Michelson, David. Forthcoming. Zazie dans le métro: Raymond Queneau, linguiste des parigots et la belle langue françoise.

Miclău, Paul. 1966. Le français parlé dans les poésies de Jacques Prévert. BRPh. 5:1.120–133.

Miège, Madeleine. 1937. Le français dialectal de Lyon. Étude contemporaine. Lyon.

Migliorini, Bruno. 1933. Sui toponimi conglomerati del tipo *Mongibello*. ACIL[3] 214–218.

———. 1935. I prefissoidi. AGI 27.13–39. (Reprinted in Migliorini 1942:7–54.)

———. 1940. Il "Vocabolario cateriniano" de Girolamo Gigli. LN 1.73–80. (Reprinted in Migliorini, 1948:167–189.)

———. 1942. Saggi sulla lingua del Novecento. Firenze. (BLN no. 1.)

———. 1946. Primordî del *Lei*. LN 7.25–29. (Reprinted in Migliorini 1957:187–196.)

———. 1948. Lingua e cultura. Firenze.

———. 1949. La questione della lingua. In Momigliano (ed.) 1948–49:3.1–75.

———. 1955. Note sulla grafia italiana del Rinascimento. StFI 13.259–296. (Reprinted in Migliorini, 1957:197–225.)

———. 1956. Le lingue classiche, serbatoio lessicale delle lingue europee moderne. LN 17.33–38.

———. 1957. Saggi linguistici. Firenze.

———. 1960. Storia della lingua italiana. Firenze.

———. 1963. Lingua e dialetti. LN 24.81–87.

———. 1968. Il linguaggio maccheronico del Folengo. Ausonia 23.7–26.

———. 1970. Omofonie e omografie nella svolta ortografica italiana del Cinquecento. Mille 119–127.

———, and T. Gwynfor Griffith. 1966. The Italian language. London and New York.

Mihăescu, Haralambie. 1960. Limba latină în provinciile dunărene ale Imperiului Roman. Bucureşti.

———. 1966a. Influenţa grecească asupră limbii române pînă în secolul al XV-lea. Bucureşti.

———. 1966b. Les éléments latins de la langue albanaise. RESEE 4.5–33, 323–353.

Mihăilă, G. 1960. Împrumuturi vechi sud-slave la limba romînă. Bucureşti.

Milá y Fontanals, M. 1861. De los trovadores en España. Barcelona.

Millán Urdiales, José. 1966. El habla de Villacidayo (León). Madrid. (BAE Anejo no. 13.)

Millardet, Georges. 1910. Études de dialectologie landaise. Toulouse.

———. 1921–23. Linguistique et dialectologie romanes. RLR 61.1–160 (1921), 193–368 (1922); 62.1–157 (1923). Also sep.: Paris and Montpellier, 1923.

———. 1924. Linguistique et dialectologie romanes. Réponse à quelques critiques. RLR 62:2.377–422.

———. 1933. Sur un ancien substrat commun à la Sicile, la Corse et la Sardaigne. RLiR 9.346–369.

Millares Carlo, A. 1950. Historia de la literatura española hasta fines del siglo XV. Méjico, D.F.

Miller, Wick R. 1959–60. Spanish loanwords in Acoma. IJAL 25.147–153 (1959); 26.41–49 (1960).

Minadeo, Michele. 1955. Lessico del dialetto di Ripalimosani, in provincia di Campobasso. Torino. (PFLUT VII.3.)

Mistral, Frédéri. 1878. Lou tresor dou Felibrige, ou dictionnaire provençal-français embrassant les dialectes de la langue d'oc moderne. Aix-en-Provence. (Reprlnted Paris, 1932, and Osnabrück, 1966.)

Mørland, Henning. 1932. Die lateinischen Oribasiusübersetzungen. Oslo.

Mohrmann, Christine. 1955. Latin vulgaire; latin des chrétiens; latin médiéval. Paris.

———. 1961–65. Etudes sur le latin des chrétiens. Rome. 3 vols.

Moisy, Henri. 1889. Glossaire comparatif anglo-normand. Caen.

Molho, Maurice. 1960. Literatura sefardita de Oriente. Madrid-Barcelona.

Molíns, Mariano Roca de Togores, Marqués de. 1870. Reseña histórica de la Academia Española. MRAE 1.7–128.

Moll y Casanovas, Francisc de B. 1952. Gramatica histórica catalana. Madrid.

———. 1960. Estática y dinámica del catalán en Mallorca. PSA 17.161–175.

Momigliano, Attilio (ed.). 1948–49. Problemi ed orientamenti critici di lingua e di letteratura italiana. Milano.

Moncourt, E. 1851. De la méthode grammaticale de Vaugelas. Paris.

Monge, Felix. 1951. El habla de la Puebla de Hijar. RDyTP 7.187–241.

Monteiro, Clóvis. 1954. Ortografia da língua portuguësa. Rio de Janeiro.

Monteverdi, Àngelo. 1952. Manuale di avviamento agli studî romanzi. Milano.

Monti, Pietro. 1845. Vocabolario dei dialetti della città e diocesi di Como. Milano.

Montori, Arturo. 1916. Modificaciones populares del idioma castellano en Cuba CuC 11.232–252.

Morais-Barbosa, Jorge (ed.). 1967. Crioulos, estudos linguísticos. Reedição de artigos publicados no Boletim da Sociedade de Geografia de Lisboa, introdução e notas. Lisboa.

Morf, Heinrich (ed.). 1909. Die romanischen Literaturen und Sprachen mit Einschluss des Keltischen. Berlin:Leipzig. (2nd ed., 1925.)

———. 1911. Zur sprachlichen Gliederung Frankreichs. Berlin. (AbhBerlin 1911:2.)

———. 1912. Vom Ursprung der provenzalischen Schriftsprache. SbBerlin 45. (Reprinted in Morf: Aus Dichtung und Sprache der Romanen 3.321–356 [1922].)

Morgan, Raleigh, Jr. 1959. Structural sketch of Saint Martin Creole. AnL 1:8.20–24f.

———. 1960. The lexicon of Saint Martin Creole. AnL 2:1.7–29.

Morínigo, Marcos A. 1931. Hispanismos en el guaraní: estudio sobre la penetración de la cultura española en la guaraní, según se refleja en la lengua. Buenos Aires.

———. 1966. Diccionario de americanismos. Buenos Aires.

Morley, S. Griswold, and Courtney Bruerton. 1940. The chronology of Lope de Vega's Comedias. New York and London.

Morosi, Gaetano. 1878. Il vocalismo del dialetto leccese. AGI 4.117–144.

———. 1880. L'elemento greco nei dialetti dell'Italia meridionale. AGI 12.76–96.

Morri, Antonio. 1840. Vocabolario romagnolo-italiano. Faenza.

Moulton, William Gamwell. 1941. Swiss German dialect and Romance patois. Baltimore. (Language Dissertaion no. 34.)

Müller, Marianne. 1961. Le patois des Marécottes (Commune de Salvan, Valais). Tübingen. (ZRPh. Bhft. no. 103.)

Muljačić, Žarko. 1962. Dalmatski elementi u mletački pisanimu dubrovačkim dokumentina 14. st. Prilog ragujskoj diajkronoj fonologii i dalmatsko-mletačkoj konvergencii. JAZU-Rad 327.237–380. Also separately: Zagreb.

———. 1964. Opća fono.ogija i fonologija suvremennog talijanskog jazika. Zagreb. (Italian tr.: Fonologia generale e fonologia della lingua italiana, Bologna, 1969.)

———. 1965. La posizione del dalmatico nella Romania (per una classificazione dinamica delle lingue neolatine). ACILRii 1103–1109.

———. 1967. Die Klassifikation der romanischen Sprachen. RJb. 18.23–37.

Muller, Henri François. 1923. On the use of the expression *Lingua romana* from the first to the ninth century. ZRPh. 45.9–19.

———. 1929. A chronology of Vulgar Latin. Halle/S. (ZRPh. Bhft. no. 78.)

———. 1945. L'époque mérovingienne. New York.

———, and Pauline Taylor. 1932. A chrestomathy of Vulgar Latin. New York.

Mumford, Lewis. 1961. The city in history: its origins, its transformations, and its prospects. New York.

Muñoz Cortés, M. 1958. El español vulgar. Madrid.

Munteanu, Basil. 1943. Geschichte der neueren rumänischen Literatur. München.

Mushacke, W. 1884. Geschichtliche Entwicklung der Mundart von Montpellier. Heilbronn.

Mussafia, Adolfo. 1871. Darstellung der romagnolischen Mundart. SbWien 67.653–722.

Muzzo, Giosuè. 1953. Vocabolario dialettale sassarese-italiano e italiano-sassarese. Sàssari. 2 vols.

———, and Salvator Ruju. 1955. Supplemento al vocabolario dialettale. Parte I: Sassarese-italiano.

Nandriş, Grigore. 1951. The development and structure of Rumanian. SEER 30.7–39.

———. 1963. Phonétique historique du roumain. Paris.

Nardo Cibele, Ângela. 1900. Alcune parole usate dalla popolazione mista italiana e negra nelle "fazende" di S. Paulo nel Brasile. ASTP 19.18–24.

Nascentes, Antenor. 1932. Diccionário etimológico da língua portuguêsa. Rio de Janeiro.

———. 1953a. O linguajar carioca. Rio de Janeiro.

———. 1953b. A gíria brasileira. Rio de Janeiro.

———. 1966. Dicionário etimológico resumido. Rio de Janeiro.

Nauton, Pierre. 1948. Le patois de Saugues (Haute-Loire). Clermont-Ferrand.

———. 1957–63. Atlas linguistique et etnographique du Massif Central. Paris.

Navarro Tomás, Tomás. 1918. Manual de pronunciación española. Madrid. (3rd ed., 1926. German tr.: Handbuch der spanischen Aussprache, Leipzig, 1923.)

———. 1944. Manual de entonación española. New York. (2nd ed., 1950.)

———. 1946. Estudios de fonología española. Syracuse, N.Y.

———. 1948. El español de Puerto Rico. Río Piedras, P.R.

———. 1953. Observaciones sobre el papiamento. NRFH 7.183–189.

———, Rafael de Balbín, et al. (eds.). 1962– . Atlas lingüístico de la península ibérica (ALPI). Madrid.

———, Aurelio M. Espinosa, Jr., and Lorenzo Rodríguez Castellano. 1933. La frontera del andaluz. RFE 20.225–227.

——— and Manuel Sanchis Guarner. 1934. Análisis fonético del valenciano literario. RFE 21.113–141.

Navone, Giulio. 1922. Il dialetto di Paliano. StR 17.73–126.

Nazari, Giulio. 1873. Parallelo fra il dialetto bellunese rustico e la lingua italiana. Belluno.

———. 1884. Dizionario bellunese-italiano. Belluno-Oderzo.

Nef, John Ulric. 1954. La naissance de la civilisation industriale. Paris.

————. 1958. Cultural foundations of industrial civilisation. Cambridge (England).

Neira, Jesús. 1955. El habla de Lena. Oviedo.

Nelson, H. L. W. 1947. Petronius en zijn Vulgair-Latijn. Een stilistisch-grammatische
Studie over de zoogenaande "vulgaire dictie" in de Cena Trimalchionis. Utrecht.

————. 1966. Die Latinisierungen in den Strassburger Eiden. VR 25.193–226.

Nencioni, Giovanni. 1949. Essenza del toscano. Studî Fiorentini 367–394. Also in
RLI 62.3–21 (1958).

Neumann, Sven-Gösta. 1959. Recherches sur le français des XVᵉ et XVIᵉ siècles et
sur la codification par les théoriciens de l'époque. Lund.

Neumann (Ritter) von Spallart, A. 1904. Zur Charakteristik des Dialekts der Marche.
ZRPh. 28.273–315, 450–491, with 1 map.

————. 1907. Weitere Beiträge zur Charakteristik des Dialekts der Marche. Halle/S.
(ZRPh. Bhft. no. 11.)

Neuvonen, Eero Kalervo. 1941. Los arabismos del Español en el siglo XIII. Helsinki

Niccoli, Piere Francesco. 1901. Il dialetto di Voghera. StFR 8.197–249.

Nicolet, Nellie. 1929. Der Dialekt des Antronatales. Lautlehre, Formenlehre, Texte,
Glossar. Halle/S. (ZRPh. Bhft. no. 79.)

Niculescu, Alexandru. 1956. I problemi della lingua letteraria nella Repubblica
Popolare Rumena. ACSR⁸ 2.311–338.

————. 1965. Individualitatea limbii române între limbile romanice. Contribuţii
gramaticale. Bucureşti.

Nieri, Idelfonso. 1901. Vocabolario lucchese. Lucca.

Ninni, I. P. 1891. Materiali per un vocabolario della lingua rustica del contado di
Treviso. Venezia. 3 vols. (Reprinted, Bologna, 1964–65.)

Ninyoles, Rafael Lluìs. 1969. Conflicte lingüìstic valencià. Barcelona.

Nisard, Charles. 1872. Étude sur le langage populaire ou patois de Paris et de sa
banlieue. Paris.

————. 1876. De quelques parisianismes populaires et autres locutions non encore ou
plus ou moins imparfaitement expliquées des XVIIᵉ, XVIIIᵉ et XIXᵉ siècles. Paris.

Nittoli, Salvatore. 1873. Vocabolario di varî dialetti irpini. Nàpoli.

Nitze, William Albert, and Edwin Preston Dargan. 1922. A history of French literature. New York .(Revised ed., 1927.)

Norreri, Oscar. 1905. Avviamento allo studio dell'italiano nel comune di Castelmadama. Perugia.

Northrup, George Tyler. 1925. An introduction to Spanish literature. Chicago.
(3rd ed., revised by N. B. Adams, 1960.)

Nunes, José Joaquim. 1919. Compêndio de gramática histórica portuguêsa (fonética e
morfologia). Lisboa. (3rd ed., 1945.)

Nykl, Alois R. 1929/30. Notes on the Spanish of Yucatán, Vera Cruz and Tlaxcala.
MPh. 27.451–460. (Spanish tr.: Notas sobre el español de Yucatán, Vera Cruz y
Tlaxcala, BDH 5.207–225 [1931].)

Nyrop, Kristoffer. 1899–1930. Grammaire historique de la langue française. Copenhague.

————. 1902. Manuel phonétique du français parlé. Copenhague. (8th ed., revised by
Alf Lombard, 1963.)

Odin, Alfred. 1886. Phonologie des patois du canton de Vaud. Halle/S.

Odin, Louise. 1910. Glossaire du patois de Blonay. Lausanne.

Oliver Asín, Jaime. 1938. Introducción al estudio de la historia de la lengua española.
Pamplona.

Olivieri, Dante. 1953. Dizionario etimologico italiano, concordato coi dialetti, le lingue straniere e la topo-onomastica. Milano.

Olson, Donald. 1963. Spanish loanwords in Pame. IJAL 29.219–221.

Ondis, Lewis A. 1932. Phonology of th3 Cilentan dialect, with a word-index and dialect texts. New York.

Oroz, Rodolfo. 1966. La lengua castellana en Chile. Santiago de Chile.

Ortíz, Fernando. 1921–22. Un catauro de cubanismos. RBC 16.51–57, 65–75, 129–157, 202–232, 262–294, 328–353 (1921); 17.17–45, 87–106, 150–165, 209–231, 295–314. Also sep.: La Habana, 1923.

Ortíz Fernández, Fernando. 1924. Glosario de afronegrismos. La Habana.

Osterwalder, Th. 1933. Beiträge zur Kenntnis des Dialektes von Magland (Hochsavoyen). Zürich.

Pabst, Walter. 1952. Dante und die literarische Vielsprachigkeit der südlichen Romania. RJb. 5.161–181.

Pagani, Severino. 1945. Come parla Meneghino. Piccola grammatica del dialetto milanese. Milano.

Pagliaro, Antonino. 1930. Sommario di linguistica arioeuropea. Roma.

———. 1934. Aspetti della storia linguistica della Sicilia. AR 18.355–380.

———. 1947. La dottrina linguistica di Dante. QR 1.485–501.

Pajello, Luigi. 1896. Dizionario vicentino-italiano e italiano-vicentino preceduto da osservazioni grammaticali e da regole di ortografia applicata. Vicenza.

Palay, Maximin ("Simin"). 1932. Dictionnaire du béarnais et du gascon moderne (Bassin d l'Adour), embrassant les dialects du Béarn, de la Bigoree, du Gers, des Landes et de la Gascogne maritime. Pau. 2 vols.

Pallioppi, Zaccaria and Emil. 1895–1902. Dicziunari dels idioms romauntschs d'Engiadin ota e bassa, della Val Müstair, da Bravuogn e Filisur. Samedan. 2 vols.

Pallottino, Massimo. 1936. Elementi di lingua etrusca. Firenze.

———. 1947. L'origine degli Etruschi. Roma.

Palmer, Leonard Robert. 1954. The Latin language. London. (3rd impression, 1961.)

Panconcelli-Calzia, Guido. 1911. Italiano. Fonetica—Morfologia—Testi. Lepizig-Berlin.

Pansa, Giovanni. 1885. Saggio di uno studio sul dialetto abruzzese. Lanciano.

Pansier, Pierre. 1924–27. Histoire de la langue provençale à Avignon du XIIᵉ au XIXᵉ siècle. Avignon. 4 vols.

Paoli, Ugo Enrico. 1959. Il latino maccheronico. Firenze.

Pap, Leo. 1949. Portuguese-American speech: an outline of speech conditions among Portuguese immigrants in New England and elsewhere in the United States. New York.

Papahagi, Tache. 1925. Graiul și folklorul Maramureșului. București.

———. 1963. Dicționarul dialectului aromân general și etimologic. București.

Papanti, Giovanni. 1875. I parlari italiani in Certaldo. Livorno.

Pardo Asso, J. 1938. Nuevo diccionario etimológico aragonés. Zaragoza.

Parducci, Amos. 1947/48. Giunte al vocabolario lucchese di I. Nieri. RABologna V.1.34–61.

Parentes Fortes, Herbert. 1962. A questão da língua brasileira. Rio de Janeiro.

Pariset, Carlo. 1885–1892. Vocabolario parmigiano-italiano. Parma. 2 vols.

Parlangèli, Oronzo. 1952. Il dialetto di Loretio Aprutino. RIL II.85.113–176.

———. 1953. Sui dialetti romanzi e romaici del Salento. MIL III.35/36.93–198. (Résumé in Orbis 3.453–454 [1954].)

————. 1958. Postille e giunte al "Vocabolario dei dialetti salentini" di G. Rohlfs. RIL II.92.737–798.

————. 1960a. Storia linguistica e storia politica nell'Italia meridonale. Firenze.

————. 1960b. Ancora sulla grecità dell'Italia meridionale. ZRPh. 76.118–129.

————. 1964/65. Il sostrato linguistico in Sicilia. Kōkalos 10/11.211–244 (with discussion 245–258).

————. 1969. Considerazioni sulla classificazione dei dialetti italiani. Studî V. Pisani 715–760.

Parodi, Ernesto Giàcomo. 1905. Studî liguri. 3. Il dialetto di Genova dal secolo XVI ai giorni nostri. AGI 15.105–161, 333–365.

————. 1907. Intorno al dialetto d'Ormea. StR 5.89–122.

Parrino, Flavio. 1967. Per una carta dei dialetti delle Marche. BCDI 2.5–37.

Parry, John J. 1946. The revival of Cornish: An Dasserghyans Kernewek. PMLA 61.258–268.

Paschall, Dorothy May. 1939. The vocabulary of mental aberration in Roman comedy and Petronius. Baltimore. (Language Dissertation no. 27.)

Pascu, G. 1925. Dictionnaire étymologique macédoroumain. Bucarest. 2 vols.

Passy, Paul. 1887. Les sons du français. Paris. (English tr.: The sounds of the French language, Oxford [England], 1907.)

Pastor, José F. 1929. Las apologías de la lengua castellana en el Siglo de Oro. Madrid.

Patuzzi, Gaetano, Giorgio Bolognini, and A. Bolognini. 1901. Piccolo dizionario moderno della città Bologna. Bologna. (Facsimile edition, Bologna, 1967.)

Pautasso, Mariella. 1969. Dialetto, lingua e integrazione linguistica a Pettinengo. Torino.

Pedersen, Holger. 1930. Linguistic science in the nineteenth ceutury. Cambridge, Massachusetts. (Reprinted as: The discovery of language, Bloomington, Indiana, 1959.)

Pei, Mario A. 1932. The language of the eighth-century texts in Northern France. New York.

————. 1941. The Italian language. New York.

————. 1945. Reflections on the origin of the Romance languages. RR 36.235–239.

————. 1965. Review of Hall 1963. RR 56.60–62.

Pellegrini, Giovanni Battista. 1954/55. Schizzo fonetico dei dialetti agordini. Contributo alla conoscenza dei dialetti di transizione fra il ladino dolomitico-atesino e il veneto. AIVeneto 113.281–424.

————. 1956. Franco-veneto e veneto antico. FRom. 3.122–140.

————. 1960. Tra lingua e dialetto in Italia. SMLV 8.137–153.

————. 1961. Terminologia geografica araba in Sicilia. AION-Ling. 3.109–201. (Reprinted in Pellegrini, 1972:237–332.)

————. 1962. Contributo allo studio dell'elemento arabo nei dialetti siciliani. Trieste.

————. 1963. L'italiano regionale. CeSc. 2:5.20–29.

————. 1965. L'individualità storico-linguistica della regione veneta. SMLV 13.143–160.

————. 1972. Gli arabismi nelle lingue neolatine, con speciale riguardo all'Italia. Brescia. 2 vols.

Pellegrini, Giovanni Battista, and Aldo Luigi Prosdòcimi. 1967. La lingua venetica. Firenze.

Pellegrini, Silvio. 1960. De vulgari Eloquentiâ, libro I, capitoli 10–19. SMLV 8.155–163.

————. 1970. Di Pasolini e di Gadda. BCSic. 11.366–371.

Penny, Ralph J. 1970. El habla pasiega: ensayo de dialectología montañesa. London.

Perez, G. 1870. Vocabolario siciliano-italiano. Palermo.

Pérez Sala, Paulino. 1973. Interferencia lingüística del inglés en el español hablado en Puerto Rico. Hato Rey, P.R.

Peri, Àngelo. 1847. Vocabolario cremonese-italiano. Cremona.

Peri, Illuminato. 1950. La questione delle colonie lombarde in Sicilia. BSBS 57.253–280.

———. 1962. Il problema langobardo nella società occidentale. Palermo.

Peruzzi, Emilio. 1967. Sabinismi dell'età regia. PP 22.29–45.

Peschieri, Ilario. 1827–28. Dizionario parmigiano-italiano. Parma.

Peter, Herbert. 1969. Entstehung und Ausbildung der italienischen Eisenbahnterminologie. Wien. (WRA no. 8.)

Peter, René. 1949. L'Académie Française et le XXe siècle. Paris.

Petersen, Elmer. 1971. Tristan Tzara: Dada and surrational theorist. Princeton, N. J.

Petracco Sicardi, Giulia. 1963. Influenze genovesi nelle colonie gallo-italiche di Sicilia BCSic. 9.106–132.

———. 1965. I dialetti liguri. CP-CDI 85–92.

———. 1969. Gli elementi fonetici e morfologici "settentrionali" nelle parlate gallo-italiche del Mezzogiorno. BCSic. 10.326–358.

Petrocchi, Giorgio. 1959. La dottrina linguistica di Dante. Messina.

Petrovici, Emil. 1956. Influenţa slavă asupră sistemului fonemelor limbii române. Bucureşti.

———. 1957a. Kann das Phonemsystem einer Sprache durch fremden Einfluss umgestaltet wereden? 's Gravenhage. (JL no. 5.)

———. 1957b. Interpénétration d'une phonologie slave et d'une morphologie romane. Mélanges Linguistiques 81–89.

———. 1964. Unitatea dialectală a limbii române. StCL 15.431–443. (French tr.: L'unité dialectale de la langue roumaine. RRL 9.375–388 [1964].)

Pfändler, Otto. 1954. Wortschatz der Sportsprache Spaniens, mit besonderer Berücksichtigung der Ballsportarten. Bern. (RH no. 47.)

Pfiffig, Ambros Josef. 1960. Die etruskische Sprache. Versuch einer Gesamtdarlung. Graz.

Pfister, Max. 1958. Beitrag zur altprovenzalischen Grammatik. VR 17.281–362.

Phillips, Hosea. 1936. Étude du parler de la paroisse Évangeline (Louisiane). Paris. (SPRF no. 17.)

Piagnoli, Agide. 1904. Fonetica parmigiana. Torino.

Pianigiani, Ottorino. 1907. Vocabolario etimologico della lingua italiana. Roma-Milano.

Piazza, Filippo. 1921. Le colonie e i dialetti lombardo-siculi. Catania.

Piccio, Giuseppe. 1916. Dizionario veneziano-italiano. Venezia.

Piccitto, Giorgio. 1941. Fonetica del dialetto di Ragusa. ID 17.17–80.

———. 1959. Il siciliano dialetto italiano. Orbis 8.183–197.

———. 1967– . Vocabolario siciliano. Catania-Palermo.

———. 1969. Di alcune isoglosse più caratteristiche dei dialetti della Sicilia centrale. BCSic. 10.359–375, with 1 map.

Piccolo, Francesco. 1938–39. Il dialetto di Lucera (Foggia). ID 14.189–200 (1938); 15.83–100 (1939).

Pichardo, Estéban. 1836. Diccionario provincial casi razonado de voces cubanas. Matanzas. (4th ed., La Habana, 1875.)

Picoche, Jacqueline. 1971. Nouveau dictionnaire étymologique du français. Paris.

Piel, Joseph M. 1965/66. Sobre alguns aspectos da renovação e inovação lexicais no português do Brasil. RPF 13.1–25.

Pieri, Silvio. 1886. Note sul dialetto aretino. Pisa.

———. 1890. Fonetica del dialetto lucchese. AGI 12.107–134.

———. 1891. Fonetica del dialetto pisano. AGI 12.141–160.

———. 1904. Il dialetto della Versilia. ZRPh. 28.161–191.

Pignon, Jacques. 1960. L'évolution phonétique des parlers du Poitou (Vienne et Deux-Sèvres). Paris.

Pinguentini, Gianni. 1969. Nuovo dizionario storico etimologico fraeologico del dialetto triestino. Bologna.

Piotrovskiĭ, R. G. 1951. Slavijanskije elementy v rumynskom jazyke. VLGU 1951: 1.134–152.

Pirandello, Luigi. 1891. Laute und Lautentwicklung der Mundart von Girgenti. Halle/S.

Piron, Maurice (ed.). 1961. Turgot, Anne Robert Jacques: Étymologie. Édition critique avec notes. Brugge.

Prona, Jàcopo. 1871. Vocabolario friulano. Venezia.

Pirson, J. 1902. Das Kasseler Glossar. ZRPh. 26.521–531.

Pisani, Vittore. 1948. Grammatica latina storica e comparata. Torino.

———. 1952. Le lingue dell'Italia antica oltre il latino. Torino. (2nd ed., 1964.)

———. 1962. Storia della lingua latina. Parte prima: Le origini, e la lingua letteraria fino a Virgilio e Orazio. Torino.

Pittau, Màssimo. 1956. Il dialetto di Nuoro: il più schietto dei parlari neolatini. Bologna.

Pizzinini, Antone. 1966. Parores ladines. Vokabulare badiot-tudësk. Ergänzt und überarbeitet von Guntram Plangg. Innsbruck.

Pochettino, Giuseppe. 1947. I Langobardi nell'Italia meridionale (570–1080). Nàpoli.

Pogastcher, A. 1888. Zur Lautlehre der griechischen, lateinischen und romanischen Lehnworte im Altenglischen. Strassburg.

Poggi Salani, Teresa. 1969. La lingua rusticana di Michelangelo il Giovane: cenni di esemplificazione nella Tancia. La poesia rusticana nel Rinascimento 233–243.

———. 1971. Il lessico della Tancia di Michelangelo Buonarroti il Giovane. Firenze.

Politzer, Robert L. 1967. Beiträge zur Phonologie der Nonsberger Mundart. Innsbruck.

Polomé, Edgar G. 1966. The position of Illyrian and Venetic. In Birnbaum and Puhvel (eds.) 1966:59–76.

Pompilus, Pradel. 1961a. La langue française en Haïti. Paris.

———. 1961b. De quelques influences du Créole sur le français officiel d'Haïti. CLS 2.91–98.

Pop, Sever. 1948. Grammaire roumaine. Berne.

———. 1949/50. Magura 'hauteur, montagne' dans l'Europe centrale. RPh. 3.117–134.

———. 1950. La dialectologie. Aperçu historique et méthodes d'enquêtes linguistiques. Louvain. 2 vols.

———. 1956–57. Encyclopédie de la philologie romane: langues et dialects de la Romania. Louvain.

——— and Rodica Doina Pop. 1960. Atlas linguistiques européens: domaine roman. Répertoire alphabétique des cartes. Louvain.

——— and Emil Petrovici (eds.). 1938–42a. Atlasul linguistic român. Cluj (later Sibiu).

—— and ——. 1938–42b. Micul atlas linguistic român. Cluj (later Sibiu).

Pope, Mildred K. 1934. From Latin to Modern French, with especial consideration of Anglo-Norman phonology and morphology. Manchester (England).

Popovici, Iosif. 1905. Rumänische Dialekte. I. Die Dialekte der Munteni und Pădureni im Hunyader Komität. Halle/S.

——. 1908–14. Dialectele române din Istria. Halle/S.

Porru, Giulia. 1939. Anmerkungen über die Phonologie des Italienisches [sic]. TCLP 8.187–208.

Porru, Vincenzo Raimondo. 1832. Nou dizionariu sardu-italianu. Casteddu.

——. 1866. Dizionariu sardu-italianu. Segunda edizioni. Casteddu.

Porter, Lambert Combs. 1960. The Cantilène de Sainte Eulalie—phonology and graphemics. StP 57.587–596.

—— (ed.). 1966. Jacques Peletier du Mans: Dialogue de l'Ortografe. Genève.

Posner, Rebecca R. 1961. Consonantal dissimilation in the Romance languages. Oxford (England).

——. 1966. The Romance languages. Garden City, L.I., N.Y. (Doubleday-Anchor Books no. A-494.)

Pottier, Bernard. 1957–58. Introduction à l'étude de la philologie hispanique. Paris. 2 vols.

——. 1958. Introduction à l'étude de la morpho-syntaxe espagnole. Bordeaux. (3rd ed., Paris, 1964; "Nouvelle édition," 1966.)

——. 1961–64. Bibliographies de linguistique romane: domaine espagnol. RLiR 25.161–177 (1961); 26.224–236 (1962); 28.211–227 (1964).

Poultney, James W. 1959. The bronze tables of Iguvium. Cambridge (England) and Baltimore.

——. 1968. Review of Georgiev 1966. Language 44.334–343.

Poupardin, René. 1907. Étude sur l'histoire des principautés lombardes de l'Italie méridionale et de leurs rapports avec l'empire franc. Paris.

Poyen-Bellisle, René. 1894. Les sons et les formes du créole dans les Antilles. Baltimore.

Prader-Schucany, Silvia. 1970. Romanisch Bünden als selbständige Sprachlandschaft. Bern. (RH no. 60.)

Prati, Angèlico. 1916. L'italiano e il parlare della Valsugana. Roma (2nd ed., 1917.)

——. 1931. I vocabolarî delle parlate italiane. Roma.

——. 1951. Vocabolario etimologico italiano. Milano.

——. 1954. Dialettalismo nell'italiano. Pisa.

——. 1960. Dizionario valsuganotto. Venezia-Roma.

Praz, Mario. 1927. Un limbo del vocabolario e della letteratura. La Cultura NS.6.337–348.

——. 1929. The Italian element in English. ES 15.20–66. (Reprinted in Praz 1944: 1–62.)

——. 1944. Richerche anglo-italiane. Roma.

Pressoir, Charles-Fernand. 1947. Débats sur le créole et le folklore. Port-au-Prince.

Prete, G. 1925. Tra i dialetti pugliesi. Dialetto di Martina Franca. Martina Franca. (3rd ed., 1957.)

Prezzolini, Giuseppe. 1939. La lingua della giobba. LN 1.121–122.

Price, Glanville. 1964. The problem of modern literary Occitan. ArL 16.34–53.

——. 1965. Bibliographie de la syntaxe occitane. StN 37.279–300.

——. 1967. Influences espagnole, italienne et occitane sur la langue de Brantôme. RLiR 31.147–179.

Pucci, Piero. 1958. Lingua e dialetto in Pasolini e in Gadda. Società 14.381–398.

———. 1959. Impasto dialettale nel linguaggio del cinema. Società 15.824–831.

Puchet, René. 1965. Clés pour le français du journal. FdaM 31.18–22.

Pulgram, Ernst. 1949. Prehistory and the Italian dialects. Language 25.241–252.

———. 1950. Spoken and written Latin. Language 26.458–466.

———. 1953. Family tree, wave theory, and dialectology. Orbis 2.67–72.

———. '958. The tongues of Italy. Cambridge, Massachusetts.

Pult, Gaspard. 1897. Le parler de Senf. Lausanne.

P roti, Basilio. 1841. Vocabolario domestico napolitano e toscano. Nàpoli. (2nd ed., 1850.)

Pușcariu, Sextil. 1905. Etymologisches Wörterbuch der rumänischen Sprache. I. Lateinisches Element, mit berücksichtigung aller romanischen Sprachen. Heidelberg.

———. 1920. Locul limbii romăne între limbile romanice. București.

———. 1937. Ost- und Westromanisch im Lichte der Sprache. Die Tatwelt 13.161–168.

———. 1940. Limba romănă. București. (German tr.: Die rumänische Sprache, Leipzig, 1943.)

———, M. G. Bàrtoli, A. Balulovici, and A. Byhan. 1926–29. Studii istroromâne. București. 3 vols.

Pyles, Thomas. 1952. Words and their ways in American English. New York.

Quéval, Jean. 1960. Essai sur Raymond Queneau: bibliographie, portraits, fac-similés. Paris.

Queyrat, Louis. 1927–30. Contribution à l'étude du parler de la Creuse: le patois de la région de Chavanat. Guéret. 2 vols.

Quilis, Antonio. 1963. Fonética y fonología del español. Madrid.

Rabanales, Ambrosio. 1952/53. Observaciones a "Hispanismos en el mapuche." BFUCh. 9.133–151.

Radica, Teresa. 1943/44. I dialetti abruzzesi secondo gli studî degli ultimi decennî. RIL II.77.107–150.

Raicich, Marino. 1966. Questione della lingua e scuola (1860–1900). Belfagor 21.245–268, 369–408.

Raimundo, Jacques. 1933. O elemento afro-negro na língua portuguêsa. Rio de Janeiro.

Ramos y Duarte, Félix. 1895. Diccionario de mejicanismos. Méjico, D.F. (2nd ed., 1898.)

Rando, Gaetano. 1967. Italiano e inglese in Australia. LN 28.115–118.

———. 1968. Influenze dell'inglese sul lessico italo-australiano di Sydney. LN 29.17–22.

Ratel, Victorin. 1956. Le patois de Saint-Martin-la-Porte (Savoie). Dictionnaire. Lyon. (PILRL no. 9.)

———. 1958. Morphologie du patois de Saint-Martin-la-Porte (Savoie). Paris. (PILRL no. 13.)

Raya, Gino. 1962. La lingua del Verga. Firenze.

Raynouard, François Juste Marie. 1816. Choix des poésies originales des troubadours. Paris. 6 vols.

———. 1821. Grammaire comparée des langues de l'Europe latine dans leurs rapports avec la langue des Troubadours. Paris.

———. 1836–44. Lexique roman ou dictionnaire de la langue des Troubadours, comparée avec les autres langues de l'Europe latine, précédé de nouvelles recherches historiques et philologiques, d'un résumé de la Grammaire romane, d'un nouveau choix des poésies originales de Troubadours, et d'extraits de poèmes divers. Paris. 6 vols.

Read, William A. 1931. Louisiana-French. Baton Rouge. (Revised ed., 1963.)

Rebelo Gonçalves, F. 1930. Da influência lexical do grego no latim literario. Lisboa.

Redi, Francesco. 1928. Vocabolario di alcune voci aretine. Arezzo.

Regula, Moritz. 1955–56. Historische Grammatik des Französischen. Heidelberg. 2 vols.

———. 1957. Grammaire française explicative. Heidelberg.

———, and Jospi Jernej. 1965. Grammatica italiana descrittiva su basi storiche e psicologiche. Bern and München.

Reichenkron, Günter. 1958–60. Vorrömische Bestandteile des Rumänischen. ASNS 194.273–290 (1958); Festschrift W. von Wartburg 597–613 (1958); RJb. 9.59–105 (1958); Festschrift J. Friedrich 365–401 (1959); RJb. 11.19–53 (1960); Südost-forschungen 19.344–368 (1960).

———. 1964. Vorrömische Elemente im Rumänischen. Die Kultur Südosteuropas 237–253.

———. 1965. Historische latein-altromanische Grammatik. I. Teil: Einleitung. Das sogenannte Vulgärlatein und das Wesen der Romanisierung. Wiesbaden. [No more published.]

———. 1966. Das Dakische (rekonstruiert aus dem Rumänischen). Heidelberg.

Reinecke, John E. 1936. Marginal languages. Yale University diss.

———, and Stanley M. Tsuzaki. Forthcoming. Bibliography of pidgin and creole languages.

Remacle, Louis. 1937. Le parler de la Gleize. Bruxelles-Liège.

——— (ed.). 1953– . Atlas linguistique de la Wallonie. Liège.

Renard, Raymond. 1967. Sepharad: le monde et la langue judéo-espagnole des Sephardim. Mons (Belgium).

Renda, Umberto. 1908. Alessandro Tassoni e il vocabolario della Crusca. Misc. Tassoniana 277–324.

Rensch, Karl-Heinz. 1964. Beiträge zur Kenntnis nordkalabrischer Mundarten. Münster/W.

Reumont, Alfred. 1853–57. Beiträge zur italienischen Geschichte. Berlin. 6 vols.

Révah, I. S. 1963. La question des substrats et des superstrats dans le domaine linguistique brésilien: les parlers populaires brésiliens doivent-ils être considérés comme des parlers "créoles" ou "semi-créoles"? Rom. 84.433–450.

Reynolds, Barbara. 1950. The linguistic writings of Alessandro Manzoni. Cambridge (England).

Rheinfelder, Hans. 1937–64. Altfranzösische Grammatik. München. 2 vols.

Ribeiro, Joaquim. 1939. História da romanização de América. Rio de Janeiro.

Ribezzo, Francesco. 1911. Il dialetto apulo-salentino di Francavilla Fontana. Martina Franca. (Apulia, App. 1.)

Ricci, Vittore (ed.). 1904. Vocabolario trentino-italiano. Trento.

Rice, Frank (ed.). 1962. Study of the rôle of second languages in Asia, Africa, and Latin America. Washington, D.C.

Richter, Elise. 1933. Die Entwicklung des neuesten Französisch. Bielefeld-Leipzig.

Rickard, Peter. 1968. La langue française au XVIᵉ siècle. Étude suivie de textes. Cambridge (England).

Riley, Carroll L. 1952. Trade Spanish of the Piñaguero Panare. SiL 10.6–11.

312   COMPARATIVE ROMANCE GRAMMAR

Ringenson, Karen. 1936. *Dies* et *diurnum*. Étude de lexicographie et de stylistique. StN 10.3–53.

Ripert, Emile. 1917. La renaissance provençale (1800–1860). Paris and Aix-en-Provence.

Rivelli, F. 1924. Casa e patria, ovvero il dialetto e la lingua. Guida per i Materani. Matera.

Robe, Stanley Linn. 1960. The Spanish of rural Panamá. Berkeley and Los Angeles. (UCPL no. 20.)

Robertson, Duncan Maclaren. 1910. A history of the French Academy, 1635–1910. New York.

Robins, Robert Henry. 1951. Ancient and mediaeval grammatical theory in Europe, with particular reference to modern linguistic doctrine. London.

———. 1967. A short history of linguistics. Bloomington, Indiana.

Robson, C. A. 1963. L'Appendix Probi et la philologie latine. MA 69.37–54.

Roccella, Remigio. 1875. Vocabolario della lingua parlata in Piazza Armerina (Sicilia). Caltagirone.

Roceric-Alexandrescu, Alexandra. 1968. Fonostatica limbii române. Bucureşti.

Roche, Alphonse V. 1954. Provençal regionalism. Evanston, Illinois.

Rodrigues Lapa, M. 1952. Lições de literatura portuguêsa. Época medieval. Coimbra.

Rodríguez, Zorobabel. 1875. Diccionario de chilenismos. Santiago de Chile.

Rodríguez Castellano, Lorenzo. 1952. La variedad dialectal del Alto Aller. Oviedo.

———. 1954. Aspectos del bable occidental. Oviedo.

———. 1957. Contribución al vocabulario del bable occidental. Oviedo.

———, and Adela Palacio. 1948. Contribución al estudio del dialecto andaluz. El habla de Cabra. RDyTP 4.387–418, 570–593.

Rössler, Otto. 1962. Die lateinischen Reliktwörter im Berberischen und die Frage des Vokalsystems der afrikanischen Latinität. BNF 13.258–262.

Rohlfs, Gerhard. 1924. Griechen und Romanen in Unteritalien. Genève. (BAR II.7.) (Italian tr.: Scavi linguistici nella Magna Grecia, Roma, 1933.)

———. 1925. Der Stand der Mundartenforschung in Unteritalien (bis zum Jahre 1923). RLiR 1.278–323.

———. 1927. Baskische Kultur im Spiegel des lateinischen Lehnwortes. Festschrift Voretzsch 58–86. (Spanish tr.: La influencia latina en le lengua y cultura vasca, RIEB 24.323–348 [1933].)

———. 1931. Galloitalienische Sprachinseln in der Basilicata. ZRPh. 31.249–279.

———. 1932–38. Dizionario dialettale delle Tre Calabrie, con note etimologiche e un'introduzione sulla storia dei dialetti calabresi. Halle/S.

———. 1933. Le origini della grecità in Calabria. ASCL 3.231–258.

———. 1935. Le gascon: études de philologie pyrénéenne. Halle/S. (ZRPh. Bhft. no. 85. 2nd ed., Tübingen, 1970.)

———. 1937a. Sprachliche Berührungen zwischen Sardinien und Süditalien. Donum Natalicium Jaberg 25–75.

———. 1937b. Mundarten und Griechentum des Cilento. ZRPh. 57.421–461.

———. 1937c. La struttura linguistica dell'Italia. Leipzig. (Spanish tr.: La estructura lingüística de Itália, in Rohlfs 1952b:1–29.)

———. 1941a. Galloitalienische Sprachkolonien am Golf von Policastro (Lukanien). ZRPh. 61.79–113.

———. 1941b. L'italianità linguistica della Corsica. Roma-Vienna. (Spanish tr.: La italianidad lingüística de la Córsica, in Rohlfs 1952b:117–162.)

———. 1941c. Über eine unbekannte gotisch-langobardische Wortdublette (*zolla*, cors., elb. *tolla*). ASNS 179.34–35. (Reprinted under title "Eine unbekannte gotisch-langobardische Wortdublette" in Rohlfs 1952c:228–230.)

———. 1947a. Griechischer Sprachgeist in Unteritalien. München. (SbBayr. 1944/ 46:5.)

———. 1947b. Germanisches Spracherbe in der Romania. München. (SbBayr. 1944/ 46:8.)

———. 1947c. Geographische Streifzüge durch Italien. München. (SbBayr. 1944/ 46:3.)

———. 1949–54. Historische Grammatik der italienischen Sprache und ihrer Mundarten. Bern. (Italian tr.: Grammatica storica della lingua italiana e dei suoi dialetti, Torino, 1966–69.)

———. 1950. Historische Grammatik der unteritalienischen Gräzität. München. (SbBayr. 1949:4.)

———. 1950–52. Romanische Philologie. 2 vols. (2nd ed., 1966– .)

———. 1952a. Fränkische und franco-romanische Wanderwörter in der Romania. Festgabe Gamillscheg 111–128.

———. 1952b. Estudios sobre geografía lingüística de Itália. Granada.

———. 1952c. An den Quellen der romanischen Sprachen. Halle/S.

———. 1956–59. Vocabolario dei dialetti salentini (Terra d'Otranto.) München. 3 vols. (AbhBAW NF.41., 48., 53.)

———. 1957. Manual de filología hispánica. Guía bibliográfica, crítica y metódica. Bogotá (Colombia). (PICC no. 12.)

———. 1962a. Nuovi contributi al grecismo della Sicilia nord-orientale. BCSic. 8.119–143.

———. 1962b. Neue Beiträge zur Kenntnis der unteritalienischen Gräzität. München. (SbBayr. 1962:5.)

———. 1963. Correnti e strati di romanità in Sicilia (aspetti di geografia linguistica). BCSic. 9.74–105.

———. 1964/65. Ellenismo e latinità nella Sicilia di oggi. Kōkalos 10/11.565–578.

———. 1965–67. Vocabolario supplementare dei dialetti delle Tre Calabrie. München. 2 vols. (AbhBAW nos. 64, 66.)

———. 1967a. L'Italia dialettale (dal Piemonte in Sicilia). NArg. 5.22–28.

———. 1967b. Review of Urciolo 1965. IF 72.346–353.

Rohner, Kurt. 1938. Beschreibende Phonetik der Mundart von Cachopo (östliches Algarve). Wintherthur.

Rohr, Rupprecht. 1964. Einführung in das Studium der Romanistik. Berlin.

Rolin, Gustav. 1908. Die Mundart von Vasto in den Abruzzen. PDS 8.477–504.

Rolland, Eugène. 1873–75. Vocabulaire du patois du pays Messin tel qu'il est actuellement parlé à Rémilly (ancient département de la Moselle, canton Pange). Rom. 2.437–454 (2873); 4.189–229 (1875).

Romaguera Corrêa, J., Antonio Alvares Pereira Coruga, and Luiz Carlos de Moraes. 1964. Vocabolário sul-rio-grandense. Rio de Janeiro.

Romansky, St. 1909. Lehnwörter lateinischen Ursprungs im Bulgarischen. JbIRSL 15.89–134.

Romera Navarro, M. 1929. La defensa de la lengua española en el siglo XVI. BH 31.204–255.

Rona, José Pedro. 1958. Aspectos metodológicos de la dialectología hispànica. Montevideo.

———. 1963. La reproducción del lenguaje hablado en la literatura gauchesca. RIbL 4:4.107–119.

————. 1965. El dialecto "fronterizo" del Norte de Uruguay. Montevideo.

————. 1971. Elementos españoles, portugueses y africanos en el papiamento. Watatana 3:3.7–23.

Roncaglia, Aurelio. 1950. Review of Hall 1950a. CN 10.99–102.

————. 1959. Bilinguismo esterno e plurilinguismo interno nelle Glosse di Kassel. ACISR³ 2:1.347–358.

————. 1965. La lingua dei trovatori. Roma.

Ronjat, Jules. 1913. Essai de syntaxe des parlers provençaux modernes. Mâcon.

————. 1930–32. Grammaire istorique des parlers provençaux modernes. Montpellier. 2 vols.

Rosamani, Enrico. 1958. Vocabolario giuliano. Bologna.

Rosellini, Aldo. 1970. Essai sur la francisation de la Vallée d'Aoste des origines au XVIᵉ siècle. SMLV 18.113–215.

Rosenblat, Ángel. 1933. La lengua y la cultura de Hispanoamérica. Nosotros 79.5–27. Also sep., Jena, 1933. (Later eds.: Caracas, 1949; Paris, 1951.)

————. 1962. El castellano de España y el castellano de América. Unidad y diferenciación. Caracas. (3rd ed., 1965.)

————. 1963. Fetichismo de la letra. Caracas.

————. 1967. El criterio de corrección lingüística: unidad o pluralidad de normas en el español de España y América. Bogotá (Colombia).

Rosenquist, A. 1919. Limites administratives et divisions dialectales de la France. NM 20.87–118, with 2 maps.

Rosetti, Alexandru. 1938. Istoria limbii române. București. 2 vols. (German tr.: Geschichte der rumänischen Sprache, Bucharest, 1943.)

————. 1953. Influența limbilor slave meridionale asupră limbii române (sec. VI–XII). București.

————. 1968. Istoria limbii române de la origini pînă în secolul al XVII-lea. București. (New version of Rosetti 1938.)

————, and Boris Cazacu. 1961. Istoria limbii romîne literare. București.

Rosiello, Luigi. 1958. Il "Dizionario de' Francesismi" di Basilio Puoti. LN 19.110–118.

————. 1971. Norma, dialetto e diasistema dell'italiano regionale. L'Insegnamento dell'italiano 345–352.

————. 1967. Linguistica illuminista. Bologna.

Rossi, Giuseppe Carlo. 1953. Storia della letteratura portoghese. Firenze.

Rossi, Nelson. 1963. Atlas prévio dos falares baianos. Rio de Janeiro.

Rossi, Vittorio. 1899. Storia della letteratura italiana. Milano. 3 vols.

Rossi-Casé, Luigi. 1894. Il dialetto aquilano nella storia della sua fonetica. BSSA 6.3–58.

Rostovtseff, Mikhail Ivanović. 1926. The social and economic history of the Roman Empire. Oxford (England). 3 vols.

————. 1926–27. A history of the ancient world. Oxford (England). 2 vols.

Rothe, Wolfgang. 1957. Einführung in die historische Laut- und Formenlehre des Rumänischen. Halle/S.

Rotta, Paolo. 1910. La filosofia del linguaggio nella partistica e nella scolastica. Torino.

Roulet, Eddy. 1969. Syntaxe de la proposition nucléaire en français parlé. Étude tagmématique et transformationelle. Bruxelles.

Roumiguière, Henriette. 1926. Le français dans les relations diplomatiques. UCPM-Ph. 12.259–340. Also sep.: Berkeley, Calif.

Rousselot, Pierre-Jean. 1891–92. Les modifications du langage étudiées dans le patois d'une famille de Cellefrouin. RPGR 4.65–208 (1891); 5.209–434 (1892). Also sep.: Paris, 1891.

Roussey, Charles. 1894. Glossaire du parler de Bournois (Canton de l'Isle-sur-le-Doubs, arrondissement de Beaume les Dames). Paris.

Roux, J. 1895. Grammaire limousine. Brive.

Roz, Firmin. 1957. Le rayonnement de la langue française dans le monde. Paris.

Rubin, Joan. 1968. National bilingualism in Paraguay. The Hague. (JL-SP no. 60.)

Rubio, Antonio. 1937. La crítica del galicismo en España (1726–1832). México, D.F.

Rubio García, Luís. 1965. Estudio histórico lingüístico del antiguo condado de Ribagorza. Lérida.

Rüegg, Robert. 1956. Zur Wortgeographie der italienischen Umgangssprache. Köln. (KRA NF:7.)

Ruffini, Mario. 1962. Caracterul modern al doctrinei lingvistice a lui Dante. RFRG 6.229–242.

Ruggieri, Ruggero Maria. 1961a. I. Il francoveneto. II. Gui de Nanteuil. III. Italiano, latino, francese nel Quattrocento. Roma.

———. 1961b. Origine, struttura, caratteri del francoveneto. Orbis 10.20–30. (Reprinted in Ruggieri, 1962:159–168.)

———. 1962. Saggi di linguistica italiana e italo-romanza. Firenze. (BAR II:29.).

———. 1967. "Romanità" e "Romanicità". APh. 5.117–126.

———. 1969. La filologia romanza in Italia. Capitoli di storia retrospettiva. Milano.

Ruiz i Calonia, Joan. 1954. Història de la literatura catalana. Barcelona.

Ruppert, R. 1915. Die spanischen Lehnwörter in der französischen Schriftsprache. München.

Russu, I. I. 1959. Limba traco-dacilor. Bucureşti. (2nd ed., 1967.)

Saalfeld, G. A. E. A. 1884. Thesaurus italograecus. Ausführliches historisch-kritisches Wörterbuch der griechischen Lehn- und Fremdwörter im Lateinischen. Wien.

Saarauw, Chr. 1920. Die Italienismen in der Französischen Sprache des 16. Jahrhunderts. Borna-Leipzig.

Sabatini, Francesco. 1962. Bilancio del millennario della lingua italiana. CN 22.187–215.

———. 1963. Riflessi linguistici della dominazione longobarda nell'Italia mediana e meridionale. AAColombaria 28. (= NS.14.) 132–149.

———. 1963/64. Il glossario di Monza: il testo, la localizzazione, il compilatore. AATorino 98.51–84.

———. 1968. Dalla "scripta latina rustica" alle "scriptae" romanze. StM III.9.320–358.

Sacco, Giuseppe. 1925. Il dialetto di Sciacca e dei suoi dintorni. In Scaturro 1925:83–129.

Safford, William Edward. 1905. The Chamorro language of Guam. Washington, D.C.

Sahlin, Gunvor. 1928. César Chesneau du Marsais et son rôle dans l'évolution de la grammaire générale. Paris.

Said Ali, Manoel. 1923. Formação de palavras e syntaxe do português histórico. São Paulo.

———. 1931. Gramática histórica da língua portuguêsa. São Paulo. (3rd ed., 1964.)

Sainéan, Lazare. 1920. Le langage parisien au XIXe siècle. Paris.

Sala, Marius. 1970. Estudios sobre el judeo-español de Bucarest. México, D.F.

————. 1972. Phonétique et phonologie du judéo-espagnol de Bucarest. La Haye. (JL-SP no. 142.)

Sala, Marius, and Sanda Reinheimer. 1967–68. Bibliographies de linguistique romane: domaine francoprovençal. RLiR 31.383–429 (1967); 32.199–234 (1968).

Salinas, Pedro. 1944. Aprecio y defensa del lenguaje. Río Piedras, P.R.

Salow, Karl. 1912. Sprachgeographische Untersuchungen über den östlichen Teil des katalanischen-languedokischen Grenzgeibietes. Hamburg.

Saltarelli, Mario Donato. 1970. A phonology of Italian in a generative grammar. The Hague. (JL-SP no. 93.)

Salvá, Evelina. 1959. Il dialetto di Tortorici. RIL II.93.239–273.

Salvador, Gregorio. 1957. El habla de Cúllar-Baza. Contribución al estudio de la frontera del andaluz. RFE 41.161–252.

Salvat, Joseph. 1943. Grammaire occitane. Paris. (2nd ed., Toulouse, 1951.)

Salverda de Grave, J. J. 1906. De franse woorden in het Nederlands. Amsterdam. (VKAW NS.7.)

————. 1913. L'influence de la langue française en Hollande d'après les mots empruntés. Paris.

Salvioni, Carlo. 1884. Fonetica del dialetto moderno della città di Milano. Roma-Torino-Firenze.

————. 1906. Il dialetto di Poschiavo, a proposito di una recente descrizione. RIL II.39.477–494, 505–522, 569–586, 603–622.

————. 1907. Lingua e dialetti della Svizzera italiana. RIL II.40.719–736.

————. 1916. Dell'elemento germanico nella lingua italiana. RIL II.49.1011–1067.

Samarani, Bonifacio. 1852. Vocabolario cremasco-italiano. Crema.

Sanabria Fernández, Hernando V. 1965. El habla popular de la provincia de Vallegrande (Departamento de Santa Cruz). Santa Cruz (Bolivia).

Sánchez Sevilla, P. 1928. El habla de Cespedosa de Tormes. RFE 15.131–172, 244–282.

Sanchis Guarner, Manuel. 1936. Extensión y vitalidad del dialecto valenciano "apitxat". RFE 23.45–62.

————. 1948. Introducción a la historia lingüística de Valencia. Valencia.

————. 1949. Noticia del habla de Aguaviva en Aragón. RFE 33.15–65.

————. 1950. Gramàtica valenciana. Valencia.

————. 1956. Factores históricos de los dialectos catalanes. Estudios Menéndez Pidal 6.151–186.

————. 1960. La llengua dels Valencians. Valencia. (3rd ed., 1967.)

————. 1961. Els parlars romànics de Valencia i Mallorca anteriors a la Reconquista. Valencia.

Sandfeld (-Jansen), Kristian. 1904. Die nichtlateinischen Elemente im Rumänischen. In Gröber (ed.) 1904–06:1.524–534.

————. 1928–43. Syntaxe du français contemporain. Paris. 3 vols.

————. 1930. Linguistique balkanique: problèmes et résultats. Paris.

————, and Hedwig Olsen. 1936–62. Syntaxe roumaine. Paris, 3 vols.

Sanna, A. 1957. Introduzione agli studî di linguistica sarda. Càgliari.

Santamaría, Francisco J. 1942–43. Diccionario general de americanismos. Méjico, D.F. 3 vols.

Santàngelo, Giorgio. 1961. Pietro Bembo e la questione della lingua. In Orientamenti culturali: Letteratura italiana: I minori 1.803–840 (Milano).

Santos Coco, Francisco. 1940–44. Vocabulario extremeño. RCEE 14.65–96, 134–166 (1940); 18.243–253 (1944).

Sapir, Edward. 1921. Language. New York. (Reprinted 1955.)

Saracino, G. 1901. Lessico dialettale bitontino-italiano. Molfetta.

Saraiva, Antonio José, and Óscar Lopes. 1954. História da literatura portuguêsa. Porto and Lisbon. (5th ed., 1966.)

Sarran, F. 1920. Petite grammaire gasconne. Auch.

Sassu, Salvatore D. 1951. Il dialetto di Sassari. Sàssari.

Savini, G. 1881. La grammatica ed il lessico del dialetto teramano. Torino.

———. 1895. I dialetti della provincia di Teramo. Tèramo.

Savinian. 1882. Grammaire provençale (sous-dialecte rodanien). Avignon.

Sawyer, Jesse O. 1964/65. The implications of /r/ and /rr/ in Wappo history. RPh. 14.165–177.

Scalia, S. Eugene. 1950. Sanemagogna. LN 11.91–94.

Scano, Emanuele. 1901. Saggio critico-storico della poesia dialettale sarda. Càgliari-Sàssari.

Scanu, Pasquale. 1963. Pervivencia de la llengua catalana oficial a Alguer. Studf A. Era 353–372.

Scardigno, Rosaria. 1903. Lessico dialettale molfettese-italiano. Molfetta.

———. 1963a. Nuovo lessico molfettese-italiano. Molfetta.

———. 1963b. Molfetta allo specchio. Come appare dal suo lessico. Molfetta.

Scaturro, I. 1925. Storia della città di Sciacca. Nàpoli.

Scerbo, F. 1886. Sul dialetto calabro. Firenze.

Schädel, Bernhard. 1903. Die Mundart von Ormea. Beiträge zur Laut- und Konjugationslehre der nordwestitalienischen Sprachgruppe mit Dialektproben, Glossar und Karte. Halle/S.

———. 1908. Manual de fonética catalana. Cöthen.

———. 1909. Die katalanischen Pyrenäendialekte. RDR 1.15–98, 386–412.

Schaedel, Richard P. (ed.). 1969. Research and resources of Haiti. New York.

Schane, Sanford. 1968. French phonology and morphology. Cambridge, Mass.

Scharten, Theodora. 1942. Posizione linguistica del Poitou. StR 29.5–130, with 6 maps.

Scheludko, D. 1927. Lateinische und rumänische Elemente im Bulgarischen. BA 3.252–289.

Scherer, Wilhelm. 1884. Geschichte der deutschen Litteratur. Berlin. (Many later eds.)

Scheuermeier, Paul. 1943–56. Bauernwerk in Italian, der italienischen und rätoromanischen Schweiz. Eine sprach- und sachkundliche Darstellung landwirtschaftlicher Arbeiten und Geräte. Vol. 1: Erlenbach-Zürich, 1943. Vol. 2: Bern, 1956.

Schiaffini, Alfredo. 1928. Influsso dei dialetti centro-meridionali sul toscano e sulla lingua letteraria. ID 4.77–129.

———. 1943. Latinità e italianità nell'Europa di sud-est. CN 3.133–148.

Schiavo-Lena, A. 1908. Il dialetto del circondario di Modica. ASSO 5.107–131, 424–428.

Schlack, Siegmund. 1966. Beiträge zur Lautlehre der Abruzzendialekte unter besonderer Berücksichtigung der Mundart von Scanno. Berlin.

Schmaus, J. 1912. Geschichte und Herkunft der alten Franken. Bamberg.

Schmeck, Helmut. 1952. Probleme des korsischen Konsonantismus. Phonologische Darstellung. ZRPh. 68.49–72.

———. 1954. Zur historischen Phonetik des Korsischen: Konsonantismus. ZRPh. 70.73–85.

Schmid, Henrich.   1956.   Über Randgebiete und Sprachgrenzen. VR 15.19–80, with 6
maps.

Schmidt, W. Fritz.   1914.   Die spanischen Elemente im französischen Wortschatz.
Halle/S. (ZRPh. Bhft. no. 54.)

Schmidt-Henkel, Gerhard (ed.).   1964.   Trivialliteratur: Aufsätze. Berlin.

Schmoll, Ulrich.   1959.   Die Sprachen der vorkeltischen Indogermanen Hispaniens
und das Keltiberische. Wiesbaden.

Schneegans, Heinrich.   1888.   Laute und Lautentwicklung des sicilianischen Dialectes.
Strassburg.

Schneller, C.   1870.   Die romanischen Volksmundarten im Südtirol. Gera.

Schönthaler, Willy.   1937.   Die Mundart des Bethmale-Tales (Ariège), Laut- und Formenlehre. Tübingen.

Schorta, A.   1938.   Lautlehre der Mundart von Müstair. Zürich. (RH no. 7.)

Schroeder, K. H.   1967.   Einführung in das Studium der rumänischen Sprachwissenschaft und Literaturgeschichte. Berlin.

Schuchardt, Hugo Ernst Maria.   1882–90.   Kreolische Studien. SbWien 101.889–917;
102.799–816; 103.3–17; 105.111–150, 882–904; 116.193–226, 227–234; 122.1–256.

———.   1888–89.   Beiträge zur Kenntnis des kreolischen Romanisch. ZRPh. 12.242–
254, 301–312, 312–322; 13.463–475, 476–516, 516–524 (1889).

———.   1906.   Baskisch und Romanisch. Halle/S. (ZRPh. Bhft. no. 6.)

———.   1908.   Rom. "umsonst" aus Arab. baṭil. ZRPh. 32.465–472.

———.   1909.   Die Lingua Franca. ZRPh. 33.441–461.

———.   1918.   Die romanischen Lehnwörter im Berberischen. Wien. (SbWien 188:4.)

Schürr, Friedrich.   1917.   Romagnolische Mundarten. Sprachproben in phonetischer
Transkription auf Grund phonographischer Aufnahmen. Wien. (SbWien 181:2.)

———.   1918–19.   Romagnolische Dialektstudien. Vol. 1: Wien, 1918 (SbWien 187:4.)
Vol. 2: Wien, 1919 (SbWien 188:1.)

———.   1933.   La posizione storica del romagnolo tra i dialetti contermini. RLiR
9.203–228.

———.   1938.   La classificazione dei dialetti italiani. Leipzig.

———.   1954.   Profilo dialettologico della Romagna. Orbis 3.471–485.

———.   1963.   Die Alpenromanen. VR 22.100–126.

———.   1965.   Mundartliche Gliederungen im romagnolisch—nordumbrisch—areti-
nischen Raum. Studî Schiaffini (= RCCM 7.) 1017–1024.

Schwan, Eduard.   1888.   Grammatik des Altrranzösischen. Leipzig. (Later eds. with
Dietrich Behrens. French tr. by Oscar Bloch: Grammaire de l'ancien français,
Leipzig, 1913.)

Schwendener, Ulrich.   1923.   Der Accusativus cum Infinitivo im Italienischen. Säckin-
gen am Rhein.

Searles, Colbert (ed.).   1916.   Les sentiments de l'Académie Française sur le Cid.
Minneapolis. (UMSLL no. 3.)

Sebeok, Thomas Albert (ed.).   1966.   Portraits of Linguists. Bloomington, Indiana.

Seche, Mircea.   1966.   Schiță de istorie a lexicografiei române. București.

Seeck, Otto.   1897–1921.   Geschichte des Untergangs der antiken Welt. Berlin.

Seelmann, E.   1890.   Review of Meyer-Lübke 1887. KrJber. 1.49–53.

Séguy, Jean.   1950.   Le français parlé à Toulouse. Toulouse.

———, et al. (eds.) 1954–56. Atlas linguistique et ethnographique de la Gascogne. Paris.

Seidel, Eugen.   1958.   Elemente sintactice slave în limba romînă. București.

Seraine, Florival.   1958.   Dicionário de termos populares (registrados no Ceará). Rio de
Janeiro.

Serís, Homero. 1964. Bibliografía de la lingüística española. Bogotá (Colombia). (PICC no. 19.)

Sevilla, Alberto. 1919. Vocabulario murciano. Murcia.

Seybold, Christian Friedrich. 1886. Die arabische Sprache in den romanischen Ländern. In Gröber (ed.) 1886–88:1.398–405. (In 2nd ed.: 1.515–523.)

Sganzini, Silvio (ed.). 1952– . Vocabolario dei dialetti della Svizzera italiana. Lugano.

Shipley, William. 1962/63. Spanish elements in the indigenous languages of central California. RPh. 16.1–21.

Shipman, George R. 1953. The vowel phonemes of Meigret. Washingtoh, D.C.

Silva Neto, Serafim. 1938a. O crioulo de Surinam. Misc. Said Ali. (Reprinted in Cultura (Rio de Janeiro) 2.57–70 (1949) and in Silva Neto 1960:127–153.)

———. 1938b. Fontes do latim vulgar. Rio de Janeiro. (3rd ed., 1956.)

———. 1949. Falares crioulos. Brasilia 5.

———. 1951. Introdução ao estudo da língua portuguêsa no Brasil. Rio de Janeiro. (2nd ed., 1963.)

———. 1952. História da língua portuguêsa. Rio de Janeiro.

———. 1955. Guia para estudos dialectológicos. Florianopolis. (2nd ed., 1958.)

———. 1957. História do latim vulgar. Rio de Janeiro. (BBF no. 13.)

———. 1960. Lingua, Cultura e Civilização. Rio de Janeiro.

Simon, Hans Joachim. 1967. Beobachtungen an Mundarten Piemonts. Heidelberg.

Simoncini, Forrest. 1959. The San Francisco Italian dialect: a study. Orbis 8.342–354.

Siotto-Pintor, Giovanni. 1843–44. Storia letteraria di Sardegna. Càgliari. 4 vols. (Reprinted, Bologna, 1966.)

Sjögren, A. 1928. Mots d'emprunt norrois en normand. Rom. 54.341–412.

———. 1964– . Les parlers bas-normands de l'Île de Guernesey. Paris.

Skok, Petar. 1923. Slave et Roumain. RÉS 3.59–77.

———. 1931. Byzance comme centre d'irradiation pour les mots latins des langues balkaniques. Byzantion 6.371–378.

Sletsjoe, Leif. 1967. La position du mirandais. StN 39.150–173.

Sneyders de Vogel, K. 1927. Syntaxe historique du français. Groningen.

Soares de Azevedo, Celestino. 1928/29. A linguagem popular de Ervedosa de Douro. RLus. 27.86–197.

Sobrero, Alberto. 1971. Effetti linguistici dei mezzi di comunicazione di massa. PeM 1.167–189.

Soffietti, James Peter. 1949. Phonemic analysis of the word in Turinese. New York.

Solá-Solé, J. M. 1967/68. El artículo al- en los arabismos iberorrománicos. RPh. 21.275–285.

Solé, Carlos A. 1970. Bibliografía sobre el español en América, 1920–1967. Washington, D.C.

Southern, R. W. 1953. The making of the Middle Ages. New Haven and London.

Sozzi, Bortolo Tommaso. 1955. Aspetti e momenti della questione linguistica. Pàdova.

Spaulding, Robert K. 1943. How Spanish grew. Berkeley and Los Angeles.

Spence, Nicol C. M. 1960. A glossary of Jersey-French. Oxford (England).

Spencer, Robert F. 1947. Spanish loan-words in Keresan. SJA 3.130–146.

Spiess, Federico. 1956. Die Verwendung des Subjekt-Personalpronomens in den lombardischen Mundarten. Bern. (RH no. 59.)

Spitzer, Leo. 1922. Italienische Umgangssprache. Bonn-Leipzig.

Spoerri, Theophil. 1918. Il dialetto della Valsesia. RIL II.51.391–409, 683–698, 732–752.

Spòtti, Luigi. 1929. Vocabolarietto anconitano-italiano. Genève. (BAR II.15.)

Stampa, Gian Andrea. 1934. Der Dialekt des Bregell. Aarau.

Stefenelli, Arnulf. 1962. Die Volkssprache im Werk des Petron, in Himblick auf die romanischen Sprachen. Wien. (WRA no. 1.)

Steiger, Arnald. 1932. Contribución a la fonética del hispano-árabe y de los arabismos en el ibero-románico y el siciliano. Madrid. (RFE Anejo no. 17.)

———. 1943. Zur Sprache der Mozaraber. Sache, Ort und Wort 625–714.

———. 1963. Origin and spread of oriental words in European languages. New York.

Steinthal, Heymann. 1863. Geschichte der Sprachwissenschaft bei den Griechen und Römern. Berlin. (2nd ed., 1890–91.)

Sten, Holger. 1944. Les particularités de la langue portugaise. Copenhague. (TCLC no. 2.)

Stengel, Eduard. 1878. Die beiden ältesten provenzalischen Grammatiken. Marburg.

———. 1879. Die erstein Anleitungsschriften zur Erlernung der französischen Sprache. ZFSL 1.1–40.

Stern, Samuel Miklós. 1953. Les chansons mozarabes. Palermo. (Reprinted Oxford [England], 1964.)

Stevenson, C. H. 1970. The Spanish language today. London.

Stewart, William A. 1962. Creole languages in the Caribbean. In Rice (ed.) 1962:34–53.

Stimm, Helmut. 1952. Studien zur Entwicklungsgeschichte des Frankoprovenzalischen. Mainz. (AbhMainz 1952:6.)

Stolz, Friedrich. 1910. Geschichte der lateinischen Sprache. Berlin. (Later eds. revised by A. Debrunner, W. Schmid.) (Italian tr.: Storia della lingua latina, Bologna, 1966.)

———, and J. H. Schmalz. 1885. Lateinische Grammatik (Laut- und Formenlehre, Syntax und Stylistik). Nördlingen. (Later eds. revised by M. Leumann and others.)

Straka, Georges (ed.). 1964. Poèmes du XVIIIᵉ siècle en dialecte de Saint-Étienne (Loire). Paris. 2 vols. (PILRL nos. 22., 23.)

Strauss, Franz. 1938. Vulgärlatein und Vulgärsprache im Zusammenhang der Sprachenfrage im 16. Jahrhundert (Frankreich und Italien). Marburg. (MBRP no. 21.)

Streuber, Albert. 1964–69. Französische Grammatik und französischer Unterricht in Frankreich und Deutschland während des 16. Jahrhunderts. ZFSL 74.342–361 (1964); 75.31–50, 247–273 (1965); 77.235–267 (1967); 78.69–101 (1968); 79.172–191, 328–348 (1969).

Strohmeyer, Fr. 1929. Französische Grammatik auf sprachhistorisch-psychologischer Grundlage. Leipzig.

Stürzinger, Jakob. 1884. Orthographia gallica. Heilbronn. (Reprinted, Darmstadt, 1967.)

Sturtevant, Edgar Howard. 1917. Linguistic change. Chicago

———. 1920. The pronunciation of Greek and Latin. Chicago. (2nd ed., Philadelphia, 1940.)

Suárez, Constantino. 1921. Vocabulario cubano. La Habana and Madrid.

Suárez, Jorge A. 1966/67. Indigenismos e hispanismos, vistos desde la Argentina. RPh. 20.68–90.

Sütterlin, L. 1896. Die heutige Mundart von Nizza. RF 9.249–586.

Svennung, Josef. 1933. Wortstudien zu den spätlateinischen Oribasiusrezensionen. SSUF 1933. (= UUÅ 1933:5.) 57–146.

Svensen, Lars Owe. 1959. Les parlers du Marais vendéen. Göteborg. 2 vols. (RGoth. no. 8.)

Swann, Harvey J. 1918. French terminologies in the making: studies in conscious contributions to the vocabulary. New York.

Sylvain(-Comhaire), Suzanne. 1936. Le créole haïtien: morphologie et syntaxe. Wetteren and Port-au-Prince.

Symonds, John Addington. 1875–86. Renaissance in Italy. London. (Many later eds.)

Szemerényi Oswald. 1961/62. The study of substratum in ancient Italy. RPh. 15.301–311.

Tagliavini, Carlo. 1926. Il dialetto del Comèlico. AR 10.1–200.

———. 1933–34. Il dialetto del Livinallongo. Saggio lessicale. AAA 28.331–380 (1933); 29.53–221, 643–704 (1934). Also sep.: Bolzano, 1934.

———. 1936. Elementi di linguistica italiana. Pàdova.

———. 1942–44. Studî linguistici ladino-veneti. I. Nuovi contributi alla conoscenza dei dialetti del Comelico. AIVeneto 102.843–884 (1942/43); 103.33–67, 181–245, 287–350 (1943/44).

———. 1943. La stratificazione del lessico albanese. Bologna.

———. 1947. Le origini delle lingue neolatine. Bologna. (5th ed., 1969.)

———. 1956. It. fasullo < ebr. pâsúl. Studî Levi della Vida 2.539–552.

———. 1963. Storia della linguistica. Bologna.

Taine, Hyppolite. 1875–94. Les origines de la France contemporaine. Paris.

Tavani, Giuseppe. 1968. Preistoria e istoria delle lingue ispaniche. L'Àquila.

Taylor, Alan R. 1962/63. Spanish manteca in Alaskan Eskimo. RPh. 16.30–32.

Taylor, Douglas McR. 1947. Phonemes of Caribbean Creole. Word 2.173–179.

———. 1951. Structural outline of Caribbean Creole. Word 7.43–59.

———. 1961. New languages for old in the West Indies. CSSH 3.277–288.

———. 1962/63. Lexical borrowing in Island-Carib. RPh. 16.143–152.

Taylor, Pauline. 1932. The Latinity of the Liber Historiae Francorum. New York.

Tejeira, Gil Blas. 1964. El habla del panameño. Panamá.

Tejera, E. 1935. Palabras indígenas de la isla de Santo Domingo. Santo Domingo.

Tellenbach, Fritz. 1909. Der römische Dialekt nach den Sonetten von G. G. Belli. Zürich.

Terlingen, Johannes Hermanus. 1943. Los italianismos en español desde la formación del idioma hasta principios del siglo XVII. Amsterdam.

Terracini, Benvenuto Aron. 1910–22. Il parlare d'Usseglio. AGI 17.198–249 (1910/13); 18.105–186 (1914/22).

———. 1951. Residui di parlate giudeo-italiane raccolti a Pitigliano, Roma, Ferrara. RMI III.17.1-11, 63–72, 113–121.

———. 1952. "Quia magis videtur inniti grammatice." Mél. Roques 3.275–279. (Reprinted in Terracini, 1957:184–188.)

———. 1957. Pagine e appunti di linguistica storica. Firenze.

——— and Temistocle Franceschi (eds.). 1964– . Saggio di un atlante linguistico della Sardegna. Torino. 2 vols.

Terrera, Guillermo Alfredo. 1968. Sociología y vocabulario del habla popular argentina. Buenos Aires.

Thomas, Earl W. 1969. The syntax of spoken Brazilian Portuguese. Nashville, Tennessee.

Thomas, T. 1889. The theory and practice of Creole grammar. Port-of-Spain.

Thompson, Edward Arthur. 1969. The Goths in Spain. Oxford (England).

Thompson, R. W.   1961.   A note on some possible affinities between the Creole dialects of the Old World and those of the new. CLS 2.107–113.

Tibiletti Bruno, Maria Grazia.   1961–62.   I sabini e la loro lingua. RIL II.95.501–544 (1961); II.96.413–442, 565–640 (1963). Also sep.: Milano, 1962.

Timiras, Nicolas.   1955.   The Sicilian dialect spoken by the Monterrey (California) fishermen. Orbis 4.349–376, with 2 plates.

Tiraboschi, Antonio.   1873.   Vocabolario dei dialetti bergamaschi antichi e moderni. Bèrgamo.

———.   1879.   Appendice al vocabolario dei dialetti bergpmaschi. Bèrgamo.

Tisch, Joseph L.   1959.   French in Louisiana: a study of the historical development of the French language in Louisiana. New Orleans.

Tiscornia, Eleuterio Felipe.   1930.   La lengua de *Martín Fierro*. Buenos Aires. (BDH 3.)

Titz, Karel.   1923.   Glossy Kasselské. v Praze.

Tobler, Adolf, and Eduard Lommatzsch.   1925– .   Altfranzösisches Wörterbuch. Berlin.

Togeby, Knud.   1951.   Structure immanente de la langue française. Copehnague. (TCLC 6.)

———.   1963/64.   Qu'est-ce que la dissimilation? RPh. 17.642–667.

Tognina, Riccardo.   1967.   Lingua e cultura della Valle di Poschiavo. Basel. (SSSTP no. 47.)

Toja, Gianluigi.   1969.   La lingua di Arnaut Daniel. CN 29.56–83.

Tomasi, Silvano, and Madeline H. Engel (eds.).   1970.   The Italian experience in the United States. Staten Island, N.Y.

Tomasini, Giulio.   1957.   Profilo linguistico della regione tridentina. Trento. (2nd ed., 1960.)

Tonetti, Federico.   1894.   Dizionario del dialetto valsesiano, preceduto da un saggio di grammatica. Varallo. (Facsimile ed., Torino, 1967.)

Toni, Giuseppe.   1850.   Vocabolario compendiato tascabile del dialetto bolognese. Bologna.

Toppino, Giuseppe.   1905–29.   Il dialetto di Castellinaldo. AGI 16.517–548 (1905); StR 10.1–104 (1913); ID 1.114–160 (1925); 2.1–49 (1926); 3.94–157 (1927); 5.202–225 (1929).

Torres Fornés, C.   1903.   Sobre voces usadas en Segorbe. Valencia.

Toscano Mateus, Humberto.   1953.   El español en el Ecuador. Madrid. (FRE Anejo no. 61.)

Tovar, Antonio.   1961.   The ancient languages of Spain and Portugal. New York.

———.   1964.   A research report on Vulgar Latin and its local variations. Kratylos 9.113–134.

———.   1968.   Lo que sabemos de la lucha de lenguas en la Península Ibérica. Madrid.

Tovar, Enrique D.   1966.   Vocabulario del Oriente peruano. Lima.

Tozzoli, Giovanni.   1857.   Piccolo dizionario domestico imolese-italiano. Imola.

Trabalza, Ciro.   1908.   Storia della grammatica italiana. Milano. (Reprinted, Bologna, 1963.)

Tracconaglia, Giovanni.   1907.   Contributo allo studio dell'italianismo in Francia: Henri Estienne e gli italianismi. Lodi.

Trager, George Leonard.   1932.   The use of the Latin demonstratives (especially *ille* and *ipse*) up to 600 A.D. as the source of the Romance article. New York.

———.   1934.   On the classification of the Romance languages. RR 25.129–136

———.   1938.   The phonemes of Castillian [sic] Spanish. TCLP 8.219–222.

———.   1944.   Spanish and English loan-words in Taos. IJAL 10.144–158.

――――. 1946. Changes of emphasis in linguistics: a comment. StP 43.462–464.

――――, and G. Valdez. 1937. English loans in Colorado Spanish. AS 12.34–44.

Traina, Antonio. 1868. Nuovo vocabolario siciliano-italiano. Palermo. (2nd ed., 1890.)

Troeger, O. 1928. Namengebung und Bedeutungswandel in gerereitechnischen und gerbereichemischen Ausdrücken der französischen Sprache. Leipzig.

Trofin, Aurel. 1967. Observații cu privire la adaptarea terminologiei sportive de origine engleză în limba romnă. SUBB 12:2.125–130.

Tropea, Giovanni. 1963. Un dialetto moribondo: il galloitalico di Francavilla. BCSic. 9.133–152.

――――. 1966. Effetti di simbiosi linguistica nelle parlate galloitaliche di Aidone, Nicosia e Novara di Sicilia. BALI NS.13/14.3–50.

Tucker, R. Whitney. 1944. The Roumanian vocative. Language 20.22–27.

Turialt, J. 1874. Étude sur le langage créole de la Martinique. Brest.

Udler, R., V. Melnik, and V. Komarnicki. 1968. Atlasul linguistik moldovenesk. Kišinev.

Uhlenbeck, E. M. 1963. An appraisal of transformational theory. Lingua 12.1–18.

――――. 1967. Some further remarks on transformational theory. Lingua 17.263–316.

Urciolo, Raphael G. 1965. The intervocalic plosives in Tuscan (-p- -t- -c-). Bern. (RH no. 74.)

Urruty, Jean. 1950–51. Le patois créole de l'Île Maurice. RGua. 31., 32.

Urzí, Emma. 1962. Analisi fonematica della parlata di Ortisei (Val Gardena). QI-GUB 6.69–87.

Vacandard, Jean. 1964. Glossaire picard de Normandie. Dialecte de Melleville, canton d'Eu, Seine-Maritime. Amiens. (CSLP no. 2.)

Vaccari, Walter. 1959. Vita e tumulti di F. T. Marinetti. Milano.

Vaccaro, Gennaro. 1969. Vocabolario romanesco belliano e italiano-romanesco. Roma.

――――. 1971. Vocabolario romanesco trilussiano e italiano-romanesco. Roma.

Väänänen, Veikko. 1963. Introduction au latin vulgaire. Paris. (2nd ed., 1967. Spanish tr.: Introducción al latín vulgar, Madrid, 1968.)

――――. 1968. Autour du problème de la division du latin; apport des sources écrites, en particulier des inscriptions. TLL 6:1.141–148.

――――. 1970. Trimalcion et ses convives parlaient-ils italien? NM 70.604–611.

Valbuena Prat, Ángel. 1937. Historia de la literatura española. Barcelona. 3 vols. (7th ed., 1963.)

Valdman, Albert. 1968. Language standardization in a diglossia situation: Haiti. In Fishman, Ferguson, and Das Gupta (eds.), 1968:313–326.

――――. 1969. The language situation in Haiti. In R. Schaedel (ed.), 1969:155–203.

Valkoff, Marius. 1947. Superstrats germanique et slave. Neophilologus 31.149–153.

――――. 1964. Notes socio-linguistiques sur le parler créole de la Réunion. Neophilologus 42.169–182.

――――. 1966. Studies in Portuguese and Creole, with special reference to South Africa. Johannesburg.

――――. 1969. Du nouveau sur les dialectes créoles français. RLR 78.301–308.

van Daele, Hilaire. 1939. Petit dictionnaire de l'ancien français. Paris.

van den Besselaer, J. J. 1963. Het Portugees van Brasilië. 's Hertogenbosch. 2 vols.

van Wijk, H. L. A. 1946. Contribución al estudio del habla popular en Venezuela. Amsterdam.

————. 1958.   Orígenes y evolución del papiamento. Neophilologus 42.169–182.

Vannini, A.   1920.   Notizie intorno alla vita e all'opera di Celso Cittadini. Siena.

Vàrvaro, Alberto.   1968.   Storia, problemi e metodi della linguistica romanza. Nàpoli.

Vascenco, V.   1959.   Elemente slave răsăritene în limba romînă. StCL 10.395–408.

Vasseur, Gaston.   1963.   Dictionnaire des parlers picards du Vimeu (Somme), avec considération spéciale du dialecte de Nibas. Amiens. (CSLP no. 4.)

Vasiliu, Emanuel.   1965.   Fonologia limbii române. Bucureşti.

————. 1968.   Fonologia istorică a dialectelor dacoromâne. Bucureşti.

Vaughan, Herbert Hunter.   1915.   The dialects of central Italy. Philadelphia.

————. 1925–26.   Italian [and its] dialects in the United States. AS 1.431–435 (1925); 2.13–18 (1926).

Veiga, Amable.   1969.   Fonología gallega. Fonemática. El sistema consonántico. Oposiciones entre consonantes. Grial 24.225–230.

Velleman, Ant.   1915–24.   Grammatica teoretica, pratica ed istorica della lingua d'Engiadin' Ota. Zürig.

Vendryes, J.   1902.   De hibernicis vocabulis quae a latina lingua originem duxerunt. Lutetiae Parisiorum.

Venturini, R.   1942.   Linguaggio sportivo. LN 4.109–110.

Verdier, Roger.   1951.   Dictionnaire phonétique, étymologique et comparé du patois du Haut-Maine. Le Mans.

Vianey, Joseph.   1896.   Mathurin Régnier. Paris.

Vidal de Battini, Elena.   1949.   El habla rural de San Luís. Buenos Aires. (= BDH 7.)

————. 1954.   El español de la Argentina. Buenos Aires.

Vidos Benedék Elemér.   1931.   Contributo alla storia delle parole francesi di origine italiana. AR 15.449–479.

————. 1932.   La forza d'espansione della lingua italiana. Nijmegen.

————. 1939.   Storia delle parole marinaresche italiane passate in francese. Contributo storico-linguistico all'espansione della lingua nautica italiana. Firenze. (BAR II.24.)

————. 1956.   Handboek tot de romaanse taalkunde. Nijmegen. (Italian tr.: Manuale di linguistica romanza, Firenze, 1959. Spanish tr.: Manual de lingüística románica, Madrid, 1963. German tr.: Handbuch der romanischen Sprachwissenschaft, München, 1968.)

Vidossi(ch), Giuseppe.   1900–01.   Studî sul dialetto triestino. ATr. NS.23.239–304 (1900); NS 24.5–78 (1901).

Vieli, Ramon, and Alexi Decurtins.   1962.   Vocabulari romontsch sursilvan—tudestg. Cuera.

Vignoli, Carlo.   1911.   Il vernacolo di Castro de' Volsci. StR 7.116–196.

————. 1920.   Vernacolo e canti di Amaseno. Roma.

————. 1925.   Il vernacolo di Veroli. Roma. (DRL no. 3.)

————. 1926.   Lessico del dialetto di Amaseno. Roma.

Vigón, Braulio.   1896–98.   Vocabulario dialectológico del Concejo de Colunga. Villaviciosa. (2nd ed., Madrid, 1953; RFE Anejo no. 63.)

Villey, Pierre.   1908.   Les sources italiennes de la Deffense et Illustration de la langue française de Joachim du Bellay. Paris.

Vincent, Leon H.   1901.   The French Academy. Boston and New York.

Vincenzi, Giuseppe Carlo.   1968.   Bibliografia dialettale dell'Emilia-Romagna. BCDI 3.79–130.

Violet, E.   1932.   Le patois de Clessé en Mâconnais: lexique et textes. Paris.

————. 1936. Les patois mâconnais de la zone de transition entre le francien et le franco-provençal, en partant du patois d'Igé (Saône-et-Loire). Mâcon). Paris.

Viriglio, Alberto. 1897. Come si parla a Torino. Torino.

Viscardi, Antonio. 1952. Letteratura d'oc e d'oïl. Milano.

————, Maurizio Vitale, Anna Maria Finoli, and Carla Cremonesi. 1959. Le prefazioni ai primi grando vocabolari delle lingue eruopee. Milano.

Viscidi, F. 1944. I prestiti latini nel greco antico e bizantino. Pàdova.

Vising, Johan. 1900–02. Franska språket i England. Göteborg.

————. 1923. Anglo-Norman language and literature. London.

Vitale, Maurizio. 1960. La questione della lingua. Palermo.

————. 1964. *Purista* e *purismo*: storia di parole e motivi della loro fortuna. Acme 17.187–211.

————. 1966. La III. edizione del "Vocabolario della Crusca." Acme 19.109–155.

Vivaldi, Vincenzo. 1894–98. Le controversie intorno alla nostra lingua dal 1500 ai giorni nostri. Catanzaro. 3 vols.

Volpe, Pietro Paolo. 1869. Vocabolario napolitano-italiano tascabile. Nàpoli.

Volpi, G. 1932. Saggio di voci e maniere del parlar fiorentino. Firenze.

von Ettmayer, Karl. 1903. Bergamaskische Alpenmundarten. Leipzig.

————. 1930–36. Analytische Syntax der französischen Sprache. Halle/S. 2 vols.

von Miklosich, Franz. 1861. Die slavischen Elemente im Rumänischen. DsWien 12.1–70.

————. 1881–83. Beiträge zur Lautlehre der rumunischen Dialekte. SbWien 98.519–550 (1881); 99.5–74 (1881); 100.229–304 (1882); 101.3–94 (1882); 102.2–74 (1883).

von Raffler-Engel, Walburga. 1957. Investigation of Italo-American bilinguals. Italica 34.239–244.

von Wartburg, Walther. 1919. Zur Stellung der Bergeller Mundart zwischen dem Rätischen und dem Lombardischen. BM 1919.329–348 .(Reprinted in Spitzer (ed.), 1930:2.190–207.

————. 1928–71. Französisches etymologisches Wörterbuch: eine Darstellung des galloromanischen Sprachschatzes. Bonn (later Basel). 17 vols. With Beiheft: Ortsnamenregister, Literaturverzeichnis, Übersichtskarte (Bonn, 1929).

————. 1934a. Évolution et structure de la langue française. Leipzig. (Later eds., Berne.)

————. 1934b. Bibliographie des dictionnaires patois. Paris. (SPRF no. 8.)

————. 1934c. Die Entstehung der Sprachgrenzen im Innern der Romania. BGDSL 58.209–227.

————. 1936a. Die Ausgliederung der romanischen Sprachräume. ZRPh. 56.1–48, with 7 maps. (2nd ed.: Bern, 1950. Spanish tr.: La fragmentación lingüística de la Románia, Madrid, 1952. French tr.: La fragmentation linguistique de la Romania, Strasbourg, 1967.)

————. 1936b. La posizione della lingua italiana nel mondo neolatino. Leipzig. (2nd ed., Firenze, 1939.)

————. 1939a. Die Entstehung der romanischen Völker. Halle/S. (2nd ed., Tübingen, 1951. French tr.: Les origines des peuples romans, Paris, 1941.)

————. 1939b. Die burgundischen Wörter im Frankoprovenzalischen. ZRPh. 59.302–307.

————. 1943. Einführung in Problematik und Methodik der Sprachwissenschaft. Halle/S. (Later eds.: Tübingen. French tr.: Problèmes et méthodes de la linguistique, Paris, 1963. English tr.: Problems and methods in linguistics, Oxford [England], 1969.)

326   COMPARATIVE ROMANCE GRAMMAR

———. 1952. Die griechische Kolonisation in Südgallien und ihre sprachliche Zeugen im Westromanischen. ZRPh. 68.1–48, with 5 maps. Also separate: Tübingen. Reprinted in von Wartburg, 1956:67–126.

———. 1956. Von Sprache und Mensch. Gesammelte Aufsätze. Bern.

———, Hans-Erich Keller and R. Geuljans. 1969. Bibliographie des dictionnaires patois. (1550–1967). Nouvelle édition entièrement revue et mise à jour. Genève. (SPRF no. 103.)

——— and Paul Zumthor. 1947. Précis de syntaxe du français contemporain. Berne.

Voorhoeve, Jan. 1967. Review of Hall 1965. Lingua 18.101–105.

Vossler, Karl. 1904. Positivismus und Idealismus in der Sprachwissenschaft. Heidelberg.

———. 1913. Frankreichs Kultur im Spiegel seiner Sprachentwicklung. Heidelberg. (Later eds. under title: Frankreichs Kultur und Sprache. French tr.: Langue et culture de la France, Paris, 1952.)

———. 1955. Einführung ins Vulgärlatein. München.

Wacker, Gertrud. 1916. Über das Verhältnis von Dialekt und Schriftsprache im Altfranzösischen. Halle/S. (BGRSL no. 11.)

Wagner, Max Leopold. 1907. Lautlehre der südsardischen Mundarten, mit besonderer Berücksightigung der um den Gennargentu gesprochenen Variaten. Halle/S.

———. 1909. Die Sprache der spanischen Juden. RDR 1.487–502.

———. 1914. Beiträge zur Kenntnis des Judenspanischen von Konstantinopel. Wien.

———. 1920. Spanisch-Amerikanisch und Vulgärlatein. ZRPh. 40.286–312, 385–404. (Reprinted in Spitzer (ed.), 1930:208–263. Spanish tr.: El español de América y el latín vulgar, CIF 1.45–110 [1924].)

———. 1921. Das Ländliche Leben Sardiniens im Spiegel der Sprache. Kulturhistorisch-sprachliche Untersuchungen. Heidelberg. (Italian tr.: La vita rustica della Sardegna rispecchiata nella sua lingua, Càgilari, 1928.)

———. 1927. El supuesto andalucismo de América y la teoría climatológica. RFE 14.20–32.

———. 1930. Caracteres generales del judeo-español de Oriente. Madrid. (FRE Anejo no. 12.)

———. 1931. Zum Judenspanischen von Morokko. VKR 4.221–245.

———. 1936a. Restos de latinidad en el Norte de África. Coimbra.

———. 1936b. Sic. dàgala. ZRPh. 56 374–376.

———. 1938–39. Flessione nominale e verbale del sardo antico e moderno. ID 14.93–170 (1938); 15.1–29 (1939).

———. 1939. Das peruanische Spanisch. VKR 11.48–68.

———. 1941. Historische Lautlehre des Sardischen. Halle/S. (ZRPh. Bhft. no. 93.)

———. 1944. Siz. mafarata. ZRPh. 64.573–576.

———. 1947. Il Cocoliche, lingua del lavoratore italiano nelle città del Río de la Plata. LE 12.22–24.

———. 1949. Lingua e dialetti dell'America spagnola. Firenze.

———. 1951. La lingua sarda: storia, spirito e forme. Berna.

———. 1952. Historische Wortbildungslehre des Sardischen. Bern. (RH no. 39.)

———. 1960–64. Dizionario etimologico sardo. Heidelberg.

Wagner, Robert-Léon. 1947. Introduction à la linguistique française. Lille-Genève. (2nd ed., Genève, 1955.)

Wahlgren, Ernst G. 1936. Evoluzione semasiologica di alcune parole dotte nell' italiano. Uppsala-Stockholm.

Walberg, Emanuel. 1907. Saggio sulla fonetica del parlare di Celerina-Cresta (alta Engadina). Lund.

Walser, E. 1914. Poggius Florentinus. Leipzig.

Walser, W. 1936. Zur Charakteristik der Mundart des Aosta-Tales. Aarau.

Warren, Larissa Bonfante. 1970. Roman triumphs and Etruscan kings: the Latin word *triumphus*. In Lugton and Salzer (eds.), 1970:108–120.

Walterman, John T. 1963. Perspectives in linguistics. Chicago.

———. 1966. A history of the German language. Seattle-London.

Weigand, Gustav. 1888. Die Sprache der Olympo-Walachen nebst einer Einleitung über Land und Leute. Leipzig.

———. 1894–95. Die Aromunen. Leipzig. 2 vols.

———. 1896. Körösch- und Maroschdialekte. JbIRSL 3.250–336.

———. 1897. Der Banater Dialekt. JbIRSL 4.198–332.

———. 1898–1909. Linguistischer Atlas des daco-rumänischen Sprachgebietes. Leipzig. 3 vols.

———. 1899. Samosch- und Theissdialekte. JbIRSL 6.1–85.

———. 1900. Die rumänischen Dialekte der kleinen Walachei, Serbiens und Bulgariens. JbIRSL 7.1–92.

———. 1901. Dialekte der grossen Walachei. JbIRSL 8.234–324.

———. 1902. Die Dialekte der Moldau und Dobrudscha. JbIRSL 9.138–236.

———. 1904. Die Dialekte der Bukovina und Bassarabiens. Leipzig.

———. 1907. Rumänen und Aromunen in Bosnien. JbIRSL 14.171–197.

Weigold, Hermann. 1943. Untersuchungen zur Sprachgrenze am Nordufer des Bielersees. Winterthur. (2nd ed.: Bern, 1948.)

Weise, O. 1882. Die griechischen Wörter im Latein. Leipzig.

Wengler, Heinrich. 1915. Die heutige Mundart von Zara in Dalmatien. Halle/S.

Wexler, Peter J. 1955. La formation du vocabulaire des chemins de fer en France (1778–1842). Genève-Lille.

Whatmough, Joshua. 1937. The foundations of Roman Italy. London.

———. 1944. KEΛTIKÄ. Cambridge, Massachusetts.

———. 1970. The dialects of ancient Gaul. Cambridge, Massachusetts.

Whinnom, Keith. 1956. Spanish contact vernaculars in the Philippine Islands. Hong Kong.

———. 1965. The origin of the European-based Creoles and Pidgins. Orbis 14.510–527.

White, Lynn, Jr. 1962. Mediaeval technology and social change. Oxford (England) and New York.

Whitfield, John Humphreys. 1960. A short history of Italian literature. Harmondsworth (England) and Baltimore. (Pelican Books no. A-455.)

Widmer, Ambros. 1965. Das Rätoromanische in Graubünden. Orbis 14.560–571.

———. 1966. Der Stand der bündnerromanischen Linguistik. Orbis 15.560–574.

Wilkins, Ernest Hatch. 1954. A history of Italian literature. Cambridge, Massachusetts.

Williams, Edwin Bucher. 1938. From Latin to Portuguese. Historical phonology and morphology of the Portuguese language. Philadelphia. ("Second edition" [unchanged reprint], 1968.)

Wilson, Richard Middlewood. 1952. The lost literature of mediaeval England. London.

Wilson, W. A. A. 1962. The Crioulo of Guiné. Johannesburg.

Wind, Bartina Harmina. 1928. Les mots italiens introduits en français au XVI. siècle. Deventer.

Windisch, Ernst. 1886–88. Keltische Sprache. In Gröber (ed.) 1886–88:1.283–312. (In 2nd ed.: 1.371–404.)

Wis, Marjatta. 1955. Richerche sopra gli italianismi nella lingua tedesca dalla metà del secolo XIV alla fine del secolo XVI. Helsinki. (MSNH 17.)

Wolterstorff, G. 1919. Entwickelung von *ille* zum bestimmten Artikel. Glotta 10.62–93.

Wood, Richard E. 1972. New light on the origins of Papiamentu: an eighteenth-century letter. Neophilologus 56.18–30.

Wrede, Ferdinant. 1886. Uber die Sprache der Wandalen. Leipzig.

———. 1891. Uber die Sprache der Ostgoten in Italien. Strassburg. (GFSCGV no. 68.)

Wuest, Jakob. 1969. Sprachgrenzen im Poitou. VR 28.14–58.

Wunderli, Peter. 1965. Die ältesten romanischen Texte unter dem Gesichtswinkel von Protokoll und Vorlesen. VR 24.44–63.

———. 1966. Zur Regression des Bündnerromanischen. VR 25.56–81, with 9 maps.

———. 1968. Deutsch und Italienisch im Tessin. VR 27.301–318.

Zaccaria, Enrico. 1905. Contributo allo studio degl'iberismi in Italia e della Wechselbeziehung fra la lingue romanze ossia voci e frasi spagnuole e portoghesi nel Sassetti aggiuntevi quelle del Carletti e del Magalotti. Torino.

———. 1908. Il parao, il maroma e il cabrestante ecc. ossia la ripercussione del linguaggio nautico sp. port. in Italia. Iberismi nautici o ignorati o bistrattati dai lessicografi e dai filologi. Bologna.

———. 1927. L'elemento iberico nella lingua italiana. Bologna.

Zambaldi, Francesco. 1889. Vocabolario etimologico italiano. Città di Castello.

———. 1892. Delle teorie ortografiche in Italia. AIVeneto 50.323–368.

Zamora Vicente, Alonso. 1943. El habla de Mérida y sus cercanías. Madrid. (RFE Anejo no. 29.)

———. 1953. Léxico rural asturiano: palabras y cosas de Libardón (Colunga). Granada.

———. 1960. Dialectología española. Madrid. (3rd ed., 1967.)

Zanchi Alberti, Costanza. 1937–39. Lessico del dialetto di Sansepolcro (Arezzo). ID 13.207–224 (1937); 15.137–148 (1939).

Zanette, Emilio. 1955. Dizionario del dialetto di Vittorio Veneto. Treviso.

Zannoni, Giovanni Battista. 1848. Storia della Accademia della Crusca. Firenze.

Zappettini, Stefano. 1859. Vocabolario bergamasco-italiano. Bèrgamo.

Zastrow, Dieter. 1963. Entstehung und Ausbildung des französischen Vokabulars der Luftfahrt mit Fahrzeugen "leichter als Luft" (Ballon, Luftschiff) von den Anfägnen bis 1910. Tübingen. (ZRPh. Bhft. no. 105.)

Zaun, Otto. 1917. Die Mundart von Aniane (Hérault) in alter und neuer Zeit. Halle/ S. (ZRPh. Bhft. no. 61.)

Zauner, Adolf. 1900. Romanische Sprachwissenschaft. Berlin-Leipzig. 2 vols. (Sammlung Göschen no. 128. 4th ed., 1921–26. Italian tr.: Glottologia romanza, Torino, 1904.)

Zehnder, Joseph. 1938. Les "Origini della lingua italiana" de Gilles Ménage. Paris.

Zeiller, Jacques. 1929. L'apparition du mot *Romania* chez les écrivains latins. RÉL 7.194–198.

Zéliqzon, Léon. 1922–24. Dictionnaire des patois romans de la Moselle. Strasbourg and New York. 3 vols.

Ziccardi, Giovanni. 1910. Il dialetto di Agnone. La fonetica e la flessione. ZRPh. 34.405–436.

Zimmerli, Jakob. 1891–99. Die deutsch-französische Sprachgrenze in der Schweiz. Basel and Geneva. 3 vols.

Zingarelli, Nicola. 1899–1901. Il dialetto di Cerignola. AGI 15.83–96, 226–235.

Zolli, Paolo. 1971. L'influsso francese sul veneziano del XVIII secolo. Venezia.

Zuccagni-Orlandini, Attilio. 1864. Raccolta di dialetti italiani, con illustrazioni etnologiche. Firenze.

Zumthor, Paul. 1953. Le français créole de Haïti. LT 1953.6–16.

———. 1954. Histoire littéraire de la France médiévale (VIe–XIVe siècle). Paris.

Zwanenburg, W. 1968. État actuel de la description du français parlé. LT 1968.82–89.

INDEX

Subjects and names of persons, literary or other works, and places are listed in strict alphabetical order. Material contained in the notes to each chapter is indexed only if it is not mentioned in the body of the text.